Family Maps
of
Howell County, Missouri
Deluxe Edition

With Homesteads, Roads, Waterways, Towns, Cemeteries, Railroads, and More

Family Maps
of
Howell County, Missouri
Deluxe Edition

With Homesteads, Roads, Waterways, Towns, Cemeteries, Railroads, and More

3 *Maps Per Township ...*

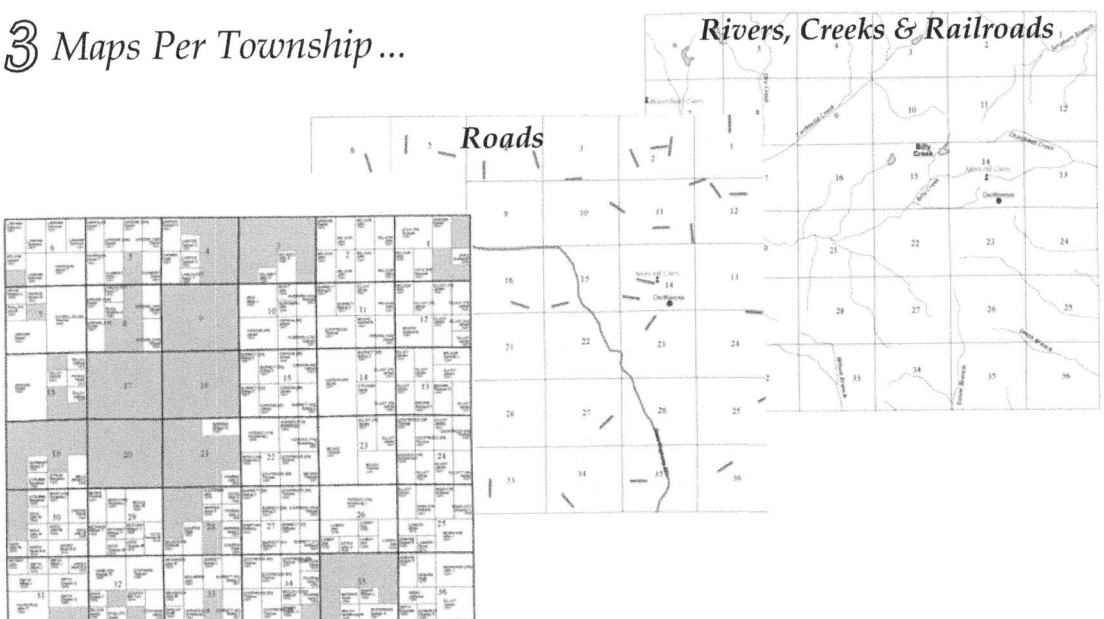

by Gregory A. Boyd, J.D.

Arphax Publishing Co.
www.arphax.com

Family Maps of Howell County, Missouri, Deluxe Edition: With Homesteads, Roads, Waterways, Towns, Cemeteries, Railroads, and More.
by Gregory A. Boyd, J.D.

ISBN 1-4203-2061-0

Published by Arphax Publishing Co., 2210 Research Park Blvd., Norman, Oklahoma, USA 73069
www.arphax.com

First Edition

ATTENTION HISTORICAL & GENEALOGICAL SOCIETIES, UNIVERSITIES, COLLEGES, CORPORATIONS, FAMILY REUNION COORDINATORS, AND PROFESSIONAL ORGANIZATIONS: Quantity discounts are available on bulk purchases of this book. For information, please contact Arphax Publishing Co., at the address listed above, or at (405) 366-6181, or visit our web-site at www.arphax.com and contact us through the "Bulk Sales" link.

—LEGAL—

Editor: Vicki Boyd

This book is dedicated to my wonderful family:

Vicki, Jordan, & Amy Boyd

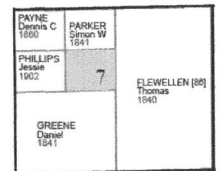

Contents

- Part I -

The Big Picture

- Part II -

Township Map Groups

(each Map Group contains a Patent Index, Patent Map, Road Map, & Historical Map)

Appendices

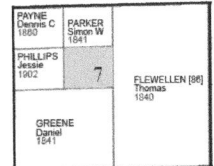

Preface

The quest for the discovery of my ancestors' origins, migrations, beliefs, and life-ways has brought me rewards that I could never have imagined. The *Family Maps* series of books is my first effort to share with historical and genealogical researchers, some of the tools that I have developed to achieve my research goals. I firmly believe that this effort will allow many people to reap the same sorts of treasures that I have.

Our Federal government's General Land Office of the Bureau of Land Management (the "GLO") has given genealogists and historians an incredible gift by virtue of its enormous database housed on its web-site at glorecords.blm.gov. Here, you can search for and find millions of parcels of land purchased by our ancestors in about thirty states.

This GLO web-site is one of the best FREE on-line tools available to family researchers. But, it is not for the faint of heart, nor is it for those unwilling or unable to to sift through and analyze the thousands of records that exist for most counties.

My immediate goal with this series is to spare you the hundreds of hours of work that it would take you to map the Land Patents for this county. Every Howell County homestead or land patent that I have gleaned from public GLO databases is mapped here. Consequently, I can usually show you in an instant, where your ancestor's land is located, as well as the names of nearby land-owners.

Originally, that was my primary goal. But after speaking to other genealogists, it became clear that there was much more that they wanted. Taking their advice set me back almost a full year, but I think you will agree it was worth the wait. Because now, you can learn so much more.

Now, this book answers these sorts of questions:

- Are there any variant spellings for surnames that I have missed in searching GLO records?
- Where is my family's traditional home-place?
- What cemeteries are near Grandma's house?
- My Granddad used to swim in such-and-such-Creek—where is that?
- How close is this little community to that one?
- Are there any other people with the same surname who bought land in the county?
- How about cousins and in-laws—did they buy land in the area?

And these are just for starters!

The rules for using the *Family Maps* books are simple, but the strategies for success are many. Some techniques are apparent on first use, but many are gained with time and experience. Please take the time to notice the roads, cemeteries, creek-names, family names, and unique first-names throughout the whole county. You cannot imagine what YOU might be the first to discover.

I hope to learn that many of you have answered age-old research questions within these pages or that you have discovered relationships previously not even considered. When these sorts of things happen to you, will you please let me hear about it? I would like nothing better. My contact information can always be found at www.arphax.com.

One more thing: please read the "How To Use This Book" chapter; it starts on the next page. This will give you the very best chance to find the treasures that lie within these pages.

My family and I wish you the very best of luck, both in life, and in your research.   Greg Boyd

How to Use This Book - A Graphical Summary

Part I
"The Big Picture"

Map A ► *Counties in the State*
Map B ► *Surrounding Counties*
Map C ► *Congressional Townships (Map Groups) in the County*
Map D ► *Cities & Towns in the County*
Map E ► *Cemeteries in the County*
Surnames in the County ► *Number of Land-Parcels for Each Surname*
Surname/Township Index ► *Directs you to Township Map Groups in Part II*

The <u>Surname/Township Index</u> can direct you to any number of **Township Map Groups**

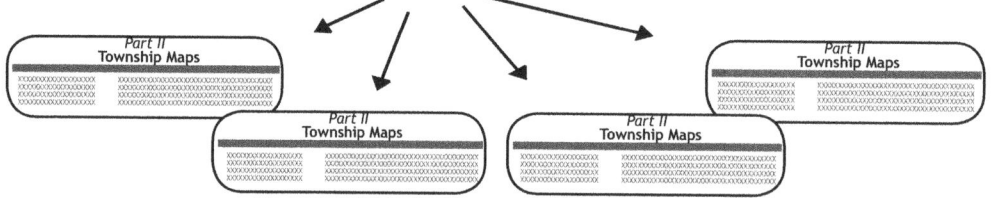

Part II
Township Map Groups
(1 for each Township in the County)

Each Township Map Group contains all four of of the following tools . . .

Land Patent Index ► *Every-name Index of Patents Mapped in this Township*
Land Patent Map ► *Map of Patents as listed in above Index*
Road Map ► *Map of Roads, City-centers, and Cemeteries in the Township*
Historical Map ► *Map of Railroads, Lakes, Rivers, Creeks, City-Centers, and Cemeteries*

Appendices

Appendix A ► *Congressional Authority enabling Patents within our Maps*
Appendix B ► *Section-Parts / Aliquot Parts (a comprehensive list)*
Appendix C ► *Multi-patentee Groups (Individuals within Buying Groups)*

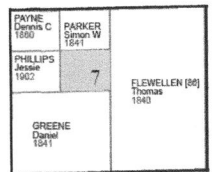

How to Use This Book

The two "Parts" of this *Family Maps* volume seek to answer two different types of questions. Part I deals with broad questions like: what counties surround Howell County, are there any ASHCRAFTs in Howell County, and if so, in which Townships or Maps can I find them? Ultimately, though, Part I should point you to a particular Township Map Group in Part II.

Part II concerns itself with details like: where exactly is this family's land, who else bought land in the area, and what roads and streams run through the land, or are located nearby. The Chart on the opposite page, and the remainder of this chapter attempt to convey to you the particulars of these two "parts", as well as how best to use them to achieve your research goals.

Part I
"The Big Picture"

Within Part I, you will find five "Big Picture" maps and two county-wide surname tools.

These include:

• Map A - Where Howell County lies within the state
• Map B - Counties that surround Howell County
• Map C - Congressional Townships of Howell County (+ Map Group Numbers)
• Map D - Cities & Towns of Howell County (with Index)
• Map E - Cemeteries of Howell County (with Index)
• Surnames in Howell County Patents (with Parcel-counts for each surname)
• Surname/Township Index (with Parcel-counts for each surname by Township)

The five "Big-Picture" Maps are fairly self-explanatory, yet should not be overlooked. This is particularly true of Maps "C", "D", and "E", all of which show Howell County and its Congressional Townships (and their assigned Map Group Numbers).

Let me briefly explain this concept of Map Group Numbers. These are a device completely of our own invention. They were created to help you quickly locate maps without having to remember the full legal name of the various Congressional Townships. It is simply easier to remember "Map Group 1" than a legal name like: "Township 9-North Range 6-West, 5th Principal Meridian." But the fact is that the TRUE legal name for these Townships IS terribly important. These are the designations that others will be familiar with and you will need to accurately record them in your notes. This is why both Map Group numbers AND legal descriptions of Townships are almost always displayed together.

Map "C" will be your first intoduction to "Map Group Numbers", and that is all it contains: legal Township descriptions and their assigned Map Group Numbers. Once you get further into your research, and more immersed in the details, you will likely want to refer back to Map "C" from time to time, in order to regain your bearings on just where in the county you are researching.

Remember, township boundaries are a completely artificial device, created to standardize land descriptions. But do not let them become a boundary in your mind when choosing which townships to research. Your relative's in-laws, children, cousins, siblings, and mamas and papas, might just as easily have lived in the township next to the one your grandfather lived in—rather than in the one where he actually lived. So Map "C" can be your guide to which other Townships/ Map Groups you likewise ought to analyze.

Of course, the same holds true for County lines; this is the purpose behind Map "B". It shows you surrounding counties that you may want to consider for further reserarch.

Map "D", the Cities and Towns map, is the first map with an index. Map "E" is the second (Cemeteries). Both, Maps "D" and "E" give you broad views of City (or Cemetery) locations in the County. But they go much further by pointing you toward pertinent Township Map Groups so you can locate the patents, roads, and waterways located near a particular city or cemetery.

Once you are familiar with these *Family Maps* volumes and the county you are researching, the "Surnames In Howell County" chapter (or its sister chapter in other volumes) is where you'll likely start your future research sessions. Here, you can quickly scan its few pages and see if anyone in the county possesses the surnames you are researching. The "Surnames in Howell County" list shows only two things: surnames and the number of parcels of land we have located for that surname in Howell County. But whether or not you immediately locate the surnames you are researching, please do not go any further without taking a few moments to scan ALL the surnames in these very few pages.

You cannot imagine how many lost ancestors are waiting to be found by someone willing to take just a little longer to scan the "Surnames In Howell County" list. Misspellings and typographical errors abound in most any index of this sort. Don't miss out on finding your Kinard that was written Rynard or Cox that was written Lox. If it looks funny or wrong, it very often is. And one of those little errors may well be your relative.

Now, armed with a surname and the knowledge that it has one or more entries in this book, you are ready for the "Surname/Township Index." Unlike the "Surnames In Howell County", which has only one line per Surname, the "Surname/Township Index" contains one line-item for each Township Map Group in which each surname is found. In other words, each line represents a different Township Map Group that you will need to review.

Specifically, each line of the Surname/Township Index contains the following four columns of in-formation:

1. Surname
2. Township Map Group Number (these Map Groups are found in Part II)
3. Parcels of Land (number of them with the given Surname within the Township)
4. Meridian/Township/Range (the legal description for this Township Map Group)

The key column here is that of the Township Map Group Number. While you should definitely record the Meridian, Township, and Range, you can do that later. Right now, you need to dig a little deeper. That Map Group Number tells you where in Part II that you need to start digging.

But before you leave the "Surname/Township Index", do the same thing that you did with the "Surnames in Howell County" list: take a moment to scan the pages of the Index and see if there are similarly spelled or misspelled surnames that deserve your attention. Here again, is an easy opportunity to discover grossly misspelled family names with very little effort. Now you are ready to turn to . . .

Part II
"Township Map Groups"

You will normally arrive here in Part II after being directed to do so by one or more "Map Group Numbers" in the Surname/Township Index of Part I.

Each Map Group represents a set of four tools dedicated to a single Congressional Township that is either wholly or partially within the county. If you are trying to learn all that you can about a particular family or their land, then these tools should usually be viewed in the order they are presented.

These four tools include:

1. a Land Patent Index
2. a Land Patent Map
3. a Road Map, and
4. an Historical Map

As I mentioned earlier, each grouping of this sort is assigned a Map Group Number. So, let's now move on to a discussion of the four tools that make up one of these Township Map Groups.

Land Patent Index

Each Township Map Group's Index begins with a title, something along these lines:

MAP GROUP 1: Index to Land Patents
Township 16-North Range 5-West (2ⁿᵈ PM)

The Index contains seven (7) columns. They are:

1. ID (a unique ID number for this Individual and a corresponding Parcel of land in this Township)
2. Individual in Patent (name)
3. Sec. (Section), and
4. Sec. Part (Section Part, or Aliquot Part)
5. Date Issued (Patent)
6. Other Counties (often means multiple counties were mentioned in GLO records, or the section lies within multiple counties).
7. For More Info . . . (points to other places within this index or elsewhere in the book where you can find more information)

While most of the seven columns are self-explanatory, I will take a few moments to explain the "Sec. Part." and "For More Info" columns.

The "Sec. Part" column refers to what surveryors and other land professionals refer to as an Aliquot Part. The origins and use of such a term mean little to a non-surveyor, and I have chosen to simply call these sub-sections of land what they are: a "Section Part". No matter what we call them, what we are referring to are things like a quarter-section or half-section or quarter-quarter-section. See Appendix "B" for most of the "Section Parts" you will come across (and many you will not) and what size land-parcel they represent.

The "For More Info" column of the Index may seem like a small appendage to each line, but please

recognize quickly that this is not so. And to understand the various items you might find here, you need to become familiar with the Legend that appears at the top of each Land Patent Index.

Here is a sample of the Legend . . .

LEGEND

"For More Info . . . " column

A = Authority (Legislative Act, See Appendix "A")
B = Block or Lot (location in Section unknown)
C = Cancelled Patent
F = Fractional Section
G = Group (Multi-Patentee Patent, see Appendix "C")
V = Overlaps another Parcel
R = Re-Issued (Parcel patented more than once)

Most parcels of land will have only one or two of these items in their "For More Info" columns, but when that is not the case, there is often some valuable information to be gained from further investigation. Below, I will explain what each of these items means to you you as a researcher.

A = Authority
(Legislative Act, See Appendix "A")

All Federal Land Patents were issued because some branch of our government (usually the U.S. Congress) passed a law making such a transfer of title possible. And therefore every patent within these pages will have an "A" item next to it in the index. The number after the "A" indicates which item in Appendix "A" holds the citation to the particular law which authorized the transfer of land to the public. As it stands, most of the Public Land data compiled and released by our government, and which serves as the basis for the patents mapped here, concerns itself with "Cash Sale" homesteads. So in some Counties, the law which authorized cash sales will be the primary, if not the only, entry in the Appendix.

B = Block or Lot (location in Section unknown)

A "B" designation in the Index is a tip-off that the EXACT location of the patent within the map is not apparent from the legal description. This Patent will nonetheless be noted within the proper

Section along with any other Lots purchased in the Section. Given the scope of this project (many states and many Counties are being mapped), trying to locate all relevant plats for Lots (if they even exist) and accurately mapping them would have taken one person several lifetimes. But since our primary goal from the onset has been to establish relationships between neighbors and families, very little is lost to this goal since we can still observe who all lived in which Section.

C = Cancelled Patent

A Cancelled Patent is just that: cancelled. Whether the original Patentee forfeited his or her patent due to fraud, a technicality, non-payment, or whatever, the fact remains that it is significant to know who received patents for what parcels and when. A cancellation may be evidence that the Patentee never physically re-located to the land, but does not in itself prove that point. Further evidence would be required to prove that. *See also*, Re-issued Patents, *below*.

F = Fractional Section

A Fractional Section is one that contains less than 640 acres, almost always because of a body of water. The exact size and shape of land-parcels contained in such sections may not be ascertainable, but we map them nonetheless. Just keep in mind that we are not mapping an actual parcel to scale in such instances. Another point to consider is that we have located some fractional sections that are not so designated by the Bureau of Land Management in their data. This means that not all fractional sections have been so identified in our indexes.

G = Group
(Multi-Patentee Patent, see Appendix "C")

A "G" designation means that the Patent was issued to a GROUP of people (Multi-patentees). The "G" will always be followed by a number. Some such groups were quite large and it was impractical if not impossible to display each individual in our maps without unduly affecting readability. EACH person in the group is named in the Index, but they won't all be found on the Map. You will find the name of the first person in such a Group

on the map with the Group number next to it, enclosed in [square brackets].

To find all the members of the Group you can either scan the Index for all people with the same Group Number or you can simply refer to Appendix "C" where all members of the Group are listed next to their number.

O = Overlaps another Parcel

An Overlap is one where PART of a parcel of land gets issued on more than one patent. For genealogical purposes, both transfers of title are important and both Patentees are mapped. If the ENTIRE parcel of land is re-issued, that is what we call it, a Re-Issued Patent (*see below*). The number after the "O" indicates the ID for the overlapping Patent(s) contained within the same Index. Like Re-Issued and Cancelled Patents, Overlaps may cause a map-reader to be confused at first, but for genealogical purposes, all of these parties' relationships to the underlying land is important, and therefore, we map them.

R = Re-Issued (Parcel patented more than once)

The label, "Re-issued Patent" describes Patents which were issued more than once for land with the EXACT SAME LEGAL DESCRIPTION. Whether the original patent was cancelled or not, there were a good many parcels which were patented more than once. The number after the "R" indicates the ID for the other Patent contained within the same Index that was for the same land. A quick glance at the map itself within the relevant Section will be the quickest way to find the other Patentee to whom the Parcel was transferred. They should both be mapped in the same general area.

I have gone to some length describing all sorts of anomalies either in the underlying data or in their representation on the maps and indexes in this book. Most of this will bore the most ardent reseracher, but I do this with all due respect to those researchers who will inevitably (and rightfully) ask: *"Why isn't so-and-so's name on the exact spot that the index says it should be?"*

In most cases it will be due to the existence of a Multi-Patentee Patent, a Re-issued Patent, a Cancelled Patent, or Overlapping Parcels named in separate Patents. I don't pretend that this discussion will answer every question along these lines, but I hope it will at least convince you of the complexity of the subject.

Not to despair, this book's companion web-site will offer a way to further explain "odd-ball" or errant data. Each book (County) will have its own web-page or pages to discuss such situations. You can go to www.arphax.com to find the relevant web-page for Howell County.

Land Patent Map

On the first two-page spread following each Township's Index to Land Patents, you'll find the corresponding Land Patent Map. And here lies the real heart of our work. For the first time anywhere, researchers will be able to observe and analyze, on a grand scale, most of the original land-owners for an area AND see them mapped in proximity to each one another.

We encourage you to make vigorous use of the accompanying Index described above, but then later, to abandon it, and just stare at these maps for a while. This is a great way to catch misspellings or to find collateral kin you'd not known were in the area.

Each Land Patent Map represents one Congressional Township containing approximately 36-square miles. Each of these square miles is labeled by an accompanying Section Number (1 through 36, in most cases). Keep in mind, that this book concerns itself solely with Howell County's patents. Townships which creep into one or more other counties will not be shown in their entirety in any one book. You will need to consult other books, as they become available, in order to view other countys' patents, cities, cemeteries, etc.

But getting back to Howell County: each Land Patent Map contains a Statistical Chart that looks like the following:

Township Statistics

Parcels Mapped	:	173
Number of Patents	:	163
Number of Individuals	:	152
Patentees Identified	:	151
Number of Surnames	:	137
Multi-Patentee Parcels	:	4
Oldest Patent Date	:	11/27/1820
Most Recent Patent	:	9/28/1917
Block/Lot Parcels	:	0
Parcels Re-Issued	:	3
Parcels that Overlap	:	8
Cities and Towns	:	6
Cemeteries	:	6

This information may be of more use to a social statistician or historian than a genealogist, but I think all three will find it interesting.

Most of the statistics are self-explanatory, and what is not, was described in the above discussion of the Index's Legend, but I do want to mention a few of them that may affect your understanding of the Land Patent Maps.

First of all, Patents often contain more than one Parcel of land, so it is common for there to be more Parcels than Patents. Also, the Number of Individuals will more often than not, not match the number of Patentees. A Patentee is literally the person or PERSONS named in a patent. So, a Patent may have a multi-person Patentee or a single-person patentee. Nonetheless, we account for all these individuals in our indexes.

On the lower-righthand side of the Patent Map is a Legend which describes various features in the map, including Section Boundaries, Patent (land) Boundaries, Lots (numbered), and Multi-Patentee Group Numbers. You'll also find a "Helpful Hints" Box that will assist you.

One important note: though the vast majority of Patents mapped in this series will prove to be reasonably accurate representations of their actual locations, we cannot claim this for patents lying along state and county lines, or waterways, or that have been platted (lots).

Shifting boundaries and sparse legal descriptions in the GLO data make this a reality that we have nonetheless tried to overcome by estimating these patents' locations the best that we can.

Road Map

On the two-page spread following each Patent Map you will find a Road Map covering the exact same area (the same Congressional Township).

For me, fully exploring the past means that every once in a while I must leave the library and travel to the actual locations where my ancestors once walked and worked the land. Our Township Road Maps are a great place to begin such a quest.

Keep in mind that the scaling and proportion of these maps was chosen in order to squeeze hundreds of people-names, road-names, and place-names into tinier spaces than you would traditionally see. These are not professional road-maps, and like any secondary genealogical source, should be looked upon as an entry-way to original sources— in this case, original patents and applications, professionally produced maps and surveys, etc.

Both our Road Maps and Historical Maps contain cemeteries and city-centers, along with a listing of these on the left-hand side of the map. I should note that I am showing you city center-points, rather than city-limit boundaries, because in many instances, this will represent a place where settlement began. This may be a good time to mention that many cemeteries are located on private property, Always check with a local historical or genealogical society to see if a particular cemetery is publicly accessible (if it is not obviously so). As a final point, look for your surnames among the road-names. You will often be surprised by what you find.

Historical Map

The third and final map in each Map Group is our attempt to display what each Township might have looked like before the advent of modern roads. In frontier times, people were usually more determined to settle near rivers and creeks than they were near roads, which were often few and

far between. As was the case with the Road Map, we've included the same cemeteries and city-centers. We've also included railroads, many of which came along before most roads.

While some may claim "Historical Map" to be a bit of a misnomer for this tool, we settled for this label simply because it was almost as accurate as saying "Railroads, Lakes, Rivers, Cities, and Cemeteries," and it is much easier to remember.

In Closing . . .

By way of example, here is *A Really Good Way to Use a Township Map Group.* First, find the person you are researching in the Township's Index to Land Patents, which will direct you to the proper Section and parcel on the Patent Map. But before leaving the Index, scan all the patents within it, looking for other names of interest. Now, turn to the Patent Map and locate your parcels of land. Pay special attention to the names of patent-holders who own land surrounding your person of interest. Next, turn the page and look at the same Section(s) on the Road Map. Note which roads are closest to your parcels and also the names of nearby towns and cemeteries. Using other resources, you may be able to learn of kin who have been buried here, plus, you may choose to visit these cemeteries the next time you are in the area.

Finally, turn to the Historical Map. Look once more at the same Sections where you found your research subject's land. Note the nearby streams, creeks, and other geographical features. You may be surprised to find family names were used to name them, or you may see a name you haven't heard mentioned in years and years—and a new research possibility is born.

Many more techniques for using these *Family Maps* volumes will no doubt be discovered. If from time to time, you will navigate to Howell County's web-page at www.arphax.com (use the "Research" link), you can learn new tricks as they become known (or you can share ones you have employed). But for now, you are ready to get started. So, go, and good luck.

– Part I –

The Big Picture

Map A - Where Howell County, Missouri Lies Within the State

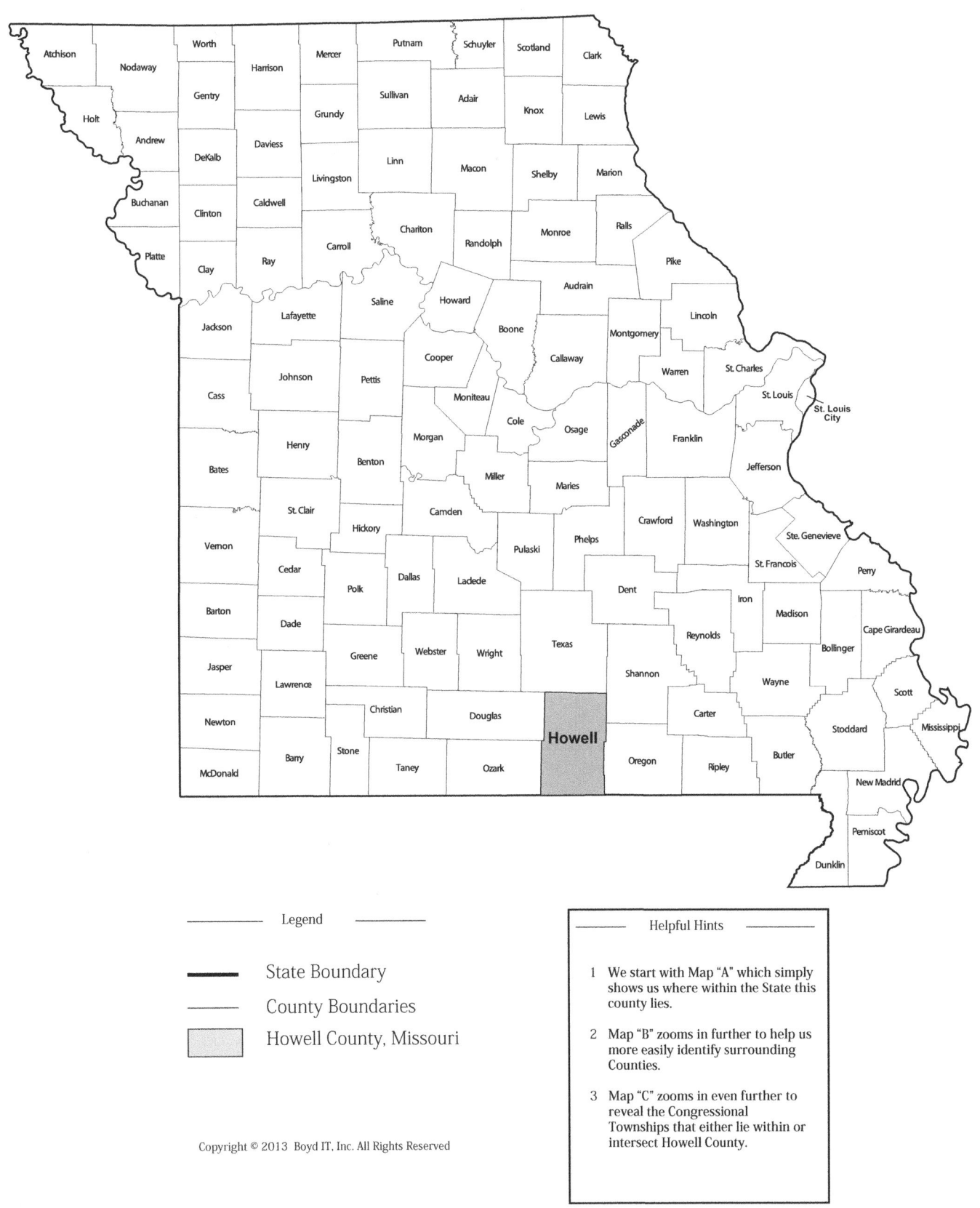

----------- Legend -----------

━━━━━━ State Boundary

───────── County Boundaries

▨ Howell County, Missouri

----------- Helpful Hints -----------

1 We start with Map "A" which simply shows us where within the State this county lies.

2 Map "B" zooms in further to help us more easily identify surrounding Counties.

3 Map "C" zooms in even further to reveal the Congressional Townships that either lie within or intersect Howell County.

Map B - Howell County, Missouri and Surrounding Counties

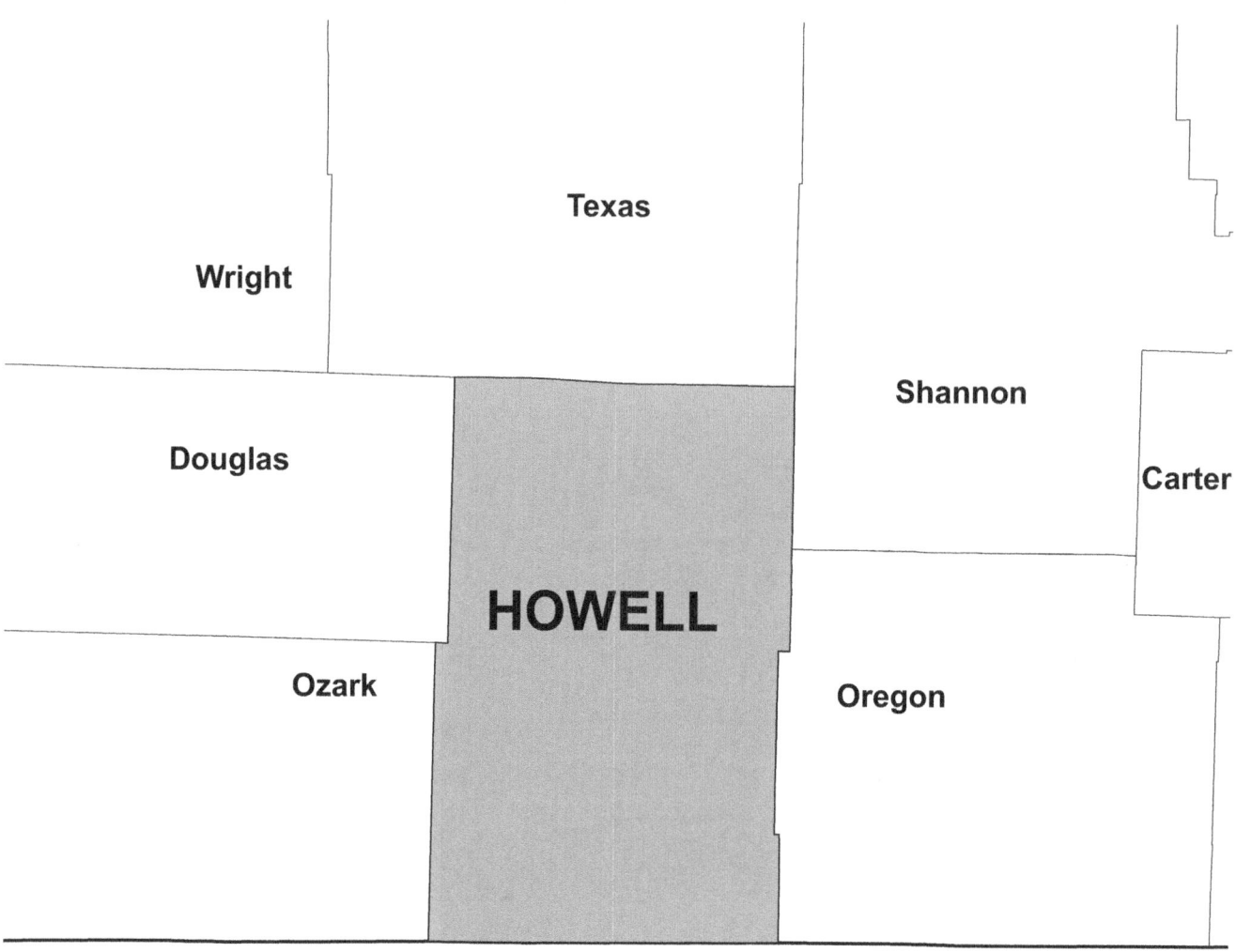

———— Legend ————

———— State Boundaries (when applicable)

———— County Boundaries

———— Helpful Hints ————

1 Many Patent-holders and their families settled across county lines. It is always a good idea to check nearby counties for your families.

2 Refer to Map "A" to see a broader view of where this County lies within the State, and Map "C" to see which Congressional Townships lie within Howell County.

Map C - Congressional Townships of Howell County, Missouri

Map Group 1 Township 27-N Range 10-W	**Map Group 2** Township 27-N Range 9-W	**Map Group 3** Township 27-N Range 8-W	**Map Group 4** Township 27-N Range 7-W
Map Group 5 Township 26-N Range 10-W	**Map Group 6** Township 26-N Range 9-W	**Map Group 7** Township 26-N Range 8-W	**Map Group 8** Township 26-N Range 7-W
Map Group 9 Township 25-N Range 10-W	**Map Group 10** Township 25-N Range 9-W	**Map Group 11** Township 25-N Range 8-W	**Map Group 12** Township 25-N Range 7-W
Map Group 13 Township 24-N Range 10-W	**Map Group 14** Township 24-N Range 9-W	**Map Group 15** Township 24-N Range 8-W	**Map Group 16** Township 24-N Range 7-W
Map Group 17 Township 23-N Range 10-W	**Map Group 18** Township 23-N Range 9-W	**Map Group 19** Township 23-N Range 8-W	**Map Group 20** Township 23-N Range 7-W
Map Group 21 Township 22-N Range 10-W	**Map Group 22** Township 22-N Range 9-W	**Map Group 23** Township 22-N Range 8-W	**Map Group 24** Township 22-N Range 7-W
Map Group 25 Township 21-N Range 10-W	**Map Group 26** Township 21-N Range 9-W	**Map Group 27** Township 21-N Range 8-W	**Map Group 28** Township 21-N Range 7-W

——— Legend ———

Howell County, Missouri

Congressional Townships

——— Helpful Hints ———

1 Many Patent-holders and their families settled across county lines. It is always a good idea to check nearby counties for your families (See Map "B").

2 Refer to Map "A" to see a broader view of where this county lies within the State, and Map "B" for a view of the counties surrounding Howell County.

Map D Index: Cities & Towns of Howell County, Missouri

The following represents the Cities and Towns of Howell County (along with the corresponding Map Group in which each is found). Cities and Towns are displayed in both the Road and Historical maps in the Group.

City/Town	Map Group No.
Amy	21
Arditta	17
Brandsville	20
Burnham	6
Carson (historical)	15
Caulfield	21
Chapel	8
Chapin	20
China	22
Cottbus	19
Crider	13
Cull	16
Cureall	17
Egypt Grove	21
Fanchon	12
Frankville	19
Fruitville	20
Globe	24
Grimmet	13
Hocomo	21
Homeland	18
Horton	9
Hutton Valley	6
Lanton	27
Lebo	22
Leota	21
Moody	21
Mott (historical)	23
Mountain View	4
Olden	10
Peace Valley	12
Pocohontas Crossing	20
Pomona	10
Pottersville	17
Siloam Springs	9
South Fork	18
Sterling	1
Summers Addition	15
Trask	3
Turnerville	4
West Plains	15
Wetherhill (historical)	21
White Church	11
Willow Springs	2

Map D - Cities & Towns of Howell County, Missouri

● Sterling

Map Group 1
Township 27-N Range 10-W

Map Group 2
Township 27-N Range 9-W

● Willow Springs

Map Group 3
Township 27-N Range 8-W

● Trask

● Turnerville

Map Group 4
Township 27-N Range 7-W

● Mountain View

Hutton Valley ●

Burnham ●

Chapel ●

Map Group 5
Township 26-N Range 10-W

Map Group 6
Township 26-N Range 9-W

Map Group 7
Township 26-N Range 8-W

Map Group 8
Township 26-N Range 7-W

● Horton

● Pomona

Map Group 10
Township 25-N Range 9-W

● Olden

White Church ●

Peace Valley ●

Map Group 9
Township 25-N Range 10-W

Map Group 11
Township 25-N Range 8-W

Map Group 12
Township 25-N Range 7-W

Siloam Springs ●

● Fanchon

Grimmet ●

Map Group 15
Township 24-N Range 8-W

West Plains ●

Map Group 13
Township 24-N Range 10-W

Map Group 14
Township 24-N Range 9-W

Summers Addition ●

Carson (historical) ●

Map Group 16
Township 24-N Range 7-W

● Cull

● Crider

Pottersville ●

Frankville ●

● Chapin

Pocohontas Crossing ●

● Cureall

Homeland ●

Map Group 19
Township 23-N Range 8-W

Map Group 20
Township 23-N Range 7-W

Brandsville ●

Map Group 17
Township 23-N Range 10-W

Map Group 18
Township 23-N Range 9-W

● Cottbus

South Fork ●

Arditta ●

● Fruitville

Caulfield ●

Egypt Grove ●

Hocomo ●

● Amy

China ●

Wetherhill (historical) ●

Mott (historical) ●

Map Group 24
Township 22-N Range 7-W

● Globe

Map Group 21
Township 22-N Range 10-W

Map Group 22
Township 22-N Range 9-W

Map Group 23
Township 22-N Range 8-W

Leota ●

Moody ●

Lebo ●

Lanton ●

Map Group 25
Township 21-N Range 10-W

Map Group 26
Township 21-N Range 9-W

Map Group 27
Township 21-N Range 8-W

Cornertown ●

Map Group 28
Township 21-N Range 7-W

───── Legend ─────

Howell County, Missouri

Congressional Townships

───── Helpful Hints ─────

1 Cities and towns are marked only at their center-points as published by the USGS and/or NationalAtlas.gov. This often enables us to more closely approximate where these might have existed when first settled.

2 To see more specifically where these Cities & Towns are located within the county, refer to both the Road and Historical maps in the Map-Group referred to above. See also, the Map "D" Index on the opposite page.

Map E Index: Cemeteries of Howell County, Missouri

The following represents many of the Cemeteries of Howell County, along with the corresponding Township Map Group in which each is found. Cemeteries are displayed in both the Road and Historical maps in the Map Groups referred to below.

Cemetery	Map Group No.
Big Spring Cemetery	21
Blue Mound Cemetery	14
Burnham Cemetery	6
Cannon Graveyard	27
Carroll Cemetery	5
Chapin Cemetery	20
Collins Cemetery	13
Cureall Cemetery	17
Davis Cemetery	22
Dripping Springs Cemetery	11
Elk Creek Cemetery	16
Epps Cemetery	6
Francis Cemetery	16
Gill Cemetery	4
Greenlawn Cemetery	4
Homeland Cemetery	18
Horton Cemetery	9
Howell County Cemetery	19
Howell Valley Cemetery	15
Jones Cemetery	1
Joyes Cemetery	21
Koellings Graveyard	28
Ledbetter Cemetery	13
Lone Pine Cemetery	14
Lost Camp Cemetery	7
McElmerry Cemetery	22
Meltabarger Cemetery	20
Mitts Cemetery	13
Moffett Graveyard	6
Mount Zion Cemetery	22
Mountain View Cemetery	4
New Hope Cemetery	12
New Liberty Cemetery	14
New Salem Cemetery	3
Nicks Cemetery	21
Oak Grove Cemetery	9
Oak Lawn Cemetery	15
Parker Cemetery	19
Pleasant Hill Cemetery	14
Pleasant View Cemetery	11
Pottersville Cemetery	17
Rowe Cemetery	3
Setzer Cemetery	17
Siloam Springs Cemetery	13
Spears Graveyard	18
Spring Valley Cemetery	1
Union Grove General Baptist Cemetery	13
Willow Springs City Cemetery	2
Youngblood Cemetery	21

Map E - Cemeteries of Howell County, Missouri

Jones Cemetery

Spring Valley Cemetery

Map Group 2
Township 27-N Range 9-W

Willow Springs City Cemetery

Map Group 1
Township 27-N Range 10-W

New Salem Cemetery

Gill Cemetery

Map Group 4
Township 27-N Range 7-W

Map Group 3
Township 27-N Range 8-W

Mountain View Cemetery

Greenlawn Cemetery

Rowe Cemetery

Moffett Graveyard

Map Group 6
Township 26-N Range 9-W

Burnham Cemetery

Map Group 7
Township 26-N Range 8-W

Lost Camp Cemetery

Map Group 5
Township 26-N Range 10-W

Carroll Cemetery

Epps Cemetery

Map Group 8
Township 26-N Range 7-W

Horton Cemetery

Oak Grove Cemetery

Map Group 11
Township 25-N Range 8-W

Map Group 12
Township 25-N Range 7-W

Map Group 9
Township 25-N Range 10-W

Map Group 10
Township 25-N Range 9-W

New Hope Cemetery

Dripping Springs Cemetery

Pleasant View Cemetery

Siloam Springs Cemetery

Collins Cemetery

Map Group 13
Township 24-N Range 10-W

Mitts Cemetery

New Liberty Cemetery

Lone Pine Cemetery

Map Group 16
Township 24-N Range 7-W

Map Group 14
Township 24-N Range 9-W

Map Group 15
Township 24-N Range 8-W

Elk Creek Cemetery

Union Grove General Baptist Cemetery

Pleasant Hill Cemetery

Oak Lawn Cemetery

Francis Cemetery

Ledbetter Cemetery

Blue Mound Cemetery

Howell Valley Cemetery

Pottersville Cemetery

Map Group 18
Township 23-N Range 9-W

Howell County Cemetery

Chapin Cemetery

Cureall Cemetery

Homeland Cemetery

Parker Cemetery

Map Group 17
Township 23-N Range 10-W

Spears Graveyard

Map Group 19
Township 23-N Range 8-W

Map Group 20
Township 23-N Range 7-W

Setzer Cemetery

Meltabarger Cemetery

Youngblood Cemetery

Map Group 21
Township 22-N Range 10-W

Mount Zion Cemetery

Big Spring Cemetery

Nicks Cemetery

Map Group 22
Township 22-N Range 9-W

Map Group 23
Township 22-N Range 8-W

Map Group 24
Township 22-N Range 7-W

Joyes Cemetery

McElmerry Cemetery

Davis Cemetery

Koellings Graveyard

Map Group 25
Township 21-N Range 10-W

Map Group 26
Township 21-N Range 9-W

Map Group 27
Township 21-N Range 8-W

Cannon Graveyard

Map Group 28 Township 21-N Range 7-W

--- Legend ---

Howell County, Missouri

Congressional Townships

--- Helpful Hints ---

1 Cemeteries are marked at locations as published by the USGS and/or NationalAtlas.gov.

2 To see more specifically where these Cemeteries are located, refer to the Road & Historical maps in the Map-Group referred to above. See also, the Map "E" Index on the opposite page to make sure you don't miss any of the Cemeteries located within this Congressional township.

Surnames in Howell County, Missouri Patents

The following list represents the surnames that we have located in Howell County, Missouri Patents and the number of parcels that we have mapped for each one. Here is a quick way to determine the existence (or not) of Patents to be found in the subsequent indexes and maps of this volume.

Surname	# of Land Parcels	Surname	# of Land Parcels	Surname	# of Land Parcels	Surname	# of Land Parcels
ABERDEEN	2	BATTERTON	3	BOYD	14	BURNET	4
ABRAMS	2	BAUMGARDNER	2	BOYSE	4	BURNETT	1
ACKLIN	4	BAY	6	BRACKETT	2	BURNHAM	2
ACREE	9	BAYS	2	BRADFORD	5	BURNS	1
ADAMS	14	BAZE	2	BRADLEY	6	BURNWORTH	2
ADEN	4	BEAMAN	2	BRADSHAW	14	BURRIS	6
ADKINS	9	BEAN	1	BRAGG	6	BURRISS	4
AKEMAN	3	BECK	2	BRAKEBILL	2	BURROUGHS	16
ALBRECHT	3	BECKER	1	BRAKEFIELD	2	BURTON	17
ALCORN	3	BECKETT	18	BRAMLETT	1	BUSSELL	6
ALESHIRE	1	BEESLEY	1	BRAND	2	BUTCHER	6
ALEXANDER	4	BEESON	1	BRANNOCK	4	BUTLER	2
ALEXANDRIA	1	BEHYMER	1	BRANSTETTER	2	BYERS	8
ALF	2	BELCHER	3	BRASSWELL	3	BYRD	3
ALFORD	1	BELEW	2	BRAY	6	CAGE	3
ALLDREDGE	3	BELL	1	BREEDLOVE	4	CALDWELL	2
ALLEN	12	BELLER	2	BRENNER	3	CALLAHAN	14
ALLRED	4	BENCH	8	BRESSLER	1	CALLISON	2
ALSOP	1	BENNETT	7	BREWINGTON	5	CAMBELL	1
ALSUP	22	BENSON	3	BREWSTER	1	CAMPBELL	41
AMERMAN	1	BENTON	4	BRIDENTHAL	3	CANNON	13
ANDERSON	5	BERRY	7	BRIDGES	19	CANTLEY	4
ANDREWS	3	BESS	6	BRIDWELL	2	CANTRELL	8
ANGLE	1	BEYER	1	BRIGGS	6	CAPIN	1
ANTHONY	2	BIBLE	3	BRILES	3	CAPPS	3
ARELL	3	BIFFLE	2	BRIMHALL	3	CAPSHAW	3
ARNOLD	3	BIGGINS	2	BRISCEY	2	CARD	1
ARVIN	2	BILLING	1	BRISCOE	2	CARGILL	4
ASHBROOK	3	BINGAMAN	13	BRITT	3	CARNER	2
ASHBY	6	BINGERMAN	1	BRIXEY	13	CARPENTER	4
ATCHISON	4	BINGHAM	2	BROOKES	4	CARR	2
ATCHLEY	2	BINKLEY	2	BROOKS	3	CARRELL	18
AUSMAN	1	BISE	8	BROONER	7	CARRIER	1
AUSTIN	4	BISHOP	2	BROTHERTON	12	CARRINGTON	2
AYERS	34	BISSEL	2	BROWER	13	CARRIS	1
BACHAR	2	BISSELL	1	BROWN	31	CARSON	10
BACHMANN	1	BISSETT	3	BROWNING	2	CARTER	13
BACON	8	BIZZELL	2	BROYLS	2	CARTMILL	9
BAILEY	4	BLACK	21	BRUNOT	1	CARTWRIGHT	2
BAILY	3	BLACKBURN	7	BRUSTER	1	CASH	2
BAIRD	1	BLACKWELL	5	BRYAN	4	CASTEEL	2
BAKER	8	BLAGG	3	BRYANT	1	CASTLEMAN	1
BALES	1	BLANKENSHIP	1	BUCHANAN	3	CASWELL	1
BALEY	4	BLEDSOE	6	BUCK	6	CATER	1
BALL	14	BLOSSOM	1	BUCKLAND	2	CATES	15
BALLARD	1	BLYTHE	4	BUCKLEW	1	CAUTLEY	1
BALLINGER	1	BOAK	9	BUCKMASTER	2	CAY	1
BARGER	5	BOATMAN	22	BUCKNER	4	CHAMBERS	2
BARKER	1	BOETTLER	2	BUFF	3	CHANDLER	12
BARKING	6	BOGARD	1	BUFORD	6	CHAPIN	11
BARNES	4	BOLERJACK	13	BUGG	1	CHAPMAN	6
BARNETT	9	BOLIN	4	BUKER	2	CHAPPELL	4
BARR	1	BOLLINGER	8	BULARD	1	CHARLES	5
BARRETT	1	BONBRIGHT	2	BULLARD	2	CHASTAIN	5
BARROWS	2	BOND	10	BUMGARNER	2	CHEATHAM	4
BARTHOLOMEW	4	BOOTMAN	5	BUMPASS	5	CHEEK	6
BARTON	12	BOSS	8	BUNCE	3	CHENEY	5
BASER	1	BOSWELL	1	BUNCH	2	CHERRY	5
BATEMAN	3	BOUCHER	2	BUNDREN	2	CHESNUT	2
BATES	6	BOWERS	1	BURDEN	6	CHESTNUT	3
BATEY	2	BOWLES	2	BURGESS	8	CHOAT	2
BATMAN	3	BOYCE	1	BURK	2	CHOWNING	17

Surname	# of Land Parcels	Surname	# of Land Parcels	Surname	# of Land Parcels	Surname	# of Land Parcels
CHRISTENSEN	3	CRAPO	3	DORRIS	4	ENO	4
CHRISTESSON	1	CRENSHAW	1	DORSEY	10	EPLEY	5
CHRISTOPHER	3	CRIDER	10	DOTY	3	EPPS	4
CHRISTY	1	CRIPE	4	DOUGHERTY	1	ERWIN	3
CHURCHILL	3	CRISP	7	DOWELL	5	ESKRIDGE	2
CLARK	42	CRISPIN	1	DOWNING	2	ESSEX	3
CLARKE	1	CRITCHER	1	DOWNS	1	ESTES	1
CLAXTON	4	CRITES	1	DRAKE	1	EVANS	17
CLAYTER	2	CRONER	1	DRENNEN	3	EVELAND	7
CLAYTON	6	CROOM	3	DRIEHAUS	1	EVERED	4
CLEARY	3	CROSS	2	DRINNON	3	EVINS	3
CLEMENT	3	CROUCH	3	DRIVER	2	EWART	1
CLEMMONES	3	CROW	6	DRUMRIGHT	4	EZELL	4
CLEMMONS	3	CROWDER	10	DRUMWRIGHT	2	FADDIS	1
CLEVELAND	4	CROWLEY	1	DRYBREAD	3	FAIR	3
CLICK	6	CRUM	4	DRYDEN	2	FALWELL	7
CLIFF	2	CRUMLEY	3	DRYER	5	FARE	3
CLIFFORD	2	CULBERTSON	4	DRYMAN	1	FARIS	1
CLIFTON	1	CULL	1	DRYMON	3	FARMER	12
CLIMER	2	CUNNINGHAM	20	DUCKERING	2	FARQUAR	2
CLINGINGSMITH	2	CURRY	14	DUDLEY	2	FARR	4
CLINKINGBEARD	3	CURTIS	3	DUKE	4	FARRAR	2
CLONINGER	7	CUTLER	2	DUNAVIN	2	FARRIS	1
CLOONEY	1	DABBS	2	DUNEHEW	1	FAST	1
CLOWNY	3	DAILY	3	DUNHAM	4	FAULCONER	1
COBB	8	DALSING	1	DUNIVAN	1	FAUROT	1
COBBS	2	DAMON	1	DUNKIN	13	FAVORITE	1
COCHRAN	9	DANIEL	9	DUNKLEBARGER	4	FEAMAN	2
COCK	7	DAUGHERTY	2	DUNLAP	6	FEATHER	5
COFFEE	8	DAVIDSON	10	DUNN	2	FEATHERINGILL	6
COFFMAN	4	DAVIES	2	DUNNE	2	FEATHERSTON	2
COFFY	2	DAVIS	48	DUNNILL	1	FEGAN	3
COLDIRON	1	DAVISON	2	DUNNING	3	FEHR	2
COLE	7	DAWSON	5	DURFEE	3	FELAND	3
COLEMAN	3	DE WITT	1	DURHAM	2	FELTS	3
COLLENS	1	DEARING	2	DURNEL	2	FERGUSON	23
COLLIER	6	DEATHERAGE	1	DURST	1	FERRELL	3
COLLINS	53	DEATON	5	DYER	2	FERRIS	1
COLMERY	2	DEBOARD	11	DYKES	2	FIELDS	5
COLTER	1	DECKER	3	EADES	3	FILES	1
COLTHARP	1	DEEMS	3	EARLS	2	FILLMAN	3
COLYER	3	DEITZ	3	EASLEY	22	FINDLEY	15
COMSTOCK	9	DEJARNATH	3	EASTERLY	1	FINE	4
CONLEY	1	DELAY	1	EASTRELY	4	FINEY	1
CONNER	4	DENGLER	1	EATON	6	FINNEY	5
COOK	21	DENNIS	1	EBLEN	9	FISCHER	5
COOPER	15	DENNY	2	EBLIN	3	FISHER	1
COOPPER	2	DENT	3	ECHOLS	2	FITE	3
COOSE	1	DENTON	6	EDELMAN	3	FITZSIMMONS	6
COPE	2	DENZEL	8	EDGAR	2	FLEMING	1
CORDES	3	DERINGER	3	EDMONSTON	2	FLESHER	3
CORDILL	8	DERRICK	1	EDMOUNDSON	4	FLINN	1
COTHRAN	1	DESITS	7	EDSON	1	FLOOD	7
COTTLE	2	DEXTER	5	EDWARDS	4	FOLEY	1
COUNTS	3	DICKSON	5	EIDSON	4	FOOTE	1
COURSEY	2	DIEHL	1	ELDER	1	FORD	12
COURTNEY	1	DIELLE	6	ELDRINGHOFF	12	FOREST	2
COVALT	3	DILL	8	ELKIN	2	FORESTER	1
COVER	1	DILLINDER	2	ELKINS	3	FOSTER	1
COVERT	2	DIXON	7	ELLEDGE	11	FOUST	5
COVINGTON	3	DOCIA	1	ELLINGTON	4	FOUTS	3
COWAN	3	DOCKERY	2	ELLIOTT	9	FOWLER	14
COX	26	DOCKEY	1	ELLIS	3	FOX	50
COZORT	1	DODD	7	ELLWOOD	3	FRAKES	3
CRABTREE	3	DODSON	3	EMERSON	4	FRANK	3
CRAFTON	1	DOERING	2	EMMONS	5	FRANKLIN	3
CRAHAN	1	DOLLENS	3	ENDECOTT	14	FRAY	3
CRAIG	11	DOLLINS	1	ENDICOTT	13	FRAYNER	5
CRAIN	1	DONNELLY	1	ENGLAND	6	FRAZEE	2
CRANE	123	DOOLEY	2	ENGLE	2	FRAZER	1

Surname	# of Land Parcels	Surname	# of Land Parcels	Surname	# of Land Parcels	Surname	# of Land Parcels
FRAZIER	3	GOODMAN	13	HARKEY	1	HOGGATT	5
FREEMAN	1	GOODMILLER	1	HARKINS	5	HOKE	1
FREEZE	1	GOODNO	3	HARLAN	3	HOKER	1
FRENCH	3	GOODWIN	2	HARLEY	3	HOLBROOK	4
FRIEND	1	GORMAN	2	HARLOW	7	HOLCOMB	3
FRISBEY	3	GOYER	9	HARMAN	4	HOLDEN	13
FRITH	4	GRAGG	1	HARMON	5	HOLEMAN	4
FRIZELL	3	GRAHAM	10	HARPER	4	HOLLAND	4
FRUSHOUR	2	GRAHNERT	1	HARREN	1	HOLLINGSHAD	3
FUDGE	1	GRAMMER	4	HARRIS	29	HOLLINGSWORTH	3
FULENWIDER	2	GRANT	2	HARRISON	9	HOLLOWAY	11
FULENWIDNER	6	GRAVES	7	HARROD	3	HOLMAN	1
FULLER	10	GRAY	1	HARSCH	4	HOLMES	3
FULLERLOVE	3	GREEN	25	HART	4	HOLT	2
FULS	6	GREENSTREET	2	HARTMAN	17	HOLZSCHEITER	3
FUNK	2	GREENWAY	3	HARVEY	5	HOMANS	4
GABBERT	1	GREENWOOD	2	HATCHER	6	HOMESLEY	2
GADBERRY	2	GREGG	1	HATFIELD	3	HON	3
GAGE	3	GREGORY	7	HATHWAY	1	HOOD	5
GAINES	6	GRIESEL	3	HAVIN	2	HOOPER	2
GALBREATH	1	GRIFFITH	25	HAWKINS	14	HOOSE	3
GALE	3	GRIMMETT	3	HAYDEN	2	HOOTEN	4
GALESBERRY	1	GRIPE	1	HAYNES	4	HOOVER	4
GALLAHER	4	GRISHAM	6	HAYS	9	HOPE	6
GALLAWAY	1	GROCE	2	HAYT	3	HOPKINS	45
GALLOWAY	9	GROFUSE	1	HEAD	1	HORN	2
GAMBER	5	GROTE	1	HEALEY	1	HORSMAN	9
GAMBLE	3	GUILLIAMS	4	HEATH	3	HORSTEN	4
GARLETTS	2	GULLEY	5	HEATON	5	HOSHOUR	3
GARNER	1	GULLY	9	HEINRICH	4	HOSKINSON	1
GAROUTTE	7	GUNDER	2	HELM	2	HOUGH	1
GARRET	3	GUNDY	3	HELMS	2	HOUGHTON	6
GARRETT	2	GUNN	3	HEMPHILL	8	HOUSE	4
GARRIGIN	3	GUNTER	9	HENDERSON	12	HOVEY	6
GARTEN	1	GUNZ	6	HENDRICK	2	HOWARD	21
GASTIAN	1	GUTHRIE	1	HENER	1	HOWELL	58
GATTON	2	GUY	2	HENRY	39	HOWERTON	1
GAYER	1	HADDOCK	4	HENSHAW	3	HOY	2
GEBBERS	1	HADLEY	1	HENSLEY	4	HOYT	1
GEISLER	6	HAGAN	3	HENSON	5	HUCKSTEP	3
GENTRY	1	HAHN	3	HERMAN	3	HUDDLESTON	2
GEYER	3	HALDEMAN	1	HERNDON	15	HUDLOW	8
GIBBS	8	HALE	9	HEROD	2	HUDSON	12
GIBSON	8	HALKYARD	4	HERREN	2	HUFF	8
GILBERT	6	HALL	39	HERRICK	1	HUFFHINES	3
GILES	2	HALLETT	7	HERRIEN	3	HUGHES	10
GILL	8	HALLOWAY	1	HERRIN	9	HUGHLETT	3
GILLELAND	1	HALSELL	3	HESTERLY	3	HUGHS	1
GILLIAM	5	HALSEY	2	HEWITT	2	HULL	9
GILLILAND	3	HALSTEAD	3	HEYING	3	HULS	2
GILLINGHAM	1	HAMBY	2	HIBBARD	2	HUMPHREY	3
GILMORE	4	HAMEL	1	HIBNER	4	HUNSPERGER	3
GIPSON	2	HAMILTON	9	HICKS	5	HUNT	15
GLADDEN	2	HAMMOND	2	HIGH	1	HUNTER	14
GLASS	3	HAMMONDS	1	HIGHTOWER	3	HUSTON	2
GLEEN	2	HAMMONS	1	HIGLEY	1	HUTCHESON	2
GLENDENING	1	HANCOCK	3	HILER	8	HUTCHINS	2
GLENN	2	HANEY	11	HILL	8	HYLTON	2
GLINN	4	HANKINS	2	HILTON	2	HYNES	3
GLOSSUP	4	HANN	5	HINDS	4	ING	1
GOBBEL	3	HANNAH	2	HINES	8	INGLE	3
GODAT	3	HANNER	3	HINKLE	1	INGOLD	9
GODDARD	5	HARBER	2	HIXON	7	INGRAM	8
GODSEY	3	HARBINSON	1	HIXSON	1	INMAN	4
GODSY	17	HARBISON	3	HOAG	3	IRVIN	4
GOLDSBERRY	11	HARDCASTLE	2	HOBBS	4	IRWIN	1
GOLESBERRY	1	HARDESTY	3	HOCUTT	2	JACKSON	19
GOOD	7	HARDIN	7	HODGES	7	JAMES	5
GOODELL	2	HARDY	1	HOEY	2	JARGENSON	4
GOODGION	1	HARGROVES	2	HOGAN	4	JARRELL	4

Surname	# of Land Parcels	Surname	# of Land Parcels	Surname	# of Land Parcels	Surname	# of Land Parcels
JAYNE	3	LANE	3	MACKEY	11	MCGEE	6
JEFFERY	1	LANG	3	MACLAIN	2	MCGINTY	7
JENKINS	17	LANGLEY	5	MACORMIC	1	MCGOLDRICK	5
JEREMIAH	3	LANGSTON	8	MADDEN	3	MCGONIGAL	3
JOHNS	12	LANNING	2	MADDOX	1	MCGOWAN	1
JOHNSON	71	LARA	3	MADES	2	MCGOWEN	1
JOHNSTON	13	LASATER	1	MAHAN	5	MCGRATH	2
JONES	74	LASSWELL	4	MAHON	2	MCGRAW	2
JORDAN	1	LAUGHERY	3	MAHONEY	2	MCGUIRE	2
JUDD	3	LAURANCE	3	MAHORNEY	2	MCHAN	9
JUDKINS	3	LAWHEAD	1	MAIN	4	MCHANN	2
JUERN	2	LAWHORN	7	MALONE	2	MCKANNA	1
JULIEN	2	LAWING	7	MANESS	1	MCKIM	4
KARR	10	LAYTON	1	MANGUM	1	MCKNIGHT	2
KAUFMAN	3	LE FORCE	2	MANNING	1	MCLAIN	2
KAY	1	LEARNARD	52	MANNIX	1	MCMAHAN	2
KEE	4	LEATHERS	1	MANNON	1	MCMAHON	2
KEELE	1	LECKRON	1	MANSFIELD	3	MCMANEMIN	2
KEELER	6	LEDBETTER	11	MANZE	2	MCMASTER	1
KEEN	2	LEE	8	MARAT	2	MCMILLIN	2
KEIRN	3	LEEDOM	3	MARITT	3	MCMURTRY	10
KEISTER	8	LEEPER	4	MARKHAM	3	MCNAY	3
KEITHLY	6	LEFEVER	2	MARONEY	1	MCNEELY	3
KEIVER	4	LELAND	1	MARRITT	1	MCRIPPEE	1
KELIN	1	LEMONS	2	MARSHALL	5	MCTHOMPSON	2
KELLUM	1	LEONARD	2	MARTIN	24	MEADOWS	3
KELLY	4	LETSINGER	2	MASON	8	MEARS	1
KELSO	2	LEWEY	3	MATLOCK	5	MEDLEY	1
KENAGA	13	LEWIS	15	MATNEY	14	MEDLIN	3
KENEGA	2	LIGETH	1	MATTHEWS	5	MEDLOCK	3
KENNEY	4	LILE	3	MAVONEY	2	MEINECKE	2
KENSLOW	6	LILES	1	MAWHINNEY	3	MELTON	3
KENT	3	LIMB	5	MAXEY	3	MENDENHALL	3
KERNOCK	5	LINDERER	8	MAXWELL	6	MEREDITH	1
KERSHNER	1	LINGO	1	MAY	3	MERIDETH	4
KIDD	1	LINTHICUM	5	MAYHEW	1	MERIDITH	2
KIDWELL	1	LIVESAY	1	MCAFEE	3	MERIEDITH	3
KIERER	1	LIVINGSTON	13	MCALLISTER	3	MERRILL	2
KILE	11	LIVSAY	3	MCANALLY	2	MERRITT	6
KILLION	6	LLOYD	3	MCBRIDE	2	MEYER	7
KILLOUGH	8	LOAGUE	2	MCCABE	3	MIDDAUGH	2
KIMBALL	1	LOCH	2	MCCALL	3	MIDDLETON	2
KIMBROUGH	3	LOCK	2	MCCALLISTER	2	MILKS	3
KINCHLOE	3	LODER	2	MCCALLON	2	MILLARD	1
KING	24	LOGAN	4	MCCAMMAN	3	MILLBANKS	3
KINGDON	2	LOGSTON	1	MCCAMMON	5	MILLER	37
KINION	6	LONG	15	MCCAMRON	2	MILLS	3
KINKEAD	3	LONGDEN	1	MCCANNON	3	MILLSAPS	2
KINSOLVING	4	LORD	3	MCCARDEL	3	MILLSPAUGH	2
KIRKPATRICK	2	LOUTHEN	3	MCCLAIN	1	MINER	1
KIRKWOOD	1	LOUTRELL	2	MCCLANAHAN	1	MIRES	1
KISER	2	LOVAN	14	MCCLELLAN	3	MITCHELL	17
KISINGER	3	LOVEL	3	MCCLINTOCK	4	MITTELSTETTER	3
KISNER	2	LOVELACE	2	MCCOLLUM	4	MITTS	3
KNIGHT	6	LOVINS	1	MCCOMB	4	MIZE	4
KNOWLTON	5	LOWREY	5	MCCOMICK	1	MOBACK	2
KNOX	4	LOWRY	3	MCCOY	6	MODRALL	12
KOLLING	1	LOY	10	MCCRACKEN	1	MOFFITT	4
KOONCE	5	LUCK	1	MCCRITE	2	MONGER	4
KRAUSE	3	LUDWIG	8	MCCULLOCH	5	MONKS	19
KROHN	5	LUKE	2	MCCULLOUGH	5	MONTGOMERY	9
KUEPEL	1	LUMBLEY	2	MCDANIEL	30	MOODY	1
KURSEY	3	LUMPS	2	MCDONAL	3	MOORE	14
LAFFOON	6	LUNG	3	MCELFATRICK	2	MOREHEAD	3
LAIR	5	LUTH	4	MCELMURRY	2	MORELAND	4
LAIRD	4	LUTHER	2	MCELRATH	2	MORGAN	13
LAMBE	3	LUTTES	2	MCEMBREE	4	MORRIS	16
LAMONS	15	LYNCH	4	MCFADDIN	6	MORRISON	3
LANCASTER	6	LYON	2	MCFALLS	3	MORROW	2
LANCE	1	MACK	9	MCFARLAND	15	MORSE	1

Surname	# of Land Parcels	Surname	# of Land Parcels	Surname	# of Land Parcels	Surname	# of Land Parcels
MORTON	2	OWINGS	2	POTTER	1	RILEY	11
MOSELEY	1	PACE	2	POTTLE	3	RINCK	4
MOSS	2	PACKMAN	2	POTTS	5	RISLEY	7
MOXLEY	2	PADGETT	10	POWELL	8	RITCHEY	4
MUHL	1	PADON	1	POWLES	1	ROACH	2
MULLANY	2	PAINE	2	PRANTL	2	ROADS	3
MULLINIX	1	PALMER	6	PRATT	37	ROBARDS	2
MULLINS	4	PANE	1	PRESLEY	3	ROBBINS	8
MURDOCK	1	PARDEW	1	PRESSLEY	5	ROBERDS	2
MURPHEY	3	PARKER	3	PRESTON	1	ROBERSON	4
MURRAY	2	PARKS	2	PREWITT	6	ROBERTS	31
MURRELL	5	PARRISH	1	PRICE	3	ROBERTSON	9
MURREY	3	PARSONS	13	PRITCHETT	3	ROBEY	2
MUSE	5	PARTNEY	1	PRIVETT	2	ROBINS	3
MUSGROVE	7	PASCALL	1	PRIVETTE	3	ROBINSON	9
MUSTION	10	PASCHAL	5	PROCK	1	ROBISON	1
MUSTON	1	PATE	4	PROFFIT	3	RODE	3
MYERS	4	PATTERSON	2	PROFFITT	13	ROEHR	3
MYRES	1	PAUL	2	PRUITT	1	ROGERS	3
MYRICK	2	PAYNE	9	PUGH	6	ROHDE	3
MYZELL	2	PAYTON	1	PURCHASE	2	ROHR	4
NAHM	3	PEACE	11	PURTEE	2	ROLLINS	6
NALE	5	PEARCE	7	QUADE	2	ROMANS	5
NANCE	7	PEARSON	12	QUEEN	1	ROMINE	6
NANEY	5	PEASE	1	QUINNAN	3	ROOP	1
NASH	8	PEAY	1	RADFORD	1	ROOT	2
NEASE	4	PEDRICK	1	RAFFERTY	2	ROOTES	1
NEEDHAM	3	PEGUES	1	RAGAN	1	ROPER	2
NELSON	4	PELTON	1	RAGSDALE	1	ROSEMBUM	1
NETTLETON	19	PENCE	8	RAINBOLT	3	ROSENBUM	4
NEWBERRY	12	PENDERGRAFT	5	RALLS	1	ROTH	1
NEWKIRK	4	PENDERGRASS	1	RAMSBURG	4	ROTHWELL	4
NEWSOM	3	PENN	2	RAMSEY	15	ROUNTREE	1
NEWTON	6	PENNINGER	1	RAND	4	ROUSH	13
NICHOLAS	23	PENNINGTON	5	RANDEL	5	ROWDEN	1
NICHOLS	3	PEOPLES	2	RANEY	4	ROWE	1
NICKELSON	3	PERKINS	10	RANKIN	2	ROWLETT	6
NICKENS	1	PERRIN	2	RATLIFF	2	ROYSE	2
NICKS	34	PERRY	9	RAULISON	2	RUBENDORF	1
NOLTE	5	PERRYMAN	2	RAY	13	RUDD	1
NORDYKE	2	PETER	2	RAYMOND	4	RUSHING	4
NORMAN	7	PETREY	3	READER	1	RUSSELL	9
NORRIS	1	PETRY	1	REAVES	4	RUTHERS	4
NORTON	1	PETTIT	3	REDDEN	3	RUTLEDGE	5
NULL	3	PETTY	1	REDMAN	2	RYAN	3
OAKES	1	PFENNIGHAUSEN	18	REED	19	RYNERSON	3
OAKS	6	PHELAN	4	REESE	15	SACKVILLE	2
OBRIEN	3	PHELPS	5	REEVES	8	SALLTOW	3
OCONNER	3	PHILLIPS	3	REICH	1	SALMON	3
ODOM	2	PHIPPS	8	REID	18	SALTSMAN	3
ODONNELL	2	PICKARD	6	REIGER	2	SAMPLE	1
OGDEN	2	PICKLE	2	REILEY	2	SANDERS	2
OGLE	1	PIERCE	2	RENFRO	3	SANMANN	1
OKELLEY	2	PIETY	2	RENFROW	1	SANTEE	1
OKES	3	PITMAN	3	RENNEKER	4	SAPP	4
OLDEN	15	PITTS	3	RENNER	2	SAPPS	1
OLIVER	1	PLANK	3	REYNOLDS	12	SARGENT	1
OLSON	3	PLAYFORTH	1	RHOADES	2	SAWYER	2
ONEY	3	PODRABSKE	4	RHOADS	3	SCALES	7
ORCHARD	3	POE	6	RHOTON	1	SCHAFLER	3
ORIELLEY	1	POKE	3	RICE	11	SCHALLER	3
ORME	1	POLK	7	RICHARD	4	SCHAUB	2
OROURKE	1	POLLOCK	2	RICHARDSON	14	SCHELL	1
ORTNER	1	POLSON	2	RICHEY	5	SCHNEIDER	7
ORVIS	2	POMEROY	1	RICHMAN	3	SCHRIVER	1
OSBORN	7	POOL	11	RIDDLE	4	SCOGGIN	18
OVERMAN	6	POOLE	1	RIDEOUT	2	SCOTT	3
OVERTON	1	POORE	1	RIDGEWAY	4	SCROGGINS	1
OWEN	1	POPE	5	RIGGS	11	SCRUGGS	2
OWENS	4	PORTER	12	RIGSBY	5	SEABORN	7

Surname	# of Land Parcels	Surname	# of Land Parcels	Surname	# of Land Parcels	Surname	# of Land Parcels
SEAL	3	SPAHR	2	TABOR	26	VEST	4
SEATS	1	SPARKS	12	TAFTON	2	VICKERS	2
SEATT	3	SPEAKER	1	TAINTER	6	VINCENT	8
SEAVER	3	SPEAKMAN	4	TALENT	2	VOEGELE	2
SEAY	16	SPEARS	20	TALLEY	2	VON BLUCHER	5
SEELY	1	SPENCE	9	TALLY	2	WADDLE	2
SEIBERLING	1	SPENCER	16	TARWATER	2	WADE	5
SELLS	11	SPRADLIN	1	TAYLOR	34	WADLEY	11
SELSOR	2	SPRADLING	9	TEDDER	1	WADLY	1
SETTLE	1	SPRENGEL	1	TENANT	2	WAID	6
SEUTEFF	3	SPRIGGS	3	TERRY	7	WALKER	41
SHADWELL	3	SPRINKEL	1	TESENMEIER	2	WALL	2
SHANKS	2	SRIVER	5	THEISSEN	4	WALLACE	8
SHARP	8	ST CLAIR	1	THEOBALD	2	WALLICE	7
SHAVER	9	STACEY	1	THOMAS	44	WALLIN	8
SHAW	7	STACY	5	THOMASSON	1	WALTER	1
SHEA	3	STAGGS	2	THOMPSON	23	WALTERS	2
SHEARHEART	1	STANBERY	2	THORNTON	7	WARCUM	6
SHEARY	1	STAPLES	1	THRASHER	3	WARD	10
SHELDON	1	STARK	3	THRELKELD	2	WARNER	7
SHELTON	6	STARKEY	5	THURMAN	1	WARREN	3
SHEPARD	6	STEELE	1	TICE	4	WASHBURN	2
SHEPPARD	2	STEELMAN	1	TILSON	13	WATERS	8
SHERLEY	2	STEGER	2	TIPTON	3	WATKINS	4
SHERRELL	3	STEIN	5	TISDALE	3	WATSON	16
SHERREY	3	STEININGER	1	TOBLER	1	WEATHERBY	3
SHERWIN	1	STEPHENS	12	TOMLINSON	12	WEATHERLY	8
SHERWOOD	1	STEPHENSON	2	TOOMEY	2	WEAVER	9
SHEWBART	2	STEPP	9	TOW	3	WEBB	15
SHINKLE	1	STEUART	2	TOWNLEY	2	WEBSTER	3
SHIPMAN	10	STEVENS	6	TRANBARGER	1	WEEKS	3
SHIPMANN	1	STEVENSON	1	TREVOR	2	WEIBEL	3
SHIRL	1	STEWARD	2	TRICHAUS	3	WEIBERT	2
SHOCKLEY	7	STEWART	10	TRIM	2	WEIR	1
SHOWERS	6	STINE	2	TRINDLE	5	WELCH	3
SHREEVE	3	STINECIPHER	3	TROLL	3	WELKER	3
SHRIVEAR	3	STOCKTON	3	TROTTER	1	WELLER	10
SHRIVER	1	STOGSDILL	2	TROUTMAN	1	WELLINGTON	2
SHULTZ	1	STOKES	7	TUCKER	3	WELLS	12
SHURLEY	3	STONE	5	TULL	4	WERKING	1
SHUTTEE	1	STORY	2	TUNE	2	WESCOTT	9
SICKLY	1	STOUT	7	TUPPER	5	WEST	15
SIDWELL	1	STOVALL	1	TURLEY	2	WESTERN	2
SIGLER	3	STRAINN	3	TURNBAUGH	4	WESTMORELAND	3
SIMMONS	9	STRANGE	2	TURNER	16	WETHERFORD	6
SIMPSON	3	STRAUSE	1	TURPEN	7	WHARTON	3
SIMS	2	STREET	7	TYREE	1	WHATLEY	3
SINGLETON	2	STRICKLAND	2	UITTS	8	WHEELER	3
SISSON	10	STRIEBEL	1	ULRICH	5	WHITAKER	2
SITZS	1	STRINGER	1	UMPHREY	2	WHITE	10
SKAGGS	2	STROTHER	2	UNDERWOOD	2	WHITLOCK	1
SKINNER	5	STROUB	1	UNGER	8	WHITNEY	2
SLATER	3	STUART	10	UPTON	8	WHITTAKER	1
SLAYBARK	2	STUBBLEFIELD	3	USHER	8	WICKER	2
SLOAN	9	STUBBS	3	UTLEY	4	WIDENER	2
SMALLEY	2	STUDDARD	2	VALENTINE	3	WIGGINS	2
SMITH	155	SUETEFF	3	VAN DERNOEF	5	WIGGS	2
SMITHER	2	SUMMERS	16	VAN METRE	2	WIKOFF	3
SMOTHERMAN	2	SUNDBYE	5	VAN VORHIS	1	WILBANKS	2
SMOTHERMON	7	SURRETT	1	VANDERHOEF	3	WILCOX	4
SMOUTHIRMAN	1	SURRITT	1	VANDERPOOL	1	WILES	2
SNEAD	1	SUSONG	1	VANDIVER	2	WILKERSON	5
SNIDER	3	SUTTLE	4	VASSAW	3	WILL	5
SNODGRASS	1	SUTTON	5	VAUGHAN	10	WILLBANKS	6
SNOWDEN	2	SWAN	5	VAUGHN	6	WILLEFORD	3
SOOTS	1	SWEARINGEN	11	VENTLE	3	WILLIAMS	62
SOUTH	2	SWECKER	2	VENUS	4	WILLIAMSON	4
SOUTHARD	1	SWIFT	4	VERBICK	5	WILLIS	6
SOWERS	4	SYMONDS	1	VERNON	5	WILSON	36
SPADLING	3	SZOPEINSKI	1	VESS	3	WINCHESTER	3

Surname	# of Land Parcels
WINDER	3
WINNINGHAM	6
WINSTON	2
WINSTRAN	6
WINTER	4
WINTERS	1
WIRE	2
WISE	1
WISEMAN	7
WISHON	1
WISNER	3
WOOD	15
WOODARD	1
WOODREL	6
WOODRELL	1
WOODRING	2
WOODROME	5
WOODS	5
WOODSIDE	8
WOODWORTH	4
WOODY	8
WOOSTER	2
WORCESTER	2
WRIGHT	32
WURL	3
WYATT	10
WYMAN	1
WYRICK	1
WYZARD	5
YARNELL	6
YATES	2
YEAGER	2
YENNEY	4
YORBER	1
YORK	3
YOUNG	12
YOUNGBLOOD	4
YOUNGS	4
ZEEBE	1
ZEEK	1
ZUMWALT	5

Surname/Township Index

This Index allows you to determine which *Township Map Group(s)* contain individuals with the following surnames. Each *Map Group* has a corresponding full-name index of all individuals who obtained patents for land within its Congressional township's borders. After each index you will find the Patent Map to which it refers, and just thereafter, you can view the township's Road Map and Historical Map, with the latter map displaying streams, railroads, and more.

So, once you find your Surname here, proceed to the Index at the beginning of the **Map Group** indicated below.

Surname	Map Group	Parcels of Land	Meridian/Township/Range		
ABERDEEN	**3**	2	5th PM	27-N	8-W
ABRAMS	**23**	2	5th PM	22-N	8-W
ACKLIN	**7**	4	5th PM	26-N	8-W
ACREE	**11**	9	5th PM	25-N	8-W
ADAMS	**17**	4	5th PM	23-N	10-W
" "	**13**	4	5th PM	24-N	10-W
" "	**18**	1	5th PM	23-N	9-W
" "	**11**	5	5th PM	25-N	8-W
ADEN	**19**	3	5th PM	23-N	8-W
" "	**12**	1	5th PM	25-N	7-W
ADKINS	**25**	3	5th PM	21-N	10-W
" "	**11**	3	5th PM	25-N	8-W
" "	**21**	3	5th PM	22-N	10-W
AKEMAN	**14**	3	5th PM	24-N	9-W
ALBRECHT	**19**	3	5th PM	23-N	8-W
ALCORN	**15**	3	5th PM	24-N	8-W
ALESHIRE	**8**	1	5th PM	26-N	7-W
ALEXANDER	**6**	3	5th PM	26-N	9-W
" "	**20**	1	5th PM	23-N	7-W
ALEXANDRIA	**18**	1	5th PM	23-N	9-W
ALF	**1**	2	5th PM	27-N	10-W
ALFORD	**21**	1	5th PM	22-N	10-W
ALLDREDGE	**4**	3	5th PM	27-N	7-W
ALLEN	**18**	3	5th PM	23-N	9-W
" "	**19**	1	5th PM	23-N	8-W
" "	**24**	5	5th PM	22-N	7-W
" "	**21**	3	5th PM	22-N	10-W
ALLRED	**13**	4	5th PM	24-N	10-W
ALSOP	**2**	1	5th PM	27-N	9-W
ALSUP	**6**	4	5th PM	26-N	9-W
" "	**2**	9	5th PM	27-N	9-W
" "	**27**	3	5th PM	21-N	8-W
" "	**18**	1	5th PM	23-N	9-W
" "	**28**	3	5th PM	21-N	7-W
" "	**9**	1	5th PM	25-N	10-W
" "	**13**	1	5th PM	24-N	10-W
AMERMAN	**18**	1	5th PM	23-N	9-W
ANDERSON	**22**	2	5th PM	22-N	9-W
" "	**21**	2	5th PM	22-N	10-W
" "	**2**	1	5th PM	27-N	9-W
ANDREWS	**15**	3	5th PM	24-N	8-W
ANGLE	**24**	1	5th PM	22-N	7-W
ANTHONY	**28**	2	5th PM	21-N	7-W
ARELL	**18**	1	5th PM	23-N	9-W

Surname	Map Group	Parcels of Land	Meridian/Township/Range		
ARELL (Cont'd)	**2**	2	5th PM	27-N	9-W
ARNOLD	**2**	1	5th PM	27-N	9-W
" "	**18**	2	5th PM	23-N	9-W
ARVIN	**23**	2	5th PM	22-N	8-W
ASHBROOK	**19**	3	5th PM	23-N	8-W
ASHBY	**2**	1	5th PM	27-N	9-W
" "	**19**	2	5th PM	23-N	8-W
" "	**3**	3	5th PM	27-N	8-W
ATCHISON	**8**	1	5th PM	26-N	7-W
" "	**12**	3	5th PM	25-N	7-W
ATCHLEY	**2**	2	5th PM	27-N	9-W
AUSMAN	**6**	1	5th PM	26-N	9-W
AUSTIN	**15**	4	5th PM	24-N	8-W
AYERS	**12**	6	5th PM	25-N	7-W
" "	**8**	28	5th PM	26-N	7-W
BACHAR	**1**	2	5th PM	27-N	10-W
BACHMANN	**19**	1	5th PM	23-N	8-W
BACON	**15**	6	5th PM	24-N	8-W
" "	**11**	2	5th PM	25-N	8-W
BAILEY	**23**	3	5th PM	22-N	8-W
" "	**19**	1	5th PM	23-N	8-W
BAILY	**21**	3	5th PM	22-N	10-W
BAIRD	**14**	1	5th PM	24-N	9-W
BAKER	**21**	3	5th PM	22-N	10-W
" "	**13**	1	5th PM	24-N	10-W
" "	**10**	2	5th PM	25-N	9-W
" "	**18**	2	5th PM	23-N	9-W
BALES	**21**	1	5th PM	22-N	10-W
BALEY	**23**	1	5th PM	22-N	8-W
" "	**16**	3	5th PM	24-N	7-W
BALL	**24**	5	5th PM	22-N	7-W
" "	**26**	8	5th PM	21-N	9-W
" "	**22**	1	5th PM	22-N	9-W
BALLARD	**14**	1	5th PM	24-N	9-W
BALLINGER	**14**	1	5th PM	24-N	9-W
BARGER	**22**	1	5th PM	22-N	9-W
" "	**23**	2	5th PM	22-N	8-W
" "	**24**	2	5th PM	22-N	7-W
BARKER	**22**	1	5th PM	22-N	9-W
BARKING	**7**	6	5th PM	26-N	8-W
BARNES	**14**	1	5th PM	24-N	9-W
" "	**11**	2	5th PM	25-N	8-W
" "	**15**	1	5th PM	24-N	8-W
BARNETT	**12**	6	5th PM	25-N	7-W
" "	**3**	1	5th PM	27-N	8-W
" "	**16**	2	5th PM	24-N	7-W
BARR	**14**	1	5th PM	24-N	9-W
BARRETT	**18**	1	5th PM	23-N	9-W
BARROWS	**18**	2	5th PM	23-N	9-W
BARTHOLOMEW	**18**	3	5th PM	23-N	9-W
" "	**19**	1	5th PM	23-N	8-W
BARTON	**12**	2	5th PM	25-N	7-W
" "	**2**	1	5th PM	27-N	9-W
" "	**10**	5	5th PM	25-N	9-W
" "	**11**	2	5th PM	25-N	8-W
" "	**7**	1	5th PM	26-N	8-W
" "	**8**	1	5th PM	26-N	7-W
BASER	**12**	1	5th PM	25-N	7-W
BATEMAN	**23**	1	5th PM	22-N	8-W
" "	**27**	2	5th PM	21-N	8-W

Surname	Map Group	Parcels of Land	Meridian/Township/Range		
BATES	**24**	3	5th PM	22-N	7-W
" "	**11**	2	5th PM	25-N	8-W
" "	**10**	1	5th PM	25-N	9-W
BATEY	**15**	2	5th PM	24-N	8-W
BATMAN	**24**	3	5th PM	22-N	7-W
BATTERTON	**17**	2	5th PM	23-N	10-W
" "	**21**	1	5th PM	22-N	10-W
BAUMGARDNER	**3**	2	5th PM	27-N	8-W
BAY	**8**	4	5th PM	26-N	7-W
" "	**12**	2	5th PM	25-N	7-W
BAYS	**14**	2	5th PM	24-N	9-W
BAZE	**21**	2	5th PM	22-N	10-W
BEAMAN	**21**	2	5th PM	22-N	10-W
BEAN	**22**	1	5th PM	22-N	9-W
BECK	**4**	2	5th PM	27-N	7-W
BECKER	**4**	1	5th PM	27-N	7-W
BECKETT	**5**	18	5th PM	26-N	10-W
BEESLEY	**20**	1	5th PM	23-N	7-W
BEESON	**2**	1	5th PM	27-N	9-W
BEHYMER	**23**	1	5th PM	22-N	8-W
BELCHER	**17**	3	5th PM	23-N	10-W
BELEW	**4**	2	5th PM	27-N	7-W
BELL	**6**	1	5th PM	26-N	9-W
BELLER	**4**	2	5th PM	27-N	7-W
BENCH	**28**	5	5th PM	21-N	7-W
" "	**24**	2	5th PM	22-N	7-W
" "	**27**	1	5th PM	21-N	8-W
BENNETT	**1**	3	5th PM	27-N	10-W
" "	**12**	4	5th PM	25-N	7-W
BENSON	**9**	1	5th PM	25-N	10-W
" "	**12**	1	5th PM	25-N	7-W
" "	**5**	1	5th PM	26-N	10-W
BENTON	**3**	4	5th PM	27-N	8-W
BERRY	**23**	4	5th PM	22-N	8-W
" "	**22**	3	5th PM	22-N	9-W
BESS	**19**	3	5th PM	23-N	8-W
" "	**11**	2	5th PM	25-N	8-W
" "	**24**	1	5th PM	22-N	7-W
BEYER	**21**	1	5th PM	22-N	10-W
BIBLE	**3**	3	5th PM	27-N	8-W
BIFFLE	**21**	2	5th PM	22-N	10-W
BIGGINS	**6**	2	5th PM	26-N	9-W
BILLING	**6**	1	5th PM	26-N	9-W
BINGAMAN	**15**	8	5th PM	24-N	8-W
" "	**18**	3	5th PM	23-N	9-W
" "	**14**	2	5th PM	24-N	9-W
BINGERMAN	**15**	1	5th PM	24-N	8-W
BINGHAM	**22**	2	5th PM	22-N	9-W
BINKLEY	**13**	2	5th PM	24-N	10-W
BISE	**18**	2	5th PM	23-N	9-W
" "	**22**	6	5th PM	22-N	9-W
BISHOP	**13**	2	5th PM	24-N	10-W
BISSEL	**19**	2	5th PM	23-N	8-W
BISSELL	**24**	1	5th PM	22-N	7-W
BISSETT	**18**	3	5th PM	23-N	9-W
BIZZELL	**17**	2	5th PM	23-N	10-W
BLACK	**21**	4	5th PM	22-N	10-W
" "	**18**	4	5th PM	23-N	9-W
" "	**22**	5	5th PM	22-N	9-W
" "	**6**	4	5th PM	26-N	9-W

Surname	Map Group	Parcels of Land	Meridian/Township/Range
BLACK (Cont'd)	**12**	4	5th PM 25-N 7-W
BLACKBURN	**16**	3	5th PM 24-N 7-W
" "	**3**	3	5th PM 27-N 8-W
" "	**20**	1	5th PM 23-N 7-W
BLACKWELL	**23**	1	5th PM 22-N 8-W
" "	**25**	2	5th PM 21-N 10-W
" "	**27**	1	5th PM 21-N 8-W
" "	**26**	1	5th PM 21-N 9-W
BLAGG	**28**	3	5th PM 21-N 7-W
BLANKENSHIP	**3**	1	5th PM 27-N 8-W
BLEDSOE	**24**	6	5th PM 22-N 7-W
BLOSSOM	**13**	1	5th PM 24-N 10-W
BLYTHE	**8**	2	5th PM 26-N 7-W
" "	**7**	2	5th PM 26-N 8-W
BOAK	**24**	9	5th PM 22-N 7-W
BOATMAN	**9**	5	5th PM 25-N 10-W
" "	**8**	1	5th PM 26-N 7-W
" "	**2**	5	5th PM 27-N 9-W
" "	**7**	11	5th PM 26-N 8-W
BOETTLER	**13**	2	5th PM 24-N 10-W
BOGARD	**15**	1	5th PM 24-N 8-W
BOLERJACK	**7**	6	5th PM 26-N 8-W
" "	**8**	4	5th PM 26-N 7-W
" "	**3**	3	5th PM 27-N 8-W
BOLIN	**6**	1	5th PM 26-N 9-W
" "	**7**	3	5th PM 26-N 8-W
BOLLINGER	**14**	6	5th PM 24-N 9-W
" "	**18**	2	5th PM 23-N 9-W
BONBRIGHT	**24**	2	5th PM 22-N 7-W
BOND	**18**	10	5th PM 23-N 9-W
BOOTMAN	**2**	1	5th PM 27-N 9-W
" "	**19**	4	5th PM 23-N 8-W
BOSS	**7**	3	5th PM 26-N 8-W
" "	**11**	5	5th PM 25-N 8-W
BOSWELL	**21**	1	5th PM 22-N 10-W
BOUCHER	**2**	2	5th PM 27-N 9-W
BOWERS	**1**	1	5th PM 27-N 10-W
BOWLES	**15**	2	5th PM 24-N 8-W
BOYCE	**11**	1	5th PM 25-N 8-W
BOYD	**7**	2	5th PM 26-N 8-W
" "	**16**	3	5th PM 24-N 7-W
" "	**20**	2	5th PM 23-N 7-W
" "	**9**	4	5th PM 25-N 10-W
" "	**11**	3	5th PM 25-N 8-W
BOYSE	**10**	1	5th PM 25-N 9-W
" "	**11**	3	5th PM 25-N 8-W
BRACKETT	**2**	2	5th PM 27-N 9-W
BRADFORD	**18**	5	5th PM 23-N 9-W
BRADLEY	**23**	3	5th PM 22-N 8-W
" "	**9**	2	5th PM 25-N 10-W
" "	**22**	1	5th PM 22-N 9-W
BRADSHAW	**6**	3	5th PM 26-N 9-W
" "	**18**	4	5th PM 23-N 9-W
" "	**12**	1	5th PM 25-N 7-W
" "	**11**	6	5th PM 25-N 8-W
BRAGG	**12**	1	5th PM 25-N 7-W
" "	**8**	3	5th PM 26-N 7-W
" "	**18**	2	5th PM 23-N 9-W
BRAKEBILL	**11**	2	5th PM 25-N 8-W
BRAKEFIELD	**6**	2	5th PM 26-N 9-W

Surname	Map Group	Parcels of Land	Meridian/Township/Range		
BRAMLETT	**7**	1	5th PM	26-N	8-W
BRAND	**20**	2	5th PM	23-N	7-W
BRANNOCK	**11**	1	5th PM	25-N	8-W
" "	**15**	3	5th PM	24-N	8-W
BRANSTETTER	**13**	2	5th PM	24-N	10-W
BRASSWELL	**2**	3	5th PM	27-N	9-W
BRAY	**16**	1	5th PM	24-N	7-W
" "	**6**	1	5th PM	26-N	9-W
" "	**14**	4	5th PM	24-N	9-W
BREEDLOVE	**18**	4	5th PM	23-N	9-W
BRENNER	**18**	2	5th PM	23-N	9-W
" "	**23**	1	5th PM	22-N	8-W
BRESSLER	**6**	1	5th PM	26-N	9-W
BREWINGTON	**3**	5	5th PM	27-N	8-W
BREWSTER	**10**	1	5th PM	25-N	9-W
BRIDENTHAL	**19**	3	5th PM	23-N	8-W
BRIDGES	**13**	1	5th PM	24-N	10-W
" "	**21**	3	5th PM	22-N	10-W
" "	**17**	6	5th PM	23-N	10-W
" "	**15**	3	5th PM	24-N	8-W
" "	**10**	6	5th PM	25-N	9-W
BRIDWELL	**21**	2	5th PM	22-N	10-W
BRIGGS	**13**	3	5th PM	24-N	10-W
" "	**11**	2	5th PM	25-N	8-W
" "	**17**	1	5th PM	23-N	10-W
BRILES	**4**	3	5th PM	27-N	7-W
BRIMHALL	**16**	1	5th PM	24-N	7-W
" "	**20**	2	5th PM	23-N	7-W
BRISCEY	**8**	2	5th PM	26-N	7-W
BRISCOE	**23**	2	5th PM	22-N	8-W
BRITT	**6**	3	5th PM	26-N	9-W
BRIXEY	**10**	1	5th PM	25-N	9-W
" "	**9**	5	5th PM	25-N	10-W
" "	**12**	7	5th PM	25-N	7-W
BROOKES	**4**	4	5th PM	27-N	7-W
BROOKS	**8**	3	5th PM	26-N	7-W
BROONER	**10**	1	5th PM	25-N	9-W
" "	**6**	6	5th PM	26-N	9-W
BROTHERTON	**3**	2	5th PM	27-N	8-W
" "	**10**	7	5th PM	25-N	9-W
" "	**11**	3	5th PM	25-N	8-W
BROWER	**11**	3	5th PM	25-N	8-W
" "	**16**	5	5th PM	24-N	7-W
" "	**6**	2	5th PM	26-N	9-W
" "	**10**	3	5th PM	25-N	9-W
BROWN	**19**	1	5th PM	23-N	8-W
" "	**10**	2	5th PM	25-N	9-W
" "	**15**	2	5th PM	24-N	8-W
" "	**21**	6	5th PM	22-N	10-W
" "	**8**	1	5th PM	26-N	7-W
" "	**11**	2	5th PM	25-N	8-W
" "	**16**	4	5th PM	24-N	7-W
" "	**13**	2	5th PM	24-N	10-W
" "	**12**	3	5th PM	25-N	7-W
" "	**14**	8	5th PM	24-N	9-W
BROWNING	**3**	2	5th PM	27-N	8-W
BROYLS	**12**	2	5th PM	25-N	7-W
BRUNOT	**8**	1	5th PM	26-N	7-W
BRUSTER	**6**	1	5th PM	26-N	9-W
BRYAN	**22**	1	5th PM	22-N	9-W

Surname	Map Group	Parcels of Land	Meridian/Township/Range
BRYAN (Cont'd)	**6**	3	5th PM 26-N 9-W
BRYANT	**14**	1	5th PM 24-N 9-W
BUCHANAN	**20**	3	5th PM 23-N 7-W
BUCK	**15**	6	5th PM 24-N 8-W
BUCKLAND	**2**	2	5th PM 27-N 9-W
BUCKLEW	**14**	1	5th PM 24-N 9-W
BUCKMASTER	**13**	2	5th PM 24-N 10-W
BUCKNER	**14**	4	5th PM 24-N 9-W
BUFF	**8**	1	5th PM 26-N 7-W
" "	**4**	2	5th PM 27-N 7-W
BUFORD	**7**	2	5th PM 26-N 8-W
" "	**2**	4	5th PM 27-N 9-W
BUGG	**12**	1	5th PM 25-N 7-W
BUKER	**13**	2	5th PM 24-N 10-W
BULARD	**19**	1	5th PM 23-N 8-W
BULLARD	**18**	2	5th PM 23-N 9-W
BUMGARNER	**9**	2	5th PM 25-N 10-W
BUMPASS	**28**	5	5th PM 21-N 7-W
BUNCE	**23**	3	5th PM 22-N 8-W
BUNCH	**6**	2	5th PM 26-N 9-W
BUNDREN	**13**	2	5th PM 24-N 10-W
BURDEN	**21**	6	5th PM 22-N 10-W
BURGESS	**10**	7	5th PM 25-N 9-W
" "	**15**	1	5th PM 24-N 8-W
BURK	**10**	2	5th PM 25-N 9-W
BURNET	**17**	4	5th PM 23-N 10-W
BURNETT	**10**	1	5th PM 25-N 9-W
BURNHAM	**3**	2	5th PM 27-N 8-W
BURNS	**19**	1	5th PM 23-N 8-W
BURNWORTH	**18**	2	5th PM 23-N 9-W
BURRIS	**19**	6	5th PM 23-N 8-W
BURRISS	**17**	4	5th PM 23-N 10-W
BURROUGHS	**11**	5	5th PM 25-N 8-W
" "	**12**	11	5th PM 25-N 7-W
BURTON	**18**	6	5th PM 23-N 9-W
" "	**22**	8	5th PM 22-N 9-W
" "	**24**	3	5th PM 22-N 7-W
BUSSELL	**24**	6	5th PM 22-N 7-W
BUTCHER	**16**	2	5th PM 24-N 7-W
" "	**15**	4	5th PM 24-N 8-W
BUTLER	**14**	2	5th PM 24-N 9-W
BYERS	**13**	3	5th PM 24-N 10-W
" "	**9**	3	5th PM 25-N 10-W
" "	**14**	2	5th PM 24-N 9-W
BYRD	**10**	3	5th PM 25-N 9-W
CAGE	**11**	3	5th PM 25-N 8-W
CALDWELL	**26**	2	5th PM 21-N 9-W
CALLAHAN	**6**	3	5th PM 26-N 9-W
" "	**21**	1	5th PM 22-N 10-W
" "	**13**	8	5th PM 24-N 10-W
" "	**17**	2	5th PM 23-N 10-W
CALLISON	**13**	2	5th PM 24-N 10-W
CAMBELL	**18**	1	5th PM 23-N 9-W
CAMPBELL	**4**	5	5th PM 27-N 7-W
" "	**7**	6	5th PM 26-N 8-W
" "	**22**	3	5th PM 22-N 9-W
" "	**2**	1	5th PM 27-N 9-W
" "	**8**	2	5th PM 26-N 7-W
" "	**14**	3	5th PM 24-N 9-W
" "	**10**	1	5th PM 25-N 9-W

Surname	Map Group	Parcels of Land	Meridian/Township/Range
CAMPBELL (Cont'd)	**24**	2	5th PM 22-N 7-W
" "	**15**	12	5th PM 24-N 8-W
" "	**16**	1	5th PM 24-N 7-W
" "	**18**	2	5th PM 23-N 9-W
" "	**3**	3	5th PM 27-N 8-W
CANNON	**6**	2	5th PM 26-N 9-W
" "	**13**	2	5th PM 24-N 10-W
" "	**27**	5	5th PM 21-N 8-W
" "	**23**	3	5th PM 22-N 8-W
" "	**14**	1	5th PM 24-N 9-W
CANTLEY	**19**	4	5th PM 23-N 8-W
CANTRELL	**25**	2	5th PM 21-N 10-W
" "	**21**	1	5th PM 22-N 10-W
" "	**7**	4	5th PM 26-N 8-W
" "	**6**	1	5th PM 26-N 9-W
CAPIN	**20**	1	5th PM 23-N 7-W
CAPPS	**3**	3	5th PM 27-N 8-W
CAPSHAW	**24**	3	5th PM 22-N 7-W
CARD	**1**	1	5th PM 27-N 10-W
CARGILL	**14**	4	5th PM 24-N 9-W
CARNER	**28**	2	5th PM 21-N 7-W
CARPENTER	**8**	4	5th PM 26-N 7-W
CARR	**22**	1	5th PM 22-N 9-W
" "	**23**	1	5th PM 22-N 8-W
CARRELL	**21**	16	5th PM 22-N 10-W
" "	**22**	2	5th PM 22-N 9-W
CARRIER	**13**	1	5th PM 24-N 10-W
CARRINGTON	**13**	1	5th PM 24-N 10-W
" "	**22**	1	5th PM 22-N 9-W
CARRIS	**11**	1	5th PM 25-N 8-W
CARSON	**24**	3	5th PM 22-N 7-W
" "	**1**	2	5th PM 27-N 10-W
" "	**15**	1	5th PM 24-N 8-W
" "	**22**	1	5th PM 22-N 9-W
" "	**14**	1	5th PM 24-N 9-W
" "	**23**	2	5th PM 22-N 8-W
CARTER	**4**	2	5th PM 27-N 7-W
" "	**15**	1	5th PM 24-N 8-W
" "	**8**	1	5th PM 26-N 7-W
" "	**25**	1	5th PM 21-N 10-W
" "	**16**	2	5th PM 24-N 7-W
" "	**17**	2	5th PM 23-N 10-W
" "	**21**	4	5th PM 22-N 10-W
CARTMILL	**7**	9	5th PM 26-N 8-W
CARTWRIGHT	**21**	2	5th PM 22-N 10-W
CASH	**19**	2	5th PM 23-N 8-W
CASTEEL	**8**	2	5th PM 26-N 7-W
CASTLEMAN	**9**	1	5th PM 25-N 10-W
CASWELL	**20**	1	5th PM 23-N 7-W
CATER	**19**	1	5th PM 23-N 8-W
CATES	**26**	3	5th PM 21-N 9-W
" "	**27**	4	5th PM 21-N 8-W
" "	**17**	8	5th PM 23-N 10-W
CAUTLEY	**19**	1	5th PM 23-N 8-W
CAY	**20**	1	5th PM 23-N 7-W
CHAMBERS	**19**	2	5th PM 23-N 8-W
CHANDLER	**11**	1	5th PM 25-N 8-W
" "	**21**	11	5th PM 22-N 10-W
CHAPIN	**27**	1	5th PM 21-N 8-W
" "	**20**	6	5th PM 23-N 7-W

Surname	Map Group	Parcels of Land	Meridian/Township/Range		
CHAPIN (Cont'd)	2	2	5th PM	27-N	9-W
" "	23	1	5th PM	22-N	8-W
" "	19	1	5th PM	23-N	8-W
CHAPMAN	18	6	5th PM	23-N	9-W
CHAPPELL	17	3	5th PM	23-N	10-W
" "	4	1	5th PM	27-N	7-W
CHARLES	11	3	5th PM	25-N	8-W
" "	12	2	5th PM	25-N	7-W
CHASTAIN	15	5	5th PM	24-N	8-W
CHEATHAM	12	4	5th PM	25-N	7-W
CHEEK	2	6	5th PM	27-N	9-W
CHENEY	21	5	5th PM	22-N	10-W
CHERRY	22	5	5th PM	22-N	9-W
CHESNUT	18	2	5th PM	23-N	9-W
CHESTNUT	18	3	5th PM	23-N	9-W
CHOAT	6	2	5th PM	26-N	9-W
CHOWNING	8	17	5th PM	26-N	7-W
CHRISTENSEN	19	3	5th PM	23-N	8-W
CHRISTESSON	1	1	5th PM	27-N	10-W
CHRISTOPHER	10	3	5th PM	25-N	9-W
CHRISTY	1	1	5th PM	27-N	10-W
CHURCHILL	12	3	5th PM	25-N	7-W
CLARK	6	3	5th PM	26-N	9-W
" "	21	3	5th PM	22-N	10-W
" "	16	4	5th PM	24-N	7-W
" "	15	1	5th PM	24-N	8-W
" "	19	2	5th PM	23-N	8-W
" "	22	2	5th PM	22-N	9-W
" "	14	2	5th PM	24-N	9-W
" "	13	2	5th PM	24-N	10-W
" "	26	1	5th PM	21-N	9-W
" "	20	5	5th PM	23-N	7-W
" "	7	6	5th PM	26-N	8-W
" "	3	3	5th PM	27-N	8-W
" "	18	8	5th PM	23-N	9-W
CLARKE	15	1	5th PM	24-N	8-W
CLAXTON	26	4	5th PM	21-N	9-W
CLAYTER	19	2	5th PM	23-N	8-W
CLAYTON	26	4	5th PM	21-N	9-W
" "	18	2	5th PM	23-N	9-W
CLEARY	14	3	5th PM	24-N	9-W
CLEMENT	18	2	5th PM	23-N	9-W
" "	22	1	5th PM	22-N	9-W
CLEMMONES	12	3	5th PM	25-N	7-W
CLEMMONS	12	3	5th PM	25-N	7-W
CLEVELAND	12	4	5th PM	25-N	7-W
CLICK	7	6	5th PM	26-N	8-W
CLIFF	4	2	5th PM	27-N	7-W
CLIFFORD	22	2	5th PM	22-N	9-W
CLIFTON	20	1	5th PM	23-N	7-W
CLIMER	10	2	5th PM	25-N	9-W
CLINGINGSMITH	3	2	5th PM	27-N	8-W
CLINKINGBEARD	17	3	5th PM	23-N	10-W
CLONINGER	18	7	5th PM	23-N	9-W
CLOONEY	20	1	5th PM	23-N	7-W
CLOWNY	16	3	5th PM	24-N	7-W
COBB	15	2	5th PM	24-N	8-W
" "	7	3	5th PM	26-N	8-W
" "	14	1	5th PM	24-N	9-W
" "	12	2	5th PM	25-N	7-W

Surname	Map Group	Parcels of Land	Meridian/Township/Range
COBBS	**2**	2	5th PM 27-N 9-W
COCHRAN	**2**	3	5th PM 27-N 9-W
" "	**25**	6	5th PM 21-N 10-W
COCK	**23**	2	5th PM 22-N 8-W
" "	**18**	5	5th PM 23-N 9-W
COFFEE	**16**	4	5th PM 24-N 7-W
" "	**15**	4	5th PM 24-N 8-W
COFFMAN	**2**	3	5th PM 27-N 9-W
" "	**6**	1	5th PM 26-N 9-W
COFFY	**16**	2 .	5th PM 24-N 7-W
COLDIRON	**19**	1	5th PM 23-N 8-W
COLE	**10**	2	5th PM 25-N 9-W
" "	**14**	1	5th PM 24-N 9-W
" "	**15**	1	5th PM 24-N 8-W
" "	**6**	1	5th PM 26-N 9-W
" "	**27**	2	5th PM 21-N 8-W
COLEMAN	**6**	3	5th PM 26-N 9-W
COLLENS	**14**	1	5th PM 24-N 9-W
COLLIER	**19**	3	5th PM 23-N 8-W
" "	**23**	1	5th PM 22-N 8-W
" "	**20**	1	5th PM 23-N 7-W
" "	**16**	1	5th PM 24-N 7-W
COLLINS	**25**	3	5th PM 21-N 10-W
" "	**23**	3	5th PM 22-N 8-W
" "	**26**	1	5th PM 21-N 9-W
" "	**21**	7	5th PM 22-N 10-W
" "	**22**	8	5th PM 22-N 9-W
" "	**9**	15	5th PM 25-N 10-W
" "	**7**	1	5th PM 26-N 8-W
" "	**13**	15	5th PM 24-N 10-W
COLMERY	**22**	2	5th PM 22-N 9-W
COLTER	**8**	1	5th PM 26-N 7-W
COLTHARP	**11**	1	5th PM 25-N 8-W
COLYER	**14**	3	5th PM 24-N 9-W
COMSTOCK	**8**	9	5th PM 26-N 7-W
CONLEY	**6**	1	5th PM 26-N 9-W
CONNER	**8**	3	5th PM 26-N 7-W
" "	**1**	1	5th PM 27-N 10-W
COOK	**12**	5	5th PM 25-N 7-W
" "	**1**	1	5th PM 27-N 10-W
" "	**15**	6	5th PM 24-N 8-W
" "	**23**	2	5th PM 22-N 8-W
" "	**18**	1	5th PM 23-N 9-W
" "	**11**	4	5th PM 25-N 8-W
" "	**17**	2	5th PM 23-N 10-W
COOPER	**16**	2	5th PM 24-N 7-W
" "	**17**	3	5th PM 23-N 10-W
" "	**18**	2	5th PM 23-N 9-W
" "	**21**	3	5th PM 22-N 10-W
" "	**22**	4	5th PM 22-N 9-W
" "	**24**	1	5th PM 22-N 7-W
COOPPER	**8**	2	5th PM 26-N 7-W
COOSE	**7**	1	5th PM 26-N 8-W
COPE	**15**	2	5th PM 24-N 8-W
CORDES	**11**	3	5th PM 25-N 8-W
CORDILL	**15**	2	5th PM 24-N 8-W
" "	**14**	3	5th PM 24-N 9-W
" "	**20**	3	5th PM 23-N 7-W
COTHRAN	**27**	1	5th PM 21-N 8-W
COTTLE	**19**	2	5th PM 23-N 8-W

Surname	Map Group	Parcels of Land	Meridian/Township/Range
COUNTS	7	1	5th PM 26-N 8-W
" "	11	2	5th PM 25-N 8-W
COURSEY	11	2	5th PM 25-N 8-W
COURTNEY	10	1	5th PM 25-N 9-W
COVALT	25	3	5th PM 21-N 10-W
COVER	10	1	5th PM 25-N 9-W
COVERT	2	2	5th PM 27-N 9-W
COVINGTON	26	3	5th PM 21-N 9-W
COWAN	11	3	5th PM 25-N 8-W
COX	26	2	5th PM 21-N 9-W
" "	27	1	5th PM 21-N 8-W
" "	17	2	5th PM 23-N 10-W
" "	20	9	5th PM 23-N 7-W
" "	7	3	5th PM 26-N 8-W
" "	3	2	5th PM 27-N 8-W
" "	2	1	5th PM 27-N 9-W
" "	12	3	5th PM 25-N 7-W
" "	6	3	5th PM 26-N 9-W
COZORT	11	1	5th PM 25-N 8-W
CRABTREE	2	3	5th PM 27-N 9-W
CRAFTON	17	1	5th PM 23-N 10-W
CRAHAN	16	1	5th PM 24-N 7-W
CRAIG	24	11	5th PM 22-N 7-W
CRAIN	12	1	5th PM 25-N 7-W
CRANE	24	27	5th PM 22-N 7-W
" "	23	73	5th PM 22-N 8-W
" "	15	9	5th PM 24-N 8-W
" "	21	1	5th PM 22-N 10-W
" "	19	13	5th PM 23-N 8-W
CRAPO	22	3	5th PM 22-N 9-W
CRENSHAW	15	1	5th PM 24-N 8-W
CRIDER	6	3	5th PM 26-N 9-W
" "	13	2	5th PM 24-N 10-W
" "	11	5	5th PM 25-N 8-W
CRIPE	4	4	5th PM 27-N 7-W
CRISP	17	3	5th PM 23-N 10-W
" "	12	3	5th PM 25-N 7-W
" "	18	1	5th PM 23-N 9-W
CRISPIN	6	1	5th PM 26-N 9-W
CRITCHER	2	1	5th PM 27-N 9-W
CRITES	15	1	5th PM 24-N 8-W
CRONER	23	1	5th PM 22-N 8-W
CROOM	25	3	5th PM 21-N 10-W
CROSS	16	2	5th PM 24-N 7-W
CROUCH	6	1	5th PM 26-N 9-W
" "	2	2	5th PM 27-N 9-W
CROW	19	3	5th PM 23-N 8-W
" "	4	3	5th PM 27-N 7-W
CROWDER	27	5	5th PM 21-N 8-W
" "	7	4	5th PM 26-N 8-W
" "	4	1	5th PM 27-N 7-W
CROWLEY	21	1	5th PM 22-N 10-W
CRUM	12	1	5th PM 25-N 7-W
" "	7	1	5th PM 26-N 8-W
" "	6	2	5th PM 26-N 9-W
CRUMLEY	21	3	5th PM 22-N 10-W
CULBERTSON	3	3	5th PM 27-N 8-W
" "	21	1	5th PM 22-N 10-W
CULL	16	1	5th PM 24-N 7-W
CUNNINGHAM	9	3	5th PM 25-N 10-W

Surname	Map Group	Parcels of Land	Meridian/Township/Range		
CUNNINGHAM (Cont'd)	**3**	4	5th PM	27-N	8-W
" "	**16**	3	5th PM	24-N	7-W
" "	**11**	3	5th PM	25-N	8-W
" "	**21**	7	5th PM	22-N	10-W
CURRY	**19**	1	5th PM	23-N	8-W
" "	**13**	1	5th PM	24-N	10-W
" "	**24**	12	5th PM	22-N	7-W
CURTIS	**16**	3	5th PM	24-N	7-W
CUTLER	**21**	2	5th PM	22-N	10-W
DABBS	**13**	2	5th PM	24-N	10-W
DAILY	**4**	3	5th PM	27-N	7-W
DALSING	**11**	1	5th PM	25-N	8-W
DAMON	**16**	1	5th PM	24-N	7-W
DANIEL	**3**	4	5th PM	27-N	8-W
" "	**15**	1	5th PM	24-N	8-W
" "	**7**	3	5th PM	26-N	8-W
" "	**8**	1	5th PM	26-N	7-W
DAUGHERTY	**12**	2	5th PM	25-N	7-W
DAVIDSON	**7**	2	5th PM	26-N	8-W
" "	**15**	2	5th PM	24-N	8-W
" "	**6**	3	5th PM	26-N	9-W
" "	**19**	3	5th PM	23-N	8-W
DAVIES	**8**	2	5th PM	26-N	7-W
DAVIS	**24**	2	5th PM	22-N	7-W
" "	**21**	3	5th PM	22-N	10-W
" "	**15**	2	5th PM	24-N	8-W
" "	**12**	3	5th PM	25-N	7-W
" "	**17**	7	5th PM	23-N	10-W
" "	**8**	2	5th PM	26-N	7-W
" "	**2**	2	5th PM	27-N	9-W
" "	**7**	3	5th PM	26-N	8-W
" "	**18**	4	5th PM	23-N	9-W
" "	**22**	4	5th PM	22-N	9-W
" "	**13**	8	5th PM	24-N	10-W
" "	**25**	3	5th PM	21-N	10-W
" "	**26**	5	5th PM	21-N	9-W
DAVISON	**20**	2	5th PM	23-N	7-W
DAWSON	**16**	1	5th PM	24-N	7-W
" "	**28**	1	5th PM	21-N	7-W
" "	**14**	3	5th PM	24-N	9-W
DE WITT	**14**	1	5th PM	24-N	9-W
DEARING	**6**	2	5th PM	26-N	9-W
DEATHERAGE	**25**	1	5th PM	21-N	10-W
DEATON	**7**	5	5th PM	26-N	8-W
DEBOARD	**8**	11	5th PM	26-N	7-W
DECKER	**17**	3	5th PM	23-N	10-W
DEEMS	**22**	3	5th PM	22-N	9-W
DEITZ	**16**	3	5th PM	24-N	7-W
DEJARNATH	**22**	3	5th PM	22-N	9-W
DELAY	**19**	1	5th PM	23-N	8-W
DENGLER	**28**	1	5th PM	21-N	7-W
DENNIS	**14**	1	5th PM	24-N	9-W
DENNY	**22**	2	5th PM	22-N	9-W
DENT	**17**	3	5th PM	23-N	10-W
DENTON	**12**	1	5th PM	25-N	7-W
" "	**11**	3	5th PM	25-N	8-W
" "	**8**	2	5th PM	26-N	7-W
DENZEL	**7**	8	5th PM	26-N	8-W
DERINGER	**7**	3	5th PM	26-N	8-W
DERRICK	**21**	1	5th PM	22-N	10-W

Surname	Map Group	Parcels of Land	Meridian/Township/Range		
DESITS	9	1	5th PM	25-N	10-W
" "	24	1	5th PM	22-N	7-W
" "	15	1	5th PM	24-N	8-W
" "	12	4	5th PM	25-N	7-W
DEXTER	20	1	5th PM	23-N	7-W
" "	16	4	5th PM	24-N	7-W
DICKSON	20	5	5th PM	23-N	7-W
DIEHL	12	1	5th PM	25-N	7-W
DIELLE	21	1	5th PM	22-N	10-W
" "	26	5	5th PM	21-N	9-W
DILL	16	8	5th PM	24-N	7-W
DILLINDER	17	2	5th PM	23-N	10-W
DIXON	2	2	5th PM	27-N	9-W
" "	10	5	5th PM	25-N	9-W
DOCIA	14	1	5th PM	24-N	9-W
DOCKERY	19	2	5th PM	23-N	8-W
DOCKEY	19	1	5th PM	23-N	8-W
DODD	25	6	5th PM	21-N	10-W
" "	15	1	5th PM	24-N	8-W
DODSON	21	3	5th PM	22-N	10-W
DOERING	4	2	5th PM	27-N	7-W
DOLLENS	9	3	5th PM	25-N	10-W
DOLLINS	9	1	5th PM	25-N	10-W
DONNELLY	16	1	5th PM	24-N	7-W
DOOLEY	19	1	5th PM	23-N	8-W
" "	18	1	5th PM	23-N	9-W
DORRIS	21	1	5th PM	22-N	10-W
" "	22	3	5th PM	22-N	9-W
DORSEY	2	2	5th PM	27-N	9-W
" "	18	5	5th PM	23-N	9-W
" "	17	3	5th PM	23-N	10-W
DOTY	23	3	5th PM	22-N	8-W
DOUGHERTY	20	1	5th PM	23-N	7-W
DOWELL	7	5	5th PM	26-N	8-W
DOWNING	21	2	5th PM	22-N	10-W
DOWNS	19	1	5th PM	23-N	8-W
DRAKE	8	1	5th PM	26-N	7-W
DRENNEN	7	3	5th PM	26-N	8-W
DRIEHAUS	11	1	5th PM	25-N	8-W
DRINNON	19	3	5th PM	23-N	8-W
DRIVER	28	2	5th PM	21-N	7-W
DRUMRIGHT	10	4	5th PM	25-N	9-W
DRUMWRIGHT	13	1	5th PM	24-N	10-W
" "	14	1	5th PM	24-N	9-W
DRYBREAD	2	3	5th PM	27-N	9-W
DRYDEN	4	2	5th PM	27-N	7-W
DRYER	11	2	5th PM	25-N	8-W
" "	12	3	5th PM	25-N	7-W
DRYMAN	3	1	5th PM	27-N	8-W
DRYMON	3	3	5th PM	27-N	8-W
DUCKERING	23	2	5th PM	22-N	8-W
DUDLEY	15	2	5th PM	24-N	8-W
DUKE	6	2	5th PM	26-N	9-W
" "	10	2	5th PM	25-N	9-W
DUNAVIN	27	2	5th PM	21-N	8-W
DUNEHEW	19	1	5th PM	23-N	8-W
DUNHAM	23	1	5th PM	22-N	8-W
" "	8	1	5th PM	26-N	7-W
" "	11	2	5th PM	25-N	8-W
DUNIVAN	2	1	5th PM	27-N	9-W

Surname	Map Group	Parcels of Land	Meridian/Township/Range		
DUNKIN	**16**	10	5th PM	24-N	7-W
" "	**8**	3	5th PM	26-N	7-W
DUNKLEBARGER	**18**	4	5th PM	23-N	9-W
DUNLAP	**7**	6	5th PM	26-N	8-W
DUNN	**22**	2	5th PM	22-N	9-W
DUNNE	**6**	2	5th PM	26-N	9-W
DUNNILL	**20**	1	5th PM	23-N	7-W
DUNNING	**6**	3	5th PM	26-N	9-W
DURFEE	**18**	3	5th PM	23-N	9-W
DURHAM	**17**	2	5th PM	23-N	10-W
DURNEL	**4**	2	5th PM	27-N	7-W
DURST	**18**	1	5th PM	23-N	9-W
DYER	**10**	2	5th PM	25-N	9-W
DYKES	**24**	1	5th PM	22-N	7-W
" "	**28**	1	5th PM	21-N	7-W
EADES	**26**	3	5th PM	21-N	9-W
EARLS	**11**	1	5th PM	25-N	8-W
" "	**2**	1	5th PM	27-N	9-W
EASLEY	**22**	3	5th PM	22-N	9-W
" "	**25**	11	5th PM	21-N	10-W
" "	**26**	3	5th PM	21-N	9-W
" "	**21**	5	5th PM	22-N	10-W
EASTERLY	**20**	1	5th PM	23-N	7-W
EASTRELY	**24**	4	5th PM	22-N	7-W
EATON	**3**	1	5th PM	27-N	8-W
" "	**4**	2	5th PM	27-N	7-W
" "	**16**	1	5th PM	24-N	7-W
" "	**14**	2	5th PM	24-N	9-W
EBLEN	**12**	9	5th PM	25-N	7-W
EBLIN	**14**	3	5th PM	24-N	9-W
ECHOLS	**10**	2	5th PM	25-N	9-W
EDELMAN	**24**	3	5th PM	22-N	7-W
EDGAR	**16**	2	5th PM	24-N	7-W
EDMONSTON	**7**	2	5th PM	26-N	8-W
EDMOUNDSON	**14**	4	5th PM	24-N	9-W
EDSON	**20**	1	5th PM	23-N	7-W
EDWARDS	**2**	3	5th PM	27-N	9-W
" "	**3**	1	5th PM	27-N	8-W
EIDSON	**2**	4	5th PM	27-N	9-W
ELDER	**21**	1	5th PM	22-N	10-W
ELDRINGHOFF	**12**	9	5th PM	25-N	7-W
" "	**8**	3	5th PM	26-N	7-W
ELKIN	**2**	2	5th PM	27-N	9-W
ELKINS	**2**	3	5th PM	27-N	9-W
ELLEDGE	**11**	11	5th PM	25-N	8-W
ELLINGTON	**15**	4	5th PM	24-N	8-W
ELLIOTT	**10**	2	5th PM	25-N	9-W
" "	**21**	2	5th PM	22-N	10-W
" "	**20**	3	5th PM	23-N	7-W
" "	**23**	2	5th PM	22-N	8-W
ELLIS	**9**	1	5th PM	25-N	10-W
" "	**15**	2	5th PM	24-N	8-W
ELLWOOD	**16**	3	5th PM	24-N	7-W
EMERSON	**6**	4	5th PM	26-N	9-W
EMMONS	**24**	5	5th PM	22-N	7-W
ENDECOTT	**13**	1	5th PM	24-N	10-W
" "	**17**	12	5th PM	23-N	10-W
" "	**21**	1	5th PM	22-N	10-W
ENDICOTT	**21**	2	5th PM	22-N	10-W
" "	**25**	3	5th PM	21-N	10-W

Surname	Map Group	Parcels of Land	Meridian/Township/Range
ENDICOTT (Cont'd)	**17**	8	5th PM 23-N 10-W
ENGLAND	**28**	1	5th PM 21-N 7-W
" "	**27**	5	5th PM 21-N 8-W
ENGLE	**23**	2	5th PM 22-N 8-W
ENO	**22**	3	5th PM 22-N 9-W
" "	**23**	1	5th PM 22-N 8-W
EPLEY	**21**	2	5th PM 22-N 10-W
" "	**14**	3	5th PM 24-N 9-W
EPPS	**6**	4	5th PM 26-N 9-W
ERWIN	**12**	3	5th PM 25-N 7-W
ESKRIDGE	**12**	2	5th PM 25-N 7-W
ESSEX	**11**	3	5th PM 25-N 8-W
ESTES	**7**	1	5th PM 26-N 8-W
EVANS	**24**	3	5th PM 22-N 7-W
" "	**19**	1	5th PM 23-N 8-W
" "	**28**	2	5th PM 21-N 7-W
" "	**6**	3	5th PM 26-N 9-W
" "	**10**	4	5th PM 25-N 9-W
" "	**7**	1	5th PM 26-N 8-W
" "	**8**	2	5th PM 26-N 7-W
" "	**14**	1	5th PM 24-N 9-W
EVELAND	**7**	7	5th PM 26-N 8-W
EVERED	**9**	2	5th PM 25-N 10-W
" "	**7**	2	5th PM 26-N 8-W
EVINS	**8**	3	5th PM 26-N 7-W
EWART	**19**	1	5th PM 23-N 8-W
EZELL	**27**	4	5th PM 21-N 8-W
FADDIS	**14**	1	5th PM 24-N 9-W
FAIR	**3**	2	5th PM 27-N 8-W
" "	**21**	1	5th PM 22-N 10-W
FALWELL	**14**	7	5th PM 24-N 9-W
FARE	**21**	3	5th PM 22-N 10-W
FARIS	**28**	1	5th PM 21-N 7-W
FARMER	**11**	5	5th PM 25-N 8-W
" "	**5**	1	5th PM 26-N 10-W
" "	**6**	5	5th PM 26-N 9-W
" "	**7**	1	5th PM 26-N 8-W
FARQUAR	**19**	2	5th PM 23-N 8-W
FARR	**15**	2	5th PM 24-N 8-W
" "	**10**	2	5th PM 25-N 9-W
FARRAR	**8**	2	5th PM 26-N 7-W
FARRIS	**15**	1	5th PM 24-N 8-W
FAST	**19**	1	5th PM 23-N 8-W
FAULCONER	**23**	1	5th PM 22-N 8-W
FAUROT	**18**	1	5th PM 23-N 9-W
FAVORITE	**3**	1	5th PM 27-N 8-W
FEAMAN	**21**	1	5th PM 22-N 10-W
" "	**22**	1	5th PM 22-N 9-W
FEATHER	**7**	5	5th PM 26-N 8-W
FEATHERINGILL	**2**	6	5th PM 27-N 9-W
FEATHERSTON	**24**	2	5th PM 22-N 7-W
FEGAN	**16**	3	5th PM 24-N 7-W
FEHR	**3**	2	5th PM 27-N 8-W
FELAND	**14**	3	5th PM 24-N 9-W
FELTS	**26**	3	5th PM 21-N 9-W
FERGUSON	**22**	3	5th PM 22-N 9-W
" "	**12**	8	5th PM 25-N 7-W
" "	**2**	5	5th PM 27-N 9-W
" "	**24**	3	5th PM 22-N 7-W
" "	**1**	4	5th PM 27-N 10-W

Surname	Map Group	Parcels of Land	Meridian/Township/Range		
FERRELL	**2**	3	5th PM	27-N	9-W
FERRIS	**4**	1	5th PM	27-N	7-W
FIELDS	**6**	2	5th PM	26-N	9-W
" "	**19**	3	5th PM	23-N	8-W
FILES	**24**	1	5th PM	22-N	7-W
FILLMAN	**4**	2	5th PM	27-N	7-W
" "	**3**	1	5th PM	27-N	8-W
FINDLEY	**2**	3	5th PM	27-N	9-W
" "	**3**	10	5th PM	27-N	8-W
" "	**7**	2	5th PM	26-N	8-W
FINE	**10**	4	5th PM	25-N	9-W
FINEY	**24**	1	5th PM	22-N	7-W
FINNEY	**24**	5	5th PM	22-N	7-W
FISCHER	**11**	5	5th PM	25-N	8-W
FISHER	**2**	1	5th PM	27-N	9-W
FITE	**21**	3	5th PM	22-N	10-W
FITZSIMMONS	**10**	5	5th PM	25-N	9-W
" "	**15**	1	5th PM	24-N	8-W
FLEMING	**4**	1	5th PM	27-N	7-W
FLESHER	**20**	3	5th PM	23-N	7-W
FLINN	**17**	1	5th PM	23-N	10-W
FLOOD	**8**	1	5th PM	26-N	7-W
" "	**4**	2	5th PM	27-N	7-W
" "	**7**	4	5th PM	26-N	8-W
FOLEY	**22**	1	5th PM	22-N	9-W
FOOTE	**2**	1	5th PM	27-N	9-W
FORD	**15**	1	5th PM	24-N	8-W
" "	**24**	3	5th PM	22-N	7-W
" "	**14**	3	5th PM	24-N	9-W
" "	**11**	5	5th PM	25-N	8-W
FOREST	**11**	1	5th PM	25-N	8-W
" "	**18**	1	5th PM	23-N	9-W
FORESTER	**21**	1	5th PM	22-N	10-W
FOSTER	**17**	1	5th PM	23-N	10-W
FOUST	**15**	1	5th PM	24-N	8-W
" "	**18**	4	5th PM	23-N	9-W
FOUTS	**4**	3	5th PM	27-N	7-W
FOWLER	**23**	1	5th PM	22-N	8-W
" "	**21**	11	5th PM	22-N	10-W
" "	**19**	2	5th PM	23-N	8-W
FOX	**13**	42	5th PM	24-N	10-W
" "	**17**	5	5th PM	23-N	10-W
" "	**14**	2	5th PM	24-N	9-W
" "	**21**	1	5th PM	22-N	10-W
FRAKES	**4**	3	5th PM	27-N	7-W
FRANK	**4**	1	5th PM	27-N	7-W
" "	**22**	2	5th PM	22-N	9-W
FRANKLIN	**15**	3	5th PM	24-N	8-W
FRAY	**20**	3	5th PM	23-N	7-W
FRAYNER	**20**	4	5th PM	23-N	7-W
" "	**16**	1	5th PM	24-N	7-W
FRAZEE	**6**	2	5th PM	26-N	9-W
FRAZER	**4**	1	5th PM	27-N	7-W
FRAZIER	**18**	1	5th PM	23-N	9-W
" "	**11**	2	5th PM	25-N	8-W
FREEMAN	**10**	1	5th PM	25-N	9-W
FREEZE	**19**	1	5th PM	23-N	8-W
FRENCH	**3**	3	5th PM	27-N	8-W
FRIEND	**22**	1	5th PM	22-N	9-W
FRISBEY	**8**	3	5th PM	26-N	7-W

Surname	Map Group	Parcels of Land	Meridian/Township/Range		
FRITH	**24**	4	5th PM	22-N	7-W
FRIZELL	**13**	3	5th PM	24-N	10-W
FRUSHOUR	**6**	2	5th PM	26-N	9-W
FUDGE	**21**	1	5th PM	22-N	10-W
FULENWIDER	**16**	2	5th PM	24-N	7-W
FULENWIDNER	**16**	6	5th PM	24-N	7-W
FULLER	**24**	4	5th PM	22-N	7-W
" "	**28**	1	5th PM	21-N	7-W
" "	**12**	5	5th PM	25-N	7-W
FULLERLOVE	**15**	3	5th PM	24-N	8-W
FULS	**18**	3	5th PM	23-N	9-W
" "	**17**	3	5th PM	23-N	10-W
FUNK	**21**	2	5th PM	22-N	10-W
GABBERT	**22**	1	5th PM	22-N	9-W
GADBERRY	**22**	2	5th PM	22-N	9-W
GAGE	**20**	3	5th PM	23-N	7-W
GAINES	**24**	6	5th PM	22-N	7-W
GALBREATH	**7**	1	5th PM	26-N	8-W
GALE	**12**	3	5th PM	25-N	7-W
GALESBERRY	**6**	1	5th PM	26-N	9-W
GALLAHER	**1**	4	5th PM	27-N	10-W
GALLAWAY	**15**	1	5th PM	24-N	8-W
GALLOWAY	**15**	5	5th PM	24-N	8-W
" "	**23**	2	5th PM	22-N	8-W
" "	**11**	2	5th PM	25-N	8-W
GAMBER	**12**	5	5th PM	25-N	7-W
GAMBLE	**3**	1	5th PM	27-N	8-W
" "	**7**	2	5th PM	26-N	8-W
GARLETTS	**1**	2	5th PM	27-N	10-W
GARNER	**17**	1	5th PM	23-N	10-W
GAROUTTE	**15**	3	5th PM	24-N	8-W
" "	**8**	4	5th PM	26-N	7-W
GARRET	**20**	3	5th PM	23-N	7-W
GARRETT	**20**	2	5th PM	23-N	7-W
GARRIGIN	**16**	3	5th PM	24-N	7-W
GARTEN	**1**	1	5th PM	27-N	10-W
GASTIAN	**3**	1	5th PM	27-N	8-W
GATTON	**4**	2	5th PM	27-N	7-W
GAYER	**11**	1	5th PM	25-N	8-W
GEBBERS	**11**	1	5th PM	25-N	8-W
GEISLER	**19**	6	5th PM	23-N	8-W
GENTRY	**12**	1	5th PM	25-N	7-W
GEYER	**22**	3	5th PM	22-N	9-W
GIBBS	**22**	2	5th PM	22-N	9-W
" "	**18**	4	5th PM	23-N	9-W
" "	**20**	2	5th PM	23-N	7-W
GIBSON	**6**	4	5th PM	26-N	9-W
" "	**19**	3	5th PM	23-N	8-W
" "	**18**	1	5th PM	23-N	9-W
GILBERT	**18**	5	5th PM	23-N	9-W
" "	**14**	1	5th PM	24-N	9-W
GILES	**8**	2	5th PM	26-N	7-W
GILL	**4**	5	5th PM	27-N	7-W
" "	**21**	1	5th PM	22-N	10-W
" "	**22**	1	5th PM	22-N	9-W
" "	**3**	1	5th PM	27-N	8-W
GILLELAND	**11**	1	5th PM	25-N	8-W
GILLIAM	**12**	5	5th PM	25-N	7-W
GILLILAND	**25**	3	5th PM	21-N	10-W
GILLINGHAM	**8**	1	5th PM	26-N	7-W

Surname	Map Group	Parcels of Land	Meridian/Township/Range
GILMORE	**18**	4	5th PM 23-N 9-W
GIPSON	**18**	2	5th PM 23-N 9-W
GLADDEN	**24**	2	5th PM 22-N 7-W
GLASS	**4**	2	5th PM 27-N 7-W
" "	**17**	1	5th PM 23-N 10-W
GLEEN	**11**	2	5th PM 25-N 8-W
GLENDENING	**11**	1	5th PM 25-N 8-W
GLENN	**19**	2	5th PM 23-N 8-W
GLINN	**14**	4	5th PM 24-N 9-W
GLOSSUP	**14**	4	5th PM 24-N 9-W
GOBBEL	**7**	1	5th PM 26-N 8-W
" "	**8**	2	5th PM 26-N 7-W
GODAT	**14**	1	5th PM 24-N 9-W
" "	**13**	2	5th PM 24-N 10-W
GODDARD	**20**	5	5th PM 23-N 7-W
GODSEY	**2**	3	5th PM 27-N 9-W
GODSY	**2**	17	5th PM 27-N 9-W
GOLDSBERRY	**2**	1	5th PM 27-N 9-W
" "	**6**	1	5th PM 26-N 9-W
" "	**4**	7	5th PM 27-N 7-W
" "	**3**	2	5th PM 27-N 8-W
GOLESBERRY	**3**	1	5th PM 27-N 8-W
GOOD	**12**	5	5th PM 25-N 7-W
" "	**11**	2	5th PM 25-N 8-W
GOODELL	**11**	2	5th PM 25-N 8-W
GOODGION	**19**	1	5th PM 23-N 8-W
GOODMAN	**8**	10	5th PM 26-N 7-W
" "	**7**	3	5th PM 26-N 8-W
GOODMILLER	**15**	1	5th PM 24-N 8-W
GOODNO	**19**	2	5th PM 23-N 8-W
" "	**23**	1	5th PM 22-N 8-W
GOODWIN	**21**	2	5th PM 22-N 10-W
GORMAN	**13**	2	5th PM 24-N 10-W
GOYER	**11**	9	5th PM 25-N 8-W
GRAGG	**22**	1	5th PM 22-N 9-W
GRAHAM	**14**	2	5th PM 24-N 9-W
" "	**13**	3	5th PM 24-N 10-W
" "	**9**	3	5th PM 25-N 10-W
" "	**10**	2	5th PM 25-N 9-W
GRAHNERT	**12**	1	5th PM 25-N 7-W
GRAMMER	**18**	4	5th PM 23-N 9-W
GRANT	**19**	2	5th PM 23-N 8-W
GRAVES	**8**	2	5th PM 26-N 7-W
" "	**12**	3	5th PM 25-N 7-W
" "	**22**	2	5th PM 22-N 9-W
GRAY	**26**	1	5th PM 21-N 9-W
GREEN	**19**	2	5th PM 23-N 8-W
" "	**4**	1	5th PM 27-N 7-W
" "	**21**	1	5th PM 22-N 10-W
" "	**12**	4	5th PM 25-N 7-W
" "	**6**	1	5th PM 26-N 9-W
" "	**8**	6	5th PM 26-N 7-W
" "	**13**	1	5th PM 24-N 10-W
" "	**7**	2	5th PM 26-N 8-W
" "	**22**	4	5th PM 22-N 9-W
" "	**18**	2	5th PM 23-N 9-W
" "	**1**	1	5th PM 27-N 10-W
GREENSTREET	**19**	2	5th PM 23-N 8-W
GREENWAY	**3**	2	5th PM 27-N 8-W
" "	**7**	1	5th PM 26-N 8-W

Surname	Map Group	Parcels of Land	Meridian/Township/Range
GREENWOOD	**9**	2	5th PM 25-N 10-W
GREGG	**5**	1	5th PM 26-N 10-W
GREGORY	**9**	7	5th PM 25-N 10-W
GRIESEL	**19**	3	5th PM 23-N 8-W
GRIFFITH	**15**	10	5th PM 24-N 8-W
" "	**11**	2	5th PM 25-N 8-W
" "	**3**	4	5th PM 27-N 8-W
" "	**19**	9	5th PM 23-N 8-W
GRIMMETT	**14**	3	5th PM 24-N 9-W
GRIPE	**4**	1	5th PM 27-N 7-W
GRISHAM	**20**	6	5th PM 23-N 7-W
GROCE	**12**	2	5th PM 25-N 7-W
GROFUSE	**24**	1	5th PM 22-N 7-W
GROTE	**19**	1	5th PM 23-N 8-W
GUILLIAMS	**17**	4	5th PM 23-N 10-W
GULLEY	**7**	3	5th PM 26-N 8-W
" "	**3**	2	5th PM 27-N 8-W
GULLY	**7**	5	5th PM 26-N 8-W
" "	**2**	1	5th PM 27-N 9-W
" "	**3**	3	5th PM 27-N 8-W
GUNDER	**23**	2	5th PM 22-N 8-W
GUNDY	**23**	3	5th PM 22-N 8-W
GUNN	**28**	3	5th PM 21-N 7-W
GUNTER	**16**	3	5th PM 24-N 7-W
" "	**11**	1	5th PM 25-N 8-W
" "	**12**	5	5th PM 25-N 7-W
GUNZ	**3**	2	5th PM 27-N 8-W
" "	**4**	4	5th PM 27-N 7-W
GUTHRIE	**19**	1	5th PM 23-N 8-W
GUY	**22**	2	5th PM 22-N 9-W
HADDOCK	**11**	4	5th PM 25-N 8-W
HADLEY	**1**	1	5th PM 27-N 10-W
HAGAN	**7**	3	5th PM 26-N 8-W
HAHN	**22**	3	5th PM 22-N 9-W
HALDEMAN	**3**	1	5th PM 27-N 8-W
HALE	**7**	4	5th PM 26-N 8-W
" "	**15**	1	5th PM 24-N 8-W
" "	**3**	4	5th PM 27-N 8-W
HALKYARD	**18**	4	5th PM 23-N 9-W
HALL	**15**	1	5th PM 24-N 8-W
" "	**17**	2	5th PM 23-N 10-W
" "	**13**	3	5th PM 24-N 10-W
" "	**23**	2	5th PM 22-N 8-W
" "	**19**	21	5th PM 23-N 8-W
" "	**20**	3	5th PM 23-N 7-W
" "	**16**	1	5th PM 24-N 7-W
" "	**11**	3	5th PM 25-N 8-W
" "	**1**	3	5th PM 27-N 10-W
HALLETT	**10**	2	5th PM 25-N 9-W
" "	**6**	3	5th PM 26-N 9-W
" "	**5**	2	5th PM 26-N 10-W
HALLOWAY	**2**	1	5th PM 27-N 9-W
HALSELL	**24**	1	5th PM 22-N 7-W
" "	**18**	1	5th PM 23-N 9-W
" "	**17**	1	5th PM 23-N 10-W
HALSEY	**21**	2	5th PM 22-N 10-W
HALSTEAD	**15**	1	5th PM 24-N 8-W
" "	**8**	2	5th PM 26-N 7-W
HAMBY	**11**	2	5th PM 25-N 8-W
HAMEL	**3**	1	5th PM 27-N 8-W

Surname	Map Group	Parcels of Land	Meridian/Township/Range		
HAMILTON	**23**	3	5th PM	22-N	8-W
" "	**4**	4	5th PM	27-N	7-W
" "	**2**	2	5th PM	27-N	9-W
HAMMOND	**26**	2	5th PM	21-N	9-W
HAMMONDS	**11**	1	5th PM	25-N	8-W
HAMMONS	**2**	1	5th PM	27-N	9-W
HANCOCK	**24**	3	5th PM	22-N	7-W
HANEY	**25**	6	5th PM	21-N	10-W
" "	**4**	3	5th PM	27-N	7-W
" "	**14**	2	5th PM	24-N	9-W
HANKINS	**24**	2	5th PM	22-N	7-W
HANN	**4**	5	5th PM	27-N	7-W
HANNAH	**20**	2	5th PM	23-N	7-W
HANNER	**14**	3	5th PM	24-N	9-W
HARBER	**18**	2	5th PM	23-N	9-W
HARBINSON	**24**	1	5th PM	22-N	7-W
HARBISON	**24**	3	5th PM	22-N	7-W
HARDCASTLE	**21**	2	5th PM	22-N	10-W
HARDESTY	**18**	1	5th PM	23-N	9-W
" "	**14**	2	5th PM	24-N	9-W
HARDIN	**27**	2	5th PM	21-N	8-W
" "	**21**	1	5th PM	22-N	10-W
" "	**22**	1	5th PM	22-N	9-W
" "	**3**	3	5th PM	27-N	8-W
HARDY	**24**	1	5th PM	22-N	7-W
HARGROVES	**8**	2	5th PM	26-N	7-W
HARKEY	**2**	1	5th PM	27-N	9-W
HARKINS	**25**	2	5th PM	21-N	10-W
" "	**19**	1	5th PM	23-N	8-W
" "	**22**	2	5th PM	22-N	9-W
HARLAN	**15**	1	5th PM	24-N	8-W
" "	**11**	2	5th PM	25-N	8-W
HARLEY	**7**	3	5th PM	26-N	8-W
HARLOW	**4**	1	5th PM	27-N	7-W
" "	**7**	2	5th PM	26-N	8-W
" "	**6**	4	5th PM	26-N	9-W
HARMAN	**16**	4	5th PM	24-N	7-W
HARMON	**20**	1	5th PM	23-N	7-W
" "	**24**	3	5th PM	22-N	7-W
" "	**17**	1	5th PM	23-N	10-W
HARPER	**12**	1	5th PM	25-N	7-W
" "	**17**	3	5th PM	23-N	10-W
HARREN	**18**	1	5th PM	23-N	9-W
HARRIS	**2**	2	5th PM	27-N	9-W
" "	**1**	2	5th PM	27-N	10-W
" "	**8**	3	5th PM	26-N	7-W
" "	**4**	1	5th PM	27-N	7-W
" "	**26**	1	5th PM	21-N	9-W
" "	**20**	9	5th PM	23-N	7-W
" "	**22**	8	5th PM	22-N	9-W
" "	**19**	3	5th PM	23-N	8-W
HARRISON	**3**	1	5th PM	27-N	8-W
" "	**17**	5	5th PM	23-N	10-W
" "	**10**	3	5th PM	25-N	9-W
HARROD	**4**	3	5th PM	27-N	7-W
HARSCH	**18**	4	5th PM	23-N	9-W
HART	**16**	1	5th PM	24-N	7-W
" "	**25**	3	5th PM	21-N	10-W
HARTMAN	**17**	17	5th PM	23-N	10-W
HARVEY	**8**	3	5th PM	26-N	7-W

Surname	Map Group	Parcels of Land	Meridian/Township/Range
HARVEY (Cont'd)	**15**	2	5th PM 24-N 8-W
HATCHER	**8**	1	5th PM 26-N 7-W
" "	**14**	5	5th PM 24-N 9-W
HATFIELD	**24**	3	5th PM 22-N 7-W
HATHWAY	**12**	1	5th PM 25-N 7-W
HAVIN	**14**	2	5th PM 24-N 9-W
HAWKINS	**11**	2	5th PM 25-N 8-W
" "	**22**	3	5th PM 22-N 9-W
" "	**18**	9	5th PM 23-N 9-W
HAYDEN	**12**	2	5th PM 25-N 7-W
HAYNES	**4**	1	5th PM 27-N 7-W
" "	**8**	3	5th PM 26-N 7-W
HAYS	**14**	3	5th PM 24-N 9-W
" "	**11**	3	5th PM 25-N 8-W
" "	**15**	3	5th PM 24-N 8-W
HAYT	**20**	3	5th PM 23-N 7-W
HEAD	**8**	1	5th PM 26-N 7-W
HEALEY	**24**	1	5th PM 22-N 7-W
HEATH	**27**	3	5th PM 21-N 8-W
HEATON	**21**	5	5th PM 22-N 10-W
HEINRICH	**22**	2	5th PM 22-N 9-W
" "	**21**	2	5th PM 22-N 10-W
HELM	**20**	2	5th PM 23-N 7-W
HELMS	**14**	2	5th PM 24-N 9-W
HEMPHILL	**21**	6	5th PM 22-N 10-W
" "	**25**	2	5th PM 21-N 10-W
HENDERSON	**20**	1	5th PM 23-N 7-W
" "	**7**	2	5th PM 26-N 8-W
" "	**22**	2	5th PM 22-N 9-W
" "	**3**	7	5th PM 27-N 8-W
HENDRICK	**18**	2	5th PM 23-N 9-W
HENER	**12**	1	5th PM 25-N 7-W
HENRY	**12**	13	5th PM 25-N 7-W
" "	**11**	13	5th PM 25-N 8-W
" "	**8**	3	5th PM 26-N 7-W
" "	**2**	1	5th PM 27-N 9-W
" "	**7**	9	5th PM 26-N 8-W
HENSHAW	**11**	3	5th PM 25-N 8-W
HENSLEY	**21**	1	5th PM 22-N 10-W
" "	**6**	2	5th PM 26-N 9-W
" "	**17**	1	5th PM 23-N 10-W
HENSON	**21**	2	5th PM 22-N 10-W
" "	**25**	3	5th PM 21-N 10-W
HERMAN	**16**	3	5th PM 24-N 7-W
HERNDON	**10**	13	5th PM 25-N 9-W
" "	**15**	2	5th PM 24-N 8-W
HEROD	**6**	2	5th PM 26-N 9-W
HERREN	**14**	2	5th PM 24-N 9-W
HERRICK	**4**	1	5th PM 27-N 7-W
HERRIEN	**17**	3	5th PM 23-N 10-W
HERRIN	**14**	7	5th PM 24-N 9-W
" "	**18**	2	5th PM 23-N 9-W
HESTERLY	**14**	3	5th PM 24-N 9-W
HEWITT	**20**	2	5th PM 23-N 7-W
HEYING	**7**	2	5th PM 26-N 8-W
" "	**11**	1	5th PM 25-N 8-W
HIBBARD	**26**	2	5th PM 21-N 9-W
HIBNER	**8**	4	5th PM 26-N 7-W
HICKS	**3**	2	5th PM 27-N 8-W
" "	**13**	3	5th PM 24-N 10-W

Surname	Map Group	Parcels of Land	Meridian/Township/Range
HIGH	**21**	1	5th PM 22-N 10-W
HIGHTOWER	**8**	3	5th PM 26-N 7-W
HIGLEY	**18**	1	5th PM 23-N 9-W
HILER	**6**	8	5th PM 26-N 9-W
HILL	**14**	1	5th PM 24-N 9-W
" "	**10**	1	5th PM 25-N 9-W
" "	**18**	1	5th PM 23-N 9-W
" "	**12**	2	5th PM 25-N 7-W
" "	**6**	3	5th PM 26-N 9-W
HILTON	**24**	2	5th PM 22-N 7-W
HINDS	**6**	4	5th PM 26-N 9-W
HINES	**21**	3	5th PM 22-N 10-W
" "	**4**	2	5th PM 27-N 7-W
" "	**25**	3	5th PM 21-N 10-W
HINKLE	**1**	1	5th PM 27-N 10-W
HIXON	**21**	4	5th PM 22-N 10-W
" "	**17**	3	5th PM 23-N 10-W
HIXSON	**14**	1	5th PM 24-N 9-W
HOAG	**3**	3	5th PM 27-N 8-W
HOBBS	**4**	1	5th PM 27-N 7-W
" "	**21**	3	5th PM 22-N 10-W
HOCUTT	**19**	2	5th PM 23-N 8-W
HODGES	**17**	1	5th PM 23-N 10-W
" "	**16**	4	5th PM 24-N 7-W
" "	**7**	2	5th PM 26-N 8-W
HOEY	**10**	2	5th PM 25-N 9-W
HOGAN	**27**	1	5th PM 21-N 8-W
" "	**2**	3	5th PM 27-N 9-W
HOGGATT	**21**	2	5th PM 22-N 10-W
" "	**8**	2	5th PM 26-N 7-W
" "	**11**	1	5th PM 25-N 8-W
HOKE	**7**	1	5th PM 26-N 8-W
HOKER	**16**	1	5th PM 24-N 7-W
HOLBROOK	**18**	4	5th PM 23-N 9-W
HOLCOMB	**12**	3	5th PM 25-N 7-W
HOLDEN	**4**	2	5th PM 27-N 7-W
" "	**8**	11	5th PM 26-N 7-W
HOLEMAN	**21**	3	5th PM 22-N 10-W
" "	**25**	1	5th PM 21-N 10-W
HOLLAND	**21**	4	5th PM 22-N 10-W
HOLLINGSHAD	**14**	3	5th PM 24-N 9-W
HOLLINGSWORTH	**1**	3	5th PM 27-N 10-W
HOLLOWAY	**2**	2	5th PM 27-N 9-W
" "	**27**	9	5th PM 21-N 8-W
HOLMAN	**22**	1	5th PM 22-N 9-W
HOLMES	**22**	3	5th PM 22-N 9-W
HOLT	**14**	2	5th PM 24-N 9-W
HOLZSCHEITER	**19**	3	5th PM 23-N 8-W
HOMANS	**20**	4	5th PM 23-N 7-W
HOMESLEY	**6**	2	5th PM 26-N 9-W
HON	**21**	3	5th PM 22-N 10-W
HOOD	**3**	4	5th PM 27-N 8-W
" "	**6**	1	5th PM 26-N 9-W
HOOPER	**22**	2	5th PM 22-N 9-W
HOOSE	**15**	3	5th PM 24-N 8-W
HOOTEN	**8**	1	5th PM 26-N 7-W
" "	**12**	3	5th PM 25-N 7-W
HOOVER	**4**	4	5th PM 27-N 7-W
HOPE	**4**	3	5th PM 27-N 7-W
" "	**8**	3	5th PM 26-N 7-W

Surname	Map Group	Parcels of Land	Meridian/Township/Range		
HOPKINS	**13**	22	5th PM	24-N	10-W
" "	**9**	2	5th PM	25-N	10-W
" "	**14**	12	5th PM	24-N	9-W
" "	**17**	9	5th PM	23-N	10-W
HORN	**17**	2	5th PM	23-N	10-W
HORSMAN	**25**	2	5th PM	21-N	10-W
" "	**21**	3	5th PM	22-N	10-W
" "	**18**	4	5th PM	23-N	9-W
HORSTEN	**6**	4	5th PM	26-N	9-W
HOSHOUR	**13**	3	5th PM	24-N	10-W
HOSKINSON	**2**	1	5th PM	27-N	9-W
HOUGH	**4**	1	5th PM	27-N	7-W
HOUGHTON	**12**	5	5th PM	25-N	7-W
" "	**8**	1	5th PM	26-N	7-W
HOUSE	**11**	2	5th PM	25-N	8-W
" "	**4**	2	5th PM	27-N	7-W
HOVEY	**18**	6	5th PM	23-N	9-W
HOWARD	**21**	4	5th PM	22-N	10-W
" "	**25**	3	5th PM	21-N	10-W
" "	**9**	2	5th PM	25-N	10-W
" "	**10**	2	5th PM	25-N	9-W
" "	**22**	4	5th PM	22-N	9-W
" "	**12**	6	5th PM	25-N	7-W
HOWELL	**11**	1	5th PM	25-N	8-W
" "	**28**	2	5th PM	21-N	7-W
" "	**15**	37	5th PM	24-N	8-W
" "	**17**	1	5th PM	23-N	10-W
" "	**14**	6	5th PM	24-N	9-W
" "	**16**	11	5th PM	24-N	7-W
HOWERTON	**27**	1	5th PM	21-N	8-W
HOY	**3**	2	5th PM	27-N	8-W
HOYT	**20**	1	5th PM	23-N	7-W
HUCKSTEP	**12**	3	5th PM	25-N	7-W
HUDDLESTON	**19**	2	5th PM	23-N	8-W
HUDLOW	**15**	2	5th PM	24-N	8-W
" "	**14**	1	5th PM	24-N	9-W
" "	**8**	2	5th PM	26-N	7-W
" "	**17**	1	5th PM	23-N	10-W
" "	**13**	2	5th PM	24-N	10-W
HUDSON	**11**	12	5th PM	25-N	8-W
HUFF	**6**	4	5th PM	26-N	9-W
" "	**21**	3	5th PM	22-N	10-W
" "	**5**	1	5th PM	26-N	10-W
HUFFHINES	**15**	3	5th PM	24-N	8-W
HUGHES	**25**	3	5th PM	21-N	10-W
" "	**7**	2	5th PM	26-N	8-W
" "	**8**	2	5th PM	26-N	7-W
" "	**11**	3	5th PM	25-N	8-W
HUGHLETT	**12**	3	5th PM	25-N	7-W
HUGHS	**11**	1	5th PM	25-N	8-W
HULL	**2**	7	5th PM	27-N	9-W
" "	**19**	2	5th PM	23-N	8-W
HULS	**21**	2	5th PM	22-N	10-W
HUMPHREY	**4**	3	5th PM	27-N	7-W
HUNSPERGER	**24**	3	5th PM	22-N	7-W
HUNT	**18**	3	5th PM	23-N	9-W
" "	**15**	2	5th PM	24-N	8-W
" "	**4**	10	5th PM	27-N	7-W
HUNTER	**18**	1	5th PM	23-N	9-W
" "	**13**	2	5th PM	24-N	10-W

Surname	Map Group	Parcels of Land	Meridian/Township/Range
HUNTER (Cont'd)	**12**	2	5th PM 25-N 7-W
" "	**17**	3	5th PM 23-N 10-W
" "	**21**	1	5th PM 22-N 10-W
" "	**11**	5	5th PM 25-N 8-W
HUSTON	**13**	2	5th PM 24-N 10-W
HUTCHESON	**17**	2	5th PM 23-N 10-W
HUTCHINS	**14**	2	5th PM 24-N 9-W
HYLTON	**23**	2	5th PM 22-N 8-W
HYNES	**10**	1	5th PM 25-N 9-W
" "	**15**	2	5th PM 24-N 8-W
ING	**18**	1	5th PM 23-N 9-W
INGLE	**19**	3	5th PM 23-N 8-W
INGOLD	**13**	4	5th PM 24-N 10-W
" "	**15**	5	5th PM 24-N 8-W
INGRAM	**14**	2	5th PM 24-N 9-W
" "	**10**	6	5th PM 25-N 9-W
INMAN	**3**	2	5th PM 27-N 8-W
" "	**17**	2	5th PM 23-N 10-W
IRVIN	**10**	4	5th PM 25-N 9-W
IRWIN	**8**	1	5th PM 26-N 7-W
JACKSON	**7**	8	5th PM 26-N 8-W
" "	**8**	7	5th PM 26-N 7-W
" "	**15**	2	5th PM 24-N 8-W
" "	**10**	1	5th PM 25-N 9-W
" "	**3**	1	5th PM 27-N 8-W
JAMES	**19**	3	5th PM 23-N 8-W
" "	**17**	2	5th PM 23-N 10-W
JARGENSON	**23**	4	5th PM 22-N 8-W
JARRELL	**23**	2	5th PM 22-N 8-W
" "	**22**	1	5th PM 22-N 9-W
" "	**8**	1	5th PM 26-N 7-W
JAYNE	**11**	3	5th PM 25-N 8-W
JEFFERY	**24**	1	5th PM 22-N 7-W
JENKINS	**7**	11	5th PM 26-N 8-W
" "	**15**	4	5th PM 24-N 8-W
" "	**4**	2	5th PM 27-N 7-W
JEREMIAH	**8**	1	5th PM 26-N 7-W
" "	**7**	2	5th PM 26-N 8-W
JOHNS	**14**	12	5th PM 24-N 9-W
JOHNSON	**15**	4	5th PM 24-N 8-W
" "	**16**	2	5th PM 24-N 7-W
" "	**19**	31	5th PM 23-N 8-W
" "	**1**	1	5th PM 27-N 10-W
" "	**14**	5	5th PM 24-N 9-W
" "	**17**	3	5th PM 23-N 10-W
" "	**21**	5	5th PM 22-N 10-W
" "	**12**	3	5th PM 25-N 7-W
" "	**13**	3	5th PM 24-N 10-W
" "	**10**	1	5th PM 25-N 9-W
" "	**24**	1	5th PM 22-N 7-W
" "	**3**	1	5th PM 27-N 8-W
" "	**2**	3	5th PM 27-N 9-W
" "	**18**	3	5th PM 23-N 9-W
" "	**22**	4	5th PM 22-N 9-W
" "	**20**	1	5th PM 23-N 7-W
JOHNSTON	**14**	5	5th PM 24-N 9-W
" "	**1**	1	5th PM 27-N 10-W
" "	**19**	1	5th PM 23-N 8-W
" "	**13**	3	5th PM 24-N 10-W
" "	**18**	2	5th PM 23-N 9-W

Surname	Map Group	Parcels of Land	Meridian/Township/Range		
JOHNSTON (Cont'd)	17	1	5th PM	23-N	10-W
JONES	21	6	5th PM	22-N	10-W
" "	1	3	5th PM	27-N	10-W
" "	7	5	5th PM	26-N	8-W
" "	15	11	5th PM	24-N	8-W
" "	12	5	5th PM	25-N	7-W
" "	2	10	5th PM	27-N	9-W
" "	3	6	5th PM	27-N	8-W
" "	14	1	5th PM	24-N	9-W
" "	6	1	5th PM	26-N	9-W
" "	9	2	5th PM	25-N	10-W
" "	8	12	5th PM	26-N	7-W
" "	4	3	5th PM	27-N	7-W
" "	26	2	5th PM	21-N	9-W
" "	22	4	5th PM	22-N	9-W
" "	24	3	5th PM	22-N	7-W
JORDAN	11	1	5th PM	25-N	8-W
JUDD	23	3	5th PM	22-N	8-W
JUDKINS	19	2	5th PM	23-N	8-W
" "	18	1	5th PM	23-N	9-W
JUERN	28	2	5th PM	21-N	7-W
JULIEN	17	2	5th PM	23-N	10-W
KARR	16	2	5th PM	24-N	7-W
" "	13	7	5th PM	24-N	10-W
" "	4	1	5th PM	27-N	7-W
KAUFMAN	11	3	5th PM	25-N	8-W
KAY	22	1	5th PM	22-N	9-W
KEE	18	2	5th PM	23-N	9-W
" "	17	2	5th PM	23-N	10-W
KEELE	22	1	5th PM	22-N	9-W
KEELER	5	6	5th PM	26-N	10-W
KEEN	2	2	5th PM	27-N	9-W
KEIRN	22	1	5th PM	22-N	9-W
" "	26	2	5th PM	21-N	9-W
KEISTER	15	8	5th PM	24-N	8-W
KEITHLY	6	5	5th PM	26-N	9-W
" "	9	1	5th PM	25-N	10-W
KEIVER	20	4	5th PM	23-N	7-W
KELIN	15	1	5th PM	24-N	8-W
KELLUM	16	1	5th PM	24-N	7-W
KELLY	22	2	5th PM	22-N	9-W
" "	4	2	5th PM	27-N	7-W
KELSO	4	2	5th PM	27-N	7-W
KENAGA	8	13	5th PM	26-N	7-W
KENEGA	8	2	5th PM	26-N	7-W
KENNEY	18	1	5th PM	23-N	9-W
" "	19	3	5th PM	23-N	8-W
KENSLOW	17	1	5th PM	23-N	10-W
" "	18	4	5th PM	23-N	9-W
" "	23	1	5th PM	22-N	8-W
KENT	13	3	5th PM	24-N	10-W
KERNOCK	16	5	5th PM	24-N	7-W
KERSHNER	1	1	5th PM	27-N	10-W
KIDD	1	1	5th PM	27-N	10-W
KIDWELL	14	1	5th PM	24-N	9-W
KIERER	16	1	5th PM	24-N	7-W
KILE	7	11	5th PM	26-N	8-W
KILLION	21	6	5th PM	22-N	10-W
KILLOUGH	22	8	5th PM	22-N	9-W
KIMBALL	26	1	5th PM	21-N	9-W

Surname	Map Group	Parcels of Land	Meridian/Township/Range
KIMBROUGH	**21**	3	5th PM 22-N 10-W
KINCHLOE	**18**	3	5th PM 23-N 9-W
KING	**15**	2	5th PM 24-N 8-W
" "	**3**	4	5th PM 27-N 8-W
" "	**18**	1	5th PM 23-N 9-W
" "	**19**	3	5th PM 23-N 8-W
" "	**14**	2	5th PM 24-N 9-W
" "	**4**	1	5th PM 27-N 7-W
" "	**26**	2	5th PM 21-N 9-W
" "	**20**	5	5th PM 23-N 7-W
" "	**21**	1	5th PM 22-N 10-W
" "	**25**	3	5th PM 21-N 10-W
KINGDON	**21**	2	5th PM 22-N 10-W
KINION	**6**	5	5th PM 26-N 9-W
" "	**10**	1	5th PM 25-N 9-W
KINKEAD	**14**	3	5th PM 24-N 9-W
KINSOLVING	**17**	1	5th PM 23-N 10-W
" "	**18**	3	5th PM 23-N 9-W
KIRKPATRICK	**19**	1	5th PM 23-N 8-W
" "	**24**	1	5th PM 22-N 7-W
KIRKWOOD	**16**	1	5th PM 24-N 7-W
KISER	**12**	2	5th PM 25-N 7-W
KISINGER	**14**	3	5th PM 24-N 9-W
KISNER	**19**	2	5th PM 23-N 8-W
KNIGHT	**19**	6	5th PM 23-N 8-W
KNOWLTON	**15**	3	5th PM 24-N 8-W
" "	**12**	2	5th PM 25-N 7-W
KNOX	**17**	2	5th PM 23-N 10-W
" "	**18**	2	5th PM 23-N 9-W
KOLLING	**28**	1	5th PM 21-N 7-W
KOONCE	**8**	5	5th PM 26-N 7-W
KRAUSE	**22**	3	5th PM 22-N 9-W
KROHN	**19**	5	5th PM 23-N 8-W
KUEPEL	**4**	1	5th PM 27-N 7-W
KURSEY	**27**	2	5th PM 21-N 8-W
" "	**23**	1	5th PM 22-N 8-W
LAFFOON	**16**	6	5th PM 24-N 7-W
LAIR	**21**	5	5th PM 22-N 10-W
LAIRD	**4**	4	5th PM 27-N 7-W
LAMBE	**23**	2	5th PM 22-N 8-W
" "	**22**	1	5th PM 22-N 9-W
LAMONS	**15**	1	5th PM 24-N 8-W
" "	**23**	3	5th PM 22-N 8-W
" "	**24**	3	5th PM 22-N 7-W
" "	**19**	6	5th PM 23-N 8-W
" "	**27**	2	5th PM 21-N 8-W
LANCASTER	**24**	6	5th PM 22-N 7-W
LANCE	**2**	1	5th PM 27-N 9-W
LANE	**11**	3	5th PM 25-N 8-W
LANG	**17**	3	5th PM 23-N 10-W
LANGLEY	**22**	5	5th PM 22-N 9-W
LANGSTON	**10**	2	5th PM 25-N 9-W
" "	**19**	1	5th PM 23-N 8-W
" "	**14**	3	5th PM 24-N 9-W
" "	**17**	2	5th PM 23-N 10-W
LANNING	**13**	2	5th PM 24-N 10-W
LARA	**15**	3	5th PM 24-N 8-W
LASATER	**10**	1	5th PM 25-N 9-W
LASSWELL	**11**	4	5th PM 25-N 8-W
LAUGHERY	**14**	3	5th PM 24-N 9-W

Surname	Map Group	Parcels of Land	Meridian/Township/Range
LAURANCE	**13**	2	5th PM 24-N 10-W
" "	**17**	1	5th PM 23-N 10-W
LAWHEAD	**24**	1	5th PM 22-N 7-W
LAWHORN	**22**	4	5th PM 22-N 9-W
" "	**23**	3	5th PM 22-N 8-W
LAWING	**17**	7	5th PM 23-N 10-W
LAYTON	**16**	1	5th PM 24-N 7-W
LE FORCE	**15**	2	5th PM 24-N 8-W
LEARNARD	**1**	5	5th PM 27-N 10-W
" "	**13**	14	5th PM 24-N 10-W
" "	**2**	29	5th PM 27-N 9-W
" "	**9**	2	5th PM 25-N 10-W
" "	**5**	2	5th PM 26-N 10-W
LEATHERS	**18**	1	5th PM 23-N 9-W
LECKRON	**17**	1	5th PM 23-N 10-W
LEDBETTER	**8**	4	5th PM 26-N 7-W
" "	**13**	7	5th PM 24-N 10-W
LEE	**8**	3	5th PM 26-N 7-W
" "	**7**	4	5th PM 26-N 8-W
" "	**6**	1	5th PM 26-N 9-W
LEEDOM	**6**	3	5th PM 26-N 9-W
LEEPER	**21**	4	5th PM 22-N 10-W
LEFEVER	**22**	2	5th PM 22-N 9-W
LELAND	**11**	1	5th PM 25-N 8-W
LEMONS	**19**	2	5th PM 23-N 8-W
LEONARD	**18**	2	5th PM 23-N 9-W
LETSINGER	**21**	2	5th PM 22-N 10-W
LEWEY	**22**	3	5th PM 22-N 9-W
LEWIS	**22**	2	5th PM 22-N 9-W
" "	**4**	2	5th PM 27-N 7-W
" "	**14**	9	5th PM 24-N 9-W
" "	**8**	2	5th PM 26-N 7-W
LIGETH	**18**	1	5th PM 23-N 9-W
LILE	**8**	3	5th PM 26-N 7-W
LILES	**16**	1	5th PM 24-N 7-W
LIMB	**4**	5	5th PM 27-N 7-W
LINDERER	**6**	8	5th PM 26-N 9-W
LINGO	**21**	1	5th PM 22-N 10-W
LINTHICUM	**22**	3	5th PM 22-N 9-W
" "	**18**	2	5th PM 23-N 9-W
LIVESAY	**4**	1	5th PM 27-N 7-W
LIVINGSTON	**8**	2	5th PM 26-N 7-W
" "	**2**	4	5th PM 27-N 9-W
" "	**4**	1	5th PM 27-N 7-W
" "	**18**	1	5th PM 23-N 9-W
" "	**3**	2	5th PM 27-N 8-W
" "	**6**	3	5th PM 26-N 9-W
LIVSAY	**4**	3	5th PM 27-N 7-W
LLOYD	**17**	3	5th PM 23-N 10-W
LOAGUE	**19**	2	5th PM 23-N 8-W
LOCH	**25**	2	5th PM 21-N 10-W
LOCK	**27**	2	5th PM 21-N 8-W
LODER	**4**	2	5th PM 27-N 7-W
LOGAN	**18**	2	5th PM 23-N 9-W
" "	**17**	2	5th PM 23-N 10-W
LOGSTON	**19**	1	5th PM 23-N 8-W
LONG	**6**	3	5th PM 26-N 9-W
" "	**21**	12	5th PM 22-N 10-W
LONGDEN	**6**	1	5th PM 26-N 9-W
LORD	**7**	3	5th PM 26-N 8-W

Surname	Map Group	Parcels of Land	Meridian/Township/Range
LOUTHEN	**20**	3	5th PM 23-N 7-W
LOUTRELL	**2**	2	5th PM 27-N 9-W
LOVAN	**2**	8	5th PM 27-N 9-W
" "	**10**	1	5th PM 25-N 9-W
" "	**9**	5	5th PM 25-N 10-W
LOVEL	**6**	3	5th PM 26-N 9-W
LOVELACE	**21**	2	5th PM 22-N 10-W
LOVINS	**9**	1	5th PM 25-N 10-W
LOWREY	**11**	2	5th PM 25-N 8-W
" "	**22**	3	5th PM 22-N 9-W
LOWRY	**13**	3	5th PM 24-N 10-W
LOY	**23**	1	5th PM 22-N 8-W
" "	**22**	9	5th PM 22-N 9-W
LUCK	**8**	1	5th PM 26-N 7-W
LUDWIG	**19**	8	5th PM 23-N 8-W
LUKE	**4**	2	5th PM 27-N 7-W
LUMBLEY	**9**	2	5th PM 25-N 10-W
LUMPS	**20**	2	5th PM 23-N 7-W
LUNG	**19**	3	5th PM 23-N 8-W
LUTH	**4**	4	5th PM 27-N 7-W
LUTHER	**24**	2	5th PM 22-N 7-W
LUTTES	**13**	2	5th PM 24-N 10-W
LYNCH	**4**	1	5th PM 27-N 7-W
" "	**12**	3	5th PM 25-N 7-W
LYON	**18**	2	5th PM 23-N 9-W
MACK	**13**	3	5th PM 24-N 10-W
" "	**23**	6	5th PM 22-N 8-W
MACKEY	**11**	7	5th PM 25-N 8-W
" "	**16**	4	5th PM 24-N 7-W
MACLAIN	**14**	2	5th PM 24-N 9-W
MACORMIC	**2**	1	5th PM 27-N 9-W
MADDEN	**24**	3	5th PM 22-N 7-W
MADDOX	**15**	1	5th PM 24-N 8-W
MADES	**4**	2	5th PM 27-N 7-W
MAHAN	**13**	5	5th PM 24-N 10-W
MAHON	**13**	2	5th PM 24-N 10-W
MAHONEY	**18**	2	5th PM 23-N 9-W
MAHORNEY	**24**	2	5th PM 22-N 7-W
MAIN	**11**	4	5th PM 25-N 8-W
MALONE	**21**	2	5th PM 22-N 10-W
MANESS	**11**	1	5th PM 25-N 8-W
MANGUM	**3**	1	5th PM 27-N 8-W
MANNING	**16**	1	5th PM 24-N 7-W
MANNIX	**24**	1	5th PM 22-N 7-W
MANNON	**17**	1	5th PM 23-N 10-W
MANSFIELD	**23**	3	5th PM 22-N 8-W
MANZE	**23**	2	5th PM 22-N 8-W
MARAT	**7**	2	5th PM 26-N 8-W
MARITT	**17**	1	5th PM 23-N 10-W
" "	**13**	2	5th PM 24-N 10-W
MARKHAM	**7**	3	5th PM 26-N 8-W
MARONEY	**20**	1	5th PM 23-N 7-W
MARRITT	**18**	1	5th PM 23-N 9-W
MARSHALL	**1**	1	5th PM 27-N 10-W
" "	**24**	2	5th PM 22-N 7-W
" "	**16**	2	5th PM 24-N 7-W
MARTIN	**15**	8	5th PM 24-N 8-W
" "	**6**	3	5th PM 26-N 9-W
" "	**21**	4	5th PM 22-N 10-W
" "	**3**	3	5th PM 27-N 8-W

Surname	Map Group	Parcels of Land	Meridian/Township/Range		
MARTIN (Cont'd)	**4**	3	5th PM	27-N	7-W
" "	**13**	1	5th PM	24-N	10-W
" "	**10**	1	5th PM	25-N	9-W
" "	**8**	1	5th PM	26-N	7-W
MASON	**26**	3	5th PM	21-N	9-W
" "	**18**	1	5th PM	23-N	9-W
" "	**22**	4	5th PM	22-N	9-W
MATLOCK	**21**	5	5th PM	22-N	10-W
MATNEY	**16**	5	5th PM	24-N	7-W
" "	**23**	2	5th PM	22-N	8-W
" "	**27**	1	5th PM	21-N	8-W
" "	**22**	1	5th PM	22-N	9-W
" "	**26**	3	5th PM	21-N	9-W
" "	**12**	2	5th PM	25-N	7-W
MATTHEWS	**21**	5	5th PM	22-N	10-W
MAVONEY	**20**	2	5th PM	23-N	7-W
MAWHINNEY	**16**	3	5th PM	24-N	7-W
MAXEY	**20**	1	5th PM	23-N	7-W
" "	**11**	2	5th PM	25-N	8-W
MAXWELL	**16**	6	5th PM	24-N	7-W
MAY	**19**	2	5th PM	23-N	8-W
" "	**15**	1	5th PM	24-N	8-W
MAYHEW	**19**	1	5th PM	23-N	8-W
MCAFEE	**18**	3	5th PM	23-N	9-W
MCALLISTER	**3**	3	5th PM	27-N	8-W
MCANALLY	**19**	2	5th PM	23-N	8-W
MCBRIDE	**21**	2	5th PM	22-N	10-W
MCCABE	**16**	3	5th PM	24-N	7-W
MCCALL	**11**	3	5th PM	25-N	8-W
MCCALLISTER	**22**	2	5th PM	22-N	9-W
MCCALLON	**22**	2	5th PM	22-N	9-W
MCCAMMAN	**20**	3	5th PM	23-N	7-W
MCCAMMON	**20**	5	5th PM	23-N	7-W
MCCAMRON	**20**	2	5th PM	23-N	7-W
MCCANNON	**15**	1	5th PM	24-N	8-W
" "	**13**	2	5th PM	24-N	10-W
MCCARDEL	**4**	3	5th PM	27-N	7-W
MCCLAIN	**19**	1	5th PM	23-N	8-W
MCCLANAHAN	**7**	1	5th PM	26-N	8-W
MCCLELLAN	**6**	3	5th PM	26-N	9-W
MCCLINTOCK	**11**	4	5th PM	25-N	8-W
MCCOLLUM	**8**	3	5th PM	26-N	7-W
" "	**16**	1	5th PM	24-N	7-W
MCCOMB	**19**	2	5th PM	23-N	8-W
" "	**14**	2	5th PM	24-N	9-W
MCCOMICK	**27**	1	5th PM	21-N	8-W
MCCOY	**22**	2	5th PM	22-N	9-W
" "	**26**	2	5th PM	21-N	9-W
" "	**8**	1	5th PM	26-N	7-W
" "	**24**	1	5th PM	22-N	7-W
MCCRACKEN	**23**	1	5th PM	22-N	8-W
MCCRITE	**12**	2	5th PM	25-N	7-W
MCCULLOCH	**4**	5	5th PM	27-N	7-W
MCCULLOUGH	**2**	5	5th PM	27-N	9-W
MCDANIEL	**17**	3	5th PM	23-N	10-W
" "	**18**	3	5th PM	23-N	9-W
" "	**22**	1	5th PM	22-N	9-W
" "	**11**	1	5th PM	25-N	8-W
" "	**21**	22	5th PM	22-N	10-W
MCDONAL	**3**	3	5th PM	27-N	8-W

Surname	Map Group	Parcels of Land	Meridian/Township/Range
MCELFATRICK	**20**	2	5th PM 23-N 7-W
MCELMURRY	**22**	2	5th PM 22-N 9-W
MCELRATH	**21**	2	5th PM 22-N 10-W
MCEMBREE	**16**	4	5th PM 24-N 7-W
MCFADDIN	**22**	6	5th PM 22-N 9-W
MCFALLS	**11**	1	5th PM 25-N 8-W
" "	**10**	2	5th PM 25-N 9-W
MCFARLAND	**3**	3	5th PM 27-N 8-W
" "	**12**	5	5th PM 25-N 7-W
" "	**11**	7	5th PM 25-N 8-W
MCGEE	**21**	1	5th PM 22-N 10-W
" "	**22**	2	5th PM 22-N 9-W
" "	**15**	2	5th PM 24-N 8-W
" "	**6**	1	5th PM 26-N 9-W
MCGINTY	**23**	3	5th PM 22-N 8-W
" "	**11**	4	5th PM 25-N 8-W
MCGOLDRICK	**17**	5	5th PM 23-N 10-W
MCGONIGAL	**3**	3	5th PM 27-N 8-W
MCGOWAN	**7**	1	5th PM 26-N 8-W
MCGOWEN	**7**	1	5th PM 26-N 8-W
MCGRATH	**3**	1	5th PM 27-N 8-W
" "	**8**	1	5th PM 26-N 7-W
MCGRAW	**6**	2	5th PM 26-N 9-W
MCGUIRE	**21**	1	5th PM 22-N 10-W
" "	**7**	1	5th PM 26-N 8-W
MCHAN	**12**	6	5th PM 25-N 7-W
" "	**8**	3	5th PM 26-N 7-W
MCHANN	**8**	2	5th PM 26-N 7-W
MCKANNA	**8**	1	5th PM 26-N 7-W
MCKIM	**26**	4	5th PM 21-N 9-W
MCKNIGHT	**15**	2	5th PM 24-N 8-W
MCLAIN	**25**	2	5th PM 21-N 10-W
MCMAHAN	**9**	2	5th PM 25-N 10-W
MCMAHON	**10**	2	5th PM 25-N 9-W
MCMANEMIN	**11**	2	5th PM 25-N 8-W
MCMASTER	**19**	1	5th PM 23-N 8-W
MCMILLIN	**9**	2	5th PM 25-N 10-W
MCMURTRY	**21**	1	5th PM 22-N 10-W
" "	**7**	9	5th PM 26-N 8-W
MCNAY	**21**	3	5th PM 22-N 10-W
MCNEELY	**26**	3	5th PM 21-N 9-W
MCRIPPEE	**15**	1	5th PM 24-N 8-W
MCTHOMPSON	**21**	2	5th PM 22-N 10-W
MEADOWS	**19**	3	5th PM 23-N 8-W
MEARS	**20**	1	5th PM 23-N 7-W
MEDLEY	**2**	1	5th PM 27-N 9-W
MEDLIN	**3**	3	5th PM 27-N 8-W
MEDLOCK	**21**	3	5th PM 22-N 10-W
MEINECKE	**6**	2	5th PM 26-N 9-W
MELTON	**28**	1	5th PM 21-N 7-W
" "	**11**	2	5th PM 25-N 8-W
MENDENHALL	**24**	2	5th PM 22-N 7-W
" "	**4**	1	5th PM 27-N 7-W
MEREDITH	**24**	1	5th PM 22-N 7-W
MERIDETH	**24**	4	5th PM 22-N 7-W
MERIDITH	**24**	2	5th PM 22-N 7-W
MERIEDITH	**24**	3	5th PM 22-N 7-W
MERRILL	**5**	2	5th PM 26-N 10-W
MERRITT	**16**	6	5th PM 24-N 7-W
MEYER	**12**	3	5th PM 25-N 7-W

Surname	Map Group	Parcels of Land	Meridian/Township/Range		
MEYER (Cont'd)	**18**	4	5th PM	23-N	9-W
MIDDAUGH	**18**	1	5th PM	23-N	9-W
" "	**22**	1	5th PM	22-N	9-W
MIDDLETON	**15**	2	5th PM	24-N	8-W
MILKS	**6**	3	5th PM	26-N	9-W
MILLARD	**20**	1	5th PM	23-N	7-W
MILLBANKS	**4**	3	5th PM	27-N	7-W
MILLER	**14**	6	5th PM	24-N	9-W
" "	**17**	1	5th PM	23-N	10-W
" "	**18**	1	5th PM	23-N	9-W
" "	**15**	3	5th PM	24-N	8-W
" "	**20**	2	5th PM	23-N	7-W
" "	**7**	11	5th PM	26-N	8-W
" "	**6**	5	5th PM	26-N	9-W
" "	**24**	6	5th PM	22-N	7-W
" "	**22**	1	5th PM	22-N	9-W
" "	**2**	1	5th PM	27-N	9-W
MILLS	**21**	1	5th PM	22-N	10-W
" "	**22**	2	5th PM	22-N	9-W
MILLSAPS	**23**	2	5th PM	22-N	8-W
MILLSPAUGH	**7**	2	5th PM	26-N	8-W
MINER	**23**	1	5th PM	22-N	8-W
MIRES	**2**	1	5th PM	27-N	9-W
MITCHELL	**12**	2	5th PM	25-N	7-W
" "	**2**	3	5th PM	27-N	9-W
" "	**17**	3	5th PM	23-N	10-W
" "	**19**	3	5th PM	23-N	8-W
" "	**1**	1	5th PM	27-N	10-W
" "	**16**	5	5th PM	24-N	7-W
MITTELSTETTER	**24**	3	5th PM	22-N	7-W
MITTS	**13**	3	5th PM	24-N	10-W
MIZE	**10**	4	5th PM	25-N	9-W
MOBACK	**18**	2	5th PM	23-N	9-W
MODRALL	**11**	3	5th PM	25-N	8-W
" "	**7**	9	5th PM	26-N	8-W
MOFFITT	**2**	4	5th PM	27-N	9-W
MONGER	**11**	3	5th PM	25-N	8-W
" "	**12**	1	5th PM	25-N	7-W
MONKS	**22**	5	5th PM	22-N	9-W
" "	**15**	11	5th PM	24-N	8-W
" "	**14**	1	5th PM	24-N	9-W
" "	**23**	2	5th PM	22-N	8-W
MONTGOMERY	**22**	2	5th PM	22-N	9-W
" "	**15**	3	5th PM	24-N	8-W
" "	**14**	4	5th PM	24-N	9-W
MOODY	**21**	1	5th PM	22-N	10-W
MOORE	**19**	1	5th PM	23-N	8-W
" "	**11**	3	5th PM	25-N	8-W
" "	**15**	2	5th PM	24-N	8-W
" "	**18**	2	5th PM	23-N	9-W
" "	**3**	2	5th PM	27-N	8-W
" "	**10**	1	5th PM	25-N	9-W
" "	**21**	2	5th PM	22-N	10-W
" "	**4**	1	5th PM	27-N	7-W
MOREHEAD	**6**	1	5th PM	26-N	9-W
" "	**7**	2	5th PM	26-N	8-W
MORELAND	**22**	3	5th PM	22-N	9-W
" "	**21**	1	5th PM	22-N	10-W
MORGAN	**7**	2	5th PM	26-N	8-W
" "	**18**	3	5th PM	23-N	9-W

Surname	Map Group	Parcels of Land	Meridian/Township/Range		
MORGAN (Cont'd)	**3**	6	5th PM	27-N	8-W
" "	**13**	2	5th PM	24-N	10-W
MORRIS	**18**	2	5th PM	23-N	9-W
" "	**21**	3	5th PM	22-N	10-W
" "	**8**	2	5th PM	26-N	7-W
" "	**13**	3	5th PM	24-N	10-W
" "	**1**	3	5th PM	27-N	10-W
" "	**26**	1	5th PM	21-N	9-W
" "	**12**	1	5th PM	25-N	7-W
" "	**11**	1	5th PM	25-N	8-W
MORRISON	**19**	3	5th PM	23-N	8-W
MORROW	**25**	2	5th PM	21-N	10-W
MORSE	**1**	1	5th PM	27-N	10-W
MORTON	**21**	2	5th PM	22-N	10-W
MOSELEY	**10**	1	5th PM	25-N	9-W
MOSS	**10**	2	5th PM	25-N	9-W
MOXLEY	**1**	2	5th PM	27-N	10-W
MUHL	**20**	1	5th PM	23-N	7-W
MULLANY	**7**	2	5th PM	26-N	8-W
MULLINIX	**7**	1	5th PM	26-N	8-W
MULLINS	**10**	2	5th PM	25-N	9-W
" "	**6**	2	5th PM	26-N	9-W
MURDOCK	**20**	1	5th PM	23-N	7-W
MURPHEY	**15**	3	5th PM	24-N	8-W
MURRAY	**16**	1	5th PM	24-N	7-W
" "	**3**	1	5th PM	27-N	8-W
MURRELL	**3**	2	5th PM	27-N	8-W
" "	**9**	2	5th PM	25-N	10-W
" "	**5**	1	5th PM	26-N	10-W
MURREY	**16**	3	5th PM	24-N	7-W
MUSE	**10**	2	5th PM	25-N	9-W
" "	**11**	2	5th PM	25-N	8-W
" "	**24**	1	5th PM	22-N	7-W
MUSGROVE	**10**	7	5th PM	25-N	9-W
MUSTION	**19**	6	5th PM	23-N	8-W
" "	**15**	4	5th PM	24-N	8-W
MUSTON	**15**	1	5th PM	24-N	8-W
MYERS	**7**	3	5th PM	26-N	8-W
" "	**27**	1	5th PM	21-N	8-W
MYRES	**23**	1	5th PM	22-N	8-W
MYRICK	**22**	2	5th PM	22-N	9-W
MYZELL	**12**	1	5th PM	25-N	7-W
" "	**11**	1	5th PM	25-N	8-W
NAHM	**4**	3	5th PM	27-N	7-W
NALE	**28**	3	5th PM	21-N	7-W
" "	**24**	2	5th PM	22-N	7-W
NANCE	**4**	2	5th PM	27-N	7-W
" "	**3**	5	5th PM	27-N	8-W
NANEY	**16**	5	5th PM	24-N	7-W
NASH	**11**	3	5th PM	25-N	8-W
" "	**22**	3	5th PM	22-N	9-W
" "	**18**	2	5th PM	23-N	9-W
NEASE	**2**	4	5th PM	27-N	9-W
NEEDHAM	**3**	3	5th PM	27-N	8-W
NELSON	**22**	2	5th PM	22-N	9-W
" "	**26**	2	5th PM	21-N	9-W
NETTLETON	**1**	1	5th PM	27-N	10-W
" "	**5**	2	5th PM	26-N	10-W
" "	**6**	8	5th PM	26-N	9-W
" "	**10**	2	5th PM	25-N	9-W

Surname	Map Group	Parcels of Land	Meridian/Township/Range
NETTLETON (Cont'd)	19	6	5th PM 23-N 8-W
NEWBERRY	21	2	5th PM 22-N 10-W
" "	22	8	5th PM 22-N 9-W
" "	20	2	5th PM 23-N 7-W
NEWKIRK	26	4	5th PM 21-N 9-W
NEWSOM	4	1	5th PM 27-N 7-W
" "	8	2	5th PM 26-N 7-W
NEWTON	7	6	5th PM 26-N 8-W
NICHOLAS	25	4	5th PM 21-N 10-W
" "	22	4	5th PM 22-N 9-W
" "	21	15	5th PM 22-N 10-W
NICHOLS	11	3	5th PM 25-N 8-W
NICKELSON	8	3	5th PM 26-N 7-W
NICKENS	6	1	5th PM 26-N 9-W
NICKS	24	1	5th PM 22-N 7-W
" "	22	8	5th PM 22-N 9-W
" "	27	2	5th PM 21-N 8-W
" "	21	5	5th PM 22-N 10-W
" "	25	10	5th PM 21-N 10-W
" "	18	8	5th PM 23-N 9-W
NOLTE	11	5	5th PM 25-N 8-W
NORDYKE	11	1	5th PM 25-N 8-W
" "	10	1	5th PM 25-N 9-W
NORMAN	13	2	5th PM 24-N 10-W
" "	17	3	5th PM 23-N 10-W
" "	1	2	5th PM 27-N 10-W
NORRIS	3	1	5th PM 27-N 8-W
NORTON	22	1	5th PM 22-N 9-W
NULL	13	3	5th PM 24-N 10-W
OAKES	9	1	5th PM 25-N 10-W
OAKS	9	6	5th PM 25-N 10-W
OBRIEN	16	3	5th PM 24-N 7-W
OCONNER	16	3	5th PM 24-N 7-W
ODOM	7	2	5th PM 26-N 8-W
ODONNELL	16	1	5th PM 24-N 7-W
" "	15	1	5th PM 24-N 8-W
OGDEN	3	2	5th PM 27-N 8-W
OGLE	7	1	5th PM 26-N 8-W
OKELLEY	11	2	5th PM 25-N 8-W
OKES	7	3	5th PM 26-N 8-W
OLDEN	24	2	5th PM 22-N 7-W
" "	10	2	5th PM 25-N 9-W
" "	9	7	5th PM 25-N 10-W
" "	15	4	5th PM 24-N 8-W
OLIVER	2	1	5th PM 27-N 9-W
OLSON	19	3	5th PM 23-N 8-W
ONEY	24	3	5th PM 22-N 7-W
ORCHARD	19	3	5th PM 23-N 8-W
ORIELLEY	20	1	5th PM 23-N 7-W
ORME	16	1	5th PM 24-N 7-W
OROURKE	20	1	5th PM 23-N 7-W
ORTNER	9	1	5th PM 25-N 10-W
ORVIS	14	2	5th PM 24-N 9-W
OSBORN	10	3	5th PM 25-N 9-W
" "	16	1	5th PM 24-N 7-W
" "	14	2	5th PM 24-N 9-W
" "	2	1	5th PM 27-N 9-W
OVERMAN	14	3	5th PM 24-N 9-W
" "	7	2	5th PM 26-N 8-W
" "	11	1	5th PM 25-N 8-W

Surname	Map Group	Parcels of Land	Meridian/Township/Range
OVERTON	**20**	1	5th PM 23-N 7-W
OWEN	**23**	1	5th PM 22-N 8-W
OWENS	**1**	4	5th PM 27-N 10-W
OWINGS	**15**	2	5th PM 24-N 8-W
PACE	**19**	2	5th PM 23-N 8-W
PACKMAN	**21**	2	5th PM 22-N 10-W
PADGETT	**4**	10	5th PM 27-N 7-W
PADON	**15**	1	5th PM 24-N 8-W
PAINE	**6**	2	5th PM 26-N 9-W
PALMER	**10**	2	5th PM 25-N 9-W
" "	**20**	1	5th PM 23-N 7-W
" "	**19**	2	5th PM 23-N 8-W
" "	**22**	1	5th PM 22-N 9-W
PANE	**3**	1	5th PM 27-N 8-W
PARDEW	**6**	1	5th PM 26-N 9-W
PARKER	**20**	1	5th PM 23-N 7-W
" "	**22**	2	5th PM 22-N 9-W
PARKS	**15**	2	5th PM 24-N 8-W
PARRISH	**19**	1	5th PM 23-N 8-W
PARSONS	**13**	6	5th PM 24-N 10-W
" "	**17**	6	5th PM 23-N 10-W
" "	**14**	1	5th PM 24-N 9-W
PARTNEY	**8**	1	5th PM 26-N 7-W
PASCALL	**12**	1	5th PM 25-N 7-W
PASCHAL	**12**	5	5th PM 25-N 7-W
PATE	**12**	4	5th PM 25-N 7-W
PATTERSON	**2**	2	5th PM 27-N 9-W
PAUL	**15**	2	5th PM 24-N 8-W
PAYNE	**3**	2	5th PM 27-N 8-W
" "	**12**	7	5th PM 25-N 7-W
PAYTON	**18**	1	5th PM 23-N 9-W
PEACE	**8**	4	5th PM 26-N 7-W
" "	**12**	1	5th PM 25-N 7-W
" "	**11**	6	5th PM 25-N 8-W
PEARCE	**26**	1	5th PM 21-N 9-W
" "	**14**	6	5th PM 24-N 9-W
PEARSON	**27**	2	5th PM 21-N 8-W
" "	**8**	10	5th PM 26-N 7-W
PEASE	**24**	1	5th PM 22-N 7-W
PEAY	**16**	1	5th PM 24-N 7-W
PEDRICK	**16**	1	5th PM 24-N 7-W
PEGUES	**10**	1	5th PM 25-N 9-W
PELTON	**4**	1	5th PM 27-N 7-W
PENCE	**14**	8	5th PM 24-N 9-W
PENDERGRAFT	**17**	1	5th PM 23-N 10-W
" "	**13**	4	5th PM 24-N 10-W
PENDERGRASS	**21**	1	5th PM 22-N 10-W
PENN	**18**	2	5th PM 23-N 9-W
PENNINGER	**3**	1	5th PM 27-N 8-W
PENNINGTON	**19**	5	5th PM 23-N 8-W
PEOPLES	**19**	2	5th PM 23-N 8-W
PERKINS	**14**	3	5th PM 24-N 9-W
" "	**1**	2	5th PM 27-N 10-W
" "	**10**	5	5th PM 25-N 9-W
PERRIN	**2**	2	5th PM 27-N 9-W
PERRY	**22**	9	5th PM 22-N 9-W
PERRYMAN	**12**	2	5th PM 25-N 7-W
PETER	**23**	2	5th PM 22-N 8-W
PETREY	**5**	1	5th PM 26-N 10-W
" "	**6**	2	5th PM 26-N 9-W

Surname	Map Group	Parcels of Land	Meridian/Township/Range		
PETRY	9	1	5th PM	25-N	10-W
PETTIT	8	1	5th PM	26-N	7-W
" "	15	2	5th PM	24-N	8-W
PETTY	9	1	5th PM	25-N	10-W
PFENNIGHAUSEN	15	1	5th PM	24-N	8-W
" "	4	17	5th PM	27-N	7-W
PHELAN	22	4	5th PM	22-N	9-W
PHELPS	17	4	5th PM	23-N	10-W
" "	13	1	5th PM	24-N	10-W
PHILLIPS	19	1	5th PM	23-N	8-W
" "	24	1	5th PM	22-N	7-W
" "	18	1	5th PM	23-N	9-W
PHIPPS	4	8	5th PM	27-N	7-W
PICKARD	12	6	5th PM	25-N	7-W
PICKLE	28	2	5th PM	21-N	7-W
PIERCE	7	1	5th PM	26-N	8-W
" "	9	1	5th PM	25-N	10-W
PIETY	23	2	5th PM	22-N	8-W
PITMAN	9	3	5th PM	25-N	10-W
PITTS	7	1	5th PM	26-N	8-W
" "	18	1	5th PM	23-N	9-W
" "	9	1	5th PM	25-N	10-W
PLANK	17	3	5th PM	23-N	10-W
PLAYFORTH	9	1	5th PM	25-N	10-W
PODRABSKE	4	4	5th PM	27-N	7-W
POE	7	4	5th PM	26-N	8-W
" "	8	1	5th PM	26-N	7-W
" "	6	1	5th PM	26-N	9-W
POKE	3	3	5th PM	27-N	8-W
POLK	4	1	5th PM	27-N	7-W
" "	3	6	5th PM	27-N	8-W
POLLOCK	4	1	5th PM	27-N	7-W
" "	7	1	5th PM	26-N	8-W
POLSON	6	2	5th PM	26-N	9-W
POMEROY	19	1	5th PM	23-N	8-W
POOL	15	2	5th PM	24-N	8-W
" "	20	1	5th PM	23-N	7-W
" "	19	1	5th PM	23-N	8-W
" "	16	7	5th PM	24-N	7-W
POOLE	16	1	5th PM	24-N	7-W
POORE	12	1	5th PM	25-N	7-W
POPE	19	2	5th PM	23-N	8-W
" "	3	3	5th PM	27-N	8-W
PORTER	14	5	5th PM	24-N	9-W
" "	3	2	5th PM	27-N	8-W
" "	8	3	5th PM	26-N	7-W
" "	13	2	5th PM	24-N	10-W
POTTER	17	1	5th PM	23-N	10-W
POTTLE	6	3	5th PM	26-N	9-W
POTTS	4	2	5th PM	27-N	7-W
" "	11	3	5th PM	25-N	8-W
POWELL	22	3	5th PM	22-N	9-W
" "	24	2	5th PM	22-N	7-W
" "	26	3	5th PM	21-N	9-W
POWLES	15	1	5th PM	24-N	8-W
PRANTL	19	2	5th PM	23-N	8-W
PRATT	28	7	5th PM	21-N	7-W
" "	24	30	5th PM	22-N	7-W
PRESLEY	28	3	5th PM	21-N	7-W
PRESSLEY	28	5	5th PM	21-N	7-W

Surname	Map Group	Parcels of Land	Meridian/Township/Range		
PRESTON	1	1	5th PM	27-N	10-W
PREWITT	6	1	5th PM	26-N	9-W
" "	1	4	5th PM	27-N	10-W
" "	9	1	5th PM	25-N	10-W
PRICE	25	2	5th PM	21-N	10-W
" "	6	1	5th PM	26-N	9-W
PRITCHETT	14	3	5th PM	24-N	9-W
PRIVETT	11	1	5th PM	25-N	8-W
" "	12	1	5th PM	25-N	7-W
PRIVETTE	11	3	5th PM	25-N	8-W
PROCK	11	1	5th PM	25-N	8-W
PROFFIT	17	1	5th PM	23-N	10-W
" "	19	2	5th PM	23-N	8-W
PROFFITT	22	3	5th PM	22-N	9-W
" "	19	2	5th PM	23-N	8-W
" "	17	8	5th PM	23-N	10-W
PRUITT	6	1	5th PM	26-N	9-W
PUGH	7	3	5th PM	26-N	8-W
" "	26	3	5th PM	21-N	9-W
PURCHASE	20	2	5th PM	23-N	7-W
PURTEE	3	2	5th PM	27-N	8-W
QUADE	24	2	5th PM	22-N	7-W
QUEEN	25	1	5th PM	21-N	10-W
QUINNAN	16	3	5th PM	24-N	7-W
RADFORD	5	1	5th PM	26-N	10-W
RAFFERTY	16	2	5th PM	24-N	7-W
RAGAN	10	1	5th PM	25-N	9-W
RAGSDALE	18	1	5th PM	23-N	9-W
RAINBOLT	11	2	5th PM	25-N	8-W
" "	7	1	5th PM	26-N	8-W
RALLS	20	1	5th PM	23-N	7-W
RAMSBURG	7	4	5th PM	26-N	8-W
RAMSEY	17	2	5th PM	23-N	10-W
" "	3	1	5th PM	27-N	8-W
" "	18	7	5th PM	23-N	9-W
" "	6	5	5th PM	26-N	9-W
RAND	16	4	5th PM	24-N	7-W
RANDEL	2	3	5th PM	27-N	9-W
" "	23	2	5th PM	22-N	8-W
RANEY	22	2	5th PM	22-N	9-W
" "	2	1	5th PM	27-N	9-W
" "	6	1	5th PM	26-N	9-W
RANKIN	15	2	5th PM	24-N	8-W
RATLIFF	18	2	5th PM	23-N	9-W
RAULISON	2	2	5th PM	27-N	9-W
RAY	10	1	5th PM	25-N	9-W
" "	4	4	5th PM	27-N	7-W
" "	11	2	5th PM	25-N	8-W
" "	7	2	5th PM	26-N	8-W
" "	1	2	5th PM	27-N	10-W
" "	20	1	5th PM	23-N	7-W
" "	25	1	5th PM	21-N	10-W
RAYMOND	24	4	5th PM	22-N	7-W
READER	2	1	5th PM	27-N	9-W
REAVES	27	2	5th PM	21-N	8-W
" "	23	2	5th PM	22-N	8-W
REDDEN	2	3	5th PM	27-N	9-W
REDMAN	18	2	5th PM	23-N	9-W
REED	14	2	5th PM	24-N	9-W
" "	13	1	5th PM	24-N	10-W

Surname	Map Group	Parcels of Land	Meridian/Township/Range
REED (Cont'd)	**7**	5	5th PM 26-N 8-W
" "	**12**	6	5th PM 25-N 7-W
" "	**20**	3	5th PM 23-N 7-W
" "	**19**	2	5th PM 23-N 8-W
REESE	**4**	1	5th PM 27-N 7-W
" "	**17**	2	5th PM 23-N 10-W
" "	**3**	3	5th PM 27-N 8-W
" "	**7**	3	5th PM 26-N 8-W
" "	**8**	6	5th PM 26-N 7-W
REEVES	**13**	5	5th PM 24-N 10-W
" "	**18**	1	5th PM 23-N 9-W
" "	**14**	2	5th PM 24-N 9-W
REICH	**6**	1	5th PM 26-N 9-W
REID	**17**	17	5th PM 23-N 10-W
" "	**4**	1	5th PM 27-N 7-W
REIGER	**14**	1	5th PM 24-N 9-W
" "	**18**	1	5th PM 23-N 9-W
REILEY	**23**	2	5th PM 22-N 8-W
RENFRO	**19**	2	5th PM 23-N 8-W
" "	**15**	1	5th PM 24-N 8-W
RENFROW	**15**	1	5th PM 24-N 8-W
RENNEKER	**24**	4	5th PM 22-N 7-W
RENNER	**22**	2	5th PM 22-N 9-W
REYNOLDS	**4**	2	5th PM 27-N 7-W
" "	**10**	7	5th PM 25-N 9-W
" "	**6**	3	5th PM 26-N 9-W
RHOADES	**13**	2	5th PM 24-N 10-W
RHOADS	**22**	3	5th PM 22-N 9-W
RHOTON	**25**	1	5th PM 21-N 10-W
RICE	**14**	1	5th PM 24-N 9-W
" "	**15**	5	5th PM 24-N 8-W
" "	**22**	1	5th PM 22-N 9-W
" "	**4**	1	5th PM 27-N 7-W
" "	**18**	1	5th PM 23-N 9-W
" "	**23**	1	5th PM 22-N 8-W
" "	**19**	1	5th PM 23-N 8-W
RICHARD	**24**	4	5th PM 22-N 7-W
RICHARDSON	**14**	5	5th PM 24-N 9-W
" "	**15**	9	5th PM 24-N 8-W
RICHEY	**21**	3	5th PM 22-N 10-W
" "	**25**	2	5th PM 21-N 10-W
RICHMAN	**2**	3	5th PM 27-N 9-W
RIDDLE	**20**	2	5th PM 23-N 7-W
" "	**4**	2	5th PM 27-N 7-W
RIDEOUT	**24**	2	5th PM 22-N 7-W
RIDGEWAY	**6**	4	5th PM 26-N 9-W
RIGGS	**15**	1	5th PM 24-N 8-W
" "	**19**	4	5th PM 23-N 8-W
" "	**14**	6	5th PM 24-N 9-W
RIGSBY	**25**	5	5th PM 21-N 10-W
RILEY	**21**	1	5th PM 22-N 10-W
" "	**18**	3	5th PM 23-N 9-W
" "	**13**	3	5th PM 24-N 10-W
" "	**7**	1	5th PM 26-N 8-W
" "	**17**	1	5th PM 23-N 10-W
" "	**3**	2	5th PM 27-N 8-W
RINCK	**7**	4	5th PM 26-N 8-W
RISLEY	**22**	6	5th PM 22-N 9-W
" "	**17**	1	5th PM 23-N 10-W
RITCHEY	**18**	4	5th PM 23-N 9-W

Surname	Map Group	Parcels of Land	Meridian/Township/Range			
ROACH	**21**	1	5th PM	22-N	10-W
" "	**7**	1	5th PM	26-N	8-W
ROADS	**26**	1	5th PM	21-N	9-W
" "	**22**	1	5th PM	22-N	9-W
" "	**25**	1	5th PM	21-N	10-W
ROBARDS	**19**	2	5th PM	23-N	8-W
ROBBINS	**7**	1	5th PM	26-N	8-W
" "	**3**	2	5th PM	27-N	8-W
" "	**4**	5	5th PM	27-N	7-W
ROBERDS	**19**	1	5th PM	23-N	8-W
" "	**4**	1	5th PM	27-N	7-W
ROBERSON	**17**	4	5th PM	23-N	10-W
ROBERTS	**1**	6	5th PM	27-N	10-W
" "	**3**	3	5th PM	27-N	8-W
" "	**13**	1	5th PM	24-N	10-W
" "	**17**	2	5th PM	23-N	10-W
" "	**11**	3	5th PM	25-N	8-W
" "	**24**	3	5th PM	22-N	7-W
" "	**21**	6	5th PM	22-N	10-W
" "	**5**	1	5th PM	26-N	10-W
" "	**18**	6	5th PM	23-N	9-W
ROBERTSON	**17**	4	5th PM	23-N	10-W
" "	**5**	3	5th PM	26-N	10-W
" "	**6**	2	5th PM	26-N	9-W
ROBEY	**6**	1	5th PM	26-N	9-W
" "	**7**	1	5th PM	26-N	8-W
ROBINS	**19**	2	5th PM	23-N	8-W
" "	**23**	1	5th PM	22-N	8-W
ROBINSON	**4**	3	5th PM	27-N	7-W
" "	**21**	3	5th PM	22-N	10-W
" "	**13**	3	5th PM	24-N	10-W
ROBISON	**13**	1	5th PM	24-N	10-W
RODE	**11**	3	5th PM	25-N	8-W
ROEHR	**12**	3	5th PM	25-N	7-W
ROGERS	**11**	2	5th PM	25-N	8-W
" "	**16**	1	5th PM	24-N	7-W
ROHDE	**10**	3	5th PM	25-N	9-W
ROHR	**7**	4	5th PM	26-N	8-W
ROLLINS	**18**	6	5th PM	23-N	9-W
ROMANS	**21**	2	5th PM	22-N	10-W
" "	**17**	3	5th PM	23-N	10-W
ROMINE	**25**	1	5th PM	21-N	10-W
" "	**21**	2	5th PM	22-N	10-W
" "	**23**	3	5th PM	22-N	8-W
ROOP	**21**	1	5th PM	22-N	10-W
ROOT	**18**	2	5th PM	23-N	9-W
ROOTES	**20**	1	5th PM	23-N	7-W
ROPER	**13**	2	5th PM	24-N	10-W
ROSEMBUM	**3**	1	5th PM	27-N	8-W
ROSENBUM	**3**	4	5th PM	27-N	8-W
ROTH	**4**	1	5th PM	27-N	7-W
ROTHWELL	**7**	4	5th PM	26-N	8-W
ROUNTREE	**16**	1	5th PM	24-N	7-W
ROUSH	**8**	13	5th PM	26-N	7-W
ROWDEN	**17**	1	5th PM	23-N	10-W
ROWE	**3**	1	5th PM	27-N	8-W
ROWLETT	**6**	3	5th PM	26-N	9-W
" "	**7**	3	5th PM	26-N	8-W
ROYSE	**14**	2	5th PM	24-N	9-W
RUBENDORF	**6**	1	5th PM	26-N	9-W

Surname	Map Group	Parcels of Land	Meridian/Township/Range
RUDD	**6**	1	5th PM 26-N 9-W
RUSHING	**4**	4	5th PM 27-N 7-W
RUSSELL	**13**	1	5th PM 24-N 10-W
" "	**20**	6	5th PM 23-N 7-W
" "	**9**	2	5th PM 25-N 10-W
RUTHERS	**16**	4	5th PM 24-N 7-W
RUTLEDGE	**14**	5	5th PM 24-N 9-W
RYAN	**12**	1	5th PM 25-N 7-W
" "	**11**	2	5th PM 25-N 8-W
RYNERSON	**18**	3	5th PM 23-N 9-W
SACKVILLE	**4**	1	5th PM 27-N 7-W
" "	**3**	1	5th PM 27-N 8-W
SALLTOW	**8**	3	5th PM 26-N 7-W
SALMON	**24**	3	5th PM 22-N 7-W
SALTSMAN	**6**	2	5th PM 26-N 9-W
" "	**2**	1	5th PM 27-N 9-W
SAMPLE	**21**	1	5th PM 22-N 10-W
SANDERS	**15**	2	5th PM 24-N 8-W
SANMANN	**3**	1	5th PM 27-N 8-W
SANTEE	**2**	1	5th PM 27-N 9-W
SAPP	**21**	4	5th PM 22-N 10-W
SAPPS	**21**	1	5th PM 22-N 10-W
SARGENT	**20**	1	5th PM 23-N 7-W
SAWYER	**6**	2	5th PM 26-N 9-W
SCALES	**22**	4	5th PM 22-N 9-W
" "	**12**	3	5th PM 25-N 7-W
SCHAFLER	**22**	3	5th PM 22-N 9-W
SCHALLER	**22**	3	5th PM 22-N 9-W
SCHAUB	**4**	2	5th PM 27-N 7-W
SCHELL	**18**	1	5th PM 23-N 9-W
SCHNEIDER	**11**	2	5th PM 25-N 8-W
" "	**8**	4	5th PM 26-N 7-W
" "	**4**	1	5th PM 27-N 7-W
SCHRIVER	**23**	1	5th PM 22-N 8-W
SCOGGIN	**22**	2	5th PM 22-N 9-W
" "	**13**	3	5th PM 24-N 10-W
" "	**15**	3	5th PM 24-N 8-W
" "	**21**	1	5th PM 22-N 10-W
" "	**18**	9	5th PM 23-N 9-W
SCOTT	**2**	3	5th PM 27-N 9-W
SCROGGINS	**21**	1	5th PM 22-N 10-W
SCRUGGS	**15**	2	5th PM 24-N 8-W
SEABORN	**17**	7	5th PM 23-N 10-W
SEAL	**3**	3	5th PM 27-N 8-W
SEATS	**8**	1	5th PM 26-N 7-W
SEATT	**19**	3	5th PM 23-N 8-W
SEAVER	**3**	3	5th PM 27-N 8-W
SEAY	**18**	1	5th PM 23-N 9-W
" "	**14**	1	5th PM 24-N 9-W
" "	**15**	12	5th PM 24-N 8-W
" "	**12**	2	5th PM 25-N 7-W
SEELY	**9**	1	5th PM 25-N 10-W
SEIBERLING	**15**	1	5th PM 24-N 8-W
SELLS	**2**	10	5th PM 27-N 9-W
" "	**4**	1	5th PM 27-N 7-W
SELSOR	**3**	2	5th PM 27-N 8-W
SETTLE	**4**	1	5th PM 27-N 7-W
SEUTEFF	**19**	3	5th PM 23-N 8-W
SHADWELL	**8**	3	5th PM 26-N 7-W
SHANKS	**15**	2	5th PM 24-N 8-W

Surname	Map Group	Parcels of Land	Meridian/Township/Range
SHARP	**21**	3	5th PM 22-N 10-W
" "	**14**	1	5th PM 24-N 9-W
" "	**18**	4	5th PM 23-N 9-W
SHAVER	**24**	9	5th PM 22-N 7-W
SHAW	**13**	1	5th PM 24-N 10-W
" "	**26**	5	5th PM 21-N 9-W
" "	**15**	1	5th PM 24-N 8-W
SHEA	**20**	2	5th PM 23-N 7-W
" "	**16**	1	5th PM 24-N 7-W
SHEARHEART	**24**	1	5th PM 22-N 7-W
SHEARY	**3**	1	5th PM 27-N 8-W
SHELDON	**4**	1	5th PM 27-N 7-W
SHELTON	**8**	1	5th PM 26-N 7-W
" "	**19**	3	5th PM 23-N 8-W
" "	**4**	2	5th PM 27-N 7-W
SHEPARD	**6**	3	5th PM 26-N 9-W
" "	**18**	3	5th PM 23-N 9-W
SHEPPARD	**20**	1	5th PM 23-N 7-W
" "	**19**	1	5th PM 23-N 8-W
SHERLEY	**22**	2	5th PM 22-N 9-W
SHERRELL	**7**	3	5th PM 26-N 8-W
SHERREY	**24**	1	5th PM 22-N 7-W
" "	**28**	2	5th PM 21-N 7-W
SHERWIN	**3**	1	5th PM 27-N 8-W
SHERWOOD	**19**	1	5th PM 23-N 8-W
SHEWBART	**19**	2	5th PM 23-N 8-W
SHINKLE	**18**	1	5th PM 23-N 9-W
SHIPMAN	**3**	5	5th PM 27-N 8-W
" "	**7**	3	5th PM 26-N 8-W
" "	**9**	2	5th PM 25-N 10-W
SHIPMANN	**3**	1	5th PM 27-N 8-W
SHIRL	**25**	1	5th PM 21-N 10-W
SHOCKLEY	**10**	7	5th PM 25-N 9-W
SHOWERS	**24**	6	5th PM 22-N 7-W
SHREEVE	**3**	3	5th PM 27-N 8-W
SHRIVEAR	**17**	3	5th PM 23-N 10-W
SHRIVER	**2**	1	5th PM 27-N 9-W
SHULTZ	**8**	1	5th PM 26-N 7-W
SHURLEY	**25**	1	5th PM 21-N 10-W
" "	**21**	2	5th PM 22-N 10-W
SHUTTEE	**15**	1	5th PM 24-N 8-W
SICKLY	**20**	1	5th PM 23-N 7-W
SIDWELL	**8**	1	5th PM 26-N 7-W
SIGLER	**25**	3	5th PM 21-N 10-W
SIMMONS	**4**	7	5th PM 27-N 7-W
" "	**6**	2	5th PM 26-N 9-W
SIMPSON	**10**	3	5th PM 25-N 9-W
SIMS	**12**	2	5th PM 25-N 7-W
SINGLETON	**21**	2	5th PM 22-N 10-W
SISSON	**11**	8	5th PM 25-N 8-W
" "	**15**	2	5th PM 24-N 8-W
SITZS	**8**	1	5th PM 26-N 7-W
SKAGGS	**2**	2	5th PM 27-N 9-W
SKINNER	**15**	1	5th PM 24-N 8-W
" "	**14**	1	5th PM 24-N 9-W
" "	**19**	3	5th PM 23-N 8-W
SLATER	**6**	3	5th PM 26-N 9-W
SLAYBARK	**21**	2	5th PM 22-N 10-W
SLOAN	**27**	2	5th PM 21-N 8-W
" "	**21**	3	5th PM 22-N 10-W

Surname	Map Group	Parcels of Land	Meridian/Township/Range		
SLOAN (Cont'd)	23	4	5th PM	22-N	8-W
SMALLEY	1	2	5th PM	27-N	10-W
SMITH	9	3	5th PM	25-N	10-W
" "	14	11	5th PM	24-N	9-W
" "	17	7	5th PM	23-N	10-W
" "	7	12	5th PM	26-N	8-W
" "	22	3	5th PM	22-N	9-W
" "	25	6	5th PM	21-N	10-W
" "	6	9	5th PM	26-N	9-W
" "	1	1	5th PM	27-N	10-W
" "	26	3	5th PM	21-N	9-W
" "	12	1	5th PM	25-N	7-W
" "	13	3	5th PM	24-N	10-W
" "	24	5	5th PM	22-N	7-W
" "	19	5	5th PM	23-N	8-W
" "	2	2	5th PM	27-N	9-W
" "	18	6	5th PM	23-N	9-W
" "	3	11	5th PM	27-N	8-W
" "	21	12	5th PM	22-N	10-W
" "	15	5	5th PM	24-N	8-W
" "	10	7	5th PM	25-N	9-W
" "	11	18	5th PM	25-N	8-W
" "	5	1	5th PM	26-N	10-W
" "	4	24	5th PM	27-N	7-W
SMITHER	2	2	5th PM	27-N	9-W
SMOTHERMAN	15	2	5th PM	24-N	8-W
SMOTHERMON	4	1	5th PM	27-N	7-W
" "	15	1	5th PM	24-N	8-W
" "	8	2	5th PM	26-N	7-W
" "	19	3	5th PM	23-N	8-W
SMOUTHIRMAN	8	1	5th PM	26-N	7-W
SNEAD	19	1	5th PM	23-N	8-W
SNIDER	18	3	5th PM	23-N	9-W
SNODGRASS	6	1	5th PM	26-N	9-W
SNOWDEN	20	2	5th PM	23-N	7-W
SOOTS	7	1	5th PM	26-N	8-W
SOUTH	25	2	5th PM	21-N	10-W
SOUTHARD	13	1	5th PM	24-N	10-W
SOWERS	11	3	5th PM	25-N	8-W
" "	15	1	5th PM	24-N	8-W
SPADLING	12	3	5th PM	25-N	7-W
SPAHR	23	2	5th PM	22-N	8-W
SPARKS	25	3	5th PM	21-N	10-W
" "	21	9	5th PM	22-N	10-W
SPEAKER	18	1	5th PM	23-N	9-W
SPEAKMAN	4	3	5th PM	27-N	7-W
" "	8	1	5th PM	26-N	7-W
SPEARS	25	3	5th PM	21-N	10-W
" "	3	3	5th PM	27-N	8-W
" "	19	1	5th PM	23-N	8-W
" "	23	3	5th PM	22-N	8-W
" "	18	10	5th PM	23-N	9-W
SPENCE	1	2	5th PM	27-N	10-W
" "	5	5	5th PM	26-N	10-W
" "	15	2	5th PM	24-N	8-W
SPENCER	17	2	5th PM	23-N	10-W
" "	18	1	5th PM	23-N	9-W
" "	16	5	5th PM	24-N	7-W
" "	23	1	5th PM	22-N	8-W
" "	14	2	5th PM	24-N	9-W

Surname	Map Group	Parcels of Land	Meridian/Township/Range
SPENCER (Cont'd)	**5**	3	5th PM 26-N 10-W
" "	**22**	2	5th PM 22-N 9-W
SPRADLIN	**12**	1	5th PM 25-N 7-W
SPRADLING	**26**	2	5th PM 21-N 9-W
" "	**25**	3	5th PM 21-N 10-W
" "	**12**	1	5th PM 25-N 7-W
" "	**7**	3	5th PM 26-N 8-W
SPRENGEL	**8**	1	5th PM 26-N 7-W
SPRIGGS	**3**	3	5th PM 27-N 8-W
SPRINKEL	**15**	1	5th PM 24-N 8-W
SRIVER	**17**	5	5th PM 23-N 10-W
ST CLAIR	**18**	1	5th PM 23-N 9-W
STACEY	**16**	1	5th PM 24-N 7-W
STACY	**25**	3	5th PM 21-N 10-W
" "	**17**	2	5th PM 23-N 10-W
STAGGS	**18**	2	5th PM 23-N 9-W
STANBERY	**19**	2	5th PM 23-N 8-W
STAPLES	**6**	1	5th PM 26-N 9-W
STARK	**21**	2	5th PM 22-N 10-W
" "	**16**	1	5th PM 24-N 7-W
STARKEY	**21**	4	5th PM 22-N 10-W
" "	**22**	1	5th PM 22-N 9-W
STEELE	**13**	1	5th PM 24-N 10-W
STEELMAN	**4**	1	5th PM 27-N 7-W
STEGER	**9**	2	5th PM 25-N 10-W
STEIN	**11**	1	5th PM 25-N 8-W
" "	**12**	4	5th PM 25-N 7-W
STEININGER	**20**	1	5th PM 23-N 7-W
STEPHENS	**28**	1	5th PM 21-N 7-W
" "	**21**	4	5th PM 22-N 10-W
" "	**24**	3	5th PM 22-N 7-W
" "	**3**	3	5th PM 27-N 8-W
" "	**14**	1	5th PM 24-N 9-W
STEPHENSON	**19**	2	5th PM 23-N 8-W
STEPP	**3**	1	5th PM 27-N 8-W
" "	**4**	8	5th PM 27-N 7-W
STEUART	**22**	1	5th PM 22-N 9-W
" "	**23**	1	5th PM 22-N 8-W
STEVENS	**27**	2	5th PM 21-N 8-W
" "	**28**	1	5th PM 21-N 7-W
" "	**7**	2	5th PM 26-N 8-W
" "	**23**	1	5th PM 22-N 8-W
STEVENSON	**7**	1	5th PM 26-N 8-W
STEWARD	**14**	2	5th PM 24-N 9-W
STEWART	**22**	4	5th PM 22-N 9-W
" "	**18**	4	5th PM 23-N 9-W
" "	**6**	2	5th PM 26-N 9-W
STINE	**7**	2	5th PM 26-N 8-W
STINECIPHER	**16**	3	5th PM 24-N 7-W
STOCKTON	**7**	3	5th PM 26-N 8-W
STOGSDILL	**2**	2	5th PM 27-N 9-W
STOKES	**7**	2	5th PM 26-N 8-W
" "	**3**	2	5th PM 27-N 8-W
" "	**12**	3	5th PM 25-N 7-W
STONE	**4**	2	5th PM 27-N 7-W
" "	**10**	3	5th PM 25-N 9-W
STORY	**17**	2	5th PM 23-N 10-W
STOUT	**3**	1	5th PM 27-N 8-W
" "	**19**	6	5th PM 23-N 8-W
STOVALL	**6**	1	5th PM 26-N 9-W

Surname	Map Group	Parcels of Land	Meridian/Township/Range		
STRAINN	**4**	3	5th PM	27-N	7-W
STRANGE	**22**	1	5th PM	22-N	9-W
" "	**26**	1	5th PM	21-N	9-W
STRAUSE	**21**	1	5th PM	22-N	10-W
STREET	**19**	6	5th PM	23-N	8-W
" "	**11**	1	5th PM	25-N	8-W
STRICKLAND	**22**	1	5th PM	22-N	9-W
" "	**15**	1	5th PM	24-N	8-W
STRIEBEL	**6**	1	5th PM	26-N	9-W
STRINGER	**2**	1	5th PM	27-N	9-W
STROTHER	**18**	1	5th PM	23-N	9-W
" "	**21**	1	5th PM	22-N	10-W
STROUB	**11**	1	5th PM	25-N	8-W
STUART	**23**	7	5th PM	22-N	8-W
" "	**22**	1	5th PM	22-N	9-W
" "	**26**	2	5th PM	21-N	9-W
STUBBLEFIELD	**11**	3	5th PM	25-N	8-W
STUBBS	**9**	3	5th PM	25-N	10-W
STUDDARD	**9**	2	5th PM	25-N	10-W
SUETEFF	**19**	3	5th PM	23-N	8-W
SUMMERS	**15**	2	5th PM	24-N	8-W
" "	**19**	4	5th PM	23-N	8-W
" "	**14**	6	5th PM	24-N	9-W
" "	**22**	2	5th PM	22-N	9-W
" "	**11**	2	5th PM	25-N	8-W
SUNDBYE	**23**	5	5th PM	22-N	8-W
SURRETT	**17**	1	5th PM	23-N	10-W
SURRITT	**17**	1	5th PM	23-N	10-W
SUSONG	**3**	1	5th PM	27-N	8-W
SUTTLE	**3**	1	5th PM	27-N	8-W
" "	**13**	3	5th PM	24-N	10-W
SUTTON	**24**	5	5th PM	22-N	7-W
SWAN	**20**	1	5th PM	23-N	7-W
" "	**16**	4	5th PM	24-N	7-W
SWEARINGEN	**6**	9	5th PM	26-N	9-W
" "	**10**	2	5th PM	25-N	9-W
SWECKER	**2**	2	5th PM	27-N	9-W
SWIFT	**14**	4	5th PM	24-N	9-W
SYMONDS	**7**	1	5th PM	26-N	8-W
SZOPEINSKI	**3**	1	5th PM	27-N	8-W
TABOR	**10**	1	5th PM	25-N	9-W
" "	**14**	3	5th PM	24-N	9-W
" "	**17**	3	5th PM	23-N	10-W
" "	**13**	17	5th PM	24-N	10-W
" "	**18**	2	5th PM	23-N	9-W
TAFTON	**16**	2	5th PM	24-N	7-W
TAINTER	**23**	6	5th PM	22-N	8-W
TALENT	**3**	2	5th PM	27-N	8-W
TALLEY	**21**	2	5th PM	22-N	10-W
TALLY	**21**	2	5th PM	22-N	10-W
TARWATER	**14**	2	5th PM	24-N	9-W
TAYLOR	**9**	6	5th PM	25-N	10-W
" "	**18**	1	5th PM	23-N	9-W
" "	**15**	2	5th PM	24-N	8-W
" "	**8**	4	5th PM	26-N	7-W
" "	**7**	3	5th PM	26-N	8-W
" "	**3**	2	5th PM	27-N	8-W
" "	**14**	3	5th PM	24-N	9-W
" "	**12**	2	5th PM	25-N	7-W
" "	**17**	2	5th PM	23-N	10-W

Surname	Map Group	Parcels of Land	Meridian/Township/Range		
TAYLOR (Cont'd)	**21**	6	5th PM	22-N	10-W
" "	**4**	1	5th PM	27-N	7-W
" "	**19**	2	5th PM	23-N	8-W
TEDDER	**18**	1	5th PM	23-N	9-W
TENANT	**11**	2	5th PM	25-N	8-W
TERRY	**25**	2	5th PM	21-N	10-W
" "	**19**	2	5th PM	23-N	8-W
" "	**7**	3	5th PM	26-N	8-W
TESENMEIER	**11**	2	5th PM	25-N	8-W
THEISSEN	**11**	2	5th PM	25-N	8-W
" "	**12**	2	5th PM	25-N	7-W
THEOBALD	**15**	2	5th PM	24-N	8-W
THOMAS	**7**	6	5th PM	26-N	8-W
" "	**4**	12	5th PM	27-N	7-W
" "	**14**	2	5th PM	24-N	9-W
" "	**21**	1	5th PM	22-N	10-W
" "	**27**	2	5th PM	21-N	8-W
" "	**12**	1	5th PM	25-N	7-W
" "	**24**	5	5th PM	22-N	7-W
" "	**13**	3	5th PM	24-N	10-W
" "	**8**	1	5th PM	26-N	7-W
" "	**11**	9	5th PM	25-N	8-W
" "	**18**	2	5th PM	23-N	9-W
THOMASSON	**7**	1	5th PM	26-N	8-W
THOMPSON	**27**	1	5th PM	21-N	8-W
" "	**12**	1	5th PM	25-N	7-W
" "	**20**	3	5th PM	23-N	7-W
" "	**7**	1	5th PM	26-N	8-W
" "	**6**	2	5th PM	26-N	9-W
" "	**21**	6	5th PM	22-N	10-W
" "	**8**	1	5th PM	26-N	7-W
" "	**25**	1	5th PM	21-N	10-W
" "	**28**	7	5th PM	21-N	7-W
THORNTON	**18**	4	5th PM	23-N	9-W
" "	**8**	3	5th PM	26-N	7-W
THRASHER	**14**	3	5th PM	24-N	9-W
THRELKELD	**22**	2	5th PM	22-N	9-W
THURMAN	**19**	1	5th PM	23-N	8-W
TICE	**2**	4	5th PM	27-N	9-W
TILSON	**13**	4	5th PM	24-N	10-W
" "	**17**	9	5th PM	23-N	10-W
TIPTON	**17**	3	5th PM	23-N	10-W
TISDALE	**13**	3	5th PM	24-N	10-W
TOBLER	**17**	1	5th PM	23-N	10-W
TOMLINSON	**10**	12	5th PM	25-N	9-W
TOOMEY	**4**	2	5th PM	27-N	7-W
TOW	**6**	3	5th PM	26-N	9-W
TOWNLEY	**15**	2	5th PM	24-N	8-W
TRANBARGER	**4**	1	5th PM	27-N	7-W
TREVOR	**4**	2	5th PM	27-N	7-W
TRICHAUS	**4**	3	5th PM	27-N	7-W
TRIM	**11**	2	5th PM	25-N	8-W
TRINDLE	**3**	5	5th PM	27-N	8-W
TROLL	**4**	3	5th PM	27-N	7-W
TROTTER	**8**	1	5th PM	26-N	7-W
TROUTMAN	**2**	1	5th PM	27-N	9-W
TUCKER	**11**	2	5th PM	25-N	8-W
" "	**6**	1	5th PM	26-N	9-W
TULL	**18**	3	5th PM	23-N	9-W
" "	**14**	1	5th PM	24-N	9-W

Surname	Map Group	Parcels of Land	Meridian/Township/Range
TUNE	**20**	2	5th PM 23-N 7-W
TUPPER	**11**	3	5th PM 25-N 8-W
" "	**4**	2	5th PM 27-N 7-W
TURLEY	**19**	2	5th PM 23-N 8-W
TURNBAUGH	**8**	3	5th PM 26-N 7-W
" "	**6**	1	5th PM 26-N 9-W
TURNER	**12**	2	5th PM 25-N 7-W
" "	**9**	1	5th PM 25-N 10-W
" "	**10**	7	5th PM 25-N 9-W
" "	**15**	1	5th PM 24-N 8-W
" "	**14**	4	5th PM 24-N 9-W
" "	**23**	1	5th PM 22-N 8-W
TURPEN	**7**	7	5th PM 26-N 8-W
TYREE	**25**	1	5th PM 21-N 10-W
UITTS	**18**	7	5th PM 23-N 9-W
" "	**14**	1	5th PM 24-N 9-W
ULRICH	**7**	5	5th PM 26-N 8-W
UMPHREY	**25**	2	5th PM 21-N 10-W
UNDERWOOD	**11**	1	5th PM 25-N 8-W
" "	**20**	1	5th PM 23-N 7-W
UNGER	**22**	4	5th PM 22-N 9-W
" "	**21**	4	5th PM 22-N 10-W
UPTON	**21**	1	5th PM 22-N 10-W
" "	**18**	2	5th PM 23-N 9-W
" "	**22**	5	5th PM 22-N 9-W
USHER	**4**	8	5th PM 27-N 7-W
UTLEY	**14**	4	5th PM 24-N 9-W
VALENTINE	**18**	3	5th PM 23-N 9-W
VAN DERNOEF	**26**	5	5th PM 21-N 9-W
VAN METRE	**2**	2	5th PM 27-N 9-W
VAN VORHIS	**18**	1	5th PM 23-N 9-W
VANDERHOEF	**22**	3	5th PM 22-N 9-W
VANDERPOOL	**6**	1	5th PM 26-N 9-W
VANDIVER	**24**	2	5th PM 22-N 7-W
VASSAW	**12**	3	5th PM 25-N 7-W
VAUGHAN	**25**	4	5th PM 21-N 10-W
" "	**11**	2	5th PM 25-N 8-W
" "	**21**	3	5th PM 22-N 10-W
" "	**3**	1	5th PM 27-N 8-W
VAUGHN	**22**	1	5th PM 22-N 9-W
" "	**21**	3	5th PM 22-N 10-W
" "	**7**	2	5th PM 26-N 8-W
VENTLE	**3**	2	5th PM 27-N 8-W
" "	**7**	1	5th PM 26-N 8-W
VENUS	**22**	3	5th PM 22-N 9-W
" "	**21**	1	5th PM 22-N 10-W
VERBICK	**21**	5	5th PM 22-N 10-W
VERNON	**21**	1	5th PM 22-N 10-W
" "	**23**	1	5th PM 22-N 8-W
" "	**27**	3	5th PM 21-N 8-W
VESS	**8**	3	5th PM 26-N 7-W
VEST	**3**	4	5th PM 27-N 8-W
VICKERS	**8**	2	5th PM 26-N 7-W
VINCENT	**24**	8	5th PM 22-N 7-W
VOEGELE	**21**	2	5th PM 22-N 10-W
VON BLUCHER	**4**	5	5th PM 27-N 7-W
WADDLE	**24**	2	5th PM 22-N 7-W
WADE	**13**	2	5th PM 24-N 10-W
" "	**10**	3	5th PM 25-N 9-W
WADLEY	**13**	1	5th PM 24-N 10-W

Surname	Map Group	Parcels of Land	Meridian/Township/Range		
WADLEY (Cont'd)	**10**	9	5th PM	25-N	9-W
" "	**17**	1	5th PM	23-N	10-W
WADLY	**18**	1	5th PM	23-N	9-W
WAID	**24**	4	5th PM	22-N	7-W
" "	**28**	2	5th PM	21-N	7-W
WALKER	**20**	1	5th PM	23-N	7-W
" "	**14**	2	5th PM	24-N	9-W
" "	**7**	4	5th PM	26-N	8-W
" "	**8**	6	5th PM	26-N	7-W
" "	**16**	5	5th PM	24-N	7-W
" "	**13**	1	5th PM	24-N	10-W
" "	**4**	1	5th PM	27-N	7-W
" "	**19**	6	5th PM	23-N	8-W
" "	**5**	1	5th PM	26-N	10-W
" "	**17**	9	5th PM	23-N	10-W
" "	**3**	5	5th PM	27-N	8-W
WALL	**20**	2	5th PM	23-N	7-W
WALLACE	**17**	6	5th PM	23-N	10-W
" "	**21**	2	5th PM	22-N	10-W
WALLICE	**21**	7	5th PM	22-N	10-W
WALLIN	**6**	8	5th PM	26-N	9-W
WALTER	**8**	1	5th PM	26-N	7-W
WALTERS	**18**	2	5th PM	23-N	9-W
WARCUM	**11**	6	5th PM	25-N	8-W
WARD	**18**	3	5th PM	23-N	9-W
" "	**6**	3	5th PM	26-N	9-W
" "	**7**	3	5th PM	26-N	8-W
" "	**9**	1	5th PM	25-N	10-W
WARNER	**2**	1	5th PM	27-N	9-W
" "	**22**	5	5th PM	22-N	9-W
" "	**1**	1	5th PM	27-N	10-W
WARREN	**4**	3	5th PM	27-N	7-W
WASHBURN	**10**	2	5th PM	25-N	9-W
WATERS	**22**	8	5th PM	22-N	9-W
WATKINS	**23**	3	5th PM	22-N	8-W
" "	**14**	1	5th PM	24-N	9-W
WATSON	**17**	1	5th PM	23-N	10-W
" "	**20**	5	5th PM	23-N	7-W
" "	**12**	9	5th PM	25-N	7-W
" "	**1**	1	5th PM	27-N	10-W
WEATHERBY	**12**	3	5th PM	25-N	7-W
WEATHERLY	**12**	8	5th PM	25-N	7-W
WEAVER	**4**	5	5th PM	27-N	7-W
" "	**18**	4	5th PM	23-N	9-W
WEBB	**4**	4	5th PM	27-N	7-W
" "	**22**	3	5th PM	22-N	9-W
" "	**8**	4	5th PM	26-N	7-W
" "	**7**	2	5th PM	26-N	8-W
" "	**11**	1	5th PM	25-N	8-W
" "	**10**	1	5th PM	25-N	9-W
WEBSTER	**14**	3	5th PM	24-N	9-W
WEEKS	**14**	3	5th PM	24-N	9-W
WEIBEL	**19**	3	5th PM	23-N	8-W
WEIBERT	**7**	2	5th PM	26-N	8-W
WEIR	**18**	1	5th PM	23-N	9-W
WELCH	**12**	2	5th PM	25-N	7-W
" "	**11**	1	5th PM	25-N	8-W
WELKER	**13**	3	5th PM	24-N	10-W
WELLER	**8**	2	5th PM	26-N	7-W
" "	**4**	8	5th PM	27-N	7-W

Surname	Map Group	Parcels of Land	Meridian/Township/Range		
WELLINGTON	**22**	2	5th PM	22-N	9-W
WELLS	**14**	4	5th PM	24-N	9-W
" "	**15**	1	5th PM	24-N	8-W
" "	**16**	3	5th PM	24-N	7-W
" "	**18**	4	5th PM	23-N	9-W
WERKING	**11**	1	5th PM	25-N	8-W
WESCOTT	**17**	8	5th PM	23-N	10-W
" "	**21**	1	5th PM	22-N	10-W
WEST	**19**	2	5th PM	23-N	8-W
" "	**7**	3	5th PM	26-N	8-W
" "	**8**	4	5th PM	26-N	7-W
" "	**18**	6	5th PM	23-N	9-W
WESTERN	**18**	2	5th PM	23-N	9-W
WESTMORELAND	**21**	3	5th PM	22-N	10-W
WETHERFORD	**9**	6	5th PM	25-N	10-W
WHARTON	**26**	3	5th PM	21-N	9-W
WHATLEY	**15**	3	5th PM	24-N	8-W
WHEELER	**3**	2	5th PM	27-N	8-W
" "	**6**	1	5th PM	26-N	9-W
WHITAKER	**3**	2	5th PM	27-N	8-W
WHITE	**15**	4	5th PM	24-N	8-W
" "	**6**	4	5th PM	26-N	9-W
" "	**10**	2	5th PM	25-N	9-W
WHITLOCK	**1**	1	5th PM	27-N	10-W
WHITNEY	**22**	1	5th PM	22-N	9-W
" "	**19**	1	5th PM	23-N	8-W
WHITTAKER	**15**	1	5th PM	24-N	8-W
WICKER	**21**	1	5th PM	22-N	10-W
" "	**18**	1	5th PM	23-N	9-W
WIDENER	**14**	2	5th PM	24-N	9-W
WIGGINS	**14**	1	5th PM	24-N	9-W
" "	**22**	1	5th PM	22-N	9-W
WIGGS	**3**	2	5th PM	27-N	8-W
WIKOFF	**18**	3	5th PM	23-N	9-W
WILBANKS	**7**	2	5th PM	26-N	8-W
WILCOX	**21**	4	5th PM	22-N	10-W
WILES	**17**	2	5th PM	23-N	10-W
WILKERSON	**19**	5	5th PM	23-N	8-W
WILL	**10**	4	5th PM	25-N	9-W
" "	**6**	1	5th PM	26-N	9-W
WILLBANKS	**7**	3	5th PM	26-N	8-W
" "	**24**	3	5th PM	22-N	7-W
WILLEFORD	**4**	3	5th PM	27-N	7-W
WILLIAMS	**1**	1	5th PM	27-N	10-W
" "	**9**	8	5th PM	25-N	10-W
" "	**28**	3	5th PM	21-N	7-W
" "	**15**	2	5th PM	24-N	8-W
" "	**26**	1	5th PM	21-N	9-W
" "	**22**	1	5th PM	22-N	9-W
" "	**16**	1	5th PM	24-N	7-W
" "	**25**	1	5th PM	21-N	10-W
" "	**10**	3	5th PM	25-N	9-W
" "	**17**	16	5th PM	23-N	10-W
" "	**2**	1	5th PM	27-N	9-W
" "	**14**	2	5th PM	24-N	9-W
" "	**6**	12	5th PM	26-N	9-W
" "	**21**	3	5th PM	22-N	10-W
" "	**8**	2	5th PM	26-N	7-W
" "	**13**	1	5th PM	24-N	10-W
" "	**12**	3	5th PM	25-N	7-W

Surname	Map Group	Parcels of Land	Meridian/Township/Range
WILLIAMS (Cont'd)	**19**	1	5th PM 23-N 8-W
WILLIAMSON	**6**	3	5th PM 26-N 9-W
" "	**20**	1	5th PM 23-N 7-W
WILLIS	**3**	4	5th PM 27-N 8-W
" "	**10**	1	5th PM 25-N 9-W
" "	**15**	1	5th PM 24-N 8-W
WILSON	**17**	11	5th PM 23-N 10-W
" "	**4**	2	5th PM 27-N 7-W
" "	**2**	8	5th PM 27-N 9-W
" "	**6**	5	5th PM 26-N 9-W
" "	**15**	3	5th PM 24-N 8-W
" "	**7**	6	5th PM 26-N 8-W
" "	**5**	1	5th PM 26-N 10-W
WINCHESTER	**8**	1	5th PM 26-N 7-W
" "	**12**	2	5th PM 25-N 7-W
WINDER	**7**	3	5th PM 26-N 8-W
WINNINGHAM	**4**	6	5th PM 27-N 7-W
WINSTON	**14**	2	5th PM 24-N 9-W
WINSTRAN	**19**	1	5th PM 23-N 8-W
" "	**23**	5	5th PM 22-N 8-W
WINTER	**10**	4	5th PM 25-N 9-W
WINTERS	**18**	1	5th PM 23-N 9-W
WIRE	**23**	2	5th PM 22-N 8-W
WISE	**13**	1	5th PM 24-N 10-W
WISEMAN	**22**	1	5th PM 22-N 9-W
" "	**10**	1	5th PM 25-N 9-W
" "	**7**	3	5th PM 26-N 8-W
" "	**6**	2	5th PM 26-N 9-W
WISHON	**4**	1	5th PM 27-N 7-W
WISNER	**21**	3	5th PM 22-N 10-W
WOOD	**14**	3	5th PM 24-N 9-W
" "	**10**	5	5th PM 25-N 9-W
" "	**20**	6	5th PM 23-N 7-W
" "	**1**	1	5th PM 27-N 10-W
WOODARD	**5**	1	5th PM 26-N 10-W
WOODREL	**19**	6	5th PM 23-N 8-W
WOODRELL	**19**	1	5th PM 23-N 8-W
WOODRING	**14**	2	5th PM 24-N 9-W
WOODROME	**14**	4	5th PM 24-N 9-W
" "	**18**	1	5th PM 23-N 9-W
WOODS	**19**	3	5th PM 23-N 8-W
" "	**9**	2	5th PM 25-N 10-W
WOODSIDE	**19**	1	5th PM 23-N 8-W
" "	**18**	1	5th PM 23-N 9-W
" "	**15**	6	5th PM 24-N 8-W
WOODWORTH	**19**	4	5th PM 23-N 8-W
WOODY	**12**	3	5th PM 25-N 7-W
" "	**15**	5	5th PM 24-N 8-W
WOOSTER	**4**	2	5th PM 27-N 7-W
WORCESTER	**16**	1	5th PM 24-N 7-W
" "	**2**	1	5th PM 27-N 9-W
WRIGHT	**10**	1	5th PM 25-N 9-W
" "	**21**	6	5th PM 22-N 10-W
" "	**22**	13	5th PM 22-N 9-W
" "	**18**	7	5th PM 23-N 9-W
" "	**14**	5	5th PM 24-N 9-W
WURL	**4**	3	5th PM 27-N 7-W
WYATT	**23**	10	5th PM 22-N 8-W
WYMAN	**18**	1	5th PM 23-N 9-W
WYRICK	**13**	1	5th PM 24-N 10-W

Surname	Map Group	Parcels of Land	Meridian/Township/Range
WYZARD	**7**	5	5th PM 26-N 8-W
YARNELL	**24**	6	5th PM 22-N 7-W
YATES	**20**	1	5th PM 23-N 7-W
" "	**14**	1	5th PM 24-N 9-W
YEAGER	**6**	2	5th PM 26-N 9-W
YENNEY	**11**	4	5th PM 25-N 8-W
YORBER	**8**	1	5th PM 26-N 7-W
YORK	**7**	3	5th PM 26-N 8-W
YOUNG	**6**	1	5th PM 26-N 9-W
" "	**1**	2	5th PM 27-N 10-W
" "	**25**	1	5th PM 21-N 10-W
" "	**10**	6	5th PM 25-N 9-W
" "	**2**	2	5th PM 27-N 9-W
YOUNGBLOOD	**18**	1	5th PM 23-N 9-W
" "	**17**	3	5th PM 23-N 10-W
YOUNGS	**19**	4	5th PM 23-N 8-W
ZEEBE	**6**	1	5th PM 26-N 9-W
ZEEK	**10**	1	5th PM 25-N 9-W
ZUMWALT	**13**	5	5th PM 24-N 10-W

– Part II –

Township Map Groups

Map Group 1: Index to Land Patents

Township 27-North Range 10-West (5th PM 27-N 10-W)

After you locate an individual in this Index, take note of the Section and Section Part then proceed to the Land Patent map on the pages immediately following. You should have no difficulty locating the corresponding parcel of land.

The "For More Info" Column will lead you to more information about the underlying Patents. See the *Legend* at right, and the "How to Use this Book" chapter, for more information.

```
                    LEGEND
           "For More Info . . . " column
A = Authority (Legislative Act, See Appendix "A")
B = Block or Lot (location in Section unknown)
C = Cancelled Patent
F = Fractional Section
G = Group  (Multi-Patentee Patent, see Appendix "C")
V = Overlaps another Parcel
R = Re-Issued (Parcel patented more than once)

(A & G items require you to look in the Appendixes referred
to above. All other Letter-designations followed by a number
require you to locate line-items in this index that possess
the ID number found after the letter).
```

ID	Individual in Patent	Sec.	Sec. Part	Date Issued	Other Counties	For More Info . . .
6894	ALF, Andrew	3	1NW	1901-06-08		A7
6896	" "	3	2NW	1901-06-08		A7
1	BACHAR, John	36	W½SE	1892-04-01		A7
2	" "	36	SWNE	1892-04-01		A7
3	BENNETT, Simeon L	13	SWSW	1860-08-01		A1
5	" "	24	NWNW	1860-08-01		A1
4	" "	24	S½NW	1860-08-01		A1
6	BOWERS, George W	3	SW	1898-10-04		A7
7	CARD, Henry T	14	SW	1892-03-07		A7
8	CARSON, David	1	SESW	1873-04-01		A1
9	" "	1	NWSW	1873-04-01		A1
10	CHRISTESSON, Lafayettet	20	NESW	1898-04-06		A7
11	CHRISTY, Benjamin J	10	SE	1895-05-28		A7
12	CONNER, Samuel P	36	SW	1890-06-06		A7
13	COOK, John M	24	S½SW	1892-01-05		A7
14	FERGUSON, David S	23	E½SE	1883-08-13		A1
15	FERGUSON, Thomas J	25	SWSW	1884-11-01		A7
16	" "	26	S½SE	1884-11-01		A7
17	" "	26	SESW	1884-11-01		A7
20	GALLAHER, William	10	S½NW	1885-03-20		A1
18	" "	10	N½SW	1885-03-20		A1
19	" "	10	NE	1885-03-20		A1
21	" "	3	SESE	1885-03-20		A1
6895	GARLETTS, Alexander P	3	2NE	1892-03-07		A7
6893	" "	3	1NE	1892-03-07		A7
22	GARTEN, William T	23	SENE	1900-08-09		A7
23	GREEN, Eli H	20	W½SW	1904-07-15		A7
24	HADLEY, David W	14	NW	1895-05-28		A7
25	HALL, Charles A	13	SESW	1892-04-01		A7
26	" "	13	N½SW	1892-04-01		A7
27	HALL, James M	36	NW	1889-06-22		A7
29	HARRIS, George	14	SENW	1859-01-01		A1
28	" "	14	NESW	1859-01-01		A1
30	HINKLE, George	23	W½SE	1892-09-09		A7
33	HOLLINGSWORTH, Charles W	11	NWSE	1895-05-28		A7
32	" "	11	S½SE	1895-05-28		A7
31	" "	11	SWNE	1895-05-28		A7
34	JOHNSON, Joseph A	11	NW	1896-08-28		A7
35	JOHNSTON, William J	10	N½NW	1901-03-23		A7
36	JONES, Delilah	6	S½SE	1878-11-30		A7
37	JONES, Isaac A	5	W½SW	1885-12-19		A7
38	" "	6	NWSE	1871-02-15		A1
6891	KERSHNER, Isaiah B	1	2NE	1903-06-01		A7
39	KIDD, James A	5	NESW	1902-10-20		A7
6889	LEARNARD, Oscar E	1	1NE	1882-06-01		A1
6890	" "	1	1NW	1882-06-01		A1

ID	Individual in Patent	Sec.	Sec. Part	Date Issued	Other Counties	For More Info . . .
40	LEARNARD, Oscar E (Cont'd)	1	SWSW	1882-06-01		A1
41	" "	12	NW	1882-06-01		A1
42	" "	23	NW	1882-06-01		A1
43	MARSHALL, William H	11	SW	1895-05-28		A7
44	MITCHELL, Elzy E	24	W½SE	1892-01-05		A7
47	MORRIS, M B	11	NESE	1886-11-19		A1
46	" "	11	NENE	1886-07-20		A1
45	" "	11	SENE	1886-11-19		A1
48	MORSE, Lucius D	27	SWSW	1872-02-05		A1
49	MOXLEY, E P	3	W½SE	1885-12-19		A1
50	" "	3	NESE	1885-12-19		A1
51	NETTLETON, George H	11	NWNE	1884-10-11		A1
53	NORMAN, William E	25	NWSW	1889-01-12		A7
52	" "	25	E½SW	1889-01-12		A7
55	OWENS, Joseph	26	NWSW	1878-06-24		A7
54	" "	26	SWNW	1878-06-24		A7
57	" "	27	SENE	1878-06-24		A7
56	" "	27	NESE	1878-06-24		A7
58	PERKINS, Alexander	10	S½SW	1902-04-15		A7
59	PERKINS, James B	20	SESW	1859-09-01		A1
6913	PRESTON, Horace K	7	S21SW	1888-05-07		A1
60	PREWITT, Christian L	27	NESW	1879-12-15		A7
62	" "	27	SENW	1879-12-15		A7
63	" "	27	SWNE	1879-12-15		A7
61	" "	27	NWSE	1879-12-15		A7
6897	RAY, Samuel M	5	1NW	1892-03-07		A7
6898	" "	5	2NW	1892-03-07		A7
6909	ROBERTS, Charles H	7	2SW	1860-02-15		A6
6912	" "	7	N21SW	1860-02-15		A6
6905	" "	7	1NW	1860-02-15		A6
6906	" "	7	2NW	1860-02-15		A6
65	ROBERTS, George W	36	SENE	1879-12-15		A7
64	" "	36	E½SE	1879-12-15		A7
6902	SMALLEY, Henry H	6	W22NE	1888-07-03		A1
6901	" "	6	W21NE	1888-07-03		A1
66	SMITH, Marcus A	5	SESW	1888-05-07		A1
6900	SPENCE, John	6	E22NE	1860-08-01		A1
6899	" "	6	E21NE	1860-08-01		A1
68	WARNER, Luther H	24	NE	1860-09-10		A6
6892	WATSON, Jasper N	1	2NW	1901-03-23		A7
69	WHITLOCK, George	1	NESW	1861-02-09		A1
70	WILLIAMS, Thomas S	24	NENW	1885-03-20		A1
71	WOOD, Lorenzo D	6	NESE	1860-08-01		A1
73	YOUNG, William	36	N½NE	1882-09-30		A7 C
72	" "	36	N½NE	1899-12-18		A7

Patent Map

T27-N R10-W
5th PM 27-N 10-W Meridian

Map Group 1

Township Statistics

Parcels Mapped	:	91
Number of Patents	:	59
Number of Individuals	:	57
Patentees Identified	:	57
Number of Surnames	:	52
Multi-Patentee Parcels	:	0
Oldest Patent Date	:	1/1/1859
Most Recent Patent	:	7/15/1904
Block/Lot Parcels	:	19
Cities and Towns	:	1
Cemeteries	:	2

Lots/Tracts-Sec. 6
E21NE   SPENCE, JOHN   1860
E22NE   SPENCE, JOHN   1860
W21NE   SMALLEY, HENRY H 1888
W22NE   SMALLEY, HENRY H 1888

Lots/Tracts-Sec. 5
1NW   RAY, SAMUEL M   1892
2NW   RAY, SAMUEL M   1892

6

JONES
Isaac A
1871

WOOD
Lorenzo D
1860

JONES
Delilah
1878

5

KIDD
James A
1902

JONES
Isaac A
1885

SMITH
Marcus A
1888

4

7

Lots/Tracts-Sec. 7
1NW   ROBERTS, CHARLES H 1860
2NW   ROBERTS, CHARLES H 1860
2SW   ROBERTS, CHARLES H 1860
N21SW   ROBERTS, CHARLES H 1860
S21SW   PRESTON, HORACE K   1888

8

9

18

17

16

19

20

GREEN
Eli H
1904

CHRISTESSON
Lafayettet
1898

PERKINS
James B
1859

21

30

29

28

31

32

33

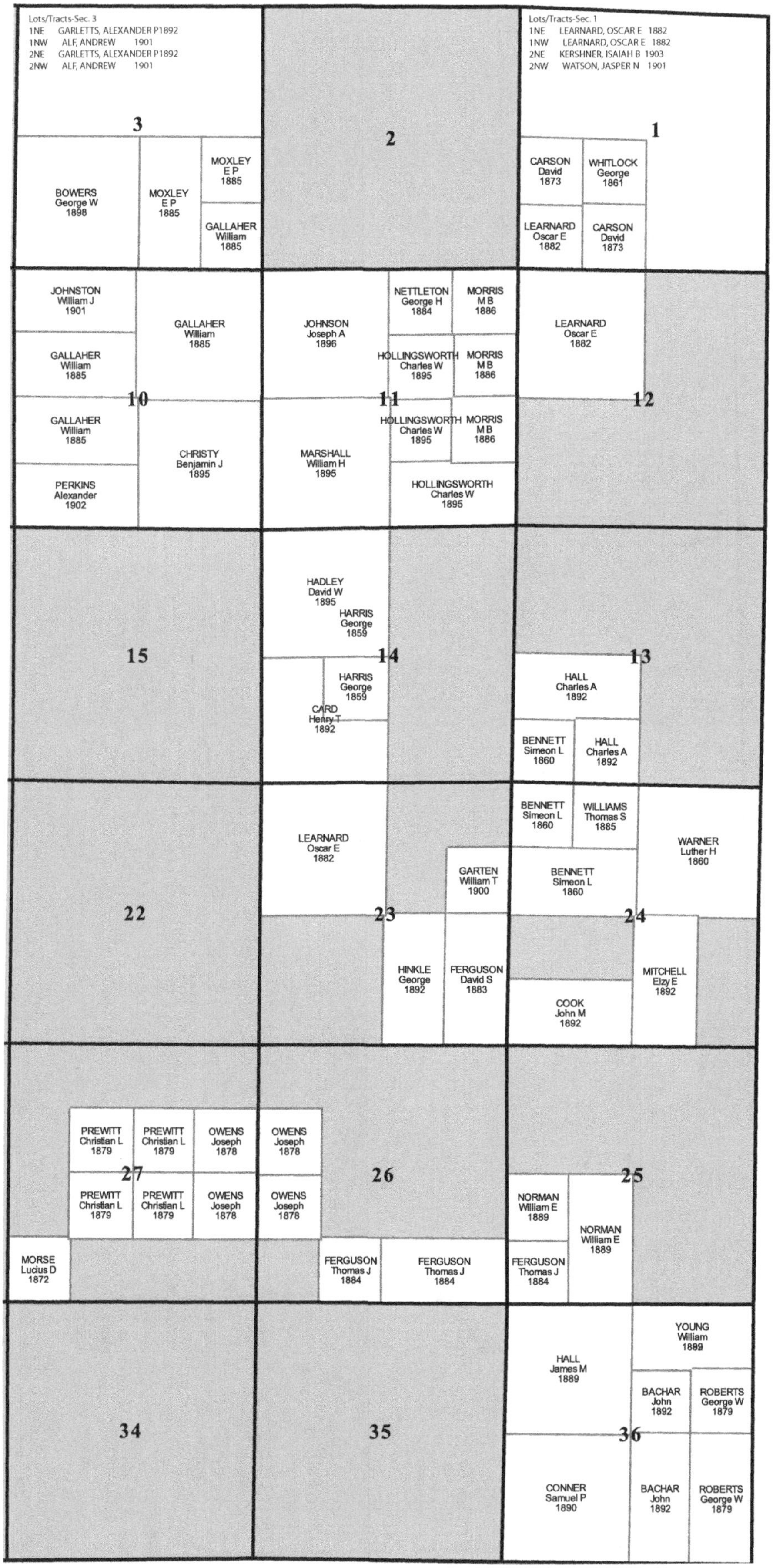

Lots/Tracts-Sec. 3
1NE   GARLETTS, ALEXANDER P1892
1NW   ALF, ANDREW   1901
2NE   GARLETTS, ALEXANDER P1892
2NW   ALF, ANDREW   1901

Lots/Tracts-Sec. 1
1NE   LEARNARD, OSCAR E 1882
1NW   LEARNARD, OSCAR E 1882
2NE   KERSHNER, ISAIAH B 1903
2NW   WATSON, JASPER N 1901

3

BOWERS
George W
1898

MOXLEY
E P
1885

MOXLEY
E P
1885

GALLAHER
William
1885

2

1

CARSON
David
1873

WHITLOCK
George
1861

LEARNARD
Oscar E
1882

CARSON
David
1873

10

JOHNSTON
William J
1901

GALLAHER
William
1885

GALLAHER
William
1885

GALLAHER
William
1885

CHRISTY
Benjamin J
1895

PERKINS
Alexander
1902

11

JOHNSON
Joseph A
1896

NETTLETON
George H
1884

MORRIS
M B
1886

HOLLINGSWORTH
Charles W
1895

MORRIS
M B
1886

HOLLINGSWORTH
Charles W
1895

MORRIS
M B
1886

MARSHALL
William H
1895

HOLLINGSWORTH
Charles W
1895

12

LEARNARD
Oscar E
1882

15

14

HADLEY
David W
1895

HARRIS
George
1859

HARRIS
George
1859

CARD
Henry T
1892

13

HALL
Charles A
1892

BENNETT
Simeon L
1860

HALL
Charles A
1892

22

23

LEARNARD
Oscar E
1882

GARTEN
William T
1900

HINKLE
George
1892

FERGUSON
David S
1883

24

BENNETT
Simeon L
1860

WILLIAMS
Thomas S
1885

WARNER
Luther H
1860

BENNETT
Simeon L
1860

COOK
John M
1892

MITCHELL
Elzy E
1892

27

PREWITT
Christian L
1879

PREWITT
Christian L
1879

OWENS
Joseph
1878

OWENS
Joseph
1878

PREWITT
Christian L
1879

PREWITT
Christian L
1879

OWENS
Joseph
1878

OWENS
Joseph
1878

MORSE
Lucius D
1872

26

FERGUSON
Thomas J
1884

FERGUSON
Thomas J
1884

25

NORMAN
William E
1889

NORMAN
William E
1889

FERGUSON
Thomas J
1884

34

35

36

HALL
James M
1889

YOUNG
William
1889

BACHAR
John
1892

ROBERTS
George W
1879

CONNER
Samuel P
1890

BACHAR
John
1892

ROBERTS
George W
1879

Helpful Hints

1. This Map's INDEX can be found on the preceding pages.

2. Refer to Map "C" to see where this Township lies within Howell County, Missouri.

3. Numbers within square brackets [ ] denote a multi-patentee land parcel (multi-owner). Refer to Appendix "C" for a full list of members in this group.

4. Areas that look to be crowded with Patentees usually indicate multiple sales of the same parcel (Re-issues) or Overlapping parcels. See this Township's Index for an explanation of these and other circumstances that might explain "odd" groupings of Patentees on this map.

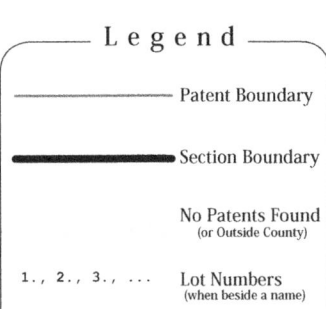

Legend

——————— Patent Boundary

━━━━━━━ Section Boundary

No Patents Found
(or Outside County)

1., 2., 3., ...   Lot Numbers
(when beside a name)

[ ]   Group Number
(see Appendix "C")

Scale: Section = 1 mile X 1 mile
(generally, with some exceptions)

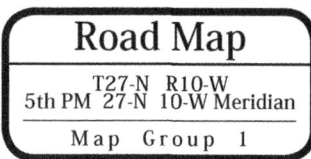

Road Map
T27-N R10-W
5th PM 27-N 10-W Meridian
Map Group 1

<u>Cities & Towns</u>
Sterling

<u>Cemeteries</u>
Jones Cemetery
Spring Valley Cemetery

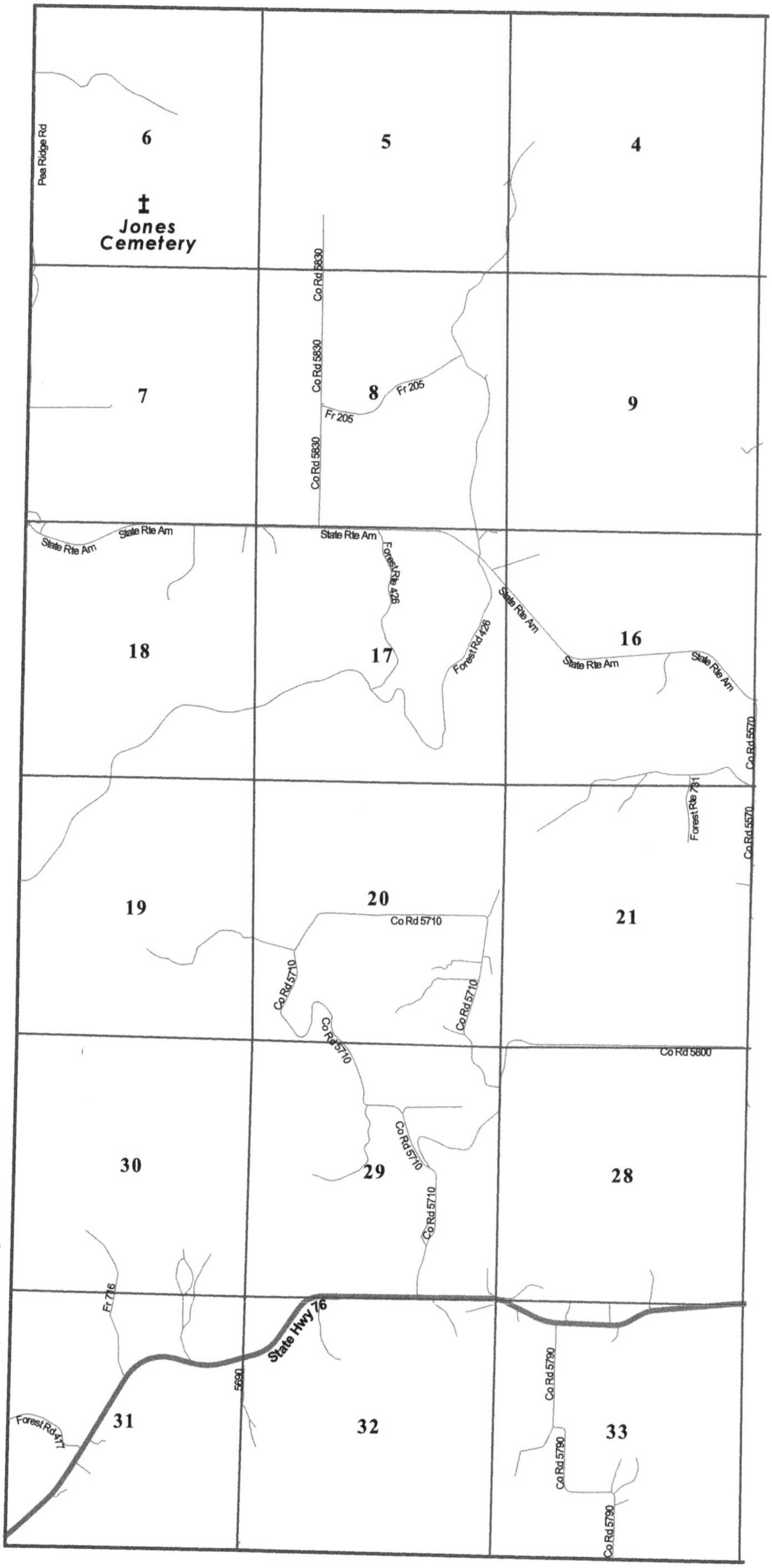

Pea Ridge Rd

6

✝
*Jones
Cemetery*

5

4

Co Rd 5830

7

Co Rd 5830

8 Fr 205

Fr 205

Co Rd 5830

9

State Rte Am

State Rte Am

State Rte Am

18

Forest Rte 426

17

Forest Rd 426

State Rte Am

16

State Rte Am

State Rte Am

Co Rd 5570

Forest Rte 751

Co Rd 5570

19

20

Co Rd 5710

Co Rd 5710

21

Co Rd 5710

Co Rd 5710

Co Rd 5800

Co Rd 5710

30

29

Co Rd 5710

Co Rd 5710

28

Fr 716

Fr 716

State Hwy 76

5690

31

Forest Rd 717

32

Co Rd 5790

33

Co Rd 5790

Co Rd 5790

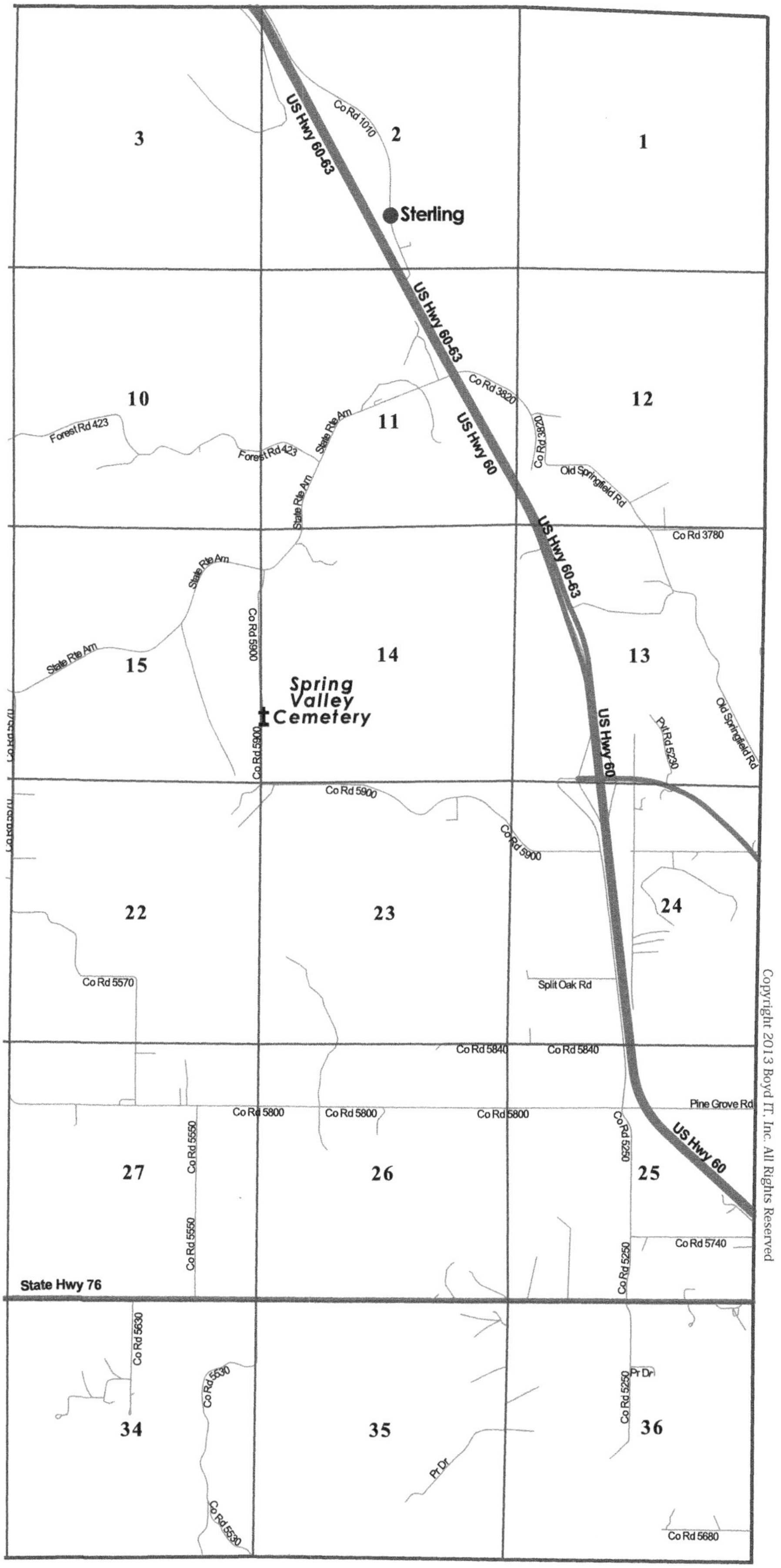

3

Co Rd 1010

2

US Hwy 60-63

● Sterling

1

US Hwy 60-63

10

Forest Rd 423

Co Rd 3820

State Rte Arn

11

Forest Rd 423

State Rte Arn

US Hwy 60

Co Rd 3830

12

Old Springfield Rd

US Hwy 60-63

Co Rd 3780

State Rte Arn

State Rte Arn

Co Rd 5900

15

14

13

Spring
Valley
Cemetery

Co Rd 5900

US Hwy 60

Pvt Rd 5250

Old Springfield Rd

Co Rd 5900

Co Rd 5900

22

23

24

Co Rd 5570

Split Oak Rd

Co Rd 5840

Co Rd 5840

Co Rd 5550

Co Rd 5800

Co Rd 5800

Co Rd 5800

Pine Grove Rd

Co Rd 5250

US Hwy 60

27

26

25

Co Rd 5550

Co Rd 5250

Co Rd 5740

State Hwy 76

Co Rd 5630

34

Co Rd 5630

35

Pr Dr

Co Rd 5250

Pr Dr

36

Pr Dr

Co Rd 5630

Co Rd 5680

Helpful Hints

1. This road map has a number of uses, but primarily it is to help you: a) find the present location of land owned by your ancestors (at least the general area), b) find cemeteries and city-centers, and c) estimate the route/roads used by Census-takers & tax-assessors.

2. If you plan to travel to Howell County to locate cemeteries or land parcels, please pick up a modern travel map for the area before you do. Mapping old land parcels on modern maps is not as exact a science as you might think. Just the slightest variations in public land survey coordinates, estimates of parcel boundaries, or road-map deviations can greatly alter a map's representation of how a road either does or doesn't cross a particular parcel of land.

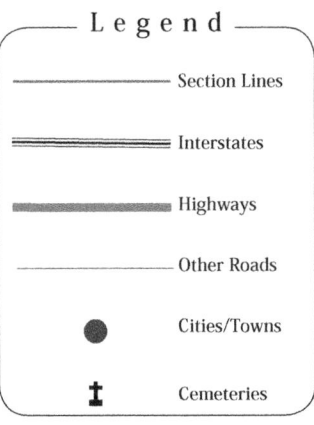

Legend

————	Section Lines
════	Interstates
▬▬▬	Highways
————	Other Roads
●	Cities/Towns
⊥	Cemeteries

Scale: Section = 1 mile X 1 mile
(generally, with some exceptions)

Historical Map

T27-N R10-W
5th PM 27-N 10-W Meridian

Map Group 1

Cities & Towns
Sterling

Cemeteries
Jones Cemetery
Spring Valley Cemetery

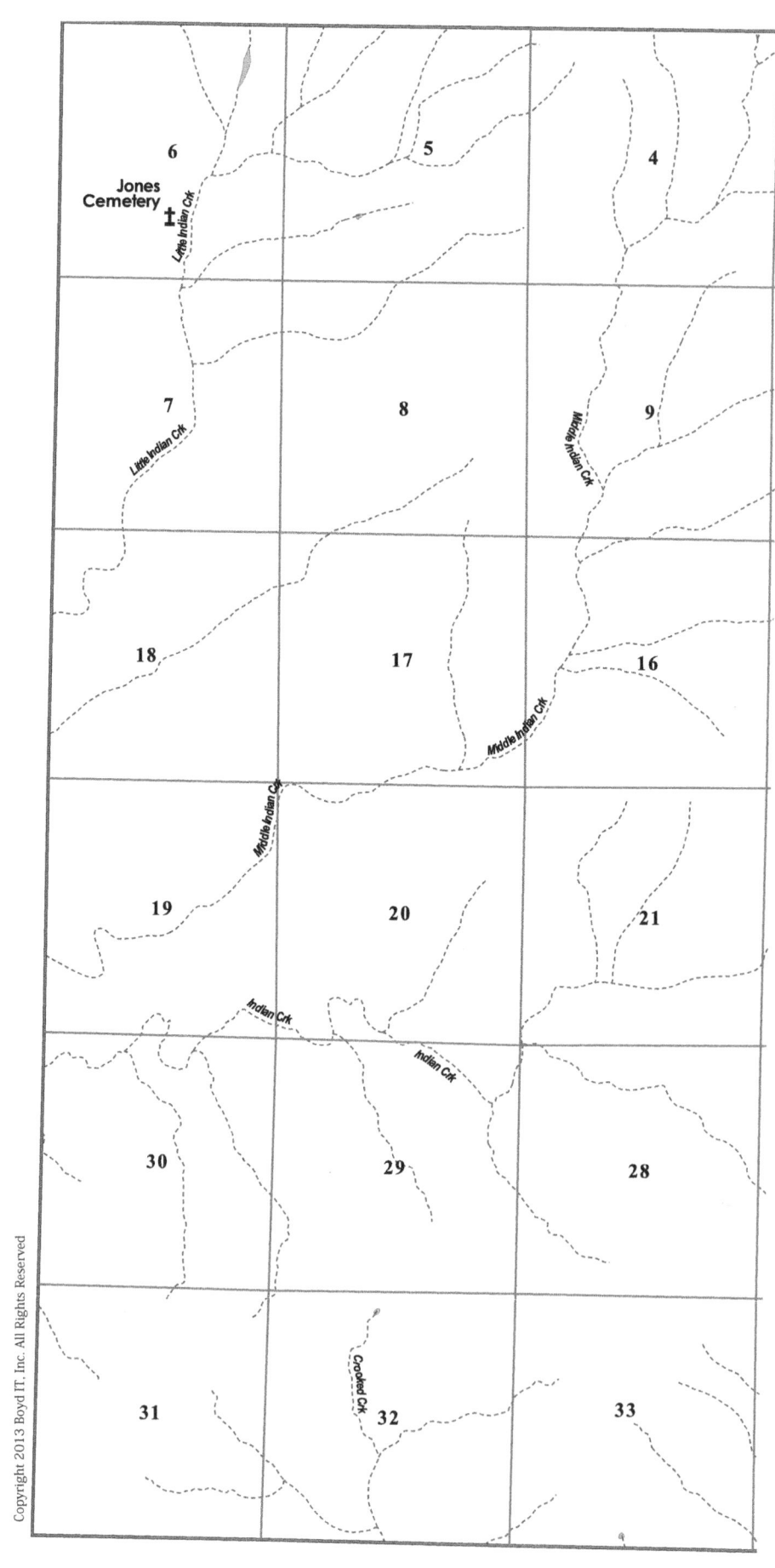

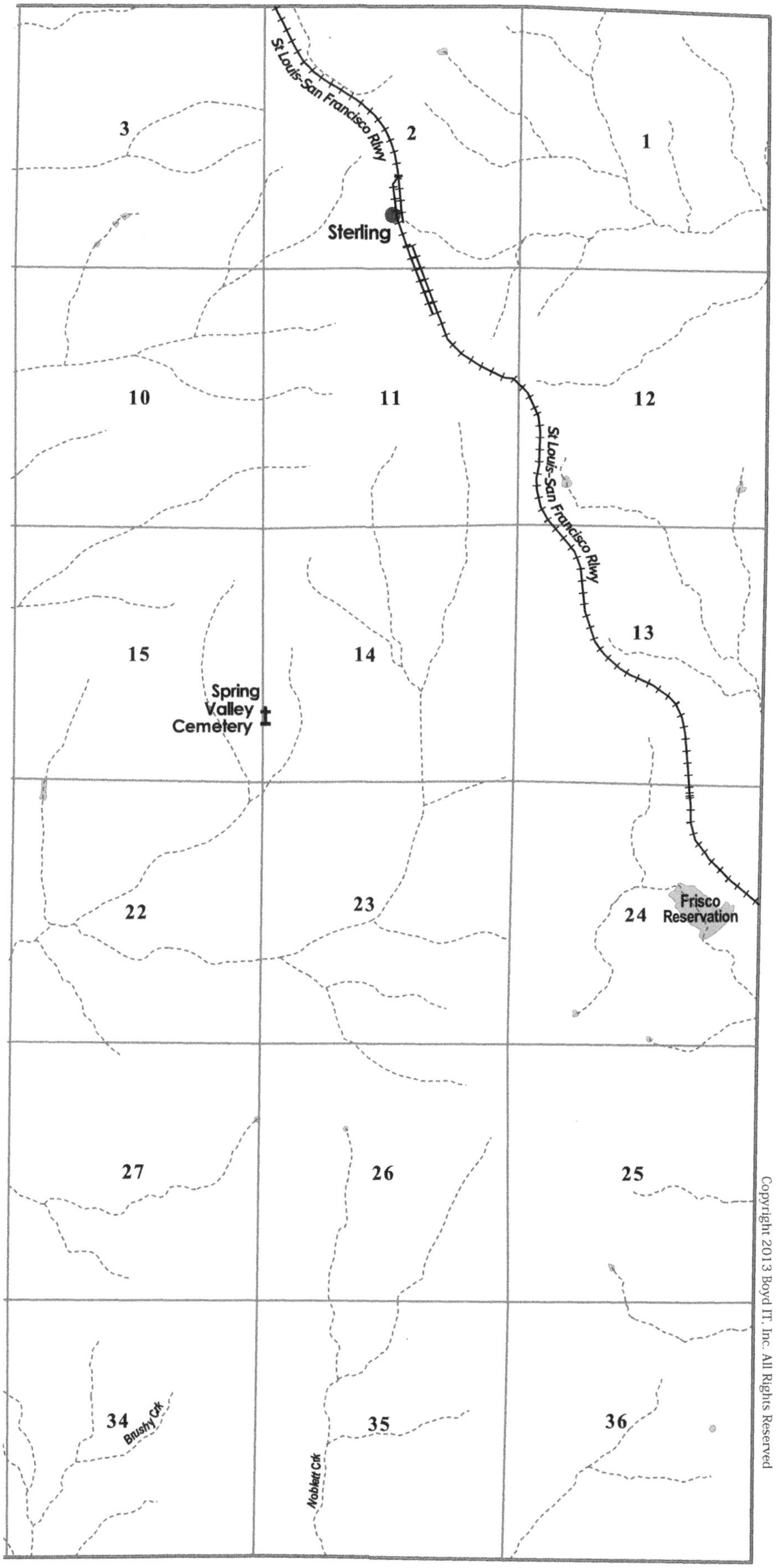

3

2

1

St Louis-San Francisco Rlwy

Sterling

10

11

12

St Louis-San Francisco Rlwy

15

14

13

Spring
Valley
Cemetery ✝

22

23

24

Frisco
Reservation

27

26

25

34

Brushy Crk

35

Noblett Crk

36

Helpful Hints

1. This Map takes a different look at the same Congressional Township displayed in the preceding two maps. It presents features that can help you better envision the historical development of the area: a) Water-bodies (lakes & ponds), b) Water-courses (rivers, streams, etc.), c) Railroads, d) City/ town center-points (where they were oftentimes located when first settled), and e) Cemeteries.

2. Using this "Historical" map in tandem with this Township's Patent Map and Road Map, may lead you to some interesting discoveries. You will often find roads, towns, cemeteries, and waterways are named after nearby landowners: sometimes those names will be the ones you are researching. See how many of these research gems you can find here in Howell County.

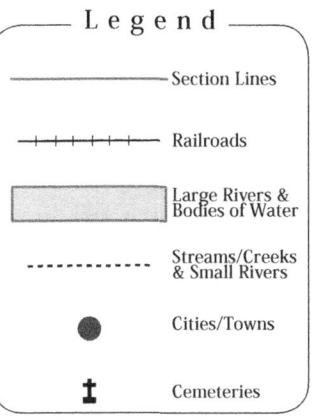

Legend

———————— Section Lines

+++++++ Railroads

▭ Large Rivers & Bodies of Water

- - - - - - - Streams/Creeks & Small Rivers

● Cities/Towns

✝ Cemeteries

Scale: Section = 1 mile X 1 mile
(there are some exceptions)

81

Map Group 2: Index to Land Patents

Township 27-North Range 9-West (5th PM 27-N 9-W)

After you locate an individual in this Index, take note of the Section and Section Part then proceed to the Land Patent map on the pages immediately following. You should have no difficulty locating the corresponding parcel of land.

The "For More Info" Column will lead you to more information about the underlying Patents. See the *Legend* at right, and the "How to Use this Book" chapter, for more information.

```
                      LEGEND
            "For More Info . . . " column
  A = Authority (Legislative Act, See Appendix "A")
  B = Block or Lot (location in Section unknown)
  C = Cancelled Patent
  F = Fractional Section
  G = Group  (Multi-Patentee Patent, see Appendix "C")
  V = Overlaps another Parcel
  R = Re-Issued (Parcel patented more than once)

  (A & G items require you to look in the Appendixes referred
  to above. All other Letter-designations followed by a number
  require you to locate line-items in this index that possess
  the ID number found after the letter).
```

ID	Individual in Patent	Sec.	Sec. Part	Date Issued	Other Counties	For More Info . . .
74	ALSOP, Benjamin	33	SESE	1854-11-15		A1
75	ALSUP, Benjamin	32	NESE	1853-08-01		A1
76	" "	32	W½NE	1853-08-01		A1
77	" "	34	S½SW	1853-08-01		A1
80	ALSUP, Martin S	32	NWSE	1873-04-10		A7
78	" "	32	SESW	1882-06-10		A1
79	" "	32	NESW	1873-04-10		A7
81	ALSUP, Zachariah	27	NWSE	1859-09-01		A1
83	ALSUP, Zachariah T	27	SWSE	1875-04-01		A7
82	" "	27	NESW	1875-04-01		A7
84	ANDERSON, Isaiah E	20	W½SW	1889-01-12		A7
85	ARELL, Joseph A	36	SENE	1904-11-01		A7
86	" "	36	NESE	1904-11-01		A7
87	ARNOLD, W W	23	NW	1889-05-29		A1
88	ASHBY, Francis A	36	NENE	1893-12-21		A7
89	ATCHLEY, Edward H	20	E½SW	1877-06-04		A7
90	" "	20	W½SE	1877-06-04		A7
91	BARTON, Anthony G	34	SWNE	1899-05-12		A7
94	BEESON, Volney W	28	NENE	1895-08-09		A1
6918	BOATMAN, James	19	N21SW	1858-12-01		A1
6923	" "	19	S21SW	1856-06-16		A8
6929	" "	30	1NW	1856-01-03		A1
6916	BOATMAN, William H	18	S22SW	1859-09-01		A1
6919	" "	19	N22NW	1859-09-01		A1
6917	BOOTMAN, William H	19	N21NW	1859-09-01		A1
95	BOUCHER, Samuel W	33	SENE	1892-10-17		A7
96	" "	33	NESE	1892-10-17		A7
97	BRACKETT, Joseph	14	E½NW	1877-08-01		A7
98	" "	14	W½NE	1877-08-01		A7
6940	BRASSWELL, Jacob B	4	W22NE	1879-12-15		A7
6936	" "	4	2NW	1879-12-15		A7
6939	" "	4	W21NW	1879-12-15		A7
99	BUCKLAND, Thomas A	7	S½NE	1872-11-15		A1
100	" "	7	NWNE	1872-11-15		A1
101	BUFORD, William	27	SESW	1858-04-01		A1
103	" "	34	W½NW	1859-10-10		A6
102	" "	34	NWSW	1859-10-10		A6
104	" "	4	NENW	1859-09-01		A1
105	CAMPBELL, Abram B	24	E½SE	1897-04-10		A7
107	CHAPIN, Ezra E	17	SESE	1892-03-07		A7
106	" "	17	N½SE	1892-03-07		A7
108	CHEEK, Nan	25	SWSE	1889-06-22		A7 G43
109	" "	36	SENW	1889-06-22		A7 G43
110	" "	36	W½NE	1889-06-22		A7 G43
111	CHEEK, Thomas J	25	SWSE	1889-06-22		A7 G43
112	" "	36	SENW	1889-06-22		A7 G43

ID	Individual in Patent	Sec.	Sec. Part	Date Issued	Other Counties	For More Info ...
113	CHEEK, Thomas J (Cont'd)	36	W½NE	1889-06-22		A7 G43
114	COBBS, Lockey	24	W½SE	1898-04-06		A7
115	" "	25	N½NE	1898-04-06		A7
117	COCHRAN, James H	27	NWNE	1893-04-29		A7
116	" "	27	N½NW	1893-04-29		A7
118	" "	27	SENW	1893-04-29		A7
119	COFFMAN, David H	36	SWSE	1867-08-20		A1
120	COFFMAN, James M	36	N½SW	1875-08-10		A7
121	" "	36	NWSE	1875-08-10		A7
122	COVERT, Jane E	27	E½SE	1900-08-09		A7 G60
123	COVERT, John R	27	E½SE	1900-08-09		A7 G60
6920	COX, Jesse N	19	N22SW	1856-10-10		A1
125	CRABTREE, Mary	5	NESE	1860-11-12		A6 G61
6943	" "	5	1NE	1860-11-12		A6 G61
6952	" "	5	E21NW	1860-11-12		A6 G61
126	CRITCHER, Charles D	33	NENW	1870-05-10		A1
127	CROUCH, Aaron	35	W½NE	1895-09-04		A7
128	" "	35	E½NW	1895-09-04		A7
129	DAVIS, James E	33	NESW	1878-04-05		A7
130	" "	33	NWSE	1878-04-05		A7
132	DIXON, James C	34	SENW	1890-11-13		A7
131	" "	34	NESW	1890-11-13		A7
133	DORSEY, Allen E	19	W½NE	1874-11-05		A7
134	" "	19	W½SE	1874-11-05		A7
135	DRYBREAD, Joseph H	31	NENE	1882-08-30		A7
136	" "	31	S½NE	1882-08-30		A7
137	" "	32	NWNW	1882-08-30		A7
138	DUNIVAN, Mary E	29	N½NW	1885-12-19		A7
6927	EARLS, William	3	E22NE	1876-05-15	Texas	A7
139	EDWARDS, Ireson	26	NENW	1895-02-15		A7
141	" "	26	SWNE	1895-02-15		A7
140	" "	26	N½NE	1895-02-15		A7
142	EIDSON, Bennett	31	NWNE	1880-11-20		A7
6933	" "	31	N21NW	1880-11-20		A7
143	EIDSON, James	33	W½NE	1877-04-05		A7
144	" "	33	SENW	1877-04-05		A7
145	ELKIN, John H	29	NESE	1860-08-01		A1
146	" "	32	NENW	1861-02-01		A1
147	ELKINS, John	32	SENW	1856-01-03		A1
148	ELKINS, John H	29	W½SE	1859-01-01		A1
149	" "	29	W½NE	1866-05-15		A6
150	FEATHERINGILL, John M	29	SWSW	1886-04-10		A7
151	" "	30	SESE	1886-04-10		A7
152	FEATHERINGILL, William	21	SWSW	1882-09-30		A1
153	" "	27	SWNE	1879-09-23		A1
154	" "	28	NWNW	1882-09-30		A1
155	" "	29	NENE	1882-09-30		A1
156	FERGUSON, Elizabeth	30	NWNE	1883-06-30		A7 G79
6930	FERGUSON, Emanuel C	30	2NW	1883-02-20		A1
157	FERGUSON, James A	29	SENE	1888-07-03		A1
158	" "	29	E½SE	1888-07-03		A1
159	FERGUSON, William M	30	NWNE	1883-06-30		A7 G79
160	FERRELL, Enoch P	6	SESE	1869-07-01		A1
161	" "	7	NENE	1869-07-01		A1
162	" "	8	NWNW	1869-07-01		A1
163	FINDLEY, John W	27	W½SW	1898-12-01		A7
164	" "	27	SWNW	1898-12-01		A7
165	" "	28	SENE	1898-12-01		A7
166	FISHER, Charles	25	SWNE	1910-04-01		A1
167	FOOTE, Elisha	35	NWNW	1898-01-26		A7
168	GODSEY, David	22	NENW	1888-05-07		A1
169	" "	22	NWNE	1888-05-07		A1
170	" "	26	NWNW	1888-05-07		A1
171	GODSY, David	23	NWSW	1888-12-06		A1
172	" "	23	SWSW	1883-06-30		A7
173	" "	27	NENE	1883-06-30		A7
175	GODSY, Emily	25	NWSW	1897-10-28		A7 G96
174	" "	25	SWNW	1897-10-28		A7 G96
176	" "	26	NESE	1897-10-28		A7 G96
177	" "	26	SENE	1897-10-28		A7 G96
179	GODSY, George A	22	E½SW	1898-07-25		A7
178	" "	22	SENW	1898-07-25		A7
180	" "	22	SWSE	1898-07-25		A7

ID	Individual in Patent	Sec.	Sec. Part	Date Issued	Other Counties	For More Info . . .
181	GODSY, John	25	NWSW	1897-10-28		A7 G96
182	" "	25	SWNW	1897-10-28		A7 G96
184	" "	26	SENE	1897-10-28		A7 G96
183	" "	26	NESE	1897-10-28		A7 G96
186	GODSY, Robert M	26	SWNW	1894-01-25		A7
185	" "	26	W½SW	1894-01-25		A7
187	" "	27	SENE	1894-01-25		A7
188	GOLDSBERRY, William H	35	S½SW	1859-10-10		A6
190	GULLY, Pleasant N	36	SESE	1867-08-20		A1
191	HALLOWAY, Richard	32	NWSW	1882-09-30		A1
192	HAMILTON, Thomas	34	N½NE	1890-11-13		A7
193	" "	34	SENE	1890-11-13		A7
194	HAMMONS, Isaac J	23	NE	1875-04-01		A7
195	HARKEY, Christopher	31	SW	1875-12-20		A7
196	HARRIS, Benjamin P	31	SE	1894-12-17		A7
197	HARRIS, James W	30	NWSE	1875-12-20		A7
198	HENRY, Mary F	17	NE	1891-06-09		A7
199	HOGAN, James H	19	E½SE	1888-12-06		A7
200	" "	19	SENE	1888-12-06		A7
201	HOGAN, John S	28	NWNE	1888-12-06		A1
203	HOLLOWAY, Richard	32	E½NE	1881-04-09		A7
202	" "	32	SWSW	1888-07-17		A1
204	HOSKINSON, Isaac	5	SWSW	1869-07-01		A1
6958	HULL, James	5	S22NW	1860-11-12		A6 C
6950	" "	5	E21NW	1860-11-12		A6 G61
205	" "	5	NESE	1860-11-12		A6 G61
6946	" "	5	2NE	1860-11-12		A6 C
6949	" "	5	2NE	1919-06-09		A6
6955	" "	5	E22NW	1919-06-09		A6
6942	" "	5	1NE	1860-11-12		A6 G61
207	JOHNSON, George W	25	SESE	1895-05-28		A7
208	" "	25	N½SE	1895-05-28		A7
206	" "	25	SENE	1895-05-28		A7
6925	JONES, Ezekiel	19	S22SW	1856-09-01		A1
212	" "	30	SENE	1856-09-01		A1
211	" "	30	SWNE	1856-01-03		A1
210	" "	30	NESE	1856-01-03		A1
213	JONES, Manuel	30	SWSE	1859-09-01		A1
214	" "	32	SWNW	1860-08-01		A1
216	JONES, Samuel	28	SESW	1859-09-01		A1
215	" "	28	SWSW	1856-01-03		A1
217	" "	33	SWSE	1856-01-03		A1
218	" "	33	W½NW	1856-01-03		A1
219	KEEN, Charles	28	E½SE	1894-05-18		A7
220	" "	33	NENE	1894-05-18		A7
221	LANCE, Henry D	33	SESW	1859-01-01		A1
222	LEARNARD, Oscar E	1		1882-06-01		A1
223	" "	10		1882-06-01		A1
224	" "	11		1882-06-01		A1
225	" "	12		1882-06-01		A1
226	" "	13		1882-06-01		A1
227	" "	14	W½NW	1882-06-01		A1
228	" "	14	E½NE	1882-06-01		A1
229	" "	14	S½	1882-06-01		A1
230	" "	15		1882-06-01		A1
231	" "	2		1882-06-01		A1
232	" "	24	N½	1882-06-01		A1
6928	" "	3	W22NE	1882-06-01		A6
6926	" "	3	1NE	1882-06-01		A1
233	" "	3	NW	1882-06-01		A1
234	" "	3	S½	1882-06-01		A1
6938	" "	4	E22NE	1882-06-01		A1
235	" "	4	S½	1882-06-01		A1
6935	" "	4	1NE	1882-06-01		A1
6937	" "	4	E21NW	1882-06-01		A1
6959	" "	5	W21NW	1919-10-15		A1
6960	" "	5	W22NW	1919-10-15		A1
236	" "	5	SESE	1919-10-15		A1
237	" "	6	N½	1882-06-01		A1
238	" "	6	SWSE	1882-06-01		A1
239	" "	8	E½NW	1882-06-01		A1
242	" "	8	E½	1882-06-01		A1
241	" "	8	SW	1882-06-01		A1

ID	Individual in Patent	Sec.	Sec. Part	Date Issued	Other Counties	For More Info . . .
240	LEARNARD, Oscar E (Cont'd)	8	SWNW	1882-06-01		A1
243	"	9		1882-06-01		A1
244	LIVINGSTON, David P	20	S½NE	1891-05-25		A7
245	" "	20	NENE	1891-05-25		A7
246	" "	21	SWNW	1891-05-25		A7
247	LIVINGSTON, John M	30	NENE	1882-12-20		A1
6915	LOUTRELL, William A	18	N22SW	1889-06-22		A7
6914	" "	18	1SW	1889-06-22		A7
248	LOVAN, Daniel R	21	SESW	1872-07-01		A7
250	" "	28	NESW	1872-07-01		A7
249	" "	28	SWNE	1882-09-30		A1
251	" "	28	E½NW	1872-07-01		A7
253	LOVAN, Goldmon L	21	NWNE	1890-12-31		A7
252	" "	21	NENW	1890-12-31		A7
254	LOVAN, James T	21	S½SE	1892-11-03		A7
255	LOVAN, William J	28	W½SE	1880-11-20		A7
256	MACORMIC, Edward	13	S½SW	1874-04-20		A7
259	MCCULLOUGH, Della	21	E½NE	1893-03-13		A1
258	" "	21	NESE	1893-03-13		A1
260	" "	22	SWNW	1893-03-13		A1
6921	MCCULLOUGH, John	19	S21NW	1882-03-30		A7
6924	" "	19	S22NW	1882-03-30		A7
261	MEDLEY, Carrie	29	S½NW	1888-12-08		A7
262	MILLER, James H	35	SESE	1860-09-10		A6
263	MIRES, J W	5	NWSW	1877-11-10		A1 G151
6934	MITCHELL, Lacy L	31	S21NW	1892-03-07		A7
265	MITCHELL, Thomas J	17	N½SW	1881-10-06		A7
264	" "	17	S½NW	1881-10-06		A7
267	MOFFITT, James H	21	SWNE	1876-01-10		A7
268	" "	21	NWSE	1876-01-10		A7
269	" "	21	NESW	1876-01-10		A7
266	" "	21	SENW	1876-01-10		A7
270	NEASE, Thomas	18	E½SE	1891-05-25		A7
271	" "	19	NENE	1891-05-25		A7
272	NEASE, William	17	N½NW	1891-05-25		A7
273	" "	18	E½NE	1891-05-25		A7
276	OLIVER, John C	20	E½SE	1892-09-09		A7
277	OSBORN, Aaron B	30	SW	1879-12-15		A7
279	PATTERSON, George	18	W½NE	1879-12-15		A7
278	" "	18	W½SE	1879-12-15		A7
281	PERRIN, Ephraim P	5	W½SE	1878-06-24		A7
280	" "	5	E½SW	1878-06-24		A7
282	RANDEL, William H	17	SWSE	1890-10-11		A7
284	" "	20	E½NW	1890-10-11		A7
283	" "	20	NWNE	1890-10-11		A7
285	RANEY, C R	22	E½SE	1898-03-21		A1
286	RAULISON, James J	21	NWSW	1890-06-04		A1
287	" "	21	NWNW	1890-06-04		A1
288	READER, Isaac T	2	NESW	1861-02-09		A1
291	REDDEN, Wiley S	22	E½NE	1873-04-10		A7
289	" "	22	NWSE	1873-04-10		A7
290	" "	22	SWNE	1873-04-10		A7
292	RICHMAN, Eli	23	E½SE	1896-03-25	/	A7
293	" "	24	SWSW	1896-03-25		A7
294	" "	25	NWNW	1896-03-25		A7
295	SALTSMAN, Daniel A	35	SWSE	1885-12-19		A1
296	SANTEE, Mary	6	N½SE	1872-02-05		A1
298	SCOTT, Samuel H	24	NWSW	1892-06-21		A7
297	" "	24	E½SW	1892-06-21		A7
299	" "	25	NENW	1892-06-21		A7
301	SELLS, Alvin	35	NESE	1888-12-06		A7
300	" "	35	E½NE	1888-12-06		A7
302	" "	36	NWNW	1888-12-06		A7
303	SELLS, Andrew J	34	N½SE	1896-03-25		A7
306	SELLS, David	26	W½SE	1891-06-09		A7
304	" "	26	SENW	1891-06-09		A7
305	" "	26	NESW	1891-06-09		A7
307	SELLS, Ephraim	26	SESW	1898-04-11		A7
308	SELLS, Peter	35	NWSW	1900-08-09		A7
309	" "	35	SWNW	1900-08-09		A7
310	SHRIVER, Harvey C	22	W½SW	1895-07-08		A7
311	SKAGGS, George W	17	S½SW	1890-10-11		A7
312	" "	20	W½NW	1890-10-11		A7

ID	Individual in Patent	Sec.	Sec. Part	Date Issued	Other Counties	For More Info . . .
313	SMITH, Andrew J	34	S½SE	1872-03-15		A7
314	SMITH, R M	36	S½SW	1885-07-27		A7
316	SMITHER, Hamilton B	35	NESW	1858-12-16		A8
315	" "	35	NWSE	1858-12-16		A8
317	STOGSDILL, Daniel	29	NWSW	1856-10-10		A1
318	" "	29	SESW	1859-01-01		A1
319	STRINGER, Finis H	36	NENW	1895-08-01		A7
320	SWECKER, Henry B	23	E½SW	1891-05-25		A7
321	" "	23	W½SE	1891-05-25		A7
323	TICE, Reuben D	25	SWSW	1872-03-15		A7
322	" "	25	SENW	1872-08-30		A1
324	" "	25	E½SW	1872-03-15		A7
325	" "	26	SESE	1872-03-15		A7
326	TROUTMAN, Henry	34	SWSW	1861-02-09		A1
329	VAN METRE, John E	28	SWNW	1901-07-09		A7
330	" "	28	NWSW	1901-07-09		A7
331	WARNER, Nancy J	36	SWNW	1892-09-09		A7
332	WILLIAMS, H M	5	NWSW	1877-11-10		A1 G151
6944	WILSON, G P	5	1NE	1860-11-12		A6 G61
333	" "	5	NESE	1860-11-12		A6 G61
6951	" "	5	E21NW	1860-11-12		A6 G61
6947	" "	5	2NE	1860-11-12		A6 C
6956	" "	5	S22NW	1860-11-12		A6 C
334	WILSON, Giles	32	S½SE	1860-02-10		A6
335	" "	33	NWSW	1856-01-03		A1
336	" "	33	SWSW	1860-02-10		A6
337	WORCESTER, Frank	22	NWNW	1890-01-30		A1
6932	YOUNG, William	31	2SW	1882-09-30		A7 C
6931	" "	31	2NW	1899-12-18		A7

Patent Map

T27-N R9-W
5th PM 27-N 9-W Meridian

Map Group 2

Township Statistics

Parcels Mapped	:	276
Number of Patents	:	171
Number of Individuals	:	145
Patentees Identified	:	139
Number of Surnames	:	109
Multi-Patentee Parcels	:	13
Oldest Patent Date	:	8/1/1853
Most Recent Patent	:	10/15/1919
Block/Lot Parcels	:	34
Cities and Town	:	1
Cemeteries	:	1

Section 6
LEARNARD Oscar E 1882

Section 5
Lots/Tracts-Sec. 5
1NE   HULL, JAMES [61]   1860
2NE   HULL, JAMES   1860
2NE   HULL, JAMES   1919
E21NW   HULL, JAMES [61]   1860
E22NW   HULL, JAMES   1919
S22NW   HULL, JAMES   1860
W21NW   LEARNARD, OSCAR E   1919
W22NW   LEARNARD, OSCAR E   1919

SANTEE Mary 1872
WILLIAMS [151] H M 1877
PERRIN Ephraim P 1878
PERRIN Ephraim P 1878
HULL [61] James 1860
LEARNARD Enoch P 1869
FERRELL Enoch P 1869
HOSKINSON Isaac 1869
LEARNARD Oscar E 1919

Section 4
BUFORD William 1859

LEARNARD Oscar E 1882

Lots/Tracts-Sec. 4
1NE   LEARNARD, OSCAR E   1882
2NW   BRASSWELL, JACOB B   1879
E21NW   LEARNARD, OSCAR E   1882
E22NE   LEARNARD, OSCAR E   1882
W21NW   BRASSWELL, JACOB B   1879
W22NE   BRASSWELL, JACOB B   1879

Section 7
LEARNARD Oscar E 1882
BUCKLAND Thomas A 1872
FERRELL Enoch P 1869
FERRELL Enoch P 1869
BUCKLAND Thomas A 1872
LEARNARD Oscar E 1882
LEARNARD Oscar E 1882

Section 8
LEARNARD Oscar E 1882
LEARNARD Oscar E 1882

Section 9
LEARNARD Oscar E 1882

Section 18
Lots/Tracts-Sec. 18
1SW   LOUTRELL, WILLIAM A   1889
N22SW   LOUTRELL, WILLIAM A   1889
S22SW   BOATMAN, WILLIAM H   1859

PATTERSON George 1879
NEASE William 1891
PATTERSON George 1879
NEASE Thomas 1891

Section 17
NEASE William 1891
MITCHELL Thomas J 1881
MITCHELL Thomas J 1881
HENRY Mary F 1891
CHAPIN Ezra E 1892
SKAGGS George W 1890
RANDEL William H 1890
CHAPIN Ezra E 1892

Section 16

Section 19
Lots/Tracts-Sec. 19
N21NW   BOATMAN, WILLIAM H   1859
N21SW   BOATMAN, JAMES   1858
N22NW   BOATMAN, WILLIAM H   1859
N22SW   COX, JESSE N   1856
S21NW   MCCULLOUGH, JOHN   1882
S21SW   BOATMAN, JAMES   1856
S22NW   MCCULLOUGH, JOHN   1882
S22SW   JONES, EZEKIEL   1856

DORSEY Allen E 1874
NEASE Thomas 1891
HOGAN James H 1888
DORSEY Allen E 1874
HOGAN James H 1888

Section 20
SKAGGS George W 1890
RANDEL William H 1890
RANDEL William H 1890
LIVINGSTON David P 1891
LIVINGSTON David P 1891
ANDERSON Isaiah E 1889
ATCHLEY Edward H 1877
ATCHLEY Edward H 1877
OLIVER John C 1892

Section 21
RAULISON James J 1890
LOVAN Goldmon L 1890
LOVAN Goldmon L 1890
MCCULLOUGH Della 1893
LIVINGSTON David P 1891
MOFFITT James H 1876
MOFFITT James H 1876
RAULISON James J 1890
MOFFITT James H 1876
MOFFITT James H 1876
MCCULLOUGH Della 1893
FEATHERINGILL William 1882
LOVAN Daniel R 1872
LOVAN James T 1892

Section 30
Lots/Tracts-Sec. 30
1NW   BOATMAN, JAMES   1856
2NW   FERGUSON, EMANUEL C   1883

FERGUSON [79] Elizabeth 1883
LIVINGSTON John M 1882
JONES Ezekiel 1856
JONES Ezekiel 1856
OSBORN Aaron B 1879
HARRIS James W 1875
JONES Ezekiel 1856
JONES Manuel 1859

Section 29
DUNIVAN Mary E 1885
MEDLEY Carrie 1888
STOGSDILL Daniel 1856
FEATHERINGILL John M 1886
STOGSDILL Daniel 1859
ELKINS John H 1859
FEATHERINGILL John M 1886
ELKINS John H 1866

Section 28
FEATHERINGILL William 1882
FEATHERINGILL William 1882
FERGUSON James A 1888
VAN METRE John E 1901
ELKIN John H 1860
VAN METRE John E 1901
FERGUSON James A 1888
LOVAN Daniel R 1872
LOVAN Daniel R 1882
LOVAN Daniel R 1872
LOVAN William J 1880
HOGAN John S 1888
BEESON Volney W 1895
FINDLEY John W 1898
KEEN Charles 1894
JONES Samuel 1856
JONES Samuel 1859

Section 31
Lots/Tracts-Sec. 31
2NW   YOUNG, WILLIAM   1899
2SW   YOUNG, WILLIAM   1882
N21NW   EIDSON, BENNETT   1880
S21NW   MITCHELL, LACY L   1892

EIDSON Bennett 1880
DRYBREAD Joseph H 1882
DRYBREAD Joseph H 1882
ELKIN John H 1861
DRYBREAD Joseph H 1882
HARKEY Christopher 1875
HARRIS Benjamin P 1894

Section 32
JONES Manuel 1860
ELKINS John 1856
ALSUP Benjamin 1853
HOLLOWAY Richard 1881
HALLOWAY Richard 1882
ALSUP Martin S 1873
ALSUP Martin S 1873
ALSUP Benjamin 1853
HOLLOWAY Richard 1888
ALSUP Martin S 1882
WILSON Giles 1860

Section 33
JONES Samuel 1856
CRITCHER Charles D 1870
EIDSON James 1877
KEEN Charles 1894
EIDSON James 1877
BOUCHER Samuel W 1892
WILSON Giles 1856
DAVIS James E 1878
DAVIS James E 1878
BOUCHER Samuel W 1892
WILSON Giles 1860
LANCE Henry D 1859
JONES Samuel 1856
ALSOP Benjamin 1854

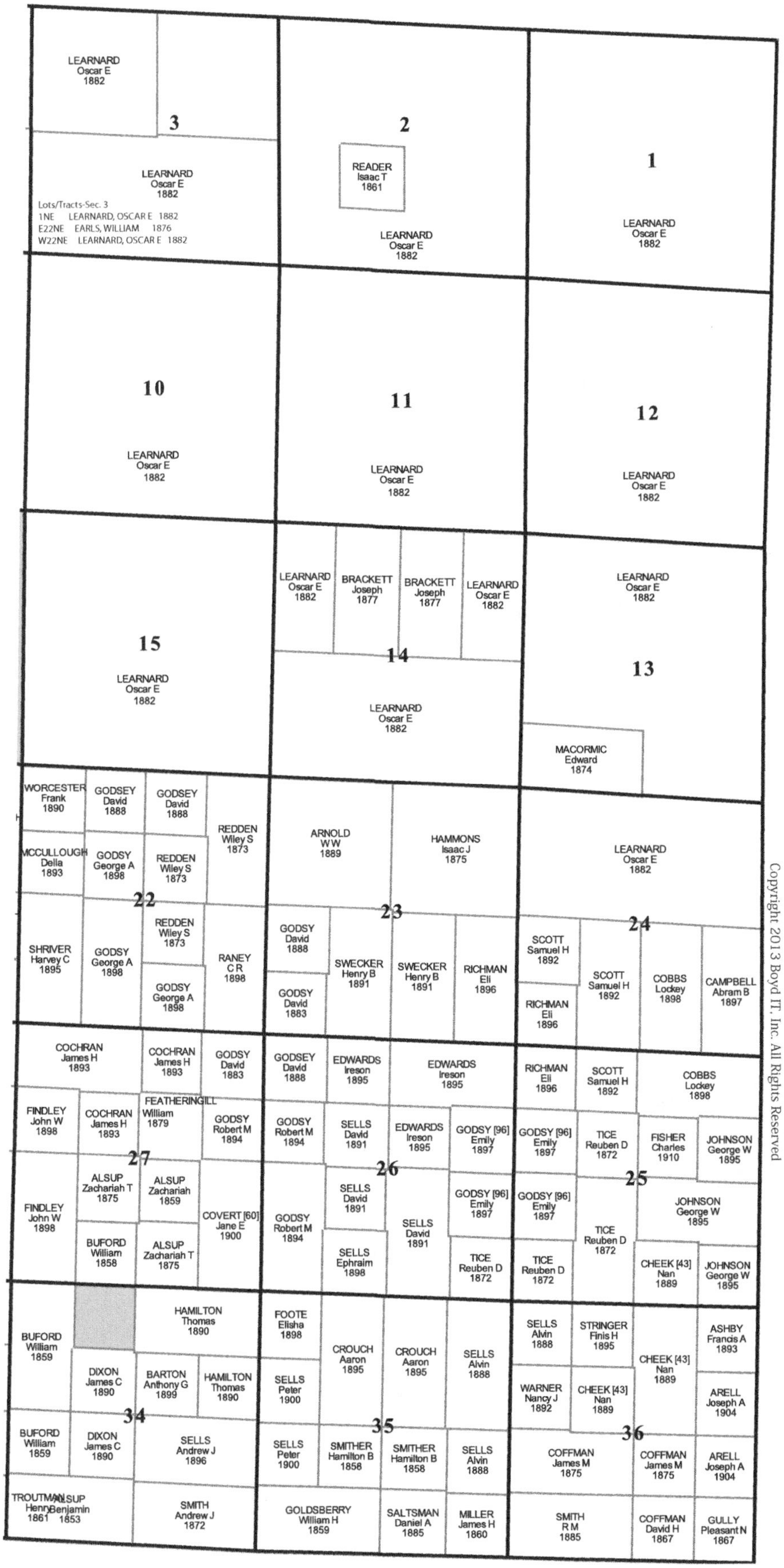

LEARNARD Oscar E 1882 **3**	**2** READER Isaac T 1861	**1**

LEARNARD
Oscar E
1882

Lots/Tracts-Sec. 3
1NE LEARNARD, OSCAR E 1882
E22NE EARLS, WILLIAM 1876
W22NE LEARNARD, OSCAR E 1882

LEARNARD
Oscar E
1882

LEARNARD
Oscar E
1882

Helpful Hints

1. This Map's INDEX can be found on the preceding pages.

2. Refer to Map "C" to see where this Township lies within Howell County, Missouri.

3. Numbers within square brackets [ ] denote a multi-patentee land parcel (multi-owner). Refer to Appendix "C" for a full list of members in this group.

4. Areas that look to be crowded with Patentees usually indicate multiple sales of the same parcel (Re-issues) or Overlapping parcels. See this Township's Index for an explanation of these and other circumstances that might explain "odd" groupings of Patentees on this map.

10 LEARNARD Oscar E 1882

11 LEARNARD Oscar E 1882

12 LEARNARD Oscar E 1882

15 LEARNARD Oscar E 1882

14 LEARNARD Oscar E 1882 / LEARNARD Oscar E 1882 / BRACKETT Joseph 1877 / BRACKETT Joseph 1877 / LEARNARD Oscar E 1882 / LEARNARD Oscar E 1882

13 LEARNARD Oscar E 1882

MACORMIC Edward 1874

Section 22:
WORCESTER Frank 1890 / GODSEY David 1888 / GODSEY David 1888
MCCULLOUGH Della 1893 / GODSY George A 1898 / REDDEN Wiley S 1873 / REDDEN Wiley S 1873
SHRIVER Harvey C 1895 / GODSY George A 1898 / REDDEN Wiley S 1873 / GODSY George A 1898 / RANEY C R 1898

Section 23:
ARNOLD W W 1889 / HAMMONS Isaac J 1875
GODSY David 1888 / GODSY David 1883 / SWECKER Henry B 1891 / SWECKER Henry B 1891 / RICHMAN Eli 1896

Section 24:
LEARNARD Oscar E 1882
SCOTT Samuel H 1892 / SCOTT Samuel H 1892 / COBBS Lockey 1898 / CAMPBELL Abram B 1897
RICHMAN Eli 1896

Section 27:
COCHRAN James H 1893 / COCHRAN James H 1893 / GODSY David 1883
FINDLEY John W 1898 / COCHRAN James H 1893 / FEATHERINGILL William 1879 / GODSY Robert M 1894
ALSUP Zachariah T 1875 / ALSUP Zachariah 1859 / COVERT [60] Jane E 1900
FINDLEY John W 1898 / BUFORD William 1858 / ALSUP Zachariah T 1875

Section 26:
GODSEY David 1888 / EDWARDS Ireson 1895 / EDWARDS Ireson 1895
GODSY Robert M 1894 / SELLS David 1891 / EDWARDS Ireson 1895 / GODSY [96] Emily 1897
GODSY Robert M 1894 / SELLS David 1891 / SELLS David 1891 / GODSY [96] Emily 1897
SELLS Ephraim 1898 / TICE Reuben D 1872

Section 25:
RICHMAN Eli 1896 / SCOTT Samuel H 1892 / COBBS Lockey 1898
GODSY [96] Emily 1897 / TICE Reuben D 1872 / FISHER Charles 1910 / JOHNSON George W 1895
GODSY [96] Emily 1897 / TICE Reuben D 1872 / JOHNSON George W 1895
TICE Reuben D 1872 / CHEEK [43] Nan 1889 / JOHNSON George W 1895

Section 34:
BUFORD William 1859 / HAMILTON Thomas 1890
DIXON James C 1890 / BARTON Anthony G 1899 / HAMILTON Thomas 1890
BUFORD William 1859 / DIXON James C 1890 / SELLS Andrew J 1896
TROUTMAN Henry 1861 / ALSUP Benjamin 1853 / SMITH Andrew J 1872

Section 35:
FOOTE Elisha 1898
CROUCH Aaron 1895 / CROUCH Aaron 1895 / SELLS Alvin 1888
SELLS Peter 1900
SELLS Peter 1900 / SMITHER Hamilton B 1858 / SMITHER Hamilton B 1858 / SELLS Alvin 1888
GOLDSBERRY William H 1859 / SALTSMAN Daniel A 1885 / MILLER James H 1860

Section 36:
SELLS Alvin 1888 / STRINGER Finis H 1895 / ASHBY Francis A 1893
CHEEK [43] Nan 1889
WARNER Nancy J 1892 / CHEEK [43] Nan 1889 / ARELL Joseph A 1904
COFFMAN James M 1875 / COFFMAN James M 1875 / ARELL Joseph A 1904
SMITH R M 1885 / COFFMAN David H 1867 / GULLY Pleasant N 1867

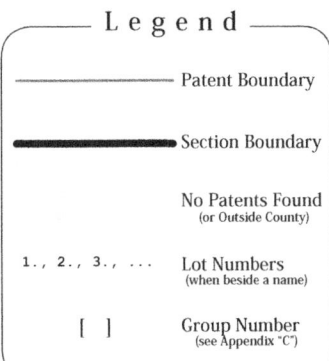

Legend

—— Patent Boundary

━━ Section Boundary

No Patents Found
(or Outside County)

1., 2., 3., ... Lot Numbers
(when beside a name)

[ ] Group Number
(see Appendix "C")

Scale: Section = 1 mile X 1 mile
(generally, with some exceptions)

Road Map

T27-N   R9-W
5th PM 27-N 9-W Meridian

Map Group 2

Cities & Towns
Willow Springs

Cemeteries
Willow Springs City Cemetery

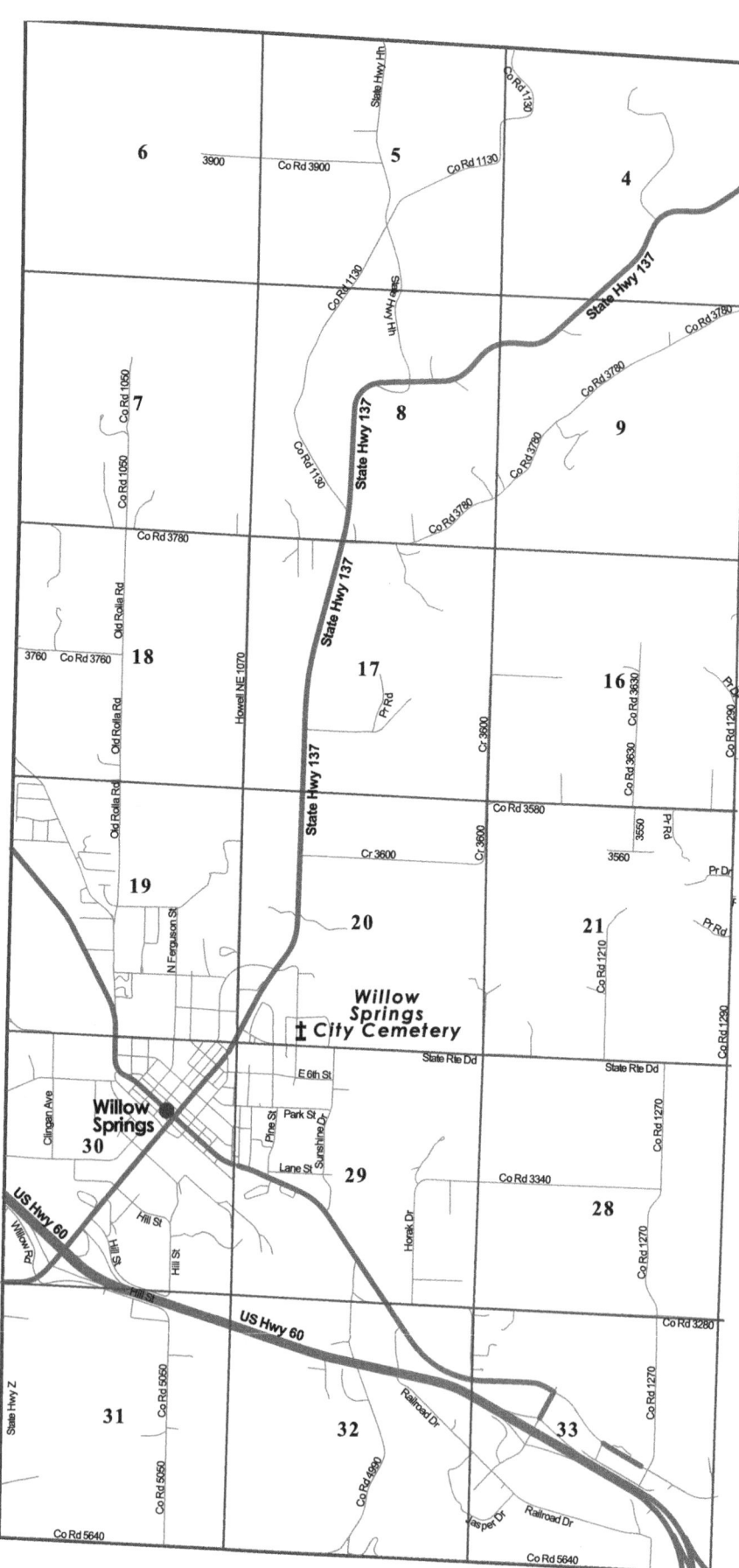

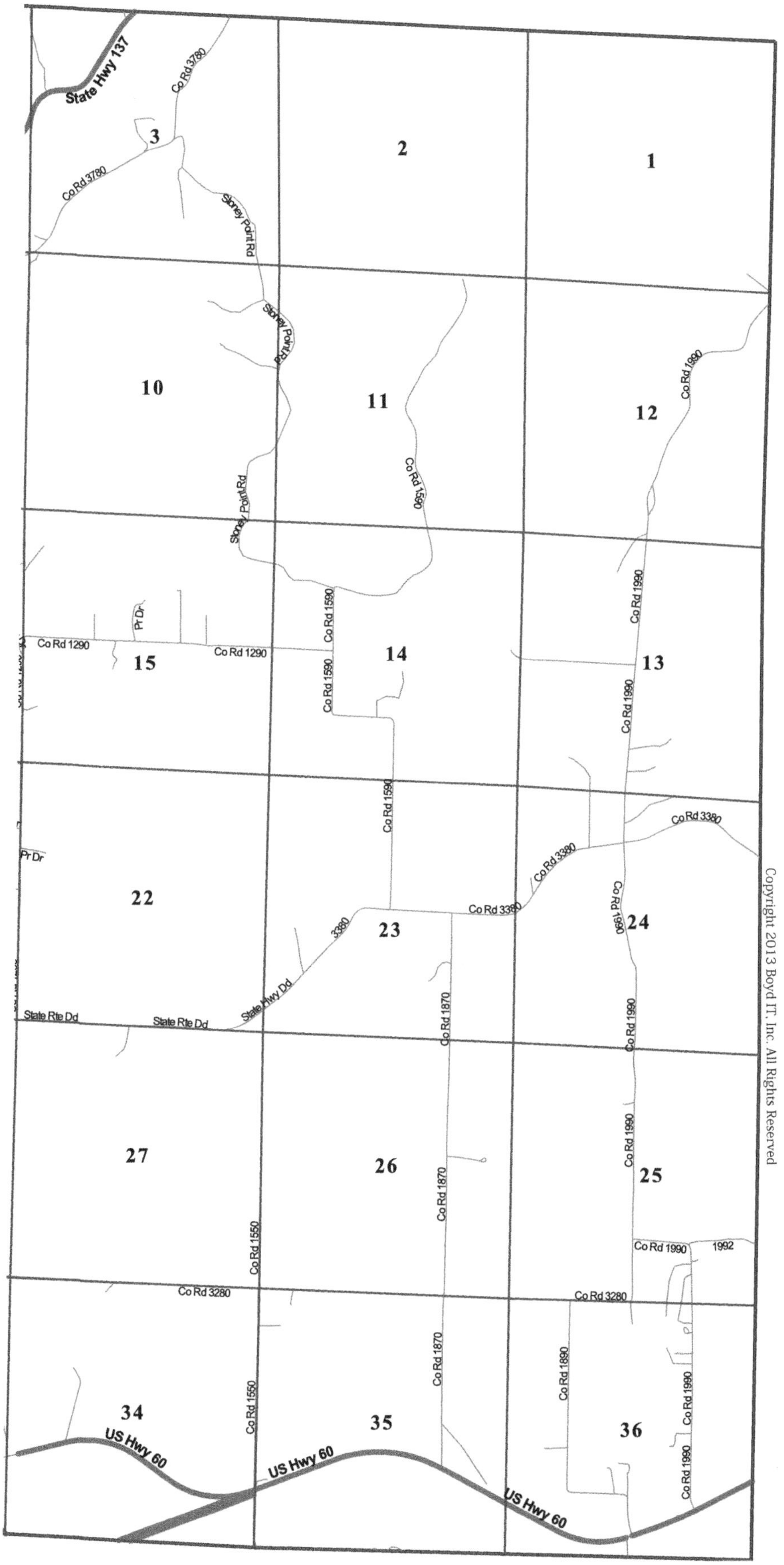

State Hwy 137

Co Rd 3780

3

2

1

Co Rd 3780

Stoney Point Rd

Co Rd 1980

10

Stoney Point Rd

11

Co Rd 1590

12

Co Rd 1990

Stoney Point Rd

Pr Dr

Co Rd 1590

15

Co Rd 1290

Co Rd 1290

Co Rd 1590

14

13

Co Rd 1990

Co Rd 1590

Pr Dr

Co Rd 3380

22

3380

Co Rd 3380

Co Rd 3380

23

Co Rd 3390

Co Rd 1990

24

State Rte Dd

State Rte Dd

State Hwy Dd

Co Rd 1870

Co Rd 1990

27

26

Co Rd 1870

Co Rd 1990

25

Co Rd 1550

Co Rd 1990

1992

Co Rd 3280

Co Rd 3280

Co Rd 1550

Co Rd 1870

Co Rd 1890

Co Rd 1990

34

35

36

US Hwy 60

US Hwy 60

US Hwy 60

Helpful Hints

1. This road map has a number of uses, but primarily it is to help you: a) find the present location of land owned by your ancestors (at least the general area), b) find cemeteries and city-centers, and c) estimate the route/roads used by Census-takers & tax-assessors.

2. If you plan to travel to Howell County to locate cemeteries or land parcels, please pick up a modern travel map for the area before you do. Mapping old land parcels on modern maps is not as exact a science as you might think. Just the slightest variations in public land survey coordinates, estimates of parcel boundaries, or road-map deviations can greatly alter a map's representation of how a road either does or doesn't cross a particular parcel of land.

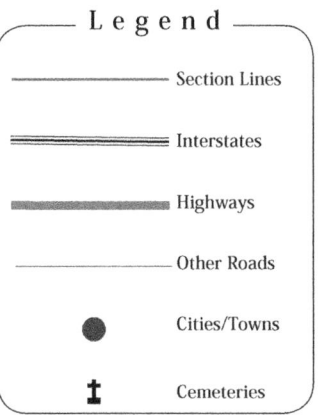

L e g e n d

———————— Section Lines

════════ Interstates

━━━━━━━━ Highways

———————— Other Roads

● Cities/Towns

☦ Cemeteries

Scale: Section = 1 mile X 1 mile
(generally, with some exceptions)

Historical Map

T27-N   R9-W
5th PM 27-N 9-W Meridian

Map Group 2

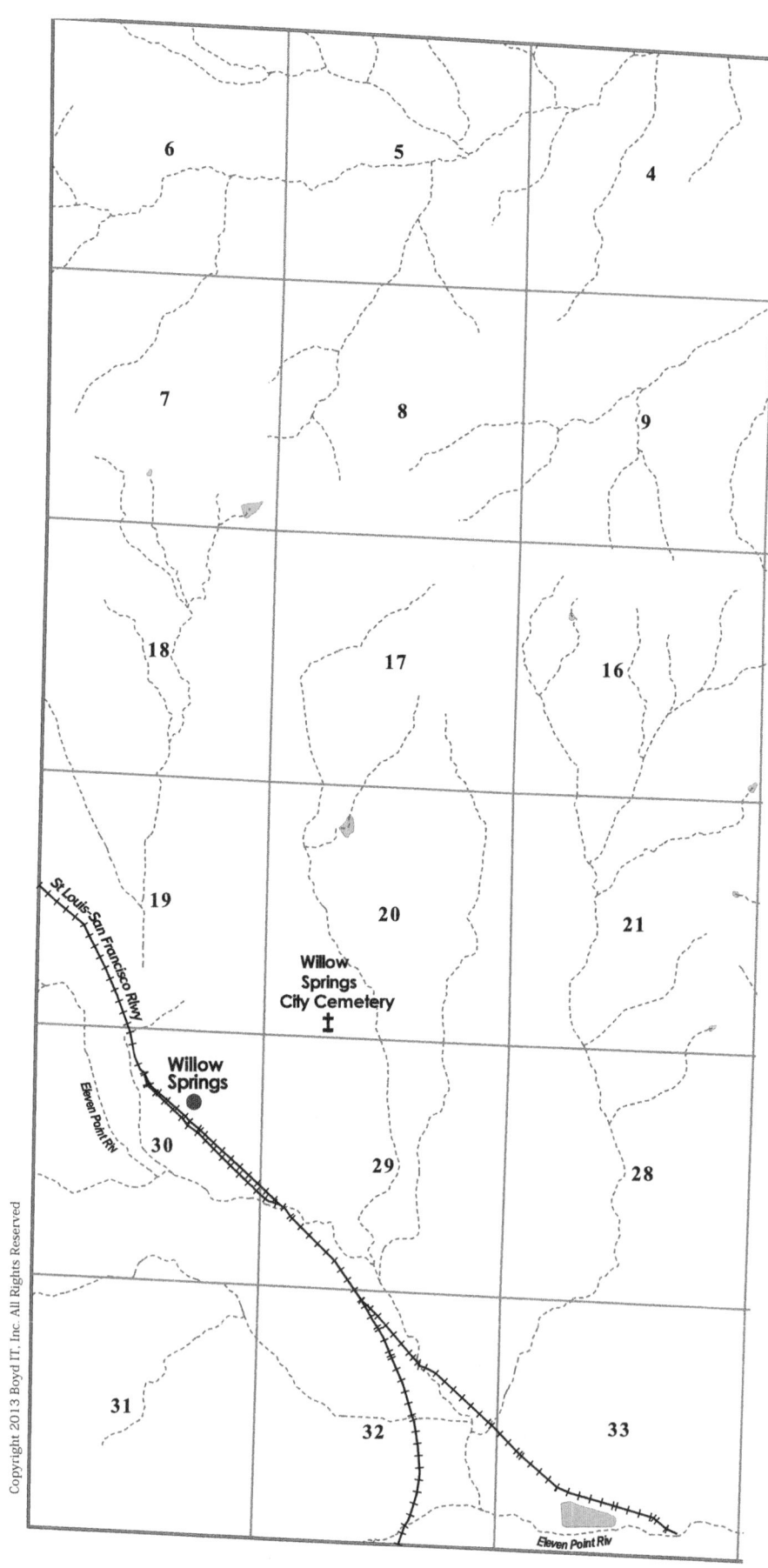

Cities & Towns

Willow Springs

Cemeteries

Willow Springs City Cemetery

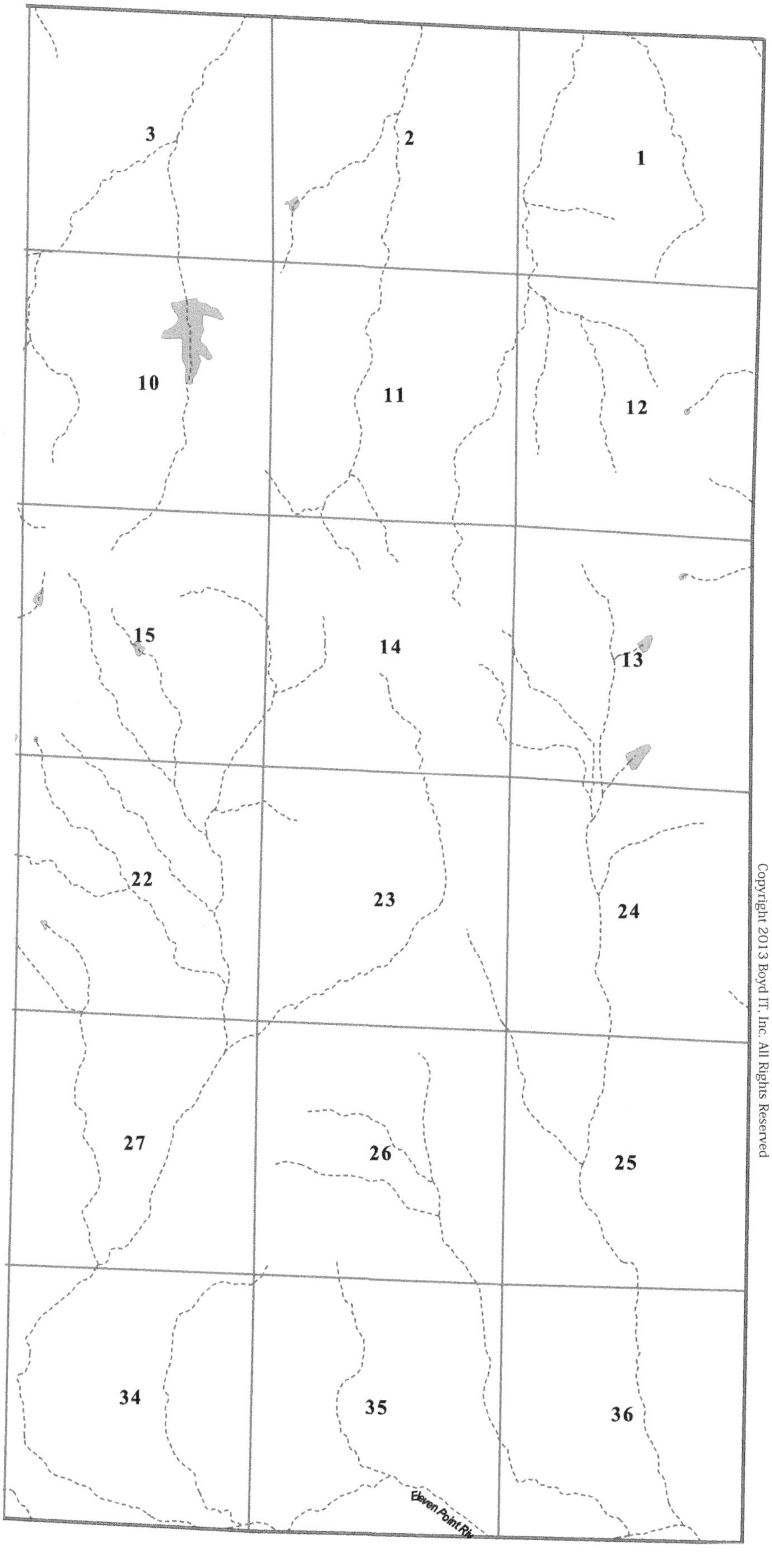

3	2	1
10	11	12
15	14	13
22	23	24
27	26	25
34	35	36

Eleven Point Riv

Helpful Hints

1. This Map takes a different look at the same Congressional Township displayed in the preceding two maps. It presents features that can help you better envision the historical development of the area: a) Water-bodies (lakes & ponds), b) Water-courses (rivers, streams, etc.), c) Railroads, d) City/town center-points (where they were oftentimes located when first settled), and e) Cemeteries.

2. Using this "Historical" map in tandem with this Township's Patent Map and Road Map, may lead you to some interesting discoveries. You will often find roads, towns, cemeteries, and waterways are named after nearby landowners: sometimes those names will be the ones you are researching. See how many of these research gems you can find here in Howell County.

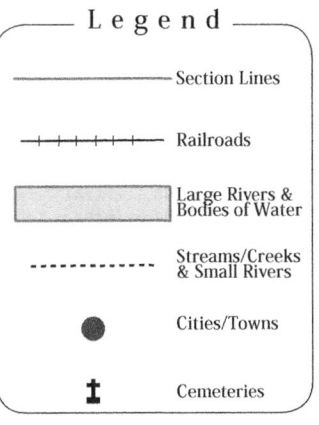

Legend

————————	Section Lines
─┼┼┼┼┼─	Railroads
▭	Large Rivers & Bodies of Water
- - - - - -	Streams/Creeks & Small Rivers
●	Cities/Towns
ⵜ	Cemeteries

Scale: Section = 1 mile X 1 mile
(there are some exceptions)

Map Group 3: Index to Land Patents

Township 27-North Range 8-West (5th PM 27-N 8-W)

After you locate an individual in this Index, take note of the Section and Section Part then proceed to the Land Patent map on the pages immediately following. You should have no difficulty locating the corresponding parcel of land.

The "For More Info" Column will lead you to more information about the underlying Patents. See the *Legend* at right, and the "How to Use this Book" chapter, for more information.

```
                    LEGEND
          "For More Info . . . " column
A = Authority (Legislative Act, See Appendix "A")
B = Block or Lot (location in Section unknown)
C = Cancelled Patent
F = Fractional Section
G = Group  (Multi-Patentee Patent, see Appendix "C")
V = Overlaps another Parcel
R = Re-Issued (Parcel patented more than once)

(A & G items require you to look in the Appendixes referred
to above. All other Letter-designations followed by a number
require you to locate line-items in this index that possess
the ID number found after the letter).
```

ID	Individual in Patent	Sec.	Sec. Part	Date Issued	Other Counties	For More Info . . .
338	ABERDEEN, Samuel F	31	S½SE	1900-02-02		A7
339	"	32	SWSW	1900-02-02		A7
6985	ASHBY, Francis A	30	S21SW	1893-12-21		A7
6989	"	31	N22NW	1893-12-21		A7
6987	"	31	N21NW	1893-12-21		A7
340	BARNETT, James D	32	NWSW	1868-07-01		A8
6961	BAUMGARDNER, Andrew J	1	2NW	1893-07-19		A7
6968	"	1	W22NE	1893-07-19		A7
343	BENTON, John	22	NWSE	1891-05-25		A7
342	"	22	SESW	1891-05-25		A7
341	"	22	N½SW	1891-05-25		A7
344	BENTON, John W	22	SENW	1894-11-22		A1
345	BIBLE, Valentine K	21	NESE	1893-12-19		A7
346	"	21	S½NE	1893-12-19		A7
347	"	22	SWNW	1893-12-19		A7
348	BLACKBURN, James H	20	SWSE	1861-08-01		A1
349	"	29	NWNE	1859-09-01		A1
350	"	29	SWNE	1859-09-10		A1
351	BLANKENSHIP, Caleb A	12	SE	1882-05-20		A7
352	BOLERJACK, Joel S	32	SESE	1894-05-18		A7
354	"	33	SWSW	1894-05-18		A7
353	"	33	E½SW	1894-05-18		A7
355	BREWINGTON, James	24	NESW	1885-12-19		A7
357	"	24	SENW	1885-12-19		A7
356	"	24	N½NW	1885-12-19		A7
358	BREWINGTON, John	23	SENE	1895-08-09		A1
359	"	24	NWSW	1895-08-09		A1
360	BROTHERTON, Moses F	35	NENW	1901-06-08		A7
361	"	35	NWNE	1901-06-08		A7
362	BROWNING, John W	23	E½NW	1894-05-23		A7
363	"	23	W½NE	1894-05-23		A7
365	BURNHAM, Charles M	32	NESW	1860-08-01		A1 G28
364	"	32	SWNW	1860-08-01		A1 G28
366	CAMPBELL, George B	1	SESE	1895-05-28		A7
6970	CAMPBELL, Henry M	19	N22SW	1897-04-10		A7
6969	"	19	N21SW	1897-04-10		A7
367	CAPPS, Henry T	33	SENE	1892-01-05		A7
368	"	34	S½NW	1892-01-05		A7
369	"	34	NESW	1892-01-05		A7
371	CLARK, Abraham J	21	S½SE	1901-08-12		A7
370	"	21	NWSE	1901-08-12		A7
372	CLARK, William	34	SESW	1898-01-26		A7
6971	CLINGINGSMITH, Leander	19	S21SW	1912-06-01		A7
6972	"	19	S22SW	1912-06-01		A7
373	COX, Daniel	20	E½SW	1861-08-01		A1
374	"	29	E½NW	1861-05-01		A1

ID	Individual in Patent	Sec.	Sec. Part	Date Issued	Other Counties	For More Info . . .
377	CULBERTSON, Charles E	14	SWNE	1906-06-30		A1
376	" "	14	E½NW	1906-06-30		A1
375	" "	14	NWNW	1906-06-30		A1
379	CUNNINGHAM, Mary M	31	SENE	1882-09-30		A1
378	" "	31	NENE	1882-09-30		A1
380	CUNNINGHAM, Wilson V	32	SWNW	1860-08-01		A1 G28
381	" "	32	NESW	1860-08-01		A1 G28
382	DANIEL, Adam T	27	SENE	1911-09-28		A7
383	DANIEL, James B	14	W½SE	1891-05-25		A7
384	" "	14	E½SW	1891-05-25		A7
385	DANIEL, William H	22	NESE	1910-03-01		A7
386	DRYMAN, John	17	SENW	1888-05-07		A1
387	DRYMON, James	17	N½NW	1898-04-11		A7
388	" "	17	SWNW	1898-04-11		A7
389	" "	18	NENE	1898-04-11		A7
390	EATON, Frank	23	W½SE	1900-08-09		A7
391	EDWARDS, James	19	NW	1895-05-28		A7
392	FAIR, James	15	S½NW	1893-12-19		A7
393	" "	15	N½SW	1893-12-19		A7
394	FAVORITE, Clarence H	25	NWSE	1907-05-10		A1
395	FEHR, Adam	1	SWSE	1895-11-13		A1
396	FEHR, Fred	1	NESE	1895-11-13		A1
397	FILLMAN, Celia B	24	E½SE	1899-05-12		A7 G80
399	FINDLEY, Jemima O	32	NESE	1901-03-23		A7 G81
398	"	32	SENE	1901-03-23		A7 G81
400	" "	33	NWSW	1901-03-23		A7 G81
402	FINDLEY, Lavada M	32	SWNE	1890-01-10		A7 G82
401	" "	32	NWSE	1890-01-10		A7 G82
403	FINDLEY, Samuel H	32	NESE	1901-03-23		A7 G81
404	" "	32	SENE	1901-03-23		A7 G81
405	" "	33	NWSW	1901-03-23		A7 G81
407	FINDLEY, William A	32	SWNE	1890-01-10		A7 G82
406	" "	32	NWSE	1890-01-10		A7 G82
408	FRENCH, William A	17	NWSW	1892-03-07		A7
410	" "	18	N½SE	1892-03-07		A7
409	" "	18	SESE	1892-03-07		A7
411	GAMBLE, James S	35	SWSW	1898-04-11		A7
412	GASTIAN, James F	17	E½SE	1886-10-11		A7
413	GILL, John C	13	NENE	1882-06-30		A7
415	GOLDSBERRY, Ignatius	33	SWSE	1859-09-01		A1
414	" "	33	NESE	1859-09-01		A1
416	GOLESBERRY, Ignatious	33	NWSE	1857-04-15		A1
417	GREENWAY, Moses M	17	S½SW	1882-11-10		A7
418	" "	20	E½NW	1882-11-10		A7
6976	GRIFFITH, Christopher M	2	E22NW	1901-06-08	Texas	A7
6979	" "	2	W22NE	1901-06-08	Texas	A7
420	GRIFFITH, John	26	W½SE	1883-06-30		A7
419	" "	26	E½SW	1883-06-30		A7
6994	GULLEY, Pleasant N	31	S22SW	1860-08-01		A1
421	" "	34	NENW	1891-08-24		A1
422	GULLY, Pleasant N	28	SESE	1890-01-30		A1
6986	" "	30	S22SW	1890-01-30		A1
6992	" "	31	S21SW	1861-02-09		A1
423	GUNZ, William	36	SENE	1898-10-04		A7
424	" "	36	NESE	1898-10-04		A7
425	HALDEMAN, Henry H	12	SWNW	1901-08-27		A1
426	HALE, Josiah	29	SWSW	1860-10-01		A1
427	" "	30	SESE	1860-10-01		A1
428	" "	32	SENW	1859-09-01		A1
429	" "	32	N½NW	1859-09-10		A1
430	HAMEL, Tice	23	SW	1895-05-28		A7
431	HARDIN, Nathan C	13	SWSW	1892-03-07		A7
432	" "	14	E½SE	1892-03-07		A7
433	" "	23	NENE	1892-03-07		A7
6963	HARRISON, Lucy E	1	E21NE	1911-11-01		A7
434	HENDERSON, Leonard E	30	NWSE	1893-03-03		A7
6981	" "	30	1NW	1893-03-03		A7
6983	" "	30	N21SW	1893-03-03		A7
435	HENDERSON, Wiley H	19	SWSE	1897-05-20		A7
438	" "	30	NESE	1886-07-20		A1
436	" "	30	SWNE	1886-07-20		A1
437	" "	30	NWNE	1897-05-20		A7
439	HICKS, David A	13	W½NW	1891-06-09		A7

ID	Individual in Patent	Sec.	Sec. Part	Date Issued	Other Counties	For More Info . . .
440	HICKS, David A (Cont'd)	14	E½NE	1891-06-09		A7
441	HOAG, William	30	SWSE	1898-04-06		A7
443	" "	31	W½NE	1898-04-06		A7
442	" "	31	NWSE	1898-04-06		A7
444	HOOD, Jesse	20	NESE	1880-11-20		A7
445	" "	21	NWSW	1880-11-20		A7
446	HOOD, William M	28	SW	1879-12-15		A7
447	" "	29	NESE	1884-10-11		A1
448	HOY, Benjamin E	32	N½NE	1912-04-25		A7
449	" "	33	W½NW	1912-04-25		A7
450	INMAN, Nancy	22	SENE	1895-07-08		A7
451	" "	23	W½NW	1895-07-08		A7
452	JACKSON, Freeman B	36	SESE	1893-09-01		A7
453	JOHNSON, Mary A	31	NESE	1894-11-22		A1
6995	JONES, Foster S	4	1NW	1892-06-21		A7
454	" "	4	NWSW	1892-06-21		A7
6999	" "	4	W22NW	1892-06-21		A7
455	JONES, James J	28	SWSE	1892-03-07		A7
457	" "	33	NENW	1892-03-07		A7
456	" "	33	N½NE	1892-03-07		A7
6990	KING, John C	31	N22SW	1900-02-02		A7
6988	" "	31	N21SW	1900-02-02		A7
6993	" "	31	S22NW	1900-02-02		A7
6991	" "	31	S21NW	1900-02-02		A7
6982	LIVINGSTON, James R	30	2NW	1895-05-28		A7
6984	" "	30	N22SW	1895-05-28		A7
458	MANGUM, George W	2	SESE	1888-07-17		A1
459	MARTIN, James	25	SWSW	1874-04-20		A7
460	" "	26	E½SE	1874-04-20		A7
461	" "	26	SENE	1874-04-20		A7
463	MCALLISTER, George W	35	W½NW	1898-04-11		A7
462	" "	35	NWSW	1898-04-11		A7
464	" "	35	SENW	1898-04-11		A7
466	MCDONAL, Rhoda	13	S½SE	1886-01-20		A7 G145
465	" "	13	SESW	1886-01-20		A7 G145
467	" "	24	NWNE	1886-01-20		A7 G145
468	MCFARLAND, Nathan	20	SESE	1897-04-10		A7
470	" "	21	NESW	1897-04-10		A7
469	" "	21	S½SW	1897-04-10		A7
471	MCGONIGAL, William E	19	SESE	1906-06-30		A7
472	" "	20	SWSW	1906-06-30		A7
473	" "	29	NWNW	1906-06-30		A7
474	MCGRATH, Frank J	11	N½SE	1908-08-17		A1
475	MEDLIN, Robert L	35	E½NE	1875-11-01		A7
476	" "	35	SWNE	1875-11-01		A7
477	" "	35	NESE	1875-11-01		A7
478	MOORE, Hugh	12	E½SW	1890-11-13		A7
479	" "	13	W½NE	1891-02-07		A7
482	MORGAN, George W	36	NWSW	1882-11-10		A7
480	" "	36	NENW	1882-11-10		A7
481	" "	36	W½NW	1882-11-10		A7
484	MORGAN, William S	36	SWNE	1898-10-04		A7
485	" "	36	SENW	1898-10-04		A7
483	" "	36	N½NE	1898-10-04		A7
486	MURRAY, Nicholas F	4	NWSE	1896-03-05		A1
487	MURRELL, George P	22	S½SE	1910-03-01		A7
488	" "	27	NENE	1910-03-01		A7
490	NANCE, Ashley	13	NESE	1888-12-06		A7
489	" "	13	SENE	1888-12-06		A7
491	NANCE, Bardin	25	SENE	1874-04-20		A7
493	" "	25	NESE	1874-04-20		A7
492	" "	25	S½SE	1874-04-20		A7
494	NEEDHAM, Thomas E	15	SWSE	1891-05-05		A7
496	" "	22	W½NE	1891-05-05		A7
495	" "	22	NENE	1891-05-05		A7
497	NORRIS, William A	25	E½SW	1891-05-25		A7
6978	OGDEN, George W	2	W21NW	1912-06-11		A1
6980	" "	2	W22NW	1912-06-11		A1
498	PANE, Daniel	24	SWNW	1861-08-01		A1
6996	PAYNE, Joseph S	4	2NE	1892-01-25	Texas	A7
6997	" "	4	E22NW	1892-01-25	Texas	A7
6998	PENNINGER, William L	4	W21NE	1888-07-17		A1
499	POKE, Richard A	23	E½SE	1887-04-20		A7

ID	Individual in Patent	Sec.	Sec. Part	Date Issued	Other Counties	For More Info . . .
500	POKE, Richard A (Cont'd)	24	SWSW	1887-04-20		A7
501	" "	26	NENE	1887-04-20		A7
502	POLK, Elias	24	W½SE	1884-02-15		A7
504	" "	24	SWNE	1884-02-15		A7
503	" "	24	SESW	1884-02-15		A7
505	POLK, John	25	SWNE	1885-05-20		A7
507	" "	25	N½NE	1885-05-20		A7
506	" "	25	NENW	1885-05-20		A7
508	POPE, Calvin L	19	E½NE	1898-06-23		A7
509	" "	19	NESE	1898-06-23		A7
510	" "	20	NWNW	1898-06-23		A7
511	PORTER, William J	20	NENE	1859-09-10		A1
512	" "	20	S½NE	1859-09-10		A1
513	PURTEE, James	26	NWSW	1895-05-28		A7
514	" "	27	NESE	1895-05-28		A7
515	RAMSEY, Alexander	8	NWSE	1903-05-25		A7
517	REESE, Elijah	29	E½SW	1859-09-10		A1
516	" "	29	S½SE	1859-09-01		A1
518	REESE, John L	20	NWSE	1859-09-01		A1
519	RILEY, James	35	S½SE	1857-04-15		A1
520	" "	36	SWSW	1859-09-01		A1
521	ROBBINS, Henry J	33	SESE	1905-05-02		A7
522	ROBBINS, John B	34	W½SW	1888-12-06		A1
6974	ROBERTS, Frank Lee	2	E21NW	1914-03-31		A7
6977	" "	2	W21NE	1914-03-31		A7
523	" "	2	N½SE	1914-03-31		A7
524	ROSEMBUM, Isiah M	34	NE	1891-05-05		A7
526	ROSENBUM, Samuel N	33	SENW	1898-05-12		A7
525	" "	33	SWNE	1898-05-12		A7
527	ROSENBUM, Thomas J	27	NWSW	1893-12-19		A7
528	" "	28	N½SE	1893-12-19		A7
529	ROWE, George W	29	NWSE	1891-08-24		A1
6965	SACKVILLE, Joseph E	1	E22NE	1888-05-07		A1
530	SANMANN, Bruno H	14	NWNE	1904-11-22		A1
531	SEAL, Rhoda	13	SESW	1886-01-20		A7 G145
532	" "	13	S½SE	1886-01-20		A7 G145
533	" "	24	NWNE	1886-01-20		A7 G145
534	SEAVER, John F	18	SWSE	1900-08-09		A7
536	" "	19	NWSE	1900-08-09		A7
535	" "	19	W½NE	1900-08-09		A7
537	SELSOR, John H	11	S½SE	1895-08-09		A1
538	" "	12	W½SW	1895-08-09		A1
539	SHEARY, George W	24	E½NE	1901-06-08		A7
6962	SHERWIN, Lucy E	1	E21NE	1911-11-01		A7
540	SHIPMAN, Daniel	27	SWSW	1859-09-01		A1
541	" "	34	NWNW	1859-09-01		A1
542	SHIPMAN, Isaac	25	W½NW	1859-09-01		A1
544	" "	25	SENW	1861-08-01		A1
543	" "	25	NWSW	1861-08-01		A1
545	SHIPMANN, Daniel	27	E½SW	1859-09-01		A1
548	SHREEVE, Saul	4	SWSE	1892-08-08		A7
546	" "	4	NESW	1892-08-08		A7
547	" "	4	S½SW	1892-08-08		A7
551	SMITH, Jacob R	26	W½NE	1892-04-23		A7
550	" "	26	E½NW	1892-04-23		A7
552	SMITH, John	13	E½NW	1892-03-07		A7
553	SMITH, John C	14	SWNW	1894-05-18		A7
555	" "	15	NWSE	1894-05-18		A7
554	" "	15	S½NE	1894-05-18		A7
556	SMITH, John L	27	W½NE	1861-05-01		A1
557	" "	27	SENW	1861-05-01		A1
558	SMITH, John T	14	W½SW	1900-08-09		A7
559	" "	15	E½SE	1900-08-09		A7
560	SMITH, Richard	13	NWSE	1859-09-01		A1
561	SPEARS, Annis	21	NW	1892-10-17		A7
562	SPEARS, James N	29	E½NE	1901-03-23		A7
563	SPEARS, Samuel J	21	N½NE	1898-04-06		A7
564	SPRIGGS, Thomas W	17	NESW	1892-03-07		A7
565	" "	17	W½SE	1892-03-07		A7
566	" "	20	NWNE	1892-03-07		A7
567	STEPHENS, John W	29	NWSW	1890-01-30		A1
568	" "	29	SWNW	1890-01-30		A1
569	" "	30	E½NE	1897-04-10		A7

ID	Individual in Patent	Sec.	Sec. Part	Date Issued	Other Counties	For More Info . . .
570	STEPP, Celia B	24	E½SE	1899-05-12		A7 G80
572	STOKES, James R	36	W½SE	1896-01-14		A7
571	" "	36	E½SW	1896-01-14		A7
573	STOUT, James	27	SE	1893-09-01		A7
574	SUSONG, David A	17	NE	1892-09-09		A7
575	SUTTLE, Nevel H	11	NWNE	1907-06-24		A1
576	SZOPEINSKI, August	12	NENW	1911-02-08		A7
578	TALENT, Joshua	32	SESW	1860-08-01		A1
577	" "	32	SWSE	1860-08-01		A1
579	TAYLOR, Joshua N	12	E½NE	1879-12-15		A7
580	TAYLOR, Noah A	34	SE	1890-06-06		A7
581	TRINDLE, Preston B	1	S½SW	1898-12-01		A7
582	" "	2	SWSE	1898-12-01		A7
584	TRINDLE, William A	11	SWNE	1896-01-14		A7
583	" "	11	E½NE	1896-01-14		A7
585	" "	12	NWNW	1896-01-14		A7
586	VAUGHAN, John H	13	N½SW	1894-05-18		A7
587	VENTLE, Rosel J	35	E½SW	1875-11-01		A7
588	" "	35	NWSE	1875-11-01		A7
589	VEST, William B	1	NWSW	1902-02-12		A7
6967	" "	1	W21NW	1902-02-12		A7
6973	" "	2	E21NE	1902-02-12		A7
6975	" "	2	E22NE	1902-02-12		A7
590	WALKER, William E	20	NWSW	1890-01-10		A7
591	" "	20	SWNW	1890-01-10		A7
592	WALKER, William J	22	SWSW	1895-05-28		A7
594	" "	27	NENW	1895-05-28		A7
593	" "	27	W½NW	1895-05-28		A7
595	WHEELER, George W	15	S½SW	1894-12-17		A7
596	" "	22	N½NW	1894-12-17		A7
598	WHITAKER, Joseph C	26	W½NW	1906-05-01		A7
597	" "	26	W½SW	1906-05-01		A7
599	WIGGS, Albert	12	SENW	1898-06-23		A7
600	" "	12	W½NE	1898-06-23		A7
602	WILLIS, James M	1	NWSE	1892-12-03		A7
601	" "	1	NESW	1892-12-03		A7
6964	" "	1	E21NW	1892-12-03		A7
6966	" "	1	W21NE	1892-12-03		A7

Patent Map

T27-N R8-W
5th PM 27-N 8-W Meridian

Map Group 3

Township Statistics

Parcels Mapped	:	291
Number of Patents	:	162
Number of Individuals	:	153
Patentees Identified	:	148
Number of Surnames	:	121
Multi-Patentee Parcels	:	11
Oldest Patent Date	:	4/15/1857
Most Recent Patent	:	3/31/1914
Block/Lot Parcels	:	38
Cities and Town	:	1
Cemeteries	:	2

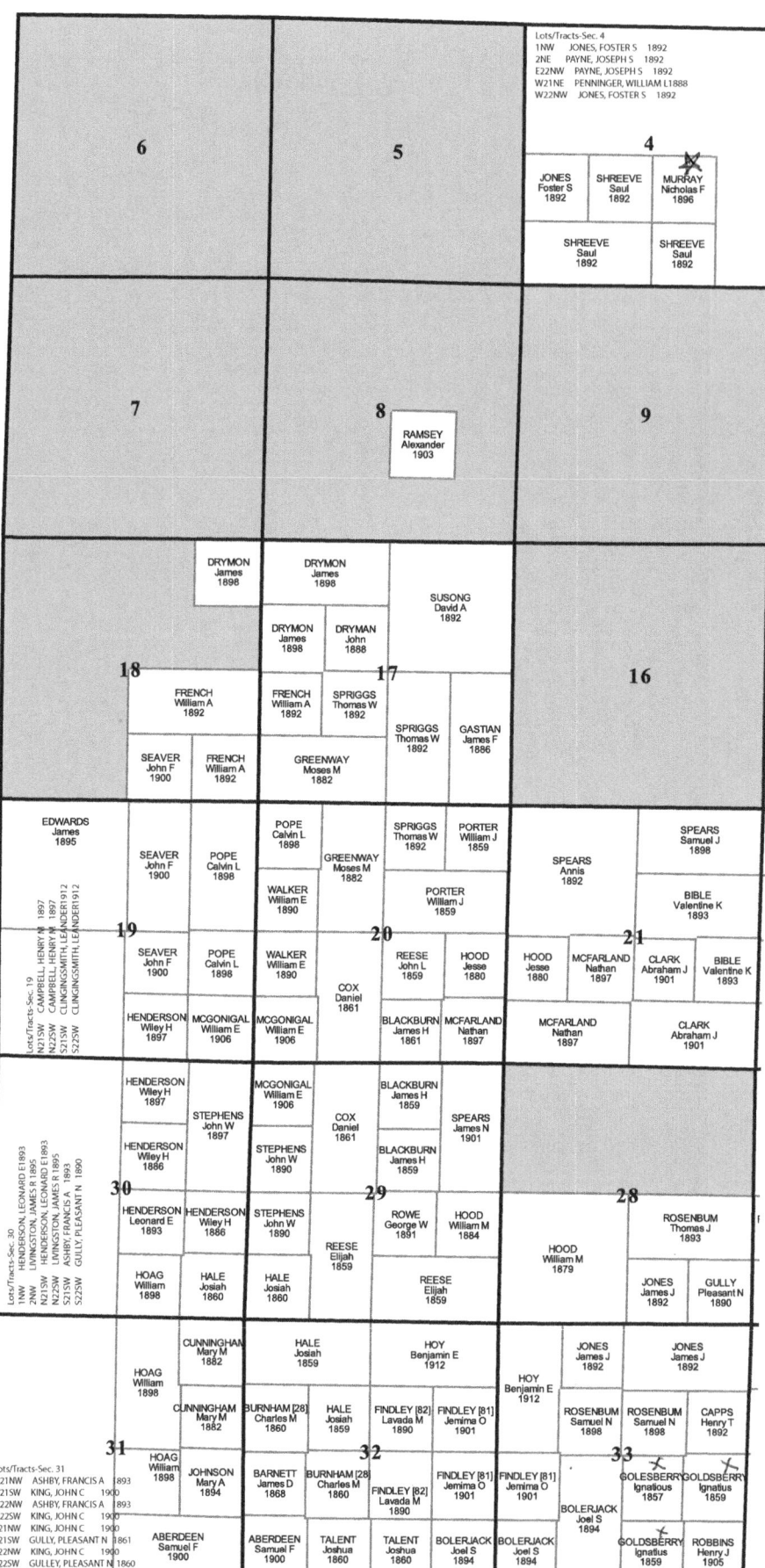

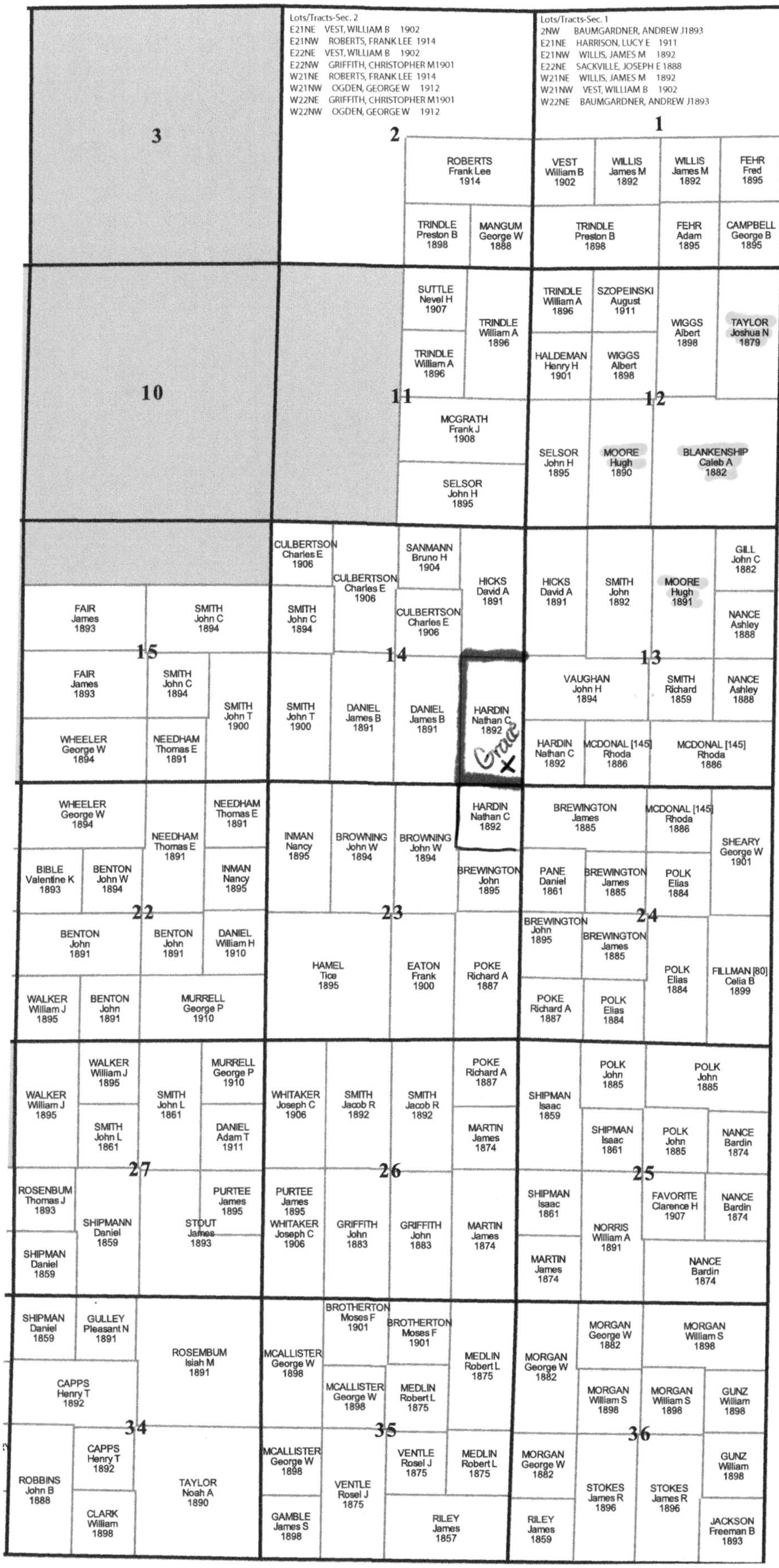

Lots/Tracts-Sec. 2
E21NE VEST, WILLIAM B   1902
E21NW ROBERTS, FRANK LEE   1914
E22NE VEST, WILLIAM B   1902
E22NW GRIFFITH, CHRISTOPHER M 1901
W21NE ROBERTS, FRANK LEE   1914
W21NW OGDEN, GEORGE W   1912
W22NE GRIFFITH, CHRISTOPHER M 1901
W22NW OGDEN, GEORGE W   1912

Lots/Tracts-Sec. 1
2NW   BAUMGARDNER, ANDREW J 1893
E21NE HARRISON, LUCY E   1911
E21NW WILLIS, JAMES M   1892
E22NE SACKVILLE, JOSEPH E 1888
W21NE WILLIS, JAMES M   1892
W21NW VEST, WILLIAM B   1902
W22NE BAUMGARDNER, ANDREW J 1893

3

2

ROBERTS Frank Lee 1914 | VEST William B 1902 | WILLIS James M 1892 | WILLIS James M 1892 | FEHR Fred 1895

TRINDLE Preston B 1898 | MANGUM George W 1888 | TRINDLE Preston B 1898 | FEHR Adam 1895 | CAMPBELL George B 1895

1

10

11

SUTTLE Nevel H 1907 | TRINDLE William A 1896 | TRINDLE William A 1896 | SZOPEINSKI August 1911 | WIGGS Albert 1898 | TAYLOR Joshua N 1879

TRINDLE William A 1896 | HALDEMAN Henry H 1901 | WIGGS Albert 1898

MCGRATH Frank J 1908 | SELSOR John H 1895 | MOORE Hugh 1890 | BLANKENSHIP Caleb A 1882

SELSOR John H 1895

12

CULBERTSON Charles E 1906 | SANMANN Bruno H 1904 | | GILL John C 1882

CULBERTSON Charles E 1906 | HICKS David A 1891 | HICKS David A 1891 | SMITH John 1892 | MOORE Hugh 1891

FAIR James 1893 | SMITH John C 1894 | SMITH John C 1894 | CULBERTSON Charles E 1906 | NANCE Ashley 1888

15

14

13

FAIR James 1893 | SMITH John C 1894 | SMITH John T 1900 | SMITH John T 1900 | DANIEL James B 1891 | DANIEL James B 1891 | HARDIN Nathan C 1892 | VAUGHAN John H 1894 | SMITH Richard 1859 | NANCE Ashley 1888

WHEELER George W 1894 | NEEDHAM Thomas E 1891 | Grace X | HARDIN Nathan C 1892 | MCDONAL [145] Rhoda 1886 | MCDONAL [145] Rhoda 1886

WHEELER George W 1894 | NEEDHAM Thomas E 1891 | NEEDHAM Thomas E 1891 | INMAN Nancy 1895 | BROWNING John W 1894 | BROWNING John W 1894 | HARDIN Nathan C 1892 | BREWINGTON James 1885 | MCDONAL [145] Rhoda 1886 | SHEARY George W 1901

BIBLE Valentine K 1893 | BENTON John W 1894 | INMAN Nancy 1895 | BREWINGTON John 1895 | PANE Daniel 1861 | BREWINGTON James 1885 | POLK Elias 1884

22

23

24

BENTON John 1891 | BENTON John 1891 | DANIEL William H 1910 | HAMEL Tice 1895 | EATON Frank 1900 | POKE Richard A 1887 | BREWINGTON John 1895 | BREWINGTON James 1885 | POLK Elias 1884 | FILLMAN [80] Celia B 1899

WALKER William J 1895 | BENTON John 1891 | MURRELL George P 1910 | POKE Richard A 1887 | POLK Elias 1884

WALKER William J 1895 | WALKER William J 1895 | MURRELL George P 1910 | WHITAKER Joseph C 1906 | SMITH Jacob R 1892 | SMITH Jacob R 1892 | POKE Richard A 1887 | POLK John 1885 | POLK John 1885

SMITH John L 1861 | DANIEL Adam T 1911 | MARTIN James 1874 | SHIPMAN Isaac 1859 | SHIPMAN Isaac 1861 | POLK John 1885 | NANCE Bardin 1874

27

26

25

ROSENBUM Thomas J 1893 | PURTEE James 1895 | PURTEE James 1895 | SHIPMAN Isaac 1861 | FAVORITE Clarence H 1907 | NANCE Bardin 1874

SHIPMANN Daniel 1859 | STOUT James 1893 | WHITAKER Joseph C 1906 | GRIFFITH John 1883 | GRIFFITH John 1883 | MARTIN James 1874 | NORRIS William A 1891 | NANCE Bardin 1874

SHIPMAN Daniel 1859 | MARTIN James 1874

SHIPMAN Daniel 1859 | GULLEY Pleasant N 1891 | BROTHERTON Moses F 1901 | BROTHERTON Moses F 1901 | MEDLIN Robert L 1875 | MORGAN George W 1882 | MORGAN George W 1882 | MORGAN William S 1898

ROSEMBUM Isiah M 1891 | MCALLISTER George W 1898 | MCALLISTER George W 1898 | MEDLIN Robert L 1875 | MORGAN George W 1882 | MORGAN William S 1898 | MORGAN William S 1898 | GUNZ William 1898

CAPPS Henry T 1892

34

35

36

CAPPS Henry T 1892 | MCALLISTER George W 1898 | VENTLE Rosel J 1875 | MEDLIN Robert L 1875 | MORGAN George W 1882 | GUNZ William 1898

ROBBINS John B 1888 | TAYLOR Noah A 1890 | VENTLE Rosel J 1875 | | STOKES James R 1896 | STOKES James R 1896

CLARK William 1898 | GAMBLE James S 1898 | RILEY James 1857 | RILEY James 1859 | JACKSON Freeman B 1893

Helpful Hints

1. This Map's INDEX can be found on the preceding pages.

2. Refer to Map "C" to see where this Township lies within Howell County, Missouri.

3. Numbers within square brackets [ ] denote a multi-patentee land parcel (multi-owner). Refer to Appendix "C" for a full list of members in this group.

4. Areas that look to be crowded with Patentees usually indicate multiple sales of the same parcel (Re-issues) or Overlapping parcels. See this Township's Index for an explanation of these and other circumstances that might explain "odd" groupings of Patentees on this map.

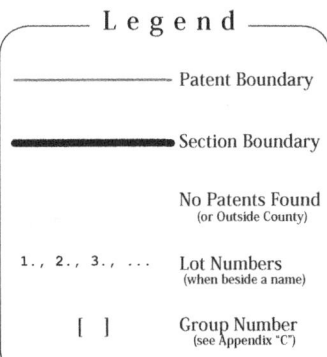

Legend

— Patent Boundary

━ Section Boundary

No Patents Found (or Outside County)

1., 2., 3., ... Lot Numbers (when beside a name)

[ ] Group Number (see Appendix "C")

Scale: Section = 1 mile X 1 mile (generally, with some exceptions)

Road Map
T27-N R8-W
5th PM 27-N 8-W Meridian
Map Group 3

Cities & Towns
Trask

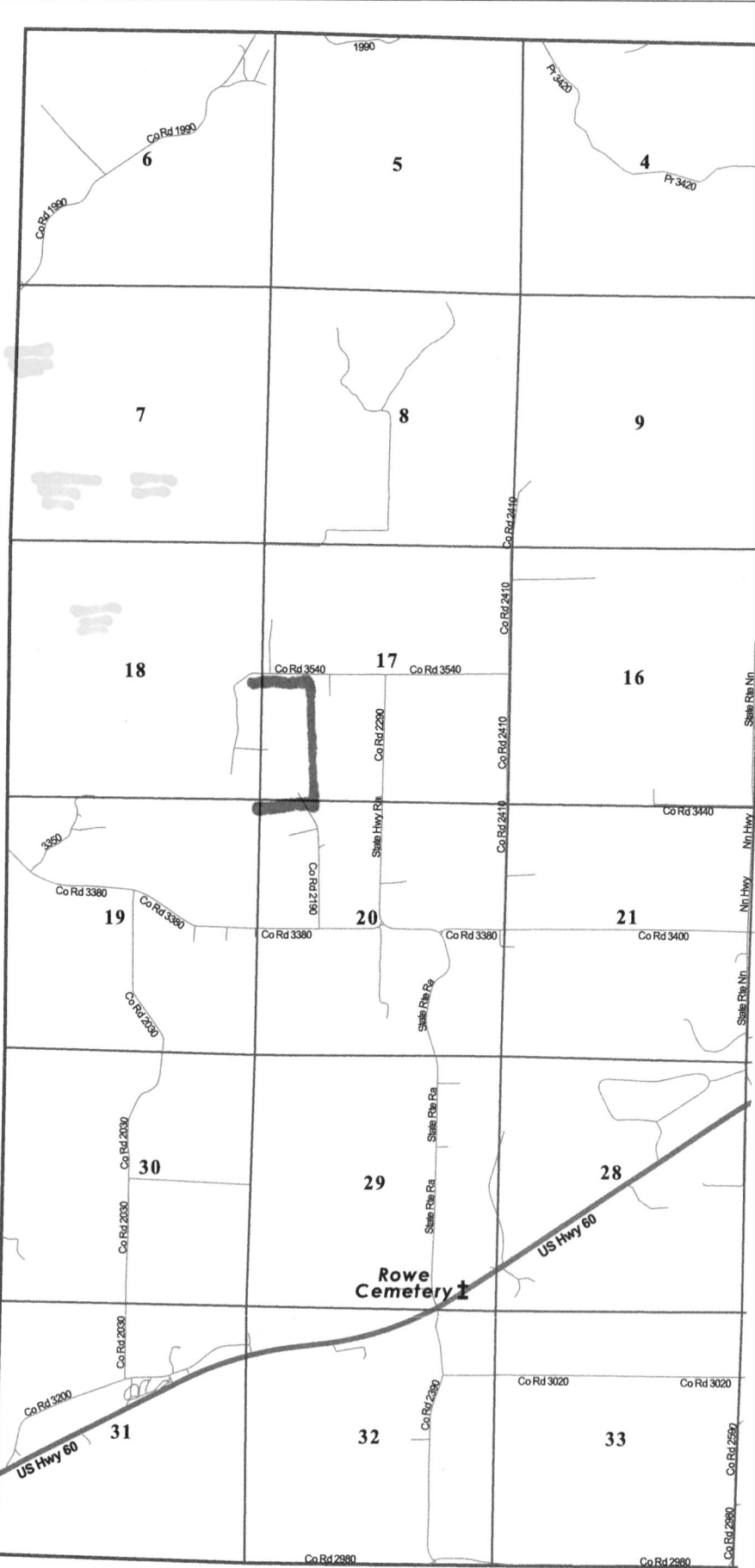

Cemeteries
New Salem Cemetery
Rowe Cemetery

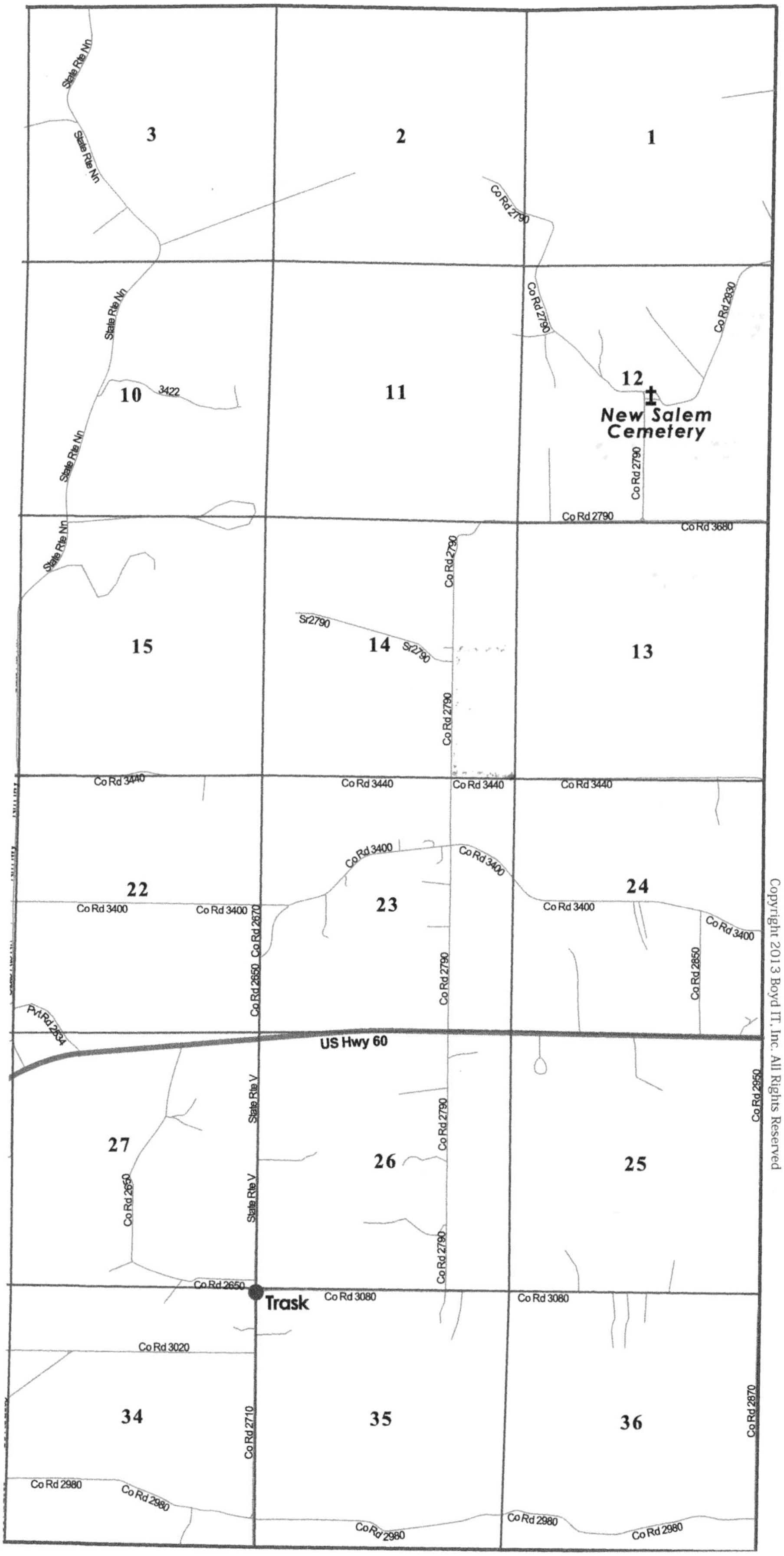

3

2

1

Co Rd 2790

Co Rd 2790

Co Rd 2830

10   3422

11

12

New Salem
Cemetery

State Rte Nn

Co Rd 2790

Co Rd 2790

Co Rd 3680

15

Sr 2790   14   Sr 2790

13

Co Rd 2790

State Rte Nn

Co Rd 3440

Co Rd 3440

Co Rd 3440

Co Rd 3440

Co Rd 3400

Co Rd 3400

22

23

24

Co Rd 3400

Co Rd 3400

Co Rd 3400

Co Rd 3400

Co Rd 2650

Co Rd 2870

Co Rd 2790

Co Rd 2850

Pvt Rd 2864

US Hwy 60

27

State Rte V

26

25

Co Rd 2650

State Rte V

Co Rd 2790

Co Rd 2790

Co Rd 2650

Trask

Co Rd 3080

Co Rd 3080

Co Rd 3020

34

Co Rd 2710

35

36

Co Rd 2870

Co Rd 2980

Co Rd 2980

Co Rd 2980

Co Rd 2980

Helpful Hints

1. This road map has a number of uses, but primarily it is to help you: a) find the present location of land owned by your ancestors (at least the general area), b) find cemeteries and city-centers, and c) estimate the route/roads used by Census-takers & tax-assessors.

2. If you plan to travel to Howell County to locate cemeteries or land parcels, please pick up a modern travel map for the area before you do. Mapping old land parcels on modern maps is not as exact a science as you might think. Just the slightest variations in public land survey coordinates, estimates of parcel boundaries, or road-map deviations can greatly alter a map's representation of how a road either does or doesn't cross a particular parcel of land.

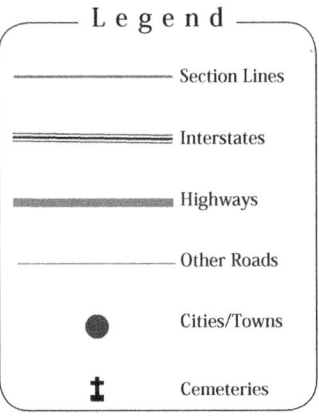

Legend

—————— Section Lines

══════ Interstates

━━━━━━ Highways

—————— Other Roads

● Cities/Towns

✝ Cemeteries

Scale: Section = 1 mile X 1 mile
(generally, with some exceptions)

Historical Map

T27-N   R8-W
5th PM 27-N 8-W Meridian

Map Group 3

Cities & Towns
Trask

Cemeteries
New Salem Cemetery
Rowe Cemetery

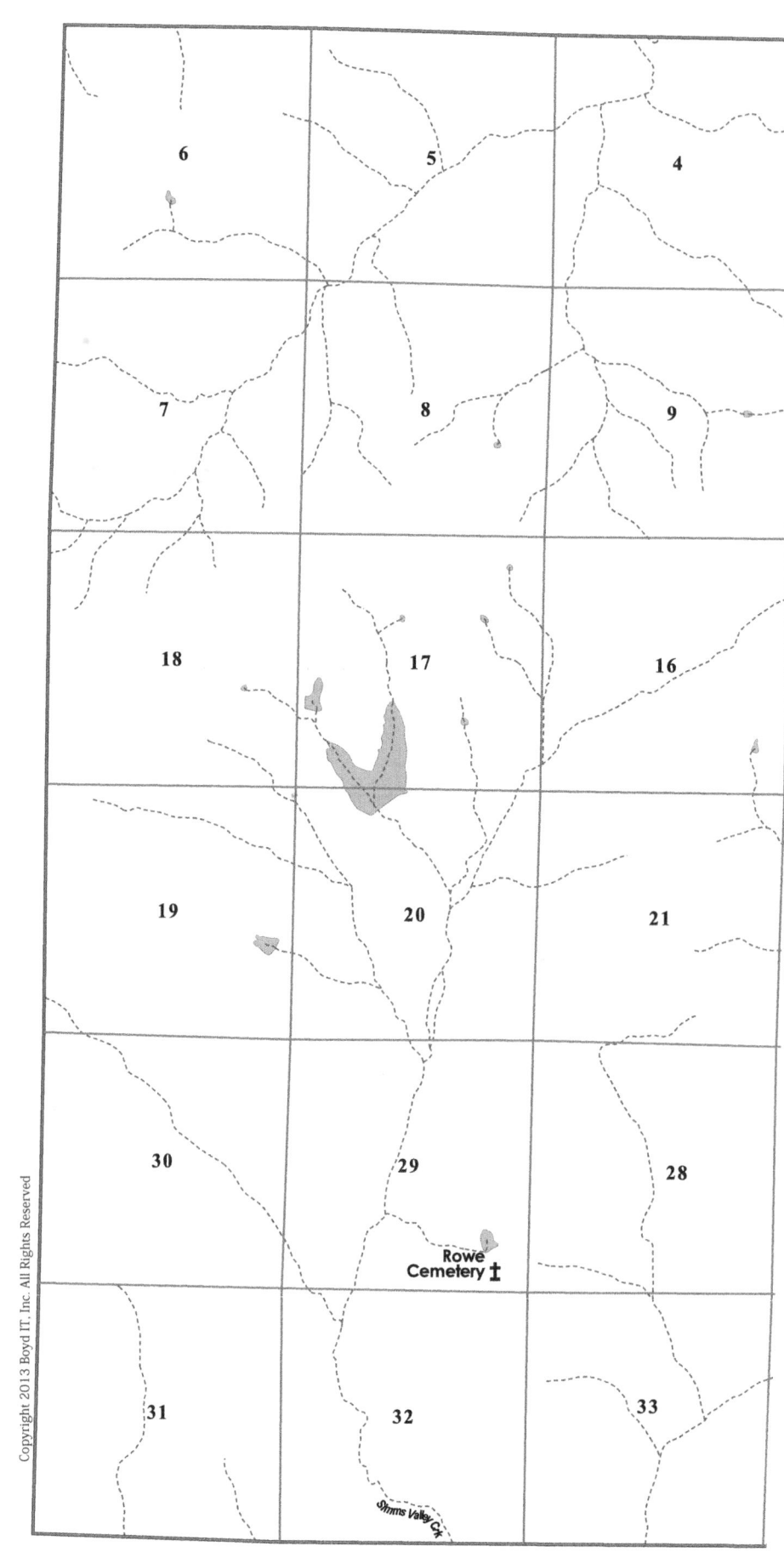

Copyright 2013 Boyd IT. Inc. All Rights Reserved

Rowe
Cemetery ‡

Simms Valley Ck

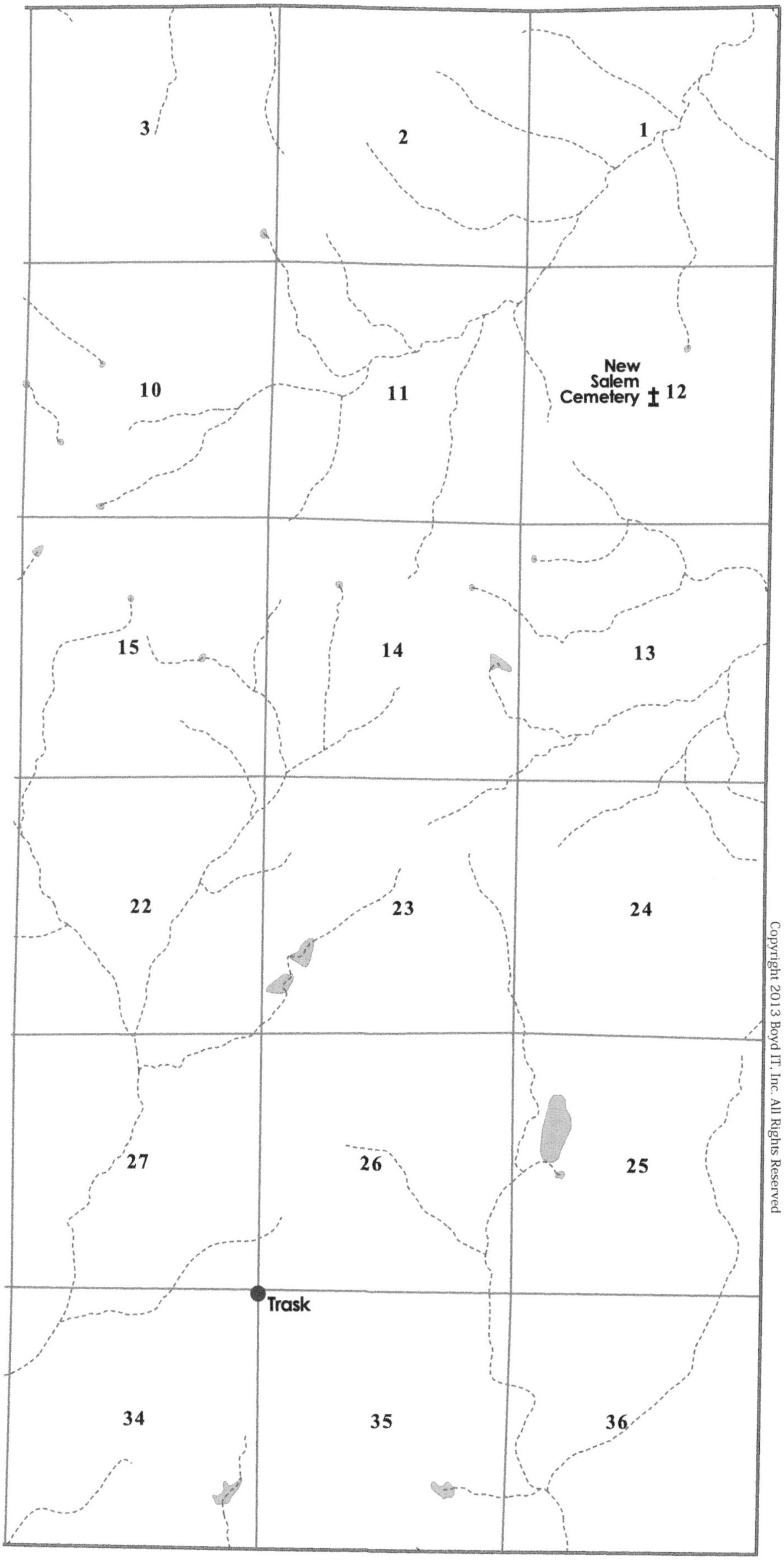

3
2
1
10
11
New Salem Cemetery
12
15
14
13
22
23
24
27
26
25
Trask
34
35
36

Helpful Hints

1. This Map takes a different look at the same Congressional Township displayed in the preceding two maps. It presents features that can help you better envision the historical development of the area: a) Water-bodies (lakes & ponds), b) Water-courses (rivers, streams, etc.), c) Railroads, d) City/town center-points (where they were oftentimes located when first settled), and e) Cemeteries.
2. Using this "Historical" map in tandem with this Township's Patent Map and Road Map, may lead you to some interesting discoveries. You will often find roads, towns, cemeteries, and waterways are named after nearby landowners: sometimes those names will be the ones you are researching. See how many of these research gems you can find here in Howell County.

Legend

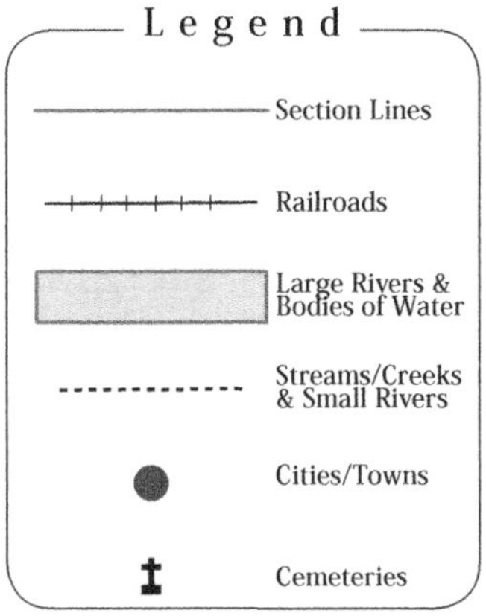

Section Lines
Railroads
Large Rivers & Bodies of Water
Streams/Creeks & Small Rivers
Cities/Towns
Cemeteries

Scale: Section = 1 mile X 1 mile
(there are some exceptions)

Map Group 4: Index to Land Patents

Township 27-North Range 7-West (5th PM 27-N 7-W)

After you locate an individual in this Index, take note of the Section and Section Part then proceed to the Land Patent map on the pages immediately following. You should have no difficulty locating the corresponding parcel of land.

The "For More Info" Column will lead you to more information about the underlying Patents. See the *Legend* at right, and the "How to Use this Book" chapter, for more information.

```
                    LEGEND
            "For More Info . . . " column
A = Authority (Legislative Act, See Appendix "A")
B = Block or Lot (location in Section unknown)
C = Cancelled Patent
F = Fractional Section
G = Group  (Multi-Patentee Patent, see Appendix "C")
V = Overlaps another Parcel
R = Re-Issued (Parcel patented more than once)

(A & G items require you to look in the Appendixes referred
to above. All other Letter-designations followed by a number
require you to locate line-items in this index that possess
the ID number found after the letter).
```

ID	Individual in Patent	Sec.	Sec. Part	Date Issued	Other Counties	For More Info . . .
603	ALLDREDGE, William	5	SWSE	1861-02-09		A1
605	" "	8	NWNE	1861-02-09		A1
604	" "	8	NENW	1861-02-09		A1
7029	BECK, William H	3	2NW	1891-11-03		A1
7045	" "	4	E22NE	1891-11-03		A1
7026	BECKER, Fred A	2	W22NE	1907-06-26		A1
606	BELEW, Joseph A	13	SENE	1891-05-25		A7
607	" "	13	NESE	1891-05-25		A7
608	BELLER, Melvin N	7	NWSE	1903-03-17		A7
609	" "	7	SWNE	1903-03-17		A7
611	BRILES, David A	20	W½SE	1893-04-29		A7
610	" "	20	SESE	1893-04-29		A7
612	" "	21	SWSW	1893-04-29		A7
613	BROOKES, Anslem	17	SWSW	1900-02-02		A7
614	" "	18	SESE	1900-02-02		A7
615	" "	19	NENE	1900-02-02		A7
616	" "	20	NWNW	1900-02-02		A7
617	BUFF, Elijah C	24	E½NW	1894-08-14		A7
618	BUFF, William M	24	NWNW	1898-04-11		A7
7064	CAMPBELL, George B	6	S22SW	1895-05-28		A7
7070	" "	7	N22NW	1895-05-28		A7
619	CAMPBELL, J J	23	SWNW	1885-02-25		A7 G34
620	CAMPBELL, Mary J	23	SWNW	1885-02-25		A7 G34
621	CAMPBELL, Robert W	22	NWNW	1903-03-17		A7
622	CARTER, Robert	32	E½SE	1888-12-08		A7
623	" "	33	NWSW	1888-12-08		A7
624	CHAPPELL, George L	14	SW	1891-05-25		A7
7050	CLIFF, Frederick	4	W22NW	1895-05-28	Texas	A7
7048	" "	4	W21NW	1895-05-28	Texas	A7
626	CRIPE, John E	10	NWNE	1900-02-02		A7
625	" "	10	NENW	1900-02-02		A7
628	" "	3	SESW	1900-02-02		A7
627	" "	3	SWSE	1900-02-02		A7
630	CROW, Azariah	29	E½SE	1892-06-21		A7
629	" "	29	SENE	1892-06-21		A7
631	" "	32	NENE	1892-06-21		A7
632	CROWDER, Jane E	31	SW	1881-10-06		A7
633	DAILY, Philip M	4	SWSE	1906-05-01		A7
634	" "	4	SESW	1906-05-01		A7
635	" "	9	E½NW	1906-05-01		A7
7024	DOERING, John	2	E22NW	1893-09-01		A7
7021	" "	2	1NW	1893-09-01		A7
636	DRYDEN, Jonathan M	5	SWSW	1899-02-13		A7
637	" "	8	W½NW	1899-02-13		A7
638	DURNEL, John W	30	E½SE	1880-11-20		A7
639	" "	31	E½NE	1880-11-20		A7

ID	Individual in Patent	Sec.	Sec. Part	Date Issued	Other Counties	For More Info . . .
640	EATON, Washington N	26	NW	1860-08-01		A1
641	" "	27	NENE	1860-08-01		A1
642	FERRIS, John C	8	E½NE	1895-10-08		A1
7014	FILLMAN, Celia B	19	N21SW	1899-05-12		A7 G80
7017	" "	19	N22SW	1899-05-12		A7 G80
643	FLEMING, Thomas W	33	NENW	1890-08-13		A1
644	FLOOD, John F	36	NESE	1897-06-02	Shannon	A7
645	" "	36	S½SE	1897-06-02	Shannon	A7
647	FOUTS, Andrew L	12	NESE	1890-01-10		A7
646	" "	12	S½SE	1890-01-10		A7
648	" "	13	NENE	1890-01-10		A7
651	FRAKES, Sarah	12	N½NE	1890-06-06		A7
649	" "	12	NENW	1890-06-06		A7
650	" "	12	SWNE	1890-06-06		A7
652	FRANK, Charles	25	NW	1860-08-01		A1
653	FRAZER, Robert	3	SWSW	1896-10-13		A1
659	GATTON, Anne	19	N½SE	1890-09-30		A6 G91
658	" "	19	SWSE	1890-09-30		A6 G91
7006	GILL, John C	18	N21NW	1882-06-30		A7
7008	" "	18	N22NW	1882-06-30		A7
7071	GILL, Martha A	7	S22NW	1879-12-15		A7
7069	" "	7	1NW	1879-12-15		A7
662	GILL, Samuel K	7	SW	1882-05-20		A7
7034	GLASS, William K	30	1SW	1877-10-10		A7
7040	" "	31	1NW	1877-10-10		A7
665	GOLDSBERRY, John	22	NWSW	1860-08-01		A1
664	" "	22	E½NW	1860-08-01		A1
663	" "	22	SWNW	1860-08-01		A1
669	GOLDSBERRY, William H	22	SWSE	1860-08-01		A1
666	" "	22	SESW	1857-10-30		A1
668	" "	22	NWSE	1859-09-01		A1
667	" "	22	NESW	1859-09-01		A1
670	GREEN, Louisa E	33	NESW	1891-05-25		A7
671	GRIPE, David	12	NWSE	1901-12-30		A7
672	GUNZ, Minnie	28	NWNW	1901-07-09		A7
673	" "	29	NENE	1901-07-09		A7
674	" "	29	W½NE	1901-07-09		A7
7042	GUNZ, William	31	S22NW	1898-10-04		A7
675	HAMILTON, Christopher B	5	NWSW	1895-05-28		A7
7059	" "	6	E21NE	1895-05-28		A7
7061	" "	6	E22NE	1895-05-28		A7
676	" "	6	NESE	1895-05-28		A7
677	HANEY, Bennett	34	SENW	1890-06-06		A7
678	" "	34	W½NE	1890-06-06		A7
679	" "	34	SENE	1890-06-06		A7
680	HANN, J J	6	NWSE	1892-08-01		A1
7065	HANN, John J	6	W21NE	1892-06-10		A7
7067	" "	6	W22NE	1892-06-10		A7
7060	" "	6	E21NW	1892-06-10		A7
7062	" "	6	E22NW	1892-06-10		A7
681	HARLOW, Reuben	29	SESW	1859-09-01		A1
682	HARRIS, Allen M	32	SESW	1861-02-01		A1
684	HARROD, Jehu	17	E½SE	1910-04-01		A1
683	" "	17	E½SE	1910-01-24		A1 C G108
685	HARROD, John	17	E½SE	1910-01-24		A1 C G108
686	HAYNES, John S	35	E½SE	1892-03-07		A7
687	HERRICK, Jerome	20	SW	1893-06-13		A7
7005	HINES, Louis J	1	W22NE	1888-12-08		A7
7001	" "	1	2NW	1888-12-08		A7
7002	HOBBS, William C	1	E21NE	1908-05-25		A1
689	HOLDEN, Wesley	35	SESW	1860-08-01		A1
688	" "	35	SWSE	1860-08-01		A1
690	HOOVER, Austin	28	W½NE	1893-04-29		A7
691	HOOVER, Walter A	10	SWSW	1906-03-31		A7
692	" "	15	W½NW	1906-03-31		A7
693	" "	9	SESE	1906-03-31		A7
694	HOPE, James A	19	SESE	1881-10-06		A7
696	" "	30	W½NE	1881-10-06		A7
695	" "	30	NENE	1881-10-06		A7
698	HOUGH, Clyde H	27	SESW	1906-06-30		A1
7055	HOUSE, James	5	W21NW	1874-04-20		A7
7057	" "	5	W22NW	1874-04-20		A7
699	HUMPHREY, James F	12	NESW	1891-05-25		A7

ID	Individual in Patent	Sec.	Sec. Part	Date Issued	Other Counties	For More Info . . .
701	HUMPHREY, James F (Cont'd)	12	W½SW	1891-05-25		A7
700	" "	12	SENW	1891-05-25		A7
703	HUNT, John	31	N½SE	1882-09-30		A7
702	" "	31	SWSE	1882-09-30		A7
704	" "	32	NWSW	1882-09-30		A7
706	HUNT, John M	32	SWNE	1893-04-08		A7 G124
705	" "	32	W½SE	1893-04-08		A7 G124
707	HUNT, Joseph G	8	SWSE	1904-06-02		A7
708	HUNT, Lulu L	32	W½SE	1893-04-08		A7 G124
709	" "	32	SWNE	1893-04-08		A7 G124
710	HUNT, Margret T	32	SWNW	1898-01-26		A7 G125
711	HUNT, William C	32	SWNW	1898-01-26		A7 G125
713	JENKINS, Douglas	17	SWNE	1893-12-09		A1
712	" "	17	NWSE	1893-12-09		A1
714	JONES, James K	1	NWSW	1894-12-17		A7
7004	" "	1	W21NE	1894-12-17		A7
7000	" "	1	1NW	1894-12-17		A7
715	KARR, John M	24	SWNW	1859-09-01		A1
716	KELLY, Levi	17	SWSE	1907-10-05		A7
717	" "	20	N½NE	1907-10-05		A7
7003	KELSO, James C	1	E22NE	1888-05-07		A1
718	" "	12	NWNW	1888-05-07		A1
7011	KING, Albert	18	S22SW	1911-02-03		A1
719	KUEPEL, Christopher	36	SW	1860-08-01		A1
7032	LAIRD, John W	3	W21NE	1892-06-21		A7
7031	" "	3	E21NW	1892-06-21		A7
721	" "	3	NESW	1892-06-21		A7
720	" "	3	NWSE	1892-06-21		A7
722	LEWIS, Augustus	33	S½SE	1861-05-01		A1
723	LEWIS, Verginia	30	SENE	1903-08-25		A7
725	LIMB, John	10	SWNE	1892-04-23		A1
727	" "	10	NESW	1892-04-23		A1
726	" "	10	NWSE	1892-04-23		A1
724	" "	10	SENW	1892-04-23		A1
7030	" "	3	E21NE	1890-01-30		A1
728	LIVESAY, John J	29	W½SE	1893-04-29		A7
729	LIVINGSTON, A H	23	NWSE	1886-10-29		A1
731	LIVSAY, George W	29	NESW	1882-11-10		A7
730	" "	29	W½SW	1882-11-10		A7
732	" "	32	NWNW	1882-11-10		A7
734	LODER, Conrad	35	NW	1860-08-01		A1
733	" "	35	W½NE	1860-08-01		A1
7027	LUKE, George	2	W22NW	1890-01-30		A1
7028	" "	3	2NE	1890-01-30		A1
7033	LUTH, Korah W	3	W21NW	1902-10-11		A7
735	" "	3	NWSW	1902-10-11		A7
736	" "	4	NESE	1902-10-11		A7
7043	" "	4	E21NE	1902-10-11		A7
737	LYNCH, George F	23	SENE	1860-08-01		A1
738	MADES, George	24	SE	1860-03-01		A1
739	" "	25	NE	1860-03-01		A1
740	MARTIN, Alfred J	17	NWNE	1900-02-02		A7
741	" "	17	E½NE	1900-02-02		A7
742	" "	8	SESE	1900-02-02		A7
743	MCCARDEL, James	11	S½SE	1860-08-01		A1
745	" "	14	SWNE	1860-08-01		A1
744	" "	14	N½NE	1860-08-01		A1
7053	MCCULLOCH, William A	5	E22NE	1892-06-21		A7
748	" "	5	SESW	1888-12-06		A1
7051	" "	5	1NE	1892-06-21		A7
747	" "	5	NWSE	1892-06-21		A7
746	" "	5	SESE	1886-11-19		A1
749	MENDENHALL, Sidney	1	SE	1891-06-09		A7
751	MILLBANKS, Larkin	28	NWSW	1879-12-15		A7
752	" "	28	E½NW	1879-12-15		A7
750	" "	28	SWNW	1879-12-15		A7
7068	MOORE, Matthew	6	W22NW	1900-05-11	Texas	A7
753	NAHM, Martin	25	E½SW	1860-08-01		A1
755	" "	36	E½NW	1860-08-01		A1
754	" "	36	NE	1860-08-01		A1
7007	NANCE, Ashley	18	N21SW	1894-11-30		A7
7009	" "	18	N22SW	1894-11-30		A7
756	NEWSOM, Mary	33	S½SW	1860-10-01		A1

ID	Individual in Patent	Sec.	Sec. Part	Date Issued	Other Counties	For More Info . . .
757	PADGETT, Abraham	28	SESE	1859-09-01		A1
758	" "	33	NENE	1859-09-01		A1
759	" "	33	SENE	1859-09-01		A1
762	" "	33	SWNE	1861-05-01		A1
761	" "	33	SENW	1861-05-01		A1
760	" "	33	NWNE	1859-09-01		A1
764	PADGETT, Robert	17	S½NW	1878-06-24		A7
763	" "	17	N½SW	1878-06-24		A7
765	PADGETT, William T	33	N½SE	1889-01-12		A7
766	" "	34	W½SW	1889-01-12		A7
767	PELTON, George A	12	SESW	1903-10-01		A7
768	PFENNIGHAUSEN, R W	1	NESE	1888-05-07		A1
770	" "	11	SWNW	1888-12-06		A1
769	" "	11	NENE	1888-05-07		A1
771	" "	12	SENE	1891-08-24		A1
772	" "	14	SWNW	1886-11-19		A1
773	" "	22	NWNE	1886-11-19		A1
774	" "	9	NWSE	1886-11-19		A1
775	PFENNIGHAUSEN, Richard W	1	S½SW	1886-11-19		A1
776	" "	11	N½NW	1886-11-19		A1
777	" "	15	SESE	1886-11-19		A1
779	" "	15	SENE	1892-09-15		A7
778	" "	15	W½SE	1892-09-15		A7
780	" "	15	NESE	1892-09-15		A7
7025	" "	2	W21NE	1886-11-19		A1
781	" "	2	S½	1886-11-19		A1
7022	" "	2	E21NE	1886-11-19		A1
7023	" "	2	E22NE	1886-11-19		A1
782	PHIPPS, James T	4	W½SW	1900-02-02		A7
783	" "	5	NESE	1900-02-02		A7
784	" "	9	NWNW	1900-02-02		A7
787	PHIPPS, John B	32	NWNE	1860-10-01		A1
788	" "	32	NENW	1860-10-01		A1
786	" "	32	SENW	1875-04-01		A7
785	" "	32	NESW	1875-04-01		A7
789	PHIPPS, William H	4	NWSE	1902-10-20		A7
792	PODRABSKE, Anthony	13	S½SE	1860-08-01		A1
790	" "	13	NWSE	1860-08-01		A1
791	" "	13	SESW	1860-08-01		A1
793	" "	24	NE	1860-08-01		A1
794	POLK, James K	23	S½SW	1890-01-10		A7
795	POLLOCK, Francis M	27	NWNW	1888-05-07		A1
796	POTTS, Thomas	10	E½SE	1895-09-04		A7
797	" "	10	E½NE	1895-09-04		A7
798	RAY, John S	5	NESW	1900-02-02		A7
7056	" "	5	W22NE	1900-02-02		A7
7054	" "	5	E22NW	1900-02-02		A7
7052	" "	5	E21NW	1900-02-02		A7
799	REESE, John L	10	SESW	1904-06-02		A7
800	REID, Andrew	21	NENE	1890-01-30		A1
802	REYNOLDS, George R	15	W½NE	1895-06-28		A7
801	" "	15	E½NW	1895-06-28		A7
803	RICE, Samuel T	22	SWSW	1857-04-01		A5
804	RIDDLE, William H	6	S½SE	1898-10-04		A7
805	" "	7	N½NE	1898-10-04		A7
807	ROBBINS, Catharine	28	N½SE	1880-11-20		A7
806	" "	28	SENE	1880-11-20		A7
808	" "	28	SWSE	1880-11-20		A7
809	ROBBINS, John B	32	SENE	1879-12-15		A7
810	" "	33	W½NW	1879-12-15		A7
811	ROBERDS, Jesse	18	N½SE	1888-11-27		A7
812	ROBINSON, William W	27	SWSW	1875-04-15		A7
814	" "	34	N½NW	1875-04-15		A7
813	" "	34	SWNW	1875-04-15		A7
815	ROTH, Frederick E	24	SW	1860-08-01		A1
816	RUSHING, Daniel E	18	SWSE	1881-10-06		A7
7010	" "	18	S21SW	1881-10-06		A7
817	" "	19	NWNE	1881-10-06		A7
7013	" "	19	N21NW	1881-10-06		A7
818	SACKVILLE, Joseph E	10	SWSE	1888-05-07		A1
819	SCHAUB, George D	10	NWSW	1908-10-26		A7 G167
820	SCHAUB, Tina	10	NWSW	1908-10-26		A7 G167
821	SCHNEIDER, Daniel	25	SE	1860-03-01		A1

ID	Individual in Patent	Sec.	Sec. Part	Date Issued	Other Counties	For More Info . . .
822	SELLS, Mary	7	SESE	1901-03-23		A7
823	SETTLE, Joseph	29	NW	1892-03-07		A7
824	SHELDON, Minor B	23	N½NW	1901-03-23		A7
825	SHELTON, John C	31	SESE	1892-06-10		A7
826	" "	32	SWSW	1892-06-10		A7
827	SIMMONS, G H	9	NESE	1890-01-30		A1
828	SIMMONS, Gilman A	10	W½NW	1893-01-07		A7
829	" "	4	SESE	1893-01-07		A7
830	" "	9	NENE	1893-01-07		A7
831	SIMMONS, William H	9	SWSE	1891-05-25		A7
832	" "	9	SWSW	1891-05-25		A7
833	" "	9	E½SW	1891-05-25		A7
834	SMITH, Abraham	18	S½NW	1874-12-20		A7
7047	SMITH, Ambrose B	4	W21NE	1859-09-01	Texas	A1
7049	" "	4	W22NE	1859-09-01	Texas	A1
7018	SMITH, James M	19	S21NW	1900-05-11		A7
835	" "	19	SWNE	1900-05-11		A7
7012	" "	19	2NW	1900-05-11		A7
836	SMITH, James W	30	W½SE	1860-08-01		A1
837	" "	31	W½NE	1861-02-01		A1
838	SMITH, Kerbey	11	SENW	1904-07-15		A7
839	SMITH, Luke	17	SESW	1901-06-08		A7
840	" "	20	NENW	1901-06-08		A7
842	SMITH, Richard	18	SENE	1872-03-15		A7
841	" "	18	W½NE	1872-03-15		A7
843	SMITH, Richard D	17	NENW	1861-02-01		A1
845	" "	7	NESE	1861-02-01		A1
844	" "	7	SENE	1861-02-01		A1
848	" "	8	NESW	1859-09-01		A1
849	" "	8	SENW	1861-02-01		A1
850	" "	8	NWSW	1861-02-01		A1
846	" "	8	SESW	1859-09-01		A1
847	" "	8	SWSW	1859-09-01		A1
851	SMITH, Richard G	7	SWSE	1873-11-01		A7
852	SMITH, Samuel H	17	NWNW	1859-09-01		A1
853	" "	18	NENE	1859-09-01		A1
854	SMOTHERMON, George W	15	SW	1879-12-15		A7
855	SPEAKMAN, William P	26	SESE	1860-08-01		A1
856	" "	35	E½NE	1860-08-01		A1
857	" "	36	W½NW	1860-08-01		A1
858	STEELMAN, Aaron	22	SWNE	1885-03-20		A1
7016	STEPP, Celia B	19	N22SW	1899-05-12		A7 G80
7015	" "	19	N21SW	1899-05-12		A7 G80
7020	STEPP, Michael	19	S22SW	1898-01-26		A7
7019	" "	19	S21SW	1898-01-26		A7
7037	" "	30	N22NW	1898-01-26		A7
7036	" "	30	N21NW	1898-01-26		A7
7038	STEPP, Wilfred E	30	S21NW	1904-03-19		A7
7039	" "	30	S22NW	1904-03-19		A7
859	STONE, Cyrus S	14	W½SE	1894-05-18		A7
860	" "	23	N½NE	1894-05-18		A7
7066	STRAINN, Thomas L	6	W21NW	1882-05-20		A7
7058	" "	6	1SW	1882-05-20		A7
7063	" "	6	N22SW	1882-05-20		A7
861	TAYLOR, Cyrus J	11	W½NE	1898-04-11		A7
862	THOMAS, Adam	11	SW	1891-05-25		A7 G178
864	THOMAS, Andrew J	23	N½SW	1860-08-01		A1
863	" "	23	SWNE	1860-08-01		A1
865	THOMAS, Elizabeth B	26	SWSE	1888-05-07		A1
866	" "	26	S½SW	1888-05-07		A1
867	THOMAS, Janey	11	SW	1891-05-25		A7 G178
868	THOMAS, John	11	SENE	1900-08-09		A7
869	" "	11	N½SE	1900-08-09		A7
870	" "	12	SWNW	1900-08-09		A7
871	THOMAS, Simpson	13	SWSW	1897-08-16		A7
872	" "	14	SENE	1897-08-16		A7
873	" "	14	E½SE	1897-08-16		A7
874	TOOMEY, Andrew J	19	SWSE	1890-09-30		A6 G91
875	" "	19	N½SE	1890-09-30		A6 G91
876	TRANBARGER, John B	36	NWSE	1905-05-09		A7
878	TREVOR, Mathew R	34	W½SE	1860-09-10		A6 G180
877	" "	34	E½SW	1860-09-10		A6 G180
879	TRICHAUS, John H	35	NESW	1860-08-01		A1

ID	Individual in Patent	Sec.	Sec. Part	Date Issued	Other Counties	For More Info . . .
881	TRICHAUS, John H (Cont'd)	35	W½SW	1860-08-01		A1
880	" "	35	NWSE	1860-08-01		A1
882	TROLL, Francis C	23	S½SE	1860-08-01		A1
883	" "	23	NESE	1860-08-01		A1
884	" "	26	NE	1860-08-01		A1
888	TUPPER, Sally	34	E½SW	1860-09-10		A6 G180
887	" "	34	W½SE	1860-09-10		A6 G180
890	USHER, Moses H	21	SWSE	1857-10-30		A1
892	" "	21	SESW	1860-08-01		A1
891	" "	21	NWSE	1859-09-01		A1
889	" "	21	SESE	1856-06-16		A1
893	" "	23	SENW	1857-04-15		A1
896	" "	28	S½SW	1859-09-01		A1
895	" "	28	NESW	1859-09-01		A1
894	" "	28	NENE	1857-10-30		A1
897	VON BLUCHER, Albert	25	W½SW	1860-08-01		A1
899	" "	26	N½SW	1860-08-01		A1
898	" "	26	N½SE	1860-08-01		A1
900	" "	27	SENE	1860-08-01		A1
901	" "	27	NESE	1860-08-01		A1
902	WALKER, Jacob L	34	E½SE	1890-01-10		A7
903	WARREN, George W	4	NESW	1891-05-05		A7
7044	" "	4	E21NW	1891-05-05		A7
7046	" "	4	E22NW	1891-05-05		A7
904	WEAVER, Daniel A	21	S½NE	1882-06-30		A7
905	" "	21	NESE	1882-06-30		A7
906	" "	21	NWNE	1882-06-30		A7
907	WEAVER, James K	22	E½SE	1876-11-03		A7
908	" "	22	E½NE	1876-11-03		A7
909	WEBB, Albert M	19	SENE	1893-04-29		A7
911	" "	20	S½NW	1893-04-29		A7
910	" "	20	SWNE	1893-04-29		A7
912	WEBB, John H	21	NW	1893-04-29		A7
913	WELLER, Charles F	27	SWNW	1888-12-06		A1
915	" "	27	N½SW	1882-05-20		A7
914	" "	27	W½SE	1882-05-20		A7
917	WELLER, John W	14	E½NW	1897-08-16		A7
916	" "	14	NWNW	1897-08-16		A7
918	" "	15	NENE	1897-08-16		A7
920	WELLER, William	27	E½NW	1872-07-01		A7
919	" "	27	W½NE	1872-07-01		A7
922	WILLEFORD, Wiley A	20	SENE	1877-08-01		A7
921	" "	20	NESE	1877-08-01		A7
923	" "	21	N½SW	1877-08-01		A7
7035	WILSON, John C	30	2SW	1893-04-08		A7
7041	" "	31	N22NW	1893-04-08		A7
924	WINNINGHAM, George W	8	SWNE	1893-12-09		A1
925	WINNINGHAM, Isaac	8	N½SE	1879-12-15		A7
928	" "	9	SWNW	1879-12-15		A7
929	" "	9	NWSW	1879-12-15		A7
926	" "	9	W½NE	1859-01-01		A1
927	" "	9	SENE	1859-09-01		A1
930	WISHON, Benjamin	3	E½SE	1856-06-16		A1
931	WOOSTER, Willard W	27	SESE	1896-08-28		A7
932	" "	34	NENE	1896-08-28		A7
935	WURL, Ernst	13	NW	1860-08-01		A1
934	" "	13	N½SW	1860-08-01		A1
933	" "	13	W½NE	1860-08-01		A1

Patent Map

T27-N R7-W
5th PM 27-N 7-W Meridian

Map Group 4

Township Statistics

Parcels Mapped	:	383
Number of Patents	:	203
Number of Individuals	:	186
Patentees Identified	:	174
Number of Surnames	:	136
Multi-Patentee Parcels	:	13
Oldest Patent Date	:	6/16/1856
Most Recent Patent	:	4/1/1910
Block/Lot Parcels	:	70
Cities and Town	:	2
Cemeteries	:	3

Lots/Tracts-Sec. 6
1SW	STRAINN, THOMAS L	1882
E21NE	HAMILTON, CHRISTOPHER B	1895
E21NW	HANN, JOHN J	1892
E22NE	HAMILTON, CHRISTOPHER B	1895
E22NW	HANN, JOHN J	1892
N22SW	STRAINN, THOMAS L	1882
S22SW	CAMPBELL, GEORGE B	1895
W21NE	HANN, JOHN J	1892
W21NW	STRAINN, THOMAS L	1882
W22NE	HANN, JOHN J	1892
W22NW	MOORE, MATTHEW	1900

Lots/Tracts-Sec. 5
1NE	MCCULLOCH, WILLIAM A	1892
E21NW	RAY, JOHN S	1900
E22NE	MCCULLOCH, WILLIAM A	1892
E22NW	RAY, JOHN S	1900
W21NW	HOUSE, JAMES	1874
W22NE	RAY, JOHN S	1900
W22NW	HOUSE, JAMES	1874

Lots/Tracts-Sec. 4
E21NE	LUTH, KORAH W	1902
E21NW	WARREN, GEORGE W	1891
E22NE	BECK, WILLIAM H	1891
E22NW	WARREN, GEORGE W	1891
W21NE	SMITH, AMBROSE B	1859
W21NW	CLIFF, FREDERICK	1895
W22NE	SMITH, AMBROSE B	1859
W22NW	CLIFF, FREDERICK	1895

Lots/Tracts-Sec. 7
1NW	GILL, MARTHA A	1879
N22NW	CAMPBELL, GEORGE B	1895
S22NW	GILL, MARTHA A	1879

Lots/Tracts-Sec. 18
N21NW	GILL, JOHN C	1882
N21SW	NANCE, ASHLEY	1894
N22NW	GILL, JOHN C	1882
N22SW	NANCE, ASHLEY	1894
S21SW	RUSHING, DANIEL E	1881
S22SW	KING, ALBERT	1911

Lots/Tracts-Sec. 19
2NW	SMITH, JAMES M	1900
N21NW	RUSHING, DANIEL E	1881
N21SW	FILLMAN, CELIA B [80]	1899
N22SW	FILLMAN, CELIA B [80]	1899
S21NW	SMITH, JAMES M	1900
S21SW	STEPP, MICHAEL	1898
S22SW	STEPP, MICHAEL	1898

Lots/Tracts-Sec. 30
1SW	GLASS, WILLIAM K	1877
2SW	WILSON, JOHN C	1893
N21NW	STEPP, MICHAEL	1898
N22NW	STEPP, MICHAEL	1898
S21NW	STEPP, WILFRED E	1904
S22NW	STEPP, WILFRED E	1904

Lots/Tracts-Sec. 31
1NW	GLASS, WILLIAM K	1877
N22NW	WILSON, JOHN C	1893
S22NW	GUNZ, WILLIAM	1898

Section 6

HANN J J 1892	HAMILTON Christopher B 1895	HAMILTON Christopher B 1895	RAY John S 1900
	RIDDLE William H 1898	DRYDEN Jonathan M 1899	

Section 5

MCCULLOCH William A 1892	PHIPPS James T 1900		
MCCULLOCH William A 1888	ALLDREDGE William 1861	MCCULLOCH William A 1886	

Section 4

WARREN George W 1891	PHIPPS William H 1902	LUTH Korah W 1902	
PHIPPS James T 1900	DAILY Philip M 1906	DAILY Philip M 1906	SIMMONS Gilman A 1893

Section 7

RIDDLE William H 1898		
BELLER Melvin N 1903	SMITH Richard D 1861	
BELLER Melvin N 1903	SMITH Richard D 1861	
GILL Samuel K 1882	SMITH Richard G 1873	SELLS Mary 1901

Section 8

DRYDEN Jonathan M 1899	ALLDREDGE William 1861	ALLDREDGE William 1861	FERRIS John C 1895
SMITH Richard D 1861	WINNINGHAM George W 1893		
SMITH Richard D 1861	SMITH Richard D 1859	WINNINGHAM Isaac 1879	
SMITH Richard D 1859	SMITH Richard D 1859	HUNT Joseph G 1904	MARTIN Alfred J 1900

Section 9

PHIPPS James T 1900	DAILY Philip M 1906	WINNINGHAM Isaac 1859	SIMMONS Gilman A 1893
WINNINGHAM Isaac 1879			WINNINGHAM Isaac 1859
WINNINGHAM Isaac 1879	SIMMONS William H 1891	PFENNIGHAUSEN R W 1886	SIMMONS G H 1890
SIMMONS William H 1891	SIMMONS William H 1891	HOOVER Walter A 1906	

Section 18

SMITH Richard 1872	SMITH Samuel H 1859	
SMITH Abraham 1874	SMITH Richard 1872	
ROBERDS Jesse 1888		
RUSHING Daniel E 1881	BROOKES Anslem 1900	

Section 17

SMITH Samuel H 1859	SMITH Richard D 1861	MARTIN Alfred J 1900
PADGETT Robert 1878	JENKINS Douglas 1893	MARTIN Alfred J 1900
PADGETT Robert 1878	JENKINS Douglas 1893	HARROD [108] John 1910
BROOKES Anslem 1900	SMITH Luke 1901	KELLY Levi 1907	HARROD Jehu 1910

Section 16

16

Section 19

RUSHING Daniel E 1881	BROOKES Anslem 1900	
SMITH James M 1900	WEBB Albert M 1893	
TOOMEY [91] Andrew J 1890		
TOOMEY [91] Andrew J 1890	HOPE James A 1881	

Section 20

BROOKES Anslem 1900	SMITH Luke 1901	KELLY Levi 1907
WEBB Albert M 1893	WEBB Albert M 1893	WILLEFORD Wiley A 1877
HERRICK Jerome 1893	BRILES David A 1893	WILLEFORD Wiley A 1877

Section 21

WEBB John H 1893	WEAVER Daniel A 1882	REID Andrew 1890
		WEAVER Daniel A 1882
WILLEFORD Wiley A 1877	USHER Moses H 1859	WEAVER Daniel A 1882
BRILES David A 1893	USHER Moses H 1860	USHER Moses H 1857	USHER Moses H 1856

Section 30

HOPE James A 1881	HOPE James A 1881	
	LEWIS Verginia 1903	
SMITH James W 1860	DURNEL John W 1880	
SMITH James W 1861	DURNEL John W 1880	

Section 29

SETTLE Joseph 1892	GUNZ Minnie 1901	
LIVSAY George W 1882		
LIVSAY George W 1882	LIVESAY John J 1893	CROW Azariah 1892
	HARLOW Reuben 1859	

Section 28

GUNZ Minnie 1901	GUNZ Minnie 1901	
CROW Azariah 1892	MILLBANKS Larkin 1879	MILLBANKS Larkin 1879	HOOVER Austin 1893
MILLBANKS Larkin 1879	USHER Moses H 1859	USHER Moses H 1857
USHER Moses H 1859	ROBBINS Catharine 1880	ROBBINS Catharine 1880
		ROBBINS Catharine 1880	PADGETT Abraham 1859

Section 31

CROWDER Jane E 1881	HUNT John 1882
	HUNT John 1882
	SHELTON John C 1892

Section 32

LIVSAY George W 1882	PHIPPS John B 1860	PHIPPS John B 1860
HUNT [125] Margret T 1898	PHIPPS John B 1875	HUNT [124] Lulu L 1893
HUNT John 1882	PHIPPS John B 1875	HUNT [124] Lulu L 1893
SHELTON John C 1892	HARRIS Allen M 1861	

Section 33

CROW Azariah 1892		
ROBBINS John B 1879	FLEMING Thomas W 1890	PADGETT Abraham 1859	PADGETT Abraham 1859
	PADGETT Abraham 1861	PADGETT Abraham 1861	PADGETT Abraham 1859
ROBBINS John B 1879	CARTER Robert 1888	GREEN Louisa E 1891	PADGETT William T 1889
CARTER Robert 1888	NEWSOM Mary 1860	LEWIS Augustus 1861

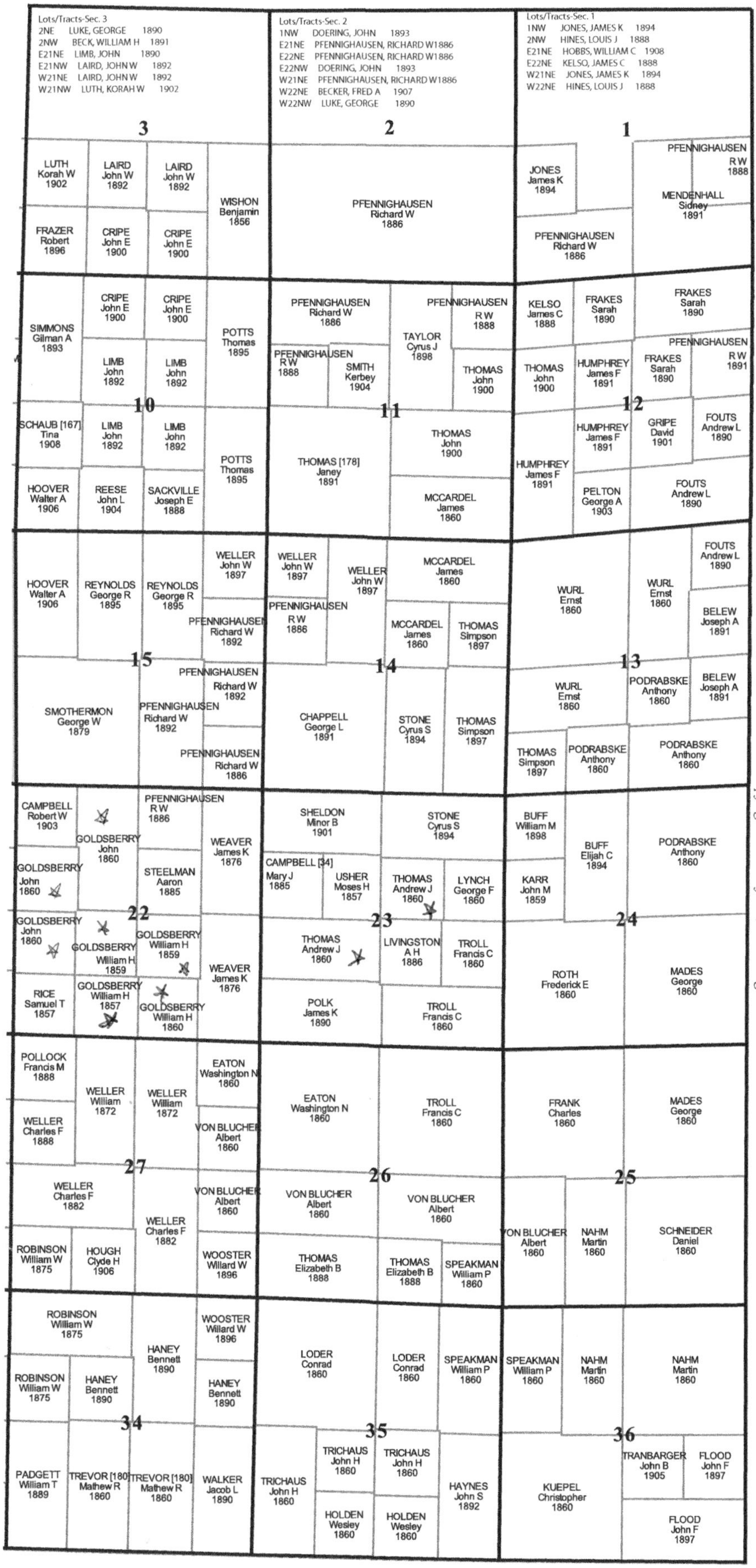

Lots/Tracts-Sec. 3
2NE   LUKE, GEORGE   1890
2NW   BECK, WILLIAM H   1891
E21NE   LIMB, JOHN   1890
E21NW   LAIRD, JOHN W   1892
W21NE   LAIRD, JOHN W   1892
W21NW   LUTH, KORAH W   1902

Lots/Tracts-Sec. 2
1NW   DOERING, JOHN   1893
E21NE   PFENNIGHAUSEN, RICHARD W 1886
E22NE   PFENNIGHAUSEN, RICHARD W 1886
E22NW   DOERING, JOHN   1893
W21NE   PFENNIGHAUSEN, RICHARD W 1886
W22NE   BECKER, FRED A   1907
W22NW   LUKE, GEORGE   1890

Lots/Tracts-Sec. 1
1NW   JONES, JAMES K   1894
2NW   HINES, LOUIS J   1888
E21NE   HOBBS, WILLIAM C   1908
E22NE   KELSO, JAMES C   1888
W21NE   JONES, JAMES K   1894
W22NE   HINES, LOUIS J   1888

3

LUTH Korah W 1902
LAIRD John W 1892
LAIRD John W 1892
WISHON Benjamin 1856

FRAZER Robert 1896
CRIPE John E 1900
CRIPE John E 1900

2

PFENNIGHAUSEN Richard W 1886

1

JONES James K 1894

PFENNIGHAUSEN R W 1888
MENDENHALL Sidney 1891

PFENNIGHAUSEN Richard W 1886

SIMMONS Gilman A 1893
CRIPE John E 1900
CRIPE John E 1900
POTTS Thomas 1895

PFENNIGHAUSEN Richard W 1886
PFENNIGHAUSEN R W 1888

TAYLOR Cyrus J 1898

KELSO James C 1888
FRAKES Sarah 1890
FRAKES Sarah 1890

LIMB John 1892
LIMB John 1892

PFENNIGHAUSEN R W 1888
SMITH Kerbey 1904

THOMAS John 1900

THOMAS John 1900
HUMPHREY James F 1891
FRAKES Sarah 1890
PFENNIGHAUSEN R W 1891

10

SCHAUB [167] Tina 1908
LIMB John 1892
LIMB John 1892

11

THOMAS John 1900

12

HUMPHREY James F 1891
GRIPE David 1901
FOUTS Andrew L 1890

HOOVER Walter A 1906
REESE John L 1904
SACKVILLE Joseph E 1888
POTTS Thomas 1895

THOMAS [178] Janey 1891

MCCARDEL James 1860

HUMPHREY James F 1891
PELTON George A 1903
FOUTS Andrew L 1890

HOOVER Walter A 1906
REYNOLDS George R 1895
REYNOLDS George R 1895

WELLER John W 1897
WELLER John W 1897
WELLER John W 1897
MCCARDEL James 1860

FOUTS Andrew L 1890

WURL Ernst 1860
WURL Ernst 1860
BELEW Joseph A 1891

15

SMOTHERMON George W 1879

PFENNIGHAUSEN Richard W 1892
PFENNIGHAUSEN Richard W 1892
PFENNIGHAUSEN Richard W 1892
PFENNIGHAUSEN Richard W 1886

PFENNIGHAUSEN R W 1892
MCCARDEL James 1860
THOMAS Simpson 1897

14

CHAPPELL George L 1891
STONE Cyrus S 1894
THOMAS Simpson 1897

WURL Ernst 1860

13

PODRABSKE Anthony 1860
BELEW Joseph A 1891

THOMAS Simpson 1897
PODRABSKE Anthony 1860
PODRABSKE Anthony 1860

CAMPBELL Robert W 1903
PFENNIGHAUSEN R W 1886

GOLDSBERRY John 1860
WEAVER James K 1876
SHELDON Minor B 1901
STONE Cyrus S 1894
BUFF William M 1898

GOLDSBERRY John 1860
STEELMAN Aaron 1885
CAMPBELL [34] Mary J 1885
USHER Moses H 1857
THOMAS Andrew J 1860
LYNCH George F 1860
BUFF Elijah C 1894
KARR John M 1859
PODRABSKE Anthony 1860

22

GOLDSBERRY John 1860
GOLDSBERRY William H 1859
GOLDSBERRY William H 1859

23

THOMAS Andrew J 1860
LIVINGSTON A H 1886
TROLL Francis C 1860

24

WEAVER James K 1876
ROTH Frederick E 1860
MADES George 1860

RICE Samuel T 1857
GOLDSBERRY William H 1857
GOLDSBERRY William H 1860
POLK James K 1890
TROLL Francis C 1860

POLLOCK Francis M 1888
EATON Washington N 1860

WELLER William 1872
WELLER William 1872
EATON Washington N 1860
TROLL Francis C 1860
FRANK Charles 1860
MADES George 1860

WELLER Charles F 1888
VON BLUCHER Albert 1860

27

WELLER Charles F 1882
VON BLUCHER Albert 1860

26

VON BLUCHER Albert 1860
VON BLUCHER Albert 1860

25

WELLER Charles F 1882

ROBINSON William W 1875
HOUGH Clyde H 1906
WOOSTER Willard W 1896
THOMAS Elizabeth B 1888
THOMAS Elizabeth B 1888
SPEAKMAN William P 1860
VON BLUCHER Albert 1860
NAHM Martin 1860
SCHNEIDER Daniel 1860

ROBINSON William W 1875
WOOSTER Willard W 1896

ROBINSON William W 1875
HANEY Bennett 1890
HANEY Bennett 1890
LODER Conrad 1860
LODER Conrad 1860
SPEAKMAN William P 1860
SPEAKMAN William P 1860
NAHM Martin 1860
NAHM Martin 1860

ROBINSON William W 1875
HANEY Bennett 1890
HANEY Bennett 1890

34

PADGETT William T 1889
TREVOR [180] Mathew R 1860
TREVOR [180] Mathew R 1860
WALKER Jacob L 1890
TRICHAUS John H 1860

35

TRICHAUS John H 1860
TRICHAUS John H 1860
HAYNES John S 1892

36

KUEPEL Christopher 1860

TRANBARGER John B 1905
FLOOD John F 1897

HOLDEN Wesley 1860
HOLDEN Wesley 1860

FLOOD John F 1897

Copyright 2013 Boyd IT, Inc. All Rights Reserved

Helpful Hints

1. This Map's INDEX can be found on the preceding pages.

2. Refer to Map "C" to see where this Township lies within Howell County, Missouri.

3. Numbers within square brackets [ ] denote a multi-patentee land parcel (multi-owner). Refer to Appendix "C" for a full list of members in this group.

4. Areas that look to be crowded with Patentees usually indicate multiple sales of the same parcel (Re-issues) or Overlapping parcels. See this Township's Index for an explanation of these and other circumstances that might explain "odd" groupings of Patentees on this map.

Legend

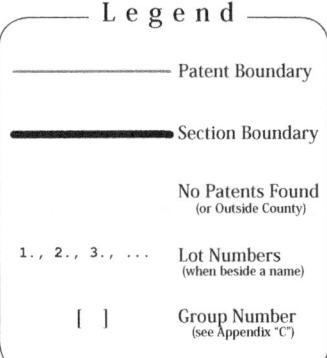

———— Patent Boundary

━━━━ Section Boundary

No Patents Found
(or Outside County)

1., 2., 3., ... Lot Numbers
(when beside a name)

[ ] Group Number
(see Appendix "C")

Scale: Section = 1 mile X 1 mile
(generally, with some exceptions)

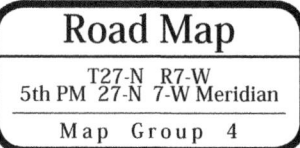

Road Map

T27-N R7-W
5th PM 27-N 7-W Meridian

Map Group 4

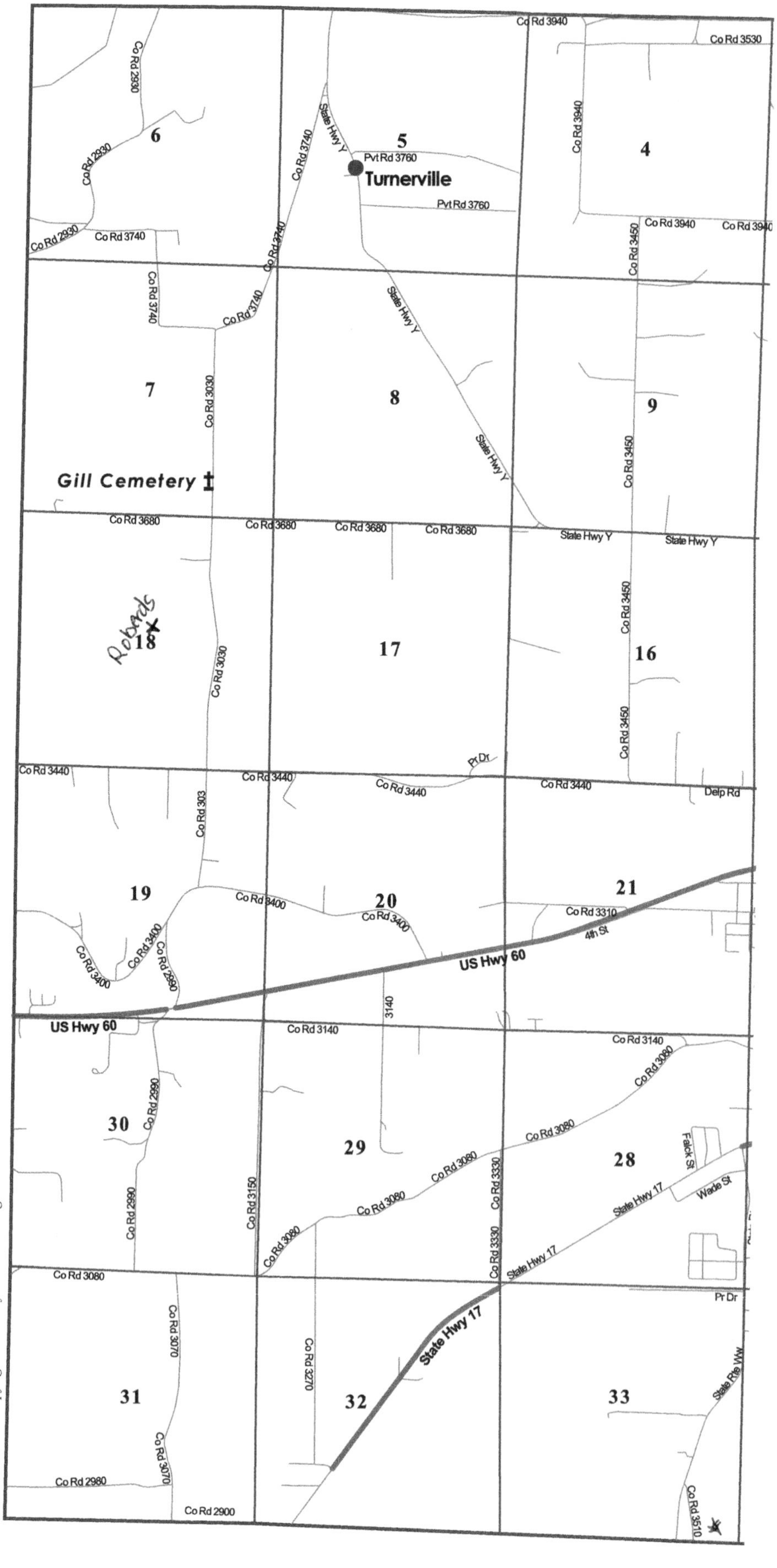

Cities & Towns
Mountain View
Turnerville

Cemeteries
Gill Cemetery
Greenlawn Cemetery
Mountain View Cemetery

Co Rd 3940

Co Rd 2930

Co Rd 3530

Co Rd 2930

6

State Hwy Y

Co Rd 3740

Pvt Rd 3760

5

Co Rd 3940

● **Turnerville**

4

Pvt Rd 3760

Co Rd 2930

Co Rd 2990

Co Rd 3740

Co Rd 3740

Co Rd 3450

Co Rd 3940   Co Rd 3940

Co Rd 3740

State Hwy Y

Co Rd 3030

7

Co Rd 3740

8

9

Co Rd 3450

State Hwy Y

Gill Cemetery ✝

Co Rd 3680   Co Rd 3680   Co Rd 3680   Co Rd 3680   State Hwy Y   State Hwy Y

Co Rd 3450

Roberts ✕
18

Co Rd 3030

17

16

Co Rd 3450

Co Rd 3450

Pr Dr

Co Rd 3440   Co Rd 3440   Co Rd 3440   Co Rd 3440   Delp Rd

Co Rd 303

19   Co Rd 3400

20

21

Co Rd 3400

Co Rd 3400

Co Rd 3310

4th St

Co Rd 2990

Co Rd 3400   Co Rd 2990

US Hwy 60

US Hwy 60

3140

Co Rd 3140

Co Rd 3140

US Hwy 60

Co Rd 2990

30

Co Rd 3150

29

Co Rd 3090

Falck St

Co Rd 3080

28

Co Rd 3090

Co Rd 3080   Co Rd 3330

State Hwy 17

Wade St

Co Rd 2990

Co Rd 3080   Co Rd 3080

Co Rd 3330

State Hwy 17

Co Rd 3080

Co Rd 3070

Co Rd 3270

Pr Dr

State Hwy 17

State Rte VW

31

Co Rd 3070

32

33

Co Rd 2980

Co Rd 2900

Co Rd 3510 ✕

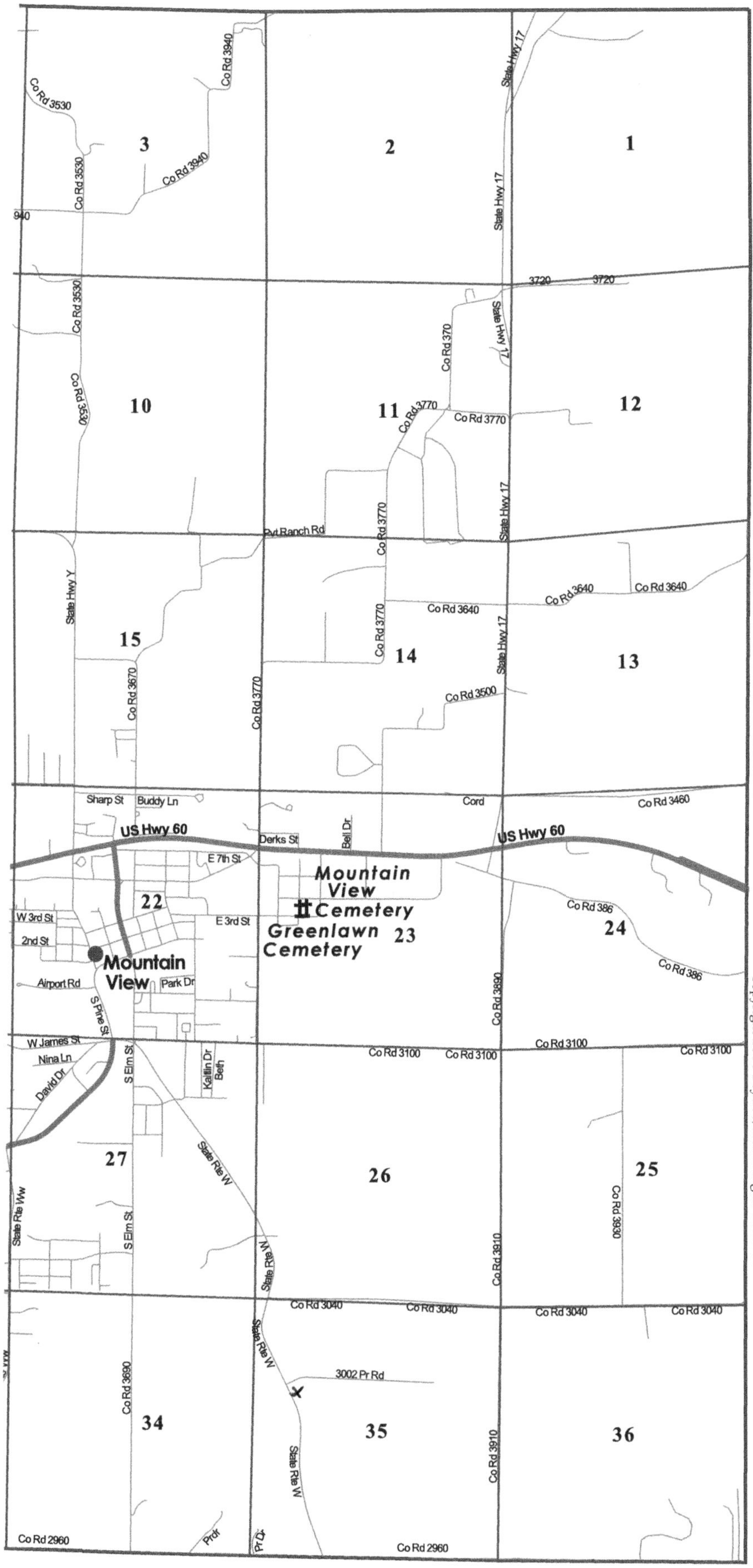

Co Rd 3530

Co Rd 3940

Co Rd 3940

3

2

1

State Hwy 17

Co Rd 3530

940

Co Rd 3530

State Hwy 17

Co Rd 370

3720   3720

Co Rd 3530

10

11

Co Rd 3770

Co Rd 3770

12

State Hwy 17

Pvt Ranch Rd

Co Rd 3770

State Hwy Y

Co Rd 3640   Co Rd 3640

Co Rd 3770

Co Rd 3640

15

Co Rd 3640

14

State Hwy 17

13

Co Rd 3670

Co Rd 3770

Co Rd 3500

Sharp St   Buddy Ln

Cord

Co Rd 3460

US Hwy 60

Derks St

Bell Dr

US Hwy 60

E 7th St

*Mountain
View*

W 3rd St

22

E 3rd St

✝*Cemetery*
Greenlawn **23**
Cemetery

Co Rd 386

24

2nd St

●**Mountain
View**

Co Rd 386

Airport Rd

Park Dr

Co Rd 3890

S Pine St

W James St

Nina Ln

Co Rd 3100   Co Rd 3100   Co Rd 3100   Co Rd 3100

David Dr

S Elm St

Kaitlin Dr

Beth

27

State Rte W

26

25

Co Rd 3930

State Rte Ww

S Elm St

Co Rd 3810

M Rte W

Co Rd 3040   Co Rd 3040   Co Rd 3040   Co Rd 3040

Co Rd 3690

State Rte W

3002 Pr Rd

✗

34

35

Co Rd 3910

36

State Rte W

Prd

Prd

Co Rd 2960   Co Rd 2960

Helpful Hints

1. This road map has a number of uses, but primarily it is to help you: a) find the present location of land owned by your ancestors (at least the general area), b) find cemeteries and city-centers, and c) estimate the route/roads used by Census-takers & tax-assessors.

2. If you plan to travel to Howell County to locate cemeteries or land parcels, please pick up a modern travel map for the area before you do. Mapping old land parcels on modern maps is not as exact a science as you might think. Just the slightest variations in public land survey coordinates, estimates of parcel boundaries, or road-map deviations can greatly alter a map's representation of how a road either does or doesn't cross a particular parcel of land.

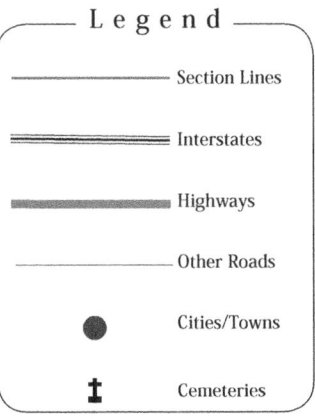

L e g e n d

———————	Section Lines
═══════	Interstates
▬▬▬▬▬	Highways
———————	Other Roads
●	Cities/Towns
✝	Cemeteries

Scale: Section = 1 mile X 1 mile
(generally, with some exceptions)

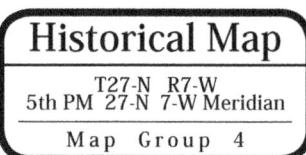

Historical Map

T27-N   R7-W
5th PM 27-N 7-W Meridian

Map Group 4

Cities & Towns
Mountain View
Turnerville

6

5
● Turnerville

4

7

8

9

Gill Cemetery ‡

18

17

16

19

20

21

Cemeteries
Gill Cemetery
Greenlawn Cemetery
Mountain View Cemetery

30

29

28

31

32

33

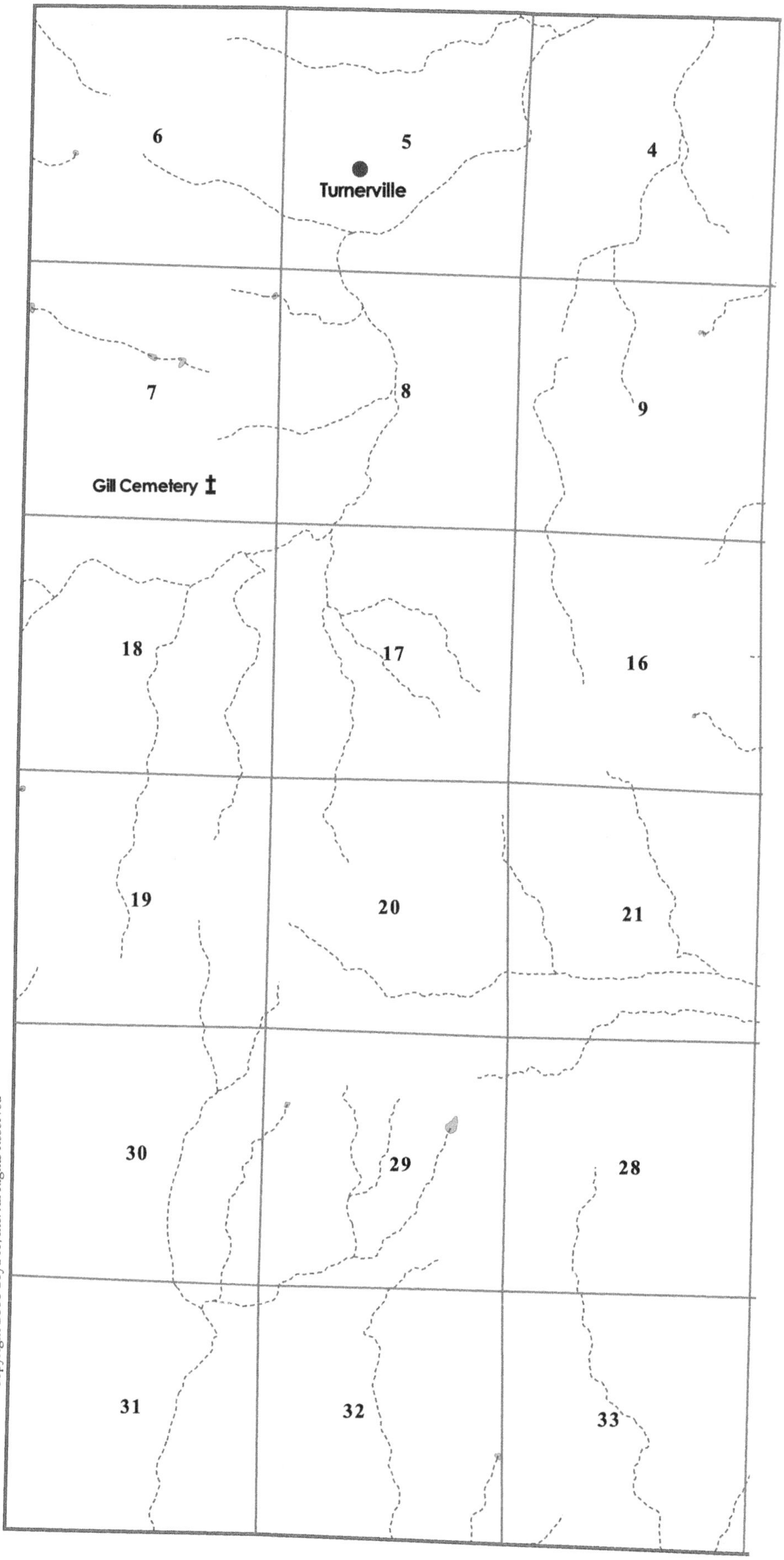

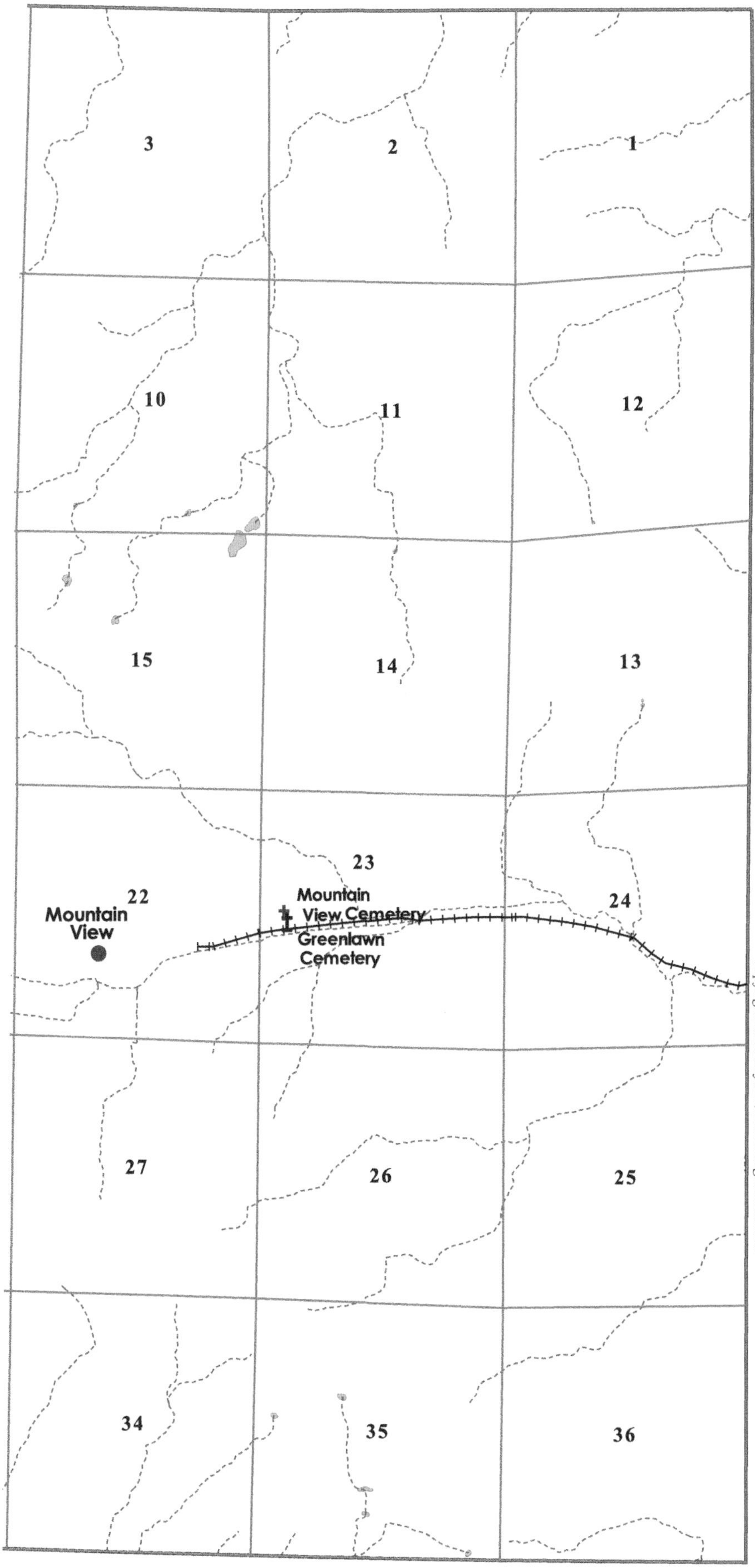

3

2

1

10

11

12

15

14

13

23

22
Mountain
View

Mountain
View Cemetery

Greenlawn
Cemetery

24

27

26

25

34

35

36

Helpful Hints

1. This Map takes a different look at the same Congressional Township displayed in the preceding two maps. It presents features that can help you better envision the historical development of the area: a) Water-bodies (lakes & ponds), b) Water-courses (rivers, streams, etc.), c) Railroads, d) City/ town center-points (where they were oftentimes located when first settled), and e) Cemeteries.

2. Using this "Historical" map in tandem with this Township's Patent Map and Road Map, may lead you to some interesting discoveries. You will often find roads, towns, cemeteries, and waterways are named after nearby landowners: sometimes those names will be the ones you are researching. See how many of these research gems you can find here in Howell County.

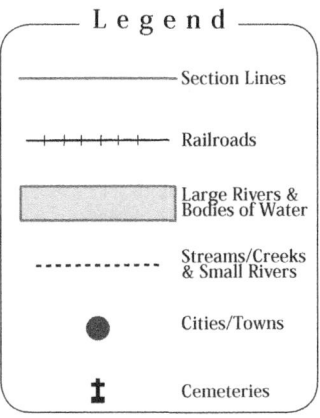

Legend

———————— Section Lines

++++++++ Railroads

Large Rivers &
Bodies of Water

----------- Streams/Creeks
& Small Rivers

● Cities/Towns

‡ Cemeteries

Scale: Section = 1 mile X 1 mile
(there are some exceptions)

Map Group 5: Index to Land Patents

Township 26-North Range 10-West (5th PM 26-N 10-W)

After you locate an individual in this Index, take note of the Section and Section Part then proceed to the Land Patent map on the pages immediately following. You should have no difficulty locating the corresponding parcel of land.

The "For More Info" Column will lead you to more information about the underlying Patents. See the *Legend* at right, and the "How to Use this Book" chapter, for more information.

```
┌─────────────────────────────────────────────────────────┐
│                         LEGEND                          │
│              "For More Info . . . " column              │
│  A = Authority (Legislative Act, See Appendix "A")      │
│  B = Block or Lot (location in Section unknown)         │
│  C = Cancelled Patent                                   │
│  F = Fractional Section                                 │
│  G = Group  (Multi-Patentee Patent, see Appendix "C")   │
│  V = Overlaps another Parcel                            │
│  R = Re-Issued (Parcel patented more than once)         │
│                                                         │
│  (A & G items require you to look in the Appendixes     │
│  referred to above. All other Letter-designations       │
│  followed by a number require you to locate line-items  │
│  in this index that possess the ID number found after   │
│  the letter).                                           │
└─────────────────────────────────────────────────────────┘
```

ID	Individual in Patent	Sec.	Sec. Part	Date Issued	Other Counties	For More Info . . .
937	BECKETT, Wiley H	1	NESW	1860-09-10		A6
938	" "	1	S½SW	1860-09-10		A6
936	" "	1	W½NE	1860-09-10		A6 G15
942	" "	11	N½NE	1860-09-10		A6
940	" "	11	S½NE	1860-09-10		A6
939	" "	11	NWSE	1860-09-10		A6
941	" "	11	S½SE	1860-09-10		A6 G16
943	" "	11	NESE	1860-09-10		A6
949	" "	12	N½SE	1860-09-10		A6 G14
944	" "	12	SENW	1860-09-10		A6
945	" "	12	SWNE	1860-09-10		A6
947	" "	12	N½NW	1860-09-10		A6
948	" "	12	SWNW	1860-09-10		A6
951	" "	12	N½SW	1860-09-10		A6
946	" "	12	N½NE	1860-09-10		A6
950	" "	12	SENE	1860-09-10		A6 G14
953	BECKETT, William H	12	SENE	1860-09-10		A6 G14
952	" "	12	N½SE	1860-09-10		A6 G14
7072	BENSON, Wilbur F	1	E21NE	1892-10-17		A7
958	FARMER, John R	34	E½SE	1888-12-04		A7
959	GREGG, Thomas	1	NWSW	1891-06-09		A7
961	HALLETT, Benjamin	36	SWNE	1877-04-05		A7
960	" "	36	E½NE	1877-04-05		A7
962	HUFF, Emma L	26	NE	1877-04-05		A7
965	KEELER, Charles H	25	NWSE	1899-05-12		A7
966	KEELER, Joseph E	35	NESE	1884-11-01		A7
967	" "	35	E½NE	1884-11-01		A7
968	" "	35	NWNE	1884-11-01		A7
969	KEELER, Smith	25	W½SW	1876-05-10		A7
970	" "	26	E½SE	1876-05-10		A7
975	LEARNARD, Oscar E	33		1882-06-01		A1
976	" "	34	W½SE	1882-06-01		A1
980	MERRILL, Franklin	36	NESW	1874-11-05		A7
979	" "	36	S½SW	1874-11-05		A7
982	MURRELL, George P	34	SENE	1900-02-02		A7
983	NETTLETON, George H	12	S½SW	1884-03-10		A1
984	" "	12	S½SE	1884-03-10		A1
987	PETREY, Silas	25	NESE	1882-03-30		A7
7074	RADFORD, John C	2	2NW	1890-01-10		A7
7073	ROBERTS, George W	1	E22NE	1879-12-15		A7
990	ROBERTSON, Moses	35	NWSE	1882-11-10		A7
989	" "	35	SWNE	1882-11-10		A7
988	" "	35	S½SE	1882-11-10		A7
992	SMITH, George H	29	SESE	1905-11-03		A1
994	SPENCE, George F	25	SWSE	1889-01-12		A7
993	" "	25	E½SW	1889-01-12		A7

ID	Individual in Patent	Sec.	Sec. Part	Date Issued	Other Counties	For More Info . . .
995	SPENCE, John	25	SESE	1860-08-01		A1
997	" "	36	SENW	1860-08-01		A1
996	" "	36	NWNE	1860-08-01		A1
1000	SPENCER, John	36	N½NW	1877-08-01		A7
999	" "	36	NWSW	1860-05-02		A6
998	" "	36	SWNW	1860-05-02		A6
1001	WALKER, Mary	1	W½NE	1860-09-10		A6 G15
1003	WILSON, William H	28	SWSW	1915-01-19		A7
1005	WOODARD, Sally	11	S½SE	1860-09-10		A6 G16

Patent Map

T26-N R10-W
5th PM 26-N 10-W Meridian

Map Group 5

Township Statistics

Parcels Mapped	:	51
Number of Patents	:	34
Number of Individuals	:	37
Patentees Identified	:	34
Number of Surnames	:	31
Multi-Patentee Parcels	:	4
Oldest Patent Date	:	5/2/1860
Most Recent Patent	:	1/19/1915
Block/Lot Parcels	:	3
Cities and Town	:	0
Cemeteries	:	1

6	5	4
7	8	9
18	17	16
19	20	21
30	29	28
31	32	33

SMITH George H 1905 · WILSON William H 1915

LEARNARD Oscar E 1882

3

2

Lots/Tracts-Sec. 1
E21NE   BENSON, WILBUR F 1892
E22NE   ROBERTS, GEORGE W 1879

BECKETT [15]
Wiley H
1860

1

GREGG
Thomas
1891

BECKETT
Wiley H
1860

BECKETT
Wiley H
1860

Lots/Tracts-Sec. 2
2NW   RADFORD, JOHN C 1890

BECKETT
Wiley H
1860

BECKETT
Wiley H
1860

BECKETT
Wiley H
1860

10

BECKETT
Wiley H
1860

BECKETT
Wiley H
1860

BECKETT
Wiley H
1860

BECKETT
Wiley H
1860

BECKETT [14]
William H
1860

11

12

BECKETT
Wiley H
1860

BECKETT
Wiley H
1860

BECKETT
Wiley H
1860

BECKETT [14]
William H
1860

BECKETT [16]
Wiley H
1860

NETTLETON
George H
1884

NETTLETON
George H
1884

15

14

13

22

23

24

HUFF
Emma L
1877

27

26

25

KEELER
Smith
1876

KEELER
Smith
1876

SPENCE
George F
1889

KEELER
Charles H
1899

PETREY
Silas
1882

SPENCE
George F
1889

SPENCE
John
1860

KEELER
Joseph E
1884

SPENCER
John
1877

SPENCE
John
1860

KEELER
Joseph E
1884

HALLETT
Benjamin
1877

MURRELL
George P
1900

ROBERTSON
Moses
1882

SPENCER
John
1860

SPENCE
John
1860

HALLETT
Benjamin
1877

34

35

36

LEARNARD
Oscar E
1882

FARMER
John R
1888

ROBERTSON
Moses
1882

KEELER
Joseph E
1884

SPENCER
John
1860

MERRILL
Franklin
1874

ROBERTSON
Moses
1882

MERRILL
Franklin
1874

Helpful Hints

1. This Map's INDEX can be found on the preceding pages.

2. Refer to Map "C" to see where this Township lies within Howell County, Missouri.

3. Numbers within square brackets [   ] denote a multi-patentee land parcel (multi-owner). Refer to Appendix "C" for a full list of members in this group.

4. Areas that look to be crowded with Patentees usually indicate multiple sales of the same parcel (Re-issues) or Overlapping parcels. See this Township's Index for an explanation of these and other circumstances that might explain "odd" groupings of Patentees on this map.

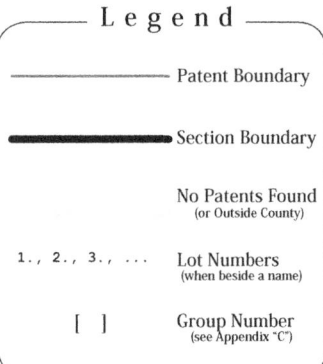

Legend

Patent Boundary

Section Boundary

No Patents Found
(or Outside County)

1., 2., 3., . . .   Lot Numbers
(when beside a name)

[   ]   Group Number
(see Appendix "C")

Scale: Section = 1 mile X 1 mile
(generally, with some exceptions)

Road Map

T26-N   R10-W
5th PM 26-N 10-W Meridian

M a p   G r o u p   5

Cities & Towns

None

Cemeteries

Carroll Cemetery

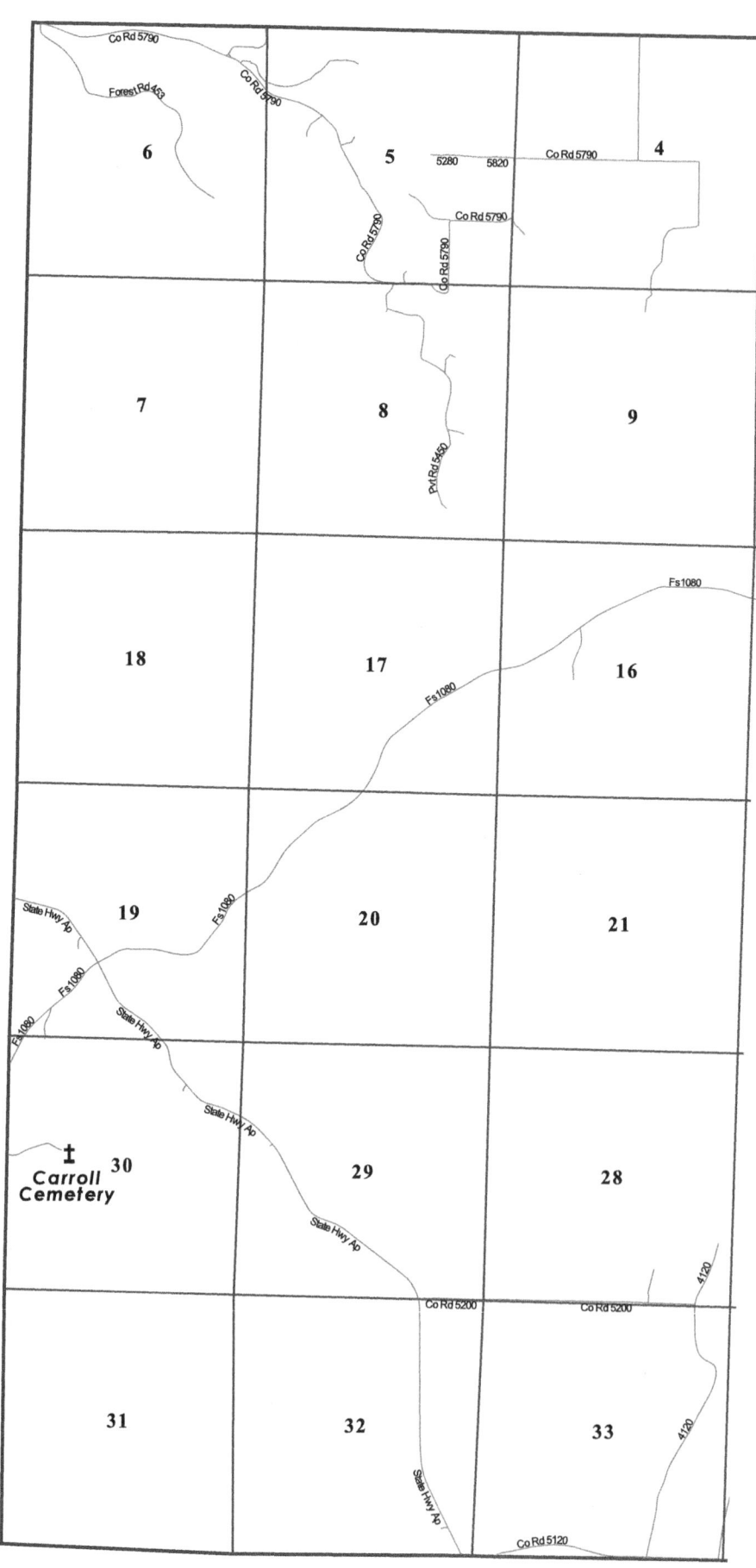

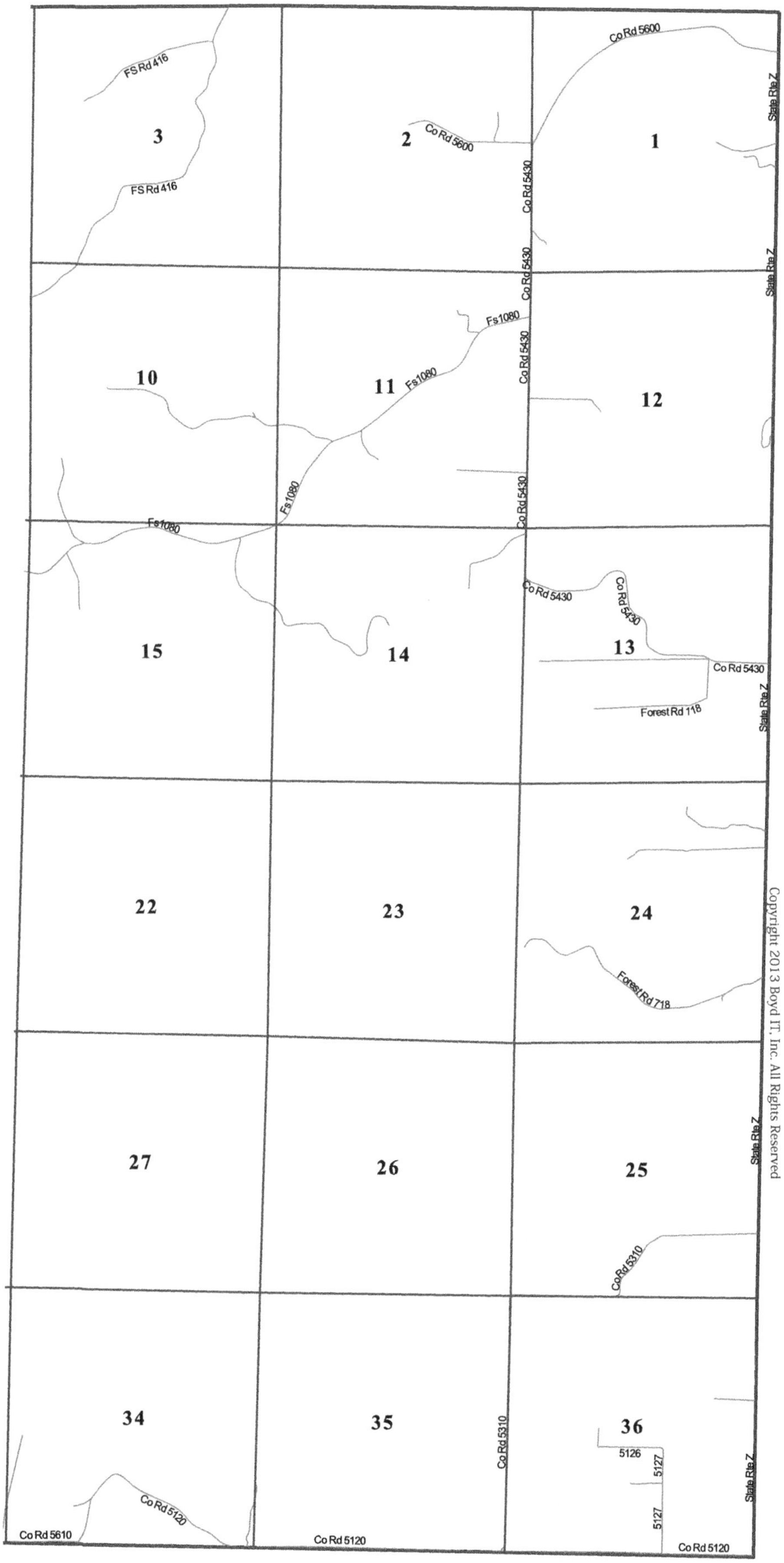

FS Rd 416

3

Co Rd 5600

2

Co Rd 5600

1

State Rte Z

Co Rd 5430

FS Rd 416

Co Rd 5430

Fs 1080

10

11 Fs 1080

Co Rd 5430

12

Fs 1080

Fs 1080

Co Rd 5430

15

14

Co Rd 5430

Co Rd 5430

13

Co Rd 5430

State Rte Z

Forest Rd 118

22

23

24

Forest Rd 718

State Rte Z

27

26

25

Co Rd 5310

34

35

Co Rd 5310

36

5126

5127

Co Rd 5120

5127

State Rte Z

Co Rd 5610

Co Rd 5120

Co Rd 5120

Helpful Hints

1. This road map has a number of uses, but primarily it is to help you: a) find the present location of land owned by your ancestors (at least the general area), b) find cemeteries and city-centers, and c) estimate the route/roads used by Census-takers & tax-assessors.

2. If you plan to travel to Howell County to locate cemeteries or land parcels, please pick up a modern travel map for the area before you do. Mapping old land parcels on modern maps is not as exact a science as you might think. Just the slightest variations in public land survey coordinates, estimates of parcel boundaries, or road-map deviations can greatly alter a map's representation of how a road either does or doesn't cross a particular parcel of land.

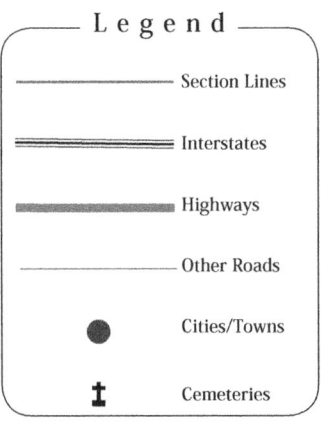

Legend

——————— Section Lines

═══════════ Interstates

━━━━━━━━━━ Highways

——————— Other Roads

● Cities/Towns

☨ Cemeteries

Scale: Section = 1 mile X 1 mile
(generally, with some exceptions)

Historical Map

T26-N R10-W
5th PM 26-N 10-W Meridian

Map Group 5

Cities & Towns
None

Cemeteries
Carroll Cemetery

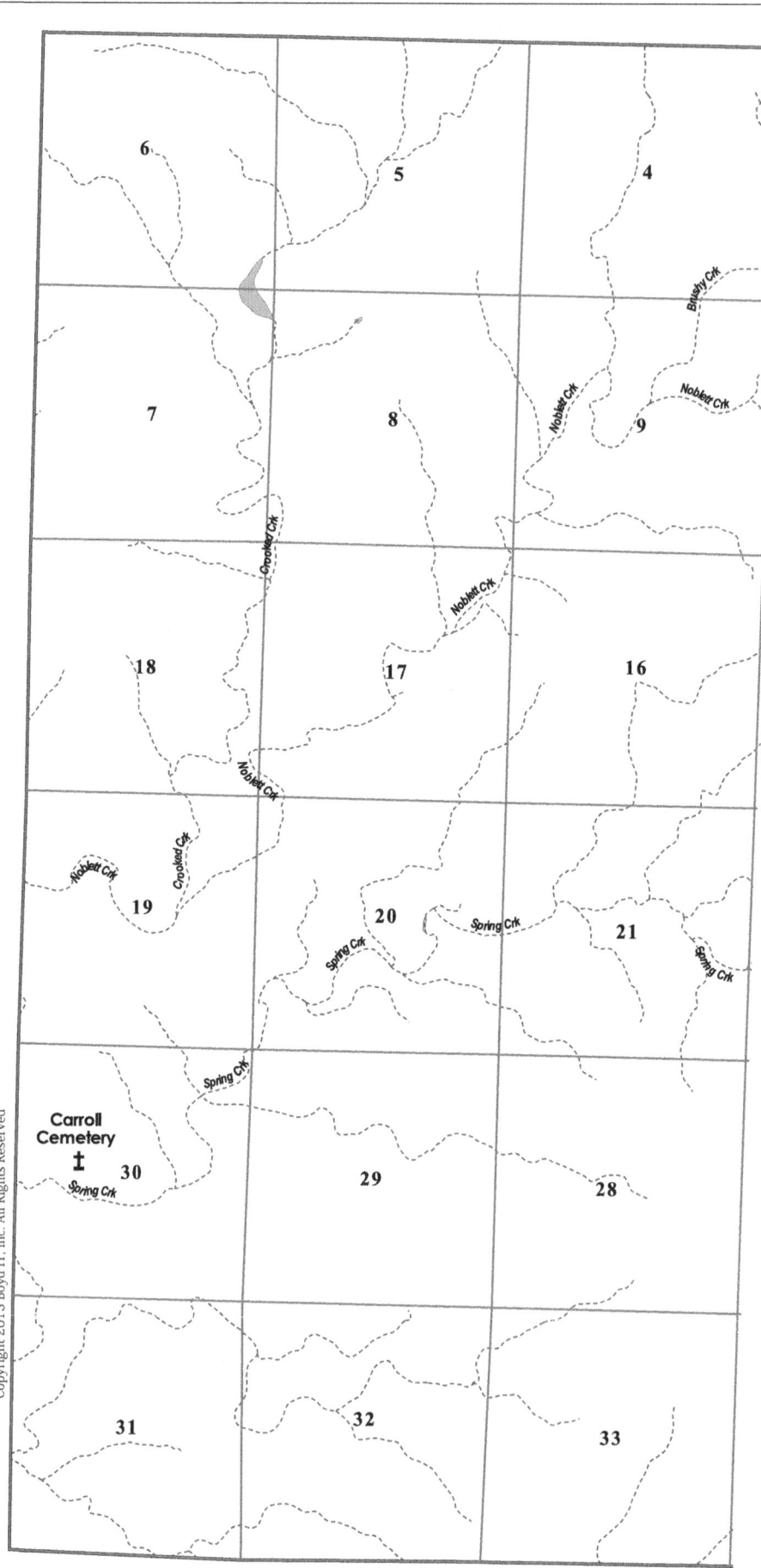

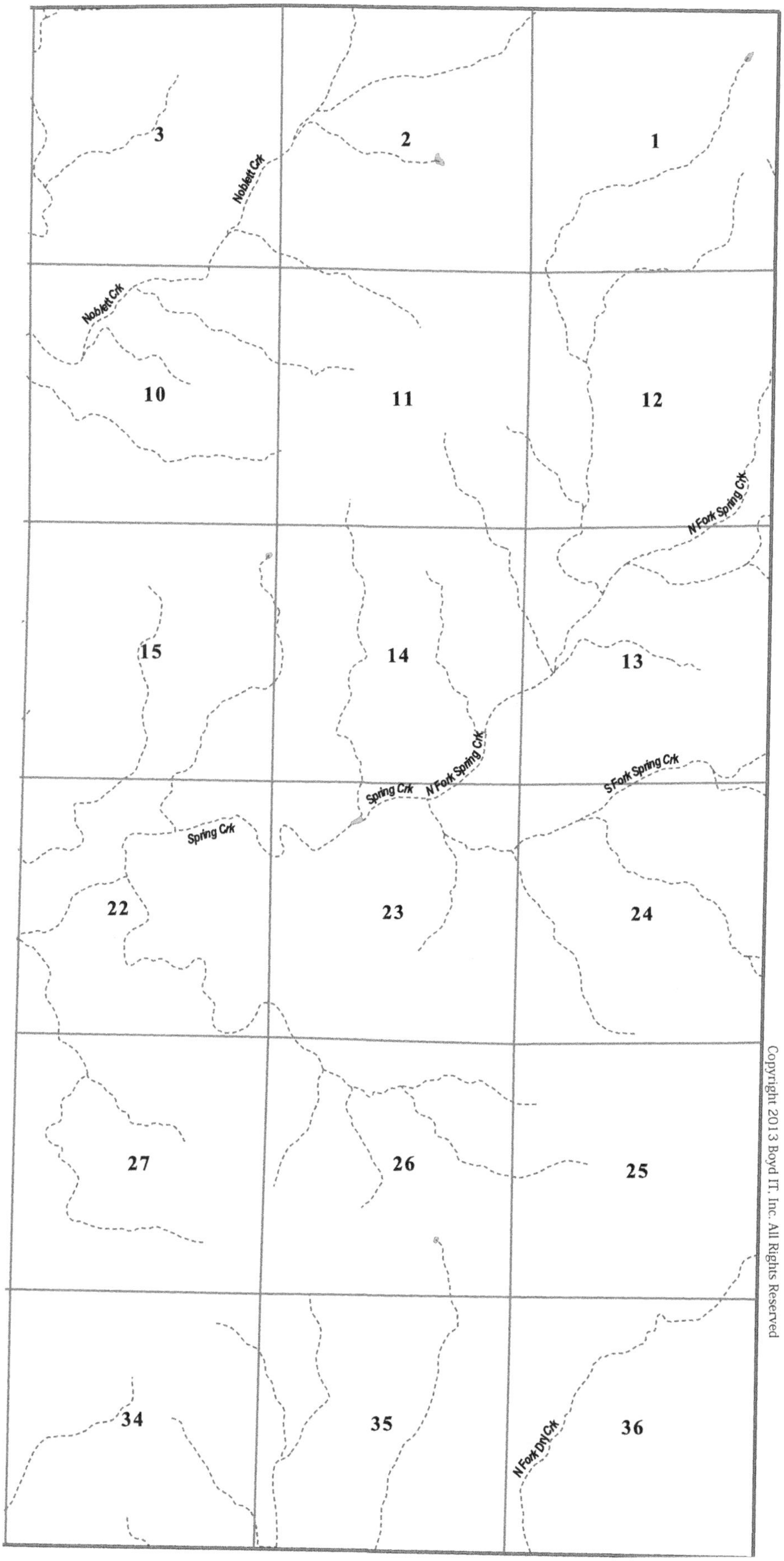

3

2

1

Noblett Crk

Noblett Crk

10

11

12

N Fork Spring Crk

15

14

13

Spring Crk   N Fork Spring Crk

S Fork Spring Crk

Spring Crk

22

23

24

27

26

25

34

35

36

N Fork Dry Crk

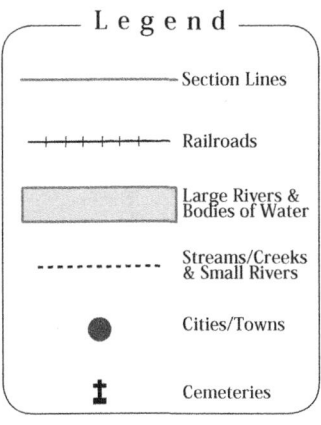

Helpful Hints

1. This Map takes a different look at the same Congressional Township displayed in the preceding two maps. It presents features that can help you better envision the historical development of the area: a) Water-bodies (lakes & ponds), b) Water-courses (rivers, streams, etc.), c) Railroads, d) City/ town center-points (where they were oftentimes located when first settled), and e) Cemeteries.

2. Using this "Historical" map in tandem with this Township's Patent Map and Road Map, may lead you to some interesting discoveries. You will often find roads, towns, cemeteries, and waterways are named after nearby landowners: sometimes those names will be the ones you are researching. See how many of these research gems you can find here in Howell County.

Legend

———————— Section Lines

+++++++++ Railroads

▭ Large Rivers & Bodies of Water

- - - - - - - Streams/Creeks & Small Rivers

● Cities/Towns

‡ Cemeteries

Scale: Section = 1 mile X 1 mile
(there are some exceptions)

Map Group 6: Index to Land Patents

Township 26-North Range 9-West (5th PM 26-N 9-W)

After you locate an individual in this Index, take note of the Section and Section Part then proceed to the Land Patent map on the pages immediately following. You should have no difficulty locating the corresponding parcel of land.

The "For More Info" Column will lead you to more information about the underlying Patents. See the *Legend* at right, and the "How to Use this Book" chapter, for more information.

```
                    LEGEND
            "For More Info . . . " column
A = Authority (Legislative Act, See Appendix "A")
B = Block or Lot (location in Section unknown)
C = Cancelled Patent
F = Fractional Section
G = Group  (Multi-Patentee Patent, see Appendix "C")
V = Overlaps another Parcel
R = Re-Issued (Parcel patented more than once)

(A & G items require you to look in the Appendixes referred
to above. All other Letter-designations followed by a number
require you to locate line-items in this index that possess
the ID number found after the letter).
```

ID	Individual in Patent	Sec.	Sec. Part	Date Issued	Other Counties	For More Info . . .
1008	ALEXANDER, Lee	17	SESE	1891-05-05		A7
1009	" "	20	NENE	1891-05-05		A7
1010	" "	21	W½NW	1891-05-05		A7
7096	ALSUP, Benjamin	3	2NW	1860-05-02		A6
7118	" "	4	E22NE	1859-09-01		A1
1011	ALSUP, James K	32	NE	1874-04-20		A7
1012	ALSUP, William	29	SWNE	1860-03-01		A1
1013	AUSMAN, Charles W	32	NWSW	1901-03-23		A7
1014	BELL, John P	12	NW	1892-03-07		A7
1015	BIGGINS, Charles	8	NWNE	1894-12-17		A7
1016	" "	8	NENW	1894-12-17		A7
1017	BILLING, Mariah	31	NE	1894-05-18		A7
1018	BLACK, James D	8	SE	1890-10-11		A7
7123	BLACK, James S	5	W22NW	1890-01-10		A7
7122	" "	5	W21NW	1890-01-10		A7
1019	" "	5	NWSW	1890-01-10		A7
7089	BOLIN, H W	2	E22NW	1872-02-05		A1
1020	BRADSHAW, Thomas L	26	S½NW	1891-05-05		A7
1021	" "	26	NWSE	1891-05-05		A7
1022	" "	26	SWNE	1891-05-05		A7
1023	BRAKEFIELD, John	5	W½SE	1891-06-09		A7
1024	" "	5	NESW	1891-06-09		A7
1025	BRAY, David M	21	W½SW	1897-10-28		A7
1026	BRESSLER, W M	1	SWSW	1893-06-24		A1
1027	BRITT, Martin V	1	SESW	1891-05-25		A7
1028	" "	1	SWSE	1891-05-25		A7
1029	" "	12	W½NE	1891-05-25		A7
1032	BROONER, Allen D	34	NESW	1898-01-26		A7
1031	" "	34	SWNE	1888-12-06		A1
1030	" "	34	S½SW	1898-01-26		A7
1033	BROONER, Henry	27	SWSE	1893-12-19		A7
1034	" "	34	N½NE	1893-12-19		A7
1035	" "	35	NWNW	1893-12-19		A7
1037	BROWER, Charles	22	N½SW	1891-08-19		A7
1036	" "	22	E½NW	1891-08-19		A7
1038	BRUSTER, Willis G	7	SE	1888-12-06		A7
1039	BRYAN, Thomas P	24	SW	1890-06-06		A7
1040	BRYAN, William E	25	NWNW	1900-08-09		A7
1041	" "	25	E½NW	1900-08-09		A7
7102	BUNCH, Joseph C	30	1SW	1874-01-05		A6
7109	" "	30	S21NW	1874-01-05		A6
1043	CALLAHAN, John L	26	SWSE	1862-10-10		A6 G32
1042	" "	26	SESW	1862-10-10		A6 G32
1044	" "	35	NWNE	1862-10-10		A6 G32
1047	CANNON, Martha	13	S½NE	1861-09-10		A6 G36
1048	" "	13	NESE	1861-09-10		A6 G36

ID	Individual in Patent	Sec.	Sec. Part	Date Issued	Other Counties	For More Info . . .
1049	CANTRELL, Thomas J	24	SE	1875-08-10		A7
1050	CHOAT, Edward	5	S½SW	1893-06-01		A7
1051	" "	8	W½NW	1893-06-01		A7
7079	CLARK, Thomas G	19	2SW	1892-03-07		A7
7085	" "	19	S22NW	1892-03-07		A7
7107	" "	30	N22NW	1892-03-07		A7
1052	COFFMAN, David H	1	NESE	1875-02-15		A7
1053	COLE, John W	32	SWSW	1892-01-25		A7
1054	COLEMAN, Fred	29	S½NW	1896-08-28		A7
1056	" "	29	NWSW	1896-08-28		A7
1055	" "	29	NWNW	1896-08-28		A7
1057	CONLEY, John T	22	SWSE	1900-11-12		A7
7078	COX, Thomas J	19	1NW	1879-12-15		A7
7082	" "	19	N22NW	1879-12-15		A7
1058	" "	19	NWNE	1879-12-15		A7
7116	CRIDER, George W	31	S21NW	1888-12-08		A7
7112	" "	31	1SW	1888-12-08		A7
7117	" "	31	S22SW	1888-12-08		A7
1059	CRISPIN, Alonzo J	13	SWNW	1901-05-08		A7
1060	CROUCH, Charles W	12	SW	1894-12-17		A7
1061	CRUM, James	13	SESE	1897-08-16		A7
1062	" "	13	W½SE	1897-08-16		A7
1063	DAVIDSON, Thomas W	1	NWSW	1894-12-17		A7
1064	" "	2	E½SE	1894-12-17		A7
7086	" "	2	E21NE	1894-12-17		A7
1065	DEARING, George B	11	NWNW	1891-05-25		A7
1066	" "	2	SWSW	1891-05-25		A7
1067	DUKE, John B	28	SESW	1894-05-23		A7
1068	" "	33	N½NE	1894-05-23		A7
1070	DUNNE, James B	11	S½NW	1885-02-25		A7
1069	" "	11	N½SW	1885-02-25		A7
1072	DUNNING, George W	17	W½SW	1890-10-11		A7
1071	" "	17	SESW	1890-10-11		A7
1073	" "	17	SWSE	1890-10-11		A7
1074	EMERSON, Lemuel H	15	N½NW	1878-03-20		A7
1075	EMERSON, Lemuel M	10	SWSW	1892-01-20		A1
1076	" "	9	SESE	1892-01-20		A1
1077	EMERSON, Marion G	10	SE	1892-09-09		A7
1078	EPPS, Newton C	22	SESW	1873-04-01		A1
1081	" "	27	SENE	1874-01-10		A7
1079	" "	27	SENW	1874-01-10		A7
1080	" "	27	W½NE	1874-01-10		A7
1082	EVANS, Perry	21	NESW	1892-03-07		A7
1083	" "	21	E½NW	1892-03-07		A7
1084	" "	21	NWSE	1892-03-07		A7
1085	FARMER, Frank	23	S½SW	1895-05-28		A7
1086	" "	26	N½NW	1895-05-28		A7
1087	FARMER, William T	27	SWSW	1882-09-30		A7
1088	" "	28	E½SE	1882-09-30		A7
1089	" "	28	SWSE	1882-09-30		A7
1091	FIELDS, Thomas J	35	NESE	1900-08-09		A7
1090	" "	35	SENE	1900-08-09		A7
1092	FRAZEE, Enson	14	NESW	1902-05-21		A7
1093	FRAZEE, James E	17	N½NE	1893-12-19		A7
1094	FRUSHOUR, John W	11	S½SW	1894-05-18		A7
1095	" "	14	N½NW	1894-05-18		A7
7098	GALESBERRY, William	3	E22NE	1853-11-01		A8
1096	GIBSON, George M	5	W½NW	1861-09-10		A6 G93
1097	" "	5	NENW	1861-09-10		A6 G93
1099	GIBSON, George W	5	W½NE	1860-09-10		A6 G94
1098	" "	5	W2NENW	1860-09-10		A6 G94
7092	GOLDSBERRY, William H	2	W22NW	1859-10-10		A6
1104	GREEN, Fannie M	9	S½SW	1897-04-02		A7
7115	HALLETT, John J	31	N22SW	1896-01-14		A7
7113	" "	31	2NW	1896-01-14		A7
7114	" "	31	N21NW	1896-01-14		A7
1105	HARLOW, Thomas	12	SESE	1875-02-15		A7
1106	" "	13	NENE	1875-02-15		A7
1108	HARLOW, William J	12	SENE	1880-11-20		A7
1107	" "	12	NESE	1880-11-20		A7
1109	HENSLEY, William S	36	NESE	1896-06-04		A7
1110	" "	36	SENE	1896-06-04		A7
1112	HEROD, James	25	S½SW	1860-09-10		A6

ID	Individual in Patent	Sec.	Sec. Part	Date Issued	Other Counties	For More Info . . .
1111	HEROD, James (Cont'd)	25	SWSE	1860-09-10		A6
1113	HILER, George W	21	SESE	1889-06-20		A7
1114	" "	27	N½NW	1889-06-20		A7
1115	" "	28	NENE	1889-06-20		A7
1116	HILER, Henry F	35	SESW	1895-09-04		A7
1117	" "	35	SWSE	1895-09-04		A7
1118	HILER, Samuel	22	SWSW	1900-10-12		A7
1119	HILER, Thomas J	21	NESE	1895-05-28		A7
1120	" "	22	SWNW	1892-07-11		A1
1121	HILL, Jasper N	28	SWSW	1890-10-11		A7
1122	" "	33	SWNW	1890-10-11		A7
1123	" "	33	N½NW	1890-10-11		A7
1125	HINDS, Joel	13	SENW	1878-04-05		A7 G117
1124	" "	13	NWNE	1878-04-05		A7 G117
1126	HINDS, Viann	13	NWNE	1878-04-05		A7 G117
1127	" "	13	SENW	1878-04-05		A7 G117
1128	HOMESLEY, Richard	11	E½SE	1890-01-10		A7
1129	" "	11	S½NE	1890-01-10		A7
7091	HOOD, Jesse	2	W22NE	1885-03-20		A1
1130	HORSTEN, Leo	5	NENW	1860-09-10		A6 G94
1133	" "	5	NENW	1861-09-10		A6 G93
1132	" "	5	W½NW	1861-09-10		A6 G93
1131	" "	5	W½NE	1860-09-10		A6 G94
1134	HUFF, William	36	NWSE	1881-10-06		A7
1137	" "	36	NESW	1881-10-06		A7
1136	" "	36	SWNE	1881-10-06		A7
1135	" "	36	SENW	1881-10-06		A7
1138	JONES, William	3	NESE	1907-08-09		A7
1139	KEITHLY, Corydon A	22	E½SE	1890-01-10		A7
1140	" "	27	NENE	1890-01-10		A7
1141	KEITHLY, Levi	14	SWSE	1896-01-14		A7
1142	" "	14	NWSW	1896-01-14		A7
1143	" "	14	S½SW	1896-01-14		A7
1144	KINION, Benjamin	27	SESW	1890-01-10		A7
1146	" "	34	N½NW	1890-01-10		A7
1145	" "	34	SENW	1890-01-10		A7
1147	KINION, Benjamin F	33	E½SE	1894-12-17		A7
1148	" "	34	NWSW	1894-12-17		A7
1151	LEE, Susan	30	NE	1874-01-05		A6 G139
1153	LEEDOM, Martin H	27	SWNW	1892-09-09		A7
1154	" "	27	NWSW	1892-09-09		A7
1155	" "	28	S½NE	1892-09-09		A7
1156	LINDERER, Frank W	10	SESW	1896-03-25		A7
1157	" "	10	N½SW	1896-03-25		A7
1158	" "	9	NESE	1896-03-25		A7
1159	LINDERER, Joseph	9	W½NE	1893-09-01		A7
1160	" "	9	E½NW	1893-09-01		A7
1161	LINDERER, Lawrence	5	E½SE	1891-05-25		A7
7119	" "	5	E21NE	1891-05-25		A7
7121	" "	5	E22NE	1891-05-25		A7
7075	LIVINGSTON, Henry B	1	1NW	1882-03-30		A7
1162	LIVINGSTON, Thomas E	2	N½SW	1876-01-10		A7
1163	" "	2	S½NW	1876-01-10		A7
1164	LONG, Ezekiel M	10	W½NE	1892-10-17		A7
1165	" "	10	NENE	1892-10-17		A7
1166	" "	3	SWSE	1892-10-17		A7
1167	LONGDEN, Willoughby	11	W½SE	1902-04-17		A7
1168	LOVEL, Juda	34	SESE	1888-12-06		A7
1170	" "	35	SWSW	1888-12-06		A7
1169	" "	35	N½SW	1888-12-06		A7
1172	MARTIN, John L	13	NESE	1861-09-10		A6 G36
1171	" "	13	S½NE	1861-09-10		A6 G36
1173	MARTIN, Richard D	13	N½NW	1873-02-01		A7
1174	MCCLELLAN, Charles S	15	S½NW	1895-05-28		A7
1175	MCCLELLAN, William H	23	N½SE	1895-05-28		A7
1176	" "	23	N½SW	1895-05-28		A7
1177	MCGEE, Margaret C	7	NE	1892-03-07		A7
1179	MCGRAW, Madison M	29	E½SW	1898-04-11		A7
1178	" "	29	SWSW	1898-04-11		A7
1180	MEINECKE, Franz	23	S½SE	1896-01-14		A7
1181	" "	26	N½NE	1896-01-14		A7
1182	MILKS, Jerome	22	S½NE	1890-10-11		A7
1183	" "	22	NWNE	1890-10-11		A7

ID	Individual in Patent	Sec.	Sec. Part	Date Issued	Other Counties	For More Info . . .
1184	MILKS, Jerome (Cont'd)	22	NWSE	1890-10-11		A7
1185	MILLER, Alfred L	12	W½SE	1894-12-17		A7
1186	MILLER, Henry L	24	NE	1892-04-23		A7
1187	MILLER, Isaac L	24	NW	1874-01-10		A7
7077	MILLER, James H	1	2NW	1860-09-10		A6
7087	" "	2	E22NE	1860-09-10		A6
1188	MOREHEAD, John D	25	SESE	1888-12-06		A1
7090	MULLINS, John W	2	W21NE	1900-08-09		A7
1189	" "	2	NWSE	1900-08-09		A7
1190	NETTLETON, George H	17	NESW	1882-09-30		A1
1192	" "	19	SENE	1884-03-10		A1
1191	" "	19	SE	1884-03-10		A1
1195	" "	20	E½NW	1884-03-10		A1
1197	" "	20	SWNW	1884-03-10		A1
1194	" "	20	SENE	1884-03-10		A1
1193	" "	20	W½NE	1884-03-10		A1
1196	" "	20	SW	1884-03-10		A1
1198	NICKENS, Mathew	17	NW	1888-12-06		A7
1199	PAINE, John W	1	NESW	1894-05-18		A7
1200	" "	1	NWSE	1894-05-18		A7
1201	PARDEW, William	8	SW	1891-06-09		A7
7104	PETREY, Silas	30	2SW	1882-03-30		A7
7111	" "	30	S22NW	1882-03-30		A7
1203	POE, Benjamin F	8	NW	1872-03-15		A7
1204	POLSON, Mary N	32	E½SE	1883-06-30		A7
1205	" "	33	W½SW	1883-06-30		A7
1207	POTTLE, Thomas	26	NESW	1874-04-20		A7
1206	" "	26	W½SW	1874-04-20		A7
1208	" "	27	NESE	1874-04-20		A7
1209	PREWITT, Abigail	14	SENW	1860-08-01		A1
1210	PRICE, J H	15	NENE	1893-12-09		A1
1211	PRUITT, Abigail	14	NENE	1859-09-01		A1
1212	RAMSEY, Francis M	33	NWSE	1890-01-10		A7
1213	" "	33	S½NE	1890-01-10		A7
1214	" "	34	SWNW	1890-01-10		A7
1215	RAMSEY, John D	32	E½SW	1894-05-23		A7
1216	" "	32	W½NE	1894-05-23		A7
1217	RANEY, C C	14	NWNE	1869-07-01		A1
1218	REICH, Charles	10	SENE	1898-04-11		A7
1219	REYNOLDS, John F	35	NWSE	1888-12-08		A7
1220	" "	35	E½NW	1888-12-08		A7
1221	" "	35	SWNE	1888-12-08		A7
1223	RIDGEWAY, Samuel	11	NWNE	1894-08-14		A7
1222	" "	11	NENW	1894-08-14		A7
1225	" "	2	SWSE	1894-08-14		A7
1224	" "	2	SESE	1894-08-14		A7
1226	ROBERTSON, John H	31	SE	1894-05-18		A7
1227	ROBERTSON, Marion	20	SE	1888-12-04		A7
1228	ROBEY, James N	36	N½NE	1888-12-06		A7
1229	ROWLETT, Newton H	15	E½SE	1892-01-05		A7
1230	" "	15	SWSE	1892-01-05		A7
1231	" "	22	NENE	1892-01-05		A7
1232	RUBENDORF, John N	9	E½NE	1888-05-07		A1
1233	RUDD, James M	23	NW	1891-05-05		A7
1234	SALTSMAN, Daniel A	25	N½SE	1875-04-01		A7
1235	" "	25	N½SW	1875-04-01		A7
1237	SAWYER, Margaret C	28	NWSE	1898-04-06		A7
1236	" "	28	NESW	1898-04-06		A7
1239	SHEPARD, Louisa P	28	W½NW	1896-08-28		A7
1240	" "	28	SENW	1896-08-28		A7
1238	" "	28	NWSW	1896-08-28		A7
1241	SIMMONS, Wesley N	15	SENE	1860-03-01		A1
7100	" "	3	W22NE	1859-09-01		A1
1242	SLATER, Samuel	21	E½NE	1892-06-21		A7
1243	" "	21	SWNE	1892-06-21		A7
1244	" "	22	NWNW	1892-06-21		A7
1245	SMITH, Andrew J	1	NE	1860-09-10		A6
1246	SMITH, George W	3	E½SE	1888-12-06		A7
7094	" "	3	1NE	1888-12-06		A7
1247	SMITH, Logan M	1	SESE	1894-05-23		A7
1248	" "	12	NENE	1894-05-23		A7
1250	SMITH, Martin L	26	SWSE	1862-10-10		A6 G32
1251	" "	26	SESW	1862-10-10		A6 G32

ID	Individual in Patent	Sec.	Sec. Part	Date Issued	Other Counties	For More Info . . .
1252	SMITH, Martin L (Cont'd)	35	NWNE	1862-10-10		A6 G32
1253	SMITH, Thomas H	32	NW	1894-05-18		A7
1254	SNODGRASS, Robert	15	SW	1892-01-05		A7
1255	STAPLES, Samuel M	11	NENE	1900-08-09		A7
1257	STEWART, John M	8	SWNE	1899-05-12		A7
1256	" "	8	SENW	1899-05-12		A7
1258	STOVALL, David W	15	NWSE	1892-11-28		A1
1259	STRIEBEL, Stephan	3	SW	1892-07-11		A7
1260	SWEARINGEN, Erasmus	35	NENE	1888-12-06		A7
1261	" "	36	W½NW	1888-12-06		A7
1262	" "	36	NWSW	1888-12-06		A7
1263	SWEARINGEN, Henry W	25	SWNW	1895-05-28		A7
1265	" "	26	SENE	1895-05-28		A7
1264	" "	26	E½SE	1895-05-28		A7
1266	SWEARINGEN, John S	34	SWSE	1895-05-28		A7
1267	SWEARINGEN, Samuel	35	SESE	1879-12-15		A7
1268	" "	36	SWSW	1879-12-15		A7
1269	THOMPSON, Malcolm	27	NESW	1901-07-09		A7
1270	" "	27	NWSE	1901-07-09		A7
1271	TOW, Riley	33	SENW	1896-09-29		A7
1272	" "	33	E½SW	1896-09-29		A7
1273	" "	33	SWSE	1896-09-29		A7
1274	TUCKER, William W	25	NE	1889-06-22		A7
7120	TURNBAUGH, John J	5	E21NW	1860-08-01		A1
1275	VANDERPOOL, Stephen G	21	NWNE	1898-04-06		A7
1277	WALLIN, Elisha	29	SENE	1878-04-05		A7
1276	" "	29	N½NE	1878-04-05		A7
1278	" "	29	NENW	1878-04-05		A7
1279	WALLIN, James	29	SE	1875-01-06		A7
1281	WALLIN, Sarah	21	SESW	1890-06-06		A7
1280	" "	21	SWSE	1890-06-06		A7
1282	" "	28	NWNE	1890-06-06		A7
1283	" "	28	NENW	1890-06-06		A7
1285	WARD, Joseph	34	SENE	1890-01-10		A7
1284	" "	34	N½SE	1890-01-10		A7
1286	" "	35	SWNW	1890-01-10		A7
1290	WHEELER, Mary C	27	SESE	1900-11-12		A7
7095	WHITE, Alice	3	1NW	1892-04-23		A1
1291	WHITE, Columbus L	14	SWNE	1888-05-07		A1
1293	WHITE, Evans	9	W½SE	1892-09-09		A7
1292	" "	9	N½SW	1892-09-09		A7
1294	WILL, Francis M	23	NE	1891-05-05		A7
7084	WILLIAMS, D H	19	S21SW	1874-01-05		A6
7080	" "	19	N21SW	1874-01-20		A8
1296	" "	30	NE	1874-01-05		A6 G139
1295	" "	30	SE	1874-01-05		A6
7110	" "	30	S21NW	1874-01-05		A6
7103	" "	30	1SW	1874-01-05		A6
7105	" "	30	N21NW	1874-01-05		A6
1298	WILLIAMS, John B	14	N½SE	1890-06-06		A7
1299	" "	14	SESE	1890-06-06		A7
1297	" "	14	SENE	1890-06-06		A7
1301	WILLIAMS, John T	17	S½NE	1890-10-11		A7
1300	" "	17	N½SE	1890-10-11		A7
1307	WILLIAMSON, Sarah	29	NESE	1853-11-01		A8
1306	" "	29	SENE	1853-11-01		A8
1305	" "	29	W½NE	1853-11-01		A8
1308	WILSON, Andrew J	14	SWNW	1872-03-15		A7
1309	" "	15	W½NE	1872-03-15		A7
1311	WILSON, William D	19	NENE	1884-10-11		A1
1310	" "	19	SWNE	1884-10-11		A1
1312	" "	20	NWNW	1884-10-11		A1
1313	WISEMAN, Joseph A	36	S½SE	1889-01-12		A7
1314	" "	36	SESW	1889-01-12		A7
1315	YEAGER, Robert L	8	E½NE	1891-05-05		A7
1316	" "	9	W½NW	1891-05-05		A7
1317	YOUNG, David W	36	NENW	1899-05-12		A7
1318	ZEEBE, Bernhard	10	NW	1896-08-28		A7

Patent Map

T26-N R9-W
5th PM 26-N 9-W Meridian
Map Group 6

Township Statistics

Parcels Mapped	:	319
Number of Patents	:	174
Number of Individuals	:	184
Patentees Identified	:	176
Number of Surnames	:	135
Multi-Patentee Parcels	:	11
Oldest Patent Date	:	11/1/1853
Most Recent Patent	:	8/9/1907
Block/Lot Parcels	:	37
Cities and Town	:	2
Cemeteries	:	3

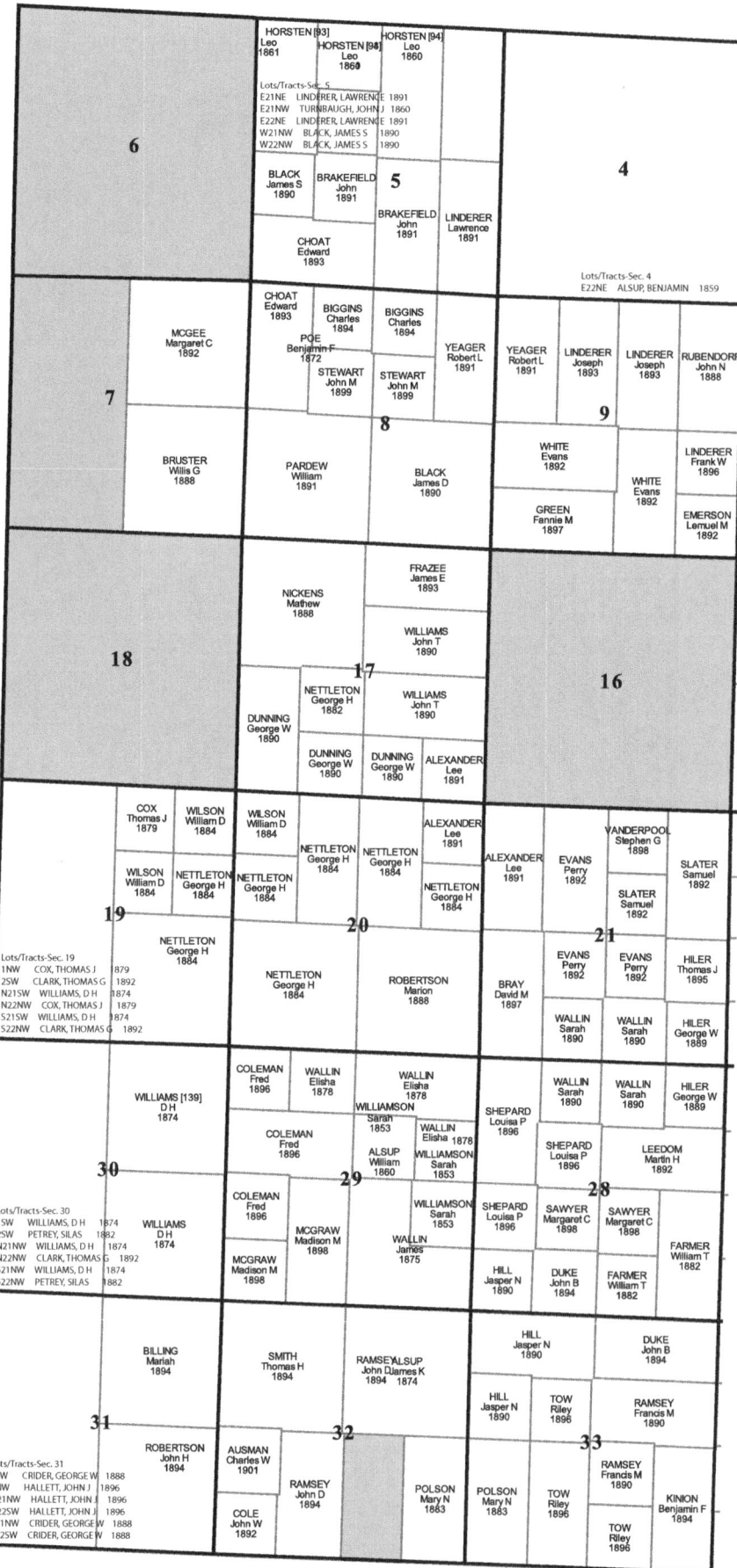

Lots/Tracts-Sec. 3
1NE   SMITH, GEORGE W   1888
1NW   WHITE, ALICE   1892
2NW   ALSUP, BENJAMIN   1860
E22NE GALESBERRY, WILLIAM 1853
W22NE SIMMONS, WESLEY N 1859

Lots/Tracts-Sec. 2
E21NE   DAVIDSON, THOMAS W 1894
E22NE   MILLER, JAMES H   1860
E22NW   BOLIN, H W   1872
W21NE   MULLINS, JOHN W   1900
W22NE   HOOD, JESSE   1885
W22NW   GOODSBERRY, WILLIAM H1859 ✓

Lots/Tracts-Sec. 1
1NW   LIVINGSTON, HENRY B 1882
2NW   MILLER, JAMES H   1860

Section 3

STRIEBEL
Stephan
1892

JONES
William
1907

SMITH
George W
1888

LONG
Ezekiel M
1892

Section 2

LIVINGSTON
Thomas E
1876

LIVINGSTON
Thomas E
1876

MULLINS
John W
1900

DAVIDSON
Thomas W
1894

DEARING
George B
1891

RIDGEWAY
Samuel
1894

RIDGEWAY
Samuel
1894

Section 1

DAVIDSON
Thomas W
1894

PAINE
John W
1894

PAINE
John W
1894

COFFMAN
David H
1875

BRESSLER
W M
1893

BRITT
Martin V
1891

BRITT
Martin V
1891

SMITH
Logan M
1894

SMITH
Andrew J
1860

Section 10

ZEEBE
Bernhard
1896

LONG
Ezekiel M
1892

LONG
Ezekiel M
1892

REICH
Charles
1898

LINDERER
Frank W
1896

EMERSON
Marion G
1892

EMERSON
Lemuel M
1892

LINDERER
Frank W
1896

Section 11

DEARING
George B
1891

RIDGEWAY
Samuel
1894

RIDGEWAY
Samuel
1894

STAPLES
Samuel M
1900

DUNNE
James B
1885

HOMESLEY
Richard
1890

DUNNE
James B
1885

LONGDEN
Willoughby
1902

HOMESLEY
Richard
1890

FRUSHOUR
John W
1894

Section 12

BELL
John P
1892

BRITT
Martin V
1891

SMITH
Logan M
1894

HARLOW
William J
1880

CROUCH
Charles W
1894

MILLER
Alfred L
1894

HARLOW
William J
1880

HARLOW
Thomas
1875

Section 15

EMERSON
Lemuel H
1878

WILSON
Andrew J
1872

PRICE
J H
1893

MCCLELLAN
Charles S
1895

SIMMONS
Wesley N
1860

SNODGRASS
Robert
1892

STOVALL
David W
1892

ROWLETT
Newton H
1892

ROWLETT
Newton H
1892

Section 14

FRUSHOUR
John W
1894

RANEY
C C
1869

PRUITT
Abigail
1859

WILSON
Andrew J
1872

PREWITT
Abigail
1860

WHITE
Columbus L
1888

WILLIAMS
John B
1890

KEITHLY
Levi
1896

FRAZEE
Enson
1902

WILLIAMS
John B
1890

KEITHLY
Levi
1896

KEITHLY
Levi
1896

WILLIAMS
John B
1890

Section 13

MARTIN
Richard D
1873

HINDS [117]
Viann
1878

HARLOW
Thomas
1875

CRISPIN
Alonzo J
1901

HINDS [117]
Viann
1878

MARTIN [36]
John L
1861

CRUM
James
1897

MARTIN [36]
John L
1861

CRUM
James
1897

Section 22

SLATER
Samuel
1892

BROWER
Charles
1891

MILKS
Jerome
1890

ROWLETT
Newton H
1892

HILER
Thomas J
1892

MILKS
Jerome
1890

BROWER
Charles
1891

MILKS
Jerome
1890

KEITHLY
Corydon A
1890

HILER
Samuel
1900

EPPS
Newton C
1873

CONLEY
John T
1900

Section 23

RUDD
James M
1891

WILL
Francis M
1891

MCCLELLAN
William H
1895

MCCLELLAN
William H
1895

FARMER
Frank
1895

MEINECKE
Franz
1896

Section 24

MILLER
Isaac L
1874

MILLER
Henry L
1892

BRYAN
Thomas P
1890

CANTRELL
Thomas J
1875

Section 27

HILER
George W
1889

EPPS
Newton C
1874

KEITHLY
Corydon A
1890

LEEDOM
Martin H
1892

EPPS
Newton C
1874

EPPS
Newton C
1874

LEEDOM
Martin H
1892

THOMPSON
Malcolm
1901

THOMPSON
Malcolm
1901

POTTLE
Thomas
1874

FARMER
William T
1882

KINION
Benjamin
1890

BROONER
Henry
1893

WHEELER
Mary C
1900

Section 26

FARMER
Frank
1895

MEINECKE
Franz
1896

BRADSHAW
Thomas L
1891

SWEARINGEN
Henry W
1895

POTTLE
Thomas
1874

BRADSHAW
Thomas L
1891

POTTLE
Thomas
1874

CALLAHAN [32]
John L
1862

SWEARINGEN
Henry W
1895

CALLAHAN [32]
John L
1862

Section 25

BRYAN
William E
1900

BRYAN
William E
1900

TUCKER
William H
1889

SWEARINGEN
Henry W
1895

SALTSMAN
Daniel A
1875

SALTSMAN
Daniel A
1875

HEROD
James
1860

HEROD
James
1860

MOREHEAD
John D
1888

Section 34

KINION
Benjamin
1890

BROONER
Henry
1893

RAMSEY
Francis M
1890

KINION
Benjamin
1890

BROONER
Allen D
1888

WARD
Joseph
1890

KINION
Benjamin F
1894

BROONER
Allen D
1898

WARD
Joseph
1890

BROONER
Allen D
1898

SWEARINGEN
John S
1895

LOVEL
Juda
1888

Section 35

BROONER
Henry
1893

REYNOLDS
John F
1888

CALLAHAN [32]
John L
1862

SWEARINGEN
Erasmus
1888

WARD
Joseph
1890

REYNOLDS
John F
1888

FIELDS
Thomas J
1900

LOVEL
Juda
1888

REYNOLDS
John F
1888

FIELDS
Thomas J
1900

LOVEL
Juda
1888

HILER
Henry F
1895

HILER
Henry F
1895

SWEARINGEN
Samuel
1879

Section 36

SWEARINGEN
Erasmus
1888

YOUNG
David W
1899

ROBEY
James N
1888

SWEARINGEN
Erasmus
1888

HUFF
William
1881

HUFF
William
1881

HENSLEY
William S
1896

SWEARINGEN
Erasmus
1888

HUFF
William
1881

HUFF
William
1881

HENSLEY
William S
1896

SWEARINGEN
Samuel
1879

WISEMAN
Joseph A
1889

WISEMAN
Joseph A
1889

Helpful Hints

1. This Map's INDEX can be found on the preceding pages.

2. Refer to Map "C" to see where this Township lies within Howell County, Missouri.

3. Numbers within square brackets [   ] denote a multi-patentee land parcel (multi-owner). Refer to Appendix "C" for a full list of members in this group.

4. Areas that look to be crowded with Patentees usually indicate multiple sales of the same parcel (Re-issues) or Overlapping parcels. See this Township's Index for an explanation of these and other circumstances that might explain "odd" groupings of Patentees on this map.

Legend

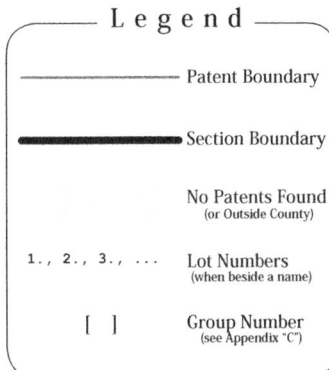

——————— Patent Boundary

━━━━━━━ Section Boundary

No Patents Found
(or Outside County)

1., 2., 3., ...   Lot Numbers
(when beside a name)

[   ]   Group Number
(see Appendix "C")

Scale: Section = 1 mile X 1 mile
(generally, with some exceptions)

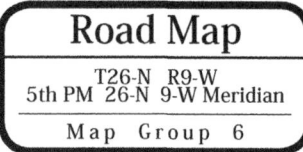

Road Map

T26-N R9-W
5th PM 26-N 9-W Meridian

Map Group 6

Cities & Towns
Burnham
Hutton Valley

Cemeteries
Burnham Cemetery
Epps Cemetery
Moffett Graveyard

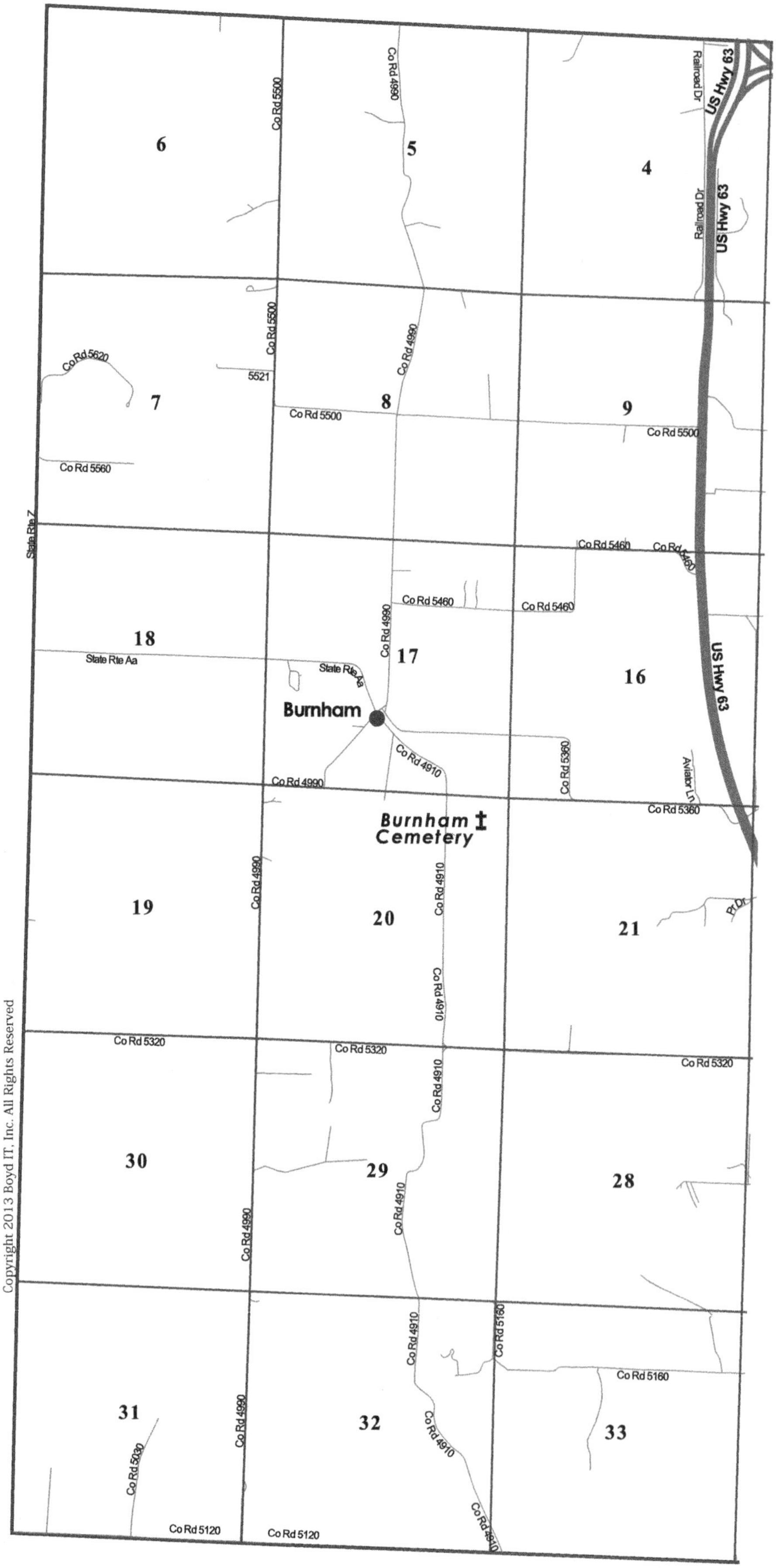

6

5

4

7

8

9

18

17

16

Burnham

Burnham ‡ Cemetery

19

20

21

30

29

28

31

32

33

Co Rd 5500

Co Rd 4990

Railroad Dr

US Hwy 63

Co Rd 5620

Co Rd 5500

5521

Co Rd 5560

Co Rd 5500

Co Rd 5500

State Rte 7

Co Rd 5460

Co Rd 4990

Co Rd 5460

Co Rd 5460

Co Rd 5460

State Rte Aa

State Rte Aa

US Hwy 63

Co Rd 4910

Co Rd 4990

Co Rd 5360

Co Rd 5360

Co Rd 4990

Co Rd 4910

Co Rd 5320

Co Rd 5320

Co Rd 4910

Co Rd 5320

Co Rd 4990

Co Rd 4910

Co Rd 4990

Co Rd 5160

Co Rd 5160

Co Rd 4910

Co Rd 5320

Co Rd 4990

Co Rd 4910

Co Rd 5120

Co Rd 5120

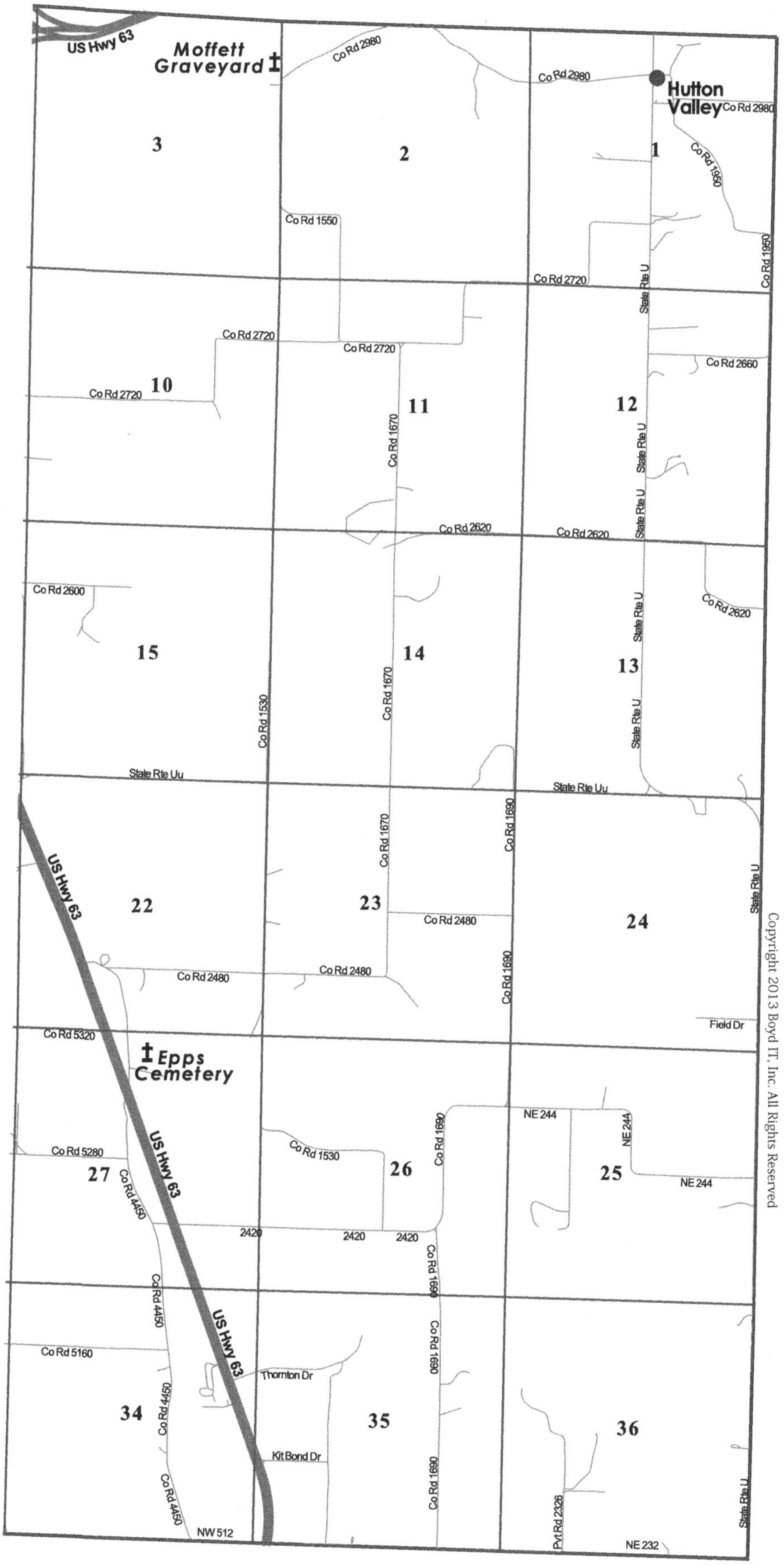

US Hwy 63

Moffett Graveyard ☩

Co Rd 2980

Co Rd 2980

Co Rd 2980

Hutton Valley Co Rd 2980

Co Rd 1950

3

2

1

Co Rd 1550

Co Rd 1950

Co Rd 2720

State Rte U

Co Rd 2720

Co Rd 2720

Co Rd 2720

Co Rd 2660

10

Co Rd 2720

11

Co Rd 1670

12

State Rte U

Co Rd 2620

Co Rd 2620

State Rte U

Co Rd 2600

Co Rd 2620

15

14

Co Rd 1670

13

Co Rd 1530

State Rte U

State Rte Uu

State Rte Uu

US Hwy 63

Co Rd 1670

Co Rd 1690

State Rte U

22

23

24

Co Rd 2480

Co Rd 1690

Co Rd 2480

Co Rd 2480

Field Dr

Co Rd 5320

☩ **Epps Cemetery**

NE 244

Co Rd 1530

NE 244

Co Rd 5280

Co Rd 1690

26

25

NE 244

27

Co Rd 4460

US Hwy 63

2420

2420

2420

Co Rd 1690

Co Rd 5160

Co Rd 4460

US Hwy 63

Co Rd 4450

Thornton Dr

Co Rd 1690

34

35

36

Kit Bond Dr

Co Rd 4460

NW 512

Pvt Rd 2326

NE 232

State Rte U

Copyright 2013 Boyd IT, Inc. All Rights Reserved

Copyright 2013 Boyd IT, Inc. All Rights Reserved

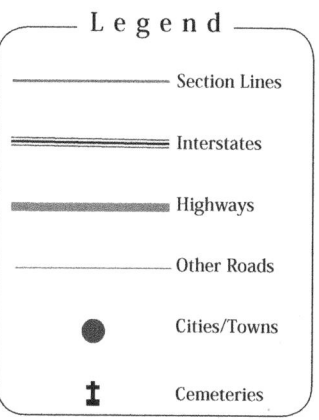

Helpful Hints

1. This road map has a number of uses, but primarily it is to help you: a) find the present location of land owned by your ancestors (at least the general area), b) find cemeteries and city-centers, and c) estimate the route/roads used by Census-takers & tax-assessors.

2. If you plan to travel to Howell County to locate cemeteries or land parcels, please pick up a modern travel map for the area before you do. Mapping old land parcels on modern maps is not as exact a science as you might think. Just the slightest variations in public land survey coordinates, estimates of parcel boundaries, or road-map deviations can greatly alter a map's representation of how a road either does or doesn't cross a particular parcel of land.

L e g e n d

——————— Section Lines

════════ Interstates

━━━━━━━ Highways

——————— Other Roads

● Cities/Towns

☩ Cemeteries

Scale: Section = 1 mile X 1 mile
(generally, with some exceptions)

Historical Map

T26-N   R9-W
5th PM 26-N 9-W Meridian

Map Group 6

Cities & Towns
Burnham
Hutton Valley

Cemeteries
Burnham Cemetery
Epps Cemetery
Moffett Graveyard

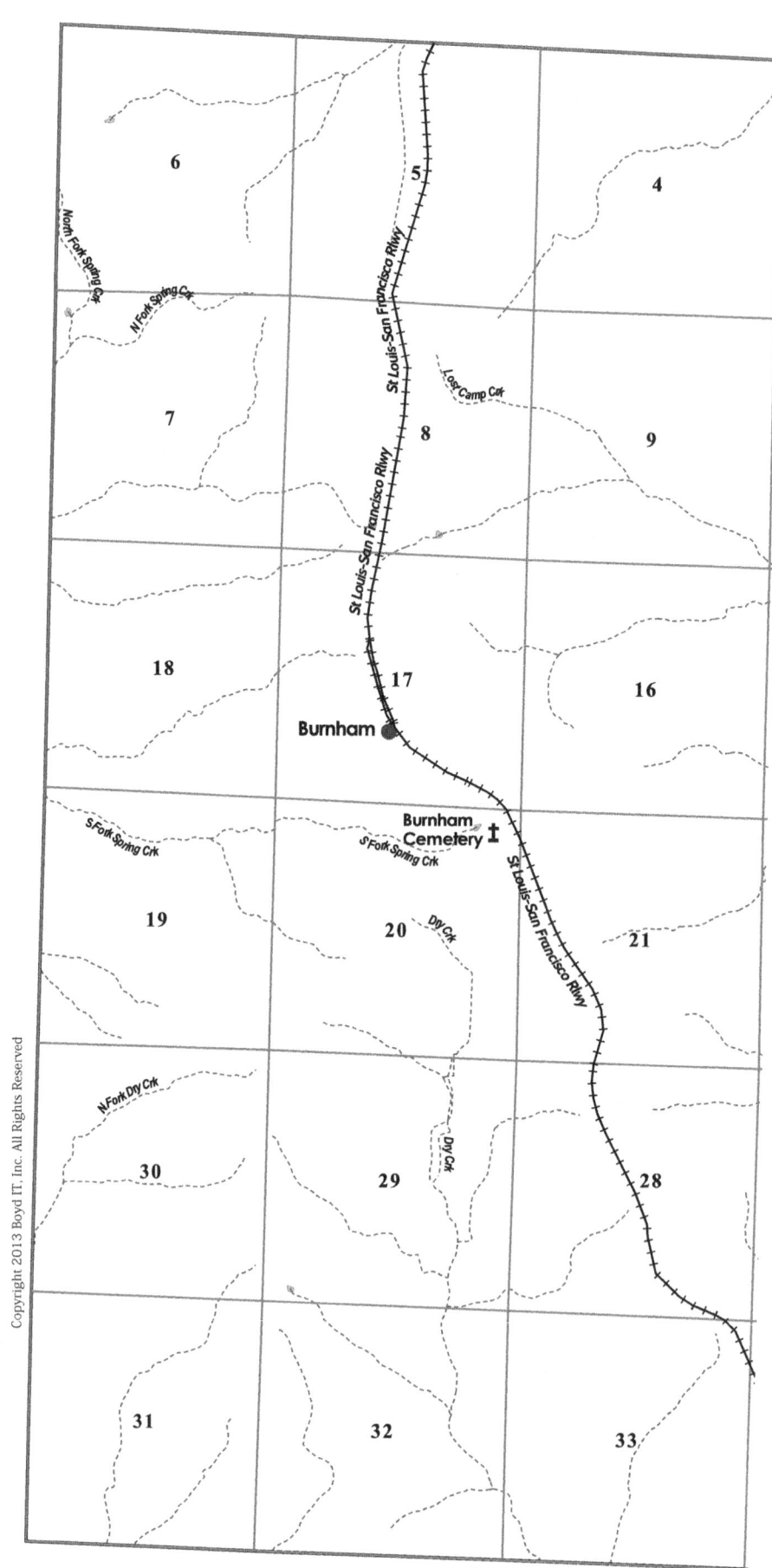

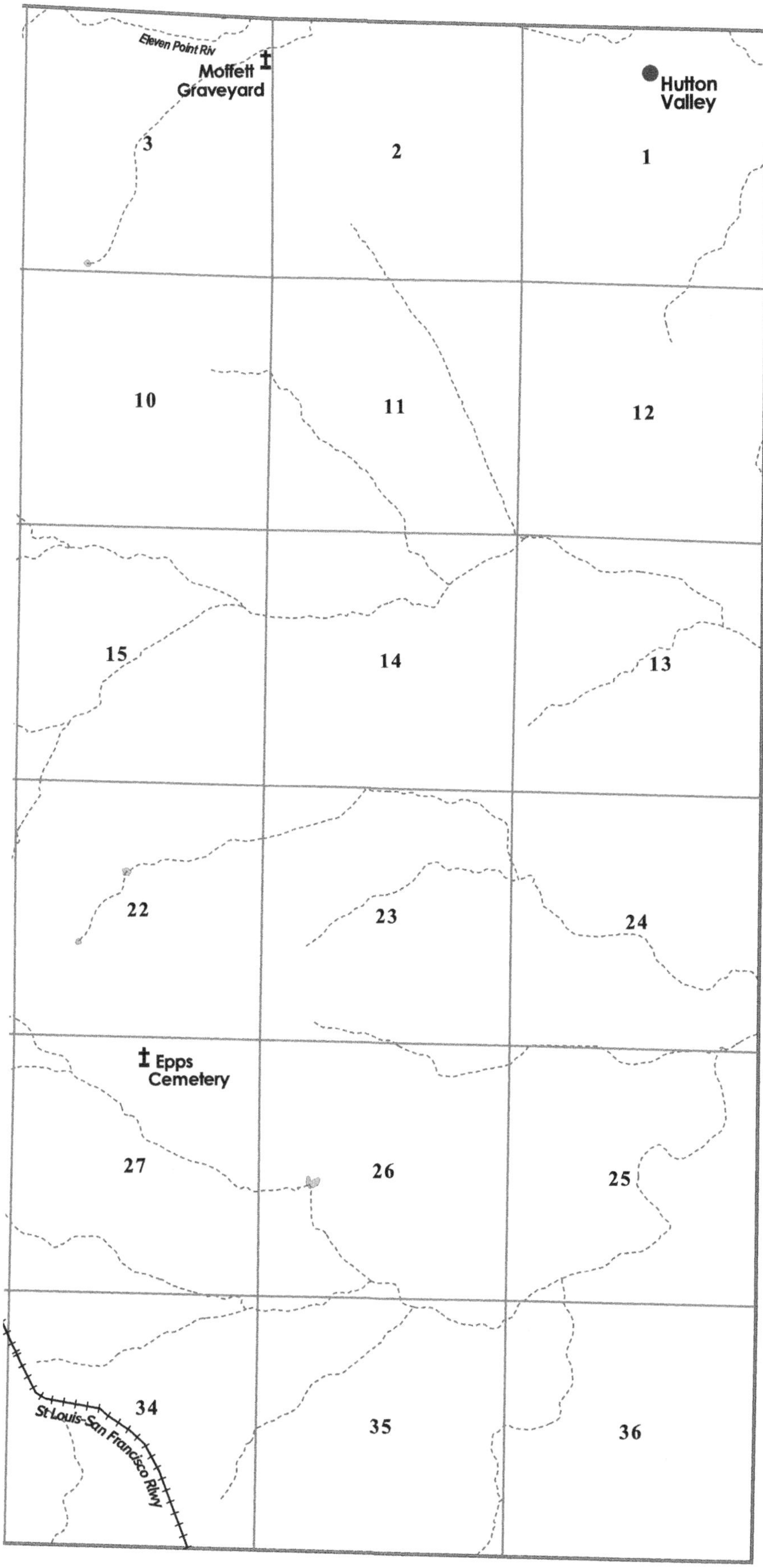

Eleven Point Riv

✝ Moffett
Graveyard

● Hutton
Valley

3

2

1

10

11

12

15

14

13

22

23

24

✝ Epps
Cemetery

27

26

25

St Louis-San Francisco Rlwy

34

35

36

Helpful Hints

1. This Map takes a different look at the same Congressional Township displayed in the preceding two maps. It presents features that can help you better envision the historical development of the area: a) Water-bodies (lakes & ponds), b) Water-courses (rivers, streams, etc.), c) Railroads, d) City/ town center-points (where they were oftentimes located when first settled), and e) Cemeteries.

2. Using this "Historical" map in tandem with this Township's Patent Map and Road Map, may lead you to some interesting discoveries. You will often find roads, towns, cemeteries, and waterways are named after nearby landowners: sometimes those names will be the ones you are researching. See how many of these research gems you can find here in Howell County.

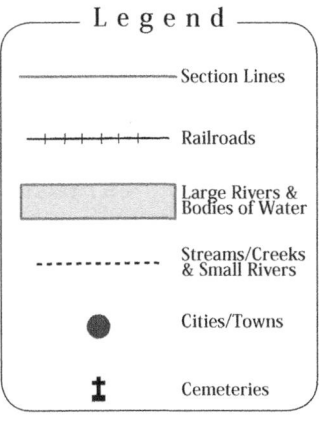

L e g e n d

———————— Section Lines

+—+—+—+—+— Railroads

▭ Large Rivers & Bodies of Water

- - - - - - - Streams/Creeks & Small Rivers

● Cities/Towns

✝ Cemeteries

Scale: Section = 1 mile X 1 mile
(there are some exceptions)

Map Group 7: Index to Land Patents

Township 26-North Range 8-West (5th PM 26-N 8-W)

After you locate an individual in this Index, take note of the Section and Section Part then proceed to the Land Patent map on the pages immediately following. You should have no difficulty locating the corresponding parcel of land.

The "For More Info" Column will lead you to more information about the underlying Patents. See the *Legend* at right, and the "How to Use this Book" chapter, for more information.

```
                        LEGEND
               "For More Info . . . " column
A = Authority (Legislative Act, See Appendix "A")
B = Block or Lot (location in Section unknown)
C = Cancelled Patent
F = Fractional Section
G = Group  (Multi-Patentee Patent, see Appendix "C")
V = Overlaps another Parcel
R = Re-Issued (Parcel patented more than once)

(A & G items require you to look in the Appendixes referred
to above. All other Letter-designations followed by a number
require you to locate line-items in this index that possess
the ID number found after the letter).
```

ID	Individual in Patent	Sec.	Sec. Part	Date Issued	Other Counties	For More Info . . .
1319	ACKLIN, Thomas H	8	NWNW	1894-11-30		A7
7176	ACKLIN, William H	4	E21NE	1896-06-04		A7
7177	" "	4	E22NE	1896-06-04		A7
1320	" "	4	E½SE	1896-06-04		A7
1322	BARKING, Herman	32	E½NE	1891-05-25		A7 G13
1321	" "	32	NESE	1891-05-25		A7 G13
1323	" "	33	NWSW	1891-05-25		A7 G13
1325	BARKING, Johannah	32	E½NE	1891-05-25		A7 G13
1324	" "	32	NESE	1891-05-25		A7 G13
1326	" "	33	NWSW	1891-05-25		A7 G13
1327	BARTON, John R	34	SESW	1895-05-28		A7
1329	BLYTHE, Martha J	13	W½NE	1885-06-20		A7 G19
1328	" "	13	E½NW	1885-06-20		A7 G19
1330	BOATMAN, Henry	25	SWSE	1859-03-01		A1
1331	" "	36	NWNE	1859-03-01		A1
1332	BOATMAN, John W	25	SESW	1885-02-25		A7
1333	" "	36	SENW	1885-02-25		A7
1334	BOATMAN, Samuel	36	NESE	1857-04-15		A1
1335	BOATMAN, Samuel J	25	SESE	1882-09-30		A1
1340	" "	36	SWNE	1861-02-01		A1
1339	" "	36	SESE	1861-02-01		A1
1338	" "	36	NWSE	1860-10-01		A1
1337	" "	36	E½NE	1876-02-01		A7
1336	" "	36	NENW	1876-03-15		A1
1343	BOLERJACK, Thomas C	12	E½NW	1884-11-01		A7
1344	" "	12	NESE	1884-11-01		A7
1345	" "	12	NWNE	1884-11-01		A7
1346	BOLERJACK, Thomas S	11	NESE	1892-09-09		A7
1347	" "	11	SENE	1892-09-09		A7
1348	" "	12	W½SW	1892-09-09		A7
1351	BOLIN, Hercules W	8	SWNE	1891-06-09		A7
1349	" "	8	S½NW	1891-06-09		A7
1350	" "	8	NESW	1891-06-09		A7
1354	BOSS, Theodore	27	SWNE	1896-01-14		A7
1353	" "	27	NESW	1896-01-14		A7
1352	" "	27	E½NW	1896-01-14		A7
1356	BOYD, William R	32	E½SW	1895-09-04		A7
1355	" "	32	SENW	1895-09-04		A7
1357	BRAMLETT, Rufus	33	NW	1889-01-12		A7
7136	BUFORD, William	18	N22SW	1859-09-01		A1
7133	" "	18	N21SW	1859-09-01		A1
1359	CAMPBELL, Susan E	29	S½NE	1891-06-09		A7 G35
1358	" "	29	SWNE	1891-06-09		A7 G35
1360	" "	29	NWSE	1891-06-09		A7 G35
1362	CAMPBELL, William	29	S½NE	1891-06-09		A7 G35
1363	" "	29	NWSE	1891-06-09		A7 G35

ID	Individual in Patent	Sec.	Sec. Part	Date Issued	Other Counties	For More Info . . .
1361	CAMPBELL, William (Cont'd)	29	SWNE	1891-06-09		A7 G35
1364	CANTRELL, Henry J	15	SW	1889-06-22		A7
1365	CANTRELL, William F	15	SWNE	1877-08-01		A7
1366	" "	15	W½NW	1877-08-01		A7
1367	" "	15	SENW	1877-08-01		A7
1368	CARTMILL, Charles	27	SWNW	1890-12-31		A7 G39
1370	" "	28	E½NE	1890-12-31		A7 G39
1369	" "	28	NESE	1890-12-31		A7 G39
1371	CARTMILL, Elzy	14	NWSE	1889-07-26		A7
1372	" "	14	SENW	1889-07-26		A7
1373	" "	14	W½NE	1889-07-26		A7
1374	CARTMILL, Emma E	27	SWNW	1890-12-31		A7 G39
1376	" "	28	NESE	1890-12-31		A7 G39
1375	" "	28	E½NE	1890-12-31		A7 G39
1380	CLARK, George	29	SWSW	1888-12-06		A1
1377	" "	29	E½SW	1889-01-12		A7
1378	" "	29	S½NW	1889-01-12		A7
1379	" "	29	NWSW	1886-11-19		A1
7157	CLARK, William	3	E22NW	1898-01-26		A7
7155	" "	3	2NE	1898-01-26		A7
1381	CLICK, George W	30	SESE	1885-02-10		A7 G49
1382	" "	31	NENE	1885-02-10		A7 G49
1383	" "	32	W½NW	1885-02-10		A7 G49
1384	CLICK, Nancy C	30	SESE	1885-02-10		A7 G49
1385	" "	31	NENE	1885-02-10		A7 G49
1386	" "	32	W½NW	1885-02-10		A7 G49
1387	COBB, John T	28	W½SE	1880-11-20		A7
1388	" "	28	SESW	1880-11-20		A7
1389	" "	33	NWNE	1880-11-20		A7
1390	COLLINS, William	24	E½SW	1910-03-10		A7
1391	COOSE, Enoch	20	SE	1894-05-18		A7
1392	COUNTS, James E	34	S½SE	1891-05-25		A7
1393	COX, James	17	NWNE	1892-09-09		A7
1395	" "	8	N½SE	1892-09-09		A7
1394	" "	8	SWSE	1892-09-09		A7
1396	CROWDER, Joshua T	13	W½NE	1885-06-20		A7 G19
1397	" "	13	E½NW	1885-06-20		A7 G19
1398	CROWDER, Martha	13	E½NW	1885-06-20		A7 G19
1399	" "	13	W½NE	1885-06-20		A7 G19
7139	CRUM, James	18	S22SW	1897-08-16		A7
1400	DANIEL, Newton W	6	S½SE	1891-06-09		A7
1401	" "	7	NWNE	1891-06-09		A7
7205	" "	7	N21NW	1891-06-09		A7
7193	DAVIDSON, David L	6	1SW	1894-05-18		A7
7194	" "	6	2SW	1894-05-18		A7
1402	DAVIS, Francis M	26	SWSW	1860-08-01		A1
1403	" "	27	SESE	1860-08-01		A1
1404	DAVIS, James A	19	SWSE	1892-10-17		A7
1406	DEATON, George M	11	E½NW	1900-08-09		A7
1405	" "	11	W½NE	1900-08-09		A7
1407	DEATON, William P	1	SWSW	1894-05-18		A7
1408	" "	11	NENE	1894-05-18		A7
1409	" "	2	S½SE	1894-05-18		A7
1410	DENZEL, Catherine	34	SENW	1900-08-09		A7 G68
1413	" "	34	NWSE	1900-08-09		A7 G68
1412	" "	34	NESW	1900-08-09		A7 G68
1411	" "	34	SWNE	1900-08-09		A7 G68
1414	DENZEL, Edward	34	SENW	1900-08-09		A7 G68
1416	" "	34	NESW	1900-08-09		A7 G68
1417	" "	34	SWNE	1900-08-09		A7 G68
1415	" "	34	NWSE	1900-08-09		A7 G68
7144	DERINGER, William	19	S21NW	1890-10-11		A7
1418	" "	19	NWSE	1890-10-11		A7
7141	" "	19	N21SW	1890-10-11		A7
1419	DOWELL, George	11	SESE	1907-08-06		A1
1420	" "	13	NWNW	1907-08-06		A1
1421	" "	14	E½NE	1907-08-06		A1
1422	DOWELL, John H	11	NESW	1912-06-27		A7
1423	" "	11	NWSE	1912-06-27		A7
1425	DRENNEN, John P	20	W½NE	1860-02-15		A6
1424	" "	20	E½NW	1860-02-15		A6
1426	" "	20	NWNW	1859-11-01		A8
1429	DUNLAP, Delila	26	S½SE	1877-10-10		A7 G70

ID	Individual in Patent	Sec.	Sec. Part	Date Issued	Other Counties	For More Info . . .
1428	DUNLAP, Delila (Cont'd)	26	SENE	1877-10-10		A7 G70
1427	" "	26	NESE	1877-10-10		A7 G70
1431	DUNLAP, R M	26	SENE	1877-10-10		A7 G70
1430	" "	26	NESE	1877-10-10		A7 G70
1432	" "	26	S½SE	1877-10-10		A7 G70
1433	EDMONSTON, Frank W	32	NENW	1898-04-06		A7
1434	" "	32	NWNE	1898-04-06		A7
7138	ESTES, Thomas J	18	S22NW	1870-11-15		A1
7175	EVANS, J C	31	S22SW	1893-12-09		A1
1438	EVELAND, James L	23	NWSE	1898-07-25		A7
1437	" "	23	SWNE	1898-07-25		A7
1436	" "	23	SENW	1898-07-25		A7
1435	" "	23	NESW	1898-07-25		A7
1439	EVELAND, William P	10	SWSE	1901-03-23		A7
1440	" "	15	NENW	1901-03-23		A7
1441	" "	15	N½NE	1901-03-23		A7
1442	EVERED, Alfred C	17	NENE	1901-06-29		A1
1443	" "	8	SESE	1901-06-29		A1
1444	FARMER, John K	32	SESE	1901-11-08		A7
1445	FEATHER, Elsie M	23	SENE	1911-05-08		A1
1446	" "	24	SWNW	1911-05-08		A1
1447	FEATHER, Nancy L	10	W½NE	1910-03-10		A7 G78
1448	" "	10	SENE	1910-03-10		A7 G78
1449	" "	11	SWNW	1910-03-10		A7 G78
7184	FINDLEY, Manuel T	5	E22NW	1896-06-04		A7
7181	" "	5	2NE	1896-06-04		A7
1450	FLOOD, Jeremiah E	1	E½SE	1889-01-12		A7
1451	FLOOD, Thomas H	10	NENE	1901-03-23		A7
1452	" "	11	NWNW	1901-03-23		A7
1453	" "	2	S½SW	1901-03-23		A7
1454	GALBREATH, Robert G	13	NESE	1888-12-06		A1
1455	GAMBLE, James S	2	W½NW	1898-04-11		A7
7156	" "	3	E21NE	1898-04-11		A7
1456	GOBBEL, John A	15	SE	1881-10-06		A7
1458	GOODMAN, Joseph R	25	S½NW	1889-01-12		A7
1459	" "	25	NESW	1889-01-12		A7
1457	" "	25	SWNE	1889-01-12		A7
1460	GREEN, George S	5	E½SW	1857-03-10		A1
1461	GREEN, Learner R	6	NESE	1857-04-15		A1
1462	GREENWAY, Coatney M	8	SENE	1894-11-22		A1
1464	GULLEY, Henry C	14	W½NW	1896-01-14		A7
1463	" "	14	NENW	1896-01-14		A7
1465	" "	15	SENE	1896-01-14		A7
7202	GULLY, Pleasant N	6	W22NE	1883-08-13		A1
7203	" "	6	W22NW	1859-09-01		A1
7183	GULLY, Robert H	5	E21NW	1883-08-13		A1
1466	" "	5	E½SE	1884-02-15		A7
7182	" "	5	E21NE	1884-02-15		A7
1467	HAGAN, John	17	SWNW	1897-04-10		A7
1468	" "	17	E½NW	1897-04-10		A7
1469	" "	18	SENE	1897-04-10		A7
1471	HALE, Nicholas L	6	NWSE	1859-09-01		A1
1470	" "	6	SWNE	1859-09-01		A1
7190	HALE, Nickolas L	6	1NW	1862-10-10		A6
7197	" "	6	E22NW	1862-10-10		A6
1472	HARLEY, James A	21	SWNE	1891-08-19		A7
1473	" "	21	N½NE	1891-08-19		A7
1474	" "	22	NWNW	1891-08-19		A7
7204	HARLOW, Thomas	7	2SW	1875-02-15		A7
1475	HARLOW, William J	18	SENW	1870-11-01		A1
7179	HENDERSON, Bradford	4	W22NE	1900-08-09		A7
7178	" "	4	W21NE	1900-08-09		A7
1476	HENRY, Elizziebeth	24	NESE	1898-04-11		A7 G115
1477	" "	24	W½SE	1898-04-11		A7 G115
1478	" "	25	NWNE	1898-04-11		A7 G115
1481	HENRY, Nimrod B	36	SESW	1872-07-01		A7
1480	" "	36	N½SW	1872-07-01		A7
1479	" "	36	SWSE	1872-07-01		A7
1483	HENRY, Osburne	24	NESE	1898-04-11		A7 G115
1482	" "	24	W½SE	1898-04-11		A7 G115
1484	" "	25	NWNE	1898-04-11		A7 G115
1485	HEYING, William A	33	E½SE	1892-10-17		A7
1486	" "	34	SWSW	1892-10-17		A7

ID	Individual in Patent	Sec.	Sec. Part	Date Issued	Other Counties	For More Info . . .
7143	HODGES, Fleming	19	N22SW	1900-08-09		A7
7146	" "	19	S22NW	1900-08-09		A7
7149	HOKE, Leroy	2	E21NW	1901-03-23		A7
7129	HUGHES, George W	1	W22NE	1895-02-15		A7
7127	" "	1	E22NW	1895-02-15		A7
1487	JACKSON, A J	33	S½NE	1893-01-07		A7 G128
1488	" "	34	NWSW	1893-01-07		A7 G128
1489	" "	34	SWNW	1893-01-07		A7 G128
7126	JACKSON, Freeman B	1	E22NE	1893-09-01		A7
7125	" "	1	E21NE	1893-09-01		A7
1490	JACKSON, Susan	33	S½NE	1893-01-07		A7 G128
1491	" "	34	NWSW	1893-01-07		A7 G128
1492	" "	34	SWNW	1893-01-07		A7 G128
1493	JENKINS, John A	34	NESE	1890-01-10		A7
1494	" "	34	SENE	1890-01-10		A7
1495	" "	35	N½SW	1890-01-10		A7
1497	JENKINS, Mary	21	SENE	1890-01-10		A7 G131
1496	" "	21	NESE	1890-01-10		A7 G131
1498	" "	22	SWNW	1890-01-10		A7 G131
1499	" "	22	NWSW	1890-01-10		A7 G131
1501	JENKINS, Thomas M	21	SENE	1890-01-10		A7 G131
1500	" "	21	NESE	1890-01-10		A7 G131
1502	" "	22	SWNW	1890-01-10		A7 G131
1503	" "	22	NWSW	1890-01-10		A7 G131
1505	JEREMIAH, Pearson A	11	SESW	1891-08-24		A1
1504	" "	11	SWSE	1891-08-24		A1
1506	JONES, Gilroy C	25	SWSW	1889-06-22		A7
1507	" "	36	NWNW	1889-06-22		A7
1508	JONES, John L	4	E½SW	1875-08-10		A7
1509	" "	4	W½SE	1875-08-10		A7
1510	JONES, Thompson	36	SWNW	1860-08-01		A1
1511	KILE, Harvey	20	SENE	1898-04-06		A7
1513	" "	21	S½NW	1898-04-06		A7
1512	" "	21	NENW	1898-04-06		A7
7135	KILE, Martha	18	N22NW	1893-12-19		A7 G135
7132	" "	18	N21NW	1893-12-19		A7 G135
1514	" "	7	SWSE	1893-12-19		A7 G135
7210	" "	7	S21SW	1893-12-19		A7 G135
7131	KILE, Walter L	18	N21NW	1893-12-19		A7 G135
7134	" "	18	N22NW	1893-12-19		A7 G135
7209	" "	7	S21SW	1893-12-19		A7 G135
1515	" "	7	SWSE	1893-12-19		A7 G135
1516	LEE, Herbert M	10	W½	1885-07-27		A1
1517	" "	9	E½NW	1885-07-27		A1
1518	" "	9	E½	1885-07-27		A1
1519	" "	9	SESW	1885-07-27		A1
1521	LORD, Tamson A	22	NENW	1889-01-12		A7 G141
1520	" "	22	N½NE	1889-01-12		A7 G141
1522	" "	23	NWNW	1889-01-12		A7 G141
1523	MARAT, William	24	SWSW	1912-08-26		A7
1524	" "	25	N½NW	1912-08-26		A7
1526	MARKHAM, Edwin C	13	SESE	1893-01-21		A1
1525	" "	13	SWSE	1893-01-21		A1
1527	" "	24	E½NE	1893-01-21		A1
1528	MCCLANAHAN, Mary C	20	E½SW	1905-03-30		A7
1529	MCGOWAN, George B	35	SENE	1860-08-01		A1
1530	MCGOWEN, George B	35	SE	1859-03-01		A1
1531	MCGUIRE, Michael R	36	SWSW	1871-10-20		A1
1532	MCMURTRY, Isaac W	14	SW	1888-11-27		A7
1534	MCMURTRY, James U	10	E½SE	1885-12-19		A7
1533	" "	10	NWSE	1885-12-19		A7
1535	" "	11	SWSW	1885-12-19		A7
1537	MCMURTRY, John J	12	W½SE	1897-04-02		A7
1536	" "	12	E½SW	1897-04-02		A7
1538	MCMURTRY, Nancy L	10	SENE	1910-03-10		A7 G78
1539	" "	10	W½NE	1910-03-10		A7 G78
1540	" "	11	SWNW	1910-03-10		A7 G78
1541	MILLER, Frank D	21	S½SW	1896-09-29		A7
1542	" "	28	W½NW	1896-09-29		A7
1543	MILLER, Harriet L	18	SE	1882-09-30		A7
1544	MILLER, Henry	19	NESE	1908-05-25		A1
7145	MILLER, James L	19	S21SW	1902-11-25		A7
7147	" "	19	S22SW	1902-11-25		A7

ID	Individual in Patent	Sec.	Sec. Part	Date Issued	Other Counties	For More Info . . .
7164	MILLER, James L (Cont'd)	30	N22NW	1902-11-25		A7
7163	" "	30	N21NW	1902-11-25		A7
1545	MILLER, William L	19	SESE	1874-01-10		A7
1546	" "	20	SWSW	1874-01-10		A7
1547	" "	30	N½NE	1874-01-10		A7
1548	MILLSPAUGH, William H	30	N½SE	1892-10-03		A1
1549	" "	30	S½NE	1892-10-03		A1
1550	MODRALL, Flora B	31	SESE	1895-05-28		A7 G152
1551	" "	32	W½SW	1895-05-28		A7 G152
1553	MODRALL, Henry W	32	W½SE	1879-12-15		A7
1552	" "	32	SWNE	1879-12-15		A7
1555	MODRALL, John R	31	NESE	1898-04-11		A7
1554	" "	31	SENE	1898-04-11		A7
1556	MODRALL, Nancy C	30	SESE	1885-02-10		A7 G49
1557	" "	31	NENE	1885-02-10		A7 G49
1558	" "	32	W½NW	1885-02-10		A7 G49
7165	MOREHEAD, John D	30	N22SW	1888-12-06		A1
7166	" "	30	S21NW	1888-12-06		A1
1559	MORGAN, Richard L	28	W½SW	1877-04-05		A7
1560	" "	29	NESE	1877-04-05		A7
1562	MULLANY, Michael	24	E½NW	1890-01-10		A7
1561	" "	24	W½NE	1890-01-10		A7
7167	MULLINIX, Abram	30	S22NW	1893-12-09		A1
7187	MYERS, John	5	W22NW	1876-07-25		A7
7186	" "	5	W21NW	1876-07-25		A7
7195	" "	6	E21NE	1876-07-25		A7
7160	NEWTON, Jonathan R	30	1SW	1894-05-18		A7 G154
7168	" "	30	S22SW	1894-05-18		A7 G154
1563	" "	30	SWSE	1894-05-18		A7 G154
7162	NEWTON, Lucy J	30	1SW	1894-05-18		A7 G154
7169	" "	30	S22SW	1894-05-18		A7 G154
1564	" "	30	SWSE	1894-05-18		A7 G154
1565	ODOM, Isaac	5	W½SW	1875-02-15		A7 G155
1566	ODOM, Mary J	5	W½SW	1875-02-15		A7 G155
7196	OGLE, Perry	6	E22NE	1882-06-10		A1
1568	OKES, Tamson A	22	NENW	1889-01-12		A7 G141
1567	" "	22	N½NE	1889-01-12		A7 G141
1569	" "	23	NWNW	1889-01-12		A7 G141
1570	OVERMAN, Flora B	31	SESE	1895-05-28		A7 G152
1571	" "	32	W½SW	1895-05-28		A7 G152
1572	PIERCE, John B	35	S½SW	1896-01-14		A7
1573	PITTS, William	13	NWSE	1901-05-27		A1
1574	POE, Jesse	24	SESE	1876-11-03		A7
1576	" "	25	E½NE	1876-11-03		A7
1575	" "	25	NWSW	1871-10-20		A1
1577	" "	35	NENE	1871-10-20		A1
1578	POLLOCK, Francis M	35	SWNE	1872-08-30		A1
7206	PUGH, John W	7	N21SW	1892-09-09		A7
1580	" "	7	NWSE	1892-09-09		A7
1579	" "	7	E½SE	1892-09-09		A7
1581	RAINBOLT, John	33	SWSW	1894-05-18		A7
7189	RAMSBURG, Edward	6	1NW	1862-10-10		A6
7198	" "	6	E22NW	1862-10-10		A6
7192	RAMSBURG, Joseph	6	1NW	`		A6 C
7200	" "	6	E22NW	`		A6 C
1582	RAY, Sarah J	31	SWSE	1902-08-22		A7 G162
1583	RAY, William R	31	SWSE	1902-08-22		A7 G162
1584	REED, Albert B	17	N½SE	1894-05-18		A7
1585	" "	17	S½NE	1894-05-18		A7
1586	REED, John L	19	E½NE	1902-02-12		A7
1587	" "	20	SWNW	1902-02-12		A7
1588	" "	20	NWSW	1902-02-12		A7
1589	REESE, J P	1	W½SE	1876-09-06		A7
1590	" "	1	E½SW	1876-09-06		A7
7180	REESE, John L	4	W22NW	1861-05-01		A1
7130	RILEY, James	1	W22NW	1860-08-01		A1
7137	RINCK, David K	18	S21SW	1892-01-05		A7
7140	" "	19	N21NW	1892-01-05		A7
7142	" "	19	N22NW	1892-01-05		A7
1591	" "	19	NWNE	1892-01-05		A7
1592	ROACH, Elijah C	1	NWSW	1860-08-01		A1
7159	ROBBINS, John B	3	W22NW	1888-12-06		A1
7173	ROBEY, James N	31	2NW	1888-12-06		A7

ID	Individual in Patent	Sec.	Sec. Part	Date Issued	Other Counties	For More Info . . .
1593	ROHR, Catherine	34	SENW	1900-08-09		A7 G68
1596	" "	34	NWSE	1900-08-09		A7 G68
1595	" "	34	SWNE	1900-08-09		A7 G68
1594	" "	34	NESW	1900-08-09		A7 G68
1597	ROTHWELL, George O	21	SESE	1907-12-05		A7
1598	" "	22	S½SW	1907-12-05		A7
1599	" "	22	SWSE	1907-12-05		A7
1600	ROTHWELL, George W	17	SW	1888-11-27		A7
1601	ROWLETT, John B	13	N½SW	1902-05-21		A7
1602	" "	13	SWNW	1902-05-21		A7
1603	" "	14	NESE	1902-05-21		A7
7124	SHERRELL, Alexander	1	1NW	1889-01-12		A7
7128	" "	1	W21NE	1889-01-12		A7
1605	SHERRELL, Isaiah	12	NW	1889-01-12		A7
1606	SHIPMAN, Daniel	7	E½NE	1894-09-18		A7
7208	" "	7	S21NW	1894-09-18		A7
1607	" "	7	SWNE	1894-09-18		A7
1608	SMITH, Jacob P	8	N½NE	1891-05-25		A7
1609	" "	8	NENW	1891-05-25		A7
1611	SMITH, Lanson H	8	S½SW	1872-07-01		A7
1610	" "	8	NWSW	1872-07-01		A7
1612	SMITH, Lawson	4	SWSW	1902-09-15		A7
1613	" "	9	NWNW	1902-09-15		A7
7207	SMITH, Logan M	7	N22NW	1894-05-23		A7
7185	SMITH, Sarah	5	W21NE	1875-08-10		A7
1614	" "	5	W½SE	1875-08-10		A7
1617	SMITH, William F	4	NENW	1893-03-03		A7
1615	" "	4	NWSW	1893-03-03		A7
1616	" "	4	S½NW	1893-03-03		A7
1618	SOOTS, John H	27	NWNW	1907-05-10		A1
1619	SPRADLING, Huston	27	W½SW	1874-04-20		A7
1620	" "	28	SESE	1874-04-20		A7
1621	" "	33	NENE	1874-04-20		A7
7154	STEVENS, Abram	3	1NW	1898-04-11		A7
7158	" "	3	W21NE	1898-04-11		A7
1622	STEVENSON, James R	2	NESE	1908-08-17		A1
1623	STINE, Thomas H	13	S½SW	1900-02-02		A7
1624	" "	14	S½SE	1900-02-02		A7
1625	STOCKTON, Harling S	9	NESW	1875-08-10		A7
1627	" "	9	W½SW	1875-08-10		A7
1626	" "	9	SWNW	1875-08-10		A7
7148	STOKES, Albert W	2	E21NE	1890-06-06		A7
7150	" "	2	E22NE	1890-06-06		A7
1628	SYMONDS, Isaac	29	E½NE	1900-08-09		A7
1629	TAYLOR, John	12	SESE	1859-09-01		A1
1631	" "	13	SENE	1860-08-01		A1
1630	" "	13	NENE	1859-09-01		A1
7170	TERRY, Lucy J	30	S22SW	1894-05-18		A7 G154
1632	" "	30	SWSE	1894-05-18		A7 G154
7161	" "	30	1SW	1894-05-18		A7 G154
1633	THOMAS, Job C	34	NENE	1891-05-25		A7
1634	THOMAS, Nathan	27	SWSE	1872-02-05		A1
1635	" "	34	NWNE	1872-02-05		A1
1636	" "	35	SENW	1872-02-05		A1
1637	" "	35	NWNE	1872-02-05		A1
1638	" "	35	W½NW	1872-02-05		A1
1639	THOMASSON, Augustine J	12	SWSW	1896-05-21		A1
1640	THOMPSON, William A	25	N½SE	1889-06-22		A7
1642	TURPEN, James U	22	SENW	1893-01-07		A7
1644	" "	22	NWSE	1893-01-07		A7
1641	" "	22	SWNE	1893-01-07		A7
1643	" "	22	NESW	1893-01-07		A7
1646	TURPEN, Martin	22	SENE	1891-05-25		A7
1645	" "	22	E½SE	1891-05-25		A7
1647	" "	23	SWNW	1891-05-25		A7
1648	ULRICH, Oren E	26	N½NW	1911-12-04		A7
1649	" "	27	N½NE	1911-12-04		A7
1650	ULRICH, Oscar E	2	NWSW	1913-01-06		A7
1651	ULRICH, William W	21	N½SW	1910-03-10		A7
1652	" "	21	W½SE	1910-03-10		A7
1653	VAUGHN, George W	33	W½SE	1892-11-03		A7
1654	" "	33	E½SW	1892-11-03		A7
7151	VENTLE, Rosel J	2	E22NW	1875-11-01		A7

ID	Individual in Patent	Sec.	Sec. Part	Date Issued	Other Counties	For More Info . . .
7153	WALKER, Helton R	2	W½NE	1881-10-06		A7
1655	" "	2	NESW	1881-10-06		A7
1656	" "	2	NWSE	1881-10-06		A7
7152	" "	2	W½NE	1881-10-06		A7
1657	WARD, John L	17	S½SE	1891-06-09		A7
1658	" "	20	NENE	1891-06-09		A7
1659	" "	21	NWNW	1891-06-09		A7
1660	WEBB, John W	31	W½NE	1875-04-01		A7
7171	" "	31	1NW	1875-04-01		A7
1661	WEIBERT, Joseph J	28	E½NW	1892-03-07		A7
1662	" "	28	W½NE	1892-03-07		A7
1663	WEST, Thomas	23	E½SE	1900-08-09		A7
1664	" "	24	NWSW	1900-08-09		A7
1665	" "	26	NENE	1900-08-09		A7
1666	WILBANKS, Paul J	29	NWNE	1897-08-09		A7
1667	" "	29	N½NW	1897-08-09		A7
1669	WILLBANKS, John H	23	S½SW	1900-08-09		A7
1668	" "	23	NWSW	1900-08-09		A7
1670	WILLBANKS, Mary E	28	NESW	1904-08-26		A7
7211	WILSON, James S	7	S½NW	1900-02-02		A7
1671	WILSON, John H	27	SESW	1906-03-31		A7
1672	" "	34	N½NW	1906-03-31		A7
1673	WILSON, William J	17	NWNW	1894-12-17		A7
1675	" "	18	W½NE	1894-12-17		A7
1674	" "	18	NENE	1894-12-17		A7
1676	WINDER, John Y	26	SWNW	1898-06-23		A7
1677	" "	27	N½SE	1898-06-23		A7
1678	" "	27	SENE	1898-06-23		A7
7172	WISEMAN, Zachariah	31	1SW	1890-01-10		A7
1679	" "	31	NWSE	1890-01-10		A7
7174	" "	31	N½SW	1890-01-10		A7
1681	WYZARD, Alexander	23	NENW	1890-12-31		A7
1680	" "	23	N½NE	1890-12-31		A7
1682	" "	24	NWNW	1890-12-31		A7
1683	WYZARD, Otto	23	SWSE	1920-06-14		A1
1684	WYZARD, William	11	NWSW	1904-06-10		A1
1685	YORK, Mary	26	SENW	1896-01-14		A7
1687	" "	26	NWSE	1896-01-14		A7
1686	" "	26	W½NE	1896-01-14		A7

Patent Map

T26-N R8-W
5th PM 26-N 8-W Meridian

Map Group 7

Township Statistics

Parcels Mapped	:	388
Number of Patents	:	194
Number of Individuals	:	205
Patentees Identified	:	184
Number of Surnames	:	138
Multi-Patentee Parcels	:	48
Oldest Patent Date	:	3/10/1857
Most Recent Patent	:	6/14/1920
Block/Lot Parcels	:	75
Cities and Town	:	0
Cemeteries	:	1

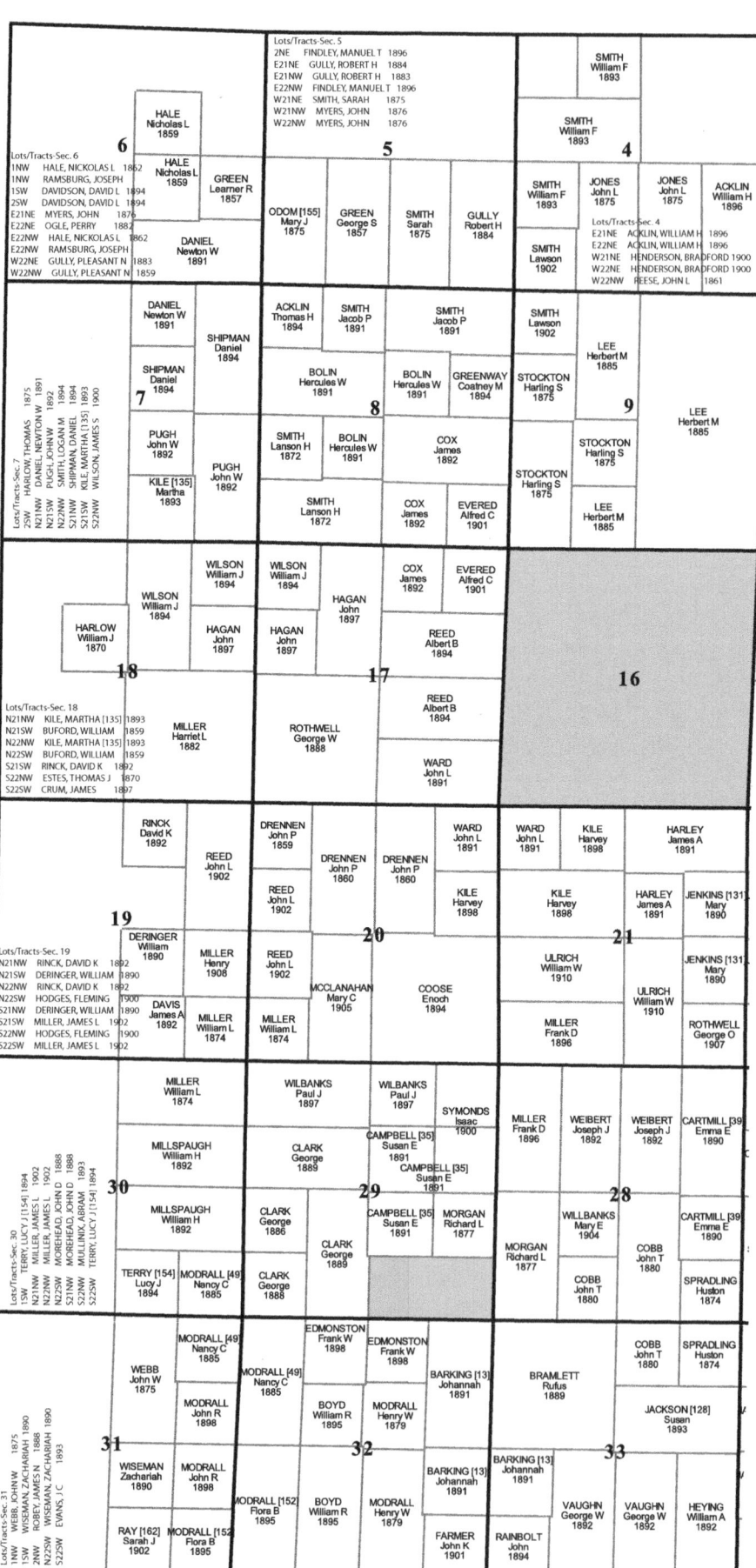

Section 3

3

Lots/Tracts-Sec. 3
1NW   STEVENS, ABRAM   1898
2NE   CLARK, WILLIAM   1898
E21NE GAMBLE, JAMES S   1898
E22NW CLARK, WILLIAM   1898
W21NE STEVENS, ABRAM   1898
W22NW ROBBINS, JOHN B   1888

Section 2

GAMBLE
James S
1898

Lots/Tracts-Sec. 2
E21NE STOKES, ALBERT W   1890
E21NW HOKE, LEROY   1901
E22NE STOKES, ALBERT W   1890
E22NW VENTLE, ROSEL J   1875
W21NE WALKER, HELTON R   1881
W22NE WALKER, HELTON R   1881

2

ULRICH
Oscar E
1913

WALKER
Helton R
1881

WALKER
Helton R
1881

STEVENSON
James S
1908

FLOOD
Thomas H
1901

DEATON
William P
1894

Section 1

Lots/Tracts-Sec. 1
1NW   SHERRELL, ALEXANDER 1889
E21NE JACKSON, FREEMAN B 1893
E22NE JACKSON, FREEMAN B 1893
E22NW HUGHES, GEORGE W   1895
W21NE SHERRELL, ALEXANDER 1889
W21NE HUGHES, GEORGE W   1895
W22NW RILEY, JAMES   1860

1

ROACH
Elijah E
1860

REESE
J P
1876

REESE
J P
1876

FLOOD
Jeremiah E
1889

DEATON
William P
1894

Section 10

LEE
Herbert M
1885

10

FEATHER [78]
Nancy L
1910

FEATHER [78]
Nancy L
1910

FEATHER [78]
Nancy L
1910

MCMURTRY
James U
1885

MCMURTRY
James U
1885

EVELAND
William P
1901

Section 11

FLOOD
Thomas H
1901

FLOOD
Thomas H
1901

DEATON
George M
1900

DEATON
George M
1900

11

WYZARD
William
1904

DOWELL
John H
1912

DOWELL
John H
1912

BOLERJACK
Thomas S
1892

MCMURTRY
James U
1885

JEREMIAH
Pearson A
1891

JEREMIAH
Pearson A
1891

DOWELL
George
1907

Section 12

DEATON
William P
1894

BOLERJACK
Thomas C
1884

BOLERJACK
Thomas C
1884

SHERRELL
Isaiah
1889

BOLERJACK
Thomas S
1892

THOMASSON
Augustine J
1896

12

BOLERJACK
Thomas S
1892

MCMURTRY
John J
1897

MCMURTRY
John J
1897

BOLERJACK
Thomas C
1884

TAYLOR
John
1859

Section 15

CANTRELL
William F
1877

15

EVELAND
William P
1901

EVELAND
William P
1901

CANTRELL
William F
1877

CANTRELL
William F
1877

GULLEY
Henry C
1896

CANTRELL
Henry J
1889

GOBBEL
John A
1881

Section 14

GULLEY
Henry C
1896

GULLEY
Henry C
1896

CARTMILL
Elzy
1889

CARTMILL
Elzy
1889

14

CARTMILL
Elzy
1889

ROWLETT
John B
1902

MCMURTRY
Isaac W
1888

STINE
Thomas H
1900

DOWELL
George
1907

Section 13

DOWELL
George
1907

BLYTHE [19]
Martha J
1885

BLYTHE [19]
Martha J
1885

ROWLETT
John B
1902

TAYLOR
John
1859

TAYLOR
John
1860

13

ROWLETT
John B
1902

PITTS
William
1901

GALBREATH
Robert G
1888

STINE
Thomas H
1900

MARKHAM
Edwin C
1893

MARKHAM
Edwin C
1893

Section 22

HARLEY
James A
1891

LORD [141]
Tamson A
1889

LORD [141]
Tamson A
1889

JENKINS [131]
Mary
1890

TURPEN
James U
1893

TURPEN
James U
1893

TURPEN
Martin
1891

22

JENKINS [131]
Mary
1890

TURPEN
James U
1893

TURPEN
James U
1893

TURPEN
Martin
1891

ROTHWELL
George O
1907

ROTHWELL
George O
1907

Section 23

LORD [141]
Tamson A
1889

WYZARD
Alexander
1890

WYZARD
Alexander
1890

TURPEN
Martin
1891

EVELAND
James L
1898

EVELAND
James L
1898

FEATHER
Elsie M
1911

23

WILLBANKS
John H
1900

EVELAND
James L
1898

EVELAND
James L
1898

WEST
Thomas
1900

WILLBANKS
John H
1900

WYZARD
Otto
1920

Section 24

WYZARD
Alexander
1890

MULLANY
Michael
1890

MULLANY
Michael
1890

MARKHAM
Edwin C
1893

FEATHER
Elsie M
1911

WEST
Thomas
1900

24

COLLINS
William
1910

HENRY [115]
Elizziebeth
1898

HENRY [115]
Elizziebeth
1898

MARAT
William
1912

POE
Jesse
1876

Section 27

SOOTS
John H
1907

BOSS
Theodore
1896

ULRICH
Oren E
1911

CARTMILL [39]
Emma E
1890

BOSS
Theodore
1896

WINDER
John Y
1898

27

SPRADLING
Huston
1874

BOSS
Theodore
1896

WINDER
John Y
1898

WILSON
John H
1906

THOMAS
Nathan
1872

DAVIS
Francis M
1860

Section 26

ULRICH
Oren E
1911

YORK
Mary
1896

WINDER
John Y
1898

YORK
Mary
1896

26

DAVIS
Francis M
1860

YORK
Mary
1896

DUNLAP [70]
Delila
1877

DUNLAP [70]
Delila
1877

Section 25

WEST
Thomas
1900

MARAT
William
1912

HENRY [115]
Elizziebeth
1898

DUNLAP [70]
Delila
1877

GOODMAN
Joseph R
1889

GOODMAN
Joseph R
1889

POE
Jesse
1876

POE
Jesse
1871

GOODMAN
Joseph R
1889

THOMPSON
William A
1889

25

JONES
Gilroy C
1889

BOATMAN
John W
1885

BOATMAN
Henry
1859

BOATMAN
Samuel J
1882

Section 34

WILSON
John H
1906

THOMAS
Nathan
1872

THOMAS
Job C
1891

THOMAS
Nathan
1872

JACKSON [128]
Susan
1893

ROHR [68]
Catherine
1900

ROHR [68]
Catherine
1900

JENKINS
John A
1890

34

JACKSON [128]
Susan
1893

ROHR [68]
Catherine
1900

ROHR [68]
Catherine
1900

JENKINS
John A
1890

HEYING
William A
1892

BARTON
John R
1895

COUNTS
James E
1891

Section 35

THOMAS
Nathan
1872

POE
Jesse
1871

JONES
Gilroy C
1889

BOATMAN
Samuel J
1876

BOATMAN
Henry
1859

THOMAS
Nathan
1872

POLLOCK
Francis M
1872

MCGOWAN
George B
1860

JONES
Thompson
1860

BOATMAN
John W
1885

BOATMAN
Samuel J
1861

35

JENKINS
John A
1890

MCGOWEN
George B
1859

PIERCE
John B
1896

Section 36

BOATMAN
Samuel J
1876

36

HENRY
Nimrod B
1872

BOATMAN
Samuel J
1860

BOATMAN
Samuel
1857

MCGUIRE
Michael R
1871

HENRY
Nimrod B
1872

HENRY
Nimrod B
1872

BOATMAN
Samuel J
1861

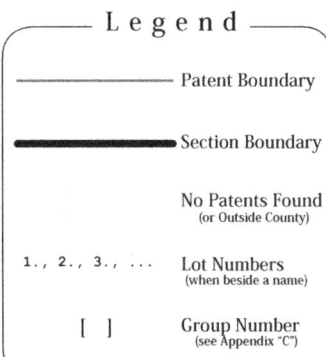

Helpful Hints

1. This Map's INDEX can be found on the preceding pages.

2. Refer to Map "C" to see where this Township lies within Howell County, Missouri.

3. Numbers within square brackets [ ] denote a multi-patentee land parcel (multi-owner). Refer to Appendix "C" for a full list of members in this group.

4. Areas that look to be crowded with Patentees usually indicate multiple sales of the same parcel (Re-issues) or Overlapping parcels. See this Township's Index for an explanation of these and other circumstances that might explain "odd" groupings of Patentees on this map.

Legend

- Patent Boundary
- Section Boundary
- No Patents Found (or Outside County)
- 1., 2., 3., ...   Lot Numbers (when beside a name)
- [ ]   Group Number (see Appendix "C")

Scale: Section = 1 mile X 1 mile (generally, with some exceptions)

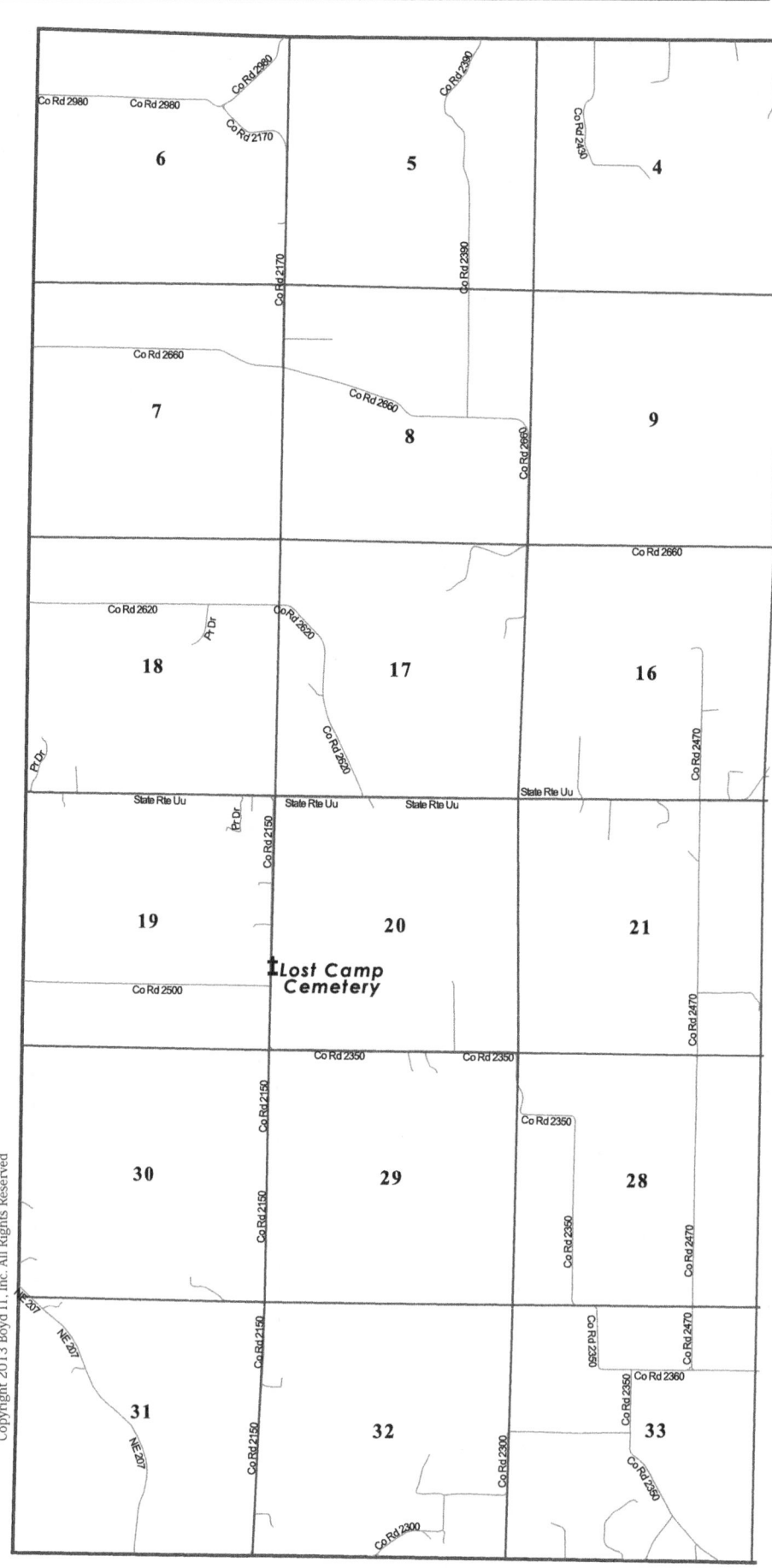

Road Map

T26-N R8-W
5th PM 26-N 8-W Meridian

Map Group 7

Cities & Towns
None

Cemeteries
Lost Camp Cemetery

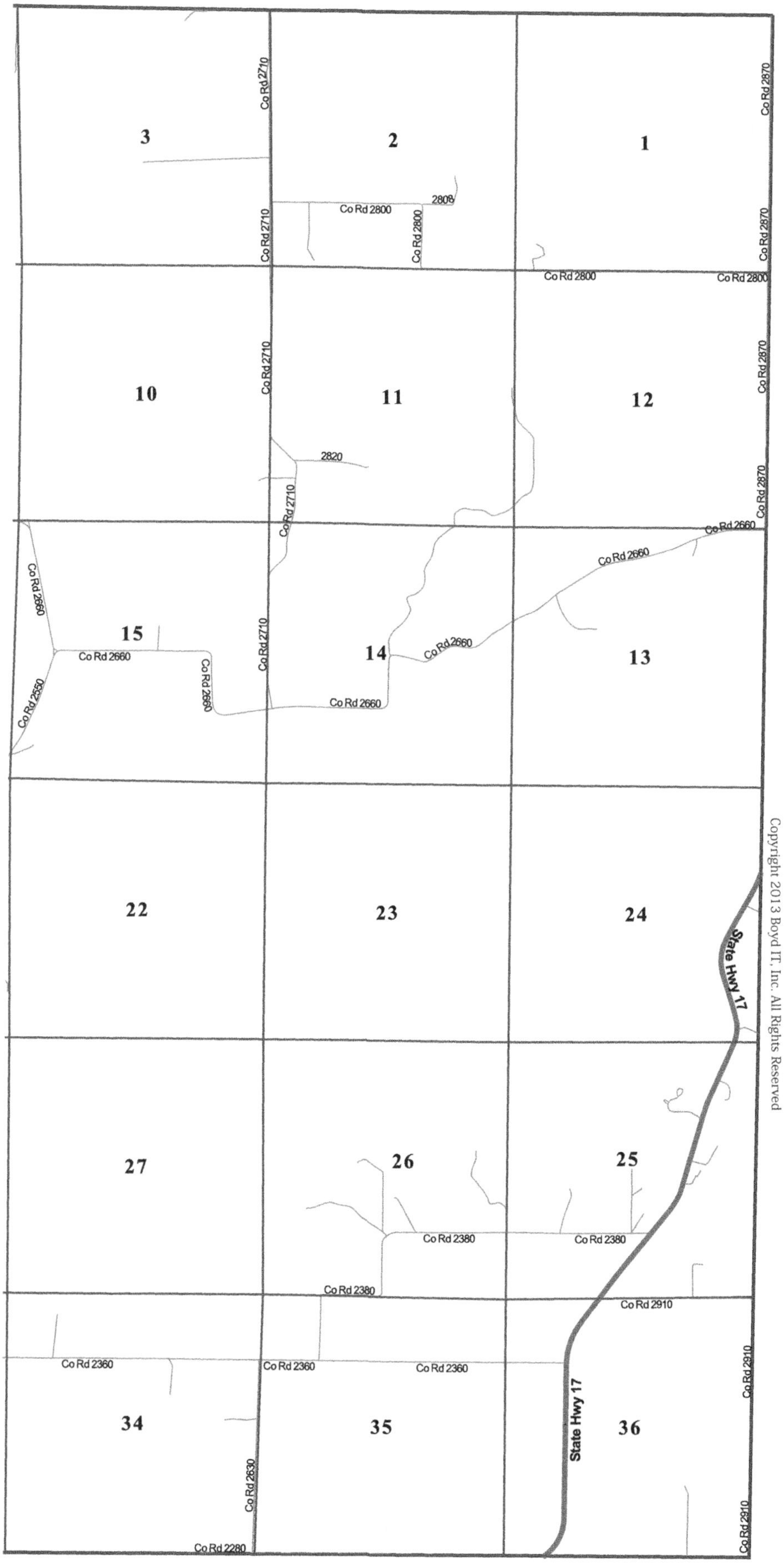

3	2	1
10	11	12
15	14	13
22	23	24
27	26	25
34	35	36

Co Rd 2710
Co Rd 2870
Co Rd 2800
2809
Co Rd 2800
Co Rd 2800
Co Rd 2800
Co Rd 2710
Co Rd 2870
2820
Co Rd 2710
Co Rd 2870
Co Rd 2660
Co Rd 2660
Co Rd 2660
Co Rd 2660
Co Rd 2660
Co Rd 2710
Co Rd 2660
Co Rd 2660
Co Rd 2660
State Hwy 17
Co Rd 2380
Co Rd 2380
Co Rd 2910
Co Rd 2360
Co Rd 2360
Co Rd 2360
Co Rd 2830
State Hwy 17
Co Rd 2310
Co Rd 2310
Co Rd 2280

Helpful Hints

1. This road map has a number of uses, but primarily it is to help you: a) find the present location of land owned by your ancestors (at least the general area), b) find cemeteries and city-centers, and c) estimate the route/roads used by Census-takers & tax-assessors.

2. If you plan to travel to Howell County to locate cemeteries or land parcels, please pick up a modern travel map for the area before you do. Mapping old land parcels on modern maps is not as exact a science as you might think. Just the slightest variations in public land survey coordinates, estimates of parcel boundaries, or road-map deviations can greatly alter a map's representation of how a road either does or doesn't cross a particular parcel of land.

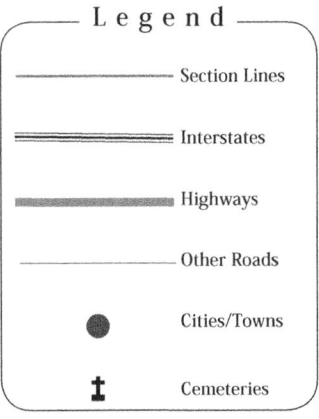

L e g e n d

——————— Section Lines

═══════ Interstates

▬▬▬▬▬▬ Highways

——————— Other Roads

● Cities/Towns

‡ Cemeteries

Scale: Section = 1 mile X 1 mile
(generally, with some exceptions)

Historical Map

T26-N   R8-W
5th PM 26-N 8-W Meridian

Map Group 7

Cities & Towns
None

Cemeteries
Lost Camp Cemetery

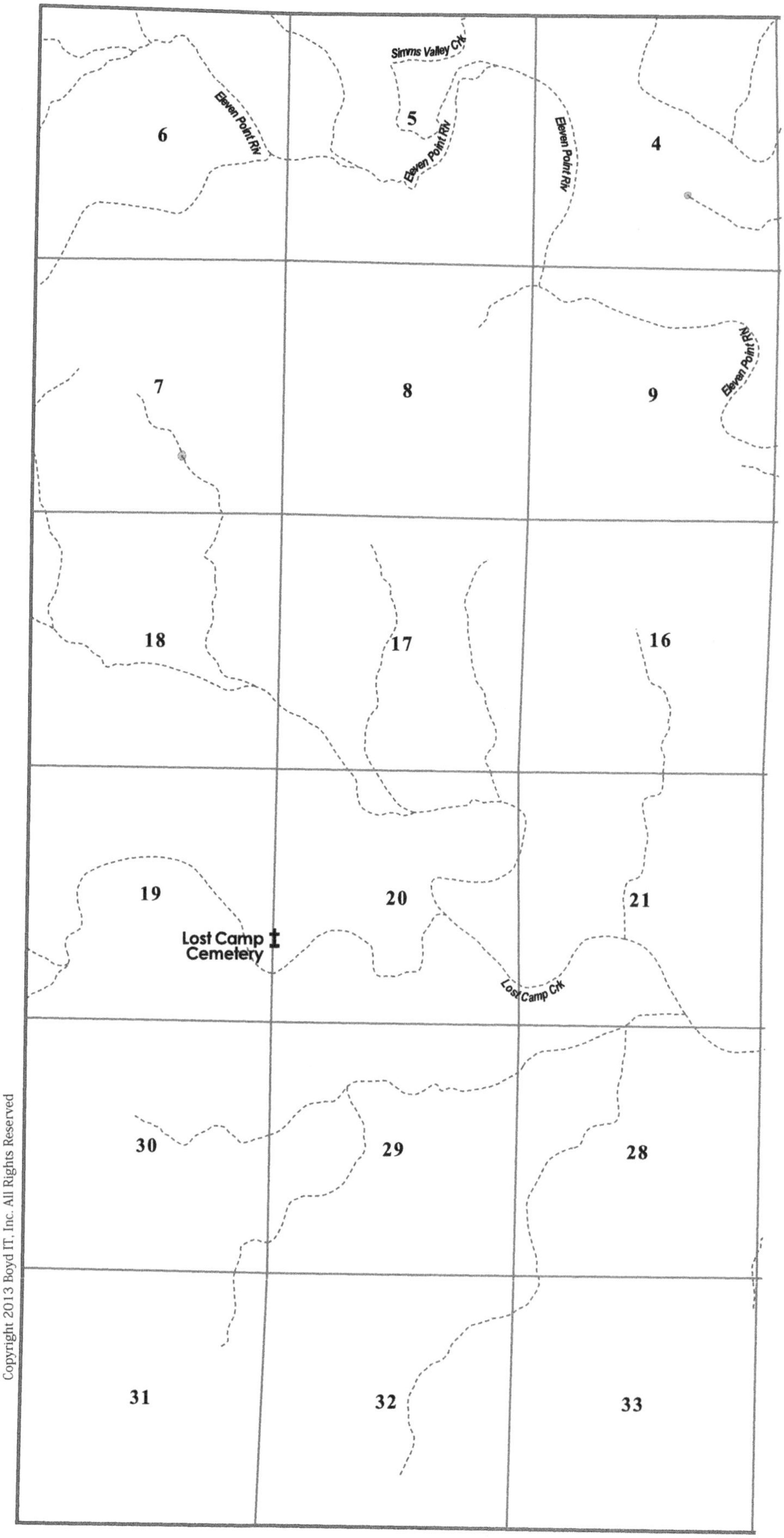

6

5

4

7

8

9

18

17

16

19

20

21

Lost Camp Cemetery

30

29

28

31

32

33

Simms Valley Crk

Eleven Point Riv

Eleven Point Riv

Eleven Point Riv

Eleven Point Riv

Lost Camp Crk

Copyright 2013 Boyd IT, Inc. All Rights Reserved

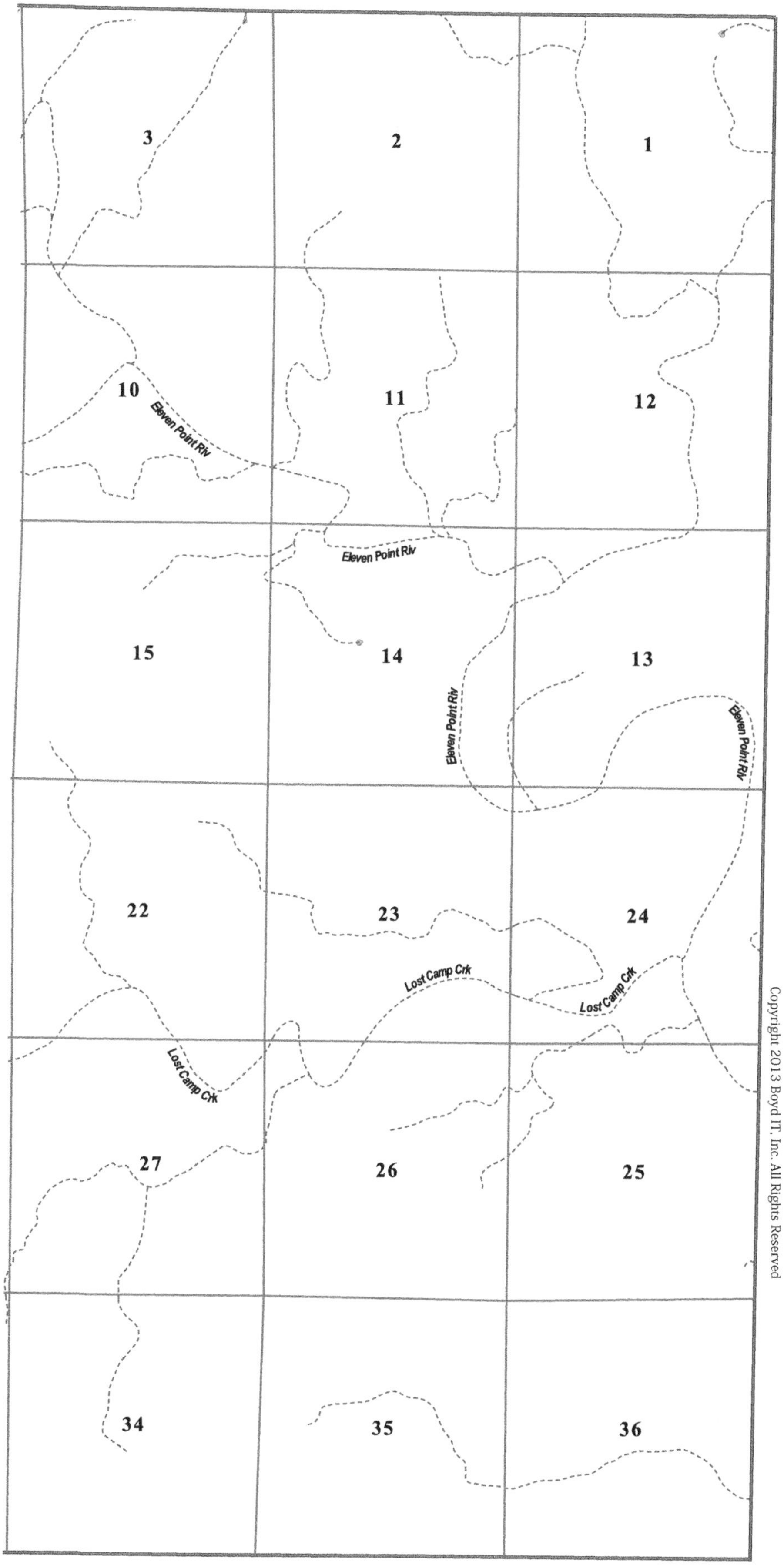

3

2

1

10

Eleven Point Riv

11

12

Eleven Point Riv

15

14

Eleven Point Riv

13

Eleven Point Riv

22

23

24

Lost Camp Crk

Lost Camp Crk

27

Lost Camp Crk

26

25

34

35

36

Helpful Hints

1. This Map takes a different look at the same Congressional Township displayed in the preceding two maps. It presents features that can help you better envision the historical development of the area: a) Water-bodies (lakes & ponds), b) Water-courses (rivers, streams, etc.), c) Railroads, d) City/ town center-points (where they were oftentimes located when first settled), and e) Cemeteries.

2. Using this "Historical" map in tandem with this Township's Patent Map and Road Map, may lead you to some interesting discoveries. You will often find roads, towns, cemeteries, and waterways are named after nearby landowners: sometimes those names will be the ones you are researching. See how many of these research gems you can find here in Howell County.

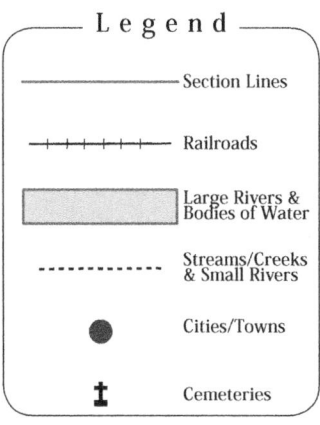

L e g e n d

——————— Section Lines

+++++++ Railroads

Large Rivers & Bodies of Water

- - - - - - - Streams/Creeks & Small Rivers

● Cities/Towns

‡ Cemeteries

Scale: Section = 1 mile X 1 mile
(there are some exceptions)

Map Group 8: Index to Land Patents

Township 26-North Range 7-West (5th PM 26-N 7-W)

After you locate an individual in this Index, take note of the Section and Section Part then proceed to the Land Patent map on the pages immediately following. You should have no difficulty locating the corresponding parcel of land.

The "For More Info" Column will lead you to more information about the underlying Patents. See the *Legend* at right, and the "How to Use this Book" chapter, for more information.

```
                    LEGEND
            "For More Info . . . " column
A = Authority (Legislative Act, See Appendix "A")
B = Block or Lot (location in Section unknown)
C = Cancelled Patent
F = Fractional Section
G = Group  (Multi-Patentee Patent, see Appendix "C")
V = Overlaps another Parcel
R = Re-Issued (Parcel patented more than once)

(A & G items require you to look in the Appendixes referred
to above. All other Letter-designations followed by a number
require you to locate line-items in this index that possess
the ID number found after the letter).
```

ID	Individual in Patent	Sec.	Sec. Part	Date Issued	Other Counties	For More Info . . .
1688	ALESHIRE, Joseph H	25	SENW	1908-11-19		A1
1689	ATCHISON, Sarah	31	SWSE	1882-11-10		A7
1691	AYERS, Alexander M	15	SESW	1882-12-20		A1
1690	" "	15	S½SE	1882-12-20		A1
7234	" "	19	S22SW	1882-12-20		A1
7232	" "	19	S21SW	1882-12-20		A1
1692	" "	19	S½SE	1882-12-20		A1
1697	" "	22	NESE	1882-12-20		A1
1695	" "	22	S½SW	1882-12-20		A1
1696	" "	22	W½NW	1882-12-20		A1
1694	" "	22	E½NE	1882-12-20		A1
1693	" "	22	NWSW	1882-12-20		A1
1698	" "	23	SWNW	1882-12-20		A1
1699	" "	25	S½SW	1882-12-20		A1
1702	" "	26	N½SE	1882-12-20		A1
1700	" "	26	SESE	1882-12-20		A1
1701	" "	26	S½NE	1882-12-20		A1
1704	" "	27	W½	1882-12-20		A1
1703	" "	27	S½SE	1882-12-20		A1
1705	" "	29	NW	1882-12-20		A1
1706	" "	30	NE	1882-12-20		A1
1707	" "	33	N½NW	1882-12-20		A1
1709	" "	33	S½NW	1882-12-20		A1
1710	" "	33	S½NE	1882-12-20		A1
1708	" "	33	N½NE	1882-12-20		A1
1713	" "	34	NWNE	1882-12-20		A1
1711	" "	34	N½NW	1882-12-20		A1
1712	" "	34	SWNE	1882-12-20		A1
1714	" "	34	S½NW	1882-12-20		A1
1715	" "	36	S½	1882-12-20		A1
1716	BARTON, William H	33	SESE	1892-03-07		A7
1717	BAY, John W	28	NWNE	1914-03-28		A1
1718	BAY, Ninian L	36	SWNW	1893-01-07		A7
1719	" "	36	E½NW	1893-01-07		A7
1720	" "	36	SWNE	1893-01-07		A7
1721	BLYTHE, Aaron	31	E½SE	1872-07-01		A7
1722	" "	32	W½SW	1872-07-01		A7
7246	BOATMAN, Henry R	31	N22SW	1860-10-01		A1
1723	BOLERJACK, Henry J	6	S½SE	1888-11-27		A7
1724	" "	7	W½NE	1888-11-27		A7
7273	BOLERJACK, Marion H	7	S22NW	1884-11-01		A7
7271	" "	7	2SW	1884-11-01		A7
1725	BRAGG, Hugh T	33	N½SE	1904-06-02		A7
1726	" "	33	SWSE	1904-06-02		A7
1727	" "	33	NESW	1904-06-02		A7
1728	BRISCEY, William I	5	W½SW	1860-08-01		A1

ID	Individual in Patent	Sec.	Sec. Part	Date Issued	Other Counties	For More Info . . .
1729	BRISCEY, William I (Cont'd)	8	NWNW	1860-08-01		A1
1730	BROOKS, Jacob	21	SESE	1888-12-06		A7
1731	" "	28	NESE	1888-12-06		A7
1732	" "	28	E½NE	1888-12-06		A7
1733	BROWN, Jonathan	3	NWSW	1898-07-25		A7
1734	BRUNOT, Felix R	15	S½SW	1860-05-02		A6
1735	BUFF, Harvey A	1	NE	1890-01-10		A7
1736	CAMPBELL, Lewis B	5	E½SE	1892-12-09		A7
1737	" "	8	E½NE	1892-12-09		A7
1738	CARPENTER, Ira	11	N½SE	1875-02-15		A7
1739	" "	11	S½NE	1875-02-15		A7
1740	" "	12	NWNW	1872-08-30		A1
1741	" "	3	NESW	1861-05-01		A1
1742	CARTER, Nannie	35	S½SE	1901-08-12		A7
1743	CASTEEL, William H	21	N½NE	1888-12-08		A7
1744	" "	21	N½NW	1888-12-08		A7
1746	CHOWNING, Austin	23	SENE	1888-12-04		A7
1745	" "	23	NESE	1888-12-04		A7
1747	" "	24	W½NW	1888-12-04		A7
1749	CHOWNING, Charles L	24	N½SE	1901-12-17		A7
1748	" "	24	S½NE	1901-12-17		A7
1750	CHOWNING, Isaac	24	NESW	1860-08-01		A1
1751	" "	24	W½SW	1860-08-01		A1
1753	" "	24	SENW	1860-08-01		A1
1752	" "	24	NENW	1860-08-01		A1
1754	CHOWNING, Jasper E	13	S½SE	1875-02-15		A7
1755	" "	24	N½NE	1875-02-15		A7
1756	CHOWNING, Leander	26	SWNW	1882-08-30		A7
1758	" "	27	E½NE	1882-08-30		A7
1757	" "	27	NESE	1882-08-30		A7
1759	CHOWNING, Levi	22	SWSE	1890-01-10		A7
1760	" "	27	NWSE	1890-01-10		A7
1761	" "	27	W½NE	1890-01-10		A7
1762	COLTER, Lewis T	23	N½NW	1897-04-10		A7
1765	COMSTOCK, Alwilda A	28	SESE	1892-07-11		A1
1764	" "	28	SWSE	1892-07-11		A1
1763	" "	28	E½SW	1892-07-11		A1
1766	" "	28	SWNE	1892-07-11		A1
1767	COMSTOCK, Frank	21	SENE	1892-08-01		A1
1768	" "	21	NESE	1892-08-01		A1
1769	" "	26	SWSE	1891-08-24		A1
1770	" "	28	NWSE	1891-08-24		A1
1771	" "	35	NENE	1892-04-23		A1
1773	CONNER, Andrew	10	N½SE	1890-01-10		A7
1772	" "	10	S½NE	1890-01-10		A7
1774	CONNER, Henry H	9	NENE	1911-06-05		A1
1775	COOPPER, George W	14	SWSE	1876-05-10		A7
1776	" "	23	NWNE	1876-05-10		A7
7269	DANIEL, Martin P	7	1NW	1861-05-01		A1
1777	DAVIES, Daniel	15	E½NW	1899-02-13		A7
1778	" "	15	NESW	1899-02-13		A7
1779	DAVIS, William K	34	SESW	1892-04-23		A1
1780	" "	34	NWSW	1892-04-23		A1
1781	DEBOARD, Ivy G	18	W½SE	1889-01-12		A7
1782	" "	18	SWNE	1889-01-12		A7
1783	" "	19	NWNE	1889-01-12		A7
1784	DEBOARD, Joel F	8	S½NW	1888-12-08		A7
1785	" "	8	SWNE	1888-12-08		A7
1786	" "	8	NWSW	1888-12-08		A7
1787	DEBOARD, Mary J	5	NWSE	1891-05-25		A7 G67
1788	" "	5	NESW	1891-05-25		A7 G67
1789	DEBOARD, Snowden S	17	SWNW	1899-02-25		A7
1790	DEBOARD, Wiley	5	NWSE	1891-05-25		A7 G67
1791	" "	5	NESW	1891-05-25		A7 G67
1792	DENTON, Jacob	31	SWNE	1900-11-12		A7
1793	" "	31	NWSE	1900-11-12		A7
1794	DRAKE, John	25	NENE	1903-10-01	Shannon	A7
7239	DUNHAM, Ephraim	30	N21NW	1885-06-03		A1
7214	DUNKIN, William J	18	N21NW	1888-12-08		A7
1795	" "	18	SENE	1888-12-08		A7
1796	" "	18	N½NE	1888-12-08		A7
1797	ELDRINGHOFF, John J	32	S½SE	1899-05-12		A7
1798	ELDRINGHOFF, Joseph M	32	NESE	1899-05-12		A7

ID	Individual in Patent	Sec.	Sec. Part	Date Issued	Other Counties	For More Info . . .
1799	ELDRINGHOFF, Joseph M (Cont'd)	32	SENE	1899-05-12		A7
1800	EVANS, Narcissa M	17	SWNE	1906-06-21		A7 G77
1801	EVANS, William	17	SWNE	1906-06-21		A7 G77
1802	EVINS, James R	34	NESE	1890-01-10		A7
1803	" "	34	E½NE	1890-01-10		A7
1804	" "	35	NWSW	1890-01-10		A7
7213	FARRAR, George W	1	2NW	1896-12-08		A7
7212	" "	1	1NW	1896-12-08		A7
7265	FLOOD, Jeremiah E	6	N22SW	1889-01-12		A7
1805	FRISBEY, George W	12	W½SW	1904-07-15		A7
1806	" "	13	NWNW	1904-07-15		A7
1807	" "	14	NENE	1904-07-15		A7
1808	GAROUTTE, Isaac	11	SESW	1874-06-15		A1
1809	" "	13	SWNE	1869-07-01		A8
1810	" "	20	W½NE	1861-02-09		A1
1811	" "	20	SENW	1861-02-09		A1
1812	GILES, Francis M	8	NESE	1901-06-08		A7
1813	" "	9	N½SW	1901-06-08		A7
1814	GILLINGHAM, Lewis	3	E½	1860-08-01		A1
7245	GOBBEL, John	31	1SW	1872-07-01		A7
7247	" "	31	S22SW	1872-07-01		A7
1815	GOODMAN, Henry	19	SWNE	1884-02-15		A7
1817	" "	19	NESE	1884-02-15		A7
1816	" "	19	NWSE	1884-02-15		A7
1818	" "	19	SENE	1861-02-01		A1
1819	" "	20	NWSW	1884-02-15		A7
1820	" "	20	SWNW	1861-02-01		A1
1821	GOODMAN, Pleasant H	34	SESE	1910-04-25		A7
1822	" "	35	SWNW	1906-08-16		A1
1824	" "	35	S½SW	1910-04-25		A7
1823	" "	35	NESW	1910-04-25		A7
1825	GRAVES, Roy E	29	E½NE	1911-04-24		A1
1826	" "	29	SWNE	1911-04-24		A1
1827	GREEN, Benjamin F	9	NWNE	1859-09-01		A1
1828	GREEN, Calvin	29	SWSW	1919-09-12		A7
1829	" "	31	E½NE	1919-09-12		A7
1830	" "	32	NWNW	1919-09-12		A7
1831	GREEN, Levin	4	SESE	1860-08-01		A1
1832	GREEN, Pleasant T	15	SWNE	1859-09-01		A1
1833	HALSTEAD, John	35	NESE	1893-03-13		A1
1834	" "	35	SENE	1893-03-13		A1
1835	HARGROVES, Franklin C	26	N½NW	1894-05-18		A7
1836	" "	26	SENW	1894-05-18		A7
1837	HARRIS, Allen M	5	NW	1860-10-01		A1
7257	" "	5	W22NE	1860-10-01		A1
7256	" "	5	W21NE	1860-10-01		A1
7228	HARVEY, William A	19	1NW	1899-03-03		A7
7233	" "	19	S22NW	1899-03-03		A7
7230	" "	19	N22NW	1894-09-18		A1
1838	HATCHER, John R	3	SWSW	1861-02-09		A1
7251	HAYNES, Frank M	4	E22NE	1901-07-09		A7
1839	" "	4	N½SE	1901-07-09		A7
7250	" "	4	E21NE	1901-07-09		A7
1840	HEAD, John D	1	SESE	1907-10-04		A1
1841	HENRY, Charles P	29	NWSW	1901-06-08		A7
1843	" "	30	N½SE	1901-06-08		A7
1842	" "	30	SESE	1901-06-08		A7
1844	HIBNER, Margaret	10	SESE	1908-05-18		A1
1846	" "	11	N½SW	1908-05-18		A1
1845	" "	11	SWSW	1908-05-18		A1
1847	HIBNER, William	11	N½SE	1904-06-02		A7
1848	HIGHTOWER, Andrew P	20	NWSE	1888-12-08		A7
1849	" "	20	SENE	1888-12-08		A7
1850	" "	20	E½SE	1888-12-08		A7
1852	HOGGATT, John D	32	NWSE	1886-04-10		A7
1851	" "	32	E½SW	1886-04-10		A7
1853	HOLDEN, Benjamin	11	S½SE	1860-08-01		A1
1854	" "	13	S½NW	1882-08-30		A7
1855	" "	13	W½SW	1882-08-30		A7
1856	" "	14	NWNE	1860-08-01		A1
1857	HOLDEN, Lockey S	12	S½SE	1876-12-01		A7
1858	" "	12	SESW	1876-12-01		A7
1859	" "	13	NENE	1876-12-01		A7

ID	Individual in Patent	Sec.	Sec. Part	Date Issued	Other Counties	For More Info . . .
7236	HOLDEN, Wesley	2	E22NW	1860-08-01		A1
7237	HOLDEN, Wesley R	2	W22NW	1910-10-10		A1
1861	HOLDEN, William F	1	N½SW	1896-08-28		A7
1860	" "	1	SWSW	1896-08-28		A7
1862	HOOTEN, Samuel H	32	S½NW	1898-10-04		A7
1864	HOPE, John J	4	SWSW	1889-06-22		A7
1863	" "	4	E½SW	1889-06-22		A7
1865	" "	4	SWSE	1889-06-22		A7
1866	HOUGHTON, Curtis L	35	NWSE	1905-04-05		A1
1867	HUDLOW, William B	7	W½SE	1872-07-01		A7
7270	" "	7	1SW	1872-07-01		A7
1868	HUGHES, Thomas A	15	W½NW	1875-08-10		A7
1869	" "	15	W½SW	1875-08-10		A7
1871	IRWIN, James Harvey	3	NW	1860-11-12		A6
1872	JACKSON, Jancey M	17	SENW	1882-09-30		A7 G129
1874	" "	17	NWNE	1882-09-30		A7 G129
1873	" "	17	N½NW	1882-09-30		A7 G129
1875	JACKSON, Jehiel	7	NENE	1882-05-10		A1
1877	" "	7	E½SE	1885-02-25		A7
1876	" "	7	SENE	1885-02-25		A7
1878	" "	8	SWSW	1885-02-25		A7
1879	JARRELL, Bert E	33	NWSW	1910-09-08		A1
1880	JEREMIAH, Enoch	14	N½NW	1902-09-15		A7
7244	JONES, Arthur C	30	S22SW	1910-09-15		A7
7238	JONES, Iradell H	30	1SW	1900-08-09		A7
1881	" "	30	SWSE	1900-08-09		A7
1882	" "	31	NWNE	1900-08-09		A7
1883	JONES, Jancey M	17	SENW	1882-09-30		A7 G129
1884	" "	17	N½NW	1882-09-30		A7 G129
1885	" "	17	NWNE	1882-09-30		A7 G129
1886	JONES, John	25	N½SE	1891-05-25		A7
1887	" "	25	S½NE	1891-05-25		A7
1888	JONES, Morgan	14	S½NE	1888-12-06		A7
1889	" "	14	N½SE	1888-12-06		A7
1890	JONES, Morgan W	24	SESW	1897-04-10		A7
1891	KENAGA, Mathias	20	NENE	1883-08-13		A1
1897	" "	21	SESW	1882-11-10		A7
1898	" "	21	W½SE	1882-11-10		A7
1896	" "	21	SWNE	1906-08-16		A1
1895	" "	21	NWSW	1892-07-11		A1
1894	" "	21	SWSW	1906-08-16		A1
1893	" "	21	NESW	1884-03-10		A1
1892	" "	21	SENW	1906-08-16		A1
1899	" "	22	NWNE	1901-05-27		A1
1900	" "	28	SWSW	1883-08-13		A1
1901	" "	28	NWNW	1884-03-10		A1
1902	" "	28	NWSW	1884-03-10		A1
1903	" "	28	NENW	1882-11-10		A7
1904	KENEGA, Mathias	20	NESW	1882-12-20		A1
1905	" "	21	SWNW	1886-10-29		A1
7261	KOONCE, Eligha W	6	1NW	1889-01-12		A7
7264	" "	6	N21SW	1889-01-12		A7
1906	" "	6	NWSE	1889-01-12		A7
7266	KOONCE, Robert H	6	S21SW	1898-04-11		A7
7267	KOONCE, Thomas J	6	S22SW	1896-08-28		A7
7231	LEDBETTER, James M	19	N22SW	1882-09-30		A1
7229	" "	19	N21SW	1882-09-30		A1
1907	" "	9	NW	1883-06-30		A7
1908	LEDBETTER, James R	9	S½NE	1876-09-06		A7
1909	LEE, John C	15	N½SE	1893-06-01		A7
1910	" "	15	NWNE	1893-06-01		A7
1911	LEE, William C	10	SW	1893-01-07		A7
1912	LEWIS, Aaron R	14	SESE	1861-02-09		A1
1913	" "	23	NENE	1861-02-09		A1
1914	LILE, William H	25	SESE	1879-12-15		A7
1915	" "	36	NWNE	1879-12-15		A7
1916	" "	36	E½NE	1879-12-15		A7
1918	LIVINGSTON, Archibald	10	NW	1977-12-06		A6
1920	" "	10	SW	1860-11-12		A6
1921	LUCK, Elijah	20	NENW	1860-08-01		A1
7259	MARTIN, James Calvin	6	1NE	1860-11-12		A6
1923	MCCOLLUM, Stephen B	1	N½SE	1894-05-23		A7
1922	" "	1	SWSE	1894-05-23		A7

ID	Individual in Patent	Sec.	Sec. Part	Date Issued	Other Counties	For More Info . . .
1924	MCCOLLUM, Stephen B (Cont'd)	12	NWNE	1894-05-23		A7
1925	MCCOY, John	28	S½NW	1901-12-17		A7
7254	MCGRATH, William H	5	E21NE	1908-03-05		A1
1926	MCHAN, Barna	13	N½SE	1859-09-01		A1
1927	" "	13	NESW	1860-08-01		A1
1928	MCHAN, Elbert	34	SWSW	1877-11-10		A1
7268	MCHANN, Albert	6	W22NE	1861-02-09		A1
7262	" "	6	2NW	1861-02-09		A1
1929	MCKANNA, Alfred	10	SWSE	1908-03-05		A1
1930	MORRIS, Nathaniel	2	SWSW	1904-11-15		A7
1931	MORRIS, William A	13	SENE	1907-05-10		A1
7249	NEWSOM, Mary	4	2NW	1860-10-01		A1
7255	" "	5	E22NE	1861-02-01		A1
1933	NICKELSON, Dave A	12	SWNE	1905-05-09		A7
1934	" "	12	N½SE	1905-05-09		A7
1935	" "	12	NESW	1905-05-09		A7
1936	PARTNEY, John S	3	SESW	1897-06-11		A7
1938	PEACE, Pleasant E	29	SWSE	1879-12-15		A7
1937	" "	29	SESW	1879-12-15		A7
1939	" "	32	NENW	1879-12-15		A7
1940	" "	32	NWNE	1879-12-15		A7
1941	PEARSON, Elias F	13	SESW	1890-08-13		A1
1942	" "	24	S½SE	1893-09-23		A7
1944	" "	25	NENW	1893-09-23		A7
1943	" "	25	NWNE	1893-09-23		A7
1945	PEARSON, James N	13	NWNE	1902-09-15		A7
1946	" "	13	NENW	1902-09-15		A7
1948	PEARSON, Thomas J	22	NWSE	1883-06-30		A7
1947	" "	22	SWNE	1882-09-30		A1
1950	" "	22	E½NW	1883-06-30		A7
1949	" "	22	NESW	1883-06-30		A7
1951	PETTIT, David S	35	NWNE	1890-08-13		A1
7240	POE, Jesse	30	N22NW	1876-11-03		A7
7242	PORTER, Emsley A	30	S21NW	1895-08-01		A7
7241	" "	30	N22SW	1895-08-01		A7
7243	" "	30	S22NW	1895-08-01		A7
1952	REESE, Charles S	4	NWSW	1903-05-25		A7
1953	REESE, David W	17	NENE	1892-11-28		A1
1954	REESE, Elijah	6	NESE	1861-05-01		A1
7252	REESE, James P	4	W21NE	1891-06-09		A7
7253	" "	4	W22NE	1891-06-09		A7
7248	" "	4	1NW	1891-06-09		A7
1955	ROUSH, Adam	23	S½SE	1875-02-15		A7
1956	" "	26	N½NE	1875-02-15		A7
7235	ROUSH, Andrew	2	1NW	1860-08-01		A1
1957	" "	2	N½SW	1860-08-01		A1
1960	ROUSH, Isaac F	35	SWNE	1891-05-25		A7
1958	" "	35	SENW	1891-05-25		A7
1959	" "	35	N½NW	1891-05-25		A7
1964	ROUSH, John	23	SENW	1872-07-01		A7
1961	" "	23	NWSE	1872-07-01		A7
1962	" "	23	SWNE	1872-07-01		A7
1963	" "	23	NESW	1872-07-01		A7
1965	ROUSH, William L	34	NESW	1900-02-02		A7
1966	" "	34	W½SE	1900-02-02		A7
1967	SALLTOW, John J	22	SESE	1875-01-06		A7
1969	" "	23	NWSW	1875-01-06		A7
1968	" "	23	S½SW	1875-01-06		A7
1973	SCHNEIDER, Henry	17	NESW	1860-08-01		A1
1972	" "	17	SE	1860-08-01		A1
1971	" "	17	SENE	1860-08-01		A1
1970	" "	17	S½SW	1860-08-01		A1
1974	SEATS, William R	29	NESW	1906-06-30		A7
1975	SHADWELL, Elmer	29	NWSE	1898-12-01		A7
1976	" "	29	E½SE	1898-12-01		A7
1977	" "	32	NENE	1898-12-01		A7
7263	SHELTON, John C	6	E22NE	1892-06-10		A7
7258	SHULTZ, Amos H	6	1NE	1860-11-12		A6
1978	SIDWELL, Thomas R	10	N½NE	1900-03-17		A7
1979	SITZS, Isaac M	31	NW	1888-11-27		A7
1980	SMOTHERMON, William R	14	S½NW	1879-12-15		A7
1981	" "	14	E½SW	1879-12-15		A7
1982	SMOUTHIRMAN, Curlis J	14	W½SW	1860-08-01		A1

ID	Individual in Patent	Sec.	Sec. Part	Date Issued	Other Counties	For More Info . . .
1984	SPEAKMAN, Miller S	15	E½NE	1860-10-01		A1
1985	SPRENGEL, Herman	2	NE	1860-08-01		A1
1986	TAYLOR, Alexander	8	E½SW	1860-08-01		A1
1987	" "	8	NWSE	1860-08-01		A1
7217	TAYLOR, John	18	N22NW	1860-08-01		A1
1988	TAYLOR, Riley I	17	NWSW	1860-08-01		A1
7272	THOMAS, Christopher C	7	N22NW	1908-05-21		A7
1989	THOMPSON, Henry	9	SE	1860-10-01		A1
1990	THORNTON, Walter	1	SESW	1900-02-02		A7
1992	" "	12	NENW	1900-02-02		A7
1991	" "	12	S½NW	1900-02-02		A7
1993	TROTTER, Lewis C	36	NWNW	1892-08-01		A1
1994	TURNBAUGH, Mary A	20	S½SW	1889-01-12		A7
1995	" "	20	SWSE	1889-01-12		A7
1996	" "	29	NWNE	1889-01-12		A7
1997	VESS, David M	18	E½SE	1876-06-20		A7
1998	" "	19	NENE	1876-06-20		A7
1999	" "	20	NWNW	1876-06-20		A7
2000	VICKERS, James	8	S½SE	1889-06-22		A7
2001	" "	9	S½SW	1889-06-22		A7
7226	WALKER, John	18	S22SW	1860-06-01		A8
7220	" "	18	S21NW	1860-09-10		A6
7218	" "	18	N22SW	1860-06-01		A8
7223	" "	18	S21SW	1860-06-01		A8
7224	" "	18	S22NW	1860-09-10		A6
7215	" "	18	N21SW	1860-06-01		A8
2002	WALTER, William H	32	SWNE	1861-02-01		A1
2003	WEBB, James	26	SW	1888-11-27		A7
2005	WEBB, John D	25	N½SW	1888-12-04		A7
2004	" "	25	W½NW	1888-12-04		A7
2006	WEBB, Samuel W	25	SWSE	1905-03-30		A7
2008	WELLER, William	2	SE	1860-08-01		A1
2007	" "	2	SESW	1860-08-01		A1
2010	WEST, James A	5	SWSE	1881-10-06		A7
2009	" "	5	SESW	1881-10-06		A7
2012	" "	8	NWNE	1881-10-06		A7
2011	" "	8	NENW	1881-10-06		A7
2014	WILLIAMS, Francis M	12	NENE	1859-09-01	Shannon	A1
2013	" "	12	SENE	1859-09-01	Shannon	A1
2015	WINCHESTER, Mitchell	33	S½SW	1901-03-23		A7
2016	YORBER, Andrew	11	NW	1890-10-11		A7

Patent Map

T26-N R7-W
5th PM 26-N 7-W Meridian

Map Group 8

Township Statistics

Parcels Mapped	:	372
Number of Patents	:	211
Number of Individuals	:	175
Patentees Identified	:	172
Number of Surnames	:	124
Multi-Patentee Parcels	:	6
Oldest Patent Date	:	9/1/1859
Most Recent Patent	:	12/6/1977
Block/Lot Parcels	:	54
Cities and Town	:	1
Cemeteries	:	0

Lots/Tracts-Sec. 6
1NE SHULTZ, AMOS H 1860
1NW KOONCE, ELIGHA W 1889
2NW MCHANN, ALBERT 1861
E22NE SHELTON, JOHN C 1892
N21SW KOONCE, ELIGHA W 1889
N22SW FLOOD, JEREMIAH E 1889
S21SW KOONCE, ROBERT H 1898
S22SW KOONCE, THOMAS J 1896
W22NE MCHANN, ALBERT 1861

Lots/Tracts-Sec. 5
E21NE MCGRATH, WILLIAM H 1908
E22NE NEWSOM, MARY 1861
W21NE HARRIS, ALLEN M 1860
W22NE HARRIS, ALLEN M 1860

Lots/Tracts-Sec. 4
1NE REESE, JAMES P 1891
2NW NEWSOM, MARY 1860
E21NE HAYNES, FRANK M 1901
E22NE HAYNES, FRANK M 1901
W21NE REESE, JAMES P 1891
W22NE REESE, JAMES P 1891

6

HARRIS Allen M 1860

5

4

KOONCE Eligha W 1889

REESE Elijah 1861

DEBOARD [67] Mary J 1891

DEBOARD [67] Mary J 1891

REESE Charles S 1903

HAYNES Frank M 1901

BOLERJACK Henry J 1888

BRISCEY William I 1860

CAMPBELL Lewis B 1892

HOPE John J 1889

WEST James A 1881

WEST James A 1881

HOPE John J 1889

HOPE John J 1889

GREEN Levin 1860

BOLERJACK Henry J 1888

JACKSON Jehiel 1882

BRISCEY William I 1860

WEST James A 1881

WEST James A 1881

GREEN Benjamin F 1859

CONNER Henry H 1911

JACKSON Jehiel 1885

DEBOARD Joel F 1888

DEBOARD Joel F 1888

CAMPBELL Lewis B 1892

LEDBETTER James M 1883

7

8

9

LEDBETTER James R 1876

Lots/Tracts-Sec. 7
1NW DANIEL, MARTIN P 1861
1SW HUDLOW, WILLIAM B 1872
2SW BOLERJACK, MARION H 1884
N22NW THOMAS, CHRISTOPHER C 1908
S22NW BOLERJACK, MARION H 1884

HUDLOW William B 1872

JACKSON Jehiel 1885

DEBOARD Joel F 1888

TAYLOR Alexander 1860

GILES Francis M 1901

GILES Francis M 1901

TAYLOR Alexander 1860

THOMPSON Henry 1860

JACKSON Jehiel 1885

VICKERS James 1889

VICKERS James 1889

DUNKIN William J 1888

JONES [129] Jancey M 1882

JONES [129] Jancey M 1882

REESE David W 1892

DEBOARD Ivy G 1889

DUNKIN William J 1888

DEBOARD Snowden S 1899

JONES [129] Jancey M 1882

☆ EVANS [77] Narcissa M 1906

SCHNEIDER Henry 1860

18

DEBOARD Ivy G 1889

17

16

Lots/Tracts-Sec. 18
N21NW DUNKIN, WILLIAM J 1888
N21SW WALKER, JOHN 1860
N22NW TAYLOR, JOHN 1860
N22SW WALKER, JOHN 1860
S21NW WALKER, JOHN 1860
S21SW WALKER, JOHN 1860
S22NW WALKER, JOHN 1860
S22SW WALKER, JOHN 1860

VESS David M 1876

TAYLOR Riley I 1860

SCHNEIDER Henry 1860

SCHNEIDER Henry 1860

SCHNEIDER Henry 1860

DEBOARD Ivy G 1889

VESS David M 1876

VESS David M 1876

LUCK Elijah 1860

GAROUTTE Isaac 1861

CASTEEL William H 1888

CASTEEL William H 1888

GOODMAN Henry 1884

GOODMAN Henry 1861

GOODMAN Henry 1884

GAROUTTE Isaac 1861

HIGHTOWER Andrew P 1888

KENEGA Mathias 1886

KENEGA Mathias 1906

KENEGA Mathias 1906

COMSTOCK Frank 1892

19

GOODMAN Henry 1884

20

21

Lots/Tracts-Sec. 19
1NW HARVEY, WILLIAM A 1899
N21SW LEDBETTER, JAMES M 1882
N22NW HARVEY, WILLIAM A 1891
N22SW LEDBETTER, JAMES M 1882
S21SW AYERS, ALEXANDER M 1882
S22NW HARVEY, WILLIAM A 1899
S22SW AYERS, ALEXANDER M 1882

GOODMAN Henry 1884

GOODMAN Henry 1884

KENEGA Mathias 1882

HIGHTOWER Andrew P 1888

KENEGA Mathias 1892

KENEGA Mathias 1884

KENEGA Mathias 1882

COMSTOCK Frank 1892

AYERS Alexander M 1882

TURNBAUGH Mary A 1889

TURNBAUGH Mary A 1889

HIGHTOWER Andrew P 1888

KENEGA Mathias 1906

KENEGA Mathias 1882

BROOKS Jacob 1888

Lots/Tracts-Sec. 30
1SW JONES, IRADELL H 1900
N21NW DUNHAM, EPHRAIM 1885
N22NW POE, JESSE 1876
N22SW PORTER, EMSLEY A 1895
S21NW PORTER, EMSLEY A 1895
S22NW PORTER, EMSLEY A 1895
S22SW JONES, ARTHUR C 1910

AYERS Alexander M 1882

AYERS Alexander M 1882

TURNBAUGH Mary A 1889

KENEGA Mathias 1884

KENEGA Mathias 1882

BAY John W 1914

GRAVES Roy E 1911

GRAVES Roy E 1911

MCCOY John 1901

COMSTOCK Alwilda A 1892

BROOKS Jacob 1888

30

HENRY Charles P 1901

29

HENRY Charles P 1901

SEATS William R 1906

SHADWELL Elmer 1898

KENEGA Mathias 1884

COMSTOCK Frank 1891

BROOKS Jacob 1888

SHADWELL Elmer 1898

COMSTOCK Alwilda A 1892

JONES Iradell H 1900

HENRY Charles P 1901

GREEN Calvin 1919

PEACE Pleasant E 1879

PEACE Pleasant E 1879

KENEGA Mathias 1883

COMSTOCK Alwilda A 1892

COMSTOCK Alwilda A 1892

JONES Iradell H 1900

GREEN Calvin 1919

PEACE Pleasant E 1879

PEACE Pleasant E 1879

SHADWELL Elmer 1898

AYERS Alexander M 1882

AYERS Alexander M 1882

SITZS Isaac M 1888

GREEN Calvin 1919

DENTON Jacob 1900

HOOTEN Samuel H 1898

WALTER William H 1861

ELDRINGHOFF Joseph M 1899

AYERS Alexander M 1882

AYERS Alexander M 1882

31

DENTON Jacob 1900

32

HOGGATT John D 1886

ELDRINGHOFF Joseph M 1899

JARRELL Bert E 1910

BRAGG Hugh T 1904

33

BRAGG Hugh T 1904

BLYTHE Aaron 1872

BLYTHE Aaron 1872

HOGGATT John D 1886

Lots/Tracts-Sec. 31
1SW GOBBEL, JOHN 1872
N22SW BOATMAN, HENRY R 1860
S22SW GOBBEL, JOHN 1872

ATCHISON Sarah 1882

ELDRINGHOFF John J 1899

WINCHESTER Mitchell 1901

BRAGG Hugh T 1904

BARTON William H 1892

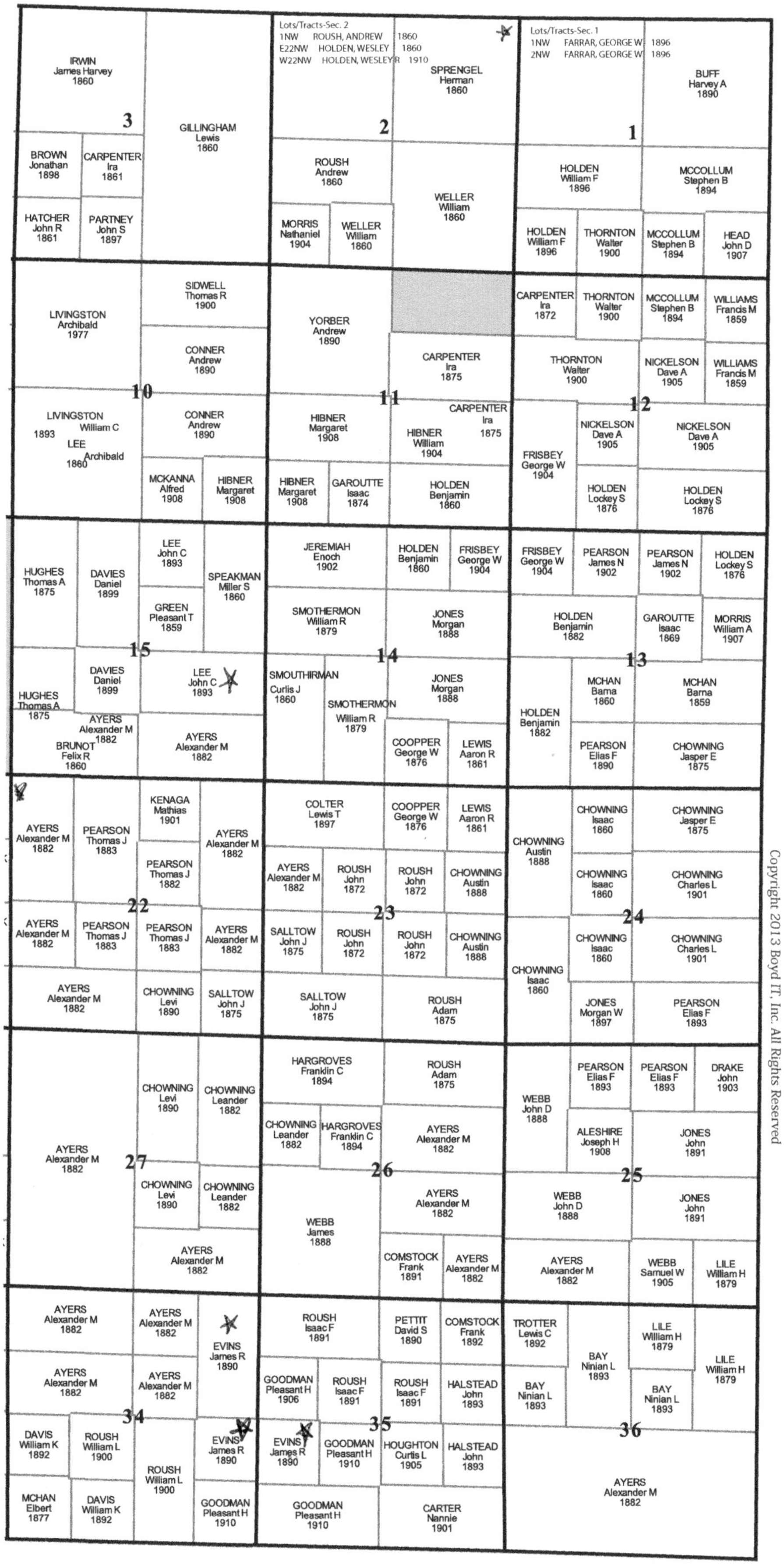

		Lots/Tracts–Sec. 2			Lots/Tracts–Sec. 1		
		1NW ROUSH, ANDREW 1860			1NW FARRAR, GEORGE W 1896		
		E22NW HOLDEN, WESLEY 1860			2NW FARRAR, GEORGE W 1896		
		W22NW HOLDEN, WESLEY R 1910					

IRWIN James Harvey 1860

3

GILLINGHAM Lewis 1860

SPRENGEL Herman 1860

2

1

BUFF Harvey A 1890

BROWN Jonathan 1898 | CARPENTER Ira 1861

ROUSH Andrew 1860

WELLER William 1860

HOLDEN William F 1896

MCCOLLUM Stephen B 1894

HATCHER John R 1861 | PARTNEY John S 1897

MORRIS Nathaniel 1904 | WELLER William 1860

HOLDEN William F 1896 | THORNTON Walter 1900 | MCCOLLUM Stephen B 1894 | HEAD John D 1907

LIVINGSTON Archibald 1977

SIDWELL Thomas R 1900

YORBER Andrew 1890

CARPENTER Ira 1872 | THORNTON Walter 1900 | MCCOLLUM Stephen B 1894 | WILLIAMS Francis M 1859

CONNER Andrew 1890

CARPENTER Ira 1875

THORNTON Walter 1900 | NICKELSON Dave A 1905 | WILLIAMS Francis M 1859

10

11

12

LIVINGSTON William C 1893 | CONNER Andrew 1890

HIBNER Margaret 1908

CARPENTER Ira 1875

NICKELSON Dave A 1905 | NICKELSON Dave A 1905

LEE Archibald 1860

HIBNER William 1904

FRISBEY George W 1904

MCKANNA Alfred 1908 | HIBNER Margaret 1908

HIBNER Margaret 1908 | GAROUTTE Isaac 1874

HOLDEN Benjamin 1860

HOLDEN Lockey S 1876 | HOLDEN Lockey S 1876

HUGHES Thomas A 1875 | DAVIES Daniel 1899

LEE John C 1893

SPEAKMAN Miller S 1860

JEREMIAH Enoch 1902

HOLDEN Benjamin 1860 | FRISBEY George W 1904

FRISBEY George W 1904 | PEARSON James N 1902 | PEARSON James N 1902 | HOLDEN Lockey S 1876

GREEN Pleasant T 1859

SMOTHERMON William R 1879

JONES Morgan 1888

HOLDEN Benjamin 1882

GAROUTTE Isaac 1869 | MORRIS William A 1907

15

14

13

DAVIES Daniel 1899

LEE John C 1893

SMOUTHIRMAN Curlis J 1860

JONES Morgan 1888

MCHAN Barna 1860 | MCHAN Barna 1859

HUGHES Thomas A 1875

SMOTHERMON William R 1879

HOLDEN Benjamin 1882

AYERS Alexander M 1882

AYERS Alexander M 1882

COOPPER George W 1876 | LEWIS Aaron R 1861

PEARSON Elias F 1890 | CHOWNING Jasper E 1875

BRUNOT Felix R 1860

KENAGA Mathias 1901

AYERS Alexander M 1882

COLTER Lewis T 1897

COOPPER George W 1876 | LEWIS Aaron R 1861

CHOWNING Austin 1888

CHOWNING Isaac 1860 | CHOWNING Jasper E 1875

AYERS Alexander M 1882 | PEARSON Thomas J 1883

PEARSON Thomas J 1882

AYERS Alexander M 1882 | ROUSH John 1872 | ROUSH John 1872 | CHOWNING Austin 1888

CHOWNING Isaac 1860 | CHOWNING Charles L 1901

22

23

24

AYERS Alexander M 1882 | PEARSON Thomas J 1883

PEARSON Thomas J 1882 | AYERS Alexander M 1882

SALLTOW John J 1875 | ROUSH John 1872 | ROUSH John 1872 | CHOWNING Austin 1888

CHOWNING Isaac 1860 | CHOWNING Charles L 1901

AYERS Alexander M 1882

CHOWNING Levi 1890 | SALLTOW John J 1875

SALLTOW John J 1875

ROUSH Adam 1875

CHOWNING Isaac 1860

JONES Morgan W 1897 | PEARSON Elias F 1893

HARGROVES Franklin C 1894

ROUSH Adam 1875

PEARSON Elias F 1893 | PEARSON Elias F 1893 | DRAKE John 1903

CHOWNING Levi 1890 | CHOWNING Leander 1882

WEBB John D 1888

CHOWNING Leander 1882 | HARGROVES Franklin C 1894

AYERS Alexander M 1882

ALESHIRE Joseph H 1908

JONES John 1891

AYERS Alexander M 1882

27

26

25

CHOWNING Levi 1890 | CHOWNING Leander 1882

AYERS Alexander M 1882

WEBB John D 1888

JONES John 1891

WEBB James 1888

AYERS Alexander M 1882

COMSTOCK Frank 1891 | AYERS Alexander M 1882

AYERS Alexander M 1882

WEBB Samuel W 1905 | LILE William H 1879

AYERS Alexander M 1882 | AYERS Alexander M 1882

EVINS James R 1890

ROUSH Isaac F 1891

PETTIT David S 1890 | COMSTOCK Frank 1892

TROTTER Lewis C 1892

LILE William H 1879

AYERS Alexander M 1882 | AYERS Alexander M 1882

GOODMAN Pleasant H 1906 | ROUSH Isaac F 1891

ROUSH Isaac F 1891 | HALSTEAD John 1893

BAY Ninian L 1893

BAY Ninian L 1893

LILE William H 1879

34

35

36

DAVIS William K 1892 | ROUSH William L 1900

EVINS James R 1890

EVINS James R 1890 | GOODMAN Pleasant H 1910

HOUGHTON Curtis L 1905 | HALSTEAD John 1893

ROUSH William L 1900

MCHAN Elbert 1877 | DAVIS William K 1892

GOODMAN Pleasant H 1910

GOODMAN Pleasant H 1910

CARTER Nannie 1901

AYERS Alexander M 1882

Helpful Hints

1. This Map's INDEX can be found on the preceding pages.

2. Refer to Map "C" to see where this Township lies within Howell County, Missouri.

3. Numbers within square brackets [ ] denote a multi-patentee land parcel (multi-owner). Refer to Appendix "C" for a full list of members in this group.

4. Areas that look to be crowded with Patentees usually indicate multiple sales of the same parcel (Re-issues) or Overlapping parcels. See this Township's Index for an explanation of these and other circumstances that might explain "odd" groupings of Patentees on this map.

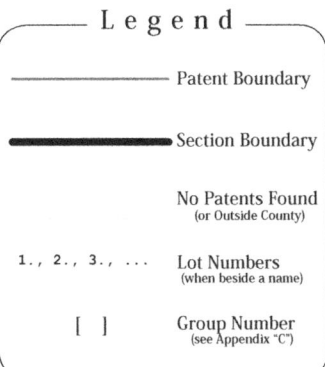

Legend

_____ Patent Boundary

━━━━━━━ Section Boundary

No Patents Found (or Outside County)

1., 2., 3., ... Lot Numbers (when beside a name)

[ ] Group Number (see Appendix "C")

Scale: Section = 1 mile X 1 mile (generally, with some exceptions)

Road Map

T26-N R7-W
5th PM 26-N 7-W Meridian

Map Group 8

Cities & Towns
Chapel

Cemeteries
None

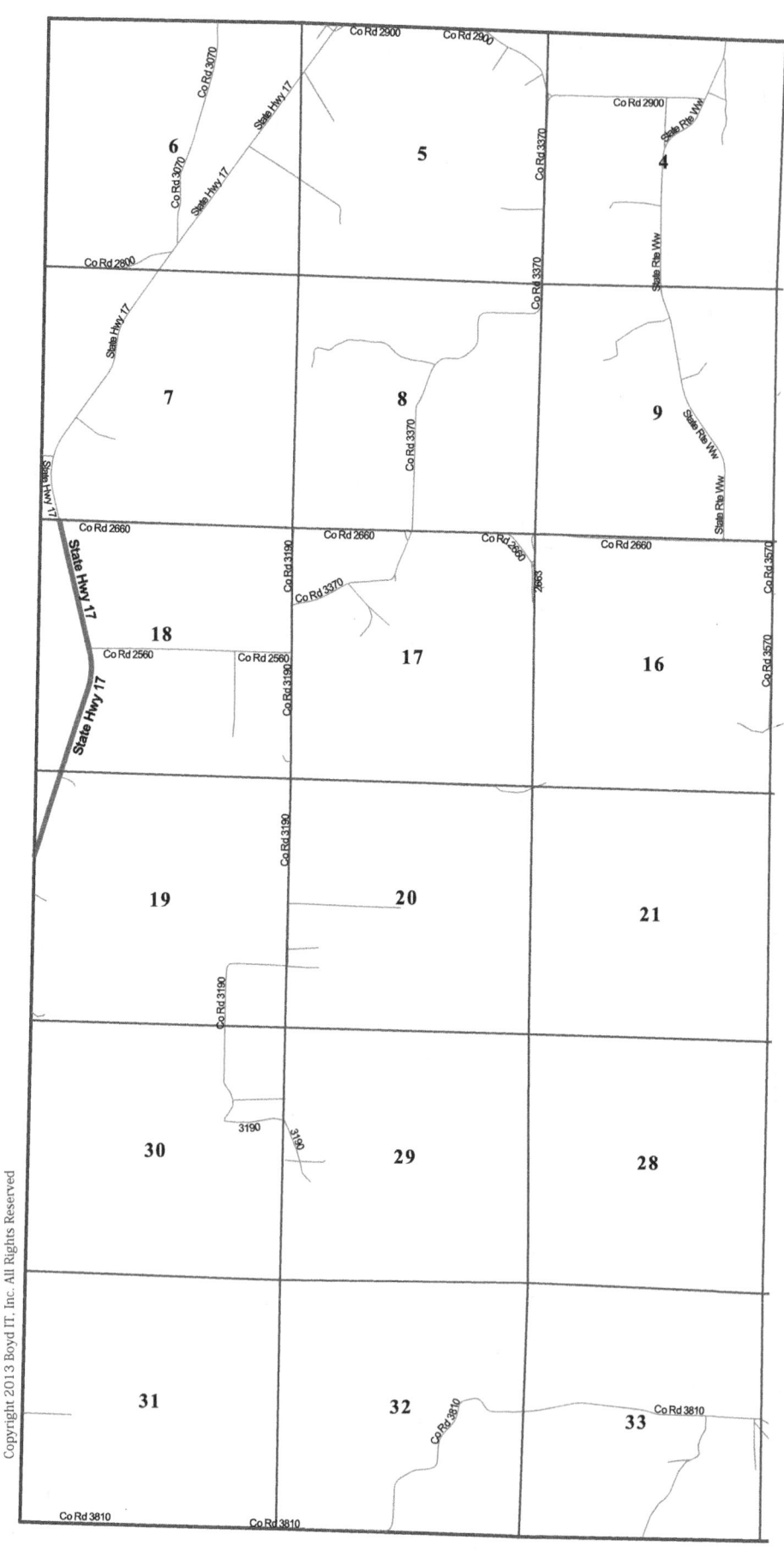

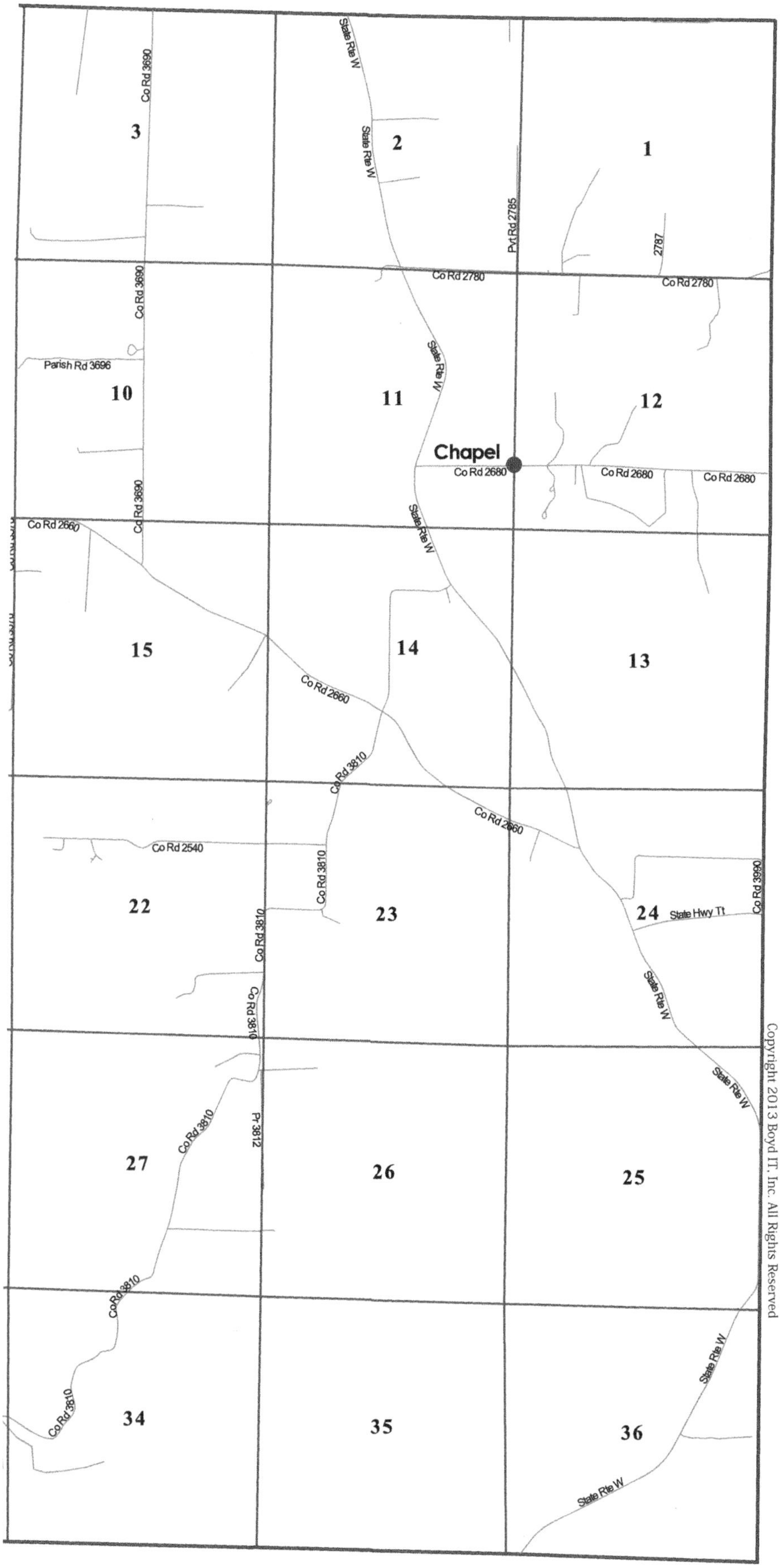

3

2

1

10

11

12

Co Rd 3690

Co Rd 3690

Parish Rd 3696

State Rte W

State Rte W

Pvt Rd 2785

2787

Co Rd 2780

Co Rd 2780

Chapel

Co Rd 2680

Co Rd 2680

Co Rd 2680

State Rte W

Co Rd 2660

Co Rd 3690

15

14

13

22

23

24

27

26

25

34

35

36

Co Rd 2660

Co Rd 3810

Co Rd 2540

Co Rd 2660

Co Rd 3810

Co Rd 3810

Co Rd 3810

Pvt 3812

Co Rd 3810

Co Rd 3810

State Hwy T1

Co Rd 3690

State Rte W

State Rte W

State Rte W

Copyright 2013 Boyd IT, Inc. All Rights Reserved

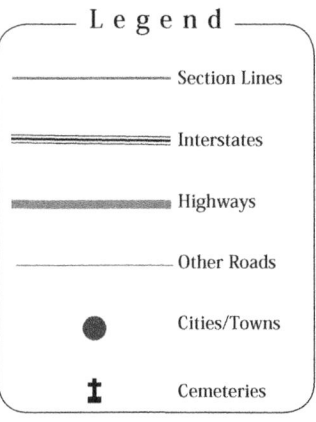

L e g e n d

——————— Section Lines

═══════ Interstates

━━━━━━━ Highways

——————— Other Roads

● Cities/Towns

☖ Cemeteries

Scale: Section = 1 mile X 1 mile
(generally, with some exceptions)

Historical Map

T26-N R7-W
5th PM 26-N 7-W Meridian

Map Group 8

Cities & Towns
Chapel

Cemeteries
None

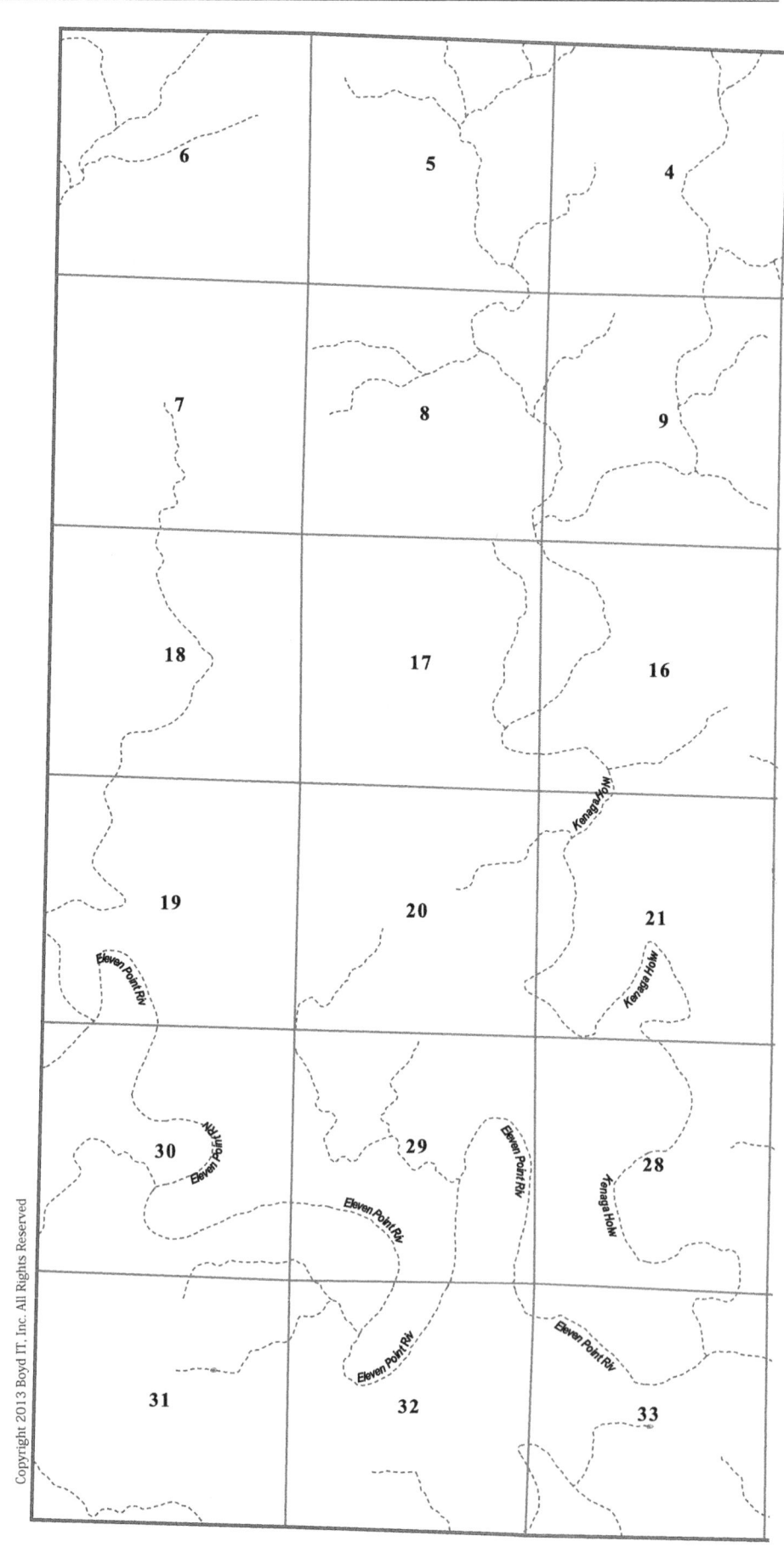

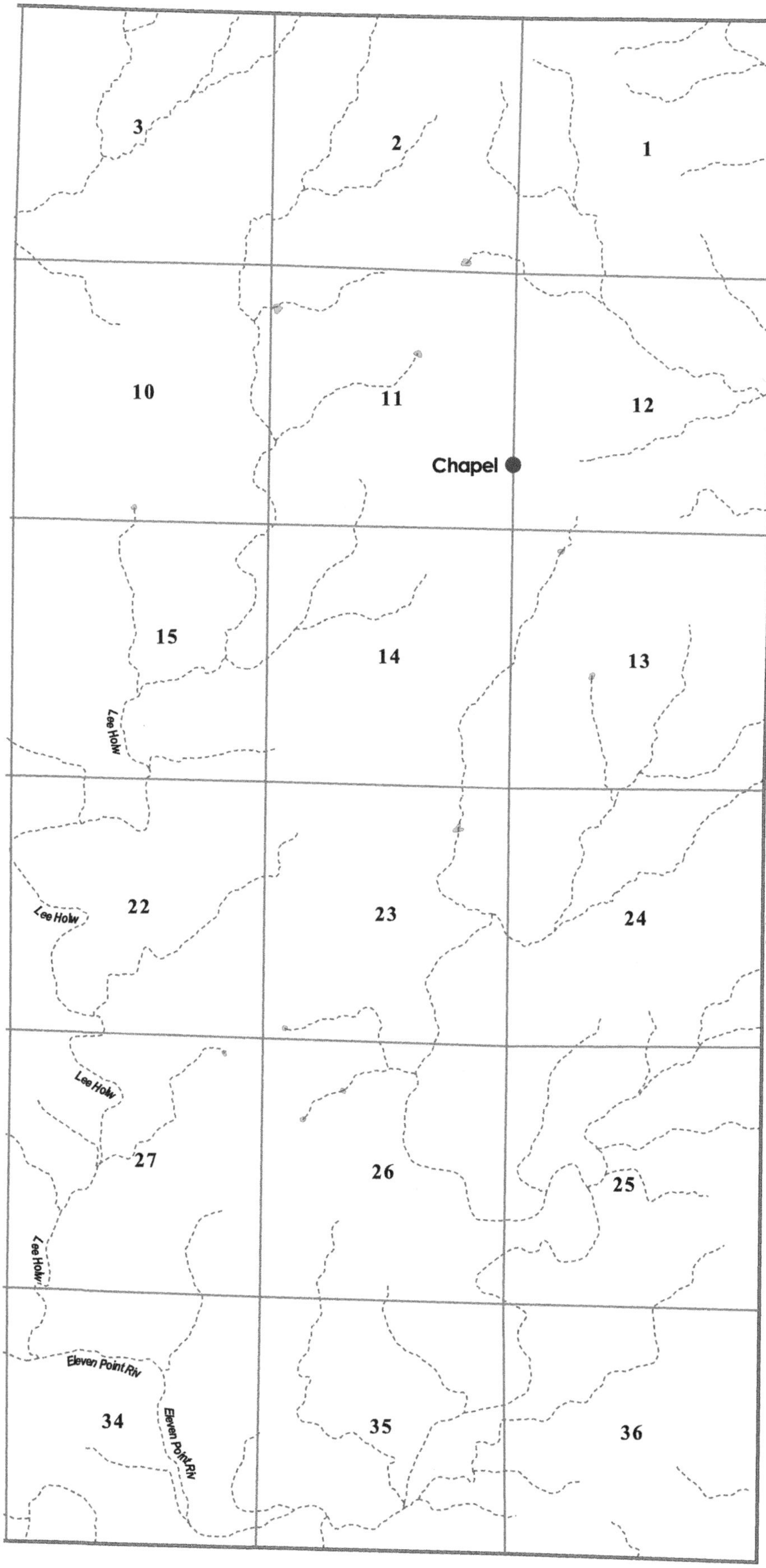

3

2

1

10

11

12

Chapel ●

15

14

13

Lee Holw

22

23

24

Lee Holw

Lee Holw

27

26

25

Lee Holw

Eleven Point Riv

34

Eleven Point Riv

35

36

Helpful Hints

1. This Map takes a different look at the same Congressional Township displayed in the preceding two maps. It presents features that can help you better envision the historical development of the area: a) Water-bodies (lakes & ponds), b) Water-courses (rivers, streams, etc.), c) Railroads, d) City/town center-points (where they were oftentimes located when first settled), and e) Cemeteries.

2. Using this "Historical" map in tandem with this Township's Patent Map and Road Map, may lead you to some interesting discoveries. You will often find roads, towns, cemeteries, and waterways are named after nearby landowners: sometimes those names will be the ones you are researching. See how many of these research gems you can find here in Howell County.

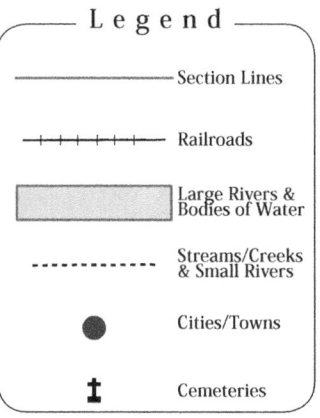

L e g e n d

——————— Section Lines

+–+–+–+–+–+ Railroads

Large Rivers & Bodies of Water

----------- Streams/Creeks & Small Rivers

● Cities/Towns

‡ Cemeteries

Scale: Section = 1 mile X 1 mile
(there are some exceptions)

Map Group 9: Index to Land Patents

Township 25-North Range 10-West (5th PM 25-N 10-W)

After you locate an individual in this Index, take note of the Section and Section Part then proceed to the Land Patent map on the pages immediately following. You should have no difficulty locating the corresponding parcel of land.

The "For More Info" Column will lead you to more information about the underlying Patents. See the *Legend* at right, and the "How to Use this Book" chapter, for more information.

```
                        LEGEND
              "For More Info . . ." column
A = Authority (Legislative Act, See Appendix "A")
B = Block or Lot (location in Section unknown)
C = Cancelled Patent
F = Fractional Section
G = Group (Multi-Patentee Patent, see Appendix "C")
V = Overlaps another Parcel
R = Re-Issued (Parcel patented more than once)

(A & G items require you to look in the Appendixes referred
to above. All other Letter-designations followed by a number
require you to locate line-items in this index that possess
the ID number found after the letter).
```

ID	Individual in Patent	Sec.	Sec. Part	Date Issued	Other Counties	For More Info . . .
2017	ALSUP, Ben M	15	NWNW	1908-03-05		A1
2018	BENSON, Marcus E	21	SWNW	1888-05-07		A1
2019	BOATMAN, Henry R	1	SE	1874-11-05		A7
2020	" "	22	NENE	1888-05-07		A1
2021	BOATMAN, Polley A	23	E½NW	1890-10-11		A7
2022	" "	23	NWNE	1890-10-11		A7
2023	" "	23	NWNW	1890-10-11		A7
2025	BOYD, Emma G	22	W½SW	1894-12-17		A7
2024	" "	22	SWNW	1894-12-17		A7
2026	" "	22	NESW	1894-12-17		A7
2027	BOYD, Robert D	15	SE	1893-09-08		A7
2028	BRADLEY, Samuel T	11	NWNE	1895-05-28		A7
2029	" "	11	NENW	1895-05-28		A7
2030	BRIXEY, Barney	36	SWNW	1912-02-15		A7
2031	BRIXEY, Samuel	35	NESE	1896-08-28		A7
2032	" "	36	NWSW	1888-12-08		A7
2033	BRIXEY, William	35	SESE	1869-07-01		A1
2034	" "	36	SWSW	1869-07-01		A1
2035	BUMGARNER, Henry	2	SESW	1901-12-17		A7
2036	" "	2	SWSE	1901-12-17		A7
2038	BYERS, Joseph A	36	SWSE	1912-03-14		A7
2039	" "	36	SESW	1912-03-14		A7
2037	" "	36	E½SE	1912-03-14		A7
2040	CASTLEMAN, Ann	35	W½SE	1861-04-01		A8 G41
2041	COLLINS, Benjamin	28	NE	1892-03-07		A7
2042	COLLINS, David	35	NESW	1883-06-30		A7
2043	COLLINS, Elec Z	21	NWNW	1890-01-30		A1
2044	" "	21	E½NW	1890-01-30		A1
2045	COLLINS, Ezekiel	15	S½SW	1890-06-04		A1
2046	" "	22	N½NW	1890-06-04		A1
2047	COLLINS, Henry	23	S½NE	1891-05-25		A7 G53
2048	" "	23	NESE	1891-05-25		A7 G53
2049	" "	23	NENE	1891-05-25		A7 G53
7285	COLLINS, James F	3	1NW	1890-01-10		A7
2050	" "	3	W½SW	1890-01-10		A7
2053	COLLINS, Polly A	23	NENE	1891-05-25		A7 G53
2052	" "	23	S½NE	1891-05-25		A7 G53
2051	" "	23	NESE	1891-05-25		A7 G53
2054	COLLINS, Thomas G	35	W½SW	1902-09-15		A7
2056	CUNNINGHAM, Hugh A	10	SWNW	1890-10-11		A7
2055	" "	10	W½SW	1890-10-11		A7
2057	" "	9	NESE	1890-10-11		A7
2058	DESITS, Malinda D	9	N½NW	1883-08-13		A1
2059	DOLLENS, John C	1	NWSW	1879-12-15		A7
2061	" "	2	N½SE	1879-12-15		A7
2060	" "	2	SESE	1879-12-15		A7

ID	Individual in Patent	Sec.	Sec. Part	Date Issued	Other Counties	For More Info . . .
2062	DOLLINS, John C	2	NESW	1885-03-20		A1
2063	ELLIS, William R	28	NESW	1897-10-28		A7
2064	EVERED, Alfred C	25	SWSE	1901-06-29		A1
2065	" "	36	NWNE	1901-06-29		A1
2067	GRAHAM, Henry	36	NESW	1900-08-09		A7
2066	" "	36	SENW	1900-08-09		A7
2068	" "	36	S½NE	1900-08-09		A7
2069	GREENWOOD, Albert	21	E½SE	1897-10-28		A7
2070	" "	21	E½NE	1897-10-28		A7
2072	GREGORY, Andrew J	23	NWSW	1900-02-02		A7
2071	" "	23	SWNW	1900-02-02		A7
2073	GREGORY, James M	23	SESE	1900-02-02		A7
2074	GREGORY, Julia A	23	W½SE	1881-10-06		A7 G98
2075	" "	23	E½SW	1881-10-06		A7 G98
2077	GREGORY, Sheriff	23	E½SW	1881-10-06		A7 G98
2076	" "	23	W½SE	1881-10-06		A7 G98
2079	HOPKINS, Jeremiah	15	N½SW	1888-12-08		A7
2078	" "	15	S½NW	1888-12-08		A7
2080	HOWARD, Harmon	35	W½SE	1861-04-01		A8 G41
7276	HOWARD, Philip J	1	W21NE	1860-08-01		A1
2081	JONES, Martin	25	NESW	1861-02-01		A1
2082	JONES, William	35	SESW	1861-02-01		A1
2083	KEITHLY, Will	10	W½NE	1906-01-30		A7
2085	LEARNARD, Oscar E	29		1882-06-01		A1
2086	" "	30		1882-06-01		A1
2087	LOVAN, James M	1	NENW	1878-11-30		A7
2089	" "	1	W½NW	1878-11-30		A7
2088	" "	1	NWNE	1878-11-30		A7
7275	LOVAN, Sterling C	1	E22NE	1892-09-09		A7
7274	" "	1	E21NE	1892-09-09		A7
2090	LOVINS, Joseph T	36	NWSE	1903-07-14		A7
2092	LUMBLEY, David	9	SWSE	1903-08-25		A7
2091	" "	9	SESW	1903-08-25		A7
2094	MCMAHAN, William N	21	W½SE	1901-04-09		A7
2093	" "	21	W½NE	1901-04-09		A7
7277	MCMILLIN, John H	2	1NE	1888-12-06		A7
7279	" "	2	E22NE	1888-12-06		A7
2096	MURRELL, Mary V	9	W½SW	1890-10-11		A7
2095	" "	9	SWNW	1890-10-11		A7
2097	OAKES, James	11	W½NW	1890-10-11		A7
2098	OAKS, Albert S	10	N½NW	1902-05-21		A7
2099	" "	3	E½SW	1902-05-21		A7
2101	OAKS, Eugene	10	SESW	1892-03-07		A7
2100	" "	10	S½SE	1892-03-07		A7
2102	" "	15	NENW	1892-03-07		A7
7284	OAKS, John M	3	1NE	1891-05-05		A7
2106	OLDEN, Benjamin F	11	NENE	1885-12-19		A1
2108	" "	11	S½NE	1885-12-19		A1
2104	" "	11	S½SW	1885-12-19		A1
2103	" "	11	SE	1885-12-19		A1
2105	" "	11	N½SW	1885-12-19		A1
2107	" "	11	SENW	1885-12-19		A1
2109	" "	15	NE	1885-07-27		A1
2110	ORTNER, George F	9	SESE	1908-03-05		A1
7287	PETRY, Nelson	3	2NW	1885-03-20		A1
7286	PETTY, Nelson	3	2NE	1889-01-12		A7
2111	PIERCE, David M	22	NWNE	1895-11-13		A1
2114	PITMAN, John	9	NESW	1890-10-11		A7
2113	" "	9	W½NE	1890-10-11		A7
2112	" "	9	SENW	1890-10-11		A7
2115	PITTS, P T	26	NENW	1884-03-10		A1
2116	PLAYFORTH, Henry	3	SE	1879-12-15		A7
2117	PREWITT, Warren	9	E½NE	1895-05-28		A7
2118	RUSSELL, Alvacinda E	28	NWSW	1888-05-07		A1
2119	" "	28	SESW	1888-05-07		A1
2120	SEELY, Walt M	9	NWSE	1908-05-25		A1
7288	SHIPMAN, James S	3	W21NW	1882-09-30		A7
2121	" "	3	NWSW	1882-09-30		A7
2122	SMITH, George	1	E½SW	1895-09-04		A7
2124	" "	1	SENW	1895-09-04		A7
2123	" "	1	SWSW	1895-09-04		A7
2125	STEGER, Robert B	10	NESW	1901-03-23		A7
2126	" "	10	SENW	1901-03-23		A7

ID	Individual in Patent	Sec.	Sec. Part	Date Issued	Other Counties	For More Info . . .
2127	STUBBS, Jacob	22	E½SE	1888-12-08		A7
2128	" "	22	SESW	1888-12-08		A7
2129	" "	22	SWSE	1888-12-08		A7
2130	STUDDARD, John A	26	SW	1875-11-01		A7
2131	STUDDARD, Joseph J	26	NWSE	1883-08-13		A1
7281	TAYLOR, John	2	W21NW	1874-11-05		A7
2132	" "	2	W½SW	1874-11-05		A7
7283	" "	2	W22NW	1874-11-05		A7
7278	TAYLOR, Travis	2	E21NW	1878-04-05		A7
7280	" "	2	E22NW	1878-04-05		A7
7282	" "	2	W22NE	1878-04-05		A7
2133	TURNER, William H	26	NE	1889-07-26		A7
2134	WARD, Samuel	28	SWSW	1901-01-10		A1
2136	WETHERFORD, Henry G	25	NWSE	1892-06-21		A7
2135	" "	25	E½SE	1892-06-21		A7
2137	" "	36	NENE	1892-06-21		A7
2138	WETHERFORD, William	22	S½NE	1881-10-06		A7
2139	" "	22	SENW	1881-10-06		A7
2140	" "	22	NWSE	1881-10-06		A7
2141	WILLIAMS, George J	23	SWSW	1892-09-09		A7
2142	" "	26	SENW	1892-09-09		A7
2143	" "	26	W½NW	1892-09-09		A7
2144	WILLIAMS, John B	25	NWSW	1892-11-03		A7
2146	" "	26	E½SE	1892-11-03		A7
2145	" "	26	SWSE	1892-11-03		A7
2147	WILLIAMS, Reuben E	25	S½SW	1894-05-18		A7
2148	" "	36	N½NW	1894-05-18		A7
2150	WOODS, Henry	10	N½SE	1888-12-08		A7
2149	" "	10	E½NE	1888-12-08		A7

Patent Map

T25-N R10-W
5th PM 25-N 10-W Meridian

Map Group 9

Township Statistics

Parcels Mapped	:	142
Number of Patents	:	80
Number of Individuals	:	79
Patentees Identified	:	75
Number of Surnames	:	55
Multi-Patentee Parcels	:	6
Oldest Patent Date	:	2/1/1861
Most Recent Patent	:	3/14/1912
Block/Lot Parcels	:	15
Cities and Town	:	2
Cemeteries	:	2

Lots/Tracts-Sec. 3
1NE	OAKS, JOHN M	1891
1NW	COLLINS, JAMES F	1890
2NE	PETTY, NELSON	1889
2NW	PETRY, NELSON	1885
W21NW	SHIPMAN, JAMES S	1882

Lots/Tracts-Sec. 2
1NE	MCMILLIN, JOHN H	1888
E21NW	TAYLOR, TRAVIS	1878
E22NE	MCMILLIN, JOHN H	1888
E22NW	TAYLOR, TRAVIS	1878
W21NW	TAYLOR, JOHN	1874
W22NE	TAYLOR, TRAVIS	1878
W22NW	TAYLOR, JOHN	1874

3

SHIPMAN James S 1882
COLLINS James F 1890
OAKS Albert S 1902
PLAYFORTH Henry 1879

2

TAYLOR John 1874
DOLLINS John C 1885
DOLLENS John C 1879
BUMGARNER Henry 1901
BUMGARNER Henry 1901
DOLLENS John C 1879

DOLLENS John C 1879
SMITH George 1895
SMITH George 1895

1

LOVAN James M 1878
LOVAN James M 1878
LOVAN James M 1878
SMITH George 1895
BOATMAN Henry R 1874

Lots/Tracts-Sec. 1
E21NE	LOVAN, STERLING C	1892
E22NE	LOVAN, STERLING C	1892
W21NE	HOWARD, PHILIP J	1860

10

OAKS Albert S 1902
KEITHLY Will 1906
WOODS Henry 1888
CUNNINGHAM Hugh A 1890
STEGER Robert B 1901
STEGER Robert B 1901
WOODS Henry 1888
CUNNINGHAM Hugh A 1890
OAKS Eugene 1892
OAKS Eugene 1892

11

OAKES James 1890
BRADLEY Samuel T 1895
BRADLEY Samuel T 1895
OLDEN Benjamin F 1885
OLDEN Benjamin F 1885
OLDEN Benjamin F 1885
OLDEN Benjamin F 1885
OLDEN Benjamin F 1885
OLDEN Benjamin F 1885

12

15

ALSUP Ben M 1908
OAKS Eugene 1892
OLDEN Benjamin F 1885
HOPKINS Jeremiah 1888
HOPKINS Jeremiah 1888
BOYD Robert D 1893
COLLINS Ezekiel 1890

14

13

22

COLLINS Ezekiel 1890
PIERCE David M 1895
BOATMAN Henry R 1888
BOYD Emma G 1894
WETHERFORD William 1881
WETHERFORD William 1881
BOYD Emma G 1894
WETHERFORD William 1881
STUBBS Jacob 1888
BOYD Emma G 1894
STUBBS Jacob 1888
STUBBS Jacob 1888

23

BOATMAN Polley A 1890
BOATMAN Polley A 1890
BOATMAN Polley A 1890
COLLINS [53] Polly A 1891
GREGORY Andrew J 1900
COLLINS [53] Polly A 1891
GREGORY Andrew J 1900
COLLINS [53] Polly A 1891
GREGORY [98] Julia A 1881
WILLIAMS George J 1892
GREGORY [98] Julia A 1881
GREGORY James M 1900

24

27

26

WILLIAMS George J 1892
PITTS P T 1884
WILLIAMS George J 1892
TURNER William H 1889
STUDDARD John A 1875
STUDDARD Joseph J 1883
WILLIAMS John B 1892
WILLIAMS John B 1892

25

WILLIAMS John B 1892
JONES Martin 1861
WETHERFORD Henry G 1892
WETHERFORD Henry G 1892
WILLIAMS Reuben E 1894
EVERED Alfred C 1901

34

35

COLLINS Thomas G 1902
COLLINS David 1883
HOWARD [41] Harmon 1861
BRIXEY Samuel 1896
JONES William 1861
BRIXEY William 1869

36

WILLIAMS Reuben E 1894
EVERED Alfred C 1901
WETHERFORD Henry G 1892
BRIXEY Barney 1912
GRAHAM Henry 1900
GRAHAM Henry 1900
BRIXEY Samuel 1888
GRAHAM Henry 1900
LOVINS Joseph T 1903
BYERS Joseph A 1912
BRIXEY William 1869
BYERS Joseph A 1912
BYERS Joseph A 1912

Helpful Hints

1. This Map's INDEX can be found on the preceding pages.

2. Refer to Map "C" to see where this Township lies within Howell County, Missouri.

3. Numbers within square brackets [ ] denote a multi-patentee land parcel (multi-owner). Refer to Appendix "C" for a full list of members in this group.

4. Areas that look to be crowded with Patentees usually indicate multiple sales of the same parcel (Re-issues) or Overlapping parcels. See this Township's Index for an explanation of these and other circumstances that might explain "odd" groupings of Patentees on this map.

Legend

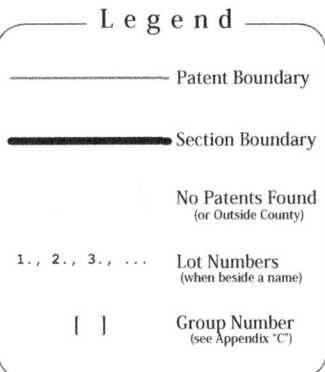

- Patent Boundary
- Section Boundary
- No Patents Found (or Outside County)
- 1., 2., 3., ... Lot Numbers (when beside a name)
- [ ] Group Number (see Appendix "C")

Scale: Section = 1 mile X 1 mile
(generally, with some exceptions)

Road Map

T25-N R10-W
5th PM 25-N 10-W Meridian

Map Group 9

Cities & Towns
Horton
Siloam Springs

Cemeteries
Horton Cemetery
Oak Grove Cemetery

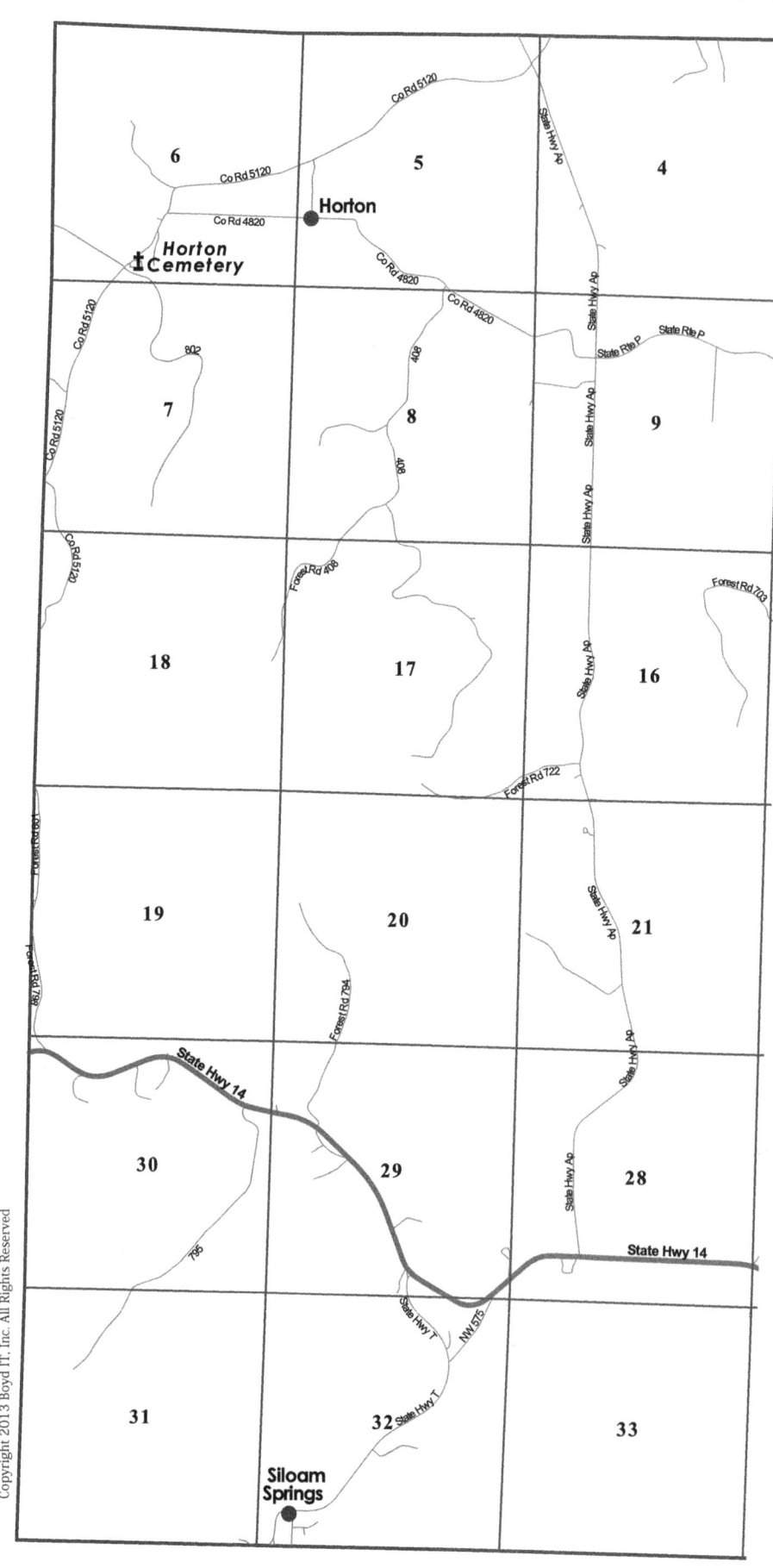

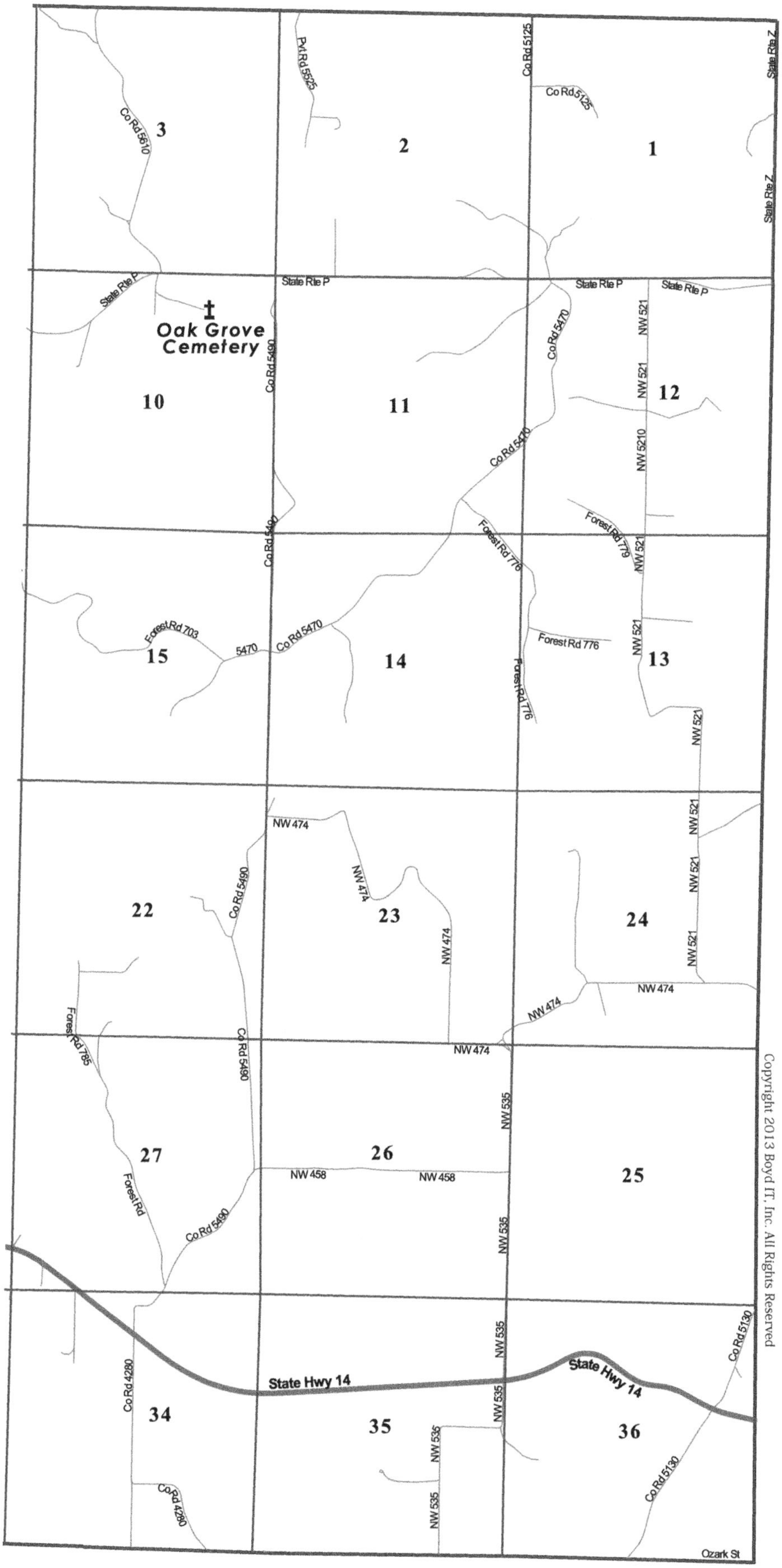

Co Rd 5610 **3**

Pvt Rd 5525 **2**

Co Rd 5125 **1**

State Rte P

Co Rd 5125

State Rte Z

State Rte P

State Rte P State Rte P

Co Rd 5470

NW 521

NW 521

✝
**Oak Grove
Cemetery**

Co Rd 5490

10

11

Co Rd 5470

12

NW 5210

Co Rd 5490

Forest Rd 776

Forest Rd 779

NW 521

Forest Rd 703

5470 Co Rd 5470

Forest Rd 776

NW 521

15

14

Forest Rd 776

NW 521

13

NW 521

NW 474

NW 474

Co Rd 5690

22

NW 474

23

NW 474

24

NW 521

NW 521

NW 521

NW 474

NW 474

Forest Rd 785

Co Rd 5490

NW 474

NW 535

27

26

NW 458 NW 458

25

Forest Rd

Co Rd 5490

NW 535

Co Rd 4280

State Hwy 14

State Hwy 14

NW 535

Co Rd 5130

34

35

36

NW 535

Co Rd 4280

NW 535

Co Rd 5130

Ozark St

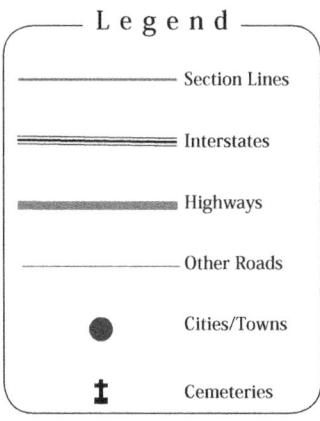

Helpful Hints

1. This road map has a number of uses, but primarily it is to help you: a) find the present location of land owned by your ancestors (at least the general area), b) find cemeteries and city-centers, and c) estimate the route/roads used by Census-takers & tax-assessors.

2. If you plan to travel to Howell County to locate cemeteries or land parcels, please pick up a modern travel map for the area before you do. Mapping old land parcels on modern maps is not as exact a science as you might think. Just the slightest variations in public land survey coordinates, estimates of parcel boundaries, or road-map deviations can greatly alter a map's representation of how a road either does or doesn't cross a particular parcel of land.

L e g e n d

——————— Section Lines

═══════ Interstates

━━━━━━━ Highways

——————— Other Roads

● Cities/Towns

✝ Cemeteries

Scale: Section = 1 mile X 1 mile
(generally, with some exceptions)

Historical Map

T25-N R10-W
5th PM 25-N 10-W Meridian

Map Group 9

Cities & Towns
Horton
Siloam Springs

Cemeteries
Horton Cemetery
Oak Grove Cemetery

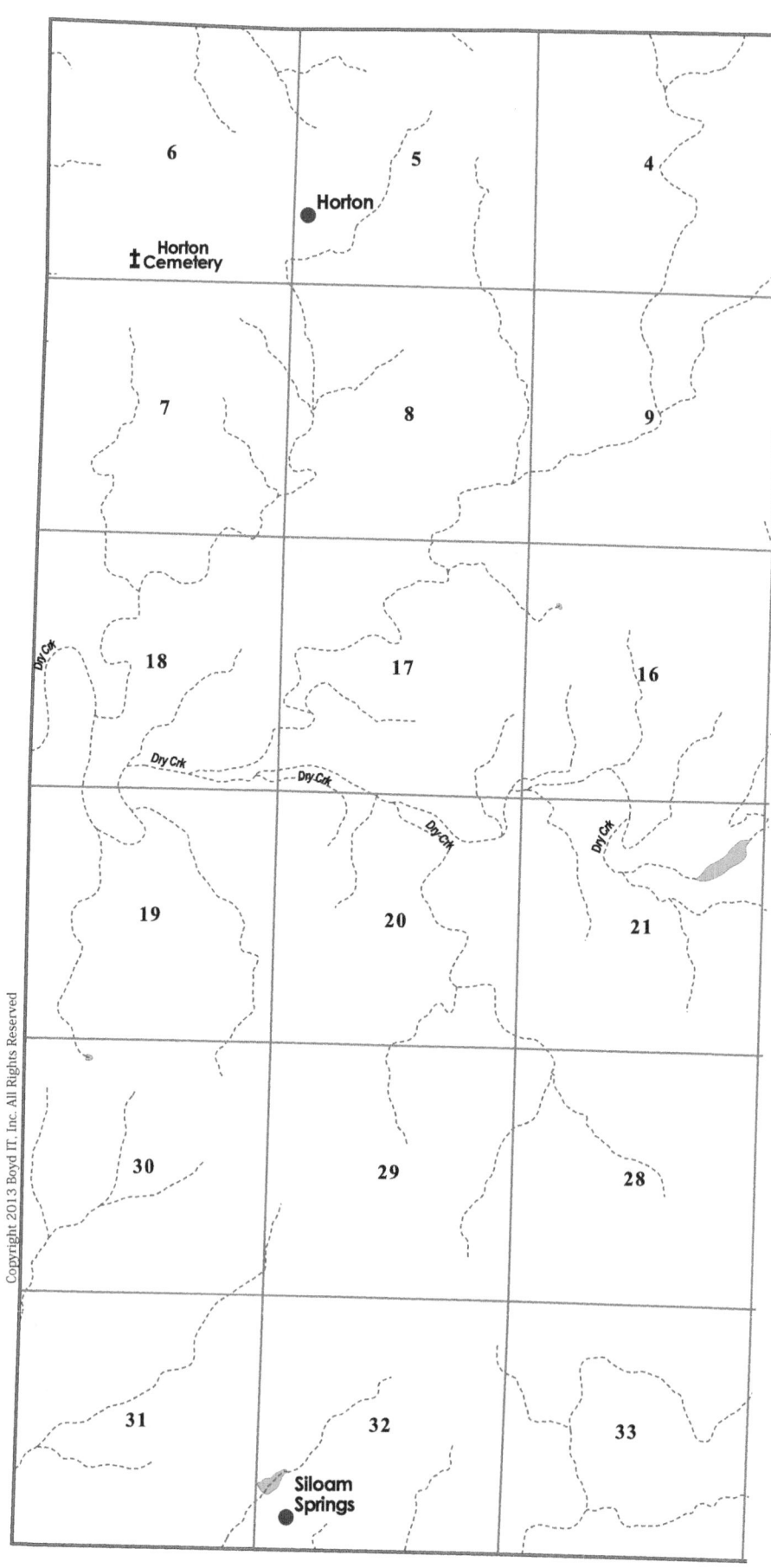

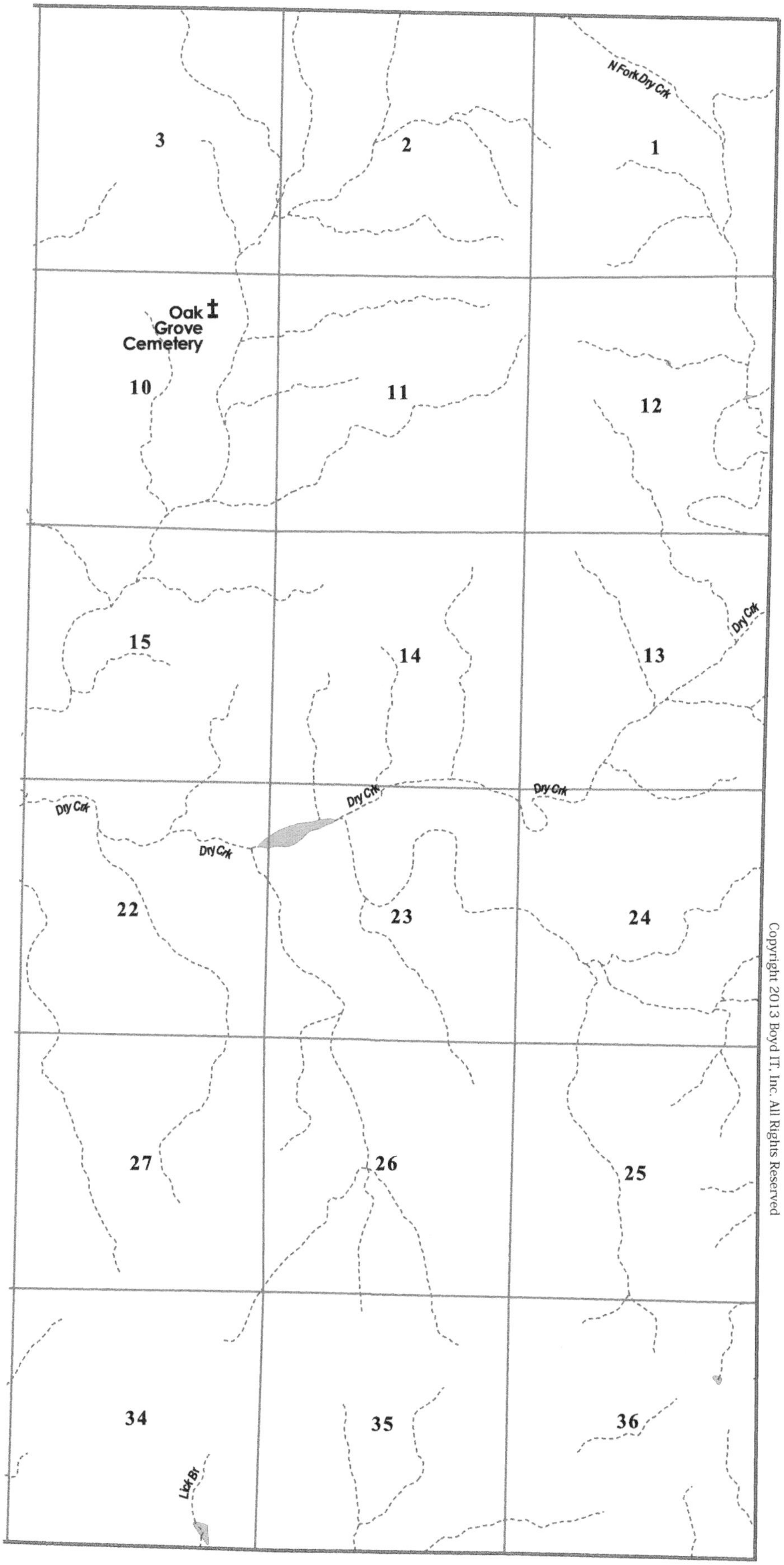

3

2

1

N Fork Dry Crk

Oak ‡
Grove
Cemetery

10

11

12

15

14

13

Dry Crk

22

Dry Crk

Dry Crk

Dry Crk

Dry Crk

Dry Crk

23

24

27

26

25

34

35

36

Lick Br

Helpful Hints

1. This Map takes a different look at
the same Congressional Township
displayed in the preceding two
maps. It presents features that
can help you better envision the
historical development of the
area: a) Water-bodies (lakes &
ponds), b) Water-courses (rivers,
streams, etc.), c) Railroads, d) City/
town center-points (where they
were oftentimes located when first
settled), and e) Cemeteries.

2. Using this "Historical" map in
tandem with this Township's
Patent Map and Road Map, may
lead you to some interesting
discoveries. You will often find
roads, towns, cemeteries, and
waterways are named after nearby
landowners: sometimes those
names will be the ones you are
researching. See how many of
these research gems you can find
here in Howell County.

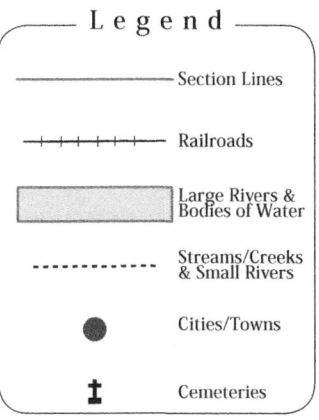

L e g e n d

——————— Section Lines

+‑+‑+‑+‑+‑+ Railroads

▭ Large Rivers &
Bodies of Water

- - - - - - - - Streams/Creeks
& Small Rivers

● Cities/Towns

‡ Cemeteries

Scale: Section = 1 mile X 1 mile
(there are some exceptions)

Map Group 10: Index to Land Patents

Township 25-North Range 9-West (5th PM 25-N 9-W)

After you locate an individual in this Index, take note of the Section and Section Part then proceed to the Land Patent map on the pages immediately following. You should have no difficulty locating the corresponding parcel of land.

The "For More Info" Column will lead you to more information about the underlying Patents. See the *Legend* at right, and the "How to Use this Book" chapter, for more information.

```
                        LEGEND
              "For More Info . . . " column
A = Authority (Legislative Act, See Appendix "A")
B = Block or Lot (location in Section unknown)
C = Cancelled Patent
F = Fractional Section
G = Group  (Multi-Patentee Patent, see Appendix "C")
V = Overlaps another Parcel
R = Re-Issued (Parcel patented more than once)

(A & G items require you to look in the Appendixes referred
to above. All other Letter-designations followed by a number
require you to locate line-items in this index that possess
the ID number found after the letter).
```

ID	Individual in Patent	Sec.	Sec. Part	Date Issued	Other Counties	For More Info . . .
7334	BAKER, Jesse P	6	S22SW	1889-01-12		A7
7333	" "	6	S21SW	1889-01-12		A7
2152	BARTON, Asa J	12	W½SE	1889-06-22		A7
2153	" "	12	SESW	1889-06-22		A7
2151	" "	12	SWNE	1889-06-22		A7
2154	BARTON, Leroy J	11	N½NW	1888-12-06		A7
2155	" "	2	E½SW	1888-12-06		A7
2156	BATES, John M	14	E½SE	1885-02-25		A7
2157	BOYSE, Marion L	12	SESE	1891-05-05		A7
2158	BREWSTER, Rollin N	14	NE	1892-01-05		A7
2160	BRIDGES, Amos E	27	SWNW	1893-12-19		A7
2159	" "	27	E½NW	1893-12-19		A7
2161	" "	28	SENE	1893-12-19		A7
2162	BRIDGES, Thomas F	27	S½SE	1888-12-06		A7
2163	" "	34	E½NE	1888-12-06		A7
2164	BRIDGES, William A	27	N½SE	1894-05-18		A7
2165	BRIXEY, Oliver H	21	SWSW	1889-01-12		A7
7313	BROONER, Allen D	3	W22NW	1898-01-26		A7
2166	BROTHERTON, Daniel C	17	E½SE	1879-12-15		A7
2167	" "	17	NWSE	1879-12-15		A7
2168	" "	17	NESW	1879-12-15		A7
2169	BROTHERTON, Hezekiah	17	N½NW	1879-12-15		A7
2170	" "	8	S½SW	1879-12-15		A7
2172	BROTHERTON, Moses	21	N½NE	1879-12-15		A7
2171	" "	21	N½NW	1879-12-15		A7
2173	BROWER, Jacob	14	SWSE	1876-01-10		A7
2175	" "	23	SENE	1876-01-10		A7
2174	" "	23	N½NE	1876-01-10		A7
2176	BROWN, John E	15	SWSW	1892-11-03		A7
2177	BROWN, Saintleger	35	E½SE	1891-05-25		A7
2178	BURGESS, Gabriel	29	S½NW	1875-11-01		A7 G27
2179	" "	30	S½NE	1875-11-01		A7 G27
2180	BURGESS, John W	29	N½NW	1893-04-29		A7
2181	" "	30	N½NE	1893-04-29		A7
2182	BURGESS, Marinda J	28	SWNW	1888-12-06		A1
2183	BURGESS, Serila A	29	S½NW	1875-11-01		A7 G27
2184	" "	30	S½NE	1875-11-01		A7 G27
2185	BURK, Richard	33	E½SE	1892-03-07		A7
2186	" "	34	S½SW	1892-03-07		A7
2187	BURNETT, John F	25	S½SE	1888-12-06		A7
2190	BYRD, Jackson C	15	S½SE	1875-11-01		A7
2188	" "	15	NWSE	1875-11-01		A7
2189	" "	15	SESW	1875-11-01		A7
2191	CAMPBELL, Judd	24	SWSE	1896-08-28		A7
7296	CHRISTOPHER, Edward	18	S21SW	1892-01-05		A7
2193	" "	18	S½SE	1892-01-05		A7

ID	Individual in Patent	Sec.	Sec. Part	Date Issued	Other Counties	For More Info . . .
2192	CHRISTOPHER, Edward (Cont'd)	18	NESE	1892-01-05		A7
2195	CLIMER, Alfred B	26	W½SE	1881-10-06		A7
2194	"	26	S½SW	1881-10-06		A7
7326	COLE, John W	5	W22NW	1892-01-25		A7
7330	" "	6	E22NE	1892-01-25		A7
2196	COURTNEY, John L	29	NE	1882-05-20		A7
7332	COVER, Jacob F	6	N22SW	1900-08-09		A7
2199	DIXON, James M	34	SENW	1874-01-10		A7
2197	" "	34	NWNE	1874-01-10		A7
2198	" "	34	N½NW	1874-01-10		A7
2200	DIXON, William T	34	N½SE	1874-01-10		A7
2201	" "	34	N½SW	1874-01-10		A7
2203	DRUMRIGHT, Richard F	33	S½NW	1883-06-30		A7
2202	" "	33	E½SW	1883-06-30		A7
2205	DRUMRIGHT, Robert J	33	W½SE	1876-01-10		A7
2204	" "	33	S½NE	1876-01-10		A7
2206	DUKE, Allen	32	SESE	1897-04-02		A7
2207	" "	33	W½SW	1897-04-02		A7
2208	DYER, John H	25	S½NE	1889-01-12		A7
2209	" "	25	N½SE	1889-01-12		A7
2210	ECHOLS, William J	8	N½SW	1892-03-07		A7
2211	" "	8	S½NW	1892-03-07		A7
2212	ELLIOTT, George	26	S½NW	1892-09-15		A7
2213	" "	26	N½SW	1892-09-15		A7
2216	EVANS, J C	14	S½NW	1885-05-25		A1
2214	" "	14	SENE	1885-03-20		A1
2215	" "	14	NESW	1885-03-20		A1
2217	" "	23	SWNE	1885-03-20		A1
2219	FARR, Isaac	35	W½SE	1879-12-15		A7
2218	" "	35	E½SW	1879-12-15		A7
2220	FINE, Franklin S	27	NE	1893-01-07		A7
2221	FINE, George S	34	SWNW	1901-08-12		A7
2222	FINE, Robert M	27	SW	1892-01-05		A7
2223	FINE, Samuel H	28	NESE	1898-04-11		A7
2224	FITZSIMMONS, William C	11	SWSE	1885-06-03		A1
2225	" "	15	W½NW	1885-05-25		A1
2228	" "	9	E½NW	1885-05-25		A1
2227	" "	9	SWNW	1885-05-25		A1
2226	" "	9	NE	1885-05-25		A1
2229	FREEMAN, William R	32	NE	1881-10-06		A7
7315	GRAHAM, Aaron	30	N22NW	1890-06-06		A7
7314	" "	30	1NW	1890-06-06		A7
7336	HALLETT, George H	6	W22NE	1877-04-05		A7
7328	" "	6	2NW	1877-04-05		A7
2230	HARRISON, Augustus	25	N½NW	1884-02-15		A7
2231	" "	26	E½NE	1884-02-15		A7
2232	HARRISON, Eva K	26	W½NE	1898-04-06		A7
7307	HERNDON, Henry W	3	1NW	1885-06-03		A1
2233	" "	3	N½SW	1885-06-03		A1
7310	" "	3	E22NW	1885-06-03		A1
7311	" "	3	W21NE	1885-06-03		A1
7312	" "	3	W22NE	1885-06-03		A1
2236	" "	4	E½SW	1885-06-03		A1
2235	" "	4	SE	1885-06-03		A1
2234	" "	4	S½NE	1885-06-03		A1
7323	" "	5	1NW	1885-06-03		A1
7325	" "	5	E22NW	1885-06-03		A1
2237	" "	5	S½	1885-06-03		A1
7322	" "	5	1NE	1885-06-03		A1
7324	" "	5	2NE	1885-06-03		A1
2238	HILL, Henry H	25	S½SW	1880-11-20		A7
2239	HOEY, John P	11	S½SW	1889-06-22		A7
2240	" "	14	N½NW	1889-06-22		A7
7331	HOWARD, Philip J	6	N21SW	1860-08-01		A1
7329	" "	6	E21NW	1860-08-01		A1
2241	HYNES, E F	28	NWSW	1872-08-30		A1
2242	INGRAM, Alfred M	11	NWNE	1876-01-10		A7
2243	" "	2	N½SE	1876-01-10		A7
2244	" "	2	SWSE	1876-01-10		A7
2245	INGRAM, Charles M	1	SWSW	1898-04-11		A7
2246	" "	12	NWNW	1898-04-11		A7
2247	" "	2	SESE	1898-04-11		A7
2250	IRVIN, Jacob	28	NESW	1878-06-24		A7

ID	Individual in Patent	Sec.	Sec. Part	Date Issued	Other Counties	For More Info . . .
2251	IRVIN, Jacob (Cont'd)	28	SWNE	1878-06-24		A7
2249	" "	28	NWSE	1878-06-24		A7
2248	" "	28	SENW	1878-06-24		A7
2252	JACKSON, Thomas	35	NW	1891-05-05		A7
2253	JOHNSON, Richard	34	SWNE	1899-02-25		A7
7299	KINION, William T	2	E21NE	1900-08-09		A7
2255	LANGSTON, Samuel J	23	E½SW	1885-05-25		A1
2254	" "	23	SWSE	1885-05-25		A1
2256	LASATER, Reuben R	26	E½SE	1870-05-10		A1
7335	LOVAN, Sterling C	6	W21NW	1892-09-09		A7
2257	MARTIN, Amplus L	32	N½NW	1896-12-08		A7
2258	MCFALLS, Andrew J	24	SESE	1892-12-09		A7
2259	" "	25	N½NE	1892-12-09		A7
2261	MCMAHON, Thomas	11	SWNW	1894-05-18		A7
2260	" "	11	NWSW	1894-05-18		A7
2263	MIZE, Jane A	19	S½SW	1874-01-10		A7
7298	" "	19	N22SW	1885-03-20		A1
7297	" "	19	N21SW	1883-08-13		A1
2262	" "	19	SWSE	1874-01-10		A7
2264	MOORE, Anderson	35	NE	1879-12-15		A7
2265	MOSELEY, Lillie O	6	SESE	1896-10-13		A1
2266	MOSS, May E	9	SW	1890-06-04		A1
2267	MOSS, Romulus A	9	SE	1889-09-27		A7
2268	MULLINS, David W	21	E½SW	1879-12-15		A7
2269	" "	28	N½NW	1879-12-15		A7
2270	MUSE, James E	12	NENE	1889-06-22		A7
2271	" "	12	NESE	1888-05-07		A1
2272	MUSGROVE, Solomon	32	SWSE	1888-12-06		A7
2273	" "	32	SESW	1888-12-06		A7
2274	" "	32	W½SW	1888-12-06		A7
2278	MUSGROVE, Thomas M	32	NESE	1888-12-06		A1
2275	" "	32	S½NW	1892-03-07		A7
2276	" "	32	NESW	1892-03-07		A7
2277	" "	32	NWSE	1892-03-07		A7
2279	NETTLETON, George H	23	NWNW	1882-09-30		A1
2280	" "	23	NWSE	1882-09-30		A1
2281	NORDYKE, Harry T	1	NWSE	1896-10-13		A1
2282	OLDEN, Benjamin F	14	SESW	1883-08-13		A1
2283	" "	23	NENW	1883-08-13		A1
2284	OSBORN, Calvin	24	E½SW	1892-03-07		A7
2286	" "	24	SWSW	1892-03-07		A7
2285	" "	24	NWSE	1892-03-07		A7
7290	PALMER, John F	1	1NW	1892-09-15		A7
2287	" "	1	N½SW	1892-09-15		A7
2288	PEGUES, John H	28	NWNE	1891-08-19		A7
2290	PERKINS, Alvin	15	N½SW	1875-11-01		A7
2289	" "	15	NENW	1875-11-01		A7
2291	PERKINS, James B	21	NWSW	1860-08-01		A1
2292	PERKINS, Sarah	21	S½NE	1877-08-01		A7
2293	" "	21	S½NW	1877-08-01		A7
2294	RAGAN, Zachariah S	24	NW	1889-02-02		A1
2295	RAY, Fannie	8	SWNE	1895-06-22		A1
7304	REYNOLDS, Cary D	2	W21NW	1889-06-22		A7
7306	" "	2	W22NW	1889-06-22		A7
7308	" "	3	E21NE	1889-06-22		A7
7309	" "	3	E22NE	1889-06-22		A7
7291	REYNOLDS, Robert L	1	E22NE	1897-04-10		A7
2296	" "	1	NESE	1897-04-10		A7
7289	" "	1	1NE	1897-04-10		A7
2298	ROHDE, Gustave A	11	SENW	1892-03-07		A7
2297	" "	11	SWNE	1892-03-07		A7
2299	" "	11	E½NE	1892-03-07		A7
2301	SHOCKLEY, Francis M	12	W½SW	1882-06-30		A7
2300	" "	12	SENW	1877-11-10		A1
2302	" "	12	NESW	1882-06-30		A7
2303	" "	12	SWNW	1882-06-30		A7
2305	SHOCKLEY, Robert J	11	SESE	1882-08-30		A7
2304	" "	11	N½SE	1882-08-30		A7
2306	" "	11	NESW	1882-08-30		A7
7319	SIMPSON, John R	4	E21NW	1879-12-15		A7
7320	" "	4	E22NW	1879-12-15		A7
7318	" "	4	2NE	1879-12-15		A7
2307	SMITH, Alwyn C	12	SENE	1894-09-18		A1

ID	Individual in Patent	Sec.	Sec. Part	Date Issued	Other Counties	For More Info . . .
2308	SMITH, Henry T	23	E½SE	1882-09-30		A1
2309	"	24	NWSW	1882-09-30		A1
2311	SMITH, Theodore A	1	SWSE	1891-05-25		A7
2310	" "	1	SESW	1891-05-25		A7
2313	" "	12	NENW	1891-05-25		A7
2312	" "	12	NWNE	1891-05-25		A7
2314	STONE, Jacob B	21	S½SE	1879-12-15		A7
2315	" "	27	NWNW	1879-12-15		A7
2316	" "	28	NENE	1879-12-15		A7
7293	SWEARINGEN, Samuel	1	W22NW	1879-12-15		A7
7301	" "	2	E22NE	1879-12-15		A7
2317	TABOR, John O	15	SENW	1857-10-30		A1
2320	TOMLINSON, Samuel J	17	S½NW	1885-06-03		A1
2322	" "	17	NWSW	1885-06-03		A1
2318	" "	17	S½SW	1885-06-03		A1
2319	" "	17	SWSE	1885-06-03		A1
2321	" "	17	NE	1885-06-03		A1
2324	" "	18	NWSE	1885-06-03		A1
7295	" "	18	N21SW	1885-06-03		A1
2323	" "	18	N½	1885-06-03		A1
7294	" "	18	2SW	1885-06-03		A1
2327	" "	19	N½SE	1885-06-03		A1
2325	" "	19	N½	1885-06-03		A1
2326	" "	19	SESE	1885-06-03		A1
2328	TURNER, Francis M	8	SWSE	1901-05-08		A7
2329	TURNER, James M	28	SESW	1883-06-30		A7
2330	" "	28	S½SE	1883-06-30		A7
2331	" "	33	NENE	1883-06-30		A7
2332	TURNER, John C	8	E½SE	1885-06-20		A7
2334	" "	8	NWSE	1885-06-20		A7
2333	" "	8	SENE	1885-06-20		A7
2335	WADE, Green	34	S½SE	1891-06-09		A7
2336	" "	35	W½SW	1891-06-09		A7
2337	WADE, Robert W	21	N½SE	1891-08-19		A7
2338	WADLEY, Jesse T	14	NWSW	1885-05-25		A1
2339	" "	15	NESE	1885-05-25		A1
2340	WADLEY, John B	14	SWSW	1883-08-13		A1
2341	WADLEY, William M	28	SWSW	1893-04-08		A7
2343	" "	33	N½NW	1893-04-08		A7
2342	" "	33	NWNE	1893-04-08		A7
2346	WADLEY, William R	24	SWNE	1876-01-10		A7
2345	" "	24	E½NE	1876-01-10		A7
2344	" "	24	NESE	1876-01-10		A7
2347	WASHBURN, John H	25	N½SW	1892-06-10		A7
2348	" "	25	S½NW	1892-06-10		A7
2349	WEBB, John M	1	SESE	1900-02-02		A7
2350	WHITE, Josie F	2	W½SW	1893-01-07		A7 G189
2351	" "	3	E½SE	1893-01-07		A7 G189
7303	WILL, Philip G	2	W21NE	1882-11-10		A7
7305	" "	2	W22NE	1882-11-10		A7
7302	" "	2	E22NW	1882-11-10		A7
7300	" "	2	E21NW	1882-11-10		A7
2352	WILLIAMS, Jefferson P	8	N½NW	1894-12-17		A7
2353	WILLIAMS, Josiah H	6	N½SE	1882-05-20		A7
7327	" "	6	1NE	1882-05-20		A7
2354	WILLIS, Armintice M	24	NWNE	1886-10-29		A1
7317	WINTER, Delila	30	S22NW	1909-02-25		A7
2355	WINTER, Felix L	23	W½SW	1885-06-03		A1
2356	" "	23	S½NW	1885-06-03		A1
7316	" "	30	S22NW	1909-02-25		A7
7292	WISEMAN, Joseph A	1	W22NE	1889-01-12		A7
7321	WOOD, Benjamin F	4	W22NW	1901-05-08		A7
2357	WOOD, Loranzia D	4	W½SW	1874-11-05		A7
2358	" "	4	SWNW	1874-11-05		A7
2359	" "	9	NWNW	1874-11-05		A7
2360	WOOD, William L	8	N½NE	1894-12-17		A7
2361	WRIGHT, Larmon Z	6	SWSE	1893-01-13		A1
2362	YOUNG, George	2	W½SW	1893-01-07		A7 G189
2363	" "	3	E½SE	1893-01-07		A7 G189
2364	YOUNG, George K	3	W½SE	1890-10-11		A7
2365	" "	3	S½SW	1890-10-11		A7
2366	YOUNG, Josie F	2	W½SW	1893-01-07		A7 G189
2367	" "	3	E½SE	1893-01-07		A7 G189

ID	Individual in Patent	Sec.	Sec. Part	Date Issued	Other Counties	For More Info . . .
2368	ZEEK, Andrew	26	N½NW	1892-06-21		A7

Patent Map

T25-N R9-W
5th PM 25-N 9-W Meridian

Map Group 10

Township Statistics

Parcels Mapped	:	259
Number of Patents	:	136
Number of Individuals	:	127
Patentees Identified	:	124
Number of Surnames	:	91
Multi-Patentee Parcels	:	4
Oldest Patent Date	:	10/30/1857
Most Recent Patent	:	8/12/1901
Block/Lot Parcels	:	47
Cities and Town	:	2
Cemeteries	:	0

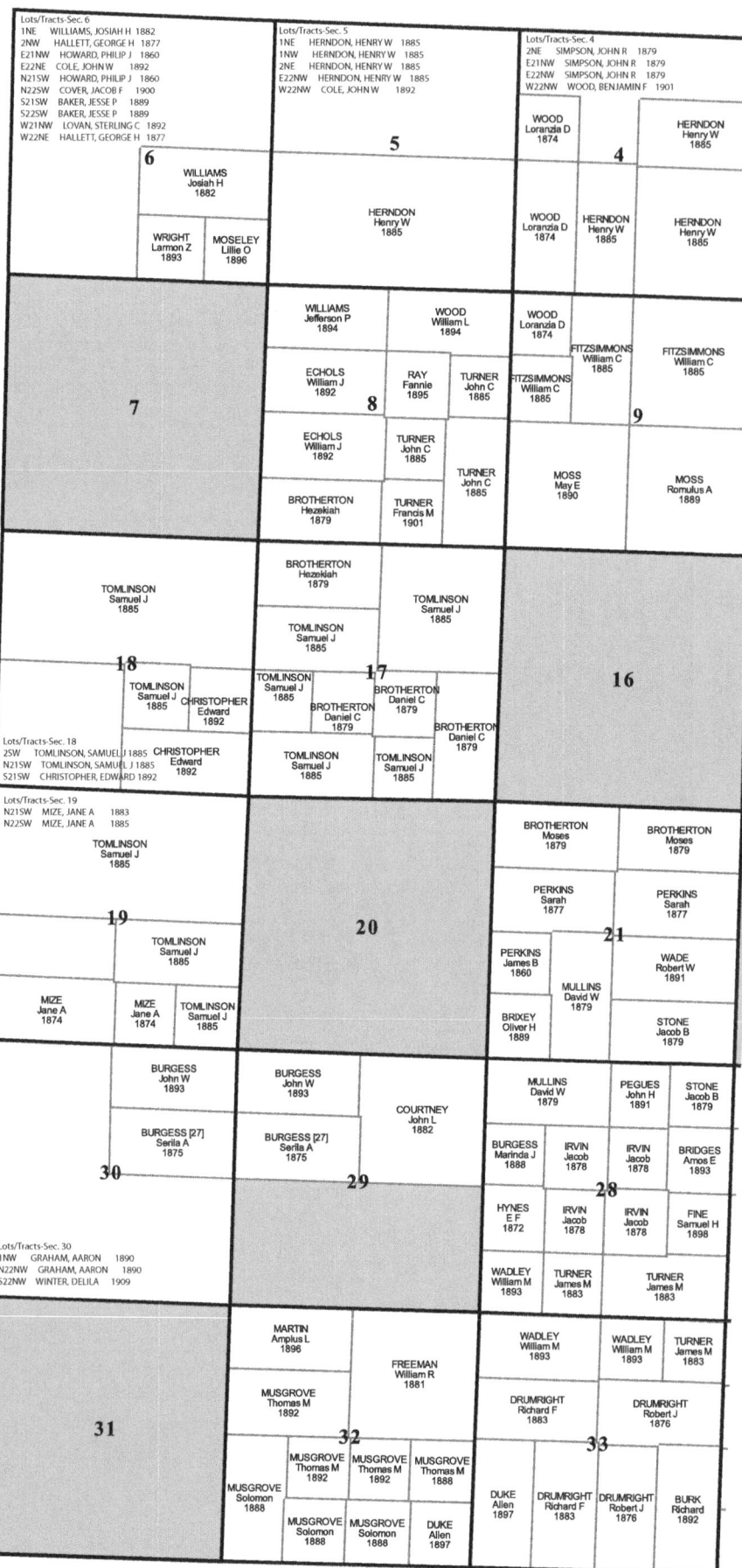

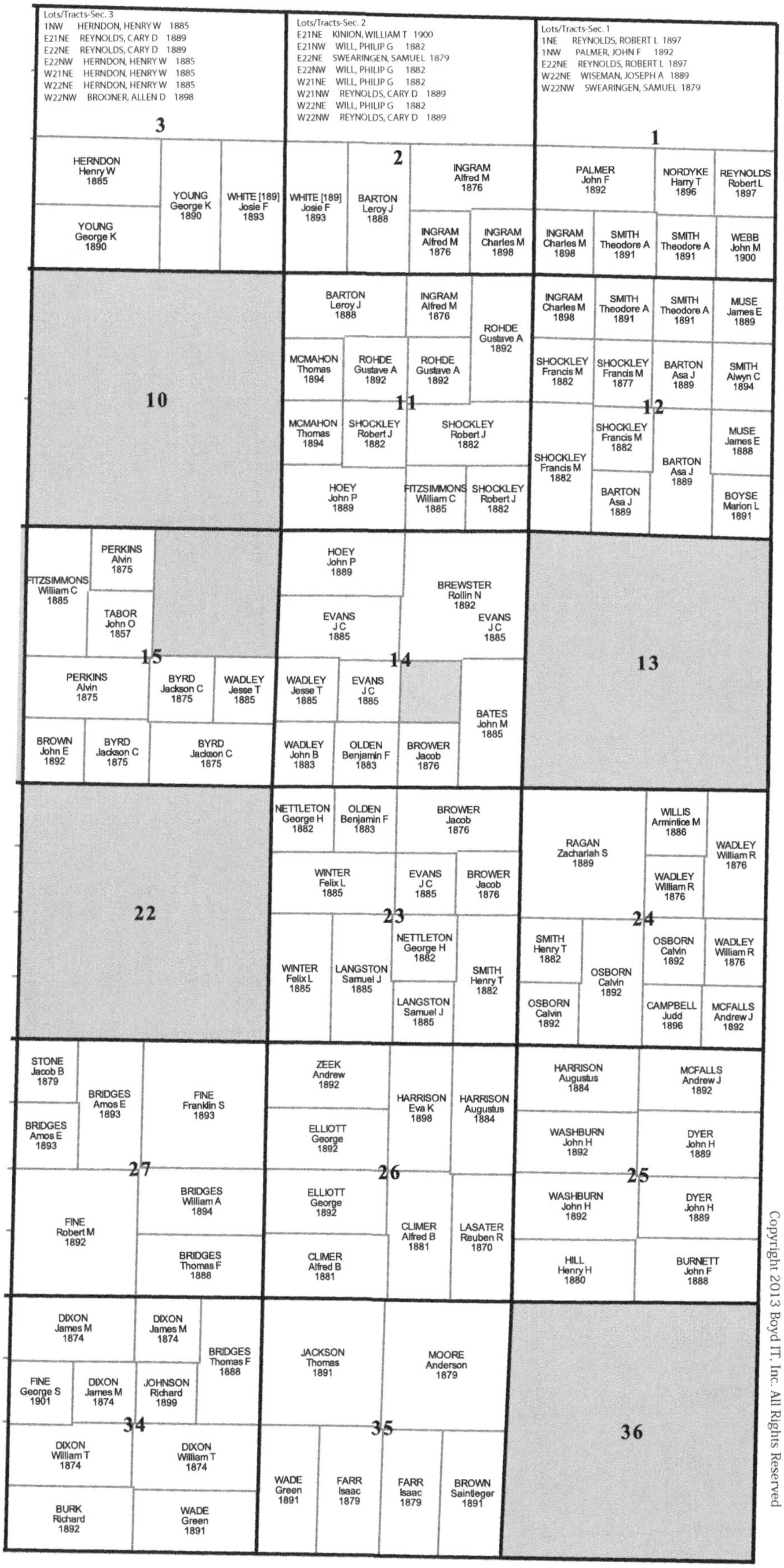

Lots/Tracts–Sec. 3
1NW HERNDON, HENRY W 1885
E21NE REYNOLDS, CARY D 1889
E22NE REYNOLDS, CARY D 1889
E22NW HERNDON, HENRY W 1885
W21NE HERNDON, HENRY W 1885
W22NE HERNDON, HENRY W 1885
W22NW BROONER, ALLEN D 1898

Lots/Tracts–Sec. 2
E21NE KINION, WILLIAM T 1900
E21NW WILL, PHILIP G 1882
E22NE SWEARINGEN, SAMUEL 1879
E22NW WILL, PHILIP G 1882
W21NE WILL, PHILIP G 1882
W21NW REYNOLDS, CARY D 1889
W22NE WILL, PHILIP G 1882
W22NW REYNOLDS, CARY D 1889

Lots/Tracts–Sec. 1
1NE REYNOLDS, ROBERT L 1897
1NW PALMER, JOHN F 1892
E22NE REYNOLDS, ROBERT L 1897
W22NE WISEMAN, JOSEPH A 1889
W22NW SWEARINGEN, SAMUEL 1879

3

2

1

HERNDON Henry W 1885
YOUNG George K 1890
WHITE [189] Josie F 1893
WHITE [189] Josie F 1893
BARTON Leroy J 1888
INGRAM Alfred M 1876
PALMER John F 1892
NORDYKE Harry T 1896
REYNOLDS Robert L 1897

YOUNG George K 1890
INGRAM Alfred M 1876
INGRAM Charles M 1898
INGRAM Charles M 1898
SMITH Theodore A 1891
SMITH Theodore A 1891
WEBB John M 1900

10

BARTON Leroy J 1888
INGRAM Alfred M 1876
ROHDE Gustave A 1892
INGRAM Charles M 1898
SMITH Theodore A 1891
SMITH Theodore A 1891
MUSE James E 1894

MCMAHON Thomas 1894
ROHDE Gustave A 1892
ROHDE Gustave A 1892
SHOCKLEY Francis M 1882
SHOCKLEY Francis M 1877
BARTON Asa J 1889
SMITH Alwyn C 1894

11

MCMAHON Thomas 1894
SHOCKLEY Robert J 1882
SHOCKLEY Robert J 1882
SHOCKLEY Francis M 1882
BARTON Asa J 1889
MUSE James E 1888

12

HOEY John P 1889
FITZSIMMONS William C 1885
SHOCKLEY Robert J 1882
SHOCKLEY Francis M 1882
BARTON Asa J 1889
BOYSE Marion L 1891

FITZSIMMONS William C 1885
PERKINS Alvin 1875
HOEY John P 1889
BREWSTER Rollin N 1892

TABOR John O 1857
EVANS J C 1885
EVANS J C 1885

15
PERKINS Alvin 1875
BYRD Jackson C 1875
WADLEY Jesse T 1885
WADLEY Jesse T 1885
EVANS J C 1885
14

13

BROWN John E 1892
BYRD Jackson C 1875
BYRD Jackson C 1875
WADLEY John B 1883
OLDEN Benjamin F 1883
BROWER Jacob 1876
BATES John M 1885

NETTLETON George H 1882
OLDEN Benjamin F 1883
BROWER Jacob 1876
WILLIS Armintice M 1886
WADLEY William R 1876

RAGAN Zachariah S 1889

WINTER Felix L 1885
EVANS J C 1885
BROWER Jacob 1876
WADLEY William R 1876

22
23
24

NETTLETON George H 1882
SMITH Henry T 1882
OSBORN Calvin 1892
WADLEY William R 1876

WINTER Felix L 1885
LANGSTON Samuel J 1885
SMITH Henry T 1882
OSBORN Calvin 1892

LANGSTON Samuel J 1885
OSBORN Calvin 1892
CAMPBELL Judd 1896
MCFALLS Andrew J 1892

STONE Jacob B 1879
ZEEK Andrew 1892
HARRISON Augustus 1884
MCFALLS Andrew J 1892

BRIDGES Amos E 1893
FINE Franklin S 1893
HARRISON Eva K 1898
HARRISON Augustus 1884

BRIDGES Amos E 1893
ELLIOTT George 1892
WASHBURN John H 1892
DYER John H 1889

27
26
25

BRIDGES William A 1894
ELLIOTT George 1892
WASHBURN John H 1892
DYER John H 1889

FINE Robert M 1892
CLIMER Alfred B 1881
LASATER Reuben R 1870

BRIDGES Thomas F 1888
CLIMER Alfred B 1881
HILL Henry H 1880
BURNETT John F 1888

DIXON James M 1874
DIXON James M 1874
BRIDGES Thomas F 1888
JACKSON Thomas 1891
MOORE Anderson 1879

FINE George S 1901
DIXON James M 1874
JOHNSON Richard 1899

34
35
36

DIXON William T 1874
DIXON William T 1874

BURK Richard 1892
WADE Green 1891
WADE Green 1891
FARR Isaac 1879
FARR Isaac 1879
BROWN Sainfeger 1891

Helpful Hints

1. This Map's INDEX can be found on the preceding pages.

2. Refer to Map "C" to see where this Township lies within Howell County, Missouri.

3. Numbers within square brackets [ ] denote a multi-patentee land parcel (multi-owner). Refer to Appendix "C" for a full list of members in this group.

4. Areas that look to be crowded with Patentees usually indicate multiple sales of the same parcel (Re-issues) or Overlapping parcels. See this Township's Index for an explanation of these and other circumstances that might explain "odd" groupings of Patentees on this map.

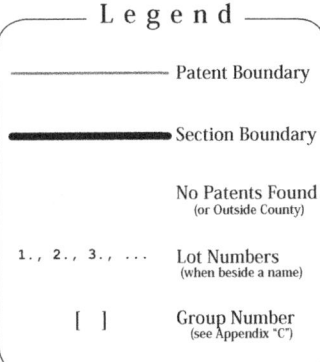

Legend

———— Patent Boundary

━━━━ Section Boundary

No Patents Found (or Outside County)

1., 2., 3., ... Lot Numbers (when beside a name)

[ ] Group Number (see Appendix "C")

Scale: Section = 1 mile X 1 mile (generally, with some exceptions)

Road Map

T25-N R9-W
5th PM 25-N 9-W Meridian

Map Group 10

Cities & Towns
Olden
Pomona

Cemeteries
None

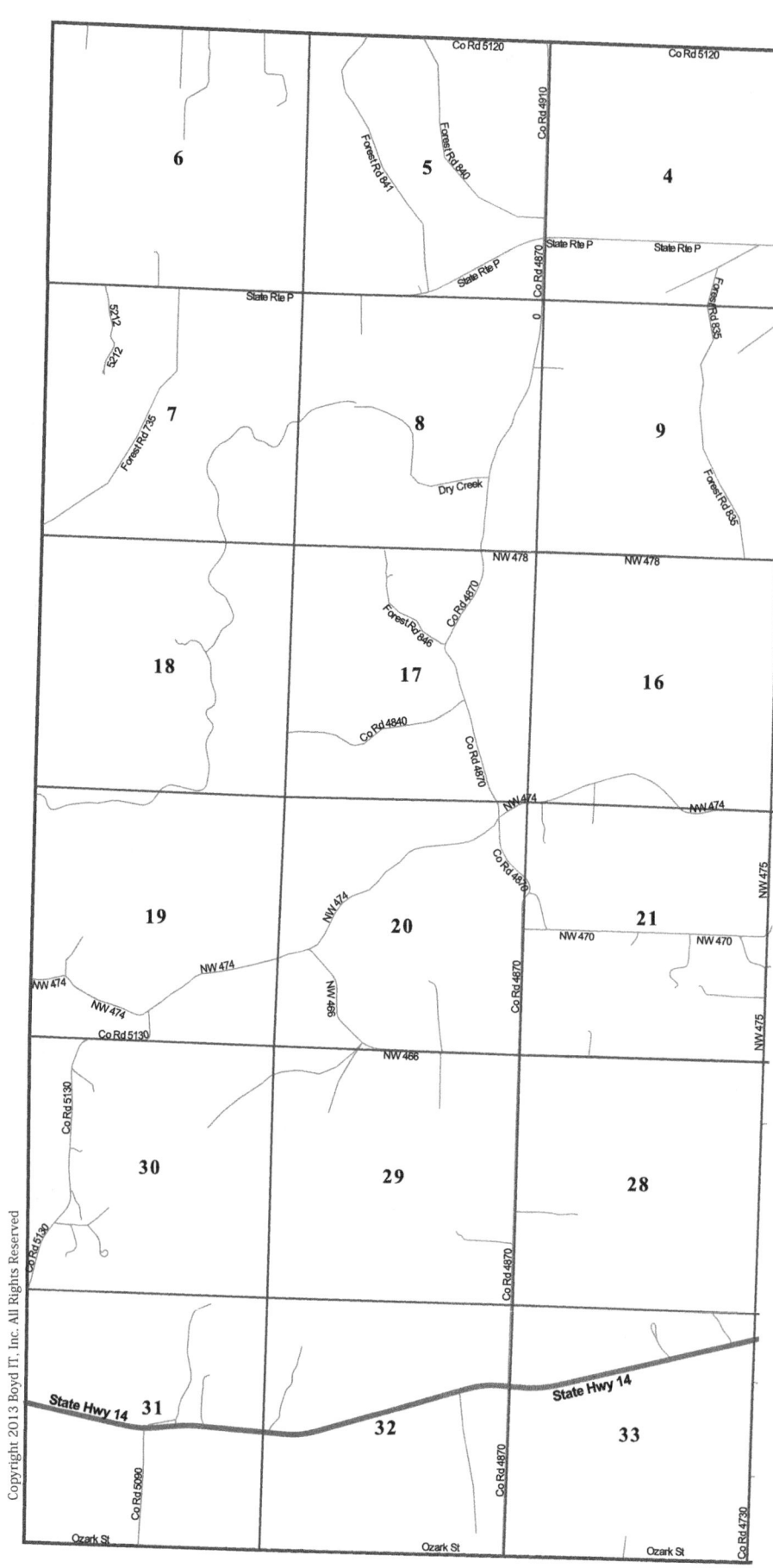

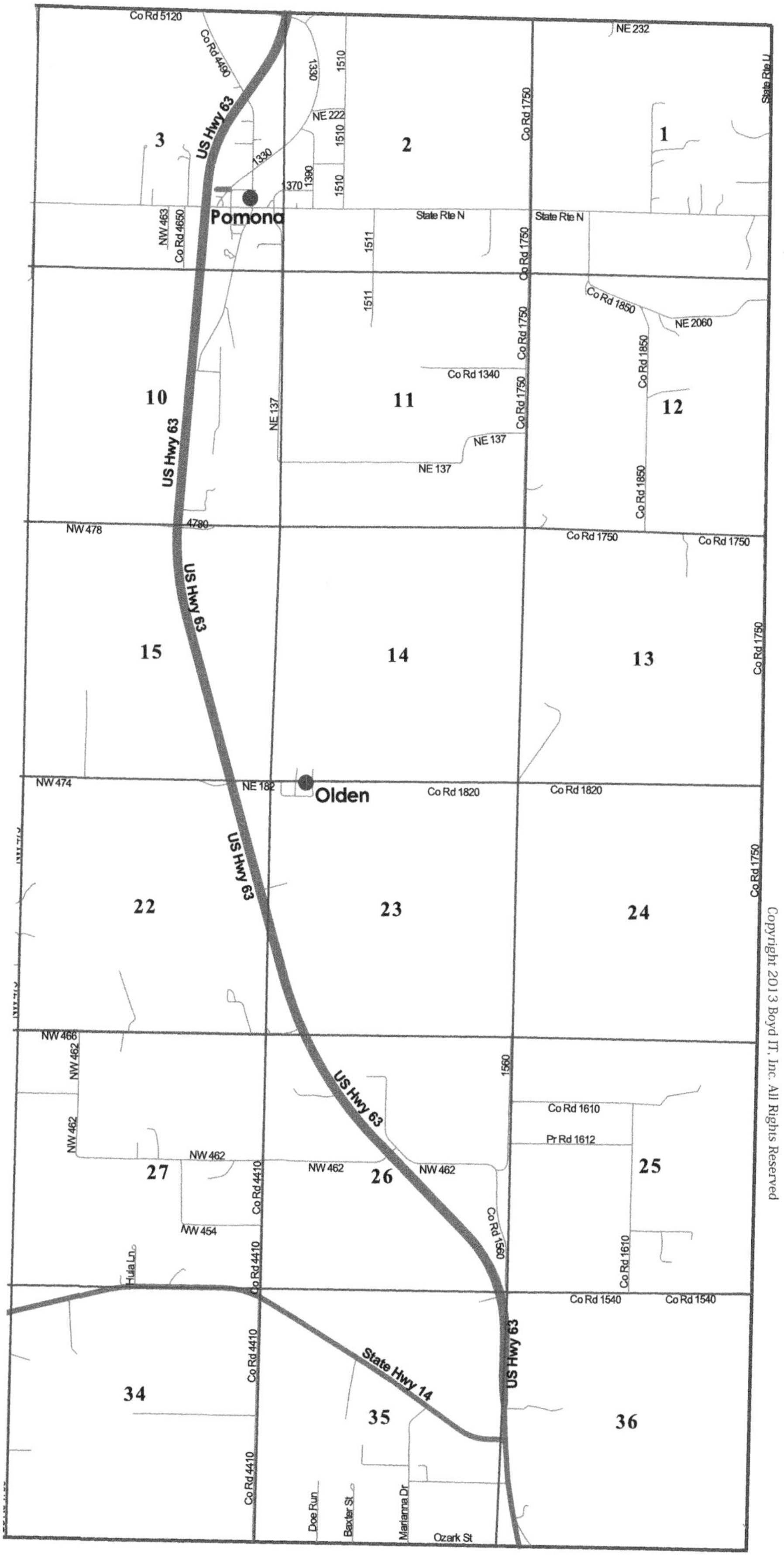

Co Rd 5120

Co Rd 4450

NE 232

State Rte

NE 222

1330

1510

US Hwy 63

3

1390

370

1390

1510

1510

2

Co Rd 1750

1

NW 463

Co Rd 4650

Pomona

State Rte N

State Rte N

1511

Co Rd 1750

1511

Co Rd 1750

Co Rd 1850

NE 2060

10

NE 137

Co Rd 1340

Co Rd 1750

11

Co Rd 1850

12

US Hwy 63

NE 137

NE 137

Co Rd 1850

NW 478

4780

Co Rd 1750

Co Rd 1750

US Hwy 63

Co Rd 1750

15

14

13

NW 474

NE 182

Olden

Co Rd 1820

Co Rd 1820

US Hwy 63

Co Rd 1750

22

23

24

NW 466

NW 462

1560

US Hwy 63

Co Rd 1610

NW 462

Pr Rd 1612

NW 462

27

Co Rd 4410

NW 462

26

NW 462

25

NW 454

Co Rd 1560

Co Rd 1610

Hula Ln

Co Rd 1540

Co Rd 1540

Co Rd 4410

US Hwy 63

State Hwy 14

34

Co Rd 4410

35

36

Doe Run

Baxter St

Marianna Dr

Ozark St

Helpful Hints

1. This road map has a number of uses, but primarily it is to help you: a) find the present location of land owned by your ancestors (at least the general area), b) find cemeteries and city-centers, and c) estimate the route/roads used by Census-takers & tax-assessors.

2. If you plan to travel to Howell County to locate cemeteries or land parcels, please pick up a modern travel map for the area before you do. Mapping old land parcels on modern maps is not as exact a science as you might think. Just the slightest variations in public land survey coordinates, estimates of parcel boundaries, or road-map deviations can greatly alter a map's representation of how a road either does or doesn't cross a particular parcel of land.

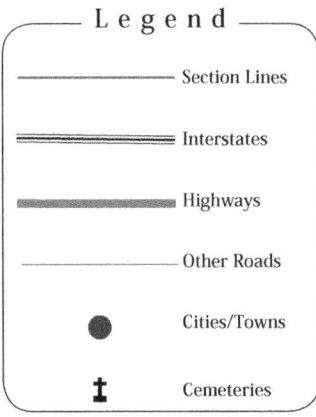

L e g e n d

———————— Section Lines

════════ Interstates

━━━━━━━━ Highways

———————— Other Roads

● Cities/Towns

✝ Cemeteries

Scale: Section = 1 mile X 1 mile
(generally, with some exceptions)

Historical Map

T25-N R9-W
5th PM 25-N 9-W Meridian

Map Group 10

Cities & Towns
Olden
Pomona

Cemeteries
None

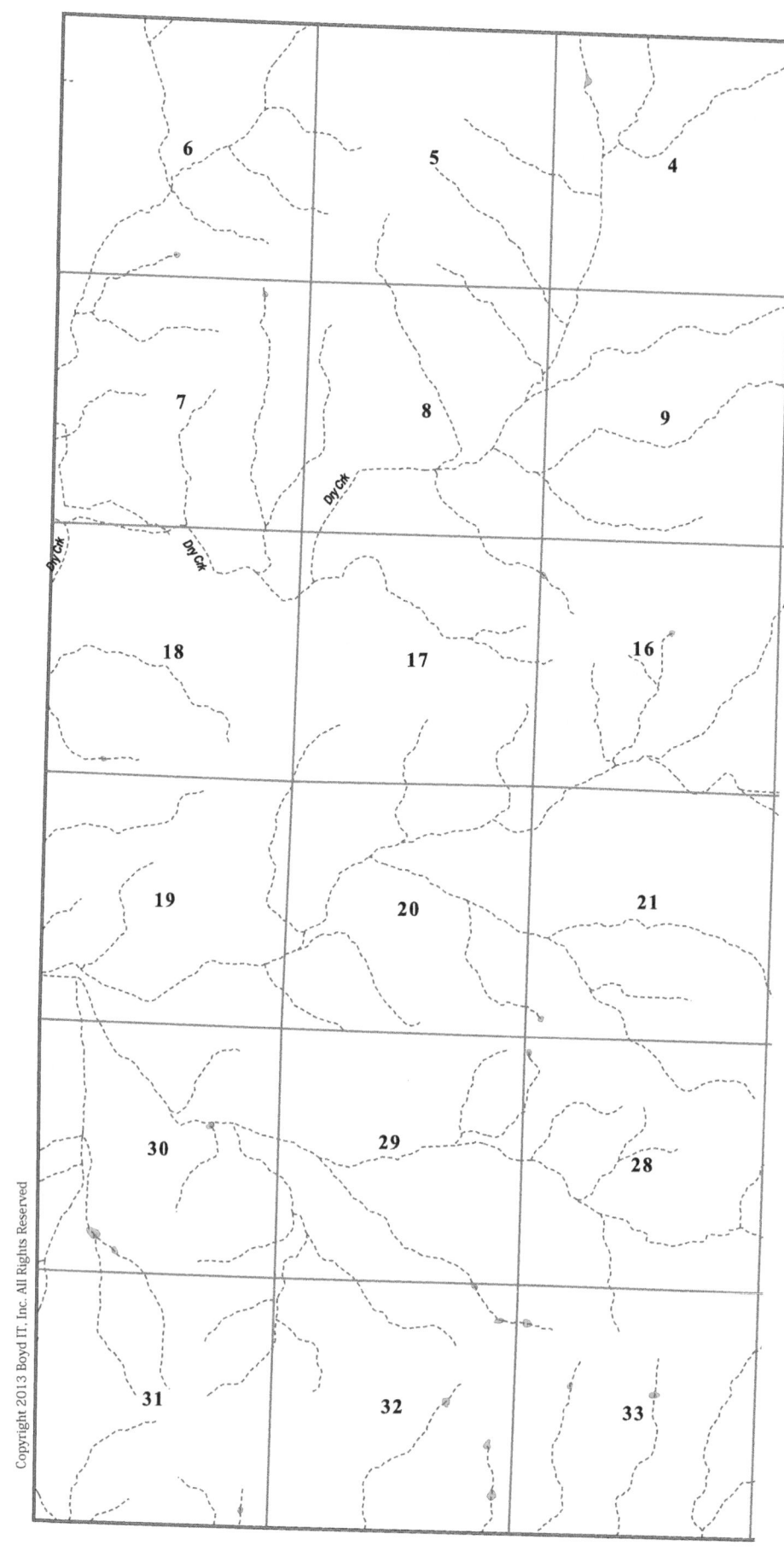

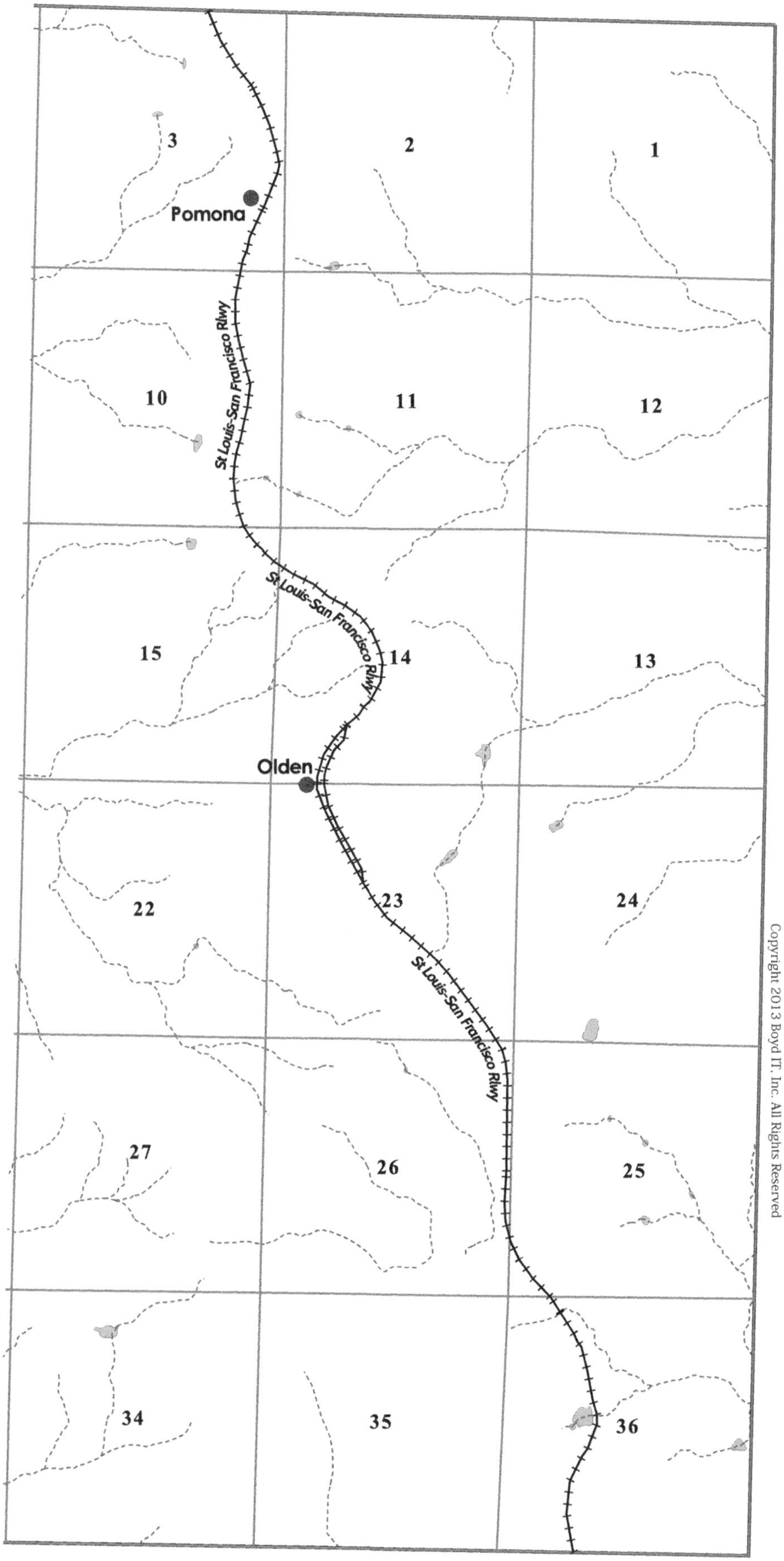

3

2

1

Pomona ●

St Louis-San Francisco Rlwy

10

11

12

St Louis-San Francisco Rlwy

15

14

13

Olden ●

22

23

24

St Louis-San Francisco Rlwy

27

26

25

34

35

36

Helpful Hints

1. This Map takes a different look at the same Congressional Township displayed in the preceding two maps. It presents features that can help you better envision the historical development of the area: a) Water-bodies (lakes & ponds), b) Water-courses (rivers, streams, etc.), c) Railroads, d) City/ town center-points (where they were oftentimes located when first settled), and e) Cemeteries.

2. Using this "Historical" map in tandem with this Township's Patent Map and Road Map, may lead you to some interesting discoveries. You will often find roads, towns, cemeteries, and waterways are named after nearby landowners: sometimes those names will be the ones you are researching. See how many of these research gems you can find here in Howell County.

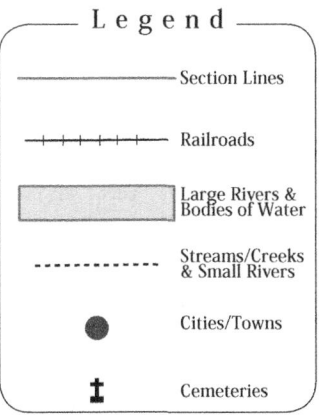

Legend

——————— Section Lines

+++++++++ Railroads

Large Rivers & Bodies of Water

---------- Streams/Creeks & Small Rivers

● Cities/Towns

‡ Cemeteries

Scale: Section = 1 mile X 1 mile
(there are some exceptions)

Map Group 11: Index to Land Patents

Township 25-North Range 8-West (5th PM 25-N 8-W)

After you locate an individual in this Index, take note of the Section and Section Part then proceed to the Land Patent map on the pages immediately following. You should have no difficulty locating the corresponding parcel of land.

The "For More Info" Column will lead you to more information about the underlying Patents. See the *Legend* at right, and the "How to Use this Book" chapter, for more information.

ID	Individual in Patent	Sec.	Sec. Part	Date Issued	Other Counties	For More Info . . .
2369	ACREE, George H	15	S½SE	1888-12-08		A7
2370	" "	15	E½SW	1888-12-08		A7
2371	ACREE, N B	15	NWNW	1889-05-29		A1
2372	" "	21	NWSE	1890-08-13		A1
2374	ACREE, Nathaniel B	14	W½NE	1888-12-06		A7
2373	" "	14	SENW	1888-12-06		A7
2375	" "	14	NENE	1888-12-06		A7
2376	" "	22	SWSW	1884-03-10		A1
2377	" "	27	W½NW	1884-03-10		A1
2379	ADAMS, Isaac	10	SWSE	1859-09-01		A1
2380	" "	10	SENE	1860-08-01		A1
2378	" "	10	N½SE	1857-10-30		A1
2381	ADAMS, John	15	SWSW	1859-09-01		A1
2382	ADAMS, Samuel	10	NESW	1859-09-01		A1
2383	ADKINS, A T	11	NWSW	1885-02-25		A7
2384	" "	11	E½SW	1885-02-25		A7
2385	" "	14	NENW	1885-02-25		A7
2386	BACON, Seth W	20	SWSW	1859-09-01		A1
2387	" "	29	NWNW	1859-09-01		A1
2388	BARNES, John H	13	SWNW	1895-09-04		A7
2389	" "	14	SENE	1895-09-04		A7
7361	BARTON, John R	3	2NW	1895-05-28		A7
7366	" "	3	W21NW	1895-05-28		A7
7371	BATES, George W	30	S22NW	1890-01-10		A7
7368	" "	30	1NW	1890-01-10		A7
2391	BESS, Christopher B	8	S½NE	1890-10-11		A7
2392	" "	9	S½NW	1890-10-11		A7
2394	BOSS, Louis	3	NWSE	1900-11-12		A7
2393	" "	3	NESW	1900-11-12		A7
7354	BOSS, Theodor	2	1NW	1891-05-25		A7
2395	" "	3	NESE	1891-05-25		A7
7362	" "	3	E21NE	1891-05-25		A7
7352	BOYCE, Jesse	19	N22NW	1860-08-01		A1
2398	BOYD, William J	23	NESW	1903-05-25		A7
2396	" "	23	SENW	1903-05-25		A7
2397	" "	23	N½NW	1903-05-25		A7
7343	BOYSE, Marion L	18	N21NW	1891-05-05		A7
7345	" "	18	N22NW	1891-05-05		A7
7406	" "	7	S22SW	1891-05-05		A7
2400	BRADSHAW, Jonathan W	8	NESW	1890-10-11		A7
2399	" "	8	N½SE	1890-10-11		A7
2401	" "	9	NWSW	1890-10-11		A7
2402	BRADSHAW, Samuel A	4	NWSW	1890-10-11		A7
2403	" "	4	S½SW	1890-10-11		A7
2404	" "	9	NENW	1890-10-11		A7
2405	BRAKEBILL, John O	35	N½SW	1895-05-28		A7

ID	Individual in Patent	Sec.	Sec. Part	Date Issued	Other Counties	For More Info . . .
2406	BRAKEBILL, John O (Cont'd)	35	S½NW	1895-05-28		A7
7375	BRANNOCK, Milton W	31	N22SW	1886-10-29		A1
7397	BRIGGS, Daniel G	6	W21NE	1859-09-01		A1
2407	" "	6	NWSE	1859-09-01		A1
2408	BROTHERTON, Abraham	33	S½NW	1892-03-07		A7
2409	" "	33	N½SW	1892-03-07		A7
2410	BROTHERTON, Bartlet	33	NE	1888-12-08		A7
7351	BROWER, Wesley T	19	1NW	1876-01-10		A7
2411	" "	19	W½NE	1876-01-10		A7
2412	BROWER, William S	19	SW	1876-01-10		A7
2413	BROWN, John A	4	S½SE	1877-10-10		A7
2414	" "	9	N½NE	1877-10-10		A7
2415	BURROUGHS, George W	11	NWNE	1873-02-01		A7
2417	" "	11	S½NW	1873-02-01		A7
2416	" "	11	NENW	1873-02-01		A7
2418	BURROUGHS, John E	10	NENE	1896-08-28		A7
2419	" "	11	NWNW	1896-08-28		A7
2421	CAGE, Adolphus A	34	SWNW	1892-02-06		A7
2420	" "	34	SESW	1892-02-06		A7
2422	" "	34	N½SW	1892-02-06		A7
2423	CARRIS, Ray B	29	SESE	1891-08-24		A1
2424	CHANDLER, William P	12	S½NE	1861-02-01		A1
2425	CHARLES, Samuel H	22	E½NW	1892-03-07		A7
2426	" "	22	SESW	1892-03-07		A7
2427	" "	27	SWNE	1892-03-07		A7
7381	COLTHARP, Williamson G	4	E21NE	1906-03-16		A1
2432	COOK, William D	19	SENE	1860-08-03		A8 G58
2430	" "	19	S½SE	1860-09-10		A6
2431	" "	19	NWSE	1860-09-10		A6
2433	" "	19	NESE	1860-08-03		A8 G58
2435	CORDES, Louis	26	W½SW	1898-01-26		A7
2436	" "	26	SWNW	1898-01-26		A7
2434	" "	26	NESW	1898-01-26		A7
7360	COUNTS, James E	2	W22NW	1891-05-25		A7
7364	" "	3	E22NE	1891-05-25		A7
2437	COURSEY, Elbert C	8	SWSE	1901-08-27		A1
2438	" "	8	SESW	1901-08-27		A1
2439	COWAN, Joseph P	26	E½NW	1892-12-09		A7
2441	" "	26	SWNE	1892-12-09		A7
2440	" "	26	NWSE	1892-12-09		A7
2444	COZORT, William A	30	N½NE	1860-08-01		A1
2445	CRIDER, Abraham	28	SENE	1897-04-10		A7
2446	CRIDER, Joseph	31	NWSE	1877-08-01		A7
7373	" "	31	N21SW	1877-08-01		A7
7376	" "	31	S21SW	1883-08-13		A1
2447	" "	31	S½NW	1878-03-20		A7
7342	CUNNINGHAM, John M	1	W21NW	1883-06-30		A7
2448	" "	1	NWSW	1883-06-30		A7
7338	" "	1	2NW	1883-06-30		A7
2449	DALSING, Bernhard	23	E½NE	1900-11-12		A7
2451	DENTON, William	13	N½NE	1859-09-01		A1
2450	" "	13	SWNE	1859-09-01		A1
2452	" "	13	SENE	1860-08-01		A1
2454	DRIEHAUS, Adolphus	21	SW	1894-05-16		A1
2455	DRYER, Conrad H	12	NWSW	1876-01-10		A1
2456	" "	25	SWNW	1886-10-29		A1
2457	DUNHAM, Gilbert C	19	NENE	1886-10-13		A1
2458	" "	20	NWNW	1886-10-13		A1
2459	EARLS, William	22	N½SW	1878-06-24		A7
2460	ELLEDGE, Isaac	17	NWNW	1859-09-01		A1
2461	" "	18	NENE	1859-01-01		A1
2462	" "	18	NWNE	1860-10-11		A1
2463	" "	7	SESW	1875-04-01		A7
2464	" "	7	S½SE	1875-04-01		A7
2465	" "	8	SWSW	1875-04-01		A7
2466	ELLEDGE, Isaac B	5	N½SW	1892-03-07		A7
7391	" "	6	E21NE	1892-03-07		A7
2467	" "	6	NESE	1892-03-07		A7
7403	ELLEDGE, James M	7	N21SW	1888-09-17		A7
7405	" "	7	S21NW	1888-09-17		A7
2469	ESSEX, Thomas	34	NWNE	1896-08-28		A7
2470	" "	34	N½NW	1896-08-28		A7
2468	" "	34	SENW	1896-08-28		A7

ID	Individual in Patent	Sec.	Sec. Part	Date Issued	Other Counties	For More Info . . .
7379	FARMER, Samuel H	4	1NW	1896-06-04		A7
2471	" "	5	NESE	1896-06-04		A7
7385	" "	5	E21NE	1896-06-04		A7
2472	FARMER, Silas	5	NWSE	1900-02-02		A7
7387	" "	5	W21NE	1900-02-02		A7
2473	FISCHER, Michael	26	SWSE	1888-11-30		A7
2474	" "	26	SESW	1888-11-30		A7
2477	" "	35	NENW	1888-11-30		A7
2476	" "	35	NWNE	1888-11-30		A7
2475	" "	35	NWNW	1891-08-24		A1
2478	FORD, Charles P	17	SE	1860-05-02		A6 G86
2480	" "	17	NENW	1860-05-02		A6
2481	" "	17	S½NW	1860-05-02		A6
2479	" "	17	NE	1860-05-02		A6
2482	FORD, Oscar H	32	SWSW	1884-10-11		A1
2483	FOREST, Benjamin F	17	N½SW	1901-03-23		A7
2486	FRAZIER, Jonathan	12	NESW	1860-09-10		A6 G87
2487	" "	12	N½SE	1860-09-10		A6 G87
2488	GALLOWAY, Samuel	36	SESE	1882-08-30		A7
2489	" "	36	SWSE	1882-08-30		A7
2490	GAYER, David P	6	SESE	1871-06-10		A1
7358	GEBBERS, George	2	W21NE	1905-11-03		A1
2491	GILLELAND, James	7	NWSE	1859-09-01		A1
7378	GLEEN, Henry	31	S22SW	1892-03-07		A7
7377	GLEEN, Louisa	31	S22SW	1892-03-07		A7
2492	GLENDENING, James E	24	NWSW	1895-06-28		A7
2493	GOOD, Joseph	36	E½NE	1890-01-10		A7
2494	" "	36	E½SE	1890-01-10		A7
2496	GOODELL, Elisha H	24	E½SW	1890-10-11		A7
2495	" "	24	W½SE	1890-10-11		A7
2497	GOYER, Daniel T	1	SESW	1857-03-10		A1
2498	" "	12	NWNE	1857-03-10		A1
2499	" "	12	N½NW	1857-03-10		A1
2500	" "	3	NWSW	1883-08-13		A1
2501	" "	3	SENW	1885-06-20		A7
2502	" "	3	SWNE	1885-06-20		A7
7367	" "	3	W22NE	1883-08-13		A1
7365	" "	3	W21NE	1885-06-20		A7
7363	" "	3	E21NW	1885-06-20		A7
2503	GRIFFITH, Elizabeth	19	SENE	1860-08-03		A8 G58
2504	" "	19	NESE	1860-08-03		A8 G58
2507	GUNTER, Samuel	24	NESE	1861-08-01		A1
2509	HADDOCK, Jesse	28	E½NW	1888-12-08		A7
2508	" "	28	W½NE	1888-12-08		A7
2510	HADDOCK, John	29	W½SW	1889-01-12		A7
2511	" "	30	E½SE	1889-01-12		A7
2514	HALL, William E	36	NESW	1893-04-29		A7
2512	" "	36	W½SW	1893-04-29		A7
2513	" "	36	SENW	1893-04-29		A7
2515	HAMBY, William	17	S½SW	1889-01-12		A7
2516	" "	18	E½SE	1889-01-12		A7
2517	HAMMONDS, James W	2	SE	1889-06-22		A7
2518	HARLAN, David B	32	SWSE	1882-05-20		A7
2519	" "	32	SESW	1882-05-20		A7
2521	HAWKINS, William A	18	W½SE	1888-11-27		A7
2520	" "	18	S½NE	1888-11-27		A7
7370	HAYS, John B	30	S21SW	1890-01-10		A7
7372	" "	31	N21NW	1890-01-10		A7
7374	" "	31	N22NW	1890-01-10		A7
7357	HENRY, Isaac P	2	E22NW	1874-04-20		A7
7356	" "	2	E22NE	1867-05-01		A1
7359	" "	2	W22NE	1874-04-20		A7
2522	HENRY, John	13	SESE	1872-07-01		A7
2523	" "	13	NESE	1860-08-01		A1
2524	HENRY, John Q	13	W½SE	1888-12-06		A7
2525	HENRY, Samuel H	1	SWSE	1872-08-30		A1
2526	" "	12	NENE	1880-11-20		A7
2527	" "	24	NE	1859-09-01		A1
7355	HENRY, Thomas H	2	E21NE	1888-05-07		A1
2528	HENRY, William I	5	SESE	1892-12-09		A7
2529	" "	8	NENE	1892-12-09		A7
2530	" "	9	NWNW	1892-12-09		A7
2531	HENSHAW, Levi	7	NESE	1893-12-19		A7

ID	Individual in Patent	Sec.	Sec. Part	Date Issued	Other Counties	For More Info . . .
2533	HENSHAW, Levi (Cont'd)	8	S½NW	1893-12-19		A7
2532	"	8	NWSW	1893-12-19		A7
7382	HEYING, William A	4	E22NE	1892-10-17		A7
7337	HOGGATT, William N	1	2NE	1875-01-06		A7
2534	HOUSE, James A	28	N½SW	1890-06-06		A7
2535	" "	28	W½NW	1890-06-06		A7
2536	HOWELL, Josiah	35	SWSW	1858-01-15		A1
2537	HUDSON, Cassandra F	10	N½NW	1900-11-12		A7
7353	" "	19	S22NW	1893-04-08		A7
2538	" "	3	SWSW	1900-11-12		A7
2539	HUDSON, Jesse F	20	SWSE	1891-10-06		A7 G122
2540	" "	20	SESW	1891-10-06		A7 G122
2541	" "	29	E½NW	1891-10-06		A7 G122
2543	HUDSON, Susan G	20	SESW	1891-10-06		A7 G122
2542	" "	20	SWSE	1891-10-06		A7 G122
2544	" "	29	E½NW	1891-10-06		A7 G122
2545	HUDSON, Thomas H	10	SWSW	1893-09-08		A7
2547	" "	9	S½SE	1893-09-08		A7
2546	" "	9	SESW	1893-09-08		A7
2548	HUGHES, Joseph M	12	SWSW	1859-09-01		A1
2549	HUGHES, Patrick H	13	SW	1859-01-01		A1
2550	" "	24	NW	1859-01-01		A1
2551	HUGHS, Joseph M	13	N½NW	1859-09-01		A1
2553	HUNTER, Andrew M	1	NWSE	1895-11-05		A7
7340	" "	1	E21NW	1895-11-05		A7
7341	" "	1	W21NE	1895-11-05		A7
2552	" "	1	NESW	1895-11-05		A7
7339	HUNTER, William W	1	E21NE	1890-01-10		A7
2554	JAYNE, Andrew J	10	NWNE	1888-12-08		A7
2556	" "	3	SESW	1888-12-08		A7
2555	" "	3	S½SE	1888-12-08		A7
2558	JORDAN, Margaret Ann	17	SE	1860-05-02		A6 G86
2559	KAUFMAN, Peter	32	SENE	1892-03-07		A7
2561	" "	32	E½SE	1892-03-07		A7
2560	" "	32	NWSE	1892-03-07		A7
2562	LANE, Franklin T	13	SENW	1890-10-11		A7
2563	LANE, Lafayette	20	N½NE	1892-06-10		A7
2564	" "	20	NENW	1892-06-10		A7
2565	LASSWELL, Julia A	15	N½SE	1895-09-04		A7 G138
2567	LASSWELL, Mary A	15	S½NE	1884-02-15		A7
2566	" "	15	NENE	1884-02-15		A7
2568	LASSWELL, William H	15	N½SE	1895-09-04		A7 G138
2569	LELAND, Oliver	32	NWNW	1888-12-06		A1
2571	LOWREY, Josiah B	11	S½NE	1890-10-11		A7
2570	" "	11	NWSE	1890-10-11		A7
7392	MACKEY, Benjamin W	6	E21NW	1880-11-20		A7
7389	" "	6	1SW	1880-11-20		A7
7402	" "	7	N21NW	1880-11-20		A7
2572	MACKEY, Thomas D	5	SWSE	1881-04-09		A7
2573	" "	5	SESW	1881-04-09		A7
2575	" "	8	NENW	1881-04-09		A7
2574	" "	8	NWNE	1881-04-09		A7
2576	MAIN, Lewis	25	SWSW	1898-07-25		A7
2577	" "	26	SESE	1898-07-25		A7
2578	" "	35	NENE	1898-07-25		A7
2579	" "	36	NWNW	1898-07-25		A7
2580	MANESS, John S	36	NENW	1882-12-20		A1
2582	MAXEY, James H	10	SWNE	1877-11-10		A1
2581	" "	10	SENW	1877-11-10		A1
2584	MCCALL, Samuel	20	N½SW	1880-11-20		A7
2583	" "	20	S½NW	1880-11-20		A7
2585	MCCALL, William H	29	SWNW	1890-01-30		A1
2587	MCCLINTOCK, Edward	27	E½SW	1885-07-27		A1
2586	" "	27	W½SW	1889-07-26		A7
2588	" "	28	S½SE	1889-07-26		A7
2589	" "	28	N½SE	1885-12-19		A1
2590	MCDANIEL, Aaron	27	NWSE	1895-02-15		A7
7369	MCFALLS, Andrew J	30	N22NW	1892-12-09		A7
7344	MCFARLAND, John L	18	N21SW	1879-12-15		A7
7346	" "	18	N22SW	1879-12-15		A7
7347	" "	18	S21NW	1879-12-15		A7
7349	" "	18	S22NW	1879-12-15		A7
2591	MCFARLAND, Tilmon M	20	SENE	1891-05-25		A7

ID	Individual in Patent	Sec.	Sec. Part	Date Issued	Other Counties	For More Info . . .
2593	MCFARLAND, Tilmon M (Cont'd)	21	E½NW	1891-05-25		A7
2592	" "	21	SWNW	1891-05-25		A7
2594	MCGINTY, William	6	SWSE	1860-10-01		A1
2595	" "	7	N½NE	1859-09-01		A1
2596	" "	7	SENE	1859-09-01		A1
2597	" "	8	NWNW	1859-09-01		A1
2599	MCMANEMIN, William	36	NWSE	1898-07-25		A7
2598	" "	36	W½NE	1898-07-25		A7
2600	MELTON, Willie C	33	E½SE	1860-03-01		A1
2601	" "	34	SWSW	1860-03-01		A1
7394	MODRALL, Flora B	6	E22NE	1895-05-28		A7 G152
7388	MODRALL, Henry W	5	W22NE	1879-12-15		A7
2602	MODRALL, Thomas P	5	NW	1890-01-10		A7
2604	MONGER, John C	29	SWSE	1890-06-06		A7
2603	" "	29	NESW	1890-06-06		A7
2605	" "	29	N½SE	1890-06-06		A7
2606	MOORE, Smith B	10	SESE	1879-12-15		A7
2607	" "	11	SWSW	1879-12-15		A7
2608	" "	14	W½NW	1879-12-15		A7
7384	MORRIS, James L	4	W22NE	1906-06-30		A1
7404	MUSE, James E	7	N22SW	1889-06-22		A7
7401	" "	7	2NW	1889-06-22		A7
2609	MYZELL, Golden S	25	E½SE	1883-02-10		A7
2611	NASH, Thomas M	20	E½SE	1891-05-25		A7
2610	" "	20	NWSE	1891-05-25		A7
2612	" "	20	SWNE	1891-05-25		A7
7398	NICHOLS, Myron G	6	W21NW	1889-01-12		A7
7390	" "	6	2NW	1889-01-12		A7
7395	" "	6	N22SW	1889-01-12		A7
2613	NOLTE, Charles	25	NWNW	1895-07-08		A7
2614	NOLTE, Emma	26	NESE	1897-05-20		A7
2615	NOLTE, Vincent	23	SESE	1886-04-10		A7
2616	" "	24	SWSW	1886-04-10		A7
2617	" "	26	E½NE	1886-04-10		A7
2618	NORDYKE, H T	7	SWNE	1894-01-27		A1
2620	OKELLEY, James N	30	S½NE	1883-06-30		A7
2619	" "	30	W½SE	1883-06-30		A7
7393	OVERMAN, Flora B	6	E22NE	1895-05-28		A7 G152
2621	PEACE, Jane E	15	SWNW	1861-02-01		A1
2622	" "	15	NWSW	1861-02-01		A1
2623	PEACE, Pleasant	29	NE	1859-09-10		A1
2624	PEACE, Pleasant E	22	W½NE	1861-02-09		A1
2625	PEACE, Pleasant M	31	E½SE	1860-03-01		A1
2626	PEACE, William R	15	NWNE	1861-05-01		A1
2628	POTTS, William L	10	SWNW	1888-12-08		A7
2627	" "	10	NWSW	1888-12-08		A7
2629	" "	9	S½NE	1888-12-08		A7
2630	PRIVETT, Alson	22	NWSE	1895-02-15		A7
2632	PRIVETTE, James P	23	W½SW	1897-11-10		A7
2631	" "	23	SWNW	1897-11-10		A7
2633	" "	26	NWNW	1897-11-10		A7
2634	PROCK, Paul J	21	NWNW	1859-09-01		A1
7380	RAINBOLT, John	4	2NW	1894-05-18		A7
7386	" "	5	E22NE	1894-05-18		A7
7399	RAY, Sarah J	6	W22NE	1902-08-22		A7 G162
7400	RAY, William R	6	W22NE	1902-08-22		A7 G162
2637	ROBERTS, George A	32	SENW	1889-01-12		A7
2638	" "	32	N½SW	1889-01-12		A7
2639	" "	32	SWNE	1889-01-12		A7
2640	RODE, Anna M	36	SWNW	1906-03-05		A1
2642	RODE, August	25	W½SE	1889-06-22		A7
2641	" "	25	E½SW	1889-06-22		A7
7350	ROGERS, Joseph A	18	S22SW	1890-10-11		A7
7348	" "	18	S21SW	1890-10-11		A7
2643	RYAN, John	28	S½SW	1892-09-09		A7
2644	" "	33	N½NW	1892-09-09		A7
2645	SCHNEIDER, Frank	34	SWNE	1885-07-27		A7
2646	" "	34	W½SE	1885-07-27		A7
2647	SISSON, Brown	21	NE	1857-10-30		A1
2648	" "	22	NW	1857-10-30		A1
2649	SISSON, Robert G	10	SESW	1860-05-02		A6
2653	" "	12	SESW	1860-05-02		A6
2650	" "	12	N½SE	1860-09-10		A6 G87

ID	Individual in Patent	Sec.	Sec. Part	Date Issued	Other Counties	For More Info . . .
2651	SISSON, Robert G (Cont'd)	12	NESW	1860-09-10		A6 G87
2652	"	12	S½SE	1860-05-02		A6
2654	"	15	E½NW	1860-05-02		A6
2655	SMITH, Hiram M	35	S½NE	1890-01-10		A7
2656	"	35	N½SE	1890-01-10		A7
2657	SMITH, James H	22	NENE	1896-08-28		A7
2658	SMITH, John	22	NESE	1888-12-08		A7
2659	"	22	SENE	1888-12-08		A7
2660	SMITH, Levi M	4	NESW	1879-12-15		A7
7383	"	4	W21NE	1879-12-15		A7
2661	"	4	N½SE	1879-12-15		A7
2662	SMITH, Mary	14	SESW	1879-12-15		A7 G170
2663	"	14	SWSE	1879-12-15		A7 G170
2664	"	23	W½NE	1879-12-15		A7 G170
2667	SMITH, Samantha A	14	W½SW	1888-12-08		A7
2665	"	14	NESW	1888-12-08		A7
2666	"	14	NWSE	1888-12-08		A7
2669	SMITH, William	14	SWSE	1879-12-15		A7 G170
2668	"	14	SESW	1879-12-15		A7 G170
2670	"	23	W½NE	1879-12-15		A7 G170
2671	SMITH, William L	27	SENE	1892-03-07		A7
2672	SOWERS, Josiah	23	SESW	1892-06-21		A7
2674	"	23	SWSE	1892-06-21		A7
2673	"	23	N½SE	1892-06-21		A7
2677	STEIN, Henry	1	SWSW	1890-12-31		A7
2678	STREET, Nancy	5	SWSW	1900-02-02		A7
2679	STROUB, Ferdinand	25	NWSW	1860-10-01		A1
2680	STUBBLEFIELD, William	21	SWSE	1883-06-30		A7
2681	"	21	E½SE	1883-06-30		A7
2682	"	28	NENE	1883-06-30		A7
2683	SUMMERS, Albro	26	NWNE	1899-02-13		A7
2684	SUMMERS, Simeon	35	S½SE	1883-02-10		A7
2685	TENANT, William	8	SESE	1860-08-01		A1
2686	"	9	SWSW	1860-08-01		A1
2687	TESENMEIER, Joseph	22	S½SE	1890-01-10		A7
2688	"	27	N½NE	1890-01-10		A7
2689	THEISSEN, Adolff	1	SESE	1898-04-11		A7
2690	THEISSEN, Gerhard	1	NESE	1890-01-10		A7
2691	THOMAS, Blackman C	11	NENE	1874-04-20		A7
2693	"	12	SWNW	1860-08-01		A1
2692	"	12	SENW	1874-04-20		A7
2694	THOMAS, John	31	SWSE	1896-03-25		A7
2695	THOMAS, Martin	34	SESE	1877-04-25		A1
2696	"	35	SESW	1860-10-01		A1
2697	THOMAS, William	27	E½SE	1880-11-20		A7
2698	"	27	SWSE	1880-11-20		A7
2699	"	34	NENE	1880-11-20		A7
2701	TRIM, James M	9	NESW	1892-03-07		A7
2700	"	9	N½SE	1892-03-07		A7
2702	TUCKER, Delpha	11	S½SE	1875-02-15		A7 G181
2703	TUCKER, Peterson	11	S½SE	1875-02-15		A7 G181
2704	TUPPER, Gilbert H	31	N½NE	1888-12-08		A7
2705	"	31	SENE	1888-12-08		A7
2706	"	32	SWNW	1888-12-08		A7
2707	UNDERWOOD, Ann	14	E½SE	1859-09-01		A1
2709	VAUGHAN, William D	33	S½SW	1892-02-08		A7
2708	"	33	W½SE	1892-02-08		A7
2710	WARCUM, Nancy E	29	SESW	1890-10-11		A7 G187
2712	"	32	N½NE	1890-10-11		A7 G187
2711	"	32	NENW	1890-10-11		A7 G187
2713	WARCUM, William H	29	SESW	1890-10-11		A7 G187
2714	"	32	NENW	1890-10-11		A7 G187
2715	"	32	N½NE	1890-10-11		A7 G187
7396	WEBB, John M	6	S22SW	1900-02-02		A7
2716	WELCH, John L	2	SW	1860-11-12		A6
2717	WERKING, James B	31	SWNE	1891-08-24		A1
2718	YENNEY, George	25	W½NE	1891-05-05		A7 G192
2719	"	25	E½NW	1891-05-05		A7 G192
2720	YENNEY, Martha	25	W½NE	1891-05-05		A7 G192
2721	"	25	E½NW	1891-05-05		A7 G192

Patent Map

T25-N R8-W
5th PM 25-N 8-W Meridian

Map Group 11

Township Statistics

Parcels Mapped	:	387
Number of Patents	:	215
Number of Individuals	:	206
Patentees Identified	:	195
Number of Surnames	:	145
Multi-Patentee Parcels	:	20
Oldest Patent Date	:	3/10/1857
Most Recent Patent	:	3/5/1906
Block/Lot Parcels	:	67
Cities and Town	:	1
Cemeteries	:	2

Lots/Tracts-Sec. 6
1SW   MACKEY, BENJAMIN W 1880
2NW   NICHOLS, MYRON G 1889
E21NE ELLEDGE, ISAAC B 1892
E21NW MACKEY, BENJAMIN W 1880
E22NE MODRALL, FLORA B [152]1895
N22SW NICHOLS, MYRON G 1889
S22SW WEBB, JOHN M 1900
W21NE BRIGGS, DANIEL G 1859
W21NW NICHOLS, MYRON G 1889
W22NE RAY, SARAH J [162] 1902

Lots/Tracts-Sec. 5
E21NE FARMER, SAMUEL H 1896
E22NE RAINBOLT, JOHN 1894
W21NE FARMER, SILAS 1900
W22NE MODRALL, HENRY W 1879

Lots/Tracts-Sec. 4
1NW   FARMER, SAMUEL H 1896
2NW   RAINBOLT, JOHN 1894
E21NE COLTHARP, WILLIAMSON G1906
E22NE HEYING, WILLIAM A 1892
W21NE SMITH, LEVI M 1879
W22NE MORRIS, JAMES L 1906

Section 6
BRIGGS Daniel G 1859
ELLEDGE Isaac B 1892
MCGINTY William 1860
GAYER David P 1871

Section 5
ELLEDGE Isaac B 1892
FARMER Silas 1900
FARMER Samuel H 1896
MODRALL Thomas P 1890
STREET Nancy 1900
MACKEY Thomas D 1881
MACKEY Thomas D 1881
HENRY William I 1892

Section 4
BRADSHAW Samuel A 1890
SMITH Levi M 1879
SMITH Levi M 1879
BRADSHAW Samuel A 1890
BROWN John A 1877

Section 7
Lots/Tracts-Sec. 7
2NW   MUSE, JAMES E 1889
N21NW MACKEY, BENJAMIN W 1880
N21SW ELLEDGE, JAMES M 1889
N22SW MUSE, JAMES E 1888
S21NW ELLEDGE, JAMES M 1888
S22SW BOYSE, MARION L 1891

MCGINTY William 1859
NORDYKE H T 1894
MCGINTY William 1859
GILLELAND James 1859
HENSHAW Levi 1893

Section 8
MCGINTY William 1859
MACKEY Thomas D 1881
MACKEY Thomas D 1881
HENRY William I 1892
HENSHAW Levi 1893
BESS Christopher B 1890
HENSHAW Levi 1893
BRADSHAW Jonathan W 1890

Section 9
HENRY William I 1892
BRADSHAW Samuel A 1890
BROWN John A 1877
BESS Christopher B 1890
POTTS William L 1888
BRADSHAW Jonathan W 1890
TRIM James M 1892
TRIM James M 1892

ELLEDGE Isaac 1875
ELLEDGE Isaac 1875
BRADSHAW Jonathan W 1890
ELLEDGE Isaac 1875
COURSEY Elbert C 1901
COURSEY Elbert C 1901
TENANT William 1860
TENANT William 1860
HUDSON Thomas H 1893
HUDSON Thomas H 1893

Section 18
Lots/Tracts-Sec. 18
N21NW BOYSE, MARION L 1891
N21SW BOYSE, MARION L 1891
N22NW BOYSE, MARION L 1891
N22SW MCFARLAND, JOHN L 1879
S21NW MCFARLAND, JOHN L 1879
S21SW MCFARLAND, JOHN L 1890
S22NW ROGERS, JOSEPH A 1890
S22SW ROGERS, JOSEPH A 1890
      MCFARLAND, JOHN L 1879
      ROGERS, JOSEPH A 1890

ELLEDGE Isaac 1860
ELLEDGE Isaac 1859
ELLEDGE Isaac 1859
HAWKINS William A 1888
HAWKINS William A 1888
HAMBY William 1889

Section 17
ELLEDGE Isaac 1859
FORD Charles P 1860
FORD Charles P 1860
FORD Charles P 1860
FORD Charles P 1860
FOREST Benjamin F 1901
FORD [86] Charles P 1860
HAMBY William 1889

Section 16
(blank shaded)

Section 19
Lots/Tracts-Sec. 19
1NW   BROWER, WESLEY T 1876
N22NW BOYCE, JESSE 1860
S22NW HUDSON, CASSANDRA F 1893

BROWER Wesley T 1876
COOK [58] William D 1860
COOK William D 1860
COOK [58] William D 1860
BROWER William S 1876
COOK William D 1860

Section 20
DUNHAM Gilbert C 1886
DUNHAM Gilbert C 1886
LANE Lafayette 1892
LANE Lafayette 1892
MCCALL Samuel 1880
NASH Thomas M 1891
MCFARLAND Tilmon M 1891
MCFARLAND Tilmon M 1891
MCCALL Samuel 1880
NASH Thomas M 1891
NASH Thomas M 1891
BACON Seth W 1859
HUDSON [122] Susan G 1891
HUDSON [122] Susan G 1891

Section 21
PROCK Paul J 1859
MCFARLAND Tilmon M 1891
SISSON Brown 1857
ACREE N B 1890
STUBBLEFIELD William 1883
DRIEHAUS Adolphus 1894
STUBBLEFIELD William 1883

Section 30
Lots/Tracts-Sec. 30
1NW   BATES, GEORGE W 1890
N22NW MCFALLS, ANDREW J 1892
S21SW HAYS, JOHN B 1890
S22NW BATES, GEORGE W 1890

COZORT William A 1860
BACON Seth W 1859
OKELLEY James N 1883
MCCALL William H 1890
OKELLEY James N 1883
HADDOCK John 1889
HADDOCK John 1889

Section 29
BACON Seth W 1859
HUDSON [122] Susan G 1891
PEACE Pleasant 1859
MONGER John C 1890
MONGER John C 1890
WARCUM [187] Nancy E 1890
MONGER John C 1890
CARRIS Ray B 1891

Section 28
HOUSE James A 1890
HADDOCK Jesse 1888
HADDOCK Jesse 1888
CRIDER Abraham 1897
STUBBLEFIELD William 1883
HOUSE James A 1890
MCCLINTOCK Edward 1885
RYAN John 1892
MCCLINTOCK Edward 1889

Section 31
Lots/Tracts-Sec. 31
N21NW HAYS, JOHN B 1890
N21SW CRIDER, JOSEPH 1877
N22NW HAYS, JOHN B 1890
N22SW BRANNOCK, MILTON W 1886
S21SW CRIDER, JOSEPH 1883
S22SW GLEEN, LOUISA 1892

TUPPER Gilbert H 1888
WERKING James B 1891
TUPPER Gilbert H 1888
CRIDER Joseph 1878
CRIDER Joseph 1877
PEACE Pleasant M 1860
THOMAS John 1896

Section 32
LELAND Oliver 1888
WARCUM [187] Nancy E 1890
WARCUM [187] Nancy E 1890
TUPPER Gilbert H 1888
ROBERTS George A 1889
ROBERTS George A 1889
KAUFMAN Peter 1892
ROBERTS George A 1889
KAUFMAN Peter 1892
KAUFMAN Peter 1892
FORD Oscar H 1884
HARLAN David B 1882
HARLAN David B 1882

Section 33
RYAN John 1892
RYAN John 1892
BROTHERTON Bartlet 1888
BROTHERTON Abraham 1892
BROTHERTON Abraham 1892
KAUFMAN Peter 1892
VAUGHAN William D 1892
MELTON Willie C 1860
VAUGHAN William D 1892

Lots/Tracts–Sec. 3
2NW   BARTON, JOHN R   1895
E21NE   BOSS, THEODOR   1891
E21NW   GOYER, DANIEL T   1885
E22NE   COUNTS, JAMES E   1891
W21NE   GOYER, DANIEL T   1885
W21NW   BARTON, JOHN R   1895
W22NE   GOYER, DANIEL T   1883

Lots/Tracts–Sec. 2
1NW   BOSS, THEODOR   1891
E21NE   HENRY, THOMAS H   1888
E22NE   HENRY, ISAAC P   1867
E22NW   HENRY, ISAAC P   1874
W21NE   GEBBERS, GEORGE   1905
W22NE   HENRY, ISAAC P   1874
W22NW   COUNTS, JAMES E   1891

Lots/Tracts–Sec. 1
2NE   HOGGATT, WILLIAM N   1875
2NW   CUNNINGHAM, JOHN M   1883
E21NE   HUNTER, WILLIAM W   1890
E21NW   HUNTER, ANDREW M   1895
W21NE   HUNTER, ANDREW M   1895
W21NW   CUNNINGHAM, JOHN M   1883

Section 3
GOYER Daniel T 1885
GOYER Daniel T 1885
GOYER Daniel T 1883
BOSS Louis 1900
BOSS Louis 1900
BOSS Theodor 1891
HUDSON Cassandra F 1900
JAYNE Andrew J 1888
JAYNE Andrew J 1888

Section 2
WELCH John L 1860
HAMMONDS James W 1889

Section 1
CUNNINGHAM John M 1883
HUNTER Andrew M 1895
HUNTER Andrew M 1895
THEISSEN Gerhard 1890
STEIN Henry 1890
GOYER Daniel T 1857
HENRY Samuel H 1872
THEISSEN Adolff 1898

Section 10
HUDSON Cassandra F 1900
JAYNE Andrew J 1888
BURROUGHS John E 1896
POTTS William L 1888
MAXEY James H 1877
MAXEY James H 1877
ADAMS Isaac 1860
POTTS William L 1888
ADAMS Samuel 1859
ADAMS Isaac 1857
HUDSON Thomas H 1893
SISSON Robert G 1860
ADAMS Isaac 1859
MOORE Smith B 1879

Section 11
BURROUGHS John E 1896
BURROUGHS George W 1873
BURROUGHS George W 1874
THOMAS Blackman C 1874
BURROUGHS George W 1873
LOWREY Josiah B 1890
ADKINS A T 1885
ADKINS A T 1885
LOWREY Josiah B 1890
MOORE Smith B 1879
TUCKER [181] Delpha 1875

Section 12
GOYER Daniel T 1857
GOYER Daniel T 1857
HENRY Samuel H 1880
THOMAS Blackman C 1860
THOMAS Blackman C 1874
CHANDLER William P 1861
DRYER Conrad H 1876
SISSON [87] Robert G 1860
SISSON [87] Robert G 1860
HUGHES Joseph M 1859
SISSON Robert G 1860
SISSON Robert G 1860

Section 15
ACREE N B 1889
PEACE William R 1861
LASSWELL Mary A 1884
SISSON Robert G 1860
PEACE Jane E 1861
LASSWELL Mary A 1884
PEACE Jane E 1861
LASSWELL [138] Julia A 1895
ACREE George H 1888
ADAMS John 1859
ACREE George H 1888

Section 14
ADKINS A T 1885
ACREE Nathaniel B 1888
MOORE Smith B 1879
ACREE Nathaniel B 1888
ACREE Nathaniel B 1888
SMITH Samantha A 1888
SMITH Samantha A 1888
SMITH Samantha A 1888
SMITH [170] Mary 1879
SMITH [170] Mary 1879

Section 13
HUGHS Joseph M 1859
DENTON William 1859
BARNES John H 1895
BARNES John H 1895
LANE Franklin T 1890
DENTON William 1859
DENTON William 1860
UNDERWOOD Ann 1859
HUGHES Patrick H 1859
HENRY John Q 1888
HENRY John 1860
HENRY John 1872

Section 22
SISSON Samuel H 1857
CHARLES Brew 1892
PEACE Pleasant E 1861
SMITH James H 1896
SMITH John 1888
EARLS William 1878
PRIVETT Alson 1895
SMITH John 1888
ACREE Nathaniel B 1884
CHARLES Samuel H 1892
TESENMEIER Joseph 1890

Section 23
BOYD William J 1903
SMITH [170] Mary 1879
PRIVETTE James P 1897
BOYD William J 1903
PRIVETTE James P 1897
BOYD William J 1903
SOWERS Josiah 1892
SOWERS Josiah 1892
SOWERS Josiah 1892
NOLTE Vincent 1886

Section 24
DALSING Bernhard 1900
HUGHES Patrick H 1859
HENRY Samuel H 1859
GLENDENING James E 1895
NOLTE Vincent 1886
GOODELL Elisha H 1890
GOODELL Elisha H 1890
GUNTER Samuel 1861

Section 27
ACREE Nathaniel B 1884
TESENMEIER Joseph 1890
ACREE Nathaniel B 1884
MCCLINTOCK Edward 1885
MCCLINTOCK Edward 1889
MCDANIEL Aaron 1895
CHARLES Samuel H 1892
SMITH William L 1892
THOMAS William 1880
THOMAS William 1880

Section 26
PRIVETTE James P 1897
SUMMERS Albro 1899
COWAN Joseph P 1892
NOLTE Vincent 1886
PRIVETTE James P 1897
CORDES Louis 1898
COWAN Joseph P 1892
CORDES Louis 1898
CORDES Louis 1898
FISCHER Michael 1888
FISCHER Michael 1888
MAIN Lewis 1898

Section 25
NOLTE Charles 1895
DRYER Conrad H 1886
YENNEY [192] Martha 1891
YENNEY [192] Martha 1891
STROUB Ferdinand 1860
MAIN Lewis 1898
RODE August 1889
RODE August 1889
MYZELL Golden S 1883

Section 34
ESSEX Thomas 1896
ESSEX Thomas 1896
THOMAS William 1880
CAGE Adolphus A 1892
ESSEX Thomas 1896
SCHNEIDER Frank 1885
CAGE Adolphus A 1892
SCHNEIDER Frank 1885
MELTON Willie C 1860
CAGE Adolphus A 1892
THOMAS Martin 1877

Section 35
FISCHER Michael 1891
FISCHER Michael 1888
FISCHER Michael 1888
MAIN Lewis 1898
BRAKEBILL John O 1895
SMITH Hiram M 1890
BRAKEBILL John O 1895
SMITH Hiram M 1890
HOWELL Josiah 1858
THOMAS Martin 1860
SUMMERS Simeon 1883

Section 36
MAIN Lewis 1898
MANESS John S 1882
MCMANEMIN William 1898
GOOD Joseph 1890
RODE Anna M 1906
HALL William E 1893
HALL William E 1893
MCMANEMIN William 1898
HALL William E 1893
GOOD Joseph 1890
GALLOWAY Samuel 1882
GALLOWAY Samuel 1882

Helpful Hints

1. This Map's INDEX can be found on the preceding pages.

2. Refer to Map "C" to see where this Township lies within Howell County, Missouri.

3. Numbers within square brackets [ ] denote a multi-patentee land parcel (multi-owner). Refer to Appendix "C" for a full list of members in this group.

4. Areas that look to be crowded with Patentees usually indicate multiple sales of the same parcel (Re-issues) or Overlapping parcels. See this Township's Index for an explanation of these and other circumstances that might explain "odd" groupings of Patentees on this map.

Legend

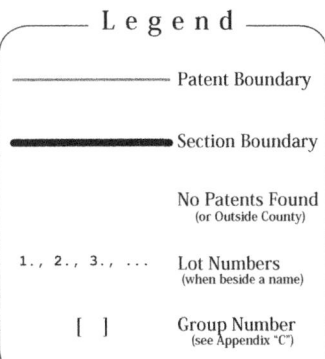

——————— Patent Boundary

━━━━━━━ Section Boundary

No Patents Found (or Outside County)

1., 2., 3., ...   Lot Numbers (when beside a name)

[ ]   Group Number (see Appendix "C")

Scale: Section = 1 mile X 1 mile (generally, with some exceptions)

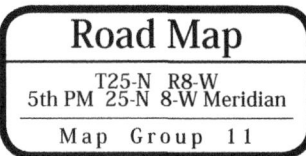

Road Map

T25-N R8-W
5th PM 25-N 8-W Meridian

Map Group 11

Cities & Towns
White Church

Cemeteries
Dripping Springs Cemetery
Pleasant View Cemetery

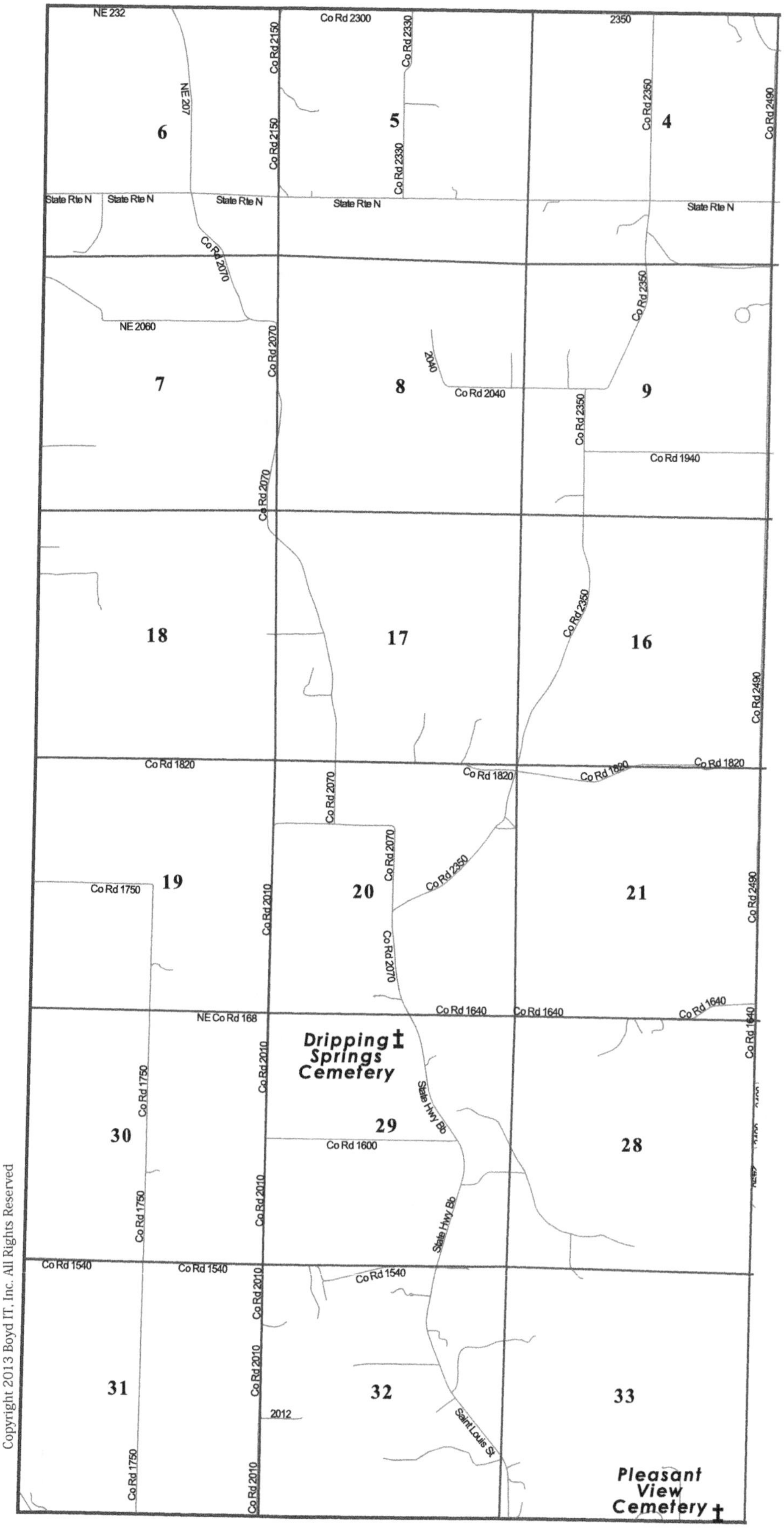

NE 232
Co Rd 2300
2350

6
5
4

State Rte N

7
8
9

Co Rd 2040
Co Rd 1940

18
17
16

Co Rd 1820
Co Rd 1690
Co Rd 1820

19
20
21

Co Rd 1750
Co Rd 1640
Co Rd 1640
Co Rd 1640

NE Co Rd 168

Dripping Springs Cemetery

30
29
28

Co Rd 1600

Co Rd 1540
Co Rd 1540
Co Rd 1540

31
32
33

2012

Pleasant View Cemetery

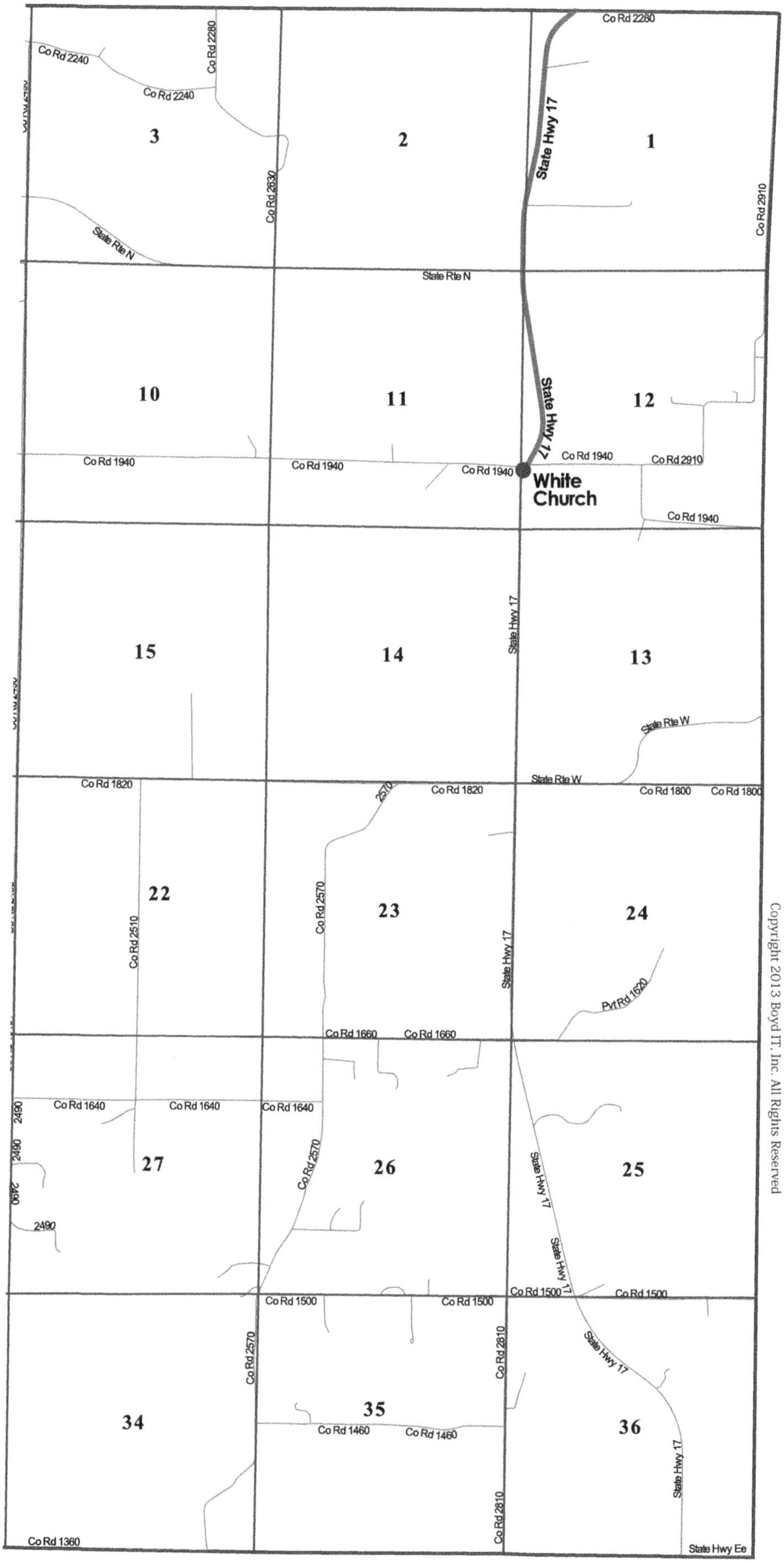

Co Rd 2280

Co Rd 2240

Co Rd 2240

Co Rd 2280

Co Rd 2830

Co Rd 2910

State Rte N

State Hwy 17

3

2

1

State Rte N

State Hwy 17

10

11

12

Co Rd 1940

Co Rd 1940

Co Rd 1940

Co Rd 1940

Co Rd 2910

White Church

Co Rd 1940

State Hwy 17

15

14

13

State Rte W

State Rte W

Co Rd 1820

Co Rd 1820

Co Rd 1800

Co Rd 1800

2570

Co Rd 2570

Co Rd 2510

22

23

24

State Hwy 17

Pvt Rd 1520

Co Rd 1660

Co Rd 1660

Co Rd 1640

Co Rd 1640

Co Rd 1640

2490

2490

Co Rd 2570

27

26

25

State Hwy 17

2490

2490

State Hwy 17

Co Rd 1500

Co Rd 1500

Co Rd 1500

Co Rd 1500

Co Rd 1500

Co Rd 2570

Co Rd 2810

State Hwy 17

34

35

36

Co Rd 1460

Co Rd 1460

Co Rd 2810

State Hwy 17

Co Rd 1360

State Hwy Ee

Helpful Hints

1. This road map has a number of uses, but primarily it is to help you: a) find the present location of land owned by your ancestors (at least the general area), b) find cemeteries and city-centers, and c) estimate the route/roads used by Census-takers & tax-assessors.

2. If you plan to travel to Howell County to locate cemeteries or land parcels, please pick up a modern travel map for the area before you do. Mapping old land parcels on modern maps is not as exact a science as you might think. Just the slightest variations in public land survey coordinates, estimates of parcel boundaries, or road-map deviations can greatly alter a map's representation of how a road either does or doesn't cross a particular parcel of land.

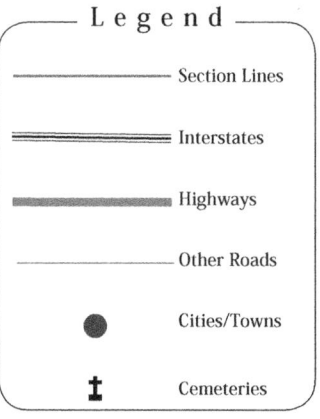

Legend

———————	Section Lines
═══════	Interstates
▬▬▬▬▬▬	Highways
———————	Other Roads
●	Cities/Towns
✝	Cemeteries

Scale: Section = 1 mile X 1 mile
(generally, with some exceptions)

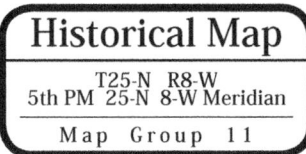

Historical Map

T25-N   R8-W
5th PM 25-N 8-W Meridian

Map Group 11

Cities & Towns
White Church

Cemeteries
Dripping Springs Cemetery
Pleasant View Cemetery

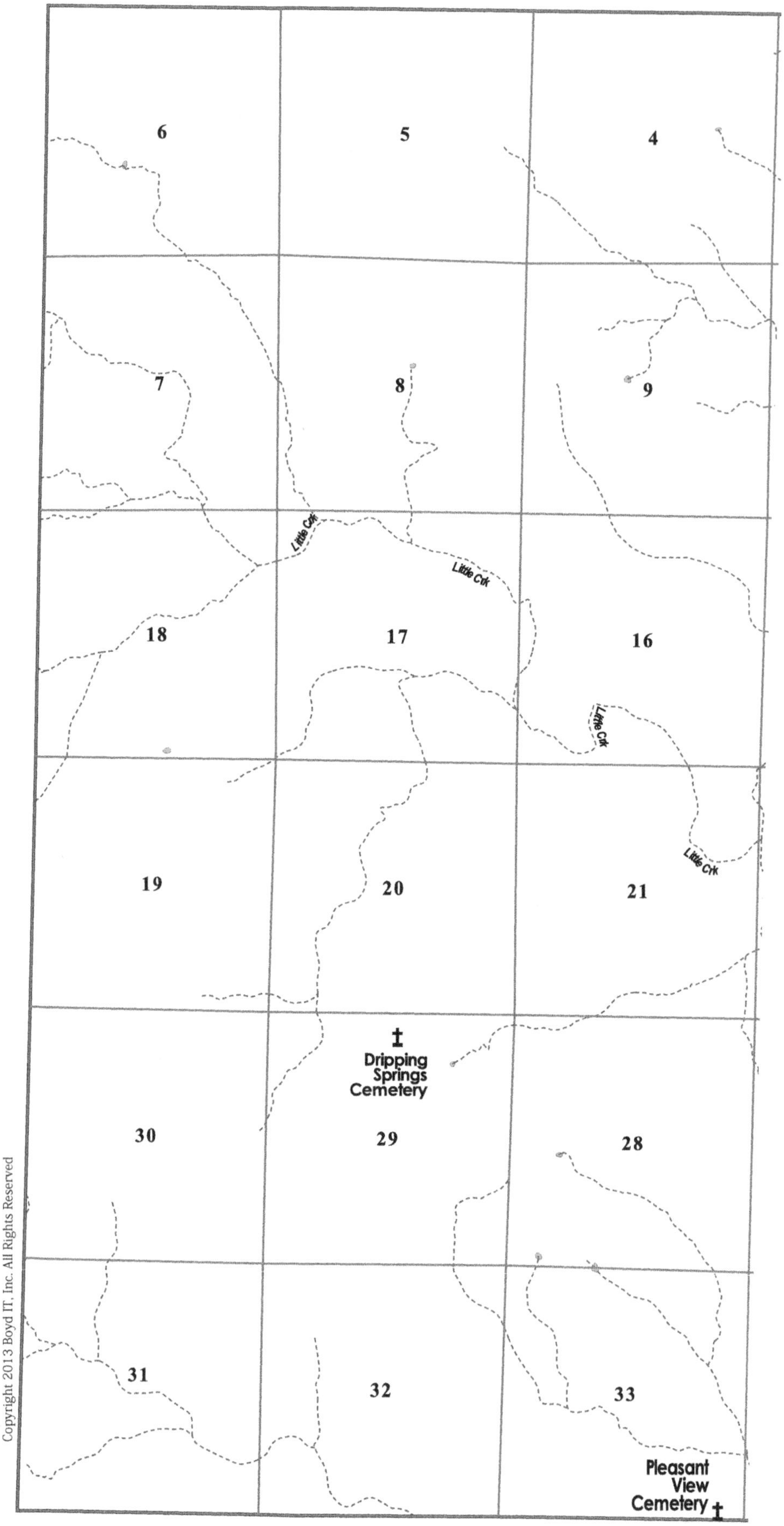

6

5

4

7

8

9

Little Crk

Little Crk

18

17

16

Little Crk

19

20

21

Little Crk

✝
Dripping
Springs
Cemetery

30

29

28

31

32

33

Pleasant
View
Cemetery ✝

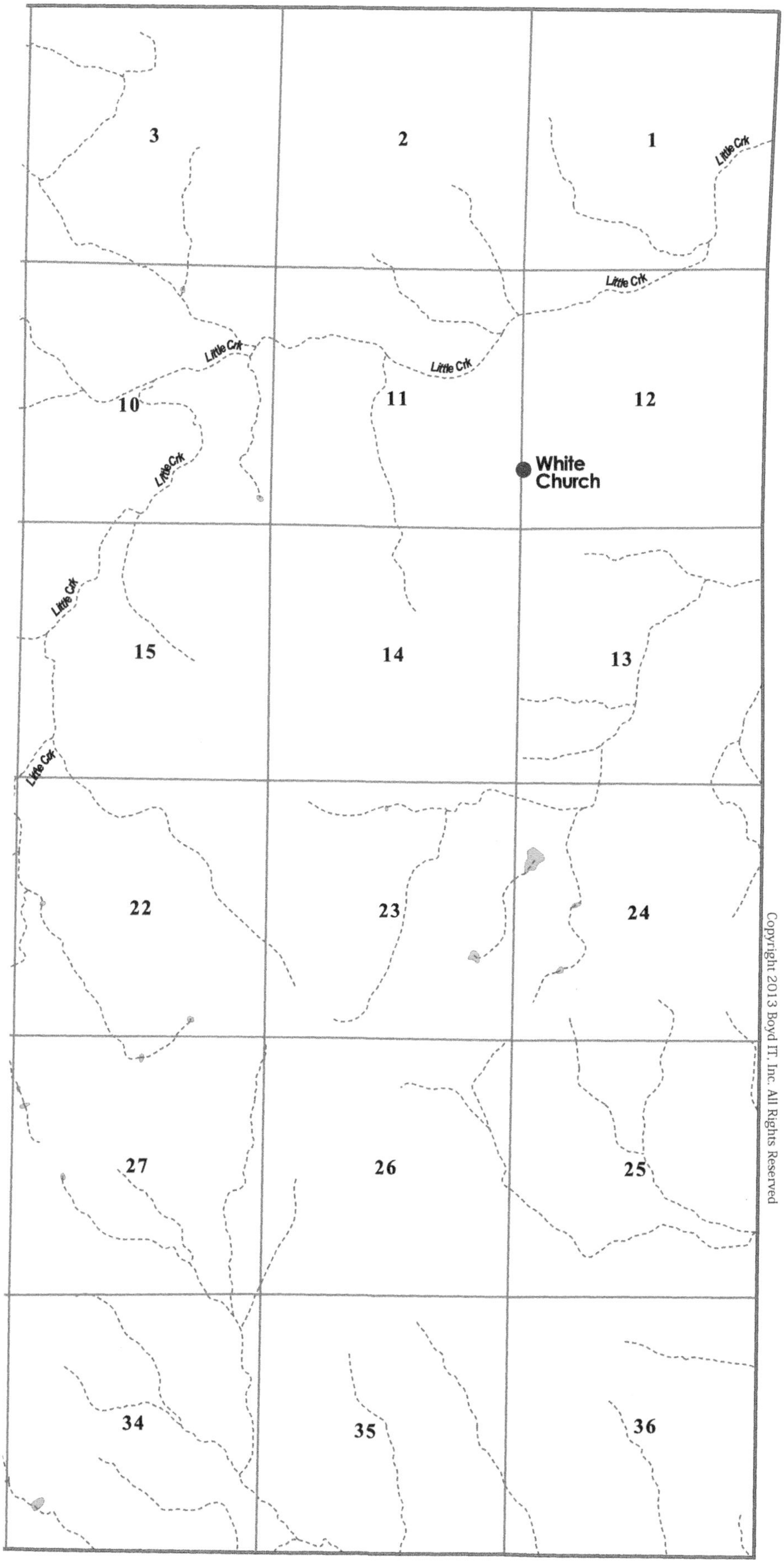

3

2

1

Little Crk

Little Crk

Little Crk

Little Crk

10

Little Crk

11

12

Little Crk

● White
Church

Little Crk

15

14

13

Little Crk

22

23

24

27

26

25

34

35

36

Helpful Hints

1. This Map takes a different look at the same Congressional Township displayed in the preceding two maps. It presents features that can help you better envision the historical development of the area: a) Water-bodies (lakes & ponds), b) Water-courses (rivers, streams, etc.), c) Railroads, d) City/ town center-points (where they were oftentimes located when first settled), and e) Cemeteries.

2. Using this "Historical" map in tandem with this Township's Patent Map and Road Map, may lead you to some interesting discoveries. You will often find roads, towns, cemeteries, and waterways are named after nearby landowners: sometimes those names will be the ones you are researching. See how many of these research gems you can find here in Howell County.

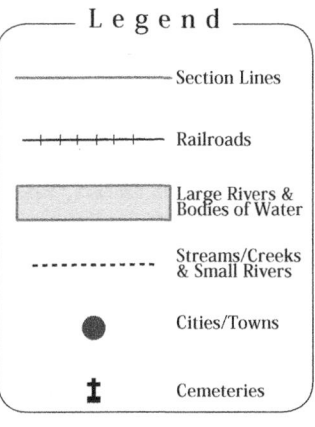

L e g e n d

——————— Section Lines

—+—+—+—+—+— Railroads

Large Rivers &
Bodies of Water

- - - - - - - - Streams/Creeks
& Small Rivers

● Cities/Towns

‡ Cemeteries

Scale: Section = 1 mile X 1 mile
(there are some exceptions)

Map Group 12: Index to Land Patents

Township 25-North Range 7-West (5th PM 25-N 7-W)

After you locate an individual in this Index, take note of the Section and Section Part then proceed to the Land Patent map on the pages immediately following. You should have no difficulty locating the corresponding parcel of land.

The "For More Info" Column will lead you to more information about the underlying Patents. See the *Legend* at right, and the "How to Use this Book" chapter, for more information.

ID	Individual in Patent	Sec.	Sec. Part	Date Issued	Other Counties	For More Info . . .
2722	ADEN, John	36	N½SW	1860-10-01		A1
7457	ATCHISON, Sarah	6	E22NW	1882-11-10		A7
7459	" "	6	W22NE	1882-11-10		A7
7458	" "	6	W21NE	1882-11-10		A7
2723	AYERS, Alexander M	1	N½	1882-12-20		A1
2724	" "	2	S½SE	1882-12-20		A1
7424	" "	2	W22NE	1882-12-20		A1
7422	" "	2	W21NE	1882-12-20		A1
7420	" "	2	E21NW	1882-12-20		A1
2725	" "	2	NESW	1882-12-20		A1
2726	BARNETT, George W	31	SESE	1882-12-20		A1
2729	BARNETT, James D	31	NWSE	1875-05-01		A7
2728	" "	31	SWNE	1875-05-01		A7
2727	" "	31	SENE	1885-06-03		A1
2730	" "	32	SWNW	1885-06-03		A1
2731	BARNETT, Obed N	32	N½SW	1877-08-01		A7
7441	BARTON, William H	4	E22NE	1892-03-07		A7
7439	" "	4	1NE	1892-03-07		A7
2732	BASER, Louis	34	SENW	1906-03-31		A7
2733	BAY, James J	11	NENE	1913-10-08		A7
2734	" "	12	NWNW	1913-10-08		A7
2736	BENNETT, Alfonzo D	32	NWSE	1898-01-26		A7
2737	" "	32	SWNE	1898-01-26		A7
2739	BENNETT, Silas M	26	E½SW	1890-10-11		A7
2738	" "	26	W½SE	1890-10-11		A7
2740	BENSON, John W	24	N½	1892-07-11		A1
2741	BLACK, James T	18	NWNE	1860-08-01		A1
2742	" "	7	S½SE	1860-08-01		A1
2743	BLACK, William P	17	NWNW	1860-08-01		A1
2744	" "	8	SWSW	1860-08-01		A1
2745	BRADSHAW, Robert W	36	NW	1901-06-08		A7
2746	BRAGG, James P	19	S½SE	1898-07-25		A7
2747	BRIXEY, J C	10	NESW	1890-01-30		A1
2749	BRIXEY, John	17	SENW	1859-09-01		A1
2748	" "	17	NE	1859-09-01		A1
2750	BRIXEY, John C	8	NESE	1875-01-06		A7
2751	" "	8	E½NE	1875-01-06		A7
2752	" "	9	NWNW	1875-01-06		A7
2753	BRIXEY, John O	4	NWSW	1915-04-12		A7
2754	BROWN, John G	8	SESW	1867-11-15		A3
2755	" "	8	N½SW	1867-11-15		A3
2756	" "	9	SW	1867-11-15		A3
2757	BROYLS, William S	10	SENW	1901-07-09		A7
2758	" "	10	SWNE	1901-07-09		A7
7435	BUGG, Robert Martin	30	S22NW	1907-08-19		A1
2759	BURROUGHS, George W	21	N½NE	1861-02-01		A1

ID	Individual in Patent	Sec.	Sec. Part	Date Issued	Other Counties	For More Info . . .
2760	BURROUGHS, James F	22	SWSE	1904-11-15		A7
2762	BURROUGHS, John F	35	SWNE	1877-10-10		A7
2761	" "	35	N½SW	1877-10-10		A7
2763	" "	35	SENW	1877-10-10		A7
2764	BURROUGHS, Joseph A	33	W½SE	1872-07-01		A7
2765	" "	33	NESE	1872-07-01		A7
2766	BURROUGHS, Mary	19	W½NE	1861-02-01		A1
2767	" "	33	SW	1873-02-01		A7
2768	BURROUGHS, Robert H	27	W½NE	1904-03-19		A7
2769	" "	27	E½NW	1904-03-19		A7
7413	CHARLES, Henry	19	1NW	1861-02-01		A1
2770	CHARLES, John W	32	NENE	1861-02-01		A1
2771	CHEATHAM, William H	3	NESE	1908-01-27		A1
7428	" "	3	E21NE	1908-01-27		A1
7450	" "	5	W21NE	1908-01-27		A1
2772	" "	5	NWSE	1908-01-27		A1
2773	CHURCHILL, H P	11	NESE	1886-11-19		A1
2774	" "	12	S½	1886-11-19		A1
2775	" "	13		1886-11-19		A1
2776	CLEMMONES, Walter D	7	E½NE	1888-12-06		A7
2777	" "	7	NESE	1888-12-06		A7
2778	" "	8	SWNW	1888-12-06		A7
7408	CLEMMONS, James W	18	N21NW	1882-11-10		A7
7462	" "	7	1SW	1882-11-10		A7
2779	" "	7	NWSE	1882-11-10		A7
2780	CLEVELAND, John A	30	SWSE	1892-01-05		A7
2781	" "	31	N½NE	1892-01-05		A7
2782	" "	32	NWNW	1892-01-05		A7
2783	CLEVELAND, Robert G	30	E½SE	1900-02-02		A7
2784	COBB, George H	25	SWSW	1907-10-11		A1
2785	" "	25	NESW	1907-10-11		A1
2786	COOK, William D	20	SWSW	1859-03-03		A8
2787	" "	21	SE	1860-05-02		A6
2788	" "	22	SW	1860-05-02		A6
2790	" "	29	SENW	1860-05-02		A6 G59
2789	" "	29	N½NW	1860-05-02		A6 G59
2793	COX, Oliver	21	S½NE	1889-02-02		A7
2791	" "	21	NESW	1889-02-02		A7
2792	" "	21	SENW	1889-02-02		A7
2794	CRAIN, John Z	25	SENE	1912-06-11		A1
2795	CRISP, Robert	31	W½NW	1875-01-06		A7
2796	" "	31	SENW	1875-01-06		A7
2797	" "	31	NESW	1875-01-06		A7
2798	CRUM, Peter	23	SENW	1905-08-08		A1
2799	DAUGHERTY, George	27	SWNW	1896-12-08		A7
2800	" "	27	N½SW	1896-12-08		A7
2802	DAVIS, George W	32	S½SW	1861-05-01		A1
2801	" "	32	SWSE	1861-05-01		A1
2803	DAVIS, Morgan	28	W½SE	1898-04-11		A7
7412	DENTON, William	18	S22SW	1859-09-01		A1
2804	DESITS, Malinda D	11	NWNE	1879-09-23		A1
2805	DESITS, Peter P	11	SENE	1873-02-01		A7
2806	" "	12	S½NW	1873-02-01		A7
2807	" "	12	SWNE	1873-05-30		A7
2808	DIEHL, John	29	E½	1860-08-01		A1
2809	DRYER, Conrad H	17	NENW	1875-02-15		A7
2810	" "	17	SWNW	1859-09-01		A1
2811	" "	18	E½NE	1859-09-01		A1
2814	EBLEN, Francis C	23	NESE	1892-04-23		A7
2812	" "	23	S½NE	1892-04-23		A7
2813	" "	23	NWNE	1892-04-23		A7
2815	EBLEN, Isaac	23	N½SW	1889-01-12		A7
2816	" "	23	NWSE	1889-01-12		A7
2817	" "	23	SWNW	1889-01-12		A7
2818	EBLEN, Isaac L	14	S½SW	1893-09-01		A7
2819	" "	23	N½NW	1893-09-01		A7
2820	" "	26	SENW	1916-06-16		A7
2822	ELDRINGHOFF, Henry B	6	W½SE	1891-06-09		A7
2821	" "	6	E½SW	1891-06-09		A7
7461	ELDRINGHOFF, Joseph	7	1NW	1888-11-06		A7
2823	" "	7	NWNE	1888-12-06		A1
2824	" "	7	SWNE	1888-11-06		A7
7465	" "	7	S22NW	1888-11-06		A7

ID	Individual in Patent	Sec.	Sec. Part	Date Issued	Other Counties	For More Info . . .
2826	ELDRINGHOFF, Theodore	10	SESW	1895-05-28		A7
2825	" "	10	W½SW	1895-05-28		A7
2827	" "	15	NWNW	1895-05-28		A7
2828	ERWIN, Austin M	12	SENE	1906-06-30		A1
2829	ERWIN, Emmet E	14	NWSW	1915-04-12		A7
7425	ERWIN, Meanda	3	1NW	1907-05-10		A1
2831	ESKRIDGE, James R	8	NWNE	1903-10-01		A7
2830	" "	8	NENW	1903-10-01		A7
2832	FERGUSON, James B	23	S½SE	1901-06-08		A7
2833	" "	24	W½SW	1901-06-08		A7
2835	FERGUSON, James M	14	SWNW	1900-02-02		A7
2836	" "	14	NESW	1900-02-02		A7
2834	" "	14	E½NW	1900-02-02		A7
2837	FERGUSON, John W	10	SESE	1888-12-08		A7
2838	" "	14	NWNW	1888-12-08		A7
2839	" "	15	N½NE	1888-12-08		A7
2840	FULLER, Joseph L	27	NWNW	1899-03-03		A7
2842	" "	28	SWNE	1899-03-03		A7
2841	" "	28	E½NE	1899-03-03		A7
2843	FULLER, Thadeous D	25	W½NW	1892-09-09		A7
2844	" "	26	N½NE	1892-09-09		A7
2847	GALE, Julius F	15	SWSE	1885-08-20		A7
2845	" "	15	NESW	1885-08-20		A7
2846	" "	15	NESE	1885-08-20		A7
2848	GAMBER, Jacob G	25	NWSE	1893-01-07		A7
2850	" "	25	SWNE	1893-01-07		A7
2849	" "	25	N½NE	1893-01-07		A7
2851	GAMBER, Michael	24	W½SE	1893-06-13		A7
2852	" "	24	E½SW	1893-06-13		A7
2853	GENTRY, Henry M	28	NWNE	1912-03-28		A1
7429	GILLIAM, Lemuel W	3	W21NE	1895-06-22		A1
7443	" "	4	W21NW	1893-12-09		A1
7440	GILLIAM, Thomas L	4	E21NW	1881-10-06		A7
2855	" "	4	E½NW	1881-10-06		A7
2854	" "	4	SWSW	1881-10-06		A7
2856	GOOD, George	27	SWSW	1890-01-10		A7
2857	" "	28	E½SE	1890-01-10		A7
2858	" "	33	NENE	1890-01-10		A7
7438	GOOD, John	31	S21SW	1890-01-10		A7
2859	" "	31	SWSE	1890-01-10		A7
2860	GRAHNERT, August	24	E½SE	1895-11-05		A7
2862	GRAVES, Robert M	1	S½SW	1894-05-18		A7
2861	" "	1	NWSW	1894-05-18		A7
2863	" "	12	NENW	1894-05-18		A7
2865	GREEN, Charles F	27	SESW	1889-06-22		A7
2864	" "	27	SWSE	1889-06-22		A7
2866	" "	34	NWNE	1889-06-22		A7
2867	" "	34	NENW	1889-06-22		A7
2868	GROCE, Pleasant	34	W½NW	1892-01-05		A7
2869	GROCE, Willis M	34	S½NE	1892-03-07		A7
7416	GUNTER, Samuel	19	N21SW	1859-09-01		A1
7417	" "	19	S21SW	1861-08-01		A1
7415	" "	19	2SW	1859-09-01		A1
2870	" "	19	NWSE	1861-08-01		A1
2871	GUNTER, William C	31	NESE	1859-09-01		A1
2872	HARPER, Lensey F	32	E½SE	1903-01-31		A7
2874	HATHWAY, William W	1	N½SE	1904-12-29		A1
2876	HAYDEN, James	32	NWNE	1896-09-29		A7
2875	" "	32	E½NW	1896-09-29		A7
2877	HENER, Conrad D	22	NW	1888-12-06		A7
2878	HENRY, C P	3	NWSE	1884-10-11		A1
2879	HENRY, Carrel	18	SWNE	1860-08-01		A1
7410	HENRY, Carrol	18	S21NW	1861-02-01		A1
2880	HENRY, George M	32	SENE	1872-07-01		A7
2882	" "	33	W½NW	1872-07-01		A7
2881	" "	33	SENW	1872-07-01		A7
2883	HENRY, Isaac	8	SESE	1860-08-01		A1
2884	HENRY, James W	20	S½NW	1885-06-20		A7
2885	" "	20	SWNE	1885-06-20		A7
7407	HENRY, John	18	2SW	1872-07-01		A7
7409	HENRY, Samuel	18	N21SW	1861-02-01		A1
7411	HENRY, William C	18	S21SW	1883-08-13		A1
2886	HENRY, William O	33	W½NE	1898-01-26		A7

ID	Individual in Patent	Sec.	Sec. Part	Date Issued	Other Counties	For More Info . . .
2887	HILL, Elverton N	21	S½SW	1893-12-19		A7
2888	" "	28	NENW	1893-12-19		A7
2889	HOLCOMB, Larkin L	14	SENE	1903-08-25		A7
2890	" "	14	NESE	1903-08-25		A7
2891	" "	14	W½SE	1903-08-25		A7
7448	HOOTEN, William R	5	E21NW	1898-10-04		A7
2892	" "	5	N½SW	1898-10-04		A7
7449	" "	5	E22NW	1898-10-04		A7
2893	HOUGHTON, Alva G	10	NENE	1901-06-08		A7
2894	" "	11	NENW	1901-06-08		A7
2895	" "	11	W½NW	1901-06-08		A7
2896	HOUGHTON, Curtis L	2	S½SW	1900-08-09		A7
2897	" "	3	S½SE	1900-08-09		A7
2898	HOWARD, John W	35	SE	1860-10-01		A1
2900	HOWARD, William	34	E½SE	1860-03-01		A1
2903	" "	34	NWSW	1860-10-01		A1
2902	" "	34	NWSE	1860-03-01		A1
2901	" "	34	SWSW	1860-03-01		A1
2899	" "	34	E½SW	1860-03-01		A1
2904	HUCKSTEP, William H	20	N½SE	1860-05-02		A6
2905	" "	20	SWSE	1860-05-02		A6
2906	" "	20	SESE	1859-05-04		A2
2907	HUGHLETT, James A	35	S½SW	1893-12-19		A7
2908	HUGHLETT, Milton B	34	NENE	1892-03-07		A7
2909	" "	35	W½NW	1892-03-07		A7
7460	HUNTER, William W	6	W22NW	1890-01-10		A7
7453	" "	6	1NW	1890-01-10		A7
2910	JOHNSON, Thomas M	18	SESE	1860-05-02		A6
2911	" "	18	W½SE	1860-05-02		A6
2912	" "	19	NENE	1860-05-02		A6
2913	JONES, James R	36	NWNE	1907-06-26		A1
2914	JONES, John M	28	S½SW	1892-12-09		A7
2915	" "	33	NENW	1892-12-09		A7
7427	JONES, Richard W	3	2NW	1902-02-12		A7
7426	" "	3	2NE	1902-02-12		A7
2916	KISER, Simeon	14	SESE	1906-06-21		A7
2917	" "	23	NENE	1906-06-21		A7
2919	KNOWLTON, Charles M	28	S½NW	1892-01-25		A7
2918	" "	28	N½SW	1892-01-25		A7
2920	LYNCH, Adam	5	SWSW	1903-10-01		A7
2921	" "	6	SESE	1903-10-01		A7
2922	" "	8	NWNW	1903-10-01		A7
2923	MATNEY, Jasper M	34	SWSE	1859-09-01		A1
2924	MATNEY, John L	33	SESE	1859-09-01		A1
2925	MCCRITE, George A	29	SWNW	1859-09-01		A1
2926	" "	30	SENE	1859-09-01		A1
2927	MCFARLAND, Francis S	27	NWSE	1885-03-20		A1
2928	MCFARLAND, William M	26	NWSW	1898-01-26		A7
2929	" "	26	SWSW	1877-04-05		A7
2931	" "	27	NESE	1898-01-26		A7
2930	" "	27	SESE	1877-04-05		A7
7421	MCHAN, Anna	2	E22NE	1881-02-10		A7
7419	" "	2	E21NE	1881-02-10		A7
7423	MCHAN, Elbert	2	W21NW	1876-12-01		A7
7418	" "	2	2NW	1876-12-01		A7
2932	" "	2	NWSW	1876-12-01		A7
2933	MCHAN, James	2	N½SE	1859-09-01		A1
2936	MEYER, Conrad	10	W½NW	1889-01-12		A7
2937	" "	10	NENW	1889-01-12		A7
2935	" "	10	NWNE	1889-01-12		A7
2938	MITCHELL, Jim O	1	S½SE	1907-08-23		A7
2939	" "	12	N½NE	1907-08-23		A7
2940	MONGER, Watson	21	NWSW	1899-05-12		A7
2941	MORRIS, Anna S	22	NWNE	1898-12-01		A7
7433	MYZELL, Golden S	30	2SW	1883-02-10		A7
2942	PASCALL, Ira T	35	SENE	1897-03-18		A1
2943	PASCHAL, Ira T	26	SESE	1892-01-05		A7
2944	" "	35	N½NE	1892-01-05		A7
2945	" "	35	NENW	1892-01-05		A7
2946	PASCHAL, John R	23	S½SW	1897-04-10		A7
2947	" "	26	N½NW	1897-04-10		A7
2949	PATE, Robert S	20	SENE	1860-08-01		A1
2948	" "	20	N½NE	1860-08-01		A1

ID	Individual in Patent	Sec.	Sec. Part	Date Issued	Other Counties	For More Info . . .
2950	PATE, Robert S (Cont'd)	21	N½NW	1860-08-01		A1
2951	" "	21	SWNW	1860-08-01		A1
2952	PAYNE, Clinton D	11	SESE	1884-02-15		A7
2953	" "	14	SWNE	1884-02-15		A7
2954	" "	14	N½NE	1884-02-15		A7
2955	PAYNE, Perleamon F	11	SWNE	1896-08-28		A7
2956	" "	11	NESW	1896-08-28		A7
2958	" "	11	NWSE	1896-08-28		A7
2957	" "	11	SENW	1896-08-28		A7
2959	PEACE, Elbert M	18	NESE	1859-09-10		A1
2960	PERRYMAN, William	17	SWSW	1888-11-27		A7
2961	" "	20	NWNW	1888-11-27		A7
2962	PICKARD, James H	15	NWSE	1861-02-01		A1
7463	PICKARD, John H	7	2SW	1859-03-01		A1
2963	PICKARD, Leonard P	17	NWSW	1859-01-01		A1
2964	" "	17	E½SW	1859-01-01		A1
2965	" "	17	SE	1859-01-01		A1
2966	" "	20	NENW	1859-01-01		A1
2967	POORE, Fred C	1	NESW	1910-09-08		A1
2968	PRIVETT, Allison I	29	E½SW	1899-05-12		A7
2969	REED, Frances	22	SESE	1894-05-18		A7 G164
2970	" "	26	SWNW	1894-05-18		A7 G164
2971	" "	27	E½NE	1894-05-18		A7 G164
2973	REED, James M	10	SWSE	1891-05-05		A7
2974	" "	10	N½SE	1891-05-05		A7
2972	" "	10	SENE	1891-05-05		A7
2977	ROEHR, August	8	SWNE	1891-06-09		A7
2975	" "	8	W½SE	1891-06-09		A7
2976	" "	8	SENW	1891-06-09		A7
2978	RYAN, Lewis	25	E½NW	1903-06-01		A7
7445	SCALES, Pleas M	4	W22NW	1901-03-23		A7
7446	" "	5	2NE	1901-03-23		A7
7447	" "	5	E21NE	1901-03-23		A7
2979	SEAY, Andrew J	15	E½NW	1889-01-12		A7
2980	" "	15	S½NE	1889-01-12		A7
2984	SIMS, Elizabeth	29	SENW	1860-05-02		A6 G59
2983	" "	29	N½NW	1860-05-02		A6 G59
2987	SMITH, Edward C	28	NWNW	1903-06-08		A7
2989	SPADLING, William A	30	SWNE	1890-10-11		A7
2988	" "	30	N½NE	1890-10-11		A7
2990	" "	30	NWSE	1890-10-11		A7
2991	SPRADLIN, Charles R	29	W½SW	1896-12-08		A7
7414	SPRADLING, John	19	2NW	1884-11-01		A7
7452	STEIN, Henry B	5	W22NW	1893-09-01		A7
7451	" "	5	W21NW	1893-09-01		A7
7456	" "	6	E22NE	1893-09-01		A7
7455	" "	6	E21NE	1893-09-01		A7
2994	STOKES, George A	15	SWNW	1893-04-29		A7
2992	" "	15	SESW	1893-04-29		A7
2993	" "	15	W½SW	1893-04-29		A7
7430	TAYLOR, Salina E	30	1NW	1890-10-11		A7
7434	" "	30	N22NW	1890-10-11		A7
7454	THEISSEN, Gerhard	6	2SW	1890-01-10		A7
7464	" "	7	N22NW	1890-01-10		A7
2995	THOMAS, Blackburn C	6	NESE	1869-07-01		A1
2996	THOMPSON, Sanford	36	SWSW	1901-10-08		A7
2998	TURNER, George V	20	N½SW	1898-04-06		A7
2997	" "	20	SESW	1898-04-06		A7
2999	VASSAW, Frances	22	SESE	1894-05-18		A7 G164
3000	" "	26	SWNW	1894-05-18		A7 G164
3001	" "	27	E½NE	1894-05-18		A7 G164
3003	WATSON, Matilda L	25	NESE	1891-06-09		A7
3004	" "	25	SESE	1891-06-09		A7
3002	" "	25	S½SE	1891-06-09		A7
3005	WATSON, Robert S	36	SESW	1891-06-09		A7
3007	" "	36	W½SE	1891-06-09		A7
3006	" "	36	SESE	1891-06-09		A7
3009	WATSON, William F	36	SWNE	1891-06-09		A7
3008	" "	36	E½NE	1891-06-09		A7
3010	" "	36	NESE	1891-06-09		A7
3011	WEATHERBY, Joseph W	25	NWSW	1877-04-05		A7
3012	" "	26	S½NE	1877-04-05		A7
3013	" "	26	NESE	1877-04-05		A7

ID	Individual in Patent	Sec.	Sec. Part	Date Issued	Other Counties	For More Info . . .
3014	WEATHERLY, Isaac H	5	SESW	1898-06-23		A7
3016	"	5	SWSE	1898-06-23		A7
3015	"	5	E½SE	1898-06-23		A7
3017	WEATHERLY, James A	15	SESE	1891-05-25		A7
3018	"	22	NESE	1891-05-25		A7
3019	"	22	E½NE	1891-05-25		A7
3021	WEATHERLY, Joseph W	22	SWNE	1885-03-20		A1
3020	"	22	NWSE	1885-03-20		A1
7431	WELCH, Thomas	30	1SW	1860-09-10		A6
7437	"	31	N21NW	1860-09-10		A6
3023	WILLIAMS, Homer	11	W½SW	1896-08-28		A7
3025	"	11	SWSE	1896-08-28		A7
3024	"	11	SESW	1896-08-28		A7
7442	WINCHESTER, Mitchell	4	E22NW	1901-03-23		A7
7444	"	4	W22NE	1901-03-23		A7
3029	WOODY, Elijah	19	NESE	1876-06-30		A7
3030	"	19	SENE	1876-06-30		A7
3031	WOODY, Elisha T	33	SENE	1905-04-05		A1

Patent Map

T25-N R7-W
5th PM 25-N 7-W Meridian
Map Group 12

Township Statistics

Parcels Mapped	:	351
Number of Patents	:	185
Number of Individuals	:	178
Patentees Identified	:	176
Number of Surnames	:	118
Multi-Patentee Parcels	:	5
Oldest Patent Date	:	1/1/1859
Most Recent Patent	:	6/16/1916
Block/Lot Parcels	:	57
Cities and Town	:	2
Cemeteries	:	1

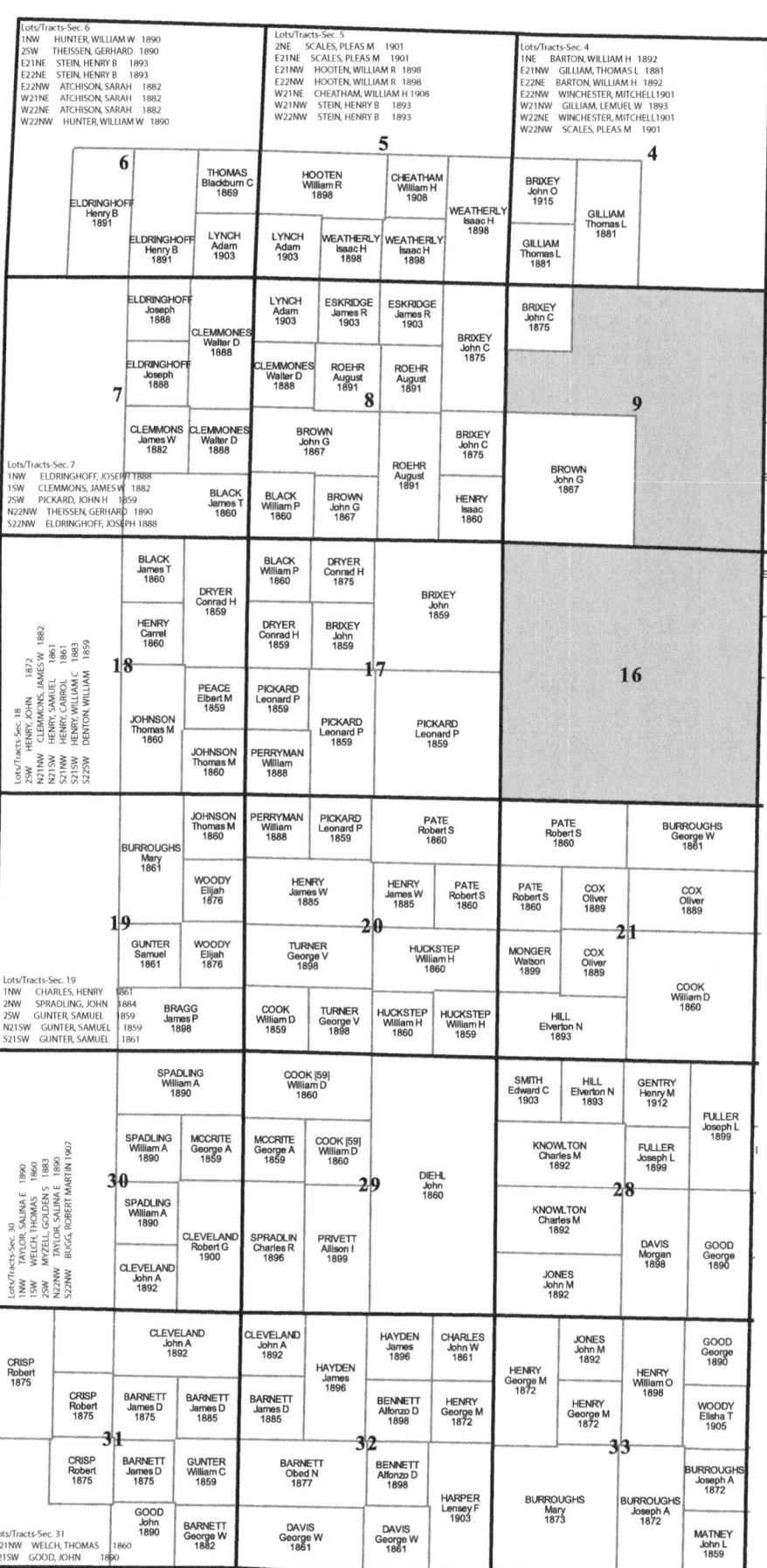

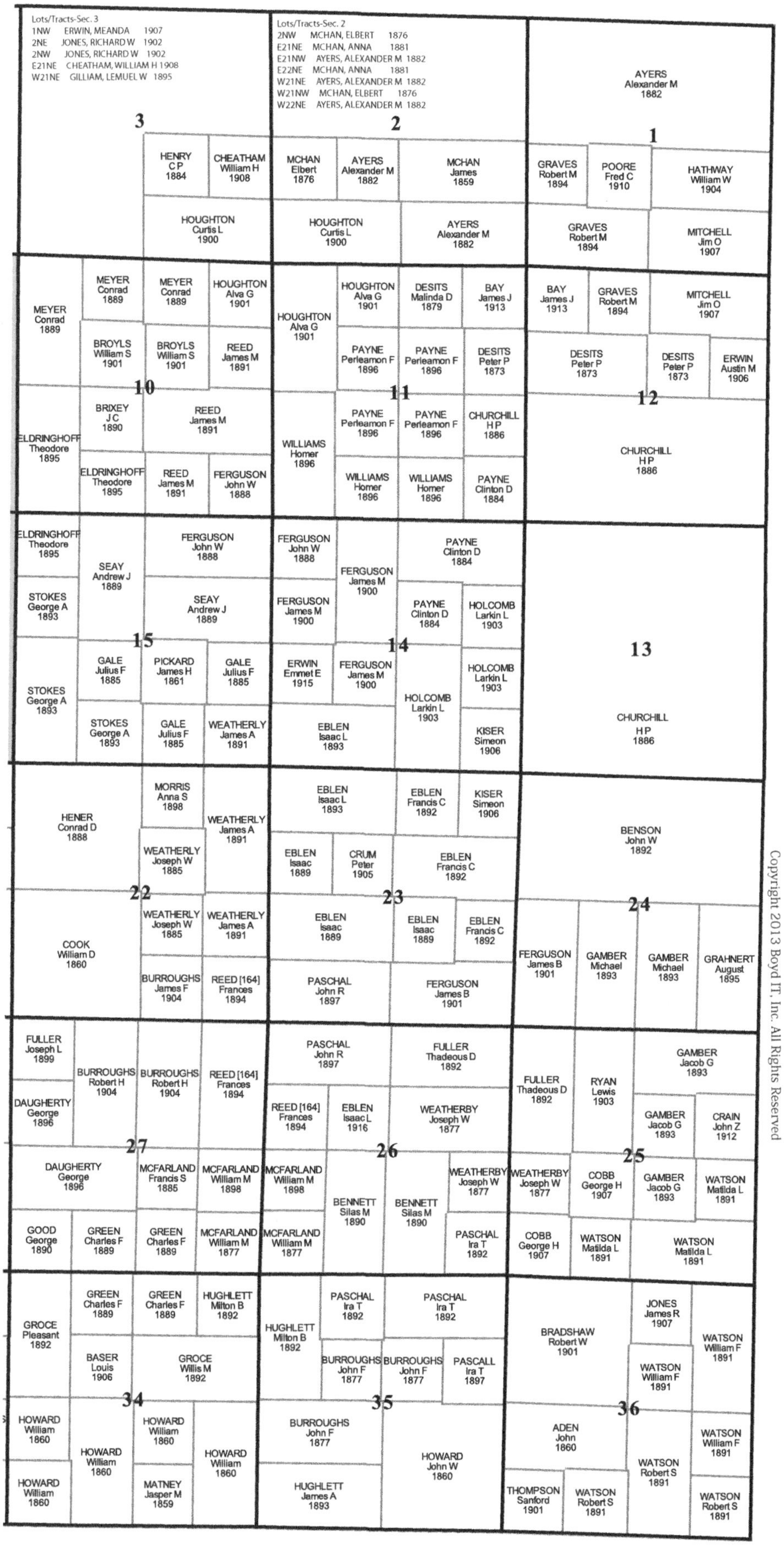

Lots/Tracts-Sec. 3
1NW ERWIN, MEANDA 1907
2NE JONES, RICHARD W 1902
2NW JONES, RICHARD W 1902
E21NE CHEATHAM, WILLIAM H 1908
W21NE GILLIAM, LEMUEL W 1895

Lots/Tracts-Sec. 2
2NW MCHAN, ELBERT 1876
E21NE MCHAN, ANNA 1881
E21NW AYERS, ALEXANDER M 1882
E22NE MCHAN, ANNA 1881
W21NE AYERS, ALEXANDER M 1882
W21NW MCHAN, ELBERT 1876
W22NE AYERS, ALEXANDER M 1882

Section 3
HENRY C P 1884 | CHEATHAM William H 1908
HOUGHTON Curtis L 1900

Section 2
MCHAN Elbert 1876 | AYERS Alexander M 1882 | MCHAN James 1859
HOUGHTON Curtis L 1900 | AYERS Alexander M 1882

Section 1
AYERS Alexander M 1882
GRAVES Robert M 1894 | POORE Fred C 1910 | HATHWAY William W 1904
GRAVES Robert M 1894 | MITCHELL Jim O 1907

Section 10
MEYER Conrad 1889
MEYER Conrad 1889 | MEYER Conrad 1889 | HOUGHTON Alva G 1901
BROYLS William S 1901 | BROYLS William S 1901 | REED James M 1891
BRIXEY J C 1890 | REED James M 1891
ELDRINGHOFF Theodore 1895
ELDRINGHOFF Theodore 1895 | REED James M 1891 | FERGUSON John W 1888

Section 11
HOUGHTON Alva G 1901
HOUGHTON Alva G 1901 | DESITS Malinda D 1879 | BAY James J 1913
PAYNE Perleamon F 1896 | PAYNE Perleamon F 1896 | DESITS Peter P 1873
PAYNE Perleamon F 1896 | PAYNE Perleamon F 1896 | CHURCHILL H P 1886
WILLIAMS Homer 1896
WILLIAMS Homer 1896 | WILLIAMS Homer 1896 | PAYNE Clinton D 1884

Section 12
BAY James J 1913 | GRAVES Robert M 1894 | MITCHELL Jim O 1907
DESITS Peter P 1873 | DESITS Peter P 1873 | ERWIN Austin M 1906
CHURCHILL H P 1886

Section 15
ELDRINGHOFF Theodore 1895
SEAY Andrew J 1889 | FERGUSON John W 1888
STOKES George A 1893 | SEAY Andrew J 1889
STOKES George A 1893 | GALE Julius F 1885 | PICKARD James H 1861 | GALE Julius F 1885
STOKES George A 1893 | GALE Julius F 1885 | WEATHERLY James A 1891

Section 14
FERGUSON John W 1888 | PAYNE Clinton D 1884
FERGUSON James M 1900
FERGUSON James M 1900 | PAYNE Clinton D 1884 | HOLCOMB Larkin L 1903
ERWIN Emmet E 1915 | FERGUSON James M 1900 | HOLCOMB Larkin L 1903
HOLCOMB Larkin L 1903
EBLEN Isaac L 1893 | KISER Simeon 1906

Section 13
CHURCHILL H P 1886

Section 22
HENER Conrad D 1888 | MORRIS Anna S 1898
WEATHERLY James A 1891
WEATHERLY Joseph W 1885
WEATHERLY Joseph W 1885 | WEATHERLY James A 1891
COOK William D 1860
BURROUGHS James F 1904 | REED [164] Frances 1894

Section 23
EBLEN Isaac L 1893 | EBLEN Francis C 1892 | KISER Simeon 1906
EBLEN Isaac 1889 | CRUM Peter 1905 | EBLEN Francis C 1892
EBLEN Isaac 1889 | EBLEN Isaac 1889 | EBLEN Francis C 1892
PASCHAL John R 1897 | FERGUSON James B 1901

Section 24
BENSON John W 1892
FERGUSON James B 1901 | GAMBER Michael 1893 | GAMBER Michael 1893 | GRAHNERT August 1895

Section 27
FULLER Joseph L 1899
BURROUGHS Robert H 1904 | BURROUGHS Robert H 1904 | REED [164] Frances 1894
DAUGHERTY George 1896
DAUGHERTY George 1896 | MCFARLAND Francis S 1885 | MCFARLAND William M 1898
GOOD George 1890 | GREEN Charles F 1889 | GREEN Charles F 1889 | MCFARLAND William M 1877

Section 26
PASCHAL John R 1897 | FULLER Thadeous D 1892
MCFARLAND William M 1898
REED [164] Frances 1894 | EBLEN Isaac L 1916 | WEATHERBY Joseph W 1877
MCFARLAND William M 1877 | BENNETT Silas M 1890 | BENNETT Silas M 1890 | PASCHAL Ira T 1892

Section 25
GAMBER Jacob G 1893
FULLER Thadeous D 1892 | RYAN Lewis 1903 | GAMBER Jacob G 1893 | CRAIN John Z 1912
WEATHERBY Joseph W 1877 | WEATHERBY Joseph W 1877 | COBB George H 1907 | GAMBER Jacob G 1893 | WATSON Matilda L 1891
COBB George H 1907 | WATSON Matilda L 1891 | WATSON Matilda L 1891

Section 34
GROCE Pleasant 1892 | GREEN Charles F 1889 | GREEN Charles F 1889 | HUGHLETT Milton B 1892
BASER Louis 1906 | GROCE Willis M 1892
HOWARD William 1860 | HOWARD William 1860 | HOWARD William 1860
HOWARD William 1860 | MATNEY Jasper M 1859

Section 35
PASCHAL Ira T 1892 | PASCHAL Ira T 1892
HUGHLETT Milton B 1892
BURROUGHS John F 1877 | BURROUGHS John F 1877 | PASCALL Ira T 1897
BURROUGHS John F 1877 | HOWARD John W 1860
HUGHLETT James A 1893

Section 36
JONES James R 1907
BRADSHAW Robert W 1901 | WATSON William F 1891
WATSON William F 1891
ADEN John 1860 | WATSON Robert S 1891 | WATSON William F 1891
THOMPSON Sanford 1901 | WATSON Robert S 1891 | WATSON Robert S 1891

Helpful Hints

1. This Map's INDEX can be found on the preceding pages.

2. Refer to Map "C" to see where this Township lies within Howell County, Missouri.

3. Numbers within square brackets [ ] denote a multi-patentee land parcel (multi-owner). Refer to Appendix "C" for a full list of members in this group.

4. Areas that look to be crowded with Patentees usually indicate multiple sales of the same parcel (Re-issues) or Overlapping parcels. See this Township's Index for an explanation of these and other circumstances that might explain "odd" groupings of Patentees on this map.

Legend

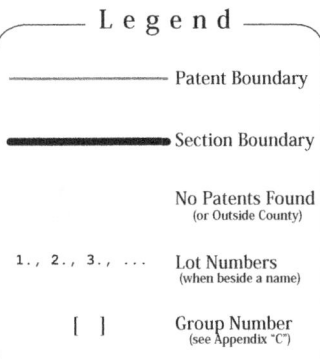

Patent Boundary
Section Boundary
No Patents Found (or Outside County)
1., 2., 3., ... Lot Numbers (when beside a name)
[ ] Group Number (see Appendix "C")

Scale: Section = 1 mile X 1 mile (generally, with some exceptions)

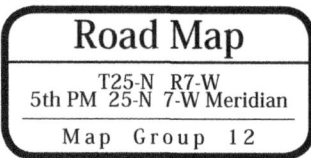

Road Map

T25-N R7-W
5th PM 25-N 7-W Meridian

Map Group 12

Cities & Towns
Fanchon
Peace Valley

Cemeteries
New Hope Cemetery

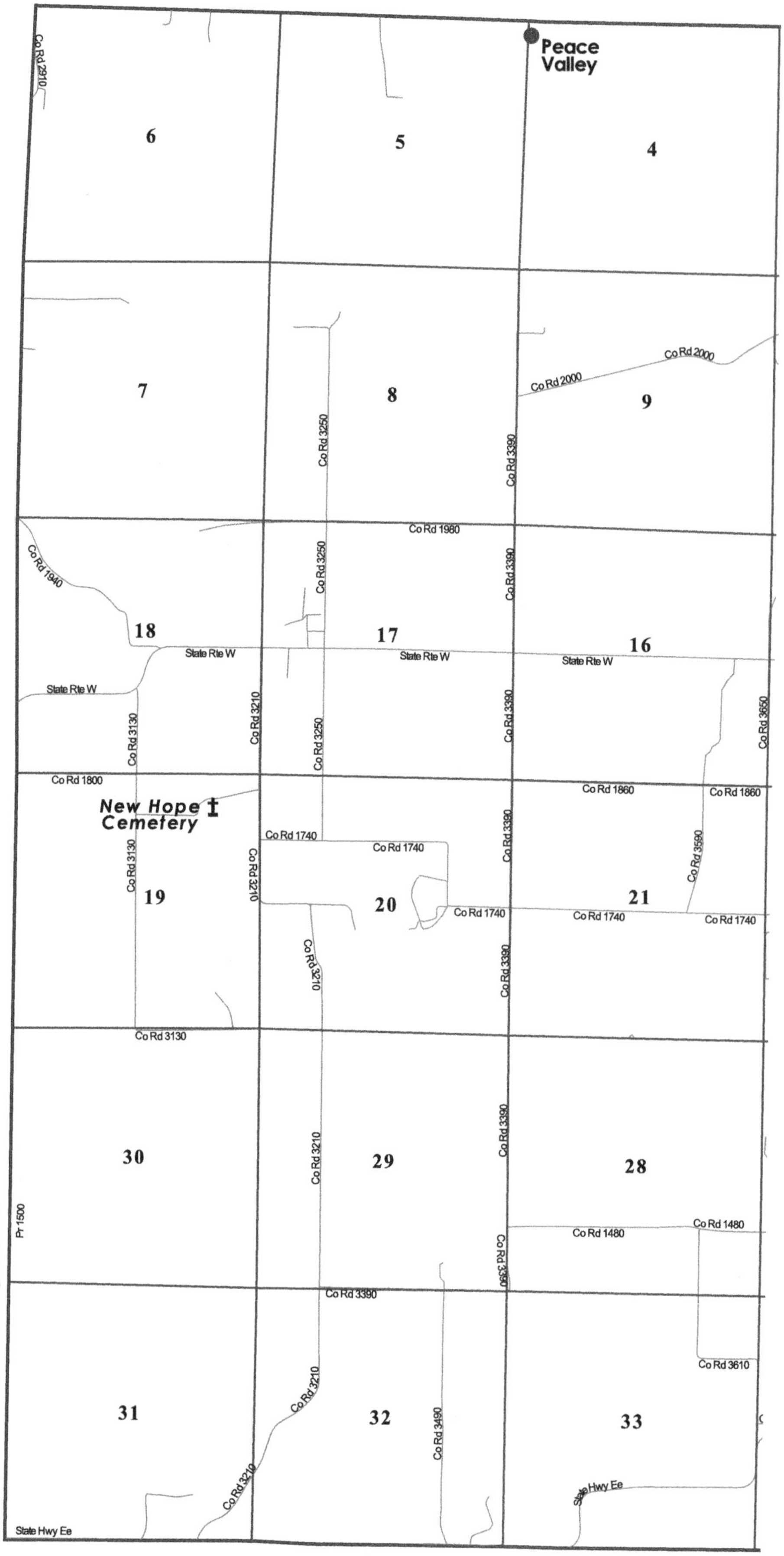

6

5

4

● Peace Valley

7

8

9

Co Rd 2910

Co Rd 3250

Co Rd 3390

Co Rd 2000

Co Rd 2000

Co Rd 1980

18

17

16

Co Rd 1940

Co Rd 3250

Co Rd 3390

Co Rd 3550

State Rte W

State Rte W

State Rte W

State Rte W

Co Rd 3130

Co Rd 3210

Co Rd 3250

Co Rd 3390

Co Rd 1800

New Hope Cemetery

Co Rd 1860

Co Rd 1860

19

20

21

Co Rd 3130

Co Rd 3210

Co Rd 1740

Co Rd 1740

Co Rd 3390

Co Rd 3590

Co Rd 1740

Co Rd 1740

Co Rd 1740

Co Rd 3210

Co Rd 3130

30

29

28

Co Rd 3210

Co Rd 3390

Pr 1500

Co Rd 1480

Co Rd 1480

Co Rd 3290

Co Rd 3390

Co Rd 3610

31

32

33

Co Rd 3210

Co Rd 3480

Co Rd 3210

State Hwy Ee

State Hwy Ee

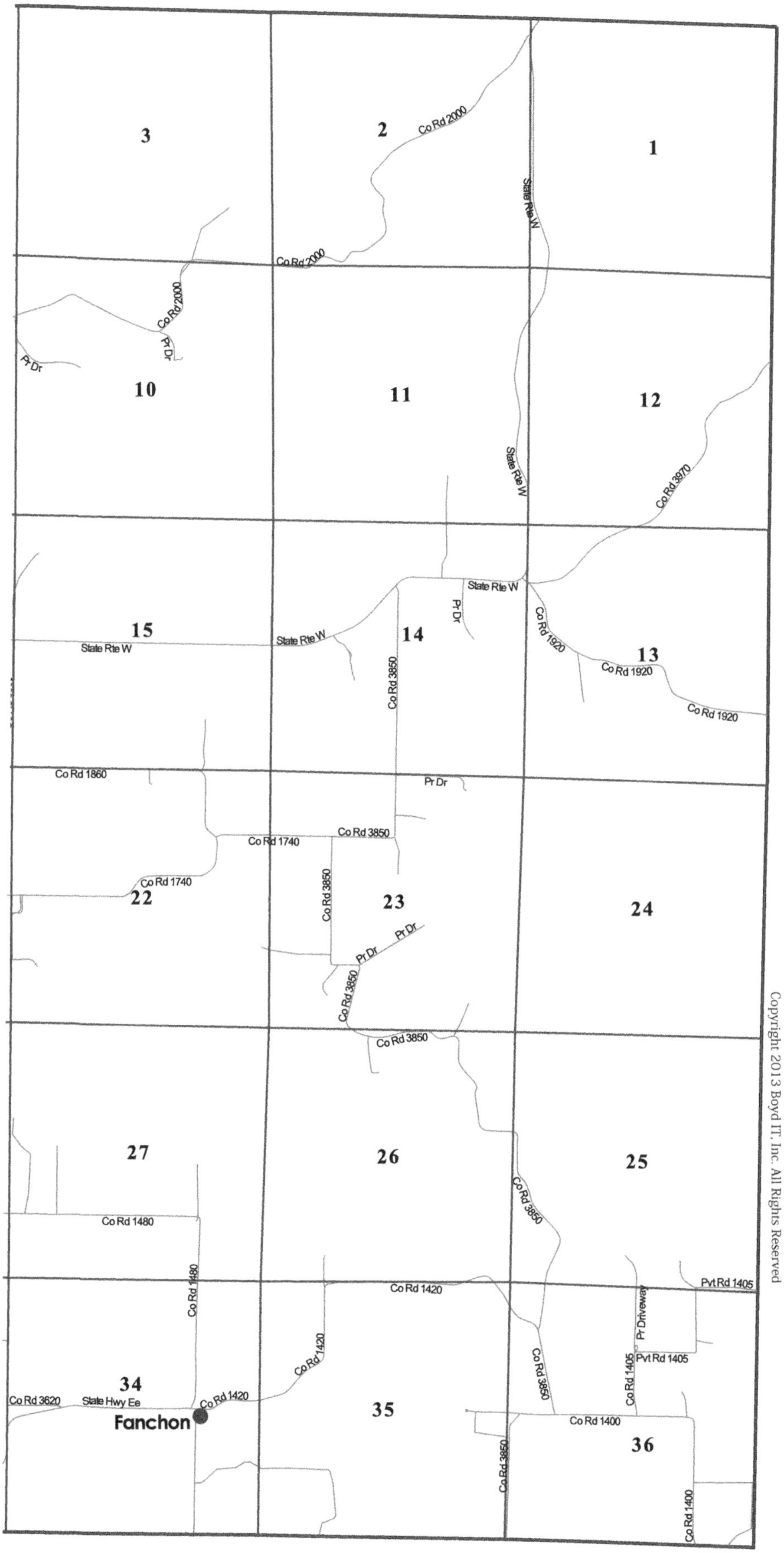

3

2   Co Rd 2000

1

State Rte W

Co Rd 2000

Co Rd 2000

Pt Dr

Pt Dr

10

11

12

State Rte W

Co Rd 3970

State Rte W

Pt Dr

15

State Rte W

State Rte W

14

Co Rd 1920

13

Co Rd 3850

Co Rd 1920

Co Rd 1920

Co Rd 1860

Pt Dr

Co Rd 3850

Co Rd 1740

Co Rd 1740

Co Rd 3850

22

23

24

Pt Dr   Pt Dr

Co Rd 3850

Co Rd 3850

27

26

25

Co Rd 3850

Co Rd 1480

Pvt Rd 1405

Co Rd 1480

Co Rd 1420

Pt Driveway

Co Rd 1420

Pvt Rd 1405

Co Rd 1405

Pvt Rd 1405

34

Co Rd 3850

Co Rd 3620   State Hwy Ee   Co Rd 1420

Fanchon

35

Co Rd 1400

36

Co Rd 3850

Co Rd 1400

Helpful Hints

1. This road map has a number of uses, but primarily it is to help you: a) find the present location of land owned by your ancestors (at least the general area), b) find cemeteries and city-centers, and c) estimate the route/roads used by Census-takers & tax-assessors.

2. If you plan to travel to Howell County to locate cemeteries or land parcels, please pick up a modern travel map for the area before you do. Mapping old land parcels on modern maps is not as exact a science as you might think. Just the slightest variations in public land survey coordinates, estimates of parcel boundaries, or road-map deviations can greatly alter a map's representation of how a road either does or doesn't cross a particular parcel of land.

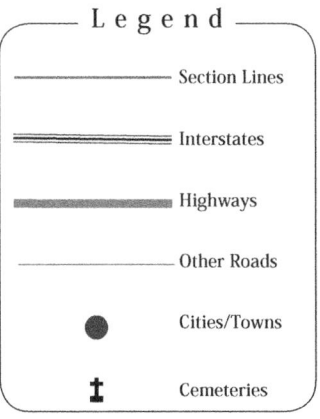

L e g e n d

Section Lines

Interstates

Highways

Other Roads

Cities/Towns

Cemeteries

Scale: Section = 1 mile X 1 mile
(generally, with some exceptions)

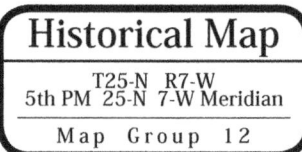

Historical Map

T25-N R7-W
5th PM 25-N 7-W Meridian

Map Group 12

Cities & Towns
Fanchon
Peace Valley

Cemeteries
New Hope Cemetery

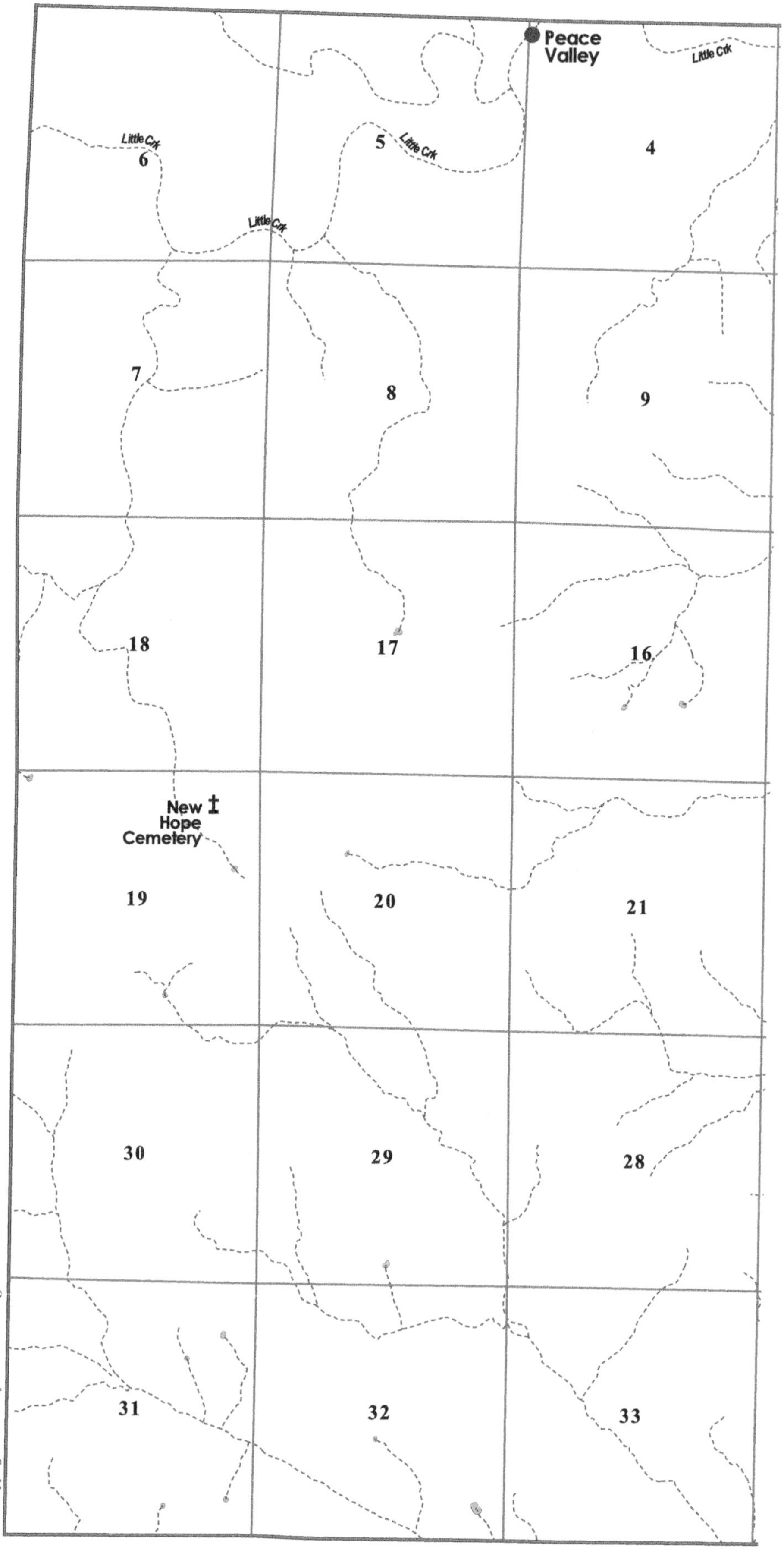

● Peace
Valley

Little Crk

6

5 *Little Crk*

4

Little Crk

Little Crk

7

8

9

18

17

16

New ✝
Hope
Cemetery

19

20

21

30

29

28

31

32

33

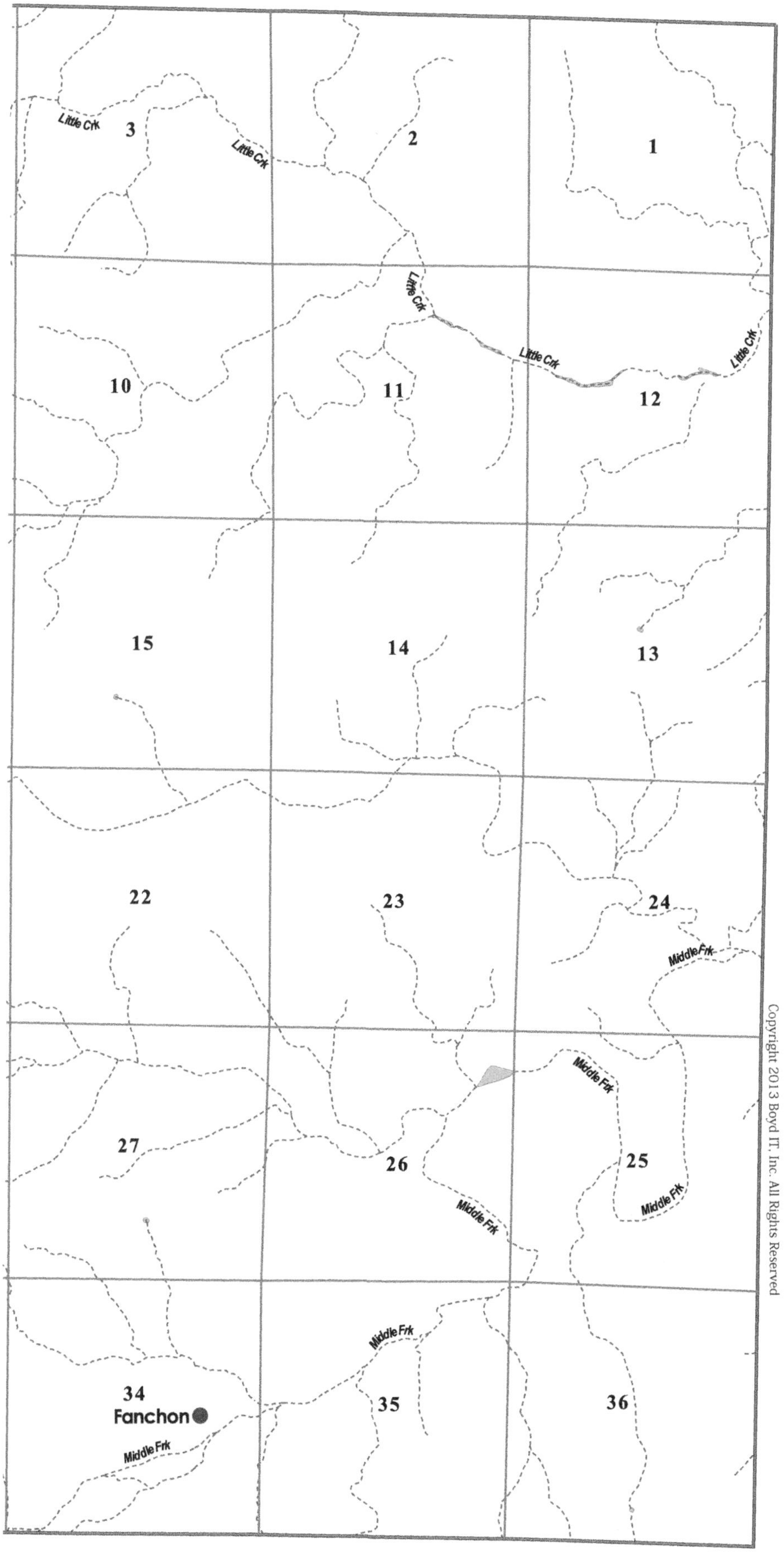

3
2
1
Little Crk
Little Crk
Little Crk
Little Crk
Little Crk
10
11
12
15
14
13
22
23
24
Middle Frk
27
26
25
Middle Frk
Middle Frk
Middle Frk
34
Fanchon
35
36
Middle Frk
Middle Frk
Copyright 2013 Boyd IT, Inc. All Rights Reserved

Helpful Hints

1. This Map takes a different look at the same Congressional Township displayed in the preceding two maps. It presents features that can help you better envision the historical development of the area: a) Water-bodies (lakes & ponds), b) Water-courses (rivers, streams, etc.), c) Railroads, d) City/town center-points (where they were oftentimes located when first settled), and e) Cemeteries.

2. Using this "Historical" map in tandem with this Township's Patent Map and Road Map, may lead you to some interesting discoveries. You will often find roads, towns, cemeteries, and waterways are named after nearby landowners: sometimes those names will be the ones you are researching. See how many of these research gems you can find here in Howell County.

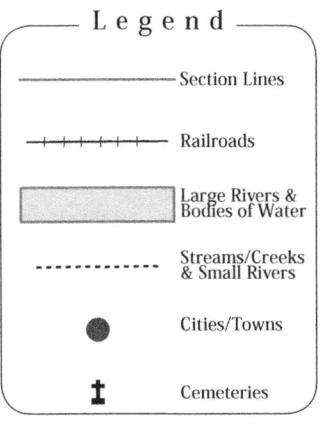

Legend
Section Lines
Railroads
Large Rivers & Bodies of Water
Streams/Creeks & Small Rivers
Cities/Towns
Cemeteries

Scale: Section = 1 mile X 1 mile
(there are some exceptions)

Map Group 13: Index to Land Patents

Township 24-North Range 10-West (5th PM 24-N 10-W)

After you locate an individual in this Index, take note of the Section and Section Part then proceed to the Land Patent map on the pages immediately following. You should have no difficulty locating the corresponding parcel of land.

The "For More Info" Column will lead you to more information about the underlying Patents. See the *Legend* at right, and the "How to Use this Book" chapter, for more information.

ID	Individual in Patent	Sec.	Sec. Part	Date Issued	Other Counties	For More Info . . .
3032	ADAMS, Benoni	36	SESE	1859-01-01		A1
3035	ADAMS, Thomas F	34	N½SW	1888-12-08		A7
3033	" "	34	NWSE	1888-12-08		A7
3034	" "	34	SWNE	1888-12-08		A7
3037	ALLRED, Richard	17	NWSW	1892-01-05		A7
3036	" "	17	SWNW	1892-01-05		A7
3038	" "	18	NESE	1892-01-05		A7
3039	" "	18	SENE	1892-01-05		A7
3040	ALSUP, Ben M	2	N½SW	1907-12-02		A1
3041	BAKER, Garret H	29	S½NW	1898-04-06		A7
3042	BINKLEY, Leonard L	12	SESE	1908-06-29		A1
3043	" "	13	NENE	1908-06-29		A1
3045	BISHOP, Henry A	24	E½SW	1885-06-03		A1
3044	" "	24	W½SE	1885-06-03		A1
3046	BLOSSOM, Maria L	17	NE	1891-05-25		A7
7496	BOETTLER, Edward	30	2NW	1893-09-08		A7
7498	" "	30	S21NW	1893-09-08		A7
3047	BRANSTETTER, Peter J	19	N½NE	1899-02-25		A7
3048	" "	19	SWNE	1899-02-25		A7
3049	BRIDGES, Joseph E	27	NENE	1860-10-01		A1
3050	BRIGGS, John F	31	NWSE	1914-01-27		A7
3051	BRIGGS, William	33	SESE	1882-12-20		A1
3052	" "	34	SWSW	1881-10-06		A7
3053	BROWN, Jonathan	27	NWNW	1871-06-10		A1
3054	BROWN, Michael	25	SE	1882-05-10		A7
3056	BUCKMASTER, Joshua	26	W½NE	1877-01-15		A7
3055	" "	26	E½NW	1877-01-15		A7
3057	BUKER, Charles H	7	S½NE	1894-12-17		A7
3058	" "	8	W½NW	1894-12-17		A7
7483	BUNDREN, George W	19	1NW	1888-11-27		A7
7484	" "	19	2NW	1888-11-27		A7
7474	BYERS, George W	1	W21NE	1882-06-30		A7
3059	" "	1	N½SW	1882-06-30		A7
3060	" "	1	NWSE	1882-06-30		A7
3061	CALLAHAN, Charles W	30	SW	1884-11-01		A7 G31
3062	CALLAHAN, John H	30	S½NE	1892-03-07		A7
3063	" "	30	NWNE	1892-03-07		A7
3064	" "	30	NWSE	1892-03-07		A7
7502	CALLAHAN, Louis F	31	N22NW	1890-01-30		A1
7499	" "	31	1NW	1890-01-10		A7
3065	" "	31	W½NE	1890-01-10		A7
3066	CALLAHAN, Sarah E	30	SW	1884-11-01		A7 G31
3067	CALLISON, George W	22	SE	1875-12-20		A7
3068	CALLISON, William	21	NW	1888-11-27		A7
3069	CANNON, Daniel M	12	NWSW	1884-03-10		A1
3070	CANNON, Sarah A	24	NE	1896-06-04		A7

ID	Individual in Patent	Sec.	Sec. Part	Date Issued	Other Counties	For More Info . . .
3071	CARRIER, Josephus	35	SESW	1890-06-06		A7
3072	CARRINGTON, Fred W	17	N½NW	1902-05-21		A7
7508	CLARK, Sarah A	5	2NE	1896-09-29		A7
7506	" "	5	1NE	1896-09-29		A7
7473	COLLINS, Aaron	1	E22NW	1861-02-01		A1
7475	" "	1	W22NW	1874-01-10		A7
7466	" "	1	1NW	1874-01-10		A7
7494	" "	2	E22NE	1874-01-10		A7
7469	COLLINS, David	1	3NE	1883-06-30		A7
7470	" "	1	3NW	1883-06-30		A7
3073	COLLINS, Leonard S	14	NWSW	1901-03-23		A7
3075	" "	15	E½SE	1901-03-23		A7
3074	" "	15	SENE	1901-03-23		A7
7468	COLLINS, Martha J	1	2NE	1892-03-07		A7 G55
3076	" "	1	NESE	1892-03-07		A7 G55
7472	" "	1	E21NE	1892-03-07		A7 G55
7471	COLLINS, William	1	E21NE	1892-03-07		A7 G55
7467	" "	1	2NE	1892-03-07		A7 G55
3077	" "	1	NESE	1892-03-07		A7 G55
7497	CRIDER, Daniel	30	N21NW	1883-08-13		A1
3078	CRIDER, Leonard S	20	N½NE	1894-01-25		A7
3079	CURRY, Thomas L	23	NESE	1908-09-01		A1
3080	DABBS, Thomas B	15	W½NW	1910-01-17		A1
3081	" "	15	NENW	1910-01-17		A1
3082	DAVIS, Eliphaz	20	S½SW	1889-01-12		A7
3083	" "	29	NWNW	1889-01-12		A7
3084	" "	30	NENE	1889-01-12		A7
3085	DAVIS, Joshua D	29	E½SE	1886-10-29		A1
3088	" "	33	SESW	1891-08-24		A1
3086	" "	33	N½SE	1892-03-07		A7
3087	" "	33	S½NE	1892-03-07		A7
3089	DAVIS, Van C	18	N½NE	1894-12-17		A7
7509	DRUMWRIGHT, Robert J	5	3NE	1880-06-30		A1
3090	ENDECOTT, Joseph	35	SENW	1859-09-01		A1
3091	FOX, Allen J	20	S½NE	1885-02-25		A7
3092	" "	20	W½SE	1885-02-25		A7
3094	FOX, Andrew J	23	W½SW	1892-03-07		A7
3093	" "	23	S½NW	1892-03-07		A7
7485	FOX, Enoch	19	N21SW	1879-09-23		A1
7486	" "	19	N22SW	1888-12-06		A1
7487	" "	19	S21SW	1879-09-23		A1
7488	" "	19	S22SW	1885-05-25		A1
3095	FOX, Esau	26	W½NW	1872-03-15		A7
3097	" "	26	NESW	1875-02-15		A7
3096	" "	26	NWSW	1872-03-15		A7
3098	" "	27	SENE	1885-03-20		A1
3100	FOX, Gastus	21	SWNE	1879-12-15		A7
3099	" "	21	E½NE	1879-12-15		A7
3101	" "	22	NWNW	1879-12-15		A7
3102	FOX, Gatus	22	NENW	1885-12-19		A1
3103	FOX, James A	26	SE	1892-06-10		A7
3105	" "	28	NESW	1892-06-30		A7
3107	" "	28	SWNE	1892-06-30		A7
3106	" "	28	NWSE	1892-06-30		A7
3104	" "	28	SENW	1892-06-30		A7
3108	FOX, John	14	W½NW	1892-06-10		A7
3109	" "	15	N½NE	1892-06-10		A7
3112	FOX, Johnson M	14	SWNE	1892-06-10		A7
3111	" "	14	NESW	1892-06-10		A7
3110	" "	14	N½SE	1892-06-10		A7
3114	FOX, Joseph S	18	SWNE	1882-09-30		A7
7480	" "	18	S21NW	1882-09-30		A7
7478	" "	18	N21SW	1882-09-30		A7
3113	" "	18	NWSE	1882-09-30		A7
3115	FOX, Joseph W	19	NWSE	1882-06-10		A1
3117	" "	33	N½SW	1901-03-23		A7
3116	" "	33	SESW	1901-03-23		A7
3118	" "	33	SWNW	1901-03-23		A7
3119	FOX, Ulisses G	23	SESW	1900-08-09		A7
3120	" "	26	SENE	1900-08-09		A7
3121	FOX, William M	32	S½SW	1898-10-04		A7
3122	FOX, William R	14	S½SW	1896-01-14		A7
3123	" "	23	N½NW	1896-01-14		A7

ID	Individual in Patent	Sec.	Sec. Part	Date Issued	Other Counties	For More Info . . .
3126	FOX, William S	22	W½NE	1890-10-11		A7
3124	" "	22	SENW	1890-10-11		A7
3125	" "	22	SENE	1890-10-11		A7
7492	FRIZELL, Jason	2	3NE	1892-06-10		A7
7493	" "	2	3NW	1892-06-10		A7
7495	" "	2	W22NE	1892-06-10		A7
3128	GODAT, Edward P	12	E½NW	1901-04-09		A7
3127	" "	12	SWNE	1901-04-09		A7
7510	GORMAN, Charles	6	1NW	1895-09-04		A7
7511	" "	6	2NW	1895-09-04		A7
3129	GRAHAM, Harvey	25	NENW	1877-04-05		A7
3130	" "	25	S½NW	1877-04-05		A7
3131	" "	26	NENE	1889-05-29		A1
3132	GREEN, Lymon J	19	S½SE	1892-09-09		A7
7512	HALL, Richard V	7	2SW	1886-04-10		A7
3133	" "	7	NWSE	1886-04-10		A7
7513	" "	7	N21SW	1886-04-10		A7
3134	HICKS, Nemier	18	S½SW	1882-06-30		A7
7481	" "	18	S21SW	1882-06-30		A7
7482	" "	18	S22SW	1882-06-30		A7
3135	HOPKINS, Benjamin F	25	SENE	1890-10-11		A7
3136	HOPKINS, George W	22	SWNW	1896-08-28		A7
3139	HOPKINS, Jacob	13	S½NW	1875-11-01		A7
3137	" "	13	NWNE	1893-01-21		A1
3138	" "	13	SWNE	1875-11-01		A7
3140	" "	14	SENE	1875-11-01		A7
3141	HOPKINS, Jacob S	22	NENE	1902-05-21		A7
3142	HOPKINS, James E	12	E½SW	1888-12-04		A7
3143	" "	12	SWSE	1888-12-04		A7
3144	" "	13	NENW	1888-12-04		A7
3145	HOPKINS, Peter P	13	NWNW	1905-03-30		A7
3146	HOPKINS, Robert L	2	NWSE	1894-08-14		A7
7489	" "	2	1NE	1894-08-14		A7
3149	HOPKINS, Thomas B	15	SENW	1875-11-01		A7
3150	" "	15	SWNE	1875-11-01		A7
3148	" "	15	NWSE	1875-11-01		A7
3147	" "	15	NESW	1875-11-01		A7
3152	HOPKINS, William F	12	NESE	1861-02-01		A1
3151	" "	12	SENE	1886-11-19		A1
3153	HOPKINS, William J	33	N½NE	1888-12-06		A7
3154	" "	34	W½NW	1888-12-06		A7
3155	HOPKINS, William T	12	NWSE	1875-11-01		A7
3158	HOSHOUR, Samuel H	15	W½SW	1884-11-17		A6 G119
3157	" "	15	SWSE	1884-11-17		A6 G119
3156	" "	15	SESW	1884-11-17		A6 G119
3159	HUDLOW, William R	32	S½SE	1892-01-05		A7
3160	" "	33	SWSW	1892-01-05		A7
3161	HUNTER, William H	36	N½SE	1888-12-08		A7
3162	" "	36	SWSE	1888-12-08		A7
3163	HUSTON, Lewis A	33	SWSE	1901-03-23		A7
3164	HUSTON, Louis A	23	N½NE	1908-11-16		A1
3166	INGOLD, Louisa	31	SENE	1892-06-21		A7 G127
3165	" "	31	NESE	1892-06-21		A7 G127
3168	" "	32	NWSW	1892-06-21		A7 G127
3167	" "	32	SWNW	1892-06-21		A7 G127
3169	JOHNSON, Benjamin N	34	SESW	1860-10-01		A1
3170	JOHNSON, James T	21	NESE	1890-10-11		A7
3171	" "	22	NWSW	1890-10-11		A7
3174	JOHNSTON, John C	28	W½SW	1891-05-05		A7
3172	" "	28	SESW	1891-05-05		A7
3173	" "	28	SWSE	1891-05-05		A7
3176	KARR, John M	19	NESE	1890-12-31		A7
3175	" "	19	SENE	1872-08-30		A1
3181	" "	20	SWNW	1892-08-01		A1
3178	" "	20	NENW	1883-02-20		A1
3179	" "	20	N½SW	1890-12-31		A7
3180	" "	20	SENW	1890-12-31		A7
3177	" "	20	NWNW	1882-12-20		A1
3182	KENT, Hollis	27	SWSW	1892-03-07		A7
3183	" "	28	E½SE	1892-03-07		A7
3184	" "	28	SENE	1892-03-07		A7
3186	LANNING, Henry W	34	E½SE	1902-11-25		A7
3185	" "	34	SENE	1902-11-25		A7

ID	Individual in Patent	Sec.	Sec. Part	Date Issued	Other Counties	For More Info . . .
3187	LAURANCE, John W	31	SWSE	1898-01-26		A7
7500	" "	31	1SW	1898-01-26		A7
3188	LEARNARD, Oscar E	10		1882-06-01		A1
3190	" "	11	N½SE	1882-06-01		A1
3191	" "	11	N½SW	1882-06-01		A1
3189	" "	11	N½	1882-06-01		A1
3192	" "	11	SWSW	1882-06-01		A1
3193	" "	3		1882-06-01		A1
3195	" "	4	S½SW	1882-06-01		A1
3194	" "	4	E½	1882-06-01		A1
3196	" "	5	NW	1882-06-01		A1
3197	" "	5	SE	1882-06-01		A1
3198	" "	5	N½SW	1882-06-01		A1
3199	" "	8	E½	1882-06-01		A1
3200	" "	8	SW	1882-06-01		A1
3201	" "	9		1882-06-01		A1
3202	LEDBETTER, James K	28	N½NW	1888-12-04		A7
3203	" "	28	SWNW	1888-12-04		A7
3204	" "	29	SENE	1888-12-04		A7
3205	LEDBETTER, Sarah	27	S½SE	1892-09-15		A7
3206	" "	34	N½NE	1892-09-15		A7
3207	LEDBETTER, Thomas S	24	W½NW	1916-09-07		A7
3208	LEDBETTER, William A	27	NENW	1890-01-30		A1
3209	LOWRY, Martin R	23	NESW	1901-05-08		A7
3210	" "	23	NWSE	1901-05-08		A7
3211	" "	23	S½NE	1901-05-08		A7
3212	LUTTES, James T	21	E½SW	1892-01-05		A7
3213	" "	21	W½SE	1892-01-05		A7
3214	MACK, James L	17	SENW	1892-09-09		A7
3215	" "	17	NESW	1892-09-09		A7
3216	" "	17	S½SW	1892-09-09		A7
3217	MAHAN, Grant	24	E½NW	1911-05-08		A1
3218	MAHAN, John	35	E½NE	1873-11-01		A7
3219	" "	36	W½NW	1873-11-01		A7
3220	MAHAN, Jonathan H	13	N½SE	1890-01-10		A7
3221	" "	13	E½SW	1890-01-10		A7
3222	MAHON, Gideon B	24	E½SE	1883-06-30		A7
3223	" "	25	N½NE	1883-06-30		A7
7501	MARITT, John W	31	2SW	1902-08-29		A7
7503	" "	31	S22NW	1902-08-29		A7
7504	MARTIN, Delia F	4	3NW	1880-06-30		A1
3224	MCCANNON, Daniel	1	S½SW	1873-05-30		A7
3225	" "	12	W½NW	1873-05-30		A7
7476	MITTS, James	18	2NW	1886-04-10		A7
7479	" "	18	N22SW	1886-04-10		A7
7477	" "	18	N21NW	1886-04-10		A7
3226	MORGAN, Benton	1	S½SE	1894-12-17		A7
3227	" "	12	N½NE	1894-12-17		A7
3228	MORRIS, Joseph J	32	SWNE	1895-05-28		A7
3229	" "	32	SENW	1895-05-28		A7
3230	" "	32	N½SE	1895-05-28		A7
7505	NORMAN, Sarah A	5	1NE	1896-09-29		A7
7507	" "	5	2NE	1896-09-29		A7
7514	NULL, John W	7	S21SW	1892-06-10		A7
3231	" "	7	E½SE	1892-06-10		A7
3232	" "	7	SWSE	1892-06-10		A7
3233	PARSONS, James A	2	E½SE	1901-03-23		A7
3234	" "	2	SWSE	1901-03-23		A7
3235	" "	2	SESW	1901-03-23		A7
3236	PARSONS, Willaim C	26	SESW	1860-11-12		A6
3237	" "	35	NENW	1860-11-12		A6
3238	PARSONS, William C	25	NWNW	1859-09-01		A1
3239	PENDERGRAFT, Jesse	31	SESE	1906-01-30		A7
3240	PENDERGRAFT, Thomas P	5	S½SW	1898-07-25		A7
3241	" "	8	E½NW	1898-07-25		A7
3242	PENDERGRAFT, William C	32	NESW	1905-03-30		A7
3243	PHELPS, Holman	36	SESW	1859-09-01		A1
3244	PORTER, John C	2	SWSW	1898-12-27		A1
3245	" "	7	NENE	1898-12-27		A1
3246	REED, John H	13	S½SE	1892-03-07		A7
3248	REEVES, James	11	SESW	1878-11-30		A7
3247	" "	11	S½SE	1878-11-30		A7
3249	" "	12	SWSW	1878-11-30		A7

ID	Individual in Patent	Sec.	Sec. Part	Date Issued	Other Counties	For More Info . . .
3250	REEVES, Sarah	13	W½SW	1897-06-11		A7
3251	"	14	S½SE	1897-06-11		A7
3252	RHOADES, Phineas S	23	S½SE	1882-05-20		A7
3253	" "	24	W½SW	1882-05-20		A7
3255	RILEY, James W	36	NWSW	1898-07-25		A7
3254	" "	36	NESW	1886-11-19		A1
3256	RILEY, Philip J	33	N½NW	1912-06-01		A7
3257	ROBERTS, John R	36	NE	1901-03-23		A7
3258	ROBINSON, James M	28	NWNE	1907-08-23		A7
3259	ROBINSON, Leander	20	E½SE	1883-06-30		A7
3260	" "	21	W½SW	1883-06-30		A7
3261	ROBISON, Leonidas	28	NENE	1886-10-29		A1
7491	ROPER, Joshua R	2	2NW	1901-05-08		A7
7490	" "	2	1NW	1901-05-08		A7
3262	RUSSELL, Santford J	21	NWNE	1886-10-29		A1
3263	SCOGGIN, Joseph N	29	SWSE	1898-04-06		A7
3264	" "	32	NENW	1898-04-06		A7
3265	" "	32	N½NE	1898-04-06		A7
3266	SHAW, James	32	SENE	1901-03-23		A7
3268	SMITH, John F	14	E½NW	1895-05-28		A7
3267	" "	14	N½NE	1895-05-28		A7
3269	SMITH, Oney	13	SENE	1878-11-30		A7
3270	SOUTHARD, Alfred	25	SW	1888-12-08		A7
3271	STEELE, Charles	25	SWNE	1893-12-09		A1
3275	SUTTLE, Maria	15	SESW	1884-11-17		A6 G119
3277	" "	15	W½SW	1884-11-17		A6 G119
3276	" "	15	SWSE	1884-11-17		A6 G119
3278	TABOR, Andrew J	26	SWSW	1889-01-12		A7
3280	" "	35	NWNE	1889-01-12		A7
3279	" "	35	NWNW	1889-01-12		A7
3281	TABOR, Andrew V	34	NESE	1886-11-19		A1
3287	" "	35	NWSE	1860-10-01		A1
3286	" "	35	NWSW	1859-09-01		A1
3285	" "	35	NESW	1856-06-16		A1
3284	" "	35	SWNW	1882-12-20		A1
3283	" "	35	NESE	1882-09-30		A1
3282	" "	35	SWNE	1873-06-05		A1
3288	" "	35	SWSW	1885-02-25		A7
3289	TABOR, John S	30	SWSE	1900-08-09		A7
3290	TABOR, Tabitha	27	N½SE	1894-05-18		A7
3291	" "	27	W½NE	1894-05-18		A7
3292	TABOR, Thomas C	34	S½SE	1882-06-30		A7
3293	TABOR, Thomas E	35	S½SE	1875-02-15		A7
3294	" "	36	SWSW	1875-02-15		A7
3295	THOMAS, Leroy	21	SESE	1890-01-10		A7
3296	" "	22	E½SW	1890-01-10		A7
3297	" "	22	SWSW	1890-01-10		A7
3298	TILSON, Louisa	31	NESE	1892-06-21		A7 G127
3299	" "	31	SENE	1892-06-21		A7 G127
3300	" "	32	SWNW	1892-06-21		A7 G127
3301	" "	32	NWSW	1892-06-21		A7 G127
3303	TISDALE, Alfred W	29	NWSE	1875-12-20		A7
3302	" "	29	SESW	1875-12-20		A7
3304	" "	29	N½SW	1875-12-20		A7
3306	WADE, Mary J	27	S½NW	1888-12-08		A7
3305	" "	27	N½SW	1888-12-08		A7
3307	WADLEY, Robert H	34	E½NW	1896-08-28		A7
3310	WALKER, Thomas J	34	SENE	1910-07-18		A7
3313	WELKER, Samuel	29	NENW	1895-05-28		A7
3312	" "	29	NENE	1895-05-28		A7
3311	" "	29	W½NE	1895-05-28		A7
3314	WILLIAMS, Perry C	27	SESW	1910-06-13		A7
3315	WISE, Lewis	17	SE	1876-12-01		A7
3316	WYRICK, Calvin	36	E½NW	1893-09-28		A7
3317	ZUMWALT, Benjamin F	29	SWSW	1882-09-30		A7
3318	" "	30	NESE	1892-08-01		A1
3319	" "	30	SESE	1882-09-30		A7
3320	" "	31	NENE	1882-09-30		A7
3321	" "	32	NWNW	1882-09-30		A7

Patent Map

T24-N R10-W
5th PM 24-N 10-W Meridian

Map Group 13

Township Statistics

Parcels Mapped	:	321
Number of Patents	:	184
Number of Individuals	:	156
Patentees Identified	:	151
Number of Surnames	:	96
Multi-Patentee Parcels	:	11
Oldest Patent Date	:	6/16/1856
Most Recent Patent	:	9/7/1916
Block/Lot Parcels	:	45
Cities and Town	:	2
Cemeteries	:	5

Section 6

Lots/Tracts-Sec. 6
1NW GORMAN, CHARLES 1895
2NW GORMAN, CHARLES 1895

Section 5

Lots/Tracts-Sec. 5
1NE NORMAN, SARAH A 1896
2NE NORMAN, SARAH A 1896
3NE DRUMWRIGHT, ROBERT J 1880

LEARNARD Oscar E 1882
LEARNARD Oscar E 1882
LEARNARD Oscar E 1882
PENDERGRAFT Thomas P 1898

Section 4

Lots/Tracts-Sec. 4
3NW MARTIN, DELIA F 1880

LEARNARD Oscar E 1882
LEARNARD Oscar E 1882

Section 7

Lots/Tracts-Sec. 7
2SW HALL, RICHARD V 1886
N21SW HALL, RICHARD V 1886
S21SW NULL, JOHN W 1892

PORTER John C 1898
BUKER Charles H 1894
HALL Richard V 1886
NULL John W 1892
NULL John W 1892

Section 8

BUKER Charles H 1894
PENDERGRAFT Thomas P 1898
LEARNARD Oscar E 1882

Section 9

LEARNARD Oscar E 1882
LEARNARD Oscar E 1882

Section 18

Lots/Tracts-Sec. 18
2NW MITTS, JAMES 1886
N21NW MITTS, JAMES 1886
N21SW FOX, JOSEPH S 1882
N22SW MITTS, JAMES 1886
S21NW FOX, JOSEPH S 1882
S21SW HICKS, NEMIER 1882
S22SW HICKS, NEMIER 1882

DAVIS Van C 1894
FOX Joseph S 1882
ALLRED Richard 1892
FOX Joseph S 1882
ALLRED Richard 1892
HICKS Nemier 1882

Section 17

CARRINGTON Fred W 1902
ALLRED Richard 1892
MACK James L 1892
BLOSSOM Maria L 1891
ALLRED Richard 1892
MACK James L 1892
MACK James L 1892
WISE Lewis 1876

Section 16

Section 19

Lots/Tracts-Sec. 19
1NW BUNDREN, GEORGE W 1888
2NW BUNDREN, GEORGE W 1888
N21SW FOX, ENOCH 1879
N22SW FOX, ENOCH 1888
S21SW FOX, ENOCH 1879
S22SW FOX, ENOCH 1885

BRANSTETTER Peter J 1899
KARR John M 1882
KARR John M 1883
BRANSTETTER Peter J 1899
KARR John M 1872
KARR John M 1892
KARR John M 1890
FOX Joseph W 1882
KARR John M 1890
KARR John M 1890
GREEN Lymon J 1892

Section 20

CRIDER Leonard S 1894
FOX Allen J 1885
FOX Allen J 1885
ROBINSON Leander 1883
DAVIS Eliphaz 1889

Section 21

RUSSELL Sanford J 1886
CALLISON William 1888
FOX Gastus 1879
FOX Gastus 1879
ROBINSON Leander 1883
LUTTES James T 1892
LUTTES James T 1892
JOHNSON James T 1890
THOMAS Leroy 1890

Section 30

Lots/Tracts-Sec. 30
2NW BOETTLER, EDWARD 1893
N21NW CRIDER, DANIEL 1883
S21NW BOETTLER, EDWARD 1893

CALLAHAN John H 1892
DAVIS Eliphaz 1889
CALLAHAN John H 1892
CALLAHAN John H 1892
CALLAHAN [31] Sarah E 1884
TABOR John S 1900

ZUMWALT Benjamin F 1892
ZUMWALT Benjamin F 1882

Section 29

DAVIS Eliphaz 1889
WELKER Samuel 1895
WELKER Samuel 1895
BAKER Garret H 1898
TISDALE Alfred W 1875
TISDALE Alfred W 1875

Section 28

WELKER Samuel 1895
LEDBETTER James K 1888
LEDBETTER James K 1888
LEDBETTER James K 1888
ROBINSON James M 1907
FOX James A 1892
FOX James A 1892
FOX James A 1892
FOX James A 1892
JOHNSTON John C 1891
JOHNSTON John C 1891
JOHNSTON John C 1891
DAVIS Joshua D 1886
ROBISON Leonidas 1886
KENT Hollis 1892
KENT Hollis 1892

TISDALE Alfred W 1875
SCOGGIN Joseph N 1898

Section 31

Lots/Tracts-Sec. 31
1NW CALLAHAN, LOUIS F 1890
1SW LAURANCE, JOHN W 1898
2SW MARITT, JOHN W 1902
N22NW CALLAHAN, LOUIS F 1890
S22NW MARITT, JOHN W 1902

CALLAHAN Louis F 1890
ZUMWALT Benjamin F 1882
ZUMWALT Benjamin F 1882
BRIGGS John F 1914
INGOLD [127] Louisa 1892
INGOLD [127] Louisa 1892
LAURANCE John W 1898
PENDERGRAFT Jesse 1906

Section 32

ZUMWALT Benjamin F 1882
SCOGGIN Joseph N 1898
SCOGGIN Joseph N 1898
INGOLD [127] Louisa 1892
MORRIS Joseph J 1895
MORRIS Joseph J 1895
SHAW James 1901
INGOLD [127] Louisa 1892
PENDERGRAFT William C 1905
MORRIS Joseph J 1895
FOX William M 1898
HUDLOW William R 1892

Section 33

RILEY Philip J 1912
HOPKINS William J 1888
FOX Joseph W 1901
DAVIS Joshua D 1892
FOX Joseph W 1901
DAVIS Joshua D 1892
HUDLOW William R 1892
FOX Joseph W 1901
DAVIS Joshua D 1891
HUSTON Lewis A 1901
BRIGGS William 1882

Lots/Tracts-Sec. 2
1NE	HOPKINS, ROBERT L 1894
1NW	ROPER, JOSHUA R 1901
2NW	ROPER, JOSHUA R 1901
3NE	FRIZELL, JASON 1892
3NW	FRIZELL, JASON 1892
E22NE	COLLINS, AARON 1874
W22NE	FRIZELL, JASON 1892

Lots/Tracts-Sec. 1
1NW	COLLINS, AARON 1874
2NE	COLLINS, MARTHA J [55]1892
3NE	COLLINS, DAVID 1883
3NW	COLLINS, DAVID 1883
E21NE	COLLINS, MARTHA J [55]1892
E22NW	COLLINS, AARON 1861
W21NE	BYERS, GEORGE W 1882
W22NW	COLLINS, AARON 1874

3
LEARNARD
Oscar E
1882

2
ALSUP Ben M 1907
HOPKINS Robert L 1894
PARSONS James A 1901
PORTER John C 1898
PARSONS James A 1901
PARSONS James A 1901

1
BYERS George W 1882
BYERS George W 1882
COLLINS [55] Martha J 1892
MCCANNON Daniel 1873
MORGAN Benton 1894

10
LEARNARD
Oscar E
1882

11
LEARNARD Oscar E 1882
LEARNARD Oscar E 1882
LEARNARD Oscar E 1882
LEARNARD Oscar E 1882
REEVES James 1878
REEVES James 1878

12
MCCANNON Daniel 1873
GODAT Edward P 1901
MORGAN Benton 1894
GODAT Edward P 1901
HOPKINS William F 1886
CANNON Daniel M 1884
HOPKINS William T 1875
HOPKINS William F 1861
HOPKINS James E 1888
REEVES James 1878
HOPKINS James E 1888
BINKLEY Leonard L 1908

15
DABBS Thomas B 1910
FOX John 1892
DABBS Thomas B 1910
HOPKINS Thomas B 1875
HOPKINS Thomas B 1875
COLLINS Leonard S 1901
HOPKINS Thomas B 1875
HOPKINS Thomas B 1875
COLLINS Leonard S 1901
HOSHOUR [119] Samuel H 1884
HOSHOUR [119] Samuel H 1884
HOSHOUR [119] Samuel H 1884

14
FOX John 1892
SMITH John F 1895
SMITH John F 1895
FOX Johnson M 1892
HOPKINS Jacob 1875
COLLINS Leonard S 1901
FOX Johnson M 1892
FOX Johnson M 1892
FOX William R 1896
REEVES Sarah 1897

13
SMITH John F 1895
HOPKINS Peter P 1905
HOPKINS James E 1888
HOPKINS Jacob 1893
BINKLEY Leonard L 1908
HOPKINS Jacob 1875
HOPKINS Jacob 1875
SMITH Oney 1878
MAHAN Jonathan H 1890
REEVES Sarah 1897
MAHAN Jonathan H 1890
REED John H 1892

22
FOX Gastus 1879
FOX Gatus 1885
FOX William S 1890
HOPKINS Jacob S 1902
HOPKINS George W 1896
FOX William S 1890
FOX William S 1890
JOHNSON James T 1890
THOMAS Leroy 1890
CALLISON George W 1875
THOMAS Leroy 1890

23
FOX William R 1896
HUSTON Louis A 1908
FOX Andrew J 1892
LOWRY Martin R 1901
LOWRY Martin R 1901
LOWRY Martin R 1901
CURRY Thomas L 1908
FOX Andrew J 1892
FOX Ulisses G 1900
RHOADES Phineas S 1882

24
LEDBETTER Thomas S 1916
MAHAN Grant 1911
CANNON Sarah A 1896
RHOADES Phineas S 1882
BISHOP Henry A 1885
BISHOP Henry A 1885
MAHON Gideon B 1883

27
BROWN Jonathan 1871
LEDBETTER William A 1890
BRIDGES Joseph E 1860
TABOR Tabitha 1894
WADE Mary J 1888
FOX Esau 1885
WADE Mary J 1888
TABOR Tabitha 1894
KENT Hollis 1892
WILLIAMS Perry C 1910
LEDBETTER Sarah 1892

26
BUCKMASTER Joshua 1877
GRAHAM Harvey 1889
FOX Esau 1872
BUCKMASTER Joshua 1877
FOX Ulisses G 1900
FOX Esau 1872
FOX Esau 1875
FOX James A 1892
TABOR Andrew J 1889
PARSONS William C 1860

25
PARSONS William C 1859
GRAHAM Harvey 1877
MAHON Gideon B 1883
GRAHAM Harvey 1877
STEELE Charles 1893
HOPKINS Benjamin F 1890
SOUTHARD Alfred 1888
BROWN Michael 1882

34
LEDBETTER Sarah 1892
HOPKINS William J 1888
WADLEY Robert H 1896
WALKER Thomas J 1910   LANNING Henry W 1902
ADAMS Thomas F 1888
ADAMS Thomas F 1888
ADAMS Thomas F 1888
TABOR Andrew V 1886   LANNING Henry W 1902
BRIGGS William 1881
JOHNSON Benjamin N 1860
TABOR Thomas C 1882

35
TABOR Andrew J 1889
PARSONS William C 1860
TABOR Andrew J 1889
TABOR Andrew V 1882
ENDECOTT Joseph 1859
TABOR Andrew V 1873
MAHAN John 1873
TABOR Andrew V 1859
TABOR Andrew V 1856
TABOR Andrew V 1860
TABOR Andrew V 1882
TABOR Andrew V 1885
CARRIER Josephus 1890
TABOR Thomas E 1875

36
MAHAN John 1873
WYRICK Calvin 1893
ROBERTS John R 1901
RILEY James W 1898
RILEY James W 1886
HUNTER William H 1888
TABOR Thomas E 1875
PHELPS Holman 1859
HUNTER William H 1888
ADAMS Benoni 1859

Helpful Hints

1. This Map's INDEX can be found on the preceding pages.

2. Refer to Map "C" to see where this Township lies within Howell County, Missouri.

3. Numbers within square brackets [ ] denote a multi-patentee land parcel (multi-owner). Refer to Appendix "C" for a full list of members in this group.

4. Areas that look to be crowded with Patentees usually indicate multiple sales of the same parcel (Re-issues) or Overlapping parcels. See this Township's Index for an explanation of these and other circumstances that might explain "odd" groupings of Patentees on this map.

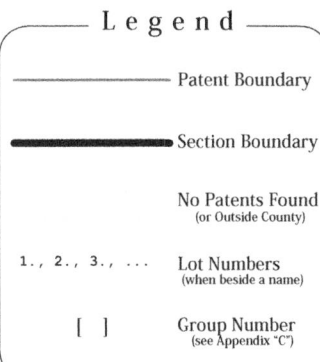

Legend

———	Patent Boundary
▬▬▬	Section Boundary
	No Patents Found (or Outside County)
1., 2., 3., . . .	Lot Numbers (when beside a name)
[ ]	Group Number (see Appendix "C")

Scale: Section = 1 mile X 1 mile
(generally, with some exceptions)

Road Map

T24-N R10-W
5th PM 24-N 10-W Meridian

Map Group 13

Cities & Towns

Crider
Grimmet

Cemeteries

Collins Cemetery
Ledbetter Cemetery
Mitts Cemetery
Siloam Springs Cemetery
Union Grove General Baptist
  Cemetery

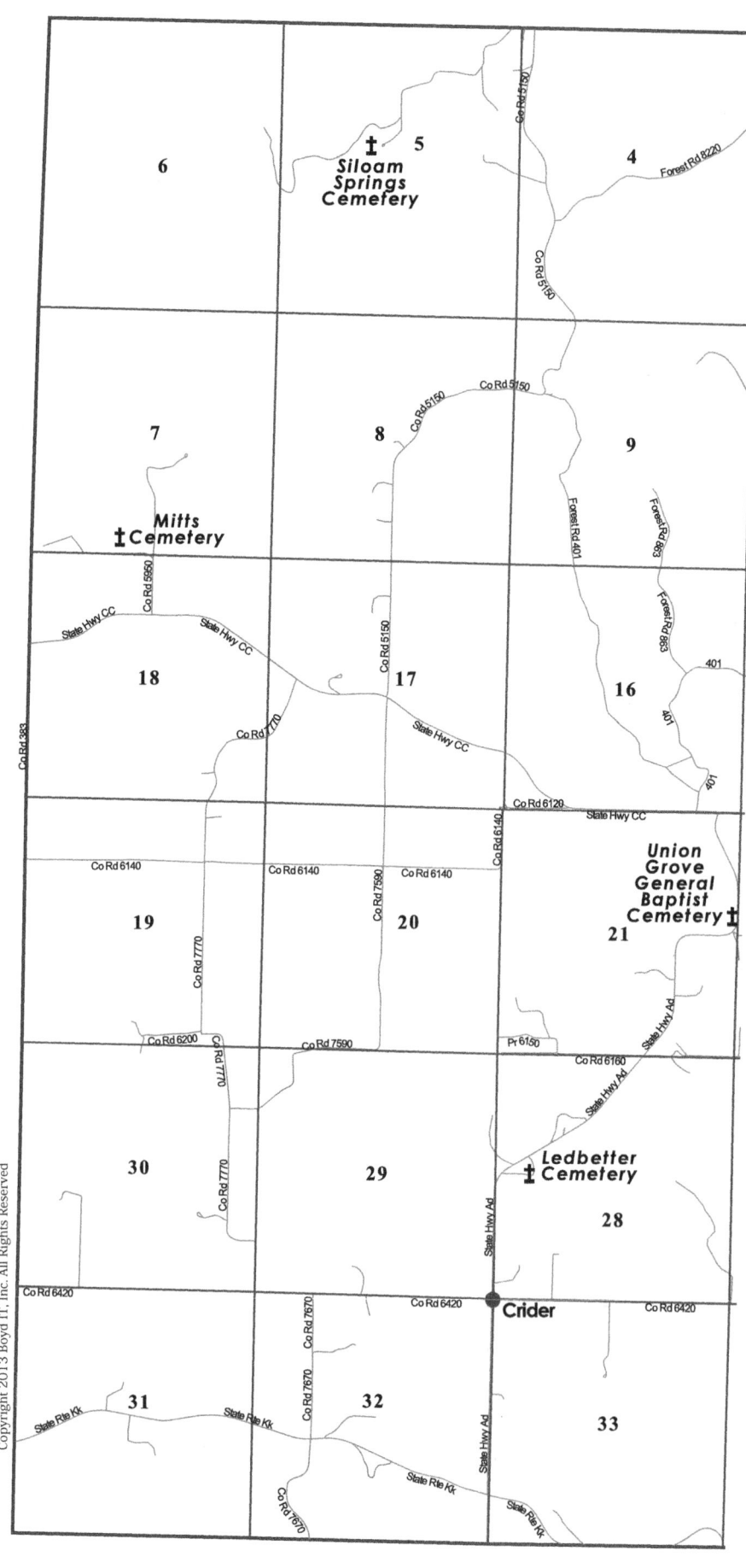

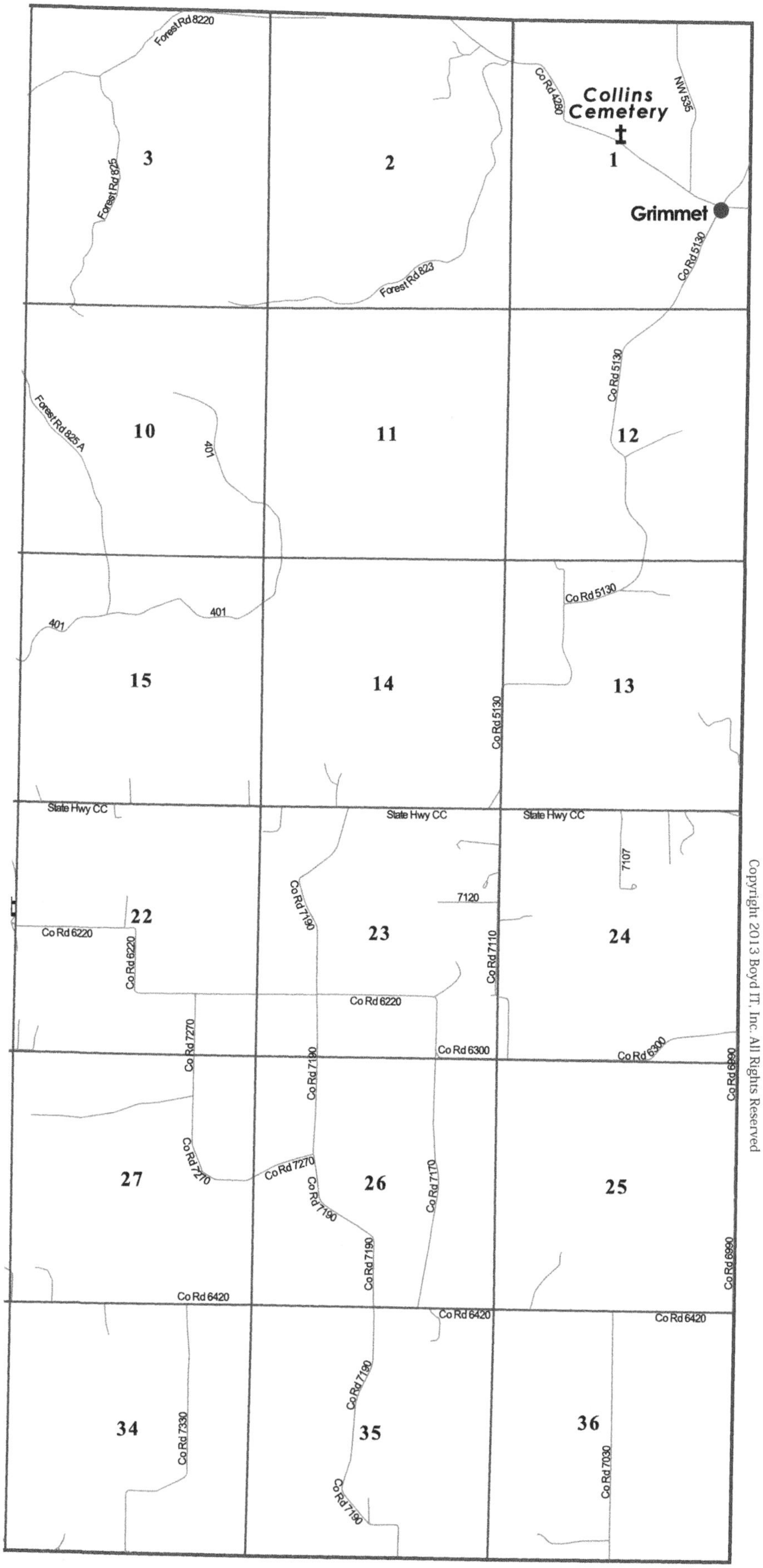

Forest Rd 8220

Forest Rd 825

3

2

Co Rd 4280

Collins
Cemetery
✝

1

NW 635

Grimmet ●

Co Rd 5130

Forest Rd 823

Forest Rd 825 A

10

401

11

12

Co Rd 5130

401

401

15

14

Co Rd 5130

Co Rd 5130

13

State Hwy CC

State Hwy CC

State Hwy CC

Co Rd 6220

22

Co Rd 6220

Co Rd 7190

23

7120

24

7107

Co Rd 7110

Co Rd 6220

Co Rd 6300

Co Rd 6300

Co Rd 6990

Co Rd 7270

Co Rd 7210

Co Rd 7270

27

Co Rd 7190

26

Co Rd 7170

Co Rd 7190

25

Co Rd 6990

Co Rd 6420

Co Rd 6420

Co Rd 6420

Co Rd 6420

34

Co Rd 7330

Co Rd 7190

35

Co Rd 7190

36

Co Rd 7030

Copyright 2013 Boyd IT, Inc. All Rights Reserved

Helpful Hints

1. This road map has a number of uses, but primarily it is to help you: a) find the present location of land owned by your ancestors (at least the general area), b) find cemeteries and city-centers, and c) estimate the route/roads used by Census-takers & tax-assessors.

2. If you plan to travel to Howell County to locate cemeteries or land parcels, please pick up a modern travel map for the area before you do. Mapping old land parcels on modern maps is not as exact a science as you might think. Just the slightest variations in public land survey coordinates, estimates of parcel boundaries, or road-map deviations can greatly alter a map's representation of how a road either does or doesn't cross a particular parcel of land.

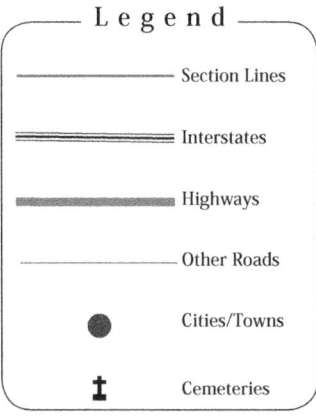

L e g e n d

———————— Section Lines

══════════ Interstates

▬▬▬▬▬▬ Highways

———————— Other Roads

● Cities/Towns

✝ Cemeteries

Scale: Section = 1 mile X 1 mile
(generally, with some exceptions)

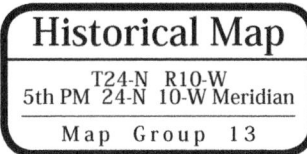

Historical Map

T24-N R10-W
5th PM 24-N 10-W Meridian

Map Group 13

6 5 4

Siloam Springs ‡Cemetery

7 8 9

‡ Mitts Cemetery

18 17 16

Tabor Crk

Union Grove General Baptist Cemetery ‡

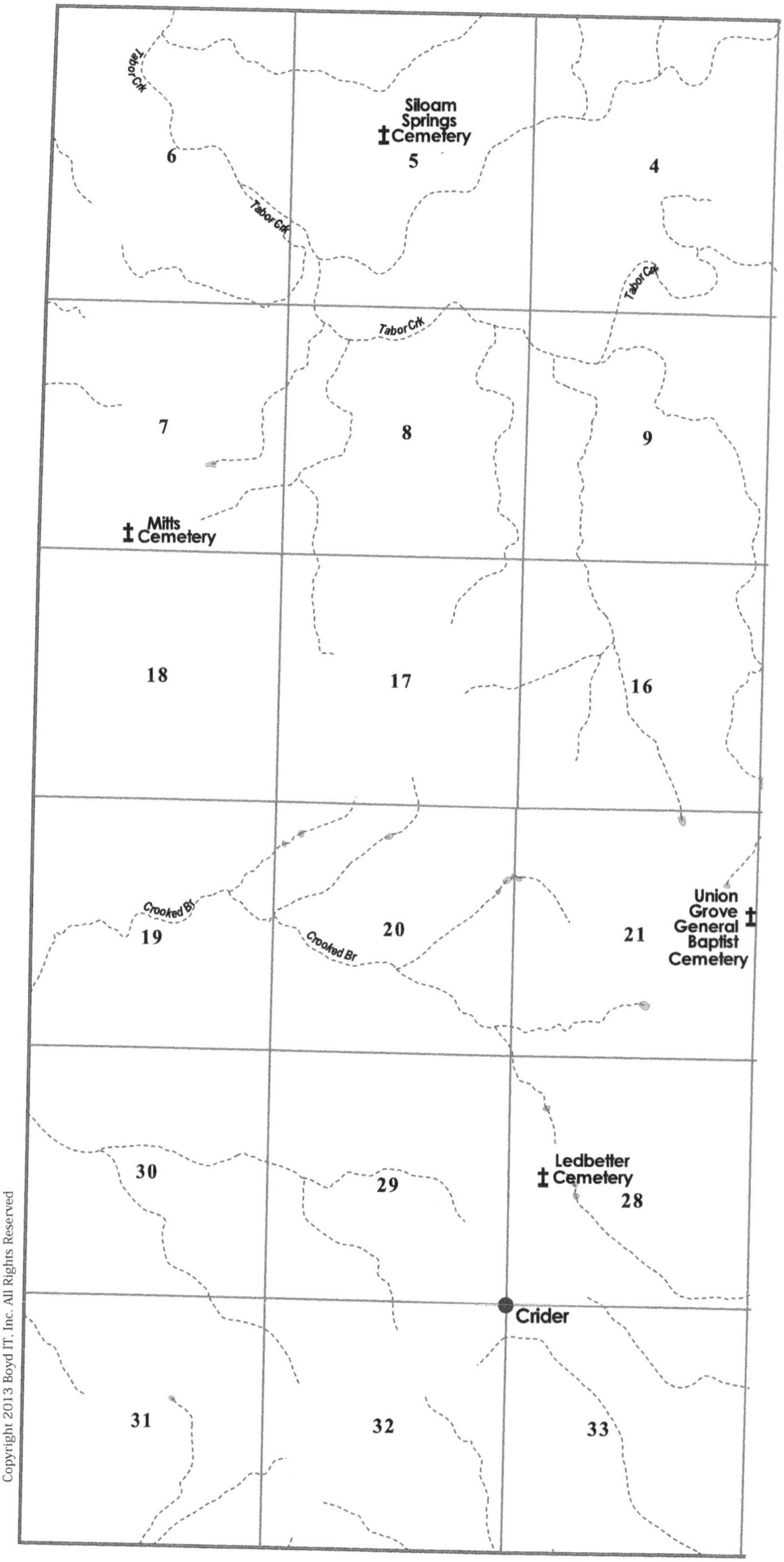

19 20 21

Crooked Br

30 29 28

Ledbetter ‡ Cemetery

● Crider

31 32 33

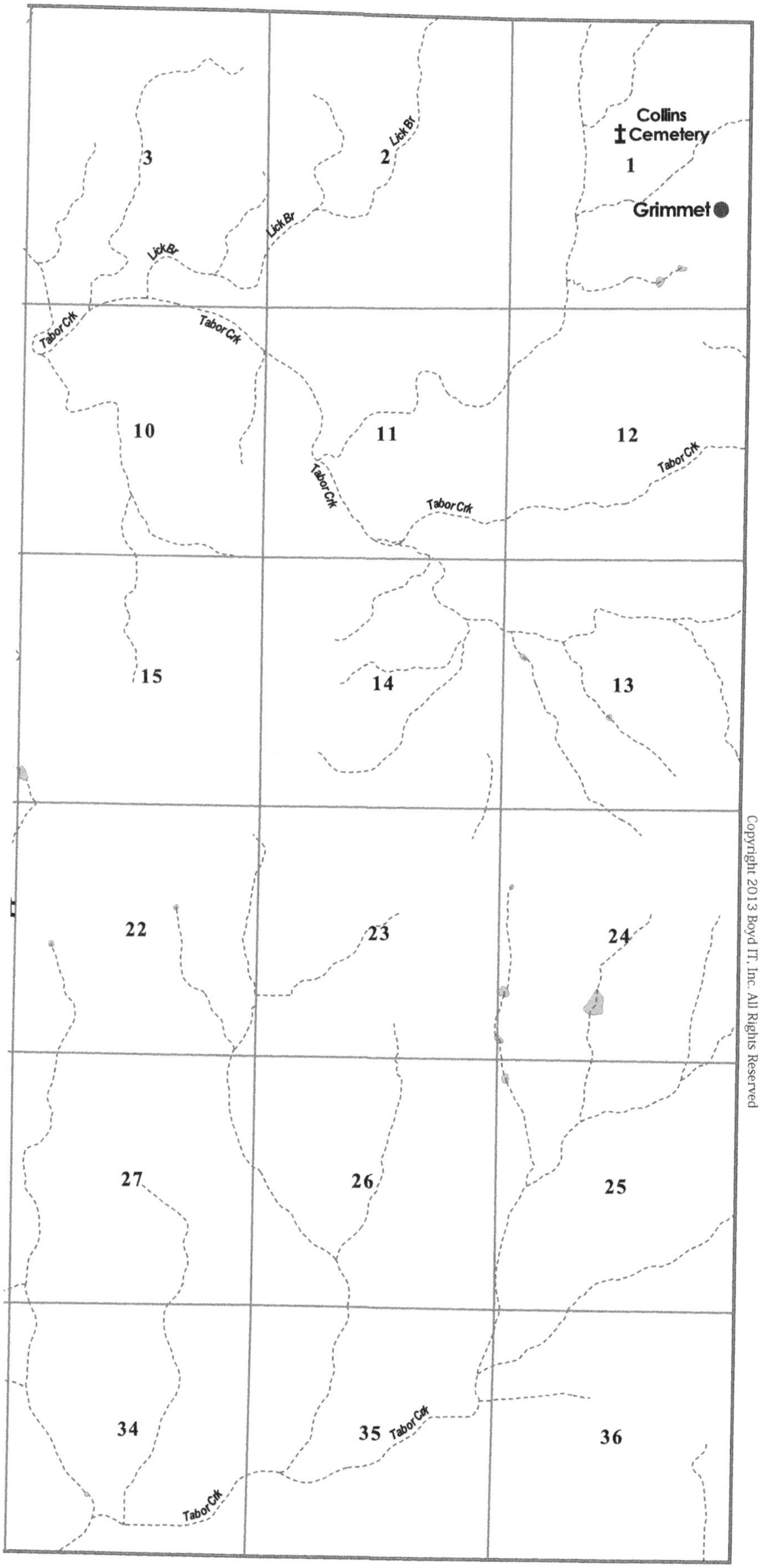

3

2

Lick Br

Lick Br

Collins
‡ Cemetery

1

Grimmet ●

Lick Br

Tabor Crk

Tabor Crk

10

11

12

Tabor Crk

Tabor Crk

Tabor Crk

Tabor Crk

15

14

13

22

23

24

27

26

25

34

35

Tabor Crk

36

Tabor Crk

Helpful Hints

1. This Map takes a different look at the same Congressional Township displayed in the preceding two maps. It presents features that can help you better envision the historical development of the area: a) Water-bodies (lakes & ponds), b) Water-courses (rivers, streams, etc.), c) Railroads, d) City/town center-points (where they were oftentimes located when first settled), and e) Cemeteries.

2. Using this "Historical" map in tandem with this Township's Patent Map and Road Map, may lead you to some interesting discoveries. You will often find roads, towns, cemeteries, and waterways are named after nearby landowners: sometimes those names will be the ones you are researching. See how many of these research gems you can find here in Howell County.

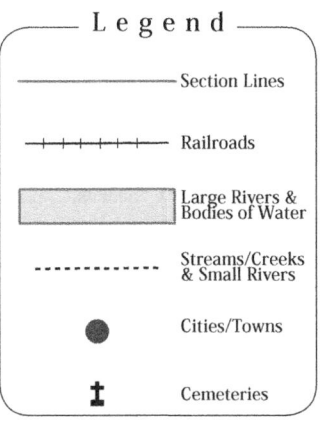

Legend

———————— Section Lines

+–+–+–+–+–+ Railroads

Large Rivers &
Bodies of Water

- - - - - - - Streams/Creeks
& Small Rivers

● Cities/Towns

‡ Cemeteries

Scale: Section = 1 mile X 1 mile
(there are some exceptions)

Map Group 14: Index to Land Patents

Township 24-North Range 9-West (5th PM 24-N 9-W)

After you locate an individual in this Index, take note of the Section and Section Part then proceed to the Land Patent map on the pages immediately following. You should have no difficulty locating the corresponding parcel of land.

The "For More Info" Column will lead you to more information about the underlying Patents. See the *Legend* at right, and the "How to Use this Book" chapter, for more information.

```
                    LEGEND
            "For More Info . . . " column
A = Authority (Legislative Act, See Appendix "A")
B = Block or Lot (location in Section unknown)
C = Cancelled Patent
F = Fractional Section
G = Group  (Multi-Patentee Patent, see Appendix "C")
V = Overlaps another Parcel
R = Re-Issued (Parcel patented more than once)

(A & G items require you to look in the Appendixes referred
to above. All other Letter-designations followed by a number
require you to locate line-items in this index that possess
the ID number found after the letter).
```

ID	Individual in Patent	Sec.	Sec. Part	Date Issued	Other Counties	For More Info . . .
3322	AKEMAN, George W	26	S½SW	1885-12-19		A7
3324	" "	26	NWSW	1885-12-19		A7
3323	" "	26	SWSE	1885-12-19		A7
3325	BAIRD, Caleb J	28	NWNE	1905-05-12		A1
3326	BALLARD, William C	25	S½NE	1886-07-20		A1
3327	BALLINGER, John	17	E½NW	1888-05-07		A1
3328	BARNES, Lucy E	13	NENE	1882-09-30		A7
3329	BARR, Leven E	35	NE	1904-04-08		A7
3330	BAYS, John	8	N½NE	1875-07-20		A7
3331	" "	9	W½NW	1875-07-20		A7
3333	BINGAMAN, Henry G	9	S½SW	1888-11-27		A7
3332	" "	9	W½SE	1888-11-27		A7
3334	BOLLINGER, Jackson C	17	NWNE	1896-01-14		A7
3336	" "	8	SESW	1896-01-14		A7
3335	" "	8	W½SE	1896-01-14		A7
3338	BOLLINGER, John	17	E½NE	1877-10-10		A7
3337	" "	17	SWNE	1877-10-10		A7
3339	" "	8	SESE	1877-10-10		A7
3340	BRAY, Emily	27	W½SW	1889-01-12		A7 G21
3341	" "	28	E½SE	1889-01-12		A7 G21
3342	BRAY, Jesse	27	W½SW	1889-01-12		A7 G21
3343	" "	28	E½SE	1889-01-12		A7 G21
3344	BROWN, Granville T	21	N½NE	1890-01-10		A7
3345	BROWN, John M	15	SWNW	1874-06-15		A1
3346	" "	15	N½SW	1881-10-06		A7
3347	" "	15	NWSE	1881-10-06		A7
3348	" "	15	SWNE	1881-10-06		A7
3349	BROWN, Thomas O	21	SENE	1873-02-01		A7
3350	" "	22	NWNW	1873-02-01		A7
3351	" "	22	S½NW	1873-02-01		A7
3352	BRYANT, Leonard L	14	SWSE	1907-12-05		A7
3353	BUCKLEW, Warren	10	N½NW	1885-07-27		A1 C
3354	BUCKNER, James R	36	N½NE	1892-10-17		A7
3356	BUCKNER, Jesse	20	NESE	1860-08-01		A1
3355	" "	20	SESE	1860-03-01		A1
3357	" "	29	NENE	1860-08-01		A1
3358	BUTLER, Frederick	7	SENE	1861-02-09		A1
3359	" "	8	NWNW	1860-08-01		A1
3361	BYERS, Samuel B	5	W½SE	1882-09-30		A7
3360	" "	5	N½SW	1882-09-30		A7
3362	CAMPBELL, James	31	SWSE	1854-11-15		A1
3364	CAMPBELL, Robert S	12	NESW	1883-02-10		A7
3363	" "	12	NWSE	1883-02-10		A7
7588	CANNON, William C	6	S22SW	1904-06-02		A7
3365	CARGILL, Samuel P	11	NENE	1882-06-30		A7
3367	" "	12	NWSW	1882-06-30		A7

ID	Individual in Patent	Sec.	Sec. Part	Date Issued	Other Counties	For More Info . . .
3366	CARGILL, Samuel P (Cont'd)	12	W½NW	1882-06-30		A7
3368	CARGILL, Thomas W	12	E½NE	1890-01-10		A7
3369	CARSON, David	36	E½SE	1874-06-15		A1
3370	CLARK, Levin	32	NWSE	1858-01-15		A1
3371	" "	32	SESW	1858-01-15		A1
3372	CLEARY, Daniel F	8	NESE	1883-02-10		A7
3374	" "	9	N½SW	1883-02-10		A7
3373	" "	9	SENE	1883-02-10		A7
3375	COBB, Elbert L	29	NESW	1872-02-05		A1
3376	COLE, Frank	36	NWSE	1885-12-19		A1
3377	COLLENS, Leonard	22	NWNE	1860-10-01		A1
3378	COLYER, Jeremiah	3	W½SW	1879-12-15		A7
3379	" "	4	SESE	1879-12-15		A7
3380	" "	9	NENE	1879-12-15		A7
3383	CORDILL, James M	10	SESE	1892-03-07		A7
3384	" "	11	W½SW	1892-03-07		A7
3385	" "	14	NWNW	1892-03-07		A7
3386	DAWSON, Richard M	34	S½NE	1888-12-06		A7
3387	" "	34	NESW	1888-12-06		A7
3388	" "	34	SENW	1888-12-06		A7
3389	DE WITT, James C	11	NW	1898-07-25		A7
3390	DENNIS, Alvin H	19	E½NE	1902-12-09		A1
3391	DOCIA, Henry	24	SENW	1896-03-25		A7
3392	DRUMWRIGHT, Squire F	17	SWNW	1910-11-25		A7
3393	EATON, Joseph	18	NWSE	1893-12-19		A7
7526	" "	18	N21SW	1893-12-19		A7
7549	EBLIN, Queen E	3	W23NW	1877-08-01		A7
7574	" "	4	W22NE	1877-08-01		A7
7575	" "	4	W23NE	1877-08-01		A7
3394	EDMOUNDSON, John S	18	SWSE	1892-08-01		A7
7529	" "	18	S21SW	1892-08-01		A7
7531	" "	19	N21NW	1892-08-01		A7
3395	" "	19	NWNE	1892-08-01		A7
3396	EPLEY, James	28	SWSE	1888-12-08		A7
3397	" "	28	S½SW	1888-12-08		A7
3398	" "	33	NWNW	1888-12-08		A7
3399	EVANS, Adam R	26	SWNW	1882-12-20		A1
3400	FADDIS, Thomas M	13	NESE	1893-01-13		A1
3401	FALWELL, Cary C	26	SWNE	1890-10-11		A7
3402	" "	26	NWSE	1890-10-11		A7
3403	" "	26	NESW	1890-10-11		A7
3404	" "	26	SENW	1890-10-11		A7
3405	FALWELL, William T	25	NWSW	1891-06-09		A7
3406	" "	26	E½SE	1891-06-09		A7
3407	" "	26	SENE	1891-06-09		A7
3408	FELAND, Lafayette F	27	SESW	1892-02-06		A7
3410	" "	34	NWNE	1892-02-06		A7
3409	" "	34	N½NW	1892-02-06		A7
3413	FORD, Joseph R	34	SESW	1877-08-01		A7
3411	" "	34	SESE	1877-08-01		A7
3412	" "	34	W½SE	1877-08-01		A7
3414	FOX, Matthew W	2	NWSE	1891-05-05		A7
3415	" "	2	NESW	1891-05-05		A7
3416	GILBERT, Horace G	23	SENE	1900-02-08		A1
3417	GLINN, James M	10	NWNW	1908-03-02		A7
3419	GLINN, James W	18	S½NE	1889-06-22		A7
3418	" "	18	NWNE	1889-06-22		A7
7525	" "	18	N21NW	1889-06-22		A7
3420	GLOSSUP, Henry D	32	SWSE	1888-07-03		A1
3421	GLOSSUP, Samuel	32	NESE	1877-10-10		A7
3423	" "	33	N½SW	1877-10-10		A7
3422	" "	33	SWSW	1877-10-10		A7
7592	GODAT, James	7	1SW	1900-08-09		A7
3424	GRAHAM, John G	15	SENW	1903-08-25		A7
3425	" "	15	NWNE	1903-08-25		A7
3426	GRIMMETT, Samuel T	10	SWNW	1881-10-06		A7
3427	" "	9	S½NE	1881-10-06		A7
3428	" "	9	SENW	1881-10-06		A7
3429	HANEY, Elijah	2	SWSE	1885-02-25		A7
3430	" "	2	SESW	1885-02-25		A7
3431	HANNER, James M	26	N½NW	1882-09-30		A7
3433	" "	27	N½NE	1882-09-30		A7
3432	" "	27	SENE	1885-03-20		A1

ID	Individual in Patent	Sec.	Sec. Part	Date Issued	Other Counties	For More Info . . .
3434	HARDESTY, Morgan M	35	S½SE	1896-09-25		A7
3435	" "	35	NWSE	1896-09-25		A7
7540	HATCHER, Aaron	3	3NE	1882-09-30		A7
7544	" "	3	E23NW	1882-09-30		A7
7543	" "	3	E22NW	1882-09-30		A7
7546	" "	3	W22NE	1888-05-07		A1
7571	" "	4	W21NW	1890-01-30		A1
3436	HAVIN, Richard	22	E½NE	1872-03-15		A7
3437	" "	23	W½NW	1872-03-15		A7
7519	HAYS, Daniel D	1	E23NE	1877-08-01		A7
7517	" "	1	2NE	1877-08-01		A7
7515	HAYS, James B	1	1NE	1877-04-05		A7
3438	HELMS, William W	4	NWSW	1875-07-20		A7
3439	" "	5	NESE	1875-07-20		A7
3440	HERREN, Josephus	32	NWNW	1884-11-01		A7
3441	HERREN, Thomas W	21	NWSW	1888-12-08		A7
3442	HERRIN, Elisha N	28	SWNW	1860-10-01		A1
3444	" "	29	SENE	1860-10-01		A1
3443	" "	29	SESW	1859-09-01		A1
3445	" "	32	E½NW	1853-04-15		A1
3448	" "	32	SWNE	1860-08-01		A1
3447	" "	32	NESW	1853-04-15		A1
3446	" "	32	SWNW	1853-04-15		A1
3451	HESTERLY, Starling J	11	NESE	1891-05-05		A7
3449	" "	11	W½NE	1891-05-05		A7
3450	" "	11	SENE	1891-05-05		A7
3452	HILL, Fletcher G	10	NENW	1901-06-08		A7
3453	HIXSON, William	7	NENE	1858-01-15		A1
3455	HOLLINGSHAD, John	13	NESW	1882-05-20		A7
3454	" "	13	S½NE	1882-05-20		A7
3456	" "	13	NWSE	1882-05-20		A7
3457	HOLT, Joseph S	3	NESW	1894-12-17		A7
3458	" "	4	NESE	1894-12-17		A7
7556	HOPKINS, Benjamin F	30	S22NW	1890-10-11		A7
7554	" "	30	N22SW	1890-10-11		A7
7555	" "	30	S21NW	1890-10-11		A7
3459	HOPKINS, Charles R	6	W½SE	1902-05-21		A7
7587	HOPKINS, Jacob	6	S21SW	1885-06-03		A1
7593	" "	7	N22NW	1882-09-30		A1
7584	HOPKINS, John	6	E22NE	1888-12-04		A7
7591	" "	7	1NW	1873-05-30		A7
3460	HOPKINS, Joseph B	6	E½SE	1860-05-02		A6
7582	" "	6	E21NE	1860-05-02		A6
7594	HOPKINS, William T	7	N22SW	1875-11-01		A7
7595	" "	7	S22NW	1875-11-01		A7
3461	HOWELL, George W	31	NWSE	1885-06-20		A7 G120
7561	" "	31	N22SW	1885-06-20		A7 G120
7559	" "	31	N21SW	1885-06-20		A7 G120
7558	HOWELL, Mary C	31	N21SW	1885-06-20		A7 G120
7560	" "	31	N22SW	1885-06-20		A7 G120
3462	" "	31	NWSE	1885-06-20		A7 G120
3463	HUDLOW, Alfred W	12	NESE	1885-02-25		A7
3465	HUTCHINS, George W	12	E½NW	1890-06-06		A7
3464	" "	12	W½NE	1890-06-06		A7
7565	INGRAM, Andrew J	4	3NW	1888-12-06		A7
7564	" "	4	2NW	1888-12-06		A7
3466	JOHNS, James A	5	SWSW	1881-04-09		A7
3467	JOHNS, John F	18	NENE	1870-11-01		A1
3468	" "	7	SWNE	1875-09-10		A7
3469	" "	7	N½SE	1875-09-10		A7
3470	" "	8	SWNW	1872-11-15		A1
3471	JOHNS, Richard C	17	NWNW	1889-01-12		A7 G132
3472	" "	7	S½SE	1889-01-12		A7 G132
3473	" "	8	SWSW	1889-01-12		A7 G132
3474	JOHNS, Susan J	17	NWNW	1889-01-12		A7 G132
3475	" "	7	S½SE	1889-01-12		A7 G132
3476	" "	8	SWSW	1889-01-12		A7 G132
3477	JOHNS, William A	7	NWNE	1892-03-07		A7
3480	JOHNSON, James	21	SWSW	1859-09-01		A1
3478	" "	21	NESW	1858-04-01		A1
3479	" "	21	SWNE	1859-01-01		A1
3481	JOHNSON, James E	21	SESW	1875-02-15		A7
3482	JOHNSON, Woodlief T	22	NENW	1866-09-01		A1

ID	Individual in Patent	Sec.	Sec. Part	Date Issued	Other Counties	For More Info . . .
3483	JOHNSTON, John P	30	E½SE	1904-11-22		A1
3484	" "	30	E½NE	1904-11-22		A1
3485	JOHNSTON, Nancy F	20	E½SW	1888-12-06		A7
3486	" "	20	W½SE	1888-12-06		A7
3487	JOHNSTON, William	17	SE	1888-12-08		A7
3488	JONES, Benjamin	13	S½SE	1878-06-24		A7
3489	KIDWELL, Sanford E	17	SW	1892-06-10		A7
3490	KING, Wilsey P	5	SESW	1860-05-02		A6
3491	" "	8	NENW	1860-05-02		A6
3492	KINKEAD, Samuel A	25	SWSW	1893-09-08		A7
3494	" "	36	SENW	1893-09-08		A7
3493	" "	36	N½NW	1893-09-08		A7
3496	KISINGER, Tilmon H	30	NWSE	1892-03-07		A7
7552	" "	30	N21NW	1892-03-07		A7
3495	" "	30	W½NE	1892-03-07		A7
3498	LANGSTON, Caleb	28	SENW	1874-01-10		A7
3499	" "	28	N½SW	1874-01-10		A7
3497	" "	28	SWNE	1874-01-10		A7
3500	LAUGHERY, Charles H	34	NENE	1892-03-07		A7
3502	" "	35	N½NW	1892-03-07		A7
3501	" "	35	SENW	1892-03-07		A7
7550	LEWIS, John R	3	W23NW	1877-08-01		A7
7577	" "	4	W23NE	1877-08-01		A7
7572	" "	4	W22NE	1877-08-01		A7
7547	LEWIS, John T	3	W22NW	1870-10-15		A1
7569	" "	4	E23NE	1861-02-09		A1
7567	" "	4	E21NW	1869-10-15		A1
7548	LEWIS, Queen E	3	W23NW	1877-08-01		A7
7576	" "	4	W23NE	1877-08-01		A7
7573	" "	4	W22NE	1877-08-01		A7
3504	MACLAIN, Thomas B	27	E½NW	1893-04-29		A7
3503	" "	27	SWNE	1893-04-29		A7
7516	MCCOMB, George H	1	1NW	1892-03-07		A7
7521	" "	1	W22NW	1892-03-07		A7
3506	MILLER, Alexander	12	S½SE	1871-11-01		A7
3507	" "	13	NWNE	1888-05-07		A1
3508	MILLER, Jacob	14	E½SW	1891-06-09		A7
3509	" "	14	E½NW	1891-06-09		A7
3510	MILLER, Jacob F	29	W½SW	1892-12-09		A7
3511	MILLER, John F	34	NESE	1859-01-01		A1
3512	MONKS, F M	32	NWSW	1869-07-01		A1
3513	MONTGOMERY, James R	27	NESE	1888-07-17		A1
3516	" "	27	NESW	1888-12-06		A7
3515	" "	27	NWSE	1888-12-06		A7
3514	" "	27	S½SE	1888-12-06		A7
3517	ORVIS, Charles W	14	SWNW	1893-12-21		A7
3518	" "	15	SENE	1893-12-21		A7
7568	OSBORN, Queen E	4	E22NE	1896-09-29		A7
3519	OSBORN, Winfield S	2	W½SW	1878-03-20		A7
3521	OVERMAN, Jacob N	3	N½SE	1873-11-01		A7
3522	" "	3	SWSE	1873-11-01		A7
3520	" "	3	SESW	1873-11-01		A7
3523	PARSONS, William C	25	SE	1890-01-10		A7
3525	PEARCE, Jackson	10	E½SW	1889-05-06		A1
3524	" "	10	W½SE	1889-05-06		A1
3526	" "	15	NENW	1885-12-19		A1
3527	PEARCE, William J	10	SENW	1890-06-06		A7
3528	" "	10	S½NE	1890-06-06		A7
3529	" "	10	NESE	1890-06-06		A7
3531	PENCE, Triplett	24	S½SW	1881-10-06		A7
3530	" "	24	NWSE	1883-08-13		A1
3534	" "	24	NESW	1886-10-29		A1
3533	" "	24	SWSE	1881-10-06		A7
3532	" "	24	NWSW	1881-10-06		A7
3537	PENCE, Upson	25	W½NW	1890-10-11		A7
3536	" "	25	NENW	1890-10-11		A7
3535	" "	25	NWNE	1890-10-11		A7
7539	PERKINS, James B	3	1NW	1889-06-22		A7
7545	" "	3	W21NE	1889-06-22		A7
7566	" "	4	E21NE	1889-06-22		A7
3538	PORTER, Lorenzo D	10	W½SW	1888-12-08		A7
3539	" "	9	E½SE	1888-12-08		A7
3540	PORTER, Thomas	15	NESE	1892-01-05		A7

ID	Individual in Patent	Sec.	Sec. Part	Date Issued	Other Counties	For More Info . . .
3542	PORTER, Thomas (Cont'd)	15	S½SE	1892-01-05		A7
3541	" "	15	SESW	1892-01-05		A7
3543	PRITCHETT, George H	23	NENE	1892-03-07		A7
3545	" "	24	SWNW	1892-03-07		A7
3544	" "	24	N½NW	1892-03-07		A7
3546	REED, George W	27	SENE	1881-10-06		A7
3547	" "	27	N½NE	1881-10-06		A7
7563	REEVES, Jesse	31	S22SW	1859-01-01		A1
7562	" "	31	S21SW	1859-09-01		A1
3548	REIGER, John A	33	N½SE	1882-09-30		A1
3549	RICE, Nancy	32	N½NE	1889-01-12		A7
7520	RICHARDSON, John G	1	E23NW	1876-07-25		A7
7523	" "	1	W23NW	1885-07-27		A7
7518	" "	1	E22NW	1876-07-25		A7
7522	" "	1	W23NE	1885-07-27		A7
3550	RICHARDSON, Thomas N	14	W½SW	1890-01-10		A7
3551	RIGGS, James C	4	SWSE	1891-05-05		A7
3552	" "	9	NWNE	1891-05-05		A7
3553	RIGGS, Okey	4	E½SE	1888-12-08		A7
3554	" "	4	NWSE	1888-12-08		A7
3555	" "	9	NENW	1888-12-08		A7
3556	RIGGS, Owen R	25	NENE	1890-10-11		A7
3558	ROYSE, Daniel	14	N½SE	1892-06-21		A7
3557	" "	14	S½NE	1892-06-21		A7
7530	RUTLEDGE, James	18	S22SW	1894-11-30		A7
7533	" "	19	N22NW	1894-11-30		A7
3559	RUTLEDGE, Lewis	18	E½SE	1893-12-19		A7
7534	RUTLEDGE, Rutha	19	N22SW	1896-08-28		A7
7537	" "	19	S22NW	1896-08-28		A7
3560	SEAY, Josiah	31	SESE	1859-01-01		A1
3561	SHARP, John	15	NENE	1884-03-10		A1
3562	SKINNER, Thomas W	36	S½NE	1888-12-08		A7
3563	SMITH, Daniel	29	NWNE	1875-02-15		A7
3564	SMITH, Joab	10	N½NE	1890-11-13		A7
3565	" "	3	SESE	1890-11-13		A7
7524	SMITH, Oney	18	2NW	1878-11-30		A7
7527	" "	18	N22SW	1878-11-30		A7
3566	SMITH, Orlena	33	E½NE	1888-12-04		A7 G171
3567	" "	34	SWNW	1888-12-04		A7 G171
3568	" "	34	NWSW	1888-12-04		A7 G171
3569	SMITH, Philip	33	E½NE	1888-12-04		A7 G171
3571	" "	34	SWNW	1888-12-04		A7 G171
3570	" "	34	NWSW	1888-12-04		A7 G171
3572	SPENCER, Alfred	11	W½SE	1889-01-12		A7
3573	" "	11	E½SW	1889-01-12		A7
7570	STEPHENS, Robert A	4	W21NE	1901-03-23		A7
3574	STEWARD, Robert	15	NWNW	1893-06-13		A7
3575	" "	15	SWSW	1893-06-13		A7
3576	SUMMERS, John	2	E½SE	1860-11-12		A6
7535	SUMMERS, Samuel F	19	S21NW	1906-05-01		A7
7532	" "	19	N21SW	1906-05-01		A7
3577	SUMMERS, Walter L	13	NWSW	1886-11-19		A1
3578	" "	13	S½SW	1886-11-19		A1
3579	" "	14	SESE	1886-11-19		A1
3580	SWIFT, Clara C	11	SESE	1893-06-13		A7 G176
3581	" "	14	N½NE	1893-06-13		A7 G176
3582	SWIFT, Franklin B	11	SESE	1893-06-13		A7 G176
3583	" "	14	N½NE	1893-06-13		A7 G176
7557	TABOR, George W	30	S22SW	1892-03-07		A7
7551	" "	30	1SW	1883-06-30		A7
3584	" "	30	SWSE	1892-03-07		A7
3585	TARWATER, James H	19	SESE	1892-12-09		A7
3586	" "	20	W½SW	1892-12-09		A7
3587	TAYLOR, Church B	4	SWSW	1901-07-09		A7
3588	" "	5	SESE	1901-07-09		A7
7581	TAYLOR, Dave E	6	3NW	1915-04-12		A7
3590	THOMAS, Lewis G	36	S½SW	1897-08-16		A7
3589	" "	36	SWSE	1897-08-16		A7
3591	THRASHER, Lucius B	35	NESE	1890-01-10		A7
3592	" "	36	SWNW	1890-01-10		A7
3593	" "	36	N½SW	1890-01-10		A7
7528	TULL, Tubman A	18	S21NW	1900-11-12		A7
7579	TURNER, John W	6	2NW	1902-10-11		A7

ID	Individual in Patent	Sec.	Sec. Part	Date Issued	Other Counties	For More Info . . .
7585	TURNER, William F	6	N21SW	1898-10-04		A7
7586	" "	6	N22SW	1898-10-04		A7
7578	" "	6	1NW	1898-10-04		A7
3594	UITTS, Johnson R	33	SESW	1886-10-29		A1
7536	UTLEY, John H	19	S21SW	1898-12-01		A7
7538	" "	19	S22SW	1898-12-01		A7
7553	" "	30	N22NW	1898-12-01		A7
3595	UTLEY, William H	29	SWNE	1888-12-08		A7
3596	WALKER, George T	27	W½NW	1889-01-12		A7
3597	" "	28	E½NE	1889-01-12		A7
3598	WATKINS, George W	28	NWSE	1900-02-02		A7
3600	WEBSTER, Tilman V	19	SWSE	1888-11-27		A7
3599	" "	19	SWNE	1888-11-27		A7
3601	" "	19	N½SE	1888-11-27		A7
3602	WEEKS, Noah	8	N½SW	1890-06-06		A7
3603	" "	8	SWNE	1890-06-06		A7
3604	" "	8	SENW	1890-06-06		A7
3605	WELLS, John	32	SENE	1882-09-30		A1
3606	" "	33	SWNW	1882-09-30		A1
3607	" "	33	S½SE	1883-08-13		A1
3608	WELLS, Samuel	24	E½SE	1875-02-15		A7
3609	WIDENER, Charles A	23	W½NE	1892-09-09		A7
3610	" "	23	E½NW	1892-09-09		A7
3611	WIGGINS, Samuel H	22	SWNE	1882-05-10		A1
3612	WILLIAMS, William A	33	W½NE	1892-01-20		A7
3613	" "	33	E½NW	1892-01-20		A7
7541	WINSTON, Sue F	3	E21NE	1894-11-22		A1
7542	" "	3	E22NE	1894-11-22		A1
7590	WOOD, James N	6	W22NE	1903-08-25		A7
7580	" "	6	3NE	1903-08-25		A7
7589	" "	6	W21NE	1903-08-25		A7
3615	WOODRING, James S	25	E½SW	1894-12-17		A7
3616	" "	25	SENW	1894-12-17		A7
3618	WOODROME, Barton C	35	S½SW	1874-01-10		A7
3620	" "	35	SWNW	1874-01-10		A7
3617	" "	35	NESW	1884-03-10		A1
3619	" "	35	NWSW	1874-01-10		A7
3621	WRIGHT, Emily	27	W½SW	1889-01-12		A7 G21
3622	" "	28	E½SE	1889-01-12		A7 G21
3623	WRIGHT, Willis M	31	NESE	1859-09-01		A1
3624	" "	32	SWSW	1860-09-01		A1
3625	" "	32	SESW	1878-04-05		A7
3626	YATES, James K	26	N½NE	1892-03-07		A7

Patent Map

T24-N R9-W
5th PM 24-N 9-W Meridian

Map Group 14

Township Statistics

Parcels Mapped	:	360
Number of Patents	:	206
Number of Individuals	:	187
Patentees Identified	:	181
Number of Surnames	:	134
Multi-Patentee Parcels	:	13
Oldest Patent Date	:	4/15/1853
Most Recent Patent	:	11/25/1910
Block/Lot Parcels	:	72
Cities and Town	:	0
Cemeteries	:	4

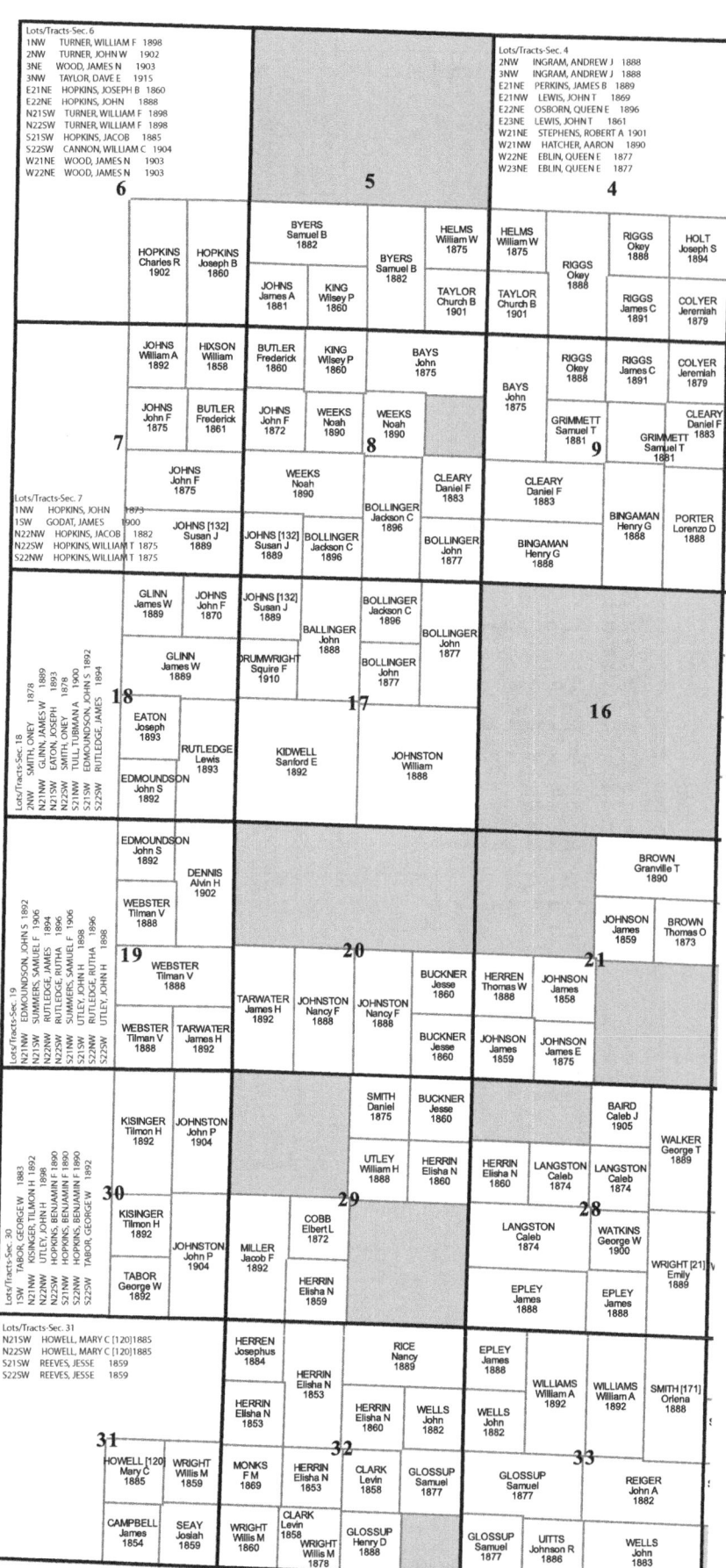

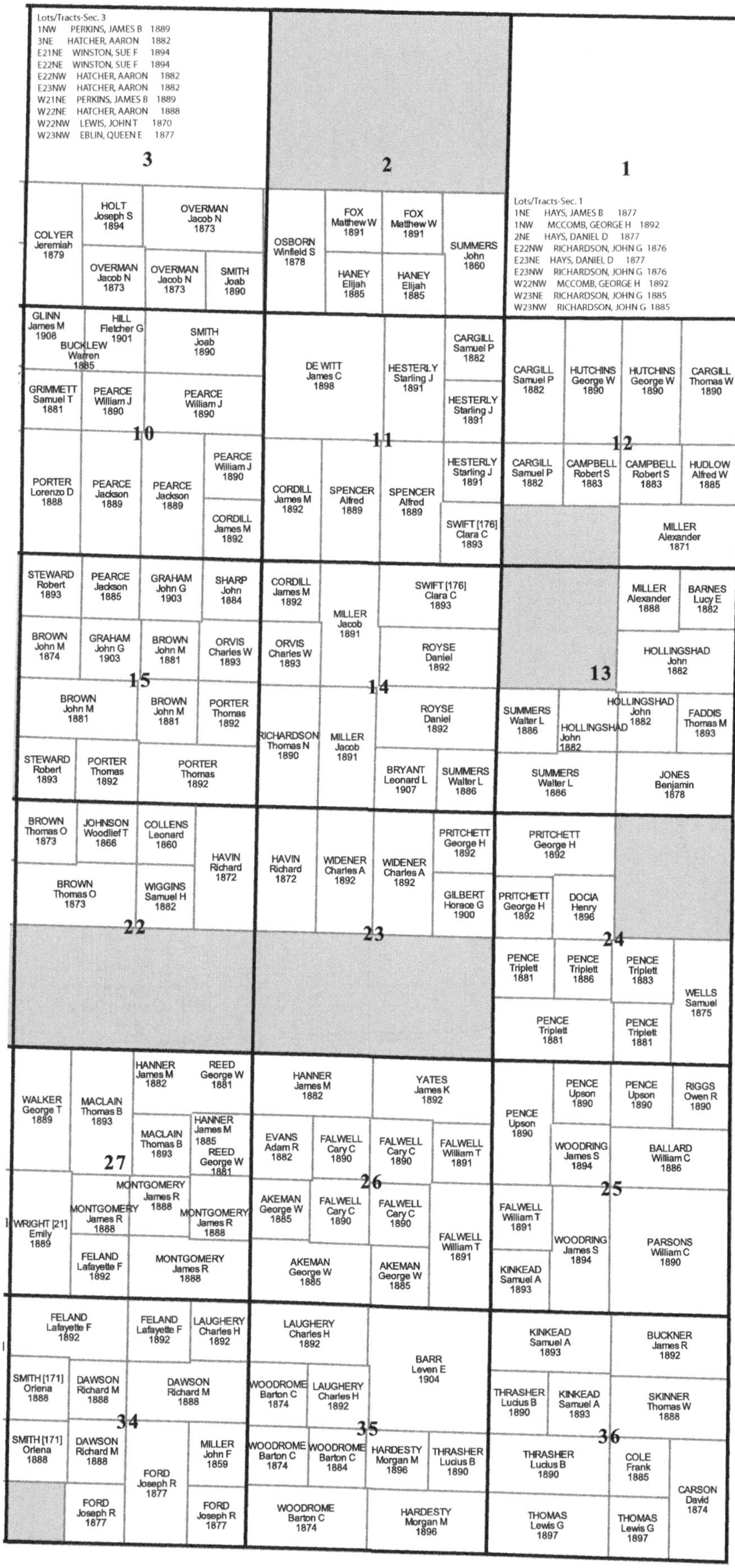

Lots/Tracts-Sec. 3

1NW	PERKINS, JAMES B	1889
3NE	HATCHER, AARON	1882
E21NE	WINSTON, SUE F	1894
E22NE	WINSTON, SUE F	1894
E22NW	HATCHER, AARON	1882
E23NW	HATCHER, AARON	1882
W21NE	PERKINS, JAMES B	1889
W22NE	HATCHER, AARON	1888
W22NW	LEWIS, JOHN T	1870
W23NW	EBLIN, QUEEN E	1877

3

2

1

Lots/Tracts-Sec. 1

1NE	HAYS, JAMES B	1877
1NW	MCCOMB, GEORGE H	1892
2NE	HAYS, DANIEL D	1877
E22NW	RICHARDSON, JOHN G	1876
E23NE	HAYS, DANIEL D	1877
E23NW	RICHARDSON, JOHN G	1876
W22NW	MCCOMB, GEORGE H	1892
W23NE	RICHARDSON, JOHN G	1885
W23NW	RICHARDSON, JOHN G	1885

Section 3 (area)

COLYER Jeremiah 1879

HOLT Joseph S 1894

OVERMAN Jacob N 1873

OVERMAN Jacob N 1873

OVERMAN Jacob N 1873

SMITH Joab 1890

Section 2 (area)

OSBORN Winfield S 1878

FOX Mathew W 1891

FOX Mathew W 1891

SUMMERS John 1860

HANEY Elijah 1885

HANEY Elijah 1885

Section 10

GLINN James M 1908

HILL Fletcher G 1901

BUCKLEW Warren 1885

SMITH Joab 1890

GRIMMETT Samuel T 1881

PEARCE William J 1890

PEARCE William J 1890

PEARCE William J 1890

PORTER Lorenzo D 1888

PEARCE Jackson 1889

PEARCE Jackson 1889

Section 11

DE WITT James C 1898

HESTERLY Starling J 1891

CORDILL James M 1892

SPENCER Alfred 1889

SPENCER Alfred 1889

CORDILL James M 1892

Section 12

CARGILL Samuel P 1882

CARGILL Samuel P 1882

HUTCHINS George W 1890

HUTCHINS George W 1890

CARGILL Thomas W 1890

HESTERLY Starling J 1891

HESTERLY Starling J 1891

CARGILL Samuel P 1882

CAMPBELL Robert S 1883

CAMPBELL Robert S 1883

HUDLOW Alfred W 1885

SWIFT [176] Clara C 1893

MILLER Alexander 1871

Section 15

STEWARD Robert 1893

PEARCE Jackson 1885

GRAHAM John G 1903

SHARP John 1884

BROWN John M 1874

GRAHAM John G 1903

BROWN John M 1881

ORVIS Charles W 1893

BROWN John M 1881

BROWN John M 1881

PORTER Thomas 1892

STEWARD Robert 1893

PORTER Thomas 1892

PORTER Thomas 1892

Section 14

CORDILL James M 1892

MILLER Jacob 1891

ORVIS Charles W 1893

SWIFT [176] Clara C 1893

ROYSE Daniel 1892

RICHARDSON Thomas N 1890

MILLER Jacob 1891

ROYSE Daniel 1892

BRYANT Leonard L 1907

SUMMERS Walter L 1886

Section 13

MILLER Alexander 1888

BARNES Lucy E 1882

HOLLINGSHAD John 1882

SUMMERS Walter L 1886

HOLLINGSHAD John 1882

HOLLINGSHAD John 1882

FADDIS Thomas M 1893

SUMMERS Walter L 1886

JONES Benjamin 1878

Section 22

BROWN Thomas O 1873

JOHNSON Woodlief T 1866

COLLENS Leonard 1860

HAVIN Richard 1872

BROWN Thomas O 1873

WIGGINS Samuel H 1882

Section 23

HAVIN Richard 1872

WIDENER Charles A 1892

WIDENER Charles A 1892

GILBERT Horace G 1900

Section 24

PRITCHETT George H 1892

PRITCHETT George H 1892

PRITCHETT George H 1892

DOCIA Henry 1896

PENCE Triplett 1881

PENCE Triplett 1886

PENCE Triplett 1883

WELLS Samuel 1875

PENCE Triplett 1881

PENCE Triplett 1881

Section 27

WALKER George T 1889

MACLAIN Thomas B 1893

HANNER James M 1882

REED George W 1881

MACLAIN Thomas B 1893

HANNER James M 1885

REED George W 1881

MONTGOMERY James R 1888

MONTGOMERY James R 1888

MONTGOMERY James R 1888

WRIGHT [21] Emily 1889

FELAND Lafayette F 1892

MONTGOMERY James R 1888

Section 26

HANNER James M 1882

YATES James K 1892

EVANS Adam R 1882

FALWELL Cary C 1890

FALWELL Cary C 1890

FALWELL William T 1891

AKEMAN George W 1885

FALWELL Cary C 1890

FALWELL Cary C 1890

FALWELL William T 1891

AKEMAN George W 1885

AKEMAN George W 1885

Section 25

PENCE Upson 1890

PENCE Upson 1890

PENCE Upson 1890

RIGGS Owen R 1890

WOODRING James S 1894

BALLARD William C 1886

FALWELL William T 1891

WOODRING James S 1894

PARSONS William C 1890

KINKEAD Samuel A 1893

Section 34

FELAND Lafayette F 1892

FELAND Lafayette F 1892

LAUGHERY Charles H 1892

SMITH [171] Orlena 1888

DAWSON Richard M 1888

DAWSON Richard M 1888

SMITH [171] Orlena 1888

DAWSON Richard M 1888

FORD Joseph R 1877

FORD Joseph R 1877

Section 35

LAUGHERY Charles H 1892

BARR Leven E 1904

WOODROME Barton C 1874

LAUGHERY Charles H 1892

MILLER John F 1859

WOODROME Barton C 1874

WOODROME Barton C 1884

HARDESTY Morgan M 1896

THRASHER Lucius B 1890

WOODROME Barton C 1874

HARDESTY Morgan M 1896

Section 36

KINKEAD Samuel A 1893

BUCKNER James R 1892

THRASHER Lucius B 1890

KINKEAD Samuel A 1893

SKINNER Thomas W 1888

THRASHER Lucius B 1890

COLE Frank 1885

CARSON David 1874

THOMAS Lewis G 1897

THOMAS Lewis G 1897

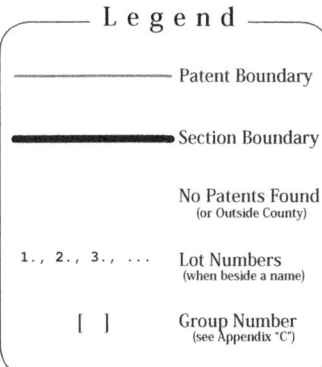

Helpful Hints

1. This Map's INDEX can be found on the preceding pages.

2. Refer to Map "C" to see where this Township lies within Howell County, Missouri.

3. Numbers within square brackets [ ] denote a multi-patentee land parcel (multi-owner). Refer to Appendix "C" for a full list of members in this group.

4. Areas that look to be crowded with Patentees usually indicate multiple sales of the same parcel (Re-issues) or Overlapping parcels. See this Township's Index for an explanation of these and other circumstances that might explain "odd" groupings of Patentees on this map.

Legend

— Patent Boundary

━ Section Boundary

No Patents Found (or Outside County)

1., 2., 3., ... Lot Numbers (when beside a name)

[ ] Group Number (see Appendix "C")

Scale: Section = 1 mile X 1 mile (generally, with some exceptions)

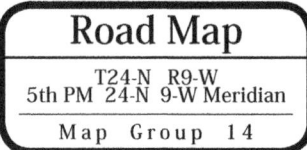

Road Map

T24-N R9-W
5th PM 24-N 9-W Meridian

Map Group 14

Cities & Towns
None

Cemeteries
Blue Mound Cemetery
Lone Pine Cemetery
New Liberty Cemetery
Pleasant Hill Cemetery

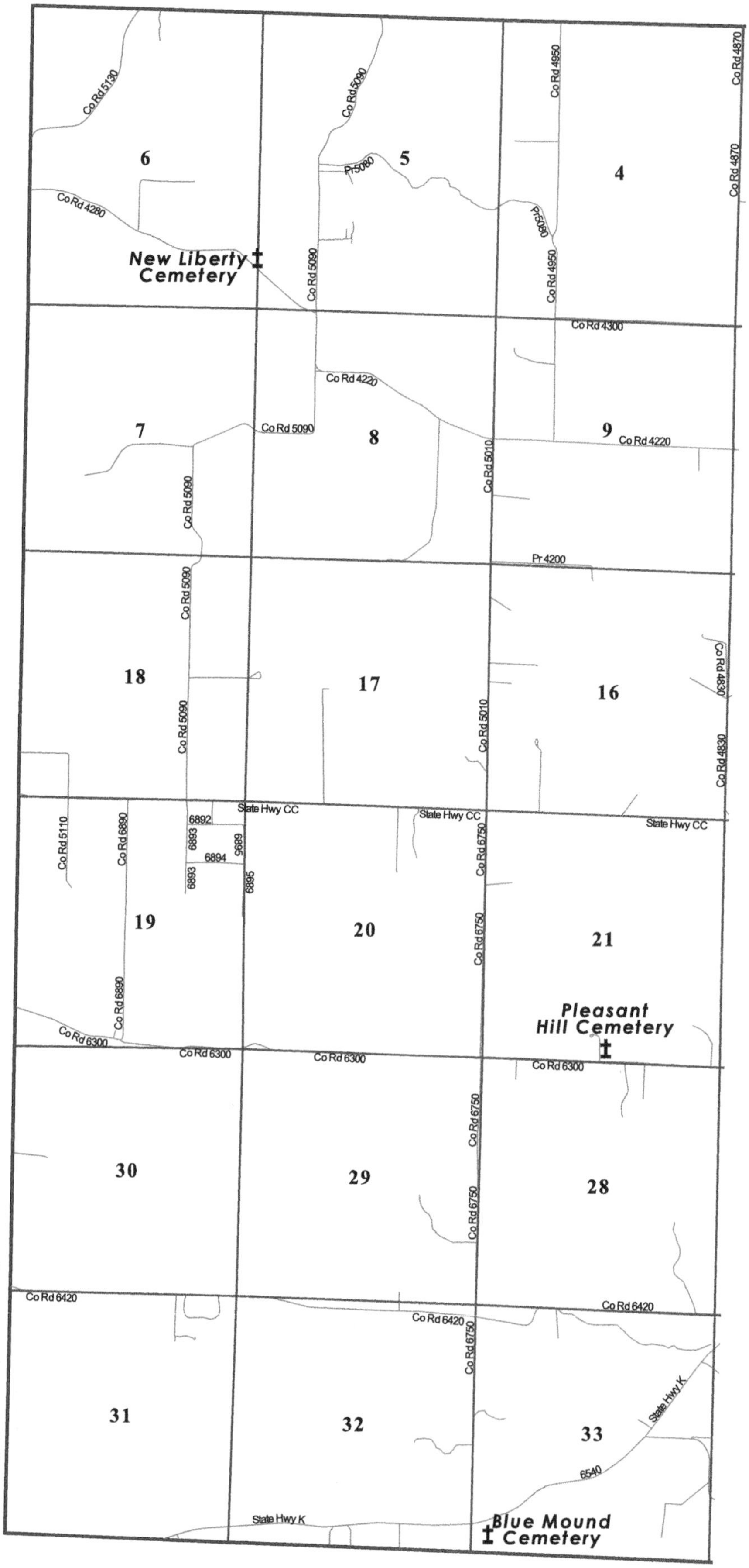

6
Co Rd 5730
Co Rd 4280

5
Co Rd 5090
Pr 5080
Pr 5060
Co Rd 5090

4
Co Rd 4950
Co Rd 4870
Co Rd 4870
Co Rd 4950

New Liberty Cemetery

Co Rd 4300

7
Co Rd 5090

8
Co Rd 4220
Co Rd 5090
Co Rd 5010

9
Co Rd 4220

Pr 4200

18
Co Rd 5090
Co Rd 5090

17

16
Co Rd 5010
Co Rd 4830
Co Rd 4830

State Hwy CC
Co Rd 5110
Co Rd 6890
6892
6893
6894
6893
6889
6894
6885
State Hwy CC
Co Rd 6750
State Hwy CC

19

20
Co Rd 6750

21
Co Rd 6750

Pleasant Hill Cemetery

Co Rd 6890
Co Rd 6300
Co Rd 6300
Co Rd 6300
Co Rd 6300

30

29

28
Co Rd 6750
Co Rd 6750

Co Rd 6420
Co Rd 6420
Co Rd 6420
Co Rd 6750

31

32

33
State Hwy K
6540

State Hwy K
Blue Mound Cemetery

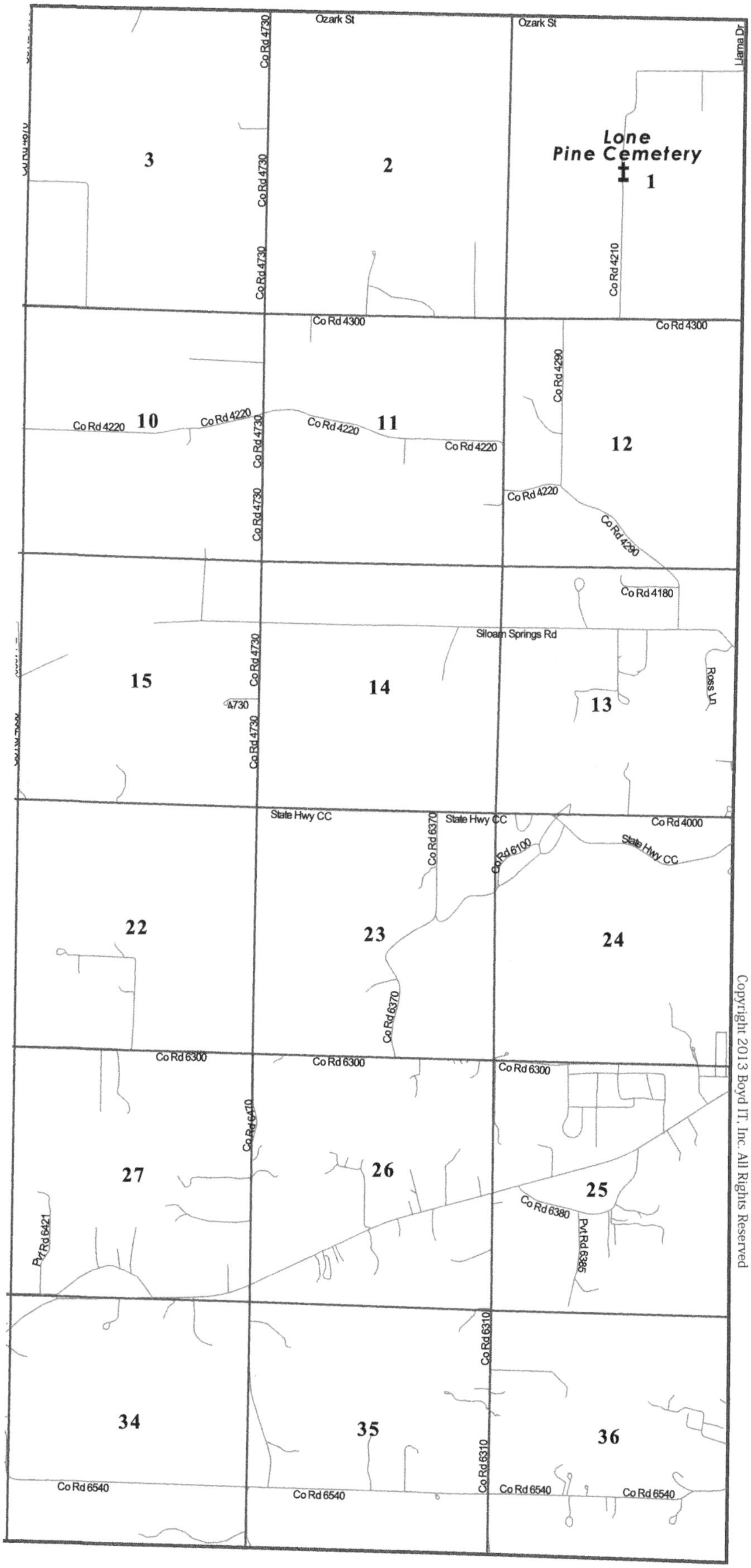

Ozark St

Ozark St

Co Rd 4730

Co Rd 4730

Co Rd 4730

Co Rd 4210

3

2

Lone
Pine Cemetery

1

Co Rd 4300

Co Rd 4300

Co Rd 4290

Co Rd 4220

10

Co Rd 4220

Co Rd 4220

Co Rd 4730

Co Rd 4220

11

Co Rd 4220

12

Co Rd 4730

Co Rd 4220

Co Rd 4280

Co Rd 4180

Co Rd 4730

Siloam Springs Rd

Ross Ln

15

A730

14

13

Co Rd 4730

State Hwy CC

State Hwy CC

Co Rd 4000

Co Rd 6370

Co Rd 6100

State Hwy CC

22

23

24

Co Rd 6370

Co Rd 6300

Co Rd 6300

Co Rd 6300

Co Rd 6410

27

26

25

Co Rd 6380

Pvt Rd 6385

Pvt Rd 6421

Co Rd 6310

34

35

36

Co Rd 6540

Co Rd 6540

Co Rd 6540

Co Rd 6540

Co Rd 6310

Helpful Hints

1. This road map has a number of uses, but primarily it is to help you: a) find the present location of land owned by your ancestors (at least the general area), b) find cemeteries and city-centers, and c) estimate the route/roads used by Census-takers & tax-assessors.

2. If you plan to travel to Howell County to locate cemeteries or land parcels, please pick up a modern travel map for the area before you do. Mapping old land parcels on modern maps is not as exact a science as you might think. Just the slightest variations in public land survey coordinates, estimates of parcel boundaries, or road-map deviations can greatly alter a map's representation of how a road either does or doesn't cross a particular parcel of land.

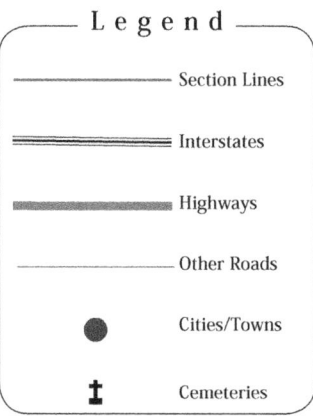

Legend

———————	Section Lines
═══════	Interstates
━━━━━━━	Highways
———————	Other Roads
●	Cities/Towns
⚱	Cemeteries

Scale: Section = 1 mile X 1 mile
(generally, with some exceptions)

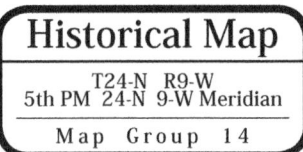

Historical Map

T24-N R9-W
5th PM 24-N 9-W Meridian

Map Group 14

Cities & Towns
None

Cemeteries
Blue Mound Cemetery
Lone Pine Cemetery
New Liberty Cemetery
Pleasant Hill Cemetery

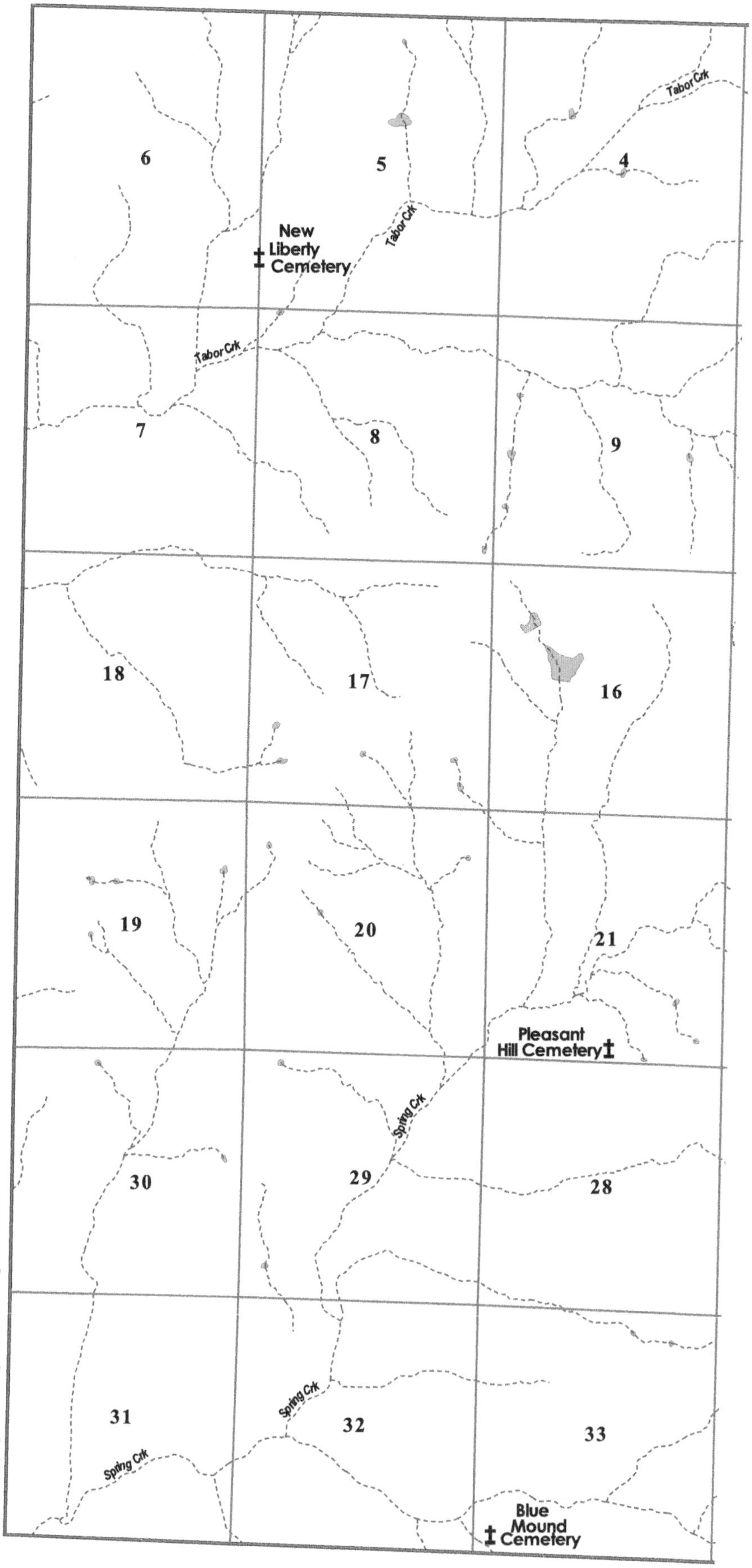

6

5

4

Tabor Crk

New
Liberty
Cemetery

Tabor Crk

7

Tabor Crk

8

9

18

17

16

19

20

21

Pleasant
Hill Cemetery

30

29

Spring Crk

28

31

Spring Crk

32

Spring Crk

33

Blue
Mound
Cemetery

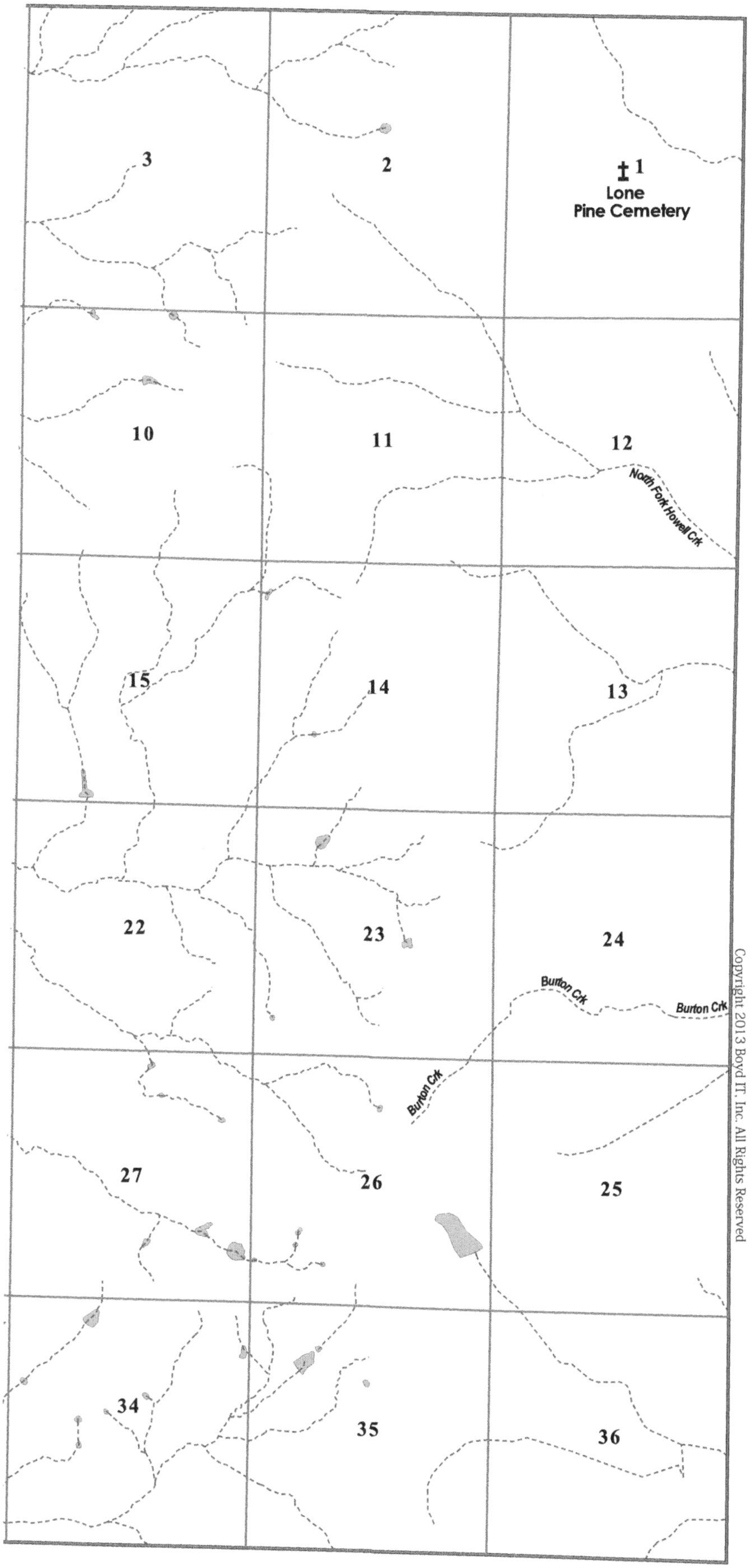

3

2

‡ 1
Lone
Pine Cemetery

10

11

12

North Fork Howell Crk

15

14

13

22

23

24

Burton Crk

Burton Crk

Burton Crk

27

26

25

34

35

36

Copyright 2013 Boyd IT, Inc. All Rights Reserved

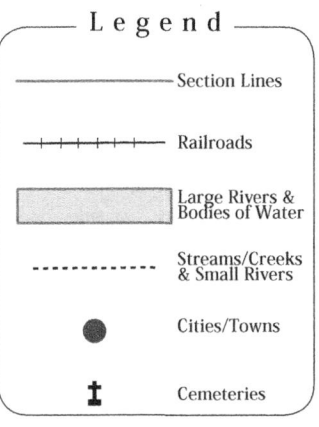

L e g e n d

——————— Section Lines

+++++++ Railroads

▭ Large Rivers & Bodies of Water

- - - - - - Streams/Creeks & Small Rivers

● Cities/Towns

‡ Cemeteries

Scale: Section = 1 mile X 1 mile
(there are some exceptions)

Map Group 15: Index to Land Patents

Township 24-North Range 8-West (5th PM 24-N 8-W)

After you locate an individual in this Index, take note of the Section and Section Part then proceed to the Land Patent map on the pages immediately following. You should have no difficulty locating the corresponding parcel of land.

The "For More Info" Column will lead you to more information about the underlying Patents. See the *Legend* at right, and the "How to Use this Book" chapter, for more information.

```
┌─────────────────────────────────────────────────────────┐
│                        LEGEND                            │
│            "For More Info . . . " column                 │
│ ───────────────────────────────────────────────         │
│ A = Authority (Legislative Act, See Appendix "A")        │
│ B = Block or Lot (location in Section unknown)           │
│ C = Cancelled Patent                                     │
│ F = Fractional Section                                   │
│ G = Group  (Multi-Patentee Patent, see Appendix "C")     │
│ V = Overlaps another Parcel                              │
│ R = Re-Issued (Parcel patented more than once)           │
│                                                          │
│ (A & G items require you to look in the Appendixes referred │
│ to above. All other Letter-designations followed by a number │
│ require you to locate line-items in this index that possess │
│ the ID number found after the letter).                   │
└─────────────────────────────────────────────────────────┘
```

ID	Individual in Patent	Sec.	Sec. Part	Date Issued	Other Counties	For More Info . . .
3627	ALCORN, Joshua	29	NWSE	1888-11-27		A7
3629	" "	29	S½SE	1888-11-27		A7
3628	" "	29	NESW	1888-11-27		A7
3630	ANDREWS, Henry J	10	SESW	1888-12-08		A7
3632	" "	15	SWNE	1888-12-08		A7
3631	" "	15	E½NW	1888-12-08		A7
3639	AUSTIN, Alexander	23	SWSW	1859-03-03		A8
3635	" "	23	SWSE	1860-05-02		A6
3637	" "	23	SESW	1860-05-02		A6
3641	" "	26	NWNW	1859-03-03		A8
7657	BACON, Daniel E	31	N22SW	1859-09-01		A1
3643	BACON, Joel W	14	W½NE	1874-01-10		A7
3645	BACON, William	7	S½SE	1894-05-18		A7
3644	" "	7	NWSE	1894-05-18		A7
3646	" "	8	SWSW	1894-05-18		A7
7628	BACON, William H	2	2NW	1874-01-10		A7
7695	BARNES, James M	7	S21SW	1889-06-22		A7
7652	BATEY, John W	30	S21NW	1874-01-10		A7
3647	" "	30	W½NE	1874-01-10		A7
3648	BINGAMAN, Peter R	19	SESE	1853-08-01		A1
3649	" "	19	SWSE	1859-01-01		A1
3650	" "	20	SWSE	1859-01-01		A1
3651	" "	20	NWSW	1859-01-01		A1
3652	" "	20	SWSW	1860-08-01		A1
3653	" "	30	NENE	1860-08-01		A1
3654	BINGAMAN, William R	19	N½SE	1889-01-12		A7
7621	" "	19	N21SW	1889-01-12		A7
3655	BINGERMAN, Peter	20	SESE	1854-11-15		A1
3656	BOGARD, William C	29	NESE	1891-08-24		A1
7645	BOWLES, Frances R	3	W23NE	1893-09-23		A1
7641	" "	3	E23NE	1893-09-23		A1
7688	BRANNOCK, Amanda E	6	W23NE	1888-12-08		A7
7678	" "	6	E22NW	1888-12-08		A7
7686	" "	6	W22NE	1888-12-08		A7
3657	BRIDGES, Sarah L	27	SESE	1879-12-15		A7 G23
3658	" "	34	NENE	1879-12-15		A7 G23
3659	" "	35	N½NW	1879-12-15		A7 G23
3660	BROWN, Elizabeth	26	SENW	1856-06-16		A8 G24
3661	BROWN, Harden	26	SENW	1856-06-16		A8 G24
3663	BUCK, Phoebe A	10	W½SW	1875-02-15		A7 G26
3664	" "	9	E½SE	1875-02-15		A7 G26
3665	BUCK, W G	10	W½SW	1875-02-15		A7 G26
3666	" "	9	E½SE	1875-02-15		A7 G26
3668	BUCK, William Z	35	NWNE	1860-08-01		A1
3667	" "	35	E½SE	1860-09-10		A6
3669	BURGESS, Nehemiah S	28	NWNW	1879-12-15		A7

ID	Individual in Patent	Sec.	Sec. Part	Date Issued	Other Counties	For More Info . . .
3670	BUTCHER, George	26	NESW	1854-11-15		A1
3672	" "	36	SENE	1859-01-01		A1
3671	" "	36	NESE	1856-10-10		A1
3673	" "	36	SWSE	1859-09-01		A1
3675	CAMPBELL, George W	6	S½SE	1889-01-12		A7 G33
3674	" "	6	NWSE	1889-01-12		A7 G33
7684	" "	6	S21SW	1889-01-12		A7 G33
7683	CAMPBELL, Harriett	6	S21SW	1889-01-12		A7 G33
3677	" "	6	S½SE	1889-01-12		A7 G33
3676	" "	6	NWSE	1889-01-12		A7 G33
7679	CAMPBELL, John V	6	E23NE	1891-06-09		A7
7677	" "	6	E22NE	1891-06-09		A7
3678	CAMPBELL, William H	15	SWSW	1859-09-01		A1
3680	" "	21	N½SW	1858-04-01		A8
3679	" "	21	SWSW	1859-01-01		A1
3681	" "	22	NWNW	1859-01-01		A1
3682	CARSON, David	35	NWSE	1873-06-05		A1
7616	CARTER, Volney	18	N22SW	1869-07-01		A1
3685	CHASTAIN, William	17	SWSW	1860-05-02		A6
3686	" "	18	SESE	1860-05-02		A6
3687	" "	5	SESW	1860-05-02		A6
3689	" "	8	NENW	1859-09-01		A1
3688	" "	8	NENW	1860-05-02		A6
3690	CLARK, Albert B	12	E½SE	1898-04-06		A7
7685	CLARKE, Madison B	6	S22SW	1892-07-11		A1
3691	COBB, James R	25	N½NW	1877-10-10		A7
3692	" "	26	E½NE	1877-10-10		A7
3693	COFFEE, Collins	25	SWSW	1853-04-15		A1
3695	" "	25	SESW	1857-10-30		A1
3694	" "	25	NWSW	1857-10-30		A1
3696	" "	36	NWNW	1858-04-01		A1
7640	COLE, John W	3	E23NE	1891-02-07		A7
3697	COOK, George N	5	NWSW	1860-09-10		A6 G57
3698	" "	6	NESE	1860-09-10		A6 G57
7675	" "	6	1NE	1860-09-10		A6 G57
3699	COOK, John L	5	NWSW	1860-09-10		A6 G57
3700	" "	6	NESE	1860-09-10		A6 G57
7673	" "	6	1NE	1860-09-10		A6 G57
7620	COPE, Martin R	19	1NW	1891-05-25		A7
7625	" "	19	S22NW	1891-05-25		A7
3701	CORDILL, James W	33	W½SE	1876-05-15		A7
3702	CORDILL, Mary M	35	S½SW	1889-01-12		A7
3703	CRANE, Albert	11	NESW	1885-05-25		A1
3704	" "	11	NWSE	1885-05-25		A1
3706	" "	12	SESW	1885-05-25		A1
3705	" "	12	W½SE	1885-05-25		A1
3707	" "	13	W½SE	1885-07-27		A1
3708	" "	15	SENE	1885-07-27		A1
3709	" "	22	NESE	1885-05-25		A1
3710	" "	30	SENE	1885-05-25		A1
3711	" "	33	SESW	1885-05-25		A1
7634	CRENSHAW, James	2	W22NE	1858-01-15		A1
3713	CRITES, James H	13	SESE	1884-10-11		A1
3715	DANIEL, Randall	32	SWNW	1871-10-20		A1
3716	DAVIDSON, Caroline	26	S½SW	1889-01-12		A7 G63
3720	DAVIDSON, William	26	S½SW	1889-01-12		A7 G63
7606	DAVIS, Solomon	1	E23NW	1859-09-01		A1
7599	DAVIS, William	1	3NE	1859-11-01		A6
3721	DESITS, Malinda D	13	NESE	1884-10-11		A1
3722	DODD, John F	10	E½NE	1889-06-22		A7
3724	DUDLEY, Stephen F W	25	NESW	1882-05-10		A6
3723	" "	25	SENW	1882-05-10		A6
3728	ELLINGTON, William	26	NWSW	1853-10-04		A2 G75
3727	" "	26	SWNW	1853-10-04		A2 G75
3729	" "	27	NESE	1853-10-04		A2 G75
3730	" "	27	SENE	1853-10-04		A2 G75
7690	ELLIS, John A	7	2NW	1877-08-01		A7
7694	" "	7	S21NW	1877-08-01		A7
7671	FARR, Morris	5	2NW	1877-08-01		A7
7670	" "	5	1NW	1877-08-01		A7
3733	FARRIS, Ezrial	35	NENE	1867-08-20		A1
7644	FITZSIMMONS, William C	3	W21NW	1885-06-03		A1
7668	FORD, Oscar H	4	W22NE	1885-03-20		A1

ID	Individual in Patent	Sec.	Sec. Part	Date Issued	Other Counties	For More Info . . .
3736	FOUST, Jacob	15	E½SW	1874-11-20		A1
3737	FRANKLIN, S Y	7	NESE	1877-08-01		A7
3739	" "	8	S½NW	1877-08-01		A7
3738	" "	8	NWSW	1877-08-01		A7
3740	FULLERLOVE, Andrew J	11	NENE	1891-05-05		A7
3741	" "	11	S½NE	1891-05-05		A7
3742	" "	12	SWNW	1891-05-05		A7
3743	GALLAWAY, George W	19	NENE	1869-07-01		A1
3744	GALLOWAY, Charles M	17	NWSW	1885-12-19		A7
3745	GALLOWAY, George W	17	SESW	1860-10-01		A1
3746	" "	19	NENW	1860-10-01		A1
3747	" "	20	NW	1860-05-02		A6
3748	GALLOWAY, James	17	SENW	1874-11-05		A7
7617	GAROUTTE, George L	18	S21NW	1892-03-07		A7
3749	" "	18	SWNE	1892-03-07		A7
7618	" "	18	S22NW	1892-03-07		A7
3752	GOODMILLER, James	28	SENW	1876-01-10		A1
3753	GRIFFITH, Lewis	21	E½SE	1858-04-10		A8 G99
3754	" "	22	NWSE	1860-03-01		A1
3755	" "	22	SWSW	1858-04-10		A8 G99
3756	" "	27	NWNW	1860-03-01		A1
3757	" "	28	NENE	1858-04-10		A8 G99
3760	GRIFFITH, Martin	36	E½NW	1853-11-01		A8 G100
3759	" "	36	NWSE	1853-11-01		A8 G100
3758	" "	36	SWNE	1853-11-01		A8 G100
3762	GRIFFITH, William	35	SWNW	1859-11-01		A6
3761	" "	35	NWSW	1859-11-01		A6
3763	HALE, Orin M	12	N½NW	1901-03-23		A7
3764	HALL, William	36	NWNE	1854-10-02		A8
7653	HALSTEAD, John	30	S22NW	1888-05-07		A1
7669	HARLAN, David B	4	W23NE	1882-05-20		A7
3766	HARVEY, William B	21	E½NE	1860-09-10		A6 G110
3767	" "	22	SWNW	1860-09-10		A6 G110
7676	HAYS, James B	6	1NW	1877-04-05		A7
7681	" "	6	N21SW	1874-06-15		A1
7682	HAYS, William A	6	N22SW	1886-11-19		A1
3770	HERNDON, Catharine	14	SWSW	1860-09-10		A6 G116
3771	" "	14	E½SW	1860-09-10		A6 G116
3778	HOOSE, Lydia	13	W½NW	1884-06-14		A6 G118
3779	" "	13	SWNE	1884-06-14		A6 G118
3777	" "	13	SENW	1884-06-14		A6 G118
3780	HOWELL, George W	20	NWNE	1860-08-01		A1
7605	HOWELL, Jasper N	1	E22NW	1861-04-01		A8
7602	" "	1	E21NW	1861-04-01		A8
3781	" "	14	NENE	1861-08-01		A1
3782	" "	22	NENW	1860-08-01		A1
3783	HOWELL, Josephus M	21	E½NE	1860-09-10		A6 G110
3788	" "	22	NWSW	1859-01-01		A1
3789	" "	22	SESE	1860-03-01		A1
3786	" "	22	SENW	1853-12-01		A1
3785	" "	22	SWSE	1853-04-12		A1
3784	" "	22	E½SW	1853-04-12		A1
3787	" "	22	SWNW	1860-09-10		A6 G110
3790	" "	27	NENW	1859-09-01		A1
3791	HOWELL, Josiah	14	SWSW	1860-09-10		A6 G116
3792	" "	14	E½SW	1860-09-10		A6 G116
3793	" "	25	S½SE	1859-11-01		A6
3794	" "	26	NWSE	1853-04-15		A1
3795	" "	26	E½SE	1853-12-01		A1
3796	" "	36	NENE	1859-11-01		A6
3797	HOWELL, Thomas H	17	SESE	1860-08-01		A1
3798	" "	20	NENE	1908-01-20		A1
3799	" "	21	W½NW	1859-01-01		A1
3800	" "	24	NENE	1853-12-01		A1
3802	HOWELL, Thomas J	21	NWSE	1859-09-01		A1
3801	" "	21	SWSE	1853-12-01		A1
3804	" "	26	NWSW	1853-10-04		A2 G75
3803	" "	26	SWNW	1853-10-04		A2 G75
3806	" "	27	SENE	1853-10-04		A2 G75
3805	" "	27	NESE	1853-10-04		A2 G75
3808	" "	28	NENW	1859-09-01		A1
3807	" "	28	NWNE	1859-01-01		A1
3809	HOWELL, Thomas Jefferson	27	N½NE	1853-11-01		A8

ID	Individual in Patent	Sec.	Sec. Part	Date Issued	Other Counties	For More Info . . .
3812	HOWELL, Wilie	20	NESE	1860-02-15		A6 G121
3811	" "	20	SWNE	1859-09-01		A1
3810	" "	20	SENE	1860-02-15		A6 G121
3813	" "	29	NWNE	1853-12-01		A1
3814	HOWELL, Wilson	29	NENE	1859-09-01		A1
7692	HUDLOW, Alfred W	7	N21SW	1885-02-25		A7
7693	" "	7	N22SW	1885-02-25		A7
7613	HUFFHINES, Jacob	18	N22NW	1860-09-10		A6 G123
3815	" "	18	NWNE	1860-09-10		A6 G123
7611	" "	18	N21NW	1860-09-10		A6 G123
3817	HUNT, Owen B	10	NESW	1892-09-09		A7
3816	" "	10	SENW	1892-09-09		A7
3818	HYNES, E F	28	S½NE	1875-07-20		A7
3819	" "	32	E½NE	1884-02-15		A7
3820	INGOLD, Dobson	10	N½SE	1888-12-04		A7
3821	" "	10	SWNE	1888-12-04		A7
3822	" "	11	NWSW	1888-12-04		A7
3824	INGOLD, William	15	NWSW	1880-11-20		A7
3823	" "	15	SWNW	1880-11-20		A7
3827	JACKSON, Joel J	5	SWSW	1875-07-20		A7
3828	" "	8	NWNW	1875-07-20		A7
3829	JENKINS, Wiliford	4	N½SE	1860-09-10		A6
7666	" "	4	W21NE	1860-09-10		A6
3830	JENKINS, William W	23	NWSW	1893-12-09		A1
3831	" "	23	SWNW	1893-12-09		A1
3833	JOHNSON, James W	27	N½SW	1888-12-08		A7
3834	" "	27	S½NW	1888-12-08		A7
3835	JOHNSON, Levi	26	SWSE	1859-09-01		A1
3836	JOHNSON, William H	27	SWNE	1859-01-01		A1
7619	JONES, Benjamin	18	S22SW	1878-06-24		A7
3841	JONES, James D	17	NWSE	1861-02-01		A1
3837	" "	17	NENW	1859-01-01		A1
3840	" "	17	SWSE	1859-01-01		A1
3839	" "	17	NESW	1859-09-01		A1
3838	" "	17	SWNW	1859-01-01		A1
7660	JONES, Murray	31	S22SW	1860-08-01		A1
3842	JONES, Murrey	29	SWSW	1860-09-10		A6 G133
3843	" "	32	NWNW	1860-09-10		A6 G133
3844	" "	32	SWNE	1860-08-01		A1
7655	JONES, Murry	31	N21SW	1860-08-01		A1
3847	KEISTER, George W	21	E½NE	1860-09-10		A6 G110
3848	" "	22	SWNE	1860-09-10		A6 G110
3849	KEISTER, Martha C	21	E½NE	1860-09-10		A6 G110
3850	" "	22	SWNW	1860-09-10		A6 G110
3851	KEISTER, Mary M	21	E½NE	1860-09-10		A6 G110
3852	" "	22	SWNW	1860-09-10		A6 G110
3853	KEISTER, Susanna	21	E½NE	1860-09-10		A6 G110
3854	" "	22	SWNW	1860-09-10		A6 G110
3855	KELIN, James S	12	NE	1890-10-11		A7
3856	KING, Wilsey P	36	SESW	1860-05-02		A6 G136
3857	" "	36	N½SW	1860-05-02		A6 G136
3860	KNOWLTON, Levi W	13	SENW	1884-06-14		A6 G118
3858	" "	13	W½NW	1884-06-14		A6 G118
3859	" "	13	SWNE	1884-06-14		A6 G118
3861	LAMONS, Henry J	35	NESW	1872-02-05		A1
3864	LARA, John O	10	W½NW	1891-05-05		A7
3862	" "	10	NWNE	1891-05-05		A7
3863	" "	10	NENW	1891-05-05		A7
7636	LE FORCE, John	3	2NE	1876-05-10		A7
7637	" "	3	2NW	1876-05-10		A7
3870	MADDOX, Mary	21	SESW	1853-12-01		A1
3871	MARTIN, Charles T	33	S½NW	1860-05-02		A6
7614	MARTIN, St George	18	N22NW	1860-09-10		A6 G123
3872	" "	18	NWNE	1860-09-10		A6 G123
7610	" "	18	N21NW	1860-09-10		A6 G123
3874	" "	34	SENE	1857-06-15		A8
3873	" "	34	NESE	1857-06-15		A8
3876	" "	34	SENW	1858-12-16		A8
3875	" "	34	SWNE	1858-12-16		A8
7654	MAY, James P	31	1NW	1891-05-25		A7
3877	MCCANNON, Mathew	36	SESE	1853-12-01		A1
7664	MCGEE, Robert D	4	E22NE	1860-09-10		A6
7661	" "	4	E21NE	1860-09-10		A6

ID	Individual in Patent	Sec.	Sec. Part	Date Issued	Other Counties	For More Info . . .
3878	MCKNIGHT, Arabella W	20	SENE	1860-02-15		A6 G121
3879	" "	20	NESE	1860-02-15		A6 G121
3882	MCRIPPEE, Milton	34	SWSE	1860-03-01		A1
3883	MIDDLETON, Alfred	10	S½SE	1882-11-10		A7
3884	" "	15	N½NE	1882-11-10		A7
7696	MILLER, Alexander	7	S22SW	1871-11-01		A7
3885	MILLER, Jesse S	23	E½SE	1890-01-10		A7
3886	" "	23	NWSE	1890-01-10		A7
3887	MONKS, Francis M	21	E½SE	1858-04-10		A8 G99
3888	" "	22	SWSW	1858-04-10		A8 G99
3889	" "	28	NENE	1858-04-10		A8 G99
3893	MONKS, James Q	21	E½SE	1858-04-10		A8 G99
3894	" "	22	SWSW	1858-04-10		A8 G99
3895	" "	28	NENE	1858-04-10		A8 G99
3896	MONKS, Nancy E	28	SWNW	1888-12-08		A7
3897	" "	29	S½NE	1888-12-08		A7
3898	MONKS, William	21	E½SE	1858-04-10		A8 G99
3899	" "	22	SWSW	1858-04-10		A8 G99
3900	" "	28	NENE	1858-04-10		A8 G99
3902	MONTGOMERY, Sarah L	27	SESE	1879-12-15		A7 G23
3903	" "	34	NENE	1879-12-15		A7 G23
3904	" "	35	N½NW	1879-12-15		A7 G23
7622	MOORE, Henry	19	N22NW	1882-09-30		A1
3905	" "	20	NWSE	1891-02-07		A7
3908	MURPHEY, Jane	36	E½NW	1853-11-01		A8 G100
3906	" "	36	SWNE	1853-11-01		A8 G100
3907	" "	36	NWSE	1853-11-01		A8 G100
3912	MUSTION, Alfred	34	SESE	1872-02-05		A1
3913	MUSTION, John W	33	SESE	1876-05-15		A7
3914	" "	34	SWSW	1876-05-15		A7
3915	MUSTION, William D	36	SWSW	1870-05-10		A1
3916	MUSTON, Alfred	34	SWNW	1860-08-01		A1
3918	ODONNELL, Patrick	11	NW	1889-06-22		A7
3919	OLDEN, Benjamin F	21	W½NE	1873-02-01		A7
7639	" "	3	E21NW	1885-03-20		A1
3920	" "	4	S½SE	1885-06-03		A1
3921	" "	9	NESW	1885-03-20		A1
7597	OWINGS, William L	1	2NE	1875-01-06		A7
7596	" "	1	1NE	1875-01-06		A7
3922	PADON, John S	21	E½NW	1874-06-15		A1
3924	PARKS, John S	12	SENW	1898-01-26		A7
3923	" "	12	NESW	1898-01-26		A7
3925	PAUL, Mary V	14	NWSW	1860-05-02		A6 G157
3926	" "	14	SWNW	1860-05-02		A6 G157
3930	PETTIT, D S	18	W½SE	1877-06-04		A7
3931	" "	18	E½SW	1877-06-04		A7
7656	PFENNIGHAUSEN, R W	31	N22NW	1886-11-19		A1
7650	POOL, John	30	N21SW	1861-05-01		A1
7648	" "	30	2	1861-05-01		A1
3932	POWLES, Daniel D	9	W½SE	1882-12-20		A1
3933	RANKIN, Lorin	9	W½SE	1884-11-01		A7 G161
3934	RANKIN, Luther	9	W½SE	1884-11-01		A7 G161
7629	RENFRO, Anna	2	3NW	1877-10-10		A7
3935	RENFROW, William	32	SENW	1884-03-10		A1
3936	RICE, Andrew J	17	NESE	1882-03-30		A7
3937	RICE, James A	14	SE	1890-10-11		A7
7626	RICE, Thomas J	19	S22SW	1873-02-01		A7
7624	" "	19	S21SW	1873-02-01		A7
7649	" "	30	N21NW	1873-02-01		A7
7646	RICHARDSON, Frances R	3	W23NE	1893-09-23		A1
7642	" "	3	E23NW	1893-09-23		A1
3938	RICHARDSON, James C	27	SWSW	1882-03-30		A7
3939	" "	27	W½SE	1882-03-30		A7
3940	" "	32	NESE	1886-01-20		A7
3941	RICHARDSON, Jeremiah	27	SESW	1871-12-06		A7
3942	" "	34	N½NW	1871-12-06		A7
3943	" "	34	NWNE	1871-12-06		A7
7672	RICHARDSON, Thomas S	5	3NW	1891-08-24		A1
7651	RIGGS, Owen R	30	N22NW	1890-10-11		A7
7647	SANDERS, William H	3	W23NW	1893-01-13		A7
7665	" "	4	E23NE	1893-01-13		A7
3945	SCOGGIN, Turpin G	35	SENW	1865-09-01		A6
3944	" "	35	S½NE	1865-09-01		A6

ID	Individual in Patent	Sec.	Sec. Part	Date Issued	Other Counties	For More Info . . .
3946	SCOGGIN, Turpin G (Cont'd)	36	SWNW	1865-09-01		A6
7689	SCRUGGS, Frank	6	W23NW	1891-05-25		A7
7687	" "	6	W22NW	1891-05-25		A7
7632	SEAY, Andrew J	2	E23NE	1860-10-01		A1
7633	SEAY, Collumbus L	2	W21NW	1893-04-29		A7
7607	SEAY, Henry S	1	W21NW	1882-08-30		A7
3947	" "	11	NWNE	1884-03-10		A1
7627	" "	2	1NE	1882-08-30		A7
7630	" "	2	E21NW	1882-08-30		A7
7635	SEAY, Josiah	2	W23NE	1860-10-01		A1
7631	" "	2	E22NE	1860-10-01		A1
3948	" "	33	S½NE	1856-06-16		A8
3949	SEAY, Thomas	29	SESW	1860-08-01		A1
3950	" "	32	NWNE	1860-05-02		A6
3951	" "	32	NENW	1860-05-02		A6
3955	SEIBERLING, Ellen	9	SESW	1882-12-20		A1
3957	SHANKS, George W	11	SWSE	1894-12-17		A7
3956	" "	11	SESW	1894-12-17		A7
7680	SHAW, George	6	E23NW	1896-03-25		A7
3958	SHUTTEE, C H	15	NWNW	1886-01-20		A1
3959	SISSON, Brown	14	NWSW	1860-05-02		A6 G157
3960	" "	14	SWNW	1860-05-02		A6 G157
7659	SKINNER, Thomas W	31	S22NW	1888-12-08		A7
3963	SMITH, Levi	32	SESE	1873-02-01		A7
3964	" "	33	SWSW	1873-02-01		A7
3965	" "	33	N½SW	1873-02-01		A7
3966	SMITH, Oscar	13	SW	1890-10-11		A7
7691	SMITH, Thomas P	7	N21NW	1892-03-07		A7
3968	SMOTHERMAN, Elmira J	33	N½NE	1882-11-10		A7
3967	" "	33	N½NW	1882-11-10		A7
3969	SMOTHERMON, Elbert A	33	NESE	1861-02-09		A1
3970	SOWERS, Calvin	14	SENE	1883-08-13		A1
3973	SPENCE, Nancy	36	N½SW	1860-05-02		A6 G136
3974	" "	36	SESW	1860-05-02		A6 G136
3976	SPRINKEL, Micajah	8	SESW	1883-08-13		A1
3977	STRICKLAND, James E	35	SWSE	1891-08-19		A7
7608	SUMMERS, William	1	W22NW	1882-09-30		A7
7609	" "	1	W23NW	1882-09-30		A7
3978	TAYLOR, Henry A	32	W½SE	1889-01-12		A7
3979	TAYLOR, John A	25	N½NE	1888-09-17		A7
3980	THEOBALD, E S	29	SWSW	1860-09-10		A6 G133
3981	" "	32	NWNW	1860-09-10		A6 G133
3984	TOWNLEY, James W	11	SWSW	1891-05-25		A7
3985	" "	14	NWNW	1891-05-25		A7
3988	TURNER, Richard	5	NESW	1894-12-17		A7
7623	WELLS, Samuel	19	N22SW	1875-02-15		A7
3991	WHATLEY, Charles	13	SENE	1890-10-11		A7
3992	" "	13	NENW	1890-10-11		A7
3990	" "	13	N½NE	1890-10-11		A7
3993	WHITE, Basil G	11	E½SE	1892-06-21		A7
3994	" "	12	W½SW	1892-06-21		A7
7638	WHITE, John	3	E21NE	1859-09-01		A1
7643	" "	3	W21NE	1860-08-01		A1
3995	WHITTAKER, Pleasant	14	E½NW	1873-02-01		A7
7658	WILLIAMS, Alexander L	31	S21SW	1893-09-01		A7
3996	WILLIAMS, Darius J	29	NWSW	1890-09-23		A1
3997	WILLIS, Thomas H	20	E½SW	1888-07-03		A1
7601	WILSON, Mary	1	E21NW	1861-04-01		A8
7604	" "	1	E22NW	1861-04-01		A8
3998	WILSON, Susan	25	SWNW	1860-03-01		A1
4001	WOODSIDE, John R	23	NESW	1859-05-04		A2
4002	" "	23	NWNW	1859-05-04		A2
4003	" "	23	E½NW	1859-05-04		A2
4005	" "	26	W½NE	1860-05-02		A6
4004	" "	26	NENW	1860-05-02		A6
4006	" "	34	SESW	1860-05-02		A6
4007	WOODY, Elijah M	17	NWNW	1877-04-05		A7
4008	" "	18	E½NE	1877-04-05		A7
4009	" "	18	NESE	1877-04-05		A7
4010	WOODY, Joseph W	25	N½SE	1861-07-01		A6
4011	" "	25	S½NE	1861-07-01		A6

Patent Map

T24-N R8-W
5th PM 24-N 8-W Meridian

Map Group 15

Township Statistics

Parcels Mapped	:	349
Number of Patents	:	235
Number of Individuals	:	233
Patentees Identified	:	204
Number of Surnames	:	155
Multi-Patentee Parcels	:	42
Oldest Patent Date	:	4/12/1853
Most Recent Patent	:	1/20/1908
Block/Lot Parcels	:	84
Cities and Town	:	3
Cemeteries	:	2

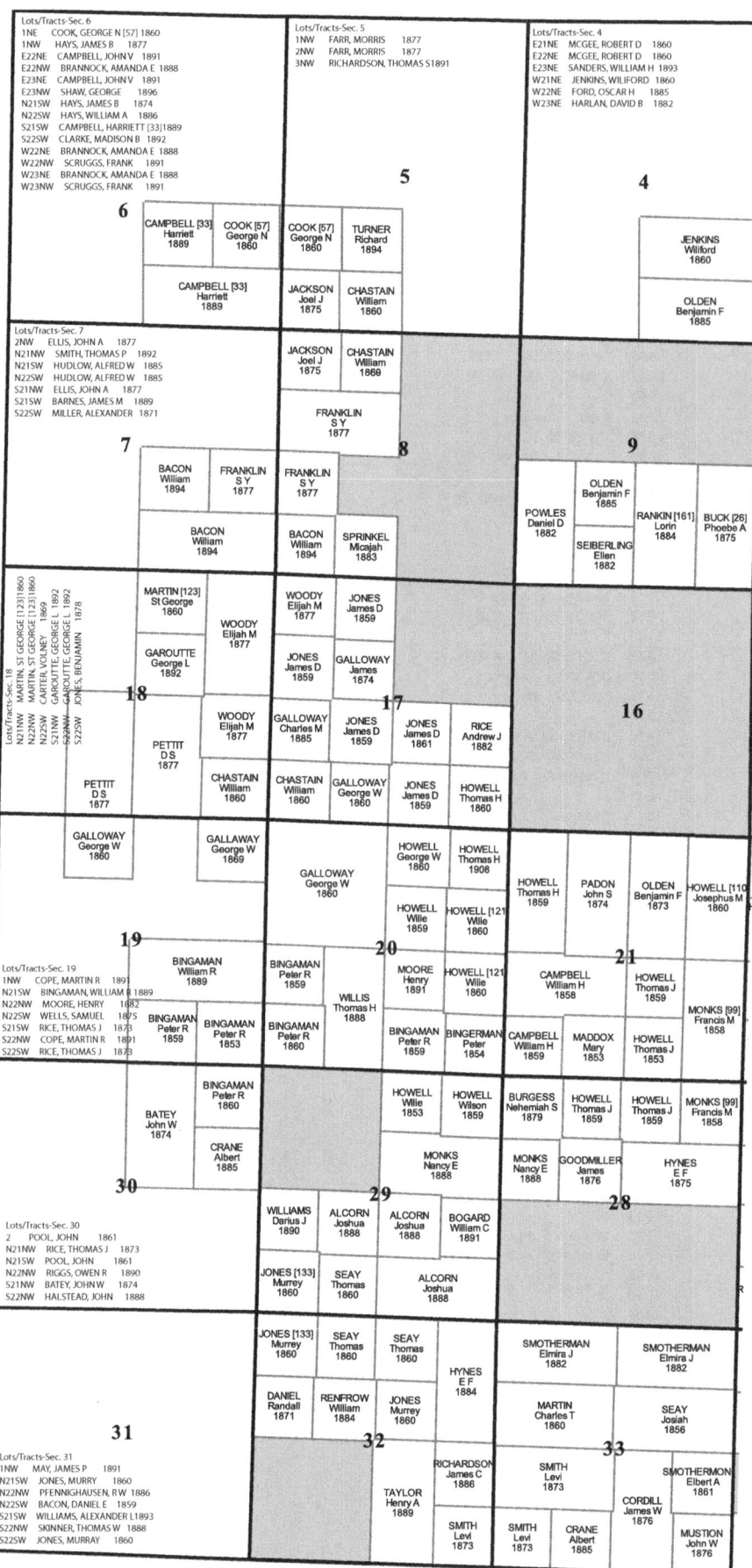

Copyright 2013 Boyd IT, Inc. All Rights Reserved

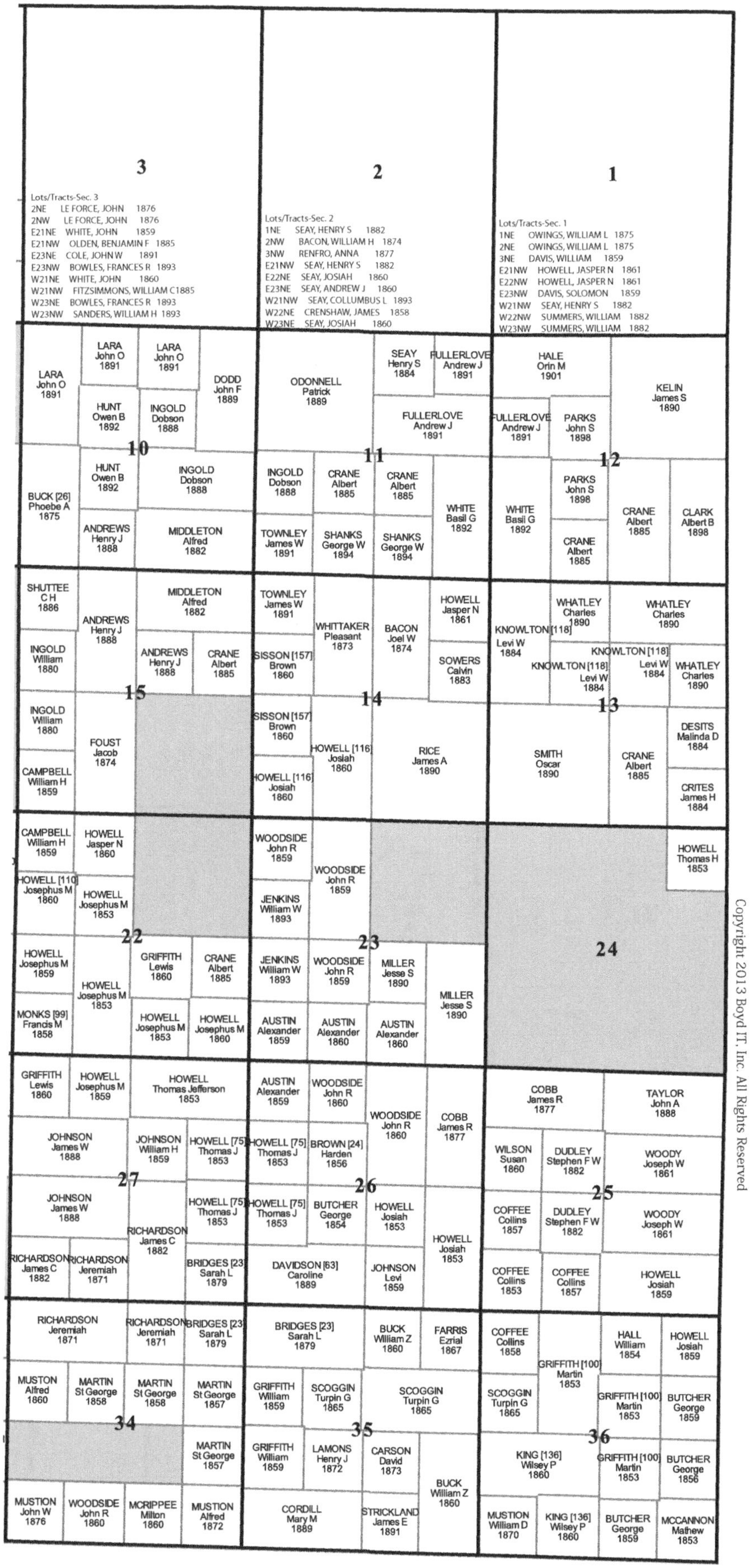

3
Lots/Tracts-Sec. 3
2NE LE FORCE, JOHN 1876
2NW LE FORCE, JOHN 1876
E21NE WHITE, JOHN 1859
E21NW OLDEN, BENJAMIN F 1885
E23NE COLE, JOHN W 1891
E23NW BOWLES, FRANCES R 1893
W21NE WHITE, JOHN 1860
W21NW FITZSIMMONS, WILLIAM C1885
W23NE BOWLES, FRANCES R 1893
W23NW SANDERS, WILLIAM H 1893
2
Lots/Tracts-Sec. 2
1NE SEAY, HENRY S 1882
2NW BACON, WILLIAM H 1874
3NW RENFRO, ANNA 1877
E21NW SEAY, HENRY S 1882
E22NE SEAY, JOSIAH 1860
E23NE SEAY, ANDREW J 1860
W21NW SEAY, COLLUMBUS L 1893
W22NE CRENSHAW, JAMES 1858
W23NE SEAY, JOSIAH 1860
1
Lots/Tracts-Sec. 1
1NE OWINGS, WILLIAM L 1875
2NE OWINGS, WILLIAM L 1875
3NE DAVIS, WILLIAM 1859
E21NW HOWELL, JASPER N 1861
E22NW HOWELL, JASPER N 1861
E23NW DAVIS, SOLOMON 1859
W21NW SEAY, HENRY S 1882
W22NW SUMMERS, WILLIAM 1882
W23NW SUMMERS, WILLIAM 1882
LARA John O 1891
LARA John O 1891
LARA John O 1891
DODD John F 1889
HUNT Owen B 1892
INGOLD Dobson 1888
10
HUNT Owen B 1892
INGOLD Dobson 1888
BUCK [26] Phoebe A 1875
ANDREWS Henry J 1888
MIDDLETON Alfred 1882
ODONNELL Patrick 1889
SEAY Henry S 1884
FULLERLOVE Andrew J 1891
FULLERLOVE Andrew J 1891
11
INGOLD Dobson 1888
CRANE Albert 1885
CRANE Albert 1885
WHITE Basil G 1892
TOWNLEY James W 1891
SHANKS George W 1894
SHANKS George W 1894
HALE Orin M 1901
KELIN James S 1890
FULLERLOVE Andrew J 1891
PARKS John S 1898
12
WHITE Basil G 1892
PARKS John S 1898
CRANE Albert 1885
CRANE Albert 1885
CLARK Albert B 1898
SHUTTEE C H 1886
MIDDLETON Alfred 1882
ANDREWS Henry J 1888
INGOLD William 1880
ANDREWS Henry J 1888
CRANE Albert 1885
15
INGOLD William 1880
FOUST Jacob 1874
CAMPBELL William H 1859
TOWNLEY James W 1891
WHITTAKER Pleasant 1873
BACON Joel W 1874
HOWELL Jasper N 1861
SISSON [157] Brown 1860
SOWERS Calvin 1883
14
SISSON [157] Brown 1860
HOWELL [116] Josiah 1860
RICE James A 1890
HOWELL [116] Josiah 1860
WHATLEY Charles 1890
WHATLEY Charles 1890
KNOWLTON [118] Levi W 1884
KNOWLTON [118] Levi W 1884
KNOWLTON [118] Levi W 1884
WHATLEY Charles 1890
13
DESITS Malinda D 1884
SMITH Oscar 1890
CRANE Albert 1885
CRITES James H 1884
CAMPBELL William H 1859
HOWELL Jasper N 1860
HOWELL [110] Josephus M 1860
HOWELL Josephus M 1853
22
HOWELL Josephus M 1859
GRIFFITH Lewis 1860
CRANE Albert 1885
HOWELL Josephus M 1853
MONKS [99] Francis M 1858
HOWELL Josephus M 1853
HOWELL Josephus M 1860
WOODSIDE John R 1859
WOODSIDE John R 1859
JENKINS William W 1893
23
JENKINS William W 1893
WOODSIDE John R 1859
MILLER Jesse S 1890
MILLER Jesse S 1890
AUSTIN Alexander 1859
AUSTIN Alexander 1860
AUSTIN Alexander 1860
HOWELL Thomas H 1853
24
GRIFFITH Lewis 1860
HOWELL Josephus M 1859
HOWELL Thomas Jefferson 1853
JOHNSON James W 1888
JOHNSON William H 1859
HOWELL [75] Thomas J 1853
27
JOHNSON James W 1888
HOWELL [75] Thomas J 1853
RICHARDSON James C 1882
RICHARDSON James C 1882
RICHARDSON Jeremiah 1871
BRIDGES [23] Sarah L 1879
AUSTIN Alexander 1859
WOODSIDE John R 1860
WOODSIDE John R 1860
COBB James R 1877
HOWELL [75] Thomas J 1853
BROWN [24] Harden 1856
26
HOWELL [75] Thomas J 1853
BUTCHER George 1854
HOWELL Josiah 1853
HOWELL Josiah 1853
DAVIDSON [63] Caroline 1889
JOHNSON Levi 1859
COBB James R 1877
TAYLOR John A 1888
WILSON Susan 1860
DUDLEY Stephen F W 1882
WOODY Joseph W 1861
25
COFFEE Collins 1857
DUDLEY Stephen F W 1882
WOODY Joseph W 1861
COFFEE Collins 1853
COFFEE Collins 1857
HOWELL Josiah 1859
RICHARDSON Jeremiah 1871
RICHARDSON Jeremiah 1871
BRIDGES [23] Sarah L 1879
MUSTON Alfred 1860
MARTIN St George 1858
MARTIN St George 1858
MARTIN St George 1857
34
MARTIN St George 1857
MUSTION John W 1876
WOODSIDE John R 1860
MCRIPPEE Milton 1860
MUSTION Alfred 1872
BRIDGES [23] Sarah L 1879
BUCK William Z 1860
FARRIS Ezrial 1867
GRIFFITH William 1859
SCOGGIN Turpin G 1865
SCOGGIN Turpin G 1865
35
GRIFFITH William 1859
LAMONS Henry J 1872
CARSON David 1873
BUCK William Z 1860
CORDILL Mary M 1889
STRICKLAND James E 1891
COFFEE Collins 1858
GRIFFITH [100] Martin 1853
HALL William 1854
HOWELL Josiah 1859
SCOGGIN Turpin G 1865
GRIFFITH [100] Martin 1853
BUTCHER George 1859
36
KING [136] Wilsey P 1860
GRIFFITH [100] Martin 1853
BUTCHER George 1856
MUSTION William D 1870
KING [136] Wilsey P 1860
BUTCHER George 1859
MCCANNON Mathew 1853

Helpful Hints

1. This Map's INDEX can be found on the preceding pages.
2. Refer to Map "C" to see where this Township lies within Howell County, Missouri.
3. Numbers within square brackets [ ] denote a multi-patentee land parcel (multi-owner). Refer to Appendix "C" for a full list of members in this group.
4. Areas that look to be crowded with Patentees usually indicate multiple sales of the same parcel (Re-issues) or Overlapping parcels. See this Township's Index for an explanation of these and other circumstances that might explain "odd" groupings of Patentees on this map.

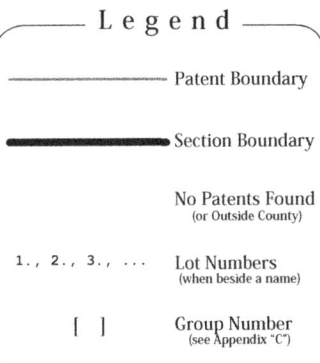

Legend

Patent Boundary

Section Boundary

No Patents Found (or Outside County)

1., 2., 3., ... Lot Numbers (when beside a name)

[ ] Group Number (see Appendix "C")

Scale: Section = 1 mile X 1 mile (generally, with some exceptions)

Road Map

T24-N R8-W
5th PM 24-N 8-W Meridian

Map Group 15

Cities & Towns
Carson (historical)
Summers Addition
West Plains

Cemeteries
Howell Valley Cemetery
Oak Lawn Cemetery

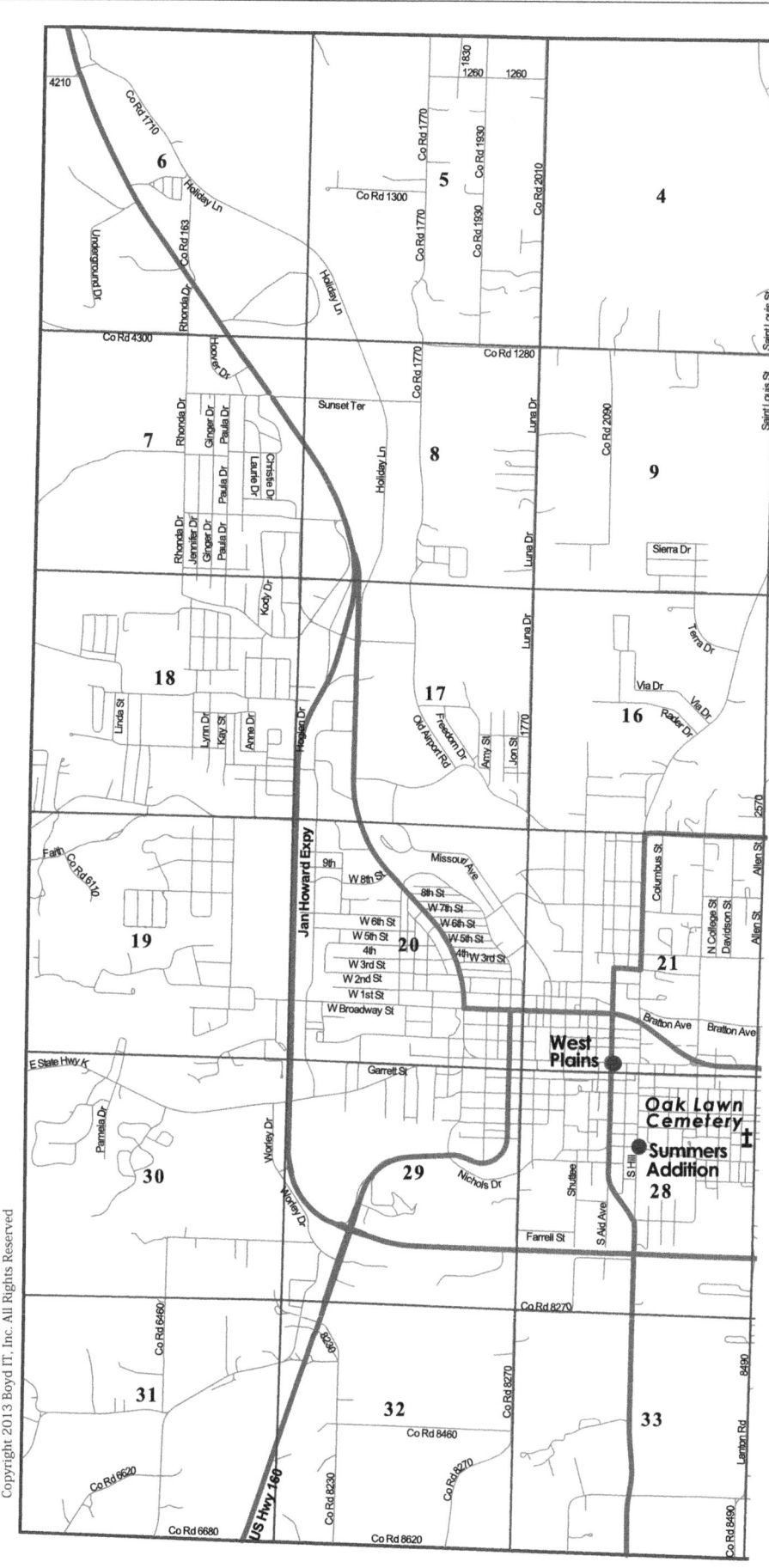

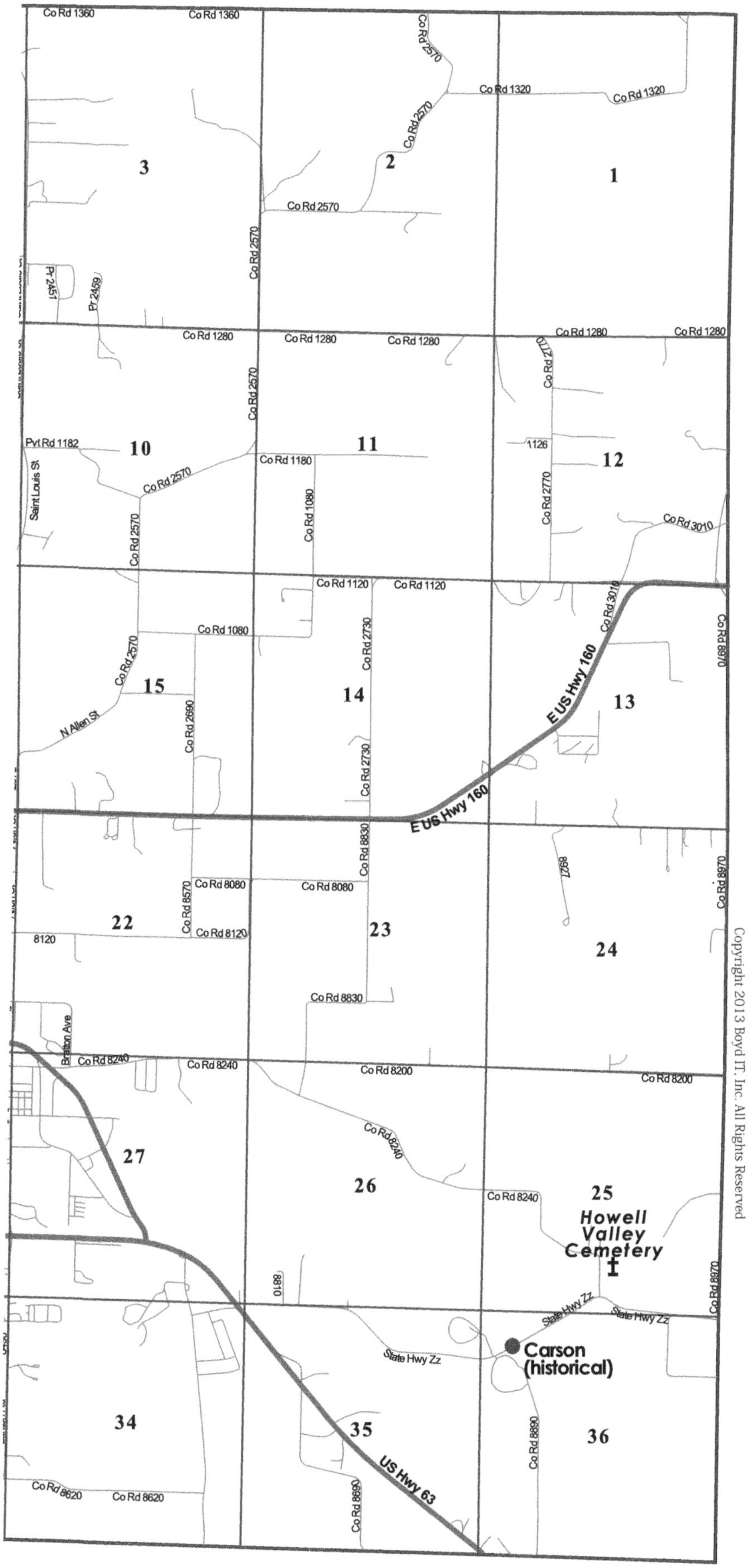

Co Rd 1360   Co Rd 1360

3

Co Rd 2570

2

Co Rd 2570

Co Rd 1320   Co Rd 1320

1

Pr 2451   Pr 2459

Co Rd 1280   Co Rd 1280   Co Rd 1280   Co Rd 1280   Co Rd 1280

Pvt Rd 1182   10   Co Rd 2570

Saint Louis St

11   Co Rd 1180

Co Rd 1080

1126   12   Co Rd 2770

Co Rd 3010

Co Rd 1120   Co Rd 1120

Co Rd 1080   Co Rd 2570

15   Co Rd 2890

N Allen St

14   Co Rd 2730

E US Hwy 160

Co Rd 3010

13

Co Rd 8970

E US Hwy 160

Co Rd 8830

Co Rd 8080   Co Rd 8080   2587

Co Rd 8570   22   Co Rd 8120

8120

23   Co Rd 8830

24

Co Rd 8070

Branson Ave

Co Rd 8240   Co Rd 8240   Co Rd 8200   Co Rd 8200

27

Co Rd 8240

26

Co Rd 8240   25

Howell
Valley
Cemetery
‡

State Hwy Zz   State Hwy Zz

0188

State Hwy Zz   ● Carson
(historical)

Co Rd 8880

Co Rd 8970

34   35   US Hwy 63   36

Co Rd 8620   Co Rd 8620   Co Rd 8890

Helpful Hints

1. This road map has a number of uses, but primarily it is to help you: a) find the present location of land owned by your ancestors (at least the general area), b) find cemeteries and city-centers, and c) estimate the route/roads used by Census-takers & tax-assessors.

2. If you plan to travel to Howell County to locate cemeteries or land parcels, please pick up a modern travel map for the area before you do. Mapping old land parcels on modern maps is not as exact a science as you might think. Just the slightest variations in public land survey coordinates, estimates of parcel boundaries, or road-map deviations can greatly alter a map's representation of how a road either does or doesn't cross a particular parcel of land.

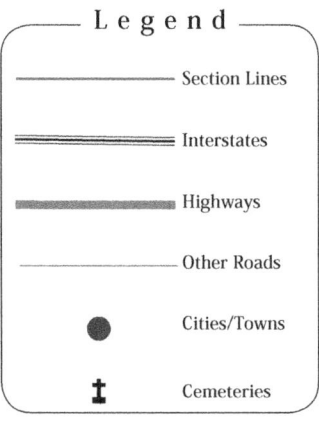

L e g e n d

———— Section Lines

════ Interstates

▬▬▬ Highways

———— Other Roads

● Cities/Towns

‡ Cemeteries

Scale: Section = 1 mile X 1 mile
(generally, with some exceptions)

Historical Map
T24-N R8-W
5th PM 24-N 8-W Meridian

Map Group 15

Cities & Towns
Carson (historical)
Summers Addition
West Plains

Cemeteries
Howell Valley Cemetery
Oak Lawn Cemetery

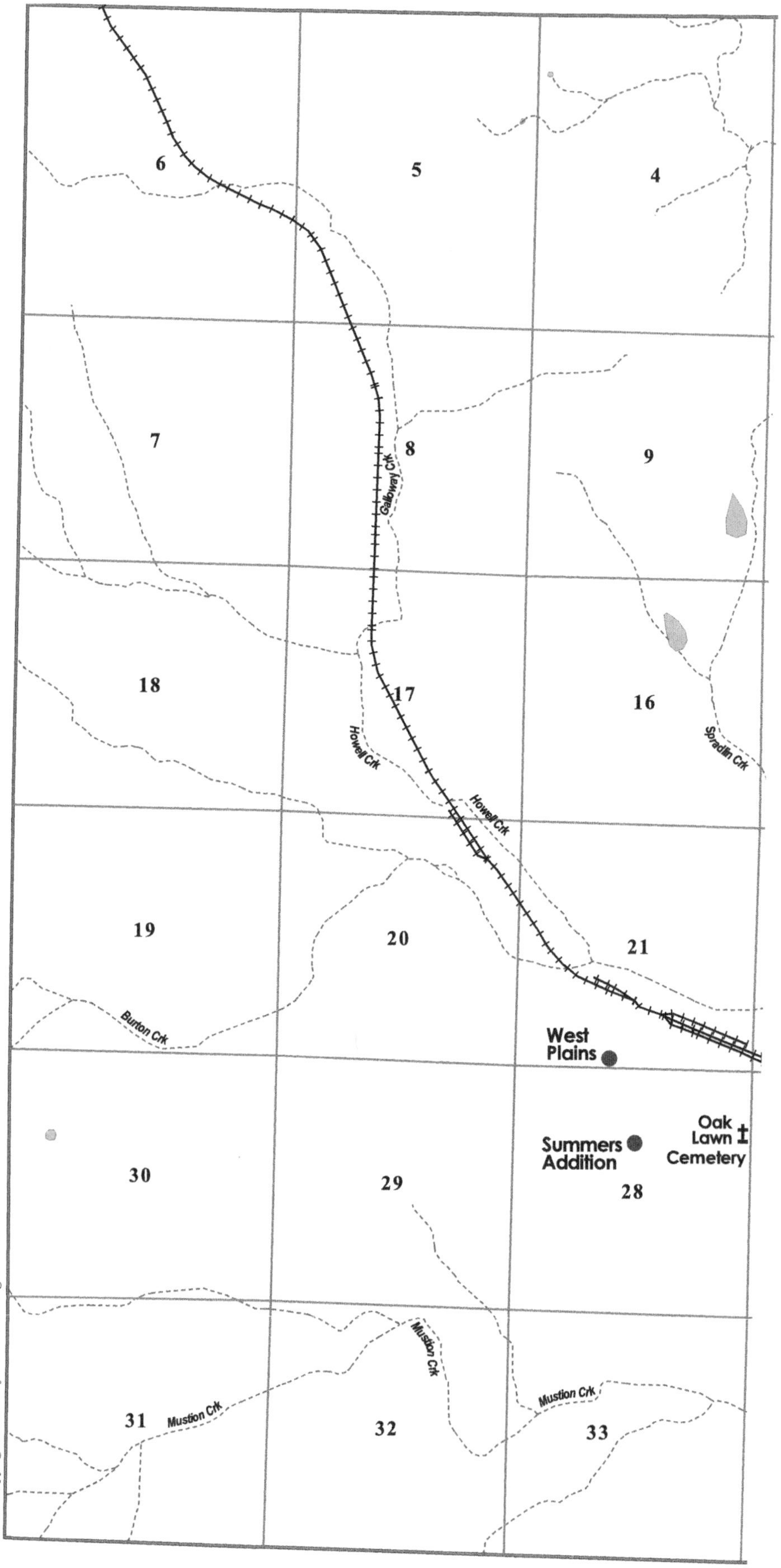

6

5

4

7

8

9

Galloway Crk

18

17

16

Howell Crk

Spradlin Crk

Howell Crk

19

20

21

Burton Crk

West
Plains ●

Oak
Lawn ✝
Cemetery

Summers ●
Addition

30

29

28

31

Mustion Crk

32

Mustion Crk

33

Mustion Crk

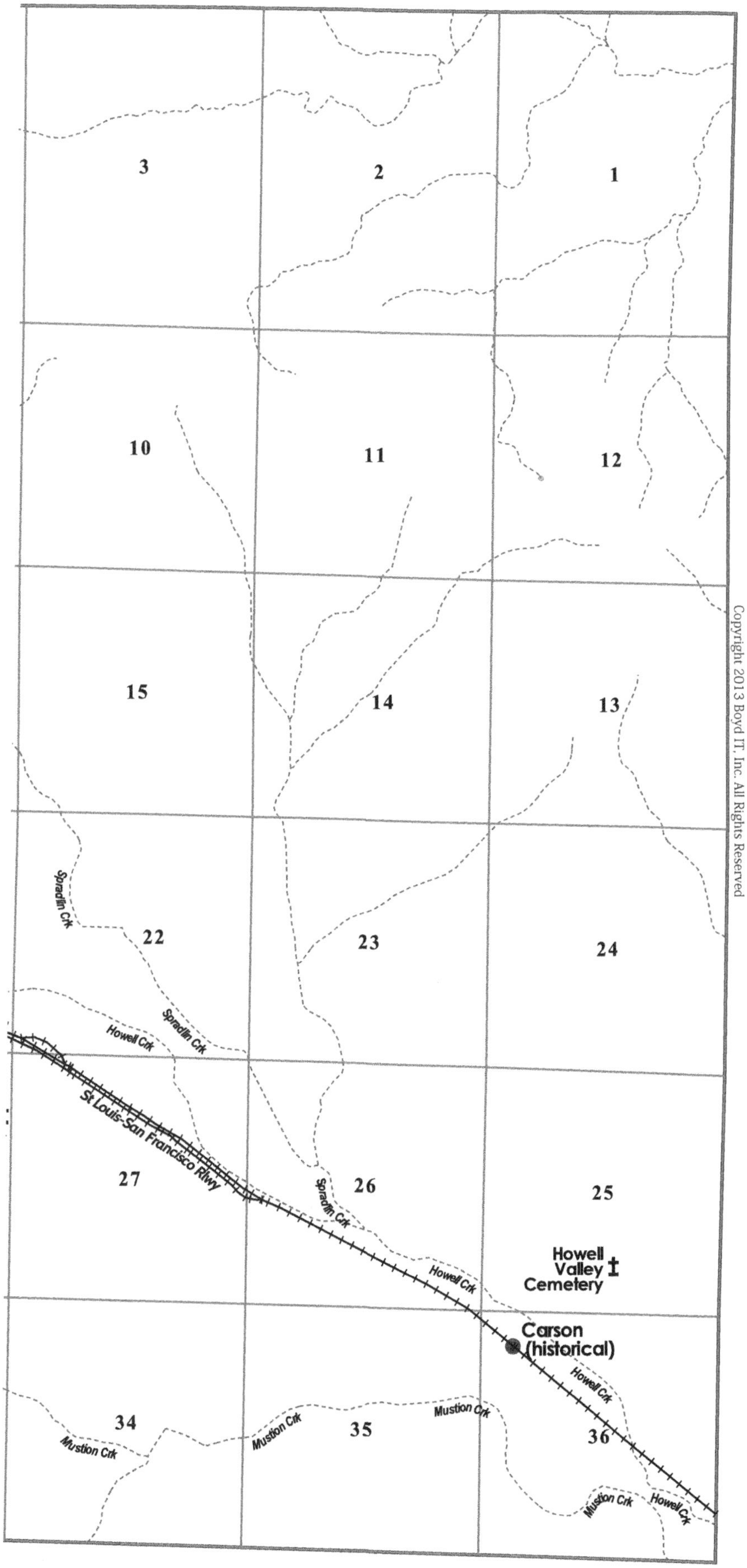

3

2

1

10

11

12

15

14

13

Spradlin Crk

22

23

24

Spradlin Crk

Howell Crk

St Louis-San Francisco Rlwy

27

Spradlin Crk

26

25

Howell Crk

Howell
Valley ‡
Cemetery

Carson
(historical)

34

Mustion Crk

35

Mustion Crk

Mustion Crk

36

Howell Crk

Mustion Crk

Howell Crk

Helpful Hints

1. This Map takes a different look at the same Congressional Township displayed in the preceding two maps. It presents features that can help you better envision the historical development of the area: a) Water-bodies (lakes & ponds), b) Water-courses (rivers, streams, etc.), c) Railroads, d) City/town center-points (where they were oftentimes located when first settled), and e) Cemeteries.

2. Using this "Historical" map in tandem with this Township's Patent Map and Road Map, may lead you to some interesting discoveries. You will often find roads, towns, cemeteries, and waterways are named after nearby landowners: sometimes those names will be the ones you are researching. See how many of these research gems you can find here in Howell County.

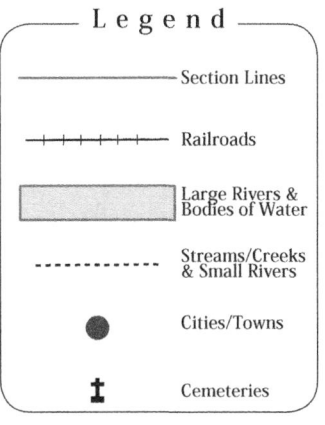

L e g e n d

——————— Section Lines

+++++++ Railroads

Large Rivers &
Bodies of Water

- - - - - - - Streams/Creeks
& Small Rivers

● Cities/Towns

‡ Cemeteries

Scale: Section = 1 mile X 1 mile
(there are some exceptions)

Map Group 16: Index to Land Patents

Township 24-North Range 7-West (5th PM 24-N 7-W)

After you locate an individual in this Index, take note of the Section and Section Part then proceed to the Land Patent map on the pages immediately following. You should have no difficulty locating the corresponding parcel of land.

The "For More Info" Column will lead you to more information about the underlying Patents. See the *Legend* at right, and the "How to Use this Book" chapter, for more information.

```
                    LEGEND
          "For More Info . . . " column
A = Authority (Legislative Act, See Appendix "A")
B = Block or Lot (location in Section unknown)
C = Cancelled Patent
F = Fractional Section
G = Group  (Multi-Patentee Patent, see Appendix "C")
V = Overlaps another Parcel
R = Re-Issued (Parcel patented more than once)

(A & G items require you to look in the Appendixes referred
to above. All other Letter-designations followed by a number
require you to locate line-items in this index that possess
the ID number found after the letter).
```

ID	Individual in Patent	Sec.	Sec. Part	Date Issued	Other Counties	For More Info . . .
4012	BALEY, William	28	W½SW	1859-09-10		A1
4014	" "	28	SWSE	1859-09-10		A1
4013	" "	28	SESW	1859-09-10		A1
7754	BARNETT, Nathaniel	5	E21NE	1860-10-01		A1
4015	" "	5	NESE	1860-10-01		A1
7711	BLACKBURN, Harvey	19	S21SW	1859-09-01		A1
7730	" "	30	N22NW	1859-09-01		A1
7728	" "	30	N21NW	1859-09-01		A1
7736	BOYD, Robert	31	1SW	1860-08-01		A1
4016	" "	31	SWSE	1860-08-01		A1
7740	" "	31	S21NW	1860-08-01		A1
4017	BRAY, Calvin	18	W½SE	1859-09-01		A1
4018	BRIMHALL, Joseph R	5	SESE	1859-09-01		A1
7713	BROWER, John E	2	2NE	1859-09-01		A1
7712	" "	2	1NE	1859-09-01		A1
7715	" "	2	E21NW	1859-09-01		A1
7716	" "	2	E22NW	1859-09-01		A1
7717	" "	2	E23NE	1859-09-01		A1
4022	BROWN, Amasa N	13	W½NE	1859-09-01		A1
4019	" "	13	NWSE	1859-09-01		A1
4020	" "	13	NW	1859-09-01		A1
4021	" "	13	NENE	1859-09-01		A1
7739	BUTCHER, George	31	N22SW	1856-10-10		A1
7741	" "	31	S22NW	1859-01-01		A1
4023	CAMPBELL, James T	13	NESE	1903-07-14		A7
7765	CARTER, Robert C	6	2SW	1903-05-25		A7
7767	CARTER, William	6	3NW	1857-03-10		A1
7746	CLARK, Lewis Y	4	E21NE	1859-09-01		A1
4026	" "	4	E½SW	1859-09-01		A1
4024	" "	4	SWSW	1859-09-01		A1
4025	" "	4	SE	1859-09-01		A1
7706	CLOWNY, James N	18	1NW	1859-09-01		A1
4027	" "	18	NE	1859-09-01		A1
4028	" "	18	E½SE	1859-09-01		A1
7710	COFFEE, Arnett	19	N21SW	1897-04-10		A7
4030	COFFEE, William	19	W½SE	1859-01-01		A1
4029	" "	19	NESE	1859-01-01		A1
4031	" "	30	NWNE	1859-01-01		A1
7731	COFFY, William	30	N22SW	1860-03-01		A1
7734	" "	30	S22NW	1860-03-01		A1
7742	COLLIER, Frederick	31	S22SW	1897-04-02		A1
4032	COOPER, William F	18	SW	1860-08-01		A1
7707	" "	18	2NW	1860-08-01		A1
4033	CRAHAN, Thomas	35	NENE	1896-12-08		A7
7726	CROSS, James K	3	E23NE	1884-11-01		A7
4034	CROSS, James P	13	NESW	1904-06-27		A1

ID	Individual in Patent	Sec.	Sec. Part	Date Issued	Other Counties	For More Info . . .
4035	CULL, David W	24	NESW	1893-09-08		A7
4036	CUNNINGHAM, Joseph	13	SWSW	1859-09-01		A1
4037	" "	13	SENE	1859-09-01		A1
4038	" "	24	NWNW	1859-09-01		A1
4039	CURTIS, Daniel R	17	SE	1859-09-01		A1
4040	" "	17	S½NE	1859-09-01		A1
4041	" "	17	E½SW	1859-09-01		A1
4042	DAMON, Osgood A	11	E½	1859-09-01		A1
4043	DAWSON, John	32	E½	1859-09-01		A1
7704	DEITZ, Lewis	1	E22NW	1859-09-01		A1
7698	" "	1	1NW	1859-09-01		A1
4044	" "	1	SW	1859-09-01		A1
4045	DEXTER, Matilda	31	E½SE	1859-09-10		A1
4046	" "	32	NESW	1859-01-01		A1
4047	" "	32	SWNW	1859-01-01		A1
4048	" "	32	NWSW	1859-09-10		A1
4049	DILL, George W	35	SENE	1859-09-01		A1
4052	" "	36	SW	1859-09-01		A1
4050	" "	36	E½NW	1859-09-01		A1
4051	" "	36	SWNW	1859-09-01		A1
4054	DILL, Zebulon	26	S½SW	1859-09-01		A1
4053	" "	26	SWSE	1859-09-01		A1
4055	" "	27	E½SE	1859-09-01		A1
4056	" "	34	NENE	1859-09-01		A1
4057	DONNELLY, Richard	15	N½	1859-09-01		A1
4058	DUNKIN, John W	24	W½SW	1859-09-01		A1
4061	DUNKIN, Levi P	24	W½SE	1859-09-01		A1
4059	" "	24	SENE	1859-09-01		A1
4060	" "	24	NESE	1859-09-01		A1
4062	DUNKIN, William M	24	SESW	1857-04-15		A1
4066	" "	25	W½SE	1859-09-01		A1
4067	" "	25	SESE	1859-09-01		A1
4065	" "	25	SWNE	1859-09-01		A1
4064	" "	25	NENW	1857-04-15		A1
4063	" "	25	NWNE	1857-04-15		A1
4068	EATON, S D	27	N½	1859-09-01		A1
4069	EDGAR, Harvey E	13	NWSW	1891-05-25		A7
4070	" "	24	SWNW	1891-05-25		A7
4071	ELLWOOD, George R	23	SENW	1860-08-01		A1
4072	" "	23	N½NW	1860-08-01		A1
4073	" "	23	NESW	1860-08-01		A1
4076	FEGAN, Patrick	7	SW	1859-09-01		A1
4075	" "	7	SESE	1859-09-01		A1
4074	" "	7	W½SE	1859-09-01		A1
4077	FRAYNER, David	12	N½	1859-09-01		A1
4078	FULENWIDER, Margaret	34	SENE	1859-09-01		A1
4079	" "	35	W½NW	1859-09-01		A1
4081	FULENWIDNER, Margaret	34	SWNE	1859-09-01		A1 C
4080	" "	34	SWNE	1912-04-11		A1
4085	" "	35	N½NE	1859-09-01		A1 C
4082	" "	35	E½NW	1912-04-11		A1
4084	" "	35	E½NW	1859-09-01		A1 C
4083	" "	35	W½NE	1912-04-11		A1
4086	GARRIGIN, Thomas	21	SE	1859-09-01		A1
4087	" "	28	E½SE	1859-09-01		A1
4088	" "	28	E½NE	1859-09-01		A1
4089	GUNTER, Heyward R	4	NWSW	1858-01-15		A1
7749	" "	4	W21NW	1858-01-15		A1
7750	" "	4	W22NW	1858-01-15		A1
4090	HALL, William A	2	S½	1859-09-01		A1
4092	HARMAN, Amos	30	E½SE	1859-09-01		A1
4091	" "	30	E½NE	1859-09-01		A1
4093	" "	31	E½NE	1859-09-01		A1
4094	" "	32	N½NW	1859-09-01		A1
4095	HART, Alfred G	17	SWNW	1905-03-30		A7
4098	HERMAN, John	33	W½SW	1860-08-01		A1
4097	" "	33	W½NW	1860-08-01		A1
4096	" "	33	SESW	1860-08-01		A1
4099	HODGES, Joseph	30	NWSE	1857-03-10		A1
7732	" "	30	S21NW	1857-03-10		A1
7729	" "	30	N21SW	1857-03-10		A1
4100	" "	30	SWNE	1857-03-10		A1
4101	HOKER, John H	9	N½	1859-09-01		A1

ID	Individual in Patent	Sec.	Sec. Part	Date Issued	Other Counties	For More Info . . .
4102	HOWELL, George W	6	SWSE	1902-02-12		A7
7735	HOWELL, Josiah	30	S22SW	1859-09-01		A1
7738	" "	31	N22NW	1859-09-01		A1
7745	" "	4	3NW	1857-10-30		A1
7748	" "	4	E22NW	1857-10-30		A1
4103	HOWELL, Thomas J	15	SESE	1859-09-01		A1
4104	" "	22	N½SE	1859-09-01		A1
4105	" "	22	E½NE	1859-09-01		A1
4106	" "	22	SWNE	1859-09-01		A1
4108	" "	23	SWNW	1859-09-01		A1
4107	" "	23	NWSW	1859-09-01		A1
4109	JOHNSON, Alfred J	34	S½	1859-09-01		A1
7708	JOHNSON, Thomas M	18	N22NW	1859-01-01		A1
4110	KARR, John M	5	NWSW	1859-09-10		A1
4111	" "	6	E½SE	1859-09-10		A1
4112	KELLUM, Samuel	9	S½	1859-09-01		A1
4114	KERNOCK, William	13	S½SE	1859-09-01		A1
4113	" "	13	SESW	1859-09-01		A1
4116	" "	24	NENE	1859-09-01		A1
4115	" "	24	E½NW	1859-09-01		A1
4117	" "	24	W½NE	1859-09-01		A1
4118	KIERER, Ernst	29	S½	1859-09-01		A1
4119	KIRKWOOD, Charles	25	E½NE	1860-08-01	Oregon	A1
4120	LAFFOON, James H	27	W½SW	1859-09-10		A1
4121	LAFFOON, James W	27	W½SE	1859-09-01		A1
4122	" "	27	E½SW	1859-09-01		A1
4123	" "	34	SENW	1899-05-05		A7
4124	" "	34	NENW	1859-09-01		A1
4125	" "	34	NWNE	1859-09-01		A1
4126	LAYTON, Abraham	8	E½NE	1859-09-01		A1
4127	LILES, Jesse	36	E½	1859-09-01		A1
7762	MACKEY, Bridget	6	1SW	1859-09-01		A1
7761	" "	6	1NW	1859-09-01		A1
7764	" "	6	2NW	1859-09-01		A1
4128	" "	6	NWSE	1859-09-01		A1
4129	MANNING, John J	35	S½	1859-09-01		A1
4130	MARSHALL, John	19	NW	1859-09-01		A1
7709	" "	19	2SW	1859-09-01		A1
7725	MATNEY, Brooks	3	3NW	1857-04-15		A1
7724	" "	3	2NW	1857-04-15		A1
7727	" "	3	W23NE	1857-04-15		A1
7744	MATNEY, Charles R	4	3NE	1857-04-15		A1
7743	" "	4	2NE	1857-04-15		A1
4132	MAWHINNEY, Sampson	33	E½SE	1857-04-15		A1
4131	" "	33	SENE	1857-04-15		A1
4133	" "	34	W½NW	1857-04-15		A1
7760	MAXWELL, John	6	1NE	1860-08-01		A1
7763	" "	6	2NE	1860-08-01		A1
4136	MAXWELL, M J	25	SW	1859-09-01		A1
4134	" "	25	W½NW	1859-09-01		A1
4135	" "	25	SENW	1859-09-01		A1
4137	" "	36	NWNW	1859-09-01		A1
4138	MCCABE, Michael J	22	SW	1859-09-01		A1
4139	" "	22	S½SE	1859-09-01		A1
4140	" "	23	S½SW	1859-09-01		A1
4141	MCCOLLUM, Joseph	8	W½NE	1859-09-01		A1
7720	MCEMBREE, Morris	2	W23NE	1859-09-01		A1
7718	" "	2	W21NW	1859-09-01		A1
7719	" "	2	W22NW	1859-09-01		A1
7714	" "	2	3NW	1859-09-01		A1
4142	MERRITT, George M	21	NE	1859-09-01		A1
4143	" "	22	NW	1859-09-01		A1
4146	MERRITT, H S	15	W½SE	1859-09-01		A1
4145	" "	15	SW	1859-09-01		A1
4144	" "	15	NESE	1859-09-01		A1
4147	" "	22	NWNE	1859-09-01		A1
4148	MITCHELL, Charles C	26	N½	1859-09-01		A1
4152	MITCHELL, Freeman	28	NW	1859-09-01		A1
4149	" "	28	W½NE	1859-09-01		A1
4150	" "	28	NWSE	1859-09-01		A1
4151	" "	28	NESW	1859-09-01		A1
4153	MURRAY, William	29	N½	1859-09-01		A1
7723	MURREY, James	3	2NE	1859-09-01		A1

ID	Individual in Patent	Sec.	Sec. Part	Date Issued	Other Counties	For More Info . . .
4154	MURREY, James (Cont'd)	3	SE	1859-09-01		A1
7721	" "	3	1NE	1859-09-01		A1
7757	NANEY, Green W	5	W21NE	1857-03-10		A1
7759	" "	5	W23NW	1857-03-10		A1
7751	" "	5	1NW	1857-03-10		A1
7758	" "	5	W22NW	1857-03-10		A1
7766	" "	6	3NE	1857-03-10		A1
7697	OBRIEN, Charles	1	1NE	1859-09-01		A1
7699	" "	1	2NE	1859-09-01		A1
4155	" "	1	SE	1859-09-01		A1
4156	OCONNER, Michael	7	NW	1859-09-01		A1
4157	" "	7	NENE	1859-09-01		A1
4158	" "	7	W½NE	1859-09-01		A1
4159	ODONNELL, Thomas	8	W½	1859-09-01		A1
4160	ORME, James T	11	W½	1859-09-01		A1
4161	OSBORN, Cyrus	14	W½	1859-09-01		A1
4162	PEAY, Thomas J	17	NENE	1897-01-07		A7
4163	PEDRICK, Thomas	10	N½	1859-09-01		A1
4164	POOL, James H	19	W½NE	1859-09-10		A1
4165	" "	32	S½SW	1857-04-15		A1
7733	POOL, John T	30	S21SW	1859-01-01		A1
4166	" "	30	SWSE	1857-03-10		A1
7737	" "	31	N21NW	1859-01-01		A1
4167	" "	31	W½NE	1857-03-10		A1
4168	" "	31	NWSE	1860-03-01		A1
7747	POOLE, Francis K	4	E21NW	1910-04-01	Barry	A1
4170	QUINNAN, Patrick	5	W½SE	1860-12-10		A1
4171	" "	5	S½SW	1860-12-10		A1
4169	" "	5	NESW	1860-12-10		A1
4173	RAFFERTY, James	7	NESE	1860-10-01		A1
4172	" "	7	SENE	1860-10-01		A1
4175	RAND, Edward B	17	NWNW	1859-09-01		A1
4176	" "	17	E½NW	1859-09-01		A1
4174	" "	17	NWNE	1859-09-01		A1
4177	" "	8	SE	1859-09-01		A1
4178	ROGERS, Levi B	21	W½	1859-09-01		A1
4179	ROUNTREE, John S	25	NESE	1893-04-29		A7
7755	RUTHERS, William	5	E22NW	1857-03-10		A1
7756	" "	5	E23NW	1857-03-10		A1
7752	" "	5	2NE	1857-03-10		A1
7753	" "	5	3NE	1857-03-10		A1
4180	SHEA, Amos K	12	S½	1859-09-01		A1
7700	SPENCER, John E	1	3NE	1859-09-01		A1
7705	" "	1	W22NW	1859-09-01		A1
7703	" "	1	4NW	1859-09-01		A1
7702	" "	1	4NE	1859-09-01		A1
7701	" "	1	3NW	1859-09-01		A1
4181	STACEY, Henry N	14	E½	1859-09-01		A1
4182	STARK, William	10	S½	1859-09-01		A1
4183	STINECIPHER, Isaac	17	W½SW	1859-09-01		A1
4184	" "	19	E½NE	1859-09-01		A1
4185	" "	20	NWNW	1859-09-01		A1
4186	SWAN, John C	19	SE	1859-09-01		A1
4187	" "	20	E½NW	1859-09-01		A1
4188	" "	20	SW	1859-09-01		A1
4189	" "	20	SWNW	1859-09-01		A1
4190	TAFTON, George	3	SW	1859-09-01		A1
7722	" "	3	1NW	1859-09-01		A1
4193	WALKER, George A	33	W½SE	1859-09-01		A1
4194	" "	33	W½NE	1859-09-01		A1
4192	" "	33	NENE	1859-09-01		A1
4191	" "	33	NESW	1859-09-01		A1
4195	" "	33	E½NW	1859-09-01		A1
4196	WELLS, Mark S	26	SESE	1859-09-01		A1
4197	" "	26	N½SE	1859-09-01		A1
4198	" "	26	N½SW	1859-09-01		A1
4199	WILLIAMS, Jesse H	23	E½	1859-09-01		A1
4200	WORCESTER, Francis	20	E½	1859-09-01		A1

Patent Map

T24-N R7-W
5th PM 24-N 7-W Meridian

Map Group 16

Township Statistics

Parcels Mapped	:	260
Number of Patents	:	120
Number of Individuals	:	109
Patentees Identified	:	109
Number of Surnames	:	94
Multi-Patentee Parcels	:	0
Oldest Patent Date	:	3/10/1857
Most Recent Patent	:	4/11/1912
Block/Lot Parcels	:	71
Cities and Town	:	1
Cemeteries	:	2

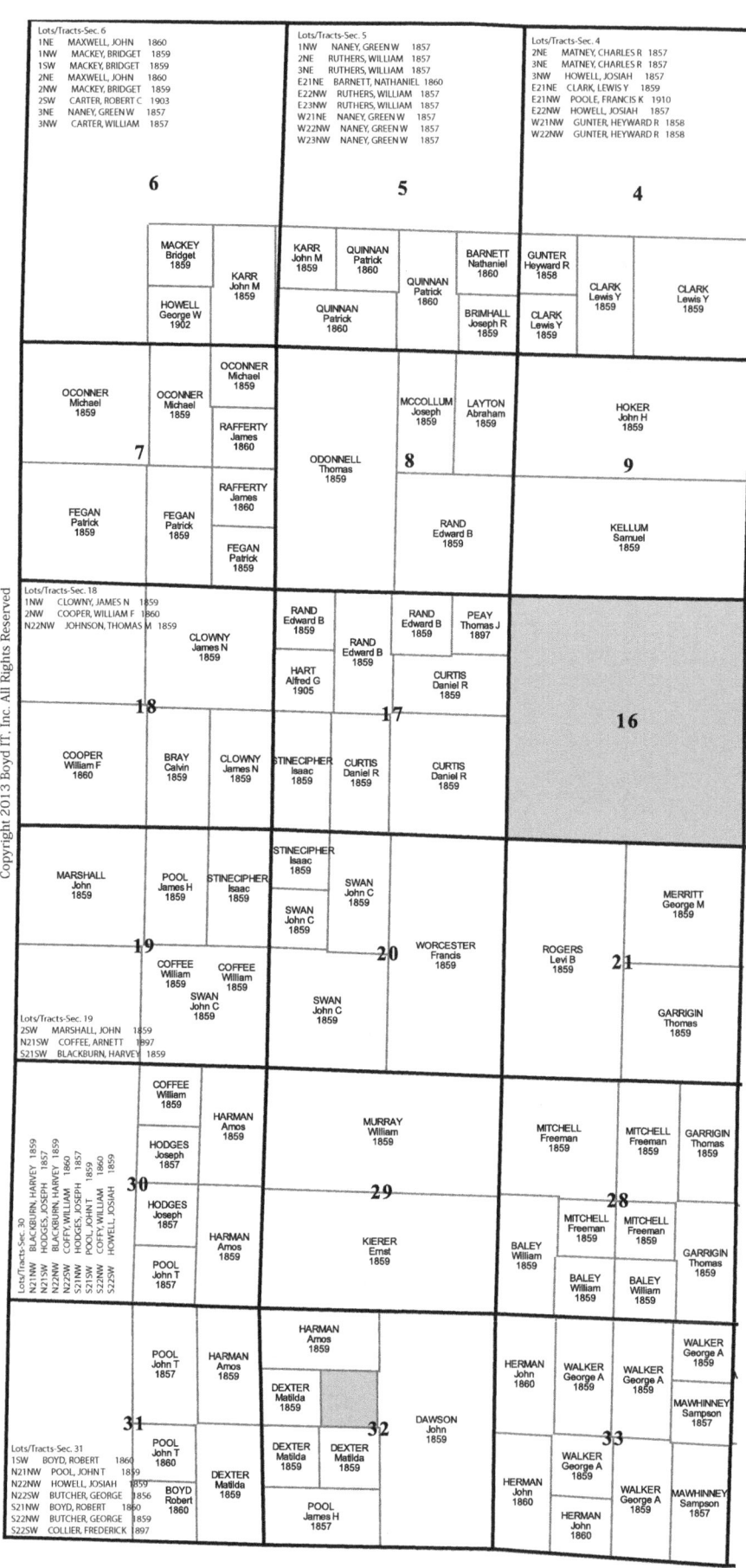

Lots/Tracts-Sec. 3
1NE MURREY, JAMES 1859
1NW TAFTON, GEORGE 1859
2NE MURREY, JAMES 1859
2NW MATNEY, BROOKS 1857
3NW MATNEY, BROOKS 1857
E23NE CROSS, JAMES K 1884
W23NE MATNEY, BROOKS 1857

Lots/Tracts-Sec. 2
1NE BROWER, JOHN E 1859
2NE BROWER, JOHN E 1859
3NW MCEMBREE, MORRIS 1859
E21NW BROWER, JOHN E 1859
E22NW BROWER, JOHN E 1859
E23NE BROWER, JOHN E 1859
W21NW MCEMBREE, MORRIS 1859
W22NW MCEMBREE, MORRIS 1859
W23NE MCEMBREE, MORRIS 1859

Lots/Tracts-Sec. 1
1NE OBRIEN, CHARLES 1859
1NW DEITZ, LEWIS 1859
2NE OBRIEN, CHARLES 1859
3NE SPENCER, JOHN E 1859
3NW SPENCER, JOHN E 1859
4NE SPENCER, JOHN E 1859
4NW SPENCER, JOHN E 1859
E22NW DEITZ, LEWIS 1859
W22NW SPENCER, JOHN E 1859

3

2

1

TAFTON George 1859

MURREY James 1859

HALL William A 1859

DEITZ Lewis 1859

OBRIEN Charles 1859

PEDRICK Thomas 1859

FRAYNER David 1859

10

ORME James T 1859

11

DAMON Osgood A 1859

12

STARK William 1859

SHEA Amos K 1859

DONNELLY Richard 1859

BROWN Amasa N 1859

BROWN Amasa N 1859

BROWN Amasa N 1859

CUNNINGHAM Joseph 1859

15

OSBORN Cyrus 1859

14

STACEY Henry N 1859

13

MERRITT H S 1859

EDGAR Harvey E 1891

CROSS James P 1904

BROWN Amasa N 1859

CAMPBELL James T 1903

MERRITT H S 1859

MERRITT H S 1859

HOWELL Thomas J 1859

CUNNINGHAM Joseph 1859

KERNOCK William 1859

KERNOCK William 1859

MERRITT H S 1859

ELLWOOD George R 1860

CUNNINGHAM Joseph 1859

KERNOCK William 1859

MERRITT George M 1859

HOWELL Thomas J 1859

HOWELL Thomas J 1859

ELLWOOD George R 1860

EDGAR Harvey E 1891

KERNOCK William 1859

KERNOCK William 1859

DUNKIN Levi P 1859

22

HOWELL Thomas J 1859

HOWELL Thomas J 1859

ELLWOOD George R 1860

23

WILLIAMS Jesse H 1859

24

MCCABE Michael J 1859

CULL David W 1893

DUNKIN Levi P 1859

MCCABE Michael J 1859

MCCABE Michael J 1859

DUNKIN John W 1859

DUNKIN Levi P 1859

DUNKIN William M 1857

EATON S D 1859

MITCHELL Charles C 1859

MAXWELL M J 1859

DUNKIN William M 1857

DUNKIN William M 1857

KIRKWOOD Charles 1860

27

26

MAXWELL M J 1859

DUNKIN William M 1859

25

LAFFOON James H 1859

LAFFOON James W 1859

LAFFOON James W 1859

DILL Zebulon 1859

WELLS Mark S 1859

WELLS Mark S 1859

ROUNTREE John S 1893

DILL Zebulon 1859

DILL Zebulon 1859

WELLS Mark S 1859

MAXWELL M J 1859

DUNKIN William M 1859

DUNKIN William M 1859

MAWHINNEY Sampson 1857

LAFFOON James W 1859

LAFFOON James W 1859

DILL Zebulon 1859

FULENWIDNER Margaret 1859

FULENWIDNER Margaret 1859

CRAHAN Thomas 1896

MAXWELL M J 1859

LAFFOON James W 1899

FULENWIDNER Margaret 1912

FULENWIDNER Margaret 1912

FULENWIDNER Margaret 1912

FULENWIDNER Margaret 1912

DILL George W 1859

DILL George W 1859

FULENWIDER Margaret 1859

DILL George W 1859

LILES Jesse 1859

34

35

36

JOHNSON Alfred J 1859

MANNING John J 1859

DILL George W 1859

Helpful Hints

1. This Map's INDEX can be found on the preceding pages.

2. Refer to Map "C" to see where this Township lies within Howell County, Missouri.

3. Numbers within square brackets [ ] denote a multi-patentee land parcel (multi-owner). Refer to Appendix "C" for a full list of members in this group.

4. Areas that look to be crowded with Patentees usually indicate multiple sales of the same parcel (Re-issues) or Overlapping parcels. See this Township's Index for an explanation of these and other circumstances that might explain "odd" groupings of Patentees on this map.

Legend

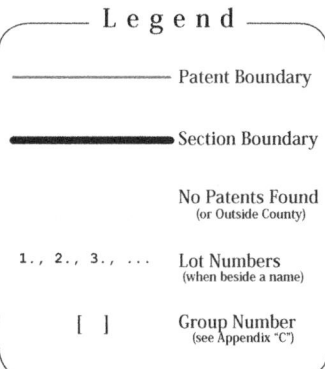

———— Patent Boundary

━━━━ Section Boundary

No Patents Found (or Outside County)

1., 2., 3., ... Lot Numbers (when beside a name)

[ ] Group Number (see Appendix "C")

Scale: Section = 1 mile X 1 mile (generally, with some exceptions)

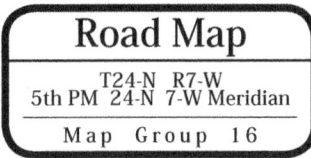

Road Map

T24-N R7-W
5th PM 24-N 7-W Meridian

Map Group 16

Cities & Towns

Cull

Cemeteries

Elk Creek Cemetery
Francis Cemetery

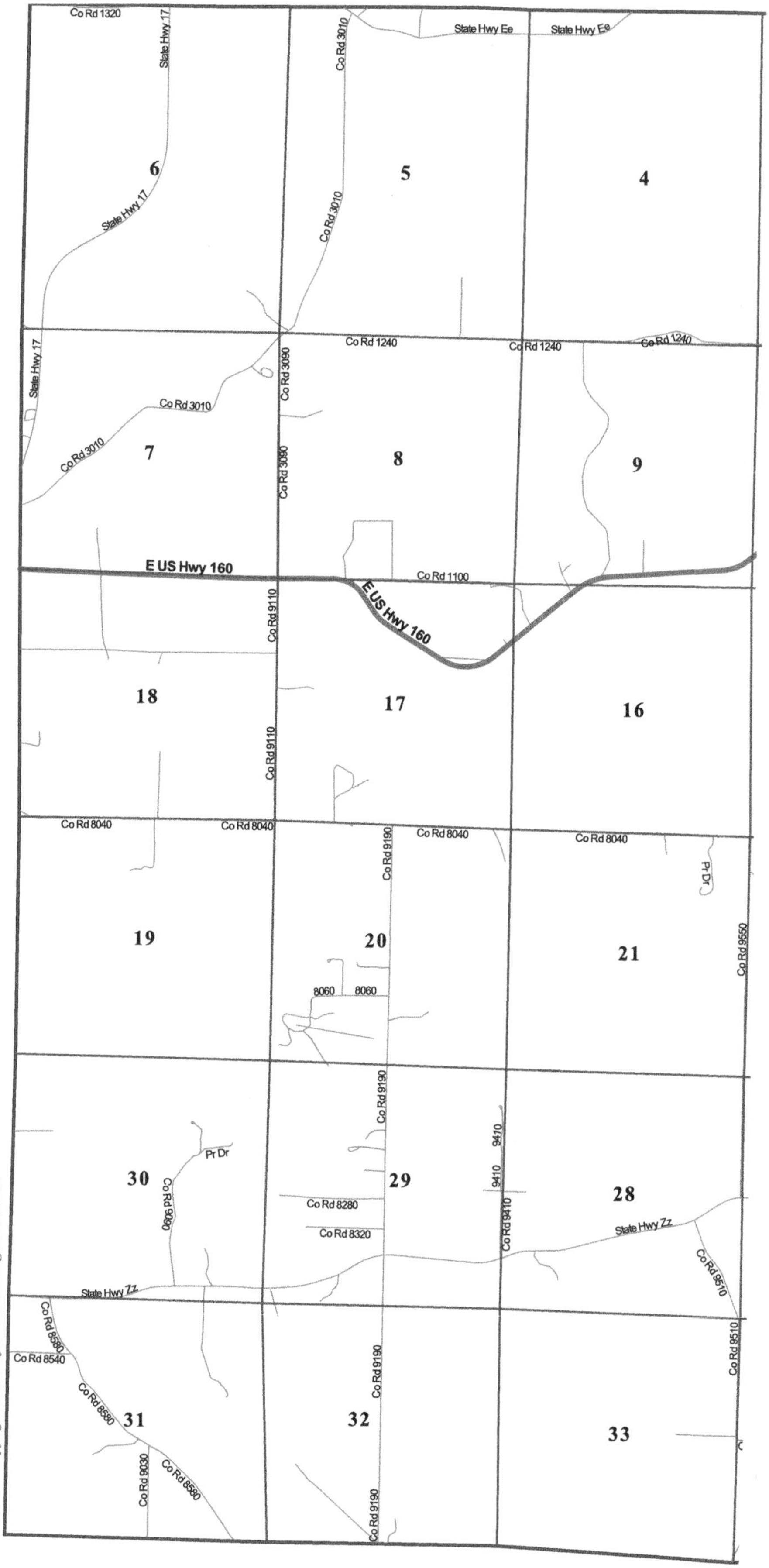

Co Rd 1320

State Hwy 17

Co Rd 3010

State Hwy Ee

State Hwy Ee

6

5

4

State Hwy 17

Co Rd 3010

Co Rd 1240

Co Rd 1240

Co Rd 1240

State Hwy 17

Co Rd 3010

Co Rd 3090

Co Rd 3010

7

Co Rd 3090

8

9

E US Hwy 160

Co Rd 1100

E US Hwy 160

Co Rd 9110

E US Hwy 160

18

17

16

Co Rd 9110

Co Rd 8040

Co Rd 8040

Co Rd 9190

Co Rd 8040

Co Rd 8040

Pr Dr

Co Rd 9550

19

20

21

8060

8060

Co Rd 9190

9410

9410

30

Pr Dr

Co Rd 9090

29

Co Rd 9410

28

Co Rd 8280

State Hwy Zz

Co Rd 8320

Co Rd 9510

State Hwy Zz

Co Rd 8540

Co Rd 8580

Co Rd 9190

Co Rd 9510

Co Rd 8580

31

32

33

Co Rd 9030

Co Rd 8580

Co Rd 9190

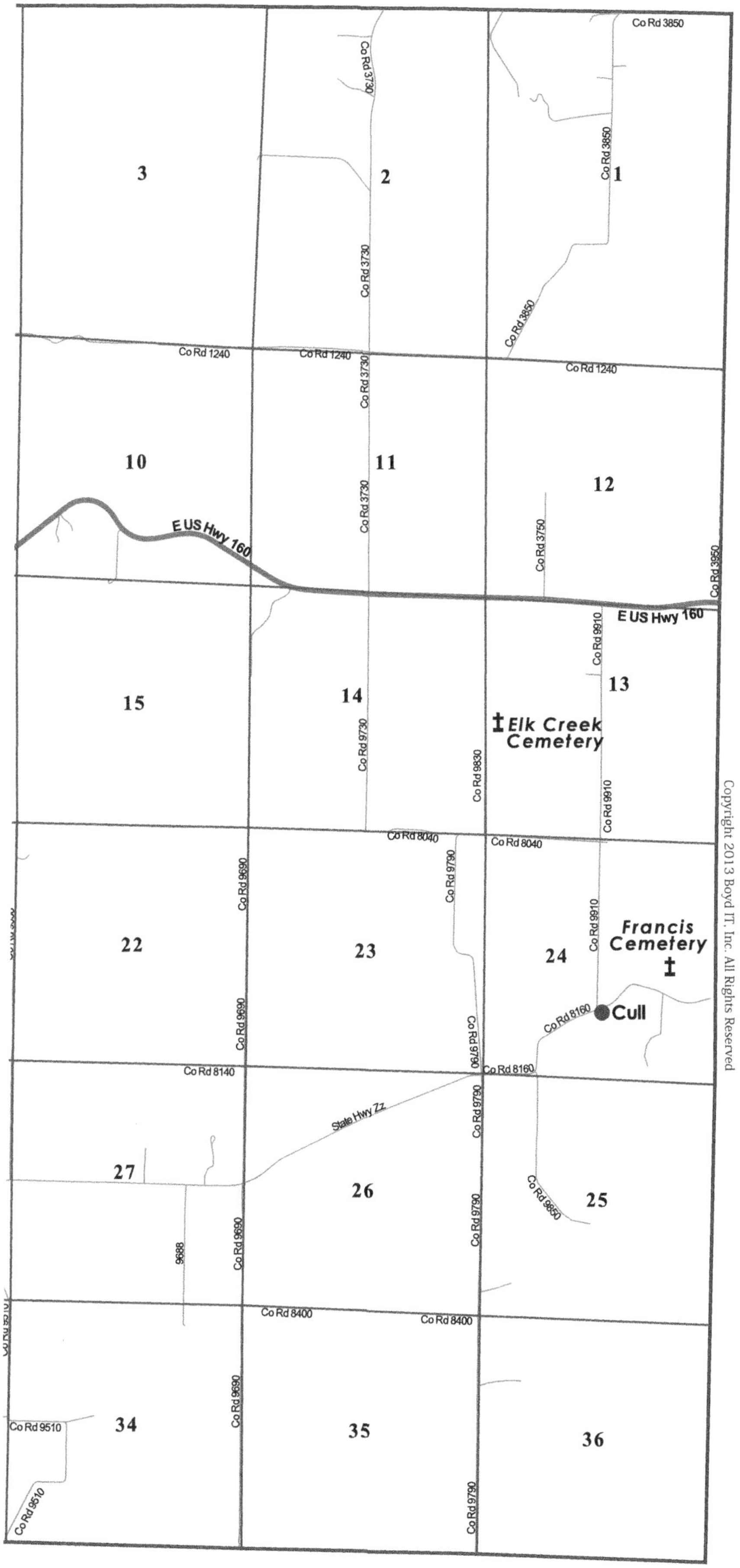

3

2

Co Rd 3850

Co Rd 3730

Co Rd 3850

1

Co Rd 1240

Co Rd 1240

Co Rd 1240

Co Rd 3730

10

11

12

E US Hwy 160

Co Rd 3730

Co Rd 3750

Co Rd 3850

E US Hwy 160

Co Rd 9910

15

14

13

‡ Elk Creek
Cemetery

Co Rd 9730

Co Rd 9830

Co Rd 9910

Co Rd 8040

Co Rd 8040

22

Co Rd 9690

Co Rd 9790

23

24

Co Rd 9910

Francis
Cemetery
‡

Co Rd 9690

Co Rd 8140

Co Rd 9790

Co Rd 8160 ● Cull

Co Rd 8160

State Hwy Zz

27

Co Rd 9690

9688

26

Co Rd 9790

Co Rd 9850

25

Co Rd 8400

Co Rd 8400

Co Rd 9690

Co Rd 9510

34

35

36

Co Rd 9510

Co Rd 9790

Helpful Hints

1. This road map has a number of uses, but primarily it is to help you: a) find the present location of land owned by your ancestors (at least the general area), b) find cemeteries and city-centers, and c) estimate the route/roads used by Census-takers & tax-assessors.

2. If you plan to travel to Howell County to locate cemeteries or land parcels, please pick up a modern travel map for the area before you do. Mapping old land parcels on modern maps is not as exact a science as you might think. Just the slightest variations in public land survey coordinates, estimates of parcel boundaries, or road-map deviations can greatly alter a map's representation of how a road either does or doesn't cross a particular parcel of land.

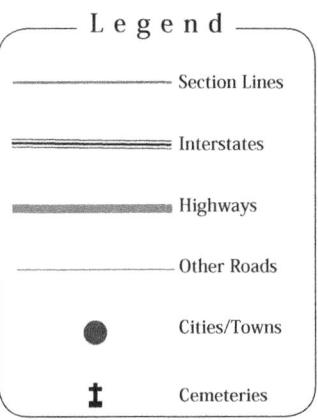

L e g e n d

——————— Section Lines

════════ Interstates

━━━━━━━ Highways

——————— Other Roads

● Cities/Towns

‡ Cemeteries

Scale: Section = 1 mile X 1 mile
(generally, with some exceptions)

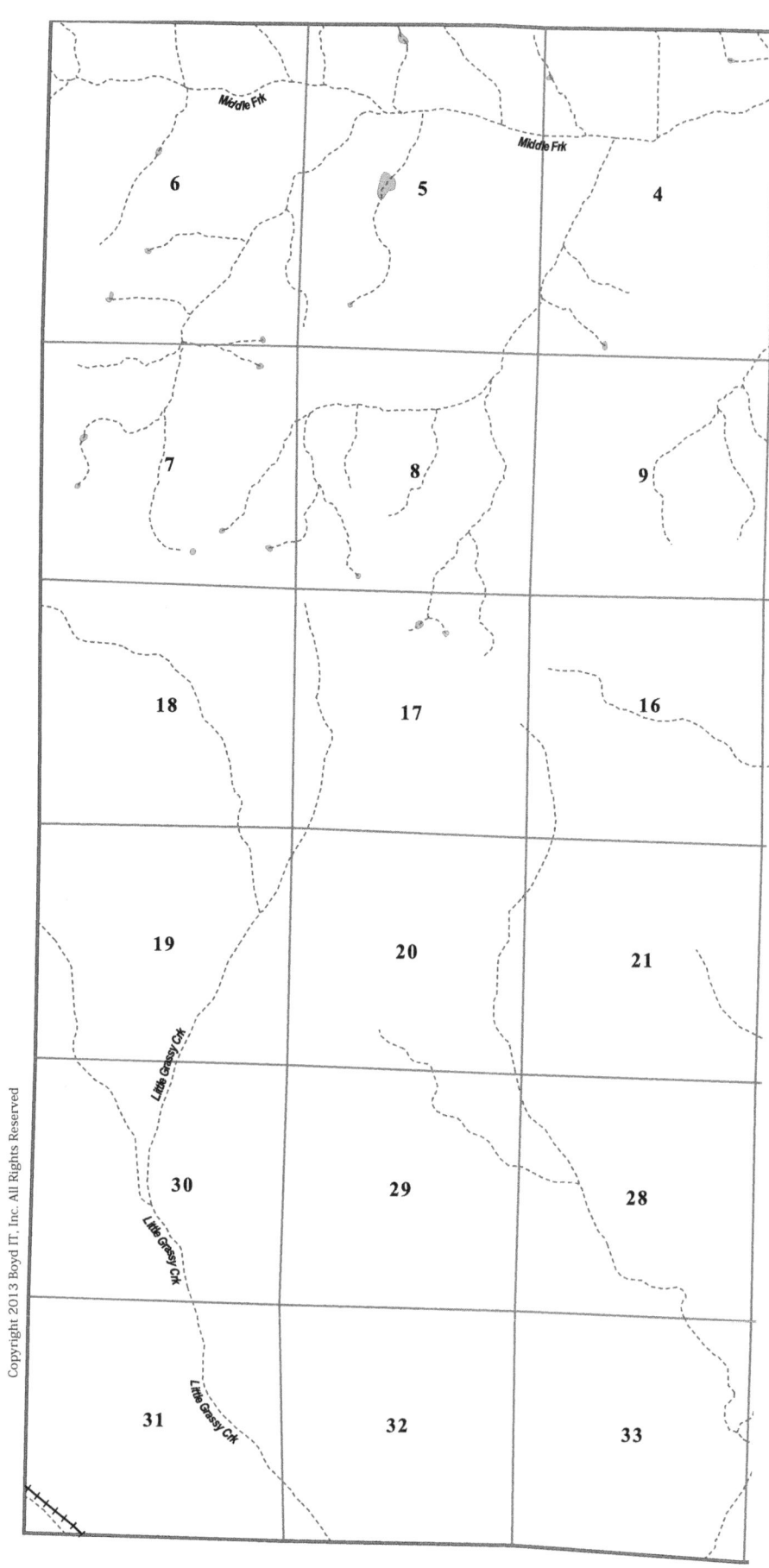

Historical Map

T24-N R7-W
5th PM 24-N 7-W Meridian

Map Group 16

Cities & Towns
Cull

Cemeteries
Elk Creek Cemetery
Francis Cemetery

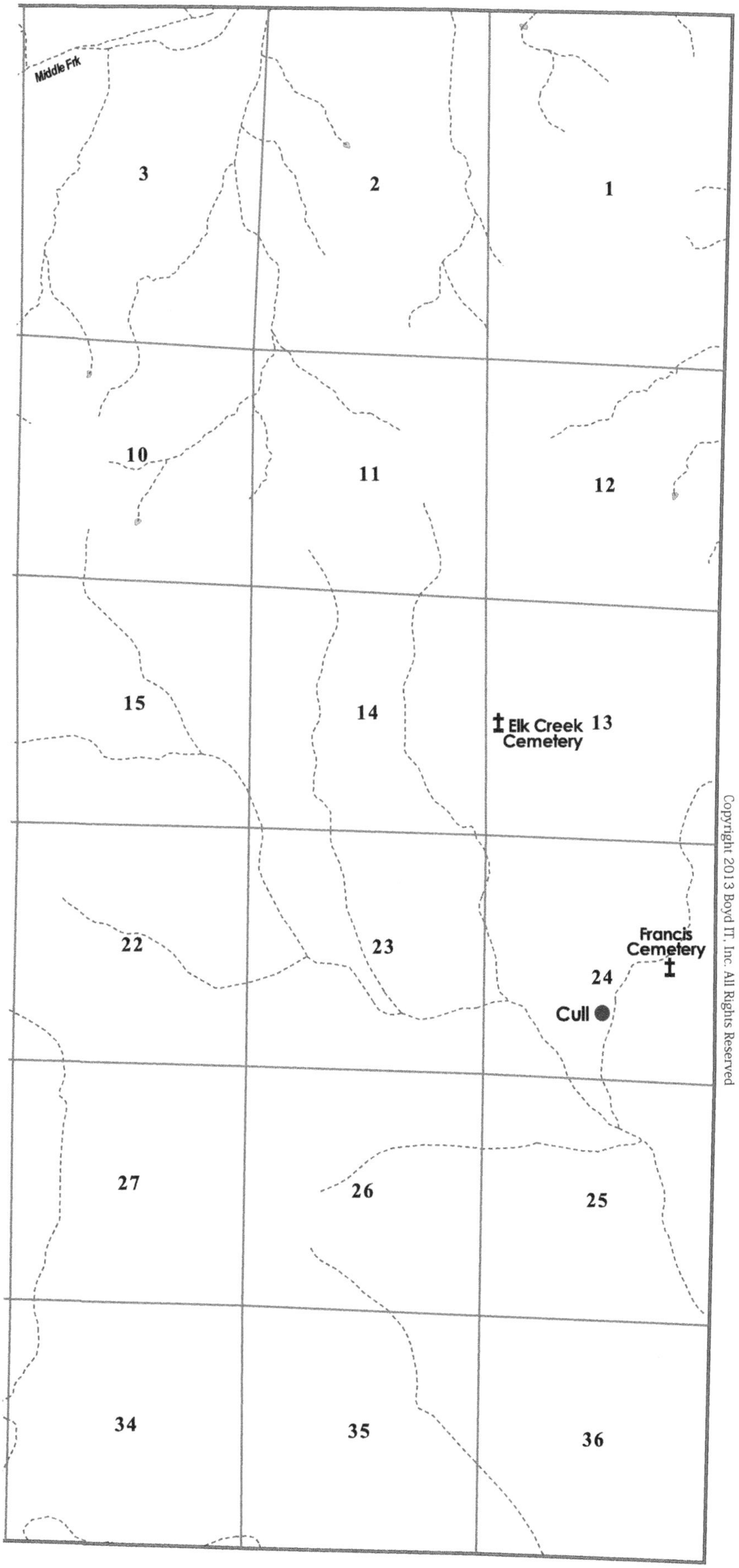

Middle Frk

3

2

1

10

11

12

15

14

‡ Elk Creek 13
Cemetery

22

23

Francis
Cemetery
24 ‡

Cull ●

27

26

25

34

35

36

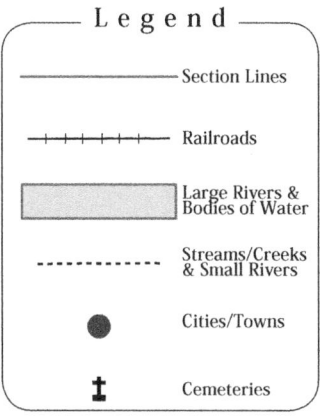

L e g e n d

——————— Section Lines

+—+—+—+—+— Railroads

[ ] Large Rivers &
Bodies of Water

- - - - - - - Streams/Creeks
& Small Rivers

● Cities/Towns

‡ Cemeteries

Scale: Section = 1 mile X 1 mile
(there are some exceptions)

Map Group 17: Index to Land Patents

Township 23-North Range 10-West (5th PM 23-N 10-W)

After you locate an individual in this Index, take note of the Section and Section Part then proceed to the Land Patent map on the pages immediately following. You should have no difficulty locating the corresponding parcel of land.

The "For More Info" Column will lead you to more information about the underlying Patents. See the *Legend* at right, and the "How to Use this Book" chapter, for more information.

```
                          LEGEND
               "For More Info . . . " column
A = Authority (Legislative Act, See Appendix "A")
B = Block or Lot (location in Section unknown)
C = Cancelled Patent
F = Fractional Section
G = Group  (Multi-Patentee Patent, see Appendix "C")
V = Overlaps another Parcel
R = Re-Issued (Parcel patented more than once)

(A & G items require you to look in the Appendixes referred
to above. All other Letter-designations followed by a number
require you to locate line-items in this index that possess
the ID number found after the letter).
```

ID	Individual in Patent	Sec.	Sec. Part	Date Issued	Other Counties	For More Info . . .
7774	ADAMS, Benoni	1	W22NE	1856-06-16		A1
7772	" "	1	W21NE	1856-06-16		A1
7768	" "	1	E21NE	1859-01-01		A1
4201	ADAMS, Edward L	1	NWSE	1859-09-01		A1
7805	BATTERTON, Alexander A	31	2SW	1894-05-18		A7
7807	" "	31	S21SW	1894-05-18		A7
4204	BELCHER, Thomas W	14	SESE	1904-08-26		A7
4205	" "	23	E½NE	1904-08-26		A7
4206	" "	23	SWNE	1904-08-26		A7
4208	BIZZELL, J L	29	S½NW	1889-06-22		A7
4207	" "	29	N½SW	1889-06-22		A7
4209	BRIDGES, John W	31	SWNE	1892-01-05		A7
7806	" "	31	N21SW	1892-01-05		A7
7803	" "	31	1NW	1892-01-05		A7
4212	BRIDGES, Orren D	30	SWNE	1888-12-06		A7
4211	" "	30	NWSE	1888-12-06		A7
4210	" "	30	S½SE	1888-12-06		A7
7798	BRIGGS, William	3	2NW	1881-10-06		A7
4213	BURNET, O J	32	NENE	1888-07-17		A1
4216	BURNET, Oswald J	32	NENW	1892-10-17		A7
4214	" "	32	S½NE	1892-10-17		A7
4215	" "	32	NWNE	1892-10-17		A7
4220	BURRISS, John	24	NWSE	1895-07-08		A7
4217	" "	24	SWNE	1895-07-08		A7
4218	" "	24	SENW	1895-07-08		A7
4219	" "	24	NESW	1895-07-08		A7
4222	CALLAHAN, George R	34	NWSE	1900-02-02		A7
4221	" "	34	N½SW	1900-02-02		A7
4223	CARTER, George H	25	SWNE	1892-08-01		A1
4224	CARTER, William M	31	S½SE	1892-01-25		A7
4225	CATES, Charley	34	SESE	1889-01-12		A7
4226	" "	35	S½SW	1889-01-12		A7
4228	CATES, Jason A	13	SWSE	1888-11-27		A7
4227	" "	13	N½SE	1888-11-27		A7
4229	" "	24	NWNE	1888-11-27		A7
4230	CATES, William	34	NESE	1888-11-27		A7
4232	" "	35	NWSE	1888-11-27		A7
4231	" "	35	N½SW	1888-11-27		A7
4233	CHAPPELL, John T	18	SWSE	1890-01-10		A7
7776	" "	18	1SW	1890-01-10		A7
4234	" "	19	NWNE	1890-01-10		A7
4235	CLINKINGBEARD, J N	20	E½SW	1877-08-01		A7
4236	" "	20	SWSE	1877-08-01		A7
4237	CLINKINGBEARD, Joel N	20	SWSW	1882-12-20		A1
4239	COOK, Giles	26	W½SW	1900-02-02		A7
4240	" "	27	E½SE	1900-02-02		A7

ID	Individual in Patent	Sec.	Sec. Part	Date Issued	Other Counties	For More Info . . .
4242	COOPER, Joel M	36	SENE	1892-10-17		A7
4243	" "	36	N½NE	1892-10-17		A7
4241	" "	36	NESE	1892-10-17		A7
4244	COX, John W	28	SENE	1907-12-05		A7
4245	COX, William D	28	SE	1892-03-07		A7
4246	CRAFTON, Aylett R	3	SWSW	1903-08-25		A7
4247	CRISP, Thomas E	14	SWSE	1896-01-14		A7
4248	" "	23	NENW	1896-01-14		A7
4249	" "	23	NWNE	1896-01-14		A7
4251	DAVIS, Caleb T	35	NWNE	1900-02-02		A7
4250	" "	35	NESE	1900-02-02		A7
4252	" "	35	S½NE	1900-02-02		A7
4255	DAVIS, George W	26	W½NE	1895-11-05		A7
4253	" "	26	SENE	1895-11-05		A7
4254	" "	26	NENW	1895-11-05		A7
4256	DAVIS, John A	2	SESW	1898-06-23		A7
4257	DECKER, Eli W	29	NWNE	1892-03-07		A7
4258	" "	29	NENW	1892-03-07		A7
4259	" "	29	S½NE	1892-03-07		A7
7797	DENT, James W	3	1NW	1893-09-01		A7
4260	" "	3	N½SW	1893-09-01		A7
4261	DENT, John C	4	NE	1873-02-01		A7
7799	DILLINDER, Martha	3	E21NE	1853-12-01		A1
7802	" "	3	W22NE	1853-12-01		A1
4262	DORSEY, Thomas J	19	SESE	1886-04-10		A7
4263	" "	19	W½SE	1886-04-10		A7
4264	" "	30	NWNE	1886-04-10		A7
4265	DURHAM, Daniel F	13	N½SW	1861-07-01		A6
4266	" "	14	NESE	1861-07-01		A6
4267	ENDECOTT, Elizabeth	4	NESW	1885-05-25		A1
4268	" "	9	NENE	1883-08-13		A1
4270	ENDECOTT, Gabriel C	9	SWSW	1888-12-08		A7
4269	" "	9	N½SW	1888-12-08		A7
4271	ENDECOTT, James M	14	SWNW	1882-05-20		A7
4272	" "	15	SENE	1882-05-20		A7
4273	ENDECOTT, Joseph	15	NESE	1859-09-01		A1
4274	" "	4	SWSE	1859-09-01		A1
4275	ENDECOTT, Samuel	14	NWSW	1860-08-01		A1
4276	" "	14	S½SW	1883-02-10		A7
4277	ENDECOTT, Samuel G	9	SWNW	1888-12-06		A1
4278	ENDECOTT, Sarah J	22	N½NW	1884-10-11		A1
4279	ENDICOTT, Elizabeth	4	NWSE	1882-11-10		A7
4280	ENDICOTT, Joseph	10	SWSW	1858-12-16		A8
4281	" "	15	SESE	1859-01-01		A1
4282	" "	15	NWNW	1858-12-16		A8
4283	ENDICOTT, Samuel	4	E½SE	1860-02-10		A6
4284	" "	9	NWNE	1888-05-07		A1
4286	ENDICOTT, Samuel G	4	SWSW	1883-08-13		A1
4285	" "	4	NWSW	1885-06-03		A1
4287	FLINN, William	2	NESE	1871-05-10		A8
7800	FOSTER, James D	3	E22NE	1860-10-01		A1
4290	FOX, William	1	E½SW	1874-12-20		A7
4289	" "	1	SWSE	1874-12-20		A7
4291	" "	12	NENW	1874-12-20		A7
7813	FOX, William M	5	E22NW	1898-10-04		A7
7816	" "	5	W22NE	1898-10-04		A7
4293	FULS, Metellus	11	SENE	1904-08-26		A7
4292	" "	11	E½SE	1904-08-26		A7
4294	" "	14	NENE	1904-08-26		A7
4295	GARNER, William S	9	S½SE	1859-09-01		A1
4298	GLASS, Nancy	13	S½NW	1863-04-20		A6 G95
4300	GUILLIAMS, Mary L	17	W½NW	1891-05-05		A7 G102
4301	" "	18	E½NE	1891-05-05		A7 G102
4302	GUILLIAMS, William M	17	W½NW	1891-05-05		A7 G102
4303	" "	18	E½NE	1891-05-05		A7 G102
7814	HALL, John T	5	W21NE	1903-06-01		A7
4304	" "	5	NWSE	1903-06-01		A7
4305	HALSELL, John E	15	E½SW	1884-02-15		A7
4306	HARMON, William	13	SESE	1859-09-01		A1
7785	HARPER, William F	19	N21SW	1899-02-13		A7
7786	" "	19	S21NW	1899-02-13		A7
4307	" "	19	S½NE	1899-02-13		A7
4308	HARRISON, John F	22	SENE	1883-02-10		A7

ID	Individual in Patent	Sec.	Sec. Part	Date Issued	Other Counties	For More Info . . .
4310	HARRISON, John F (Cont'd)	23	S½NW	1883-02-10		A7
4311	" "	23	SESW	1893-12-09		A1
4312	" "	23	NESW	1883-02-10		A7
4309	" "	23	NWSW	1879-09-23		A1
4313	HARTMAN, John A	15	W½SW	1885-05-25		A1 G109
4316	" "	17	SW	1885-05-25		A1 G109
4315	" "	17	SESE	1885-05-25		A1 G109
4314	" "	17	W½SE	1885-05-25		A1 G109
4317	" "	18	E½SE	1885-05-25		A1 G109
4320	" "	20	NE	1885-05-25		A1 G109
4318	" "	20	N½SE	1885-05-25		A1 G109
4319	" "	20	E½NW	1885-05-25		A1 G109
4323	" "	21	E½NE	1885-05-25		A1 G109
4322	" "	21	SE	1885-05-25		A1 G109
4321	" "	21	W½NW	1885-05-25		A1 G109
4324	" "	22	NWSE	1885-05-25		A1 G109
4325	" "	22	SENW	1885-05-25		A1 G109
4326	" "	22	SWSW	1885-05-25		A1 G109
4327	" "	22	W½NW	1885-05-25		A1 G109
4329	" "	22	N½SW	1885-05-25		A1 G109
4328	" "	22	SWNE	1885-05-25		A1 G109
4330	HENSLEY, William M	30	NW	1890-01-10		A7
4331	HERRIEN, John W	12	N½SW	1900-02-02		A7
4332	" "	12	SWSW	1900-02-02		A7
4333	" "	13	NWNW	1900-02-02		A7
4334	HIXON, Caleb C	27	E½SW	1906-06-21		A7
7804	HIXON, Thomas W	31	2NW	1906-06-30	Ozark	A7
4335	" "	31	NWSE	1886-11-19		A1
4336	HODGES, William J	29	SE	1892-03-07		A7
4337	HOPKINS, Andrew J	10	NENW	1888-12-06		A7
4338	" "	3	SESW	1888-12-06		A7
4339	" "	3	SESE	1886-11-19		A1
4340	HOPKINS, Henry C	26	SENW	1895-11-05		A7
4342	" "	26	N½SE	1895-11-05		A7
4341	" "	26	NESW	1895-11-05		A7
4343	HOPKINS, William W	10	NENE	1878-04-05		A7
4344	" "	10	W½NE	1878-04-05		A7
4345	" "	3	SWSE	1878-04-05		A7
7820	HORN, George W	6	2NW	1901-04-09		A7
7824	" "	6	W21NW	1901-04-09		A7
4348	HOWELL, Josephus M	14	NESW	1859-09-01		A1
7812	HUDLOW, William R	5	E22NE	1892-01-05		A7
4349	HUNTER, Nancy	25	S½SE	1877-10-10		A7
4350	" "	25	SESW	1877-10-10		A7
4351	" "	36	NENW	1877-10-10		A7
4353	HUTCHESON, Thomas W	17	NE	1860-03-01		A1
4352	" "	17	N½SE	1860-03-01		A1
7780	INMAN, Ezekiel N	18	S21NW	1891-11-23		A7
4354	" "	18	W½NE	1891-11-23		A7
4355	JAMES, John P	13	SESW	1899-05-05		A7
4356	" "	24	NENW	1899-05-05		A7
4359	JOHNSON, George W	36	SWNE	1896-07-23		A7
4357	" "	36	S½SE	1896-07-23		A7
4358	" "	36	NWSE	1896-07-23		A7
4360	JOHNSTON, William T	35	NW	1893-12-19		A7
4361	JULIEN, William	33	S½NE	1888-12-08		A7
4362	JULIEN, William S	33	N½NE	1901-12-04		A7
4363	KEE, Joseph W	24	E½SE	1899-02-13		A7
4364	" "	25	N½NE	1899-02-13		A7
4365	KENSLOW, James H	24	NENE	1879-12-15		A7
4366	KINSOLVING, William S	12	E½NE	1892-03-07		A7
4367	KNOX, Jesse F	14	E½NW	1896-10-16		A7
4368	" "	14	W½NE	1896-10-16		A7
4369	LANG, Albert	29	NWNW	1894-12-17		A7
4370	" "	30	NESE	1894-12-17		A7
4371	" "	30	E½NE	1894-12-17		A7
4372	LANGSTON, John R	1	E½SE	1892-06-10		A7
4373	" "	12	NWNE	1892-06-10		A7
7825	LAURANCE, John W	6	W22NE	1898-01-26		A7
4375	LAWING, Alfred J	10	N½SW	1882-09-30		A7
4374	" "	10	S½NW	1882-09-30		A7
7818	LAWING, Elbert A	6	1NE	1916-03-06		A7
4376	" "	6	NWSE	1916-03-06		A7

ID	Individual in Patent	Sec.	Sec. Part	Date Issued	Other Counties	For More Info . . .
7822	LAWING, Elbert A (Cont'd)	6	E21NW	1916-03-06		A7
4377	" "	9	S½NE	1885-02-25		A7
4378	" "	9	N½SE	1885-02-25		A7
4379	LECKRON, Jacob S	17	W½SW	1911-04-27	Texas	A7
4381	LLOYD, William A	31	NESE	1890-01-30		A1
4382	" "	31	SENE	1890-01-30		A1
4380	" "	31	N½NE	1890-01-30		A1
4383	LOGAN, Alexander	25	NESE	1891-05-05		A7
4384	" "	25	SENE	1891-05-05		A7
7796	MANNON, Isaac	2	W22NW	1859-09-01		A1
7801	MARITT, John W	3	W21NE	1882-09-30		A1
4385	MCDANIEL, John	32	SESW	1860-03-01		A1
4386	MCDANIEL, John M	34	SWSW	1860-08-01		A1
4387	MCDANIEL, Thomas J	34	SWSE	1860-03-01		A1
7787	MCGOLDRICK, Albert	19	S21SW	1904-12-31		A7
7783	" "	19	2SW	1904-12-31		A7
4389	MCGOLDRICK, Mary E	21	E½NW	1904-08-26		A7
4388	" "	21	W½NE	1904-08-26		A7
4390	MCGOLDRICK, Thomas W	32	SENW	1910-01-24		A1
4391	MILLER, James R	14	NWSE	1860-10-01		A1
4393	MITCHELL, Edmund H	11	NWSE	1892-01-05		A7
4392	" "	11	W½NE	1892-01-05		A7
4394	" "	2	SWSE	1892-01-05		A7
4395	NORMAN, Isaac A	11	N½NW	1892-03-07		A7
4396	" "	2	W½SW	1892-03-07		A7
4397	" "	3	NESE	1886-10-29		A1
7788	PARSONS, David	2	E21NE	1853-12-01		A1
7791	" "	2	E22NE	1853-12-01		A1
7794	PARSONS, George W	2	W21NW	1854-11-15		A1
7795	PARSONS, Simeon	2	W22NE	1854-11-15		A1
7792	" "	2	E22NW	1853-12-01		A1
7793	" "	2	W21NE	1853-12-01		A1
7823	PENDERGRAFT, Jesse	6	E22NE	1906-01-30		A7
4398	PHELPS, Holmen	1	NWSW	1859-09-01		A1
7773	PHELPS, James K	1	W21NW	1853-04-15		A1
7769	" "	1	E21NW	1859-01-01		A1
7771	PHELPS, Phelix	1	E22NW	1859-09-01		A1
4399	PLANK, John C	25	W½SW	1892-03-07		A7
4400	" "	35	NENE	1892-03-07		A7
4401	" "	36	NWNW	1892-03-07		A7
7770	POTTER, James M	1	E22NE	1853-04-12		A1
4402	PROFFITT, Henderson S	9	SESW	1876-09-06		A7
4403	PROFFITT, Nancy J	11	SWSE	1903-06-08		A7 G159
4404	" "	11	S½SW	1903-06-08		A7 G159
4405	" "	14	NWNW	1903-06-08		A7 G159
4407	PROFFITT, Riley M	11	SWSE	1903-06-08		A7 G159
4406	" "	11	S½SW	1903-06-08		A7 G159
4408	" "	14	NWNW	1903-06-08		A7 G159
4410	PROFFITT, Samuel T	9	E½NW	1884-02-15		A7
4409	" "	9	NWNW	1884-02-15		A7
4411	RAMSEY, Hiram E	24	SENE	1901-05-08		A7
4412	RAMSEY, Noel	12	SESE	1895-05-28		A7
4413	REESE, Edward	33	SW	1892-03-07		A7
4414	REESE, William	33	NW	1892-03-07		A7
4415	REID, John	15	W½SW	1885-05-25		A1 G109
4417	" "	17	SESE	1885-05-25		A1 G109
4418	" "	17	SW	1885-05-25		A1 G109
4416	" "	17	W½SE	1885-05-25		A1 G109
4419	" "	18	E½SE	1885-05-25		A1 G109
4421	" "	20	N½SE	1885-05-25		A1 G109
4422	" "	20	E½NW	1885-05-25		A1 G109
4420	" "	20	NE	1885-05-25		A1 G109
4423	" "	21	SE	1885-05-25		A1 G109
4424	" "	21	E½NE	1885-05-25		A1 G109
4425	" "	21	W½NW	1885-05-25		A1 G109
4431	" "	22	SENW	1885-05-25		A1 G109
4426	" "	22	N½SW	1885-05-25		A1 G109
4427	" "	22	W½NW	1885-05-25		A1 G109
4428	" "	22	SWNE	1885-05-25		A1 G109
4429	" "	22	SWSW	1885-05-25		A1 G109
4430	" "	22	NWSE	1885-05-25		A1 G109
4432	RILEY, Converse V	1	SWSW	1882-12-20		A1
4433	RISLEY, Charlotte F	28	S½SW	1892-04-23		A1

ID	Individual in Patent	Sec.	Sec. Part	Date Issued	Other Counties	For More Info . . .
4434	ROBERSON, Charles	10	NWNW	1885-05-25		A1
4437	ROBERSON, William R	27	SWNE	1892-03-07		A7
4435	" "	27	SENW	1892-03-07		A7
4436	" "	27	W½SE	1892-03-07		A7
4439	ROBERTS, James A	10	SENE	1908-03-02		A7
4438	" "	10	N½SE	1908-03-02		A7
4440	ROBERTSON, Charles	15	W½SE	1875-04-01		A7
4441	" "	22	N½NE	1875-04-01		A7
4443	ROBERTSON, David	5	S½SE	1890-01-10		A7
4442	" "	5	E½SW	1890-01-10		A7
4444	ROMANS, John F	13	SWSW	1914-07-29		A7
4446	" "	24	NWSW	1914-07-29		A7
4445	" "	24	W½NW	1914-07-29		A7
4447	ROWDEN, Taylor	27	SWSW	1901-08-27		A1
4454	SEABORN, Thomas	34	NENE	1885-12-19		A1
4453	" "	34	N½NW	1885-06-03		A1
4452	" "	34	SWNE	1885-12-19		A1
4451	" "	34	NWNE	1885-06-03		A1
4450	" "	34	SENW	1885-06-03		A1
4449	" "	34	SENE	1885-06-03		A1
4448	" "	34	SWNW	1885-12-19		A1
7779	SHRIVEAR, John	18	N22SW	1898-04-11		A7
7777	" "	18	2NW	1898-04-11		A7
7778	" "	18	N21NW	1898-04-11		A7
4455	SMITH, Calvin C	2	SESE	1894-05-16		A1
4456	SMITH, Elijah	11	NENE	1892-01-25		A7
4458	" "	12	SENW	1892-01-25		A7
4457	" "	12	W½NW	1892-01-25		A7
7790	SMITH, James V	2	E21NW	1860-05-02		A6
4460	" "	2	NWSE	1860-05-02		A6
4459	" "	2	NESW	1860-05-02		A6
4461	SPENCER, George W	20	SESE	1861-07-01		A6
4462	" "	29	NENE	1861-07-01		A6
4463	SRIVER, Irena	17	E½NW	1882-08-30		A7 G174
4464	" "	17	NWNE	1882-08-30		A7 G174
4466	SRIVER, Peter M	17	NWNE	1882-08-30		A7 G174
4467	" "	17	SWNE	1860-10-01		A1
4465	" "	17	E½NW	1882-08-30		A7 G174
4469	STACY, Benjamin F	11	S½NW	1892-06-10		A7
4468	" "	11	N½SW	1892-06-10		A7
4470	STORY, James H	29	S½SW	1892-01-05		A7
4471	" "	32	W½NW	1892-01-05		A7
4472	SURRETT, David	23	NWNW	1886-10-29		A1
4473	SURRITT, David E	24	SWSW	1907-12-05		A7
4474	TABOR, James P	5	NESE	1888-12-08		A7
7810	" "	5	E21NE	1888-12-08		A7
7775	TABOR, Thomas E	1	W22NW	1875-02-15		A7
7817	TAYLOR, Martha A	5	W22NW	1904-11-01		A7
7815	" "	5	W21NW	1904-11-01		A7
4477	TILSON, John A	18	NWSE	1905-03-30		A7 G179
4479	TILSON, John E	19	NENE	1888-12-06		A7
4478	" "	19	NESE	1910-01-17		A1
4481	" "	20	W½NW	1888-12-06		A7
4480	" "	20	NWSW	1888-12-06		A7
4482	TILSON, Theodore W	18	NWSE	1905-03-30		A7 G179
7781	TILSON, Thomas J	18	S22SW	1896-12-08		A7
7784	" "	19	N21NW	1896-12-08		A7
7782	" "	19	2NW	1896-12-08		A7
4485	TIPTON, John H	27	N½NW	1895-05-28		A7
4483	" "	27	NWSW	1895-05-28		A7
4484	" "	27	SWNW	1895-05-28		A7
4486	TOBLER, Jacob	13	S½NW	1863-04-20		A6 G95
4487	WADLEY, Jesse T	3	NWSE	1889-05-29		A1
4488	WALKER, Isom	5	SWSW	1911-10-23		A7
7819	WALKER, James A	6	1SW	1895-09-04		A7
7821	" "	6	2SW	1895-09-04		A7
4489	WALKER, John	17	NESE	1888-12-08		A7
4490	" "	17	E½NE	1888-12-08		A7
4491	WALKER, John H	35	S½SE	1890-10-11		A7
4492	" "	36	W½SW	1890-10-11		A7
4493	WALKER, William H	36	E½SW	1893-04-26		A7
4494	" "	36	S½NW	1893-04-26		A7
4496	WALLACE, Richard	23	NESE	1888-12-06		A1

ID	Individual in Patent	Sec.	Sec. Part	Date Issued	Other Counties	For More Info . . .
4497	WALLACE, Richard (Cont'd)	23	S½SE	1881-10-06		A7
4495	" "	23	NWSE	1880-10-01		A1
4498	" "	25	SWNW	1886-10-29		A1
4499	" "	25	NWNW	1881-10-06		A7
4500	" "	26	NENE	1881-10-06		A7
4501	WATSON, Jas S	13	S½NW	1863-04-20		A6 G95
4502	WESCOTT, Benjamin R	12	NESE	1907-10-11		A1
4503	" "	13	NENW	1907-10-11		A1
4504	" "	14	SENE	1907-10-11		A1
4505	" "	24	SWSE	1907-10-11		A1
4506	" "	24	SESW	1907-10-11		A1
4508	" "	26	S½SE	1907-10-11		A1
4509	" "	26	SWNW	1907-10-11		A1
4507	" "	26	SESW	1907-10-11		A1
4511	WILES, William S	28	NENE	1899-06-28		A7
4510	" "	28	W½NE	1899-06-28		A7
4513	WILLIAMS, Albert J	12	SWSE	1894-12-17		A7
4514	" "	12	SESW	1894-12-17		A7
4515	" "	12	NWSE	1894-12-17		A7
4512	" "	12	SWNE	1894-12-17		A7
4516	WILLIAMS, David	10	SESW	1892-01-05		A7
4517	" "	10	S½SE	1892-01-05		A7
4519	" "	15	SWNE	1888-12-06		A1
4518	" "	15	NENE	1892-01-05		A7
7811	WILLIAMS, Jane	5	E21NW	1890-01-30		A1
4520	WILLIAMS, John H	22	SWSE	1897-04-02		A7
4521	" "	27	N½NE	1897-04-02		A7
4522	" "	27	SENE	1897-04-02		A7
4523	WILLIAMS, Jonathan	22	SESW	1885-03-20		A1
4524	WILLIAMS, Joseph	15	NWNE	1875-02-15		A7
4525	" "	15	NENW	1875-02-15		A7
4526	" "	4	SESW	1885-05-25		A1
4527	WILSON, John W	5	NWSW	1892-06-10		A7
4529	" "	6	S½SE	1892-06-10		A7
4528	" "	6	NESE	1892-06-10		A7
4532	WILSON, Thomas F	25	E½NW	1892-06-10		A7
4531	" "	25	NESW	1892-06-10		A7
4530	" "	25	NWSE	1892-06-10		A7
7809	WILSON, William	4	2NW	1893-04-29		A7
7808	" "	4	1NW	1893-04-29		A7
4533	WILSON, William A	22	E½SE	1889-06-22		A7
4534	" "	23	SWSW	1889-06-22		A7
4535	" "	26	NWNW	1889-06-22		A7
4536	YOUNGBLOOD, George W	30	SW	1888-12-06		A7
4538	YOUNGBLOOD, Jonathan	32	SWSW	1885-03-20		A1
4537	" "	32	N½SW	1885-05-25		A1

Patent Map

T23-N R10-W
5th PM 23-N 10-W Meridian

Map Group 17

Township Statistics

Parcels Mapped	:	357
Number of Patents	:	194
Number of Individuals	:	179
Patentees Identified	:	172
Number of Surnames	:	116
Multi-Patentee Parcels	:	26
Oldest Patent Date	:	12/16/1858
Most Recent Patent	:	3/6/1916
Block/Lot Parcels	:	57
Cities and Town	:	3
Cemeteries	:	3

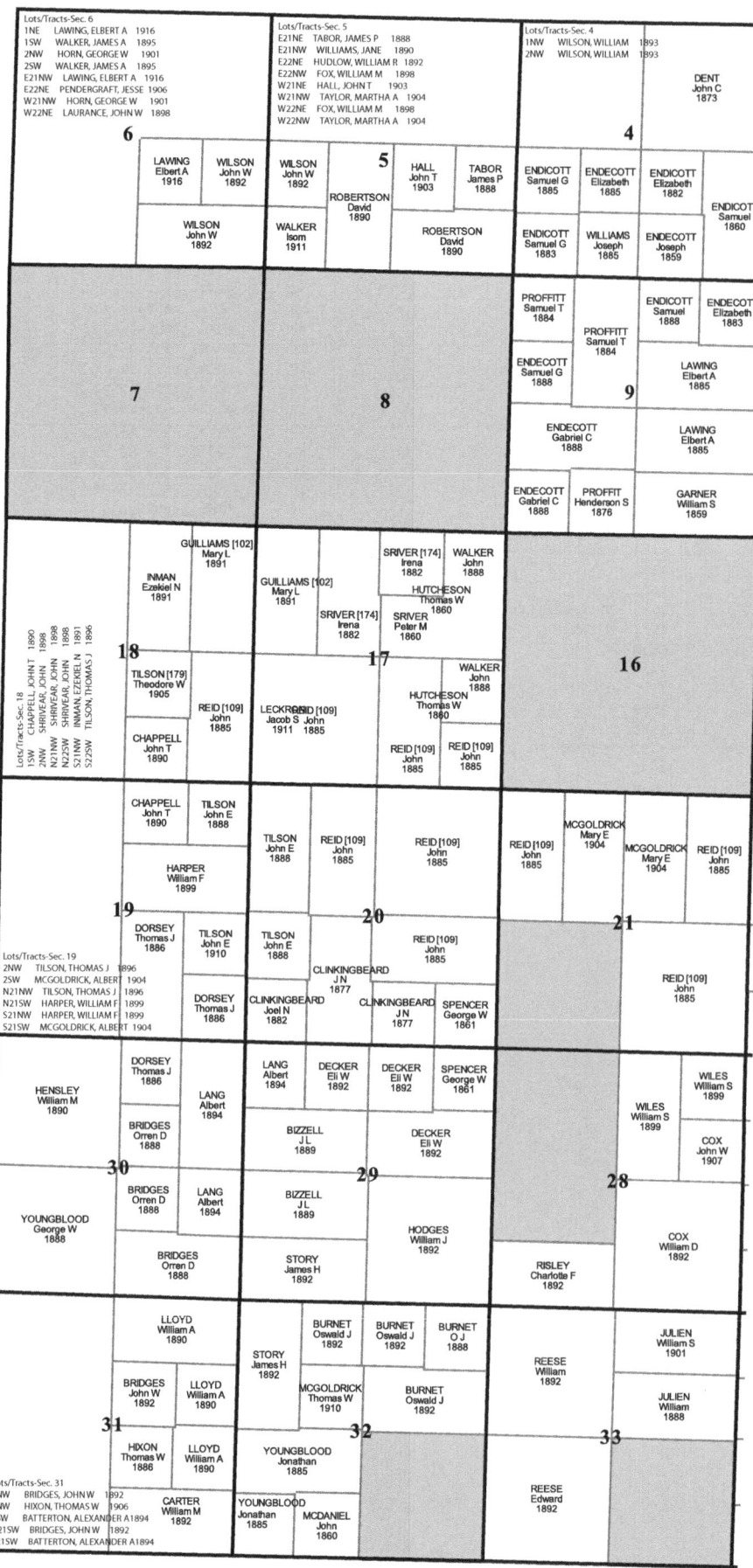

Copyright 2013 Boyd IT, Inc. All Rights Reserved

Lots/Tracts-Sec. 3
1NW	DENT, JAMES W	1893
2NW	BRIGGS, WILLIAM	1881
E21NE	DILLINDER, MARTHA	1853
E22NE	FOSTER, JAMES D	1860
W21NE	MARITT, JOHN W	1882
W22NE	DILLINDER, MARTHA	1853

Lots/Tracts-Sec. 2
E21NE	PARSONS, DAVID	1853
E21NW	SMITH, JAMES V	1860
E22NE	PARSONS, DAVID	1853
E22NW	PARSONS, SIMEON	1853
W21NE	PARSONS, SIMEON	1853
W21NW	PARSONS, GEORGE W	1854
W22NE	PARSONS, SIMEON	1854
W22NW	MANNON, ISAAC	1859

Lots/Tracts-Sec. 1
E21NE	ADAMS, BENONI	1859
E21NW	PHELPS, JAMES K	1859
E22NE	POTTER, JAMES M	1853
E22NW	PHELPS, PHELIX	1859
W21NE	ADAMS, BENONI	1856
W21NW	PHELPS, JAMES K	1853
W22NE	ADAMS, BENONI	1856
W22NW	TABOR, THOMAS E	1875

Section 3

DENT James W 1893 | WADLEY Jesse T 1889 | NORMAN Isaac A 1886
NORMAN Isaac A 1892
CRAFTON Aylett R 1903 | HOPKINS Andrew J 1888 | HOPKINS William W 1878 | HOPKINS Andrew J 1886

Section 2

SMITH James V 1860 | SMITH James V 1860 | FLINN William 1871
DAVIS John A 1898 | MITCHELL Edmund H 1892 | SMITH Calvin C 1894

Section 1

PHELPS Holmen 1859 | FOX William 1874 | ADAMS Edward L 1859 | LANGSTON John R 1892
RILEY Converse V 1882 | FOX William 1874

Section 10

ROBERSON Charles 1885 | HOPKINS Andrew J 1888 | HOPKINS William W 1878
HOPKINS William W 1878
LAWING Alfred J 1882 | ROBERTS James A 1908
LAWING Alfred J 1882 | ROBERTS James A 1908

Section 11

NORMAN Isaac A 1892
MITCHELL Edmund H 1892
STACY Benjamin F 1892
STACY Benjamin F 1892 | MITCHELL Edmund H 1892

Section 12

SMITH Elijah 1892 | FOX William 1874 | LANGSTON John R 1892
SMITH Elijah 1892 | KINSOLVING William S 1892
SMITH Elijah 1892 | WILLIAMS Albert J 1894
HERRIEN John W 1900 | WILLIAMS Albert J 1894 | WESCOTT Benjamin R 1907

Section 15

ENDICOTT Joseph 1858 | WILLIAMS David 1892 | WILLIAMS David 1892
ENDICOTT Joseph 1858 | WILLIAMS Joseph 1875 | WILLIAMS Joseph 1875 | WILLIAMS David 1892
WILLIAMS David 1888 | ENDECOTT James M 1882

Section 14

PROFFITT [159] Nancy J 1903 | PROFFITT [159] Nancy J 1903
PROFFITT [159] Nancy J 1903 | KNOX Jesse F 1896 | KNOX Jesse F 1896
ENDECOTT James M 1882

Section 13

HERRIEN John W 1900 | WILLIAMS Albert J 1894 | WILLIAMS Albert J 1894 | RAMSEY Noel 1895
FULS Metellus 1904 | HERRIEN John W 1900 | WESCOTT Benjamin R 1907
WESCOTT Benjamin R 1907 | TOBLER [95] Jacob 1863

Section 15 (lower)

REID [109] John 1885 | HALSELL John E 1884 | ROBERTSON Charles 1875
ENDECOTT Joseph 1859

Section 14 (lower)

ENDECOTT Samuel 1860 | HOWELL Josephus M 1859 | MILLER James R 1860 | DURHAM Daniel F 1861
ENDICOTT Joseph 1859 | ENDECOTT Samuel 1883 | CRISP Thomas E 1896 | BELCHER Thomas W 1904

Section 13 (lower)

DURHAM Daniel F 1861 | CATES Jason A 1888
ROMANS John F 1914 | JAMES John P 1899 | CATES Jason A 1888 | HARMON William 1859

Section 22

ENDECOTT Sarah J 1884
REID [109] John 1885
REID [109] John 1885 | REID [109] John 1885 | HARRISON John F 1883
REID [109] John 1885 | REID [109] John 1885 | WILSON William A 1889
REID [109] John 1885 | WILLIAMS Jonathan 1885 | WILLIAMS John H 1897

Section 23

ROBERTSON Charles 1875 | SURRETT David 1886 | CRISP Thomas E 1896 | CRISP Thomas E 1896
BELCHER Thomas W 1904
HARRISON John F 1883 | BELCHER Thomas W 1904
HARRISON John F 1879 | HARRISON John F 1883 | WALLACE Richard 1880 | WALLACE Richard 1888
WILSON William A 1889 | HARRISON John F 1893 | WALLACE Richard 1881

Section 24

JAMES John P 1899 | CATES Jason A 1888 | KENSLOW James H 1879
ROMANS John F 1914 | JAMES John P 1899 | CATES Jason A 1888
BURRISS John 1895 | BURRISS John 1895 | RAMSEY Hiram E 1901
ROMANS John F 1914 | BURRISS John 1895 | BURRISS John 1895 | KEE Joseph W 1899
SURRITT David E 1907 | WESCOTT Benjamin R 1907 | WESCOTT Benjamin R 1907

Section 27

TIPTON John H 1895 | WILLIAMS John H 1897
TIPTON John H 1895 | ROBERSON William R 1892 | ROBERSON William R 1892 | WILLIAMS John H 1897
TIPTON John H 1895
HIXON Caleb C 1906 | ROBERSON William R 1892 | COOK Giles 1900
ROWDEN Taylor 1901

Section 26

WILSON William A 1889 | DAVIS George W 1895 | WALLACE Richard 1881
DAVIS George W 1895
WESCOTT Benjamin R 1907 | HOPKINS Henry C 1895 | DAVIS George W 1895
HOPKINS Henry C 1895 | HOPKINS Henry C 1895
COOK Giles 1900 | WESCOTT Benjamin R 1907 | WESCOTT Benjamin R 1907

Section 25

WALLACE Richard 1881 | KEE Joseph W 1899
WILSON Thomas F 1892 | CARTER George H 1892 | LOGAN Alexander 1891
WALLACE Richard 1886 | WILSON Thomas F 1892 | WILSON Thomas F 1892 | LOGAN Alexander 1891
PLANK John C 1892 | HUNTER Nancy 1877 | HUNTER Nancy 1877

Section 34

SEABORN Thomas 1885 | SEABORN Thomas 1885 | SEABORN Thomas 1885
SEABORN Thomas 1885 | SEABORN Thomas 1885 | SEABORN Thomas 1885 | SEABORN Thomas 1885
CALLAHAN George R 1900 | CALLAHAN George R 1900 | CATES William 1888
MCDANIEL John M 1860 | MCDANIEL Thomas J 1860 | CATES Charley 1889

Section 35

JOHNSTON William T 1893
DAVIS Caleb T 1900 | PLANK John C 1892
DAVIS Caleb T 1900
CATES William 1888 | CATES William 1888 | DAVIS Caleb T 1900
CATES Charley 1889 | WALKER John H 1890

Section 36

PLANK John C 1892 | HUNTER Nancy 1877 | COOPER Joel M 1892
WALKER William H 1893 | JOHNSON George W 1896 | COOPER Joel M 1892
WALKER John H 1890 | WALKER William H 1893 | JOHNSON George W 1896 | COOPER Joel M 1892
JOHNSON George W 1896

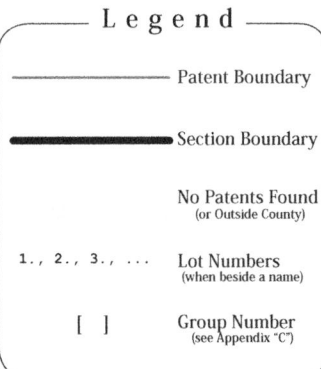

Helpful Hints

1. This Map's INDEX can be found on the preceding pages.

2. Refer to Map "C" to see where this Township lies within Howell County, Missouri.

3. Numbers within square brackets [ ] denote a multi-patentee land parcel (multi-owner). Refer to Appendix "C" for a full list of members in this group.

4. Areas that look to be crowded with Patentees usually indicate multiple sales of the same parcel (Re-issues) or Overlapping parcels. See this Township's Index for an explanation of these and other circumstances that might explain "odd" groupings of Patentees on this map.

Legend

— Patent Boundary

━━ Section Boundary

No Patents Found (or Outside County)

1., 2., 3., ...   Lot Numbers (when beside a name)

[ ]   Group Number (see Appendix "C")

Scale: Section = 1 mile X 1 mile (generally, with some exceptions)

Road Map

T23-N R10-W
5th PM 23-N 10-W Meridian

Map Group 17

Cities & Towns
Arditta
Cureall
Pottersville

Cemeteries
Cureall Cemetery
Pottersville Cemetery
Setzer Cemetery

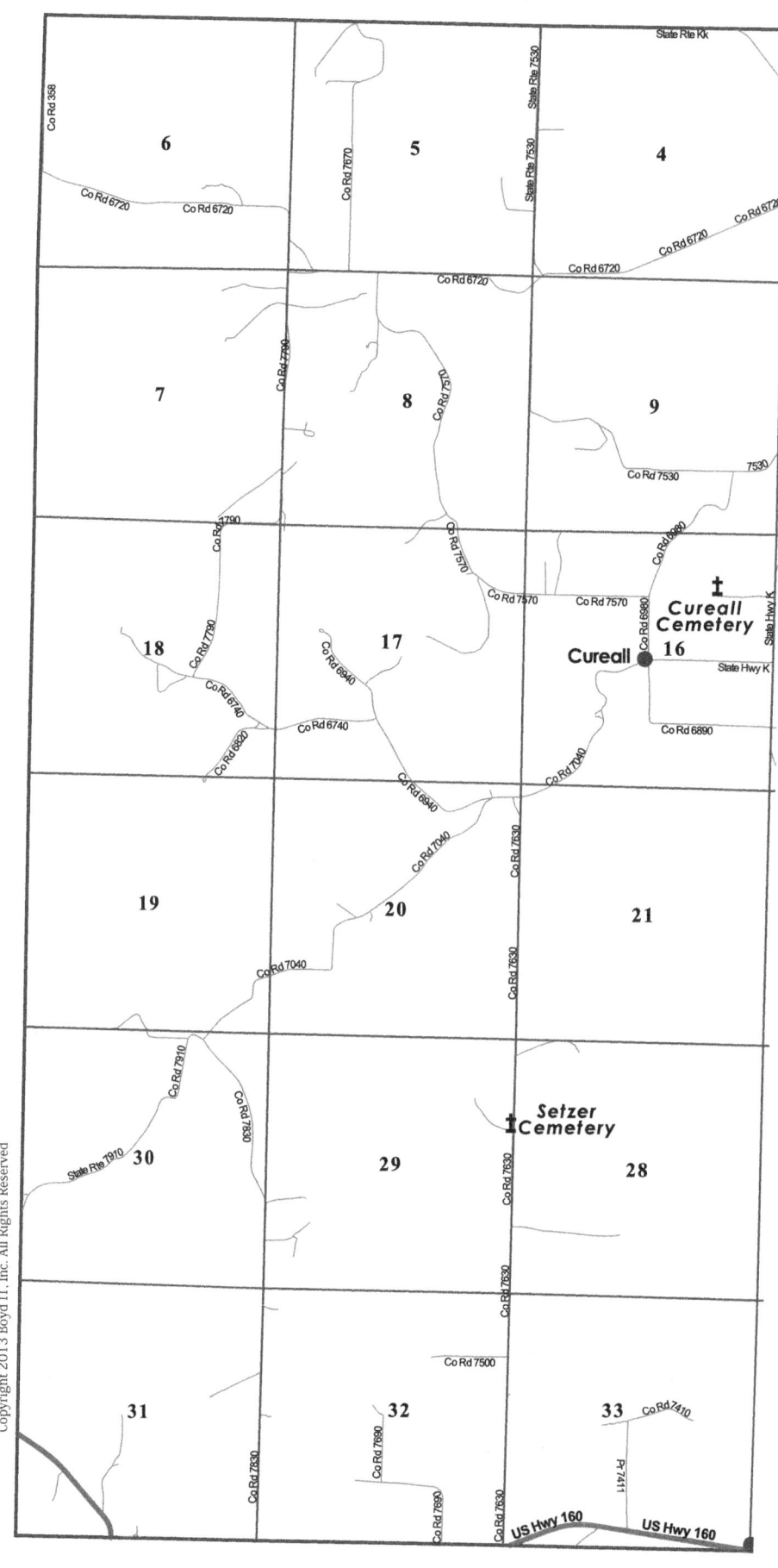

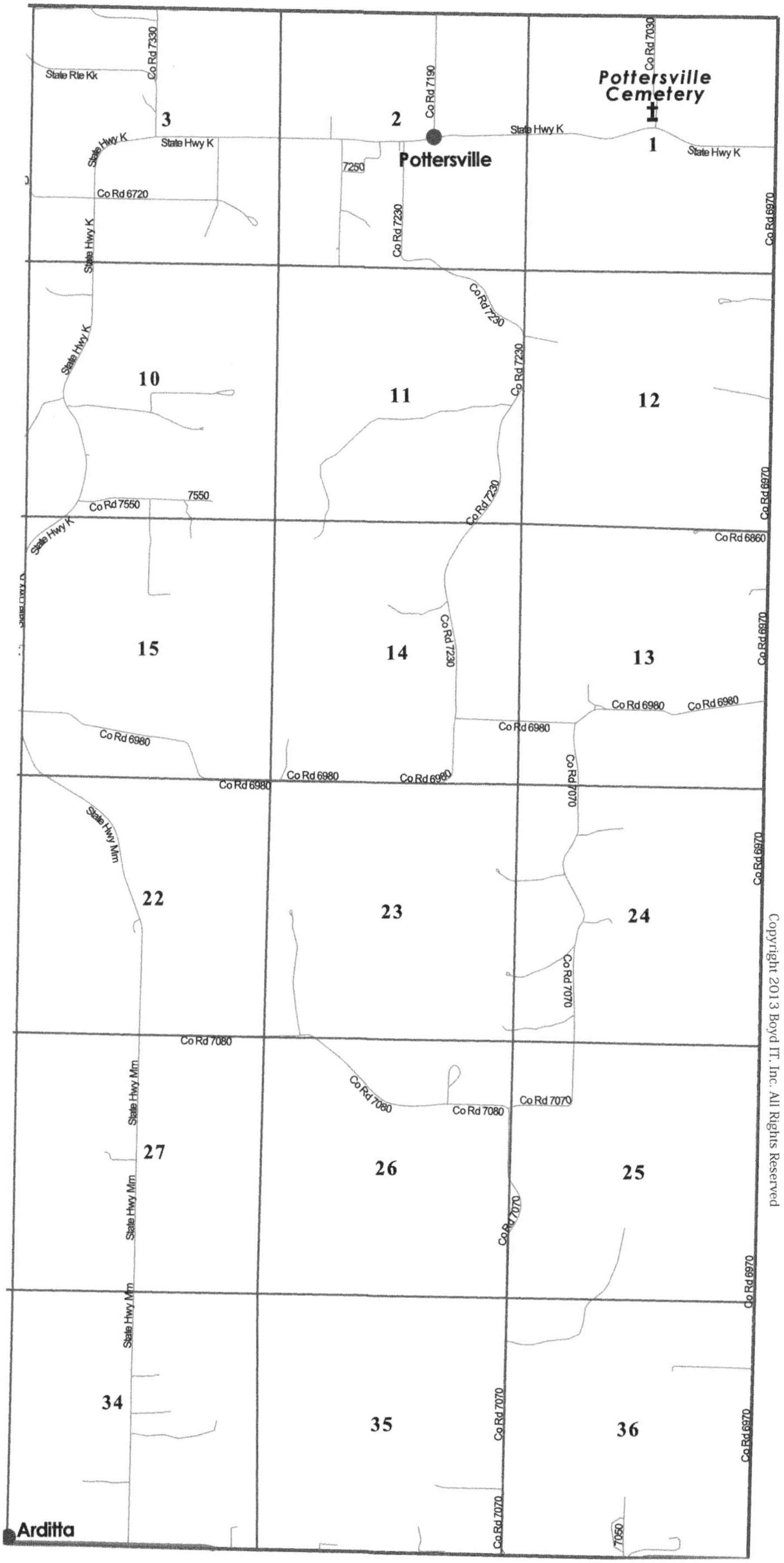

State Rte Kk

Co Rd 7330

3

State Hwy K

State Hwy K

Co Rd 6720

State Hwy K

Co Rd 7190

2

7250

Pottersville

Co Rd 7030

Pottersville Cemetery

State Hwy K

1

State Hwy K

State Hwy K

Co Rd 7230

Co Rd 7230

10

Co Rd 7230

Co Rd 7230

11

12

Co Rd 6890

Co Rd 7550

7550

15

Co Rd 7230

14

Co Rd 6860

13

Co Rd 6980

Co Rd 6980

Co Rd 6780

Co Rd 6980

Co Rd 6980

Co Rd 6980

Co Rd 6980

Co Rd 6890

State Hwy Mm

22

23

Co Rd 7070

24

Co Rd 7070

Co Rd 6970

State Hwy Mm

Co Rd 7080

Co Rd 7080

Co Rd 7080

Co Rd 7070

27

State Hwy Mm

26

Co Rd 7070

25

Co Rd 6970

State Hwy Mm

34

35

Co Rd 7070

36

Co Rd 6970

Co Rd 7070

7060

Arditta

Helpful Hints

1. This road map has a number of uses, but primarily it is to help you: a) find the present location of land owned by your ancestors (at least the general area), b) find cemeteries and city-centers, and c) estimate the route/roads used by Census-takers & tax-assessors.

2. If you plan to travel to Howell County to locate cemeteries or land parcels, please pick up a modern travel map for the area before you do. Mapping old land parcels on modern maps is not as exact a science as you might think. Just the slightest variations in public land survey coordinates, estimates of parcel boundaries, or road-map deviations can greatly alter a map's representation of how a road either does or doesn't cross a particular parcel of land.

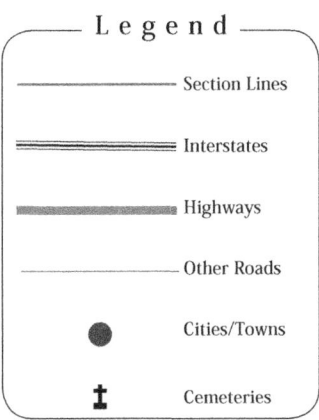

L e g e n d

——————— Section Lines

══════════ Interstates

━━━━━━━━━━ Highways

——————— Other Roads

● Cities/Towns

‡ Cemeteries

Scale: Section = 1 mile X 1 mile
(generally, with some exceptions)

Historical Map

T23-N   R10-W
5th PM   23-N   10-W Meridian

Map Group 17

<u>Cities & Towns</u>
Arditta
Cureall
Pottersville

<u>Cemeteries</u>
Cureall Cemetery
Pottersville Cemetery
Setzer Cemetery

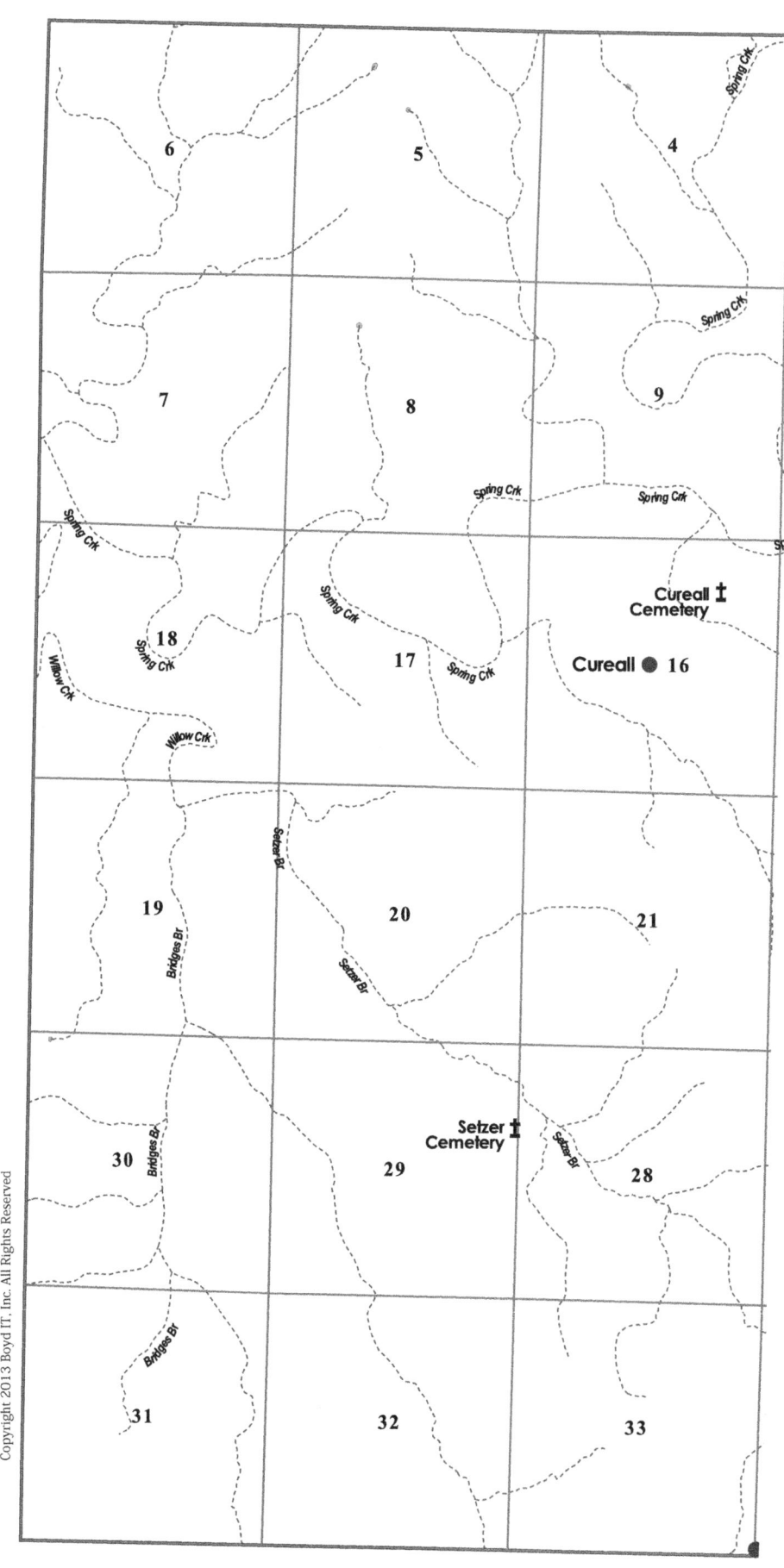

Copyright 2013 Boyd IT, Inc. All Rights Reserved

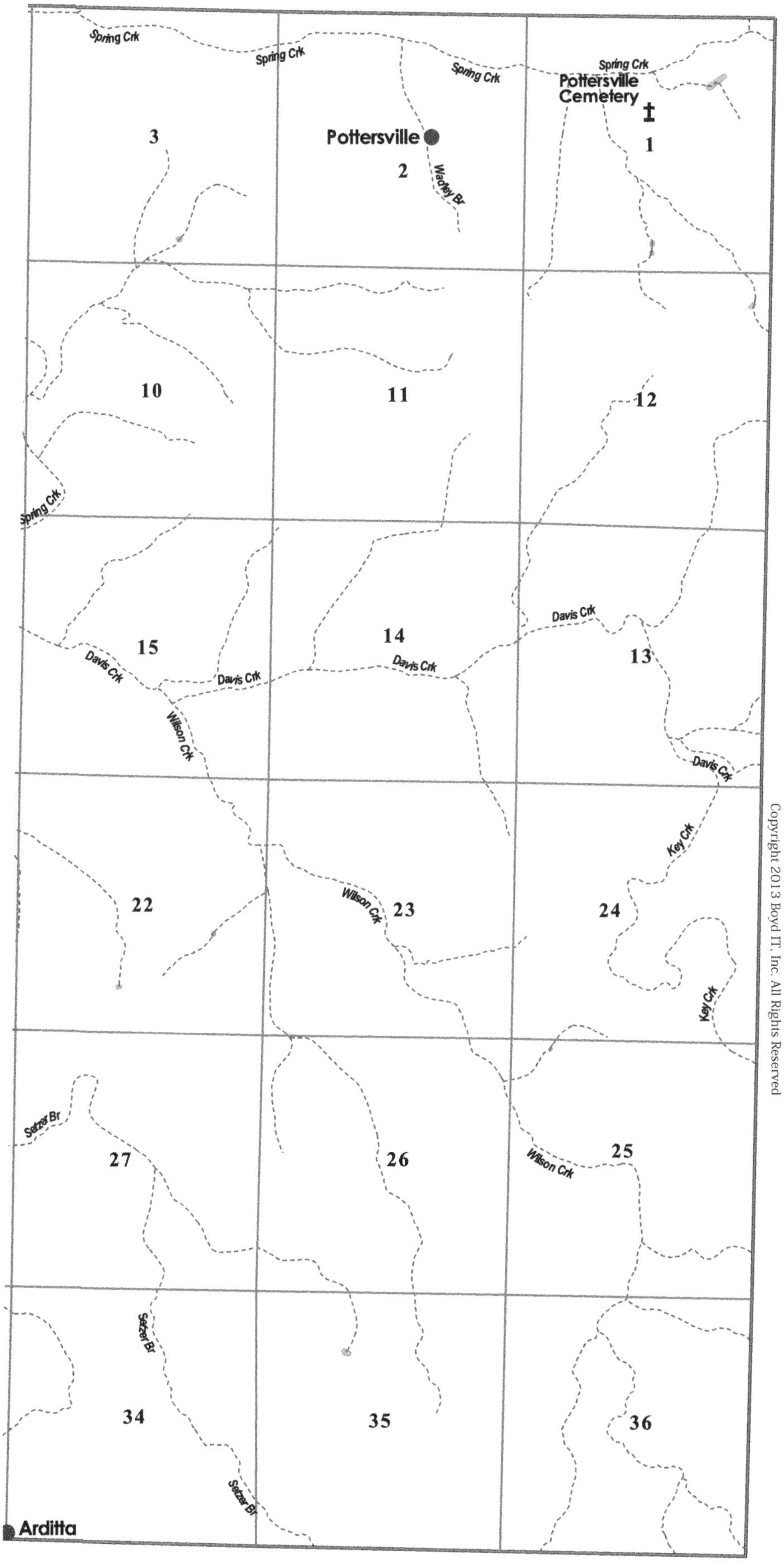

Spring Crk
Spring Crk
Spring Crk
Spring Crk
Pottersville
Cemetery ‡

3

Pottersville ●
2
Wickey Br
1

10

11

12

Spring Crk

Davis Crk

15

14

Davis Crk
Davis Crk
13

Davis Crk

Wilson Crk

Key Crk

22

Wilson Crk
23

24

Key Crk

Satzer Br

27

26

Wilson Crk
25

34

35

36

Satzer Br

Satzer Br

● Arditta

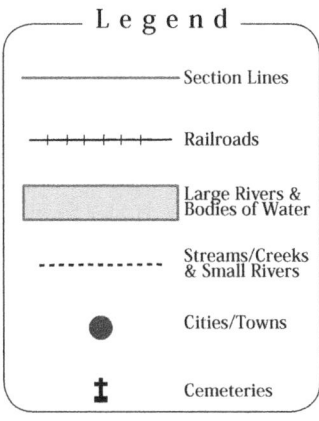

Helpful Hints

1. This Map takes a different look at the same Congressional Township displayed in the preceding two maps. It presents features that can help you better envision the historical development of the area: a) Water-bodies (lakes & ponds), b) Water-courses (rivers, streams, etc.), c) Railroads, d) City/town center-points (where they were oftentimes located when first settled), and e) Cemeteries.

2. Using this "Historical" map in tandem with this Township's Patent Map and Road Map, may lead you to some interesting discoveries. You will often find roads, towns, cemeteries, and waterways are named after nearby landowners: sometimes those names will be the ones you are researching. See how many of these research gems you can find here in Howell County.

Legend

———————— Section Lines

+++++++ Railroads

Large Rivers & Bodies of Water

- - - - - - Streams/Creeks & Small Rivers

● Cities/Towns

‡ Cemeteries

Scale: Section = 1 mile X 1 mile
(there are some exceptions)

Map Group 18: Index to Land Patents

Township 23-North Range 9-West (5th PM 23-N 9-W)

After you locate an individual in this Index, take note of the Section and Section Part then proceed to the Land Patent map on the pages immediately following. You should have no difficulty locating the corresponding parcel of land.

The "For More Info" Column will lead you to more information about the underlying Patents. See the *Legend* at right, and the "How to Use this Book" chapter, for more information.

```
                    LEGEND
            "For More Info . . . " column
A = Authority (Legislative Act, See Appendix "A")
B = Block or Lot (location in Section unknown)
C = Cancelled Patent
F = Fractional Section
G = Group  (Multi-Patentee Patent, see Appendix "C")
V = Overlaps another Parcel
R = Re-Issued (Parcel patented more than once)

(A & G items require you to look in the Appendixes referred
to above. All other Letter-designations followed by a number
require you to locate line-items in this index that possess
the ID number found after the letter).
```

ID	Individual in Patent	Sec.	Sec. Part	Date Issued	Other Counties	For More Info . . .
7903	ADAMS, Benoni	6	W½NW	1858-04-01		A1
4539	ALEXANDRIA, John G	26	E½SE	1860-09-10		A6 G1
4540	ALLEN, Achilles V	8	N½NE	1882-03-30		A7
4542	" "	8	NENW	1882-03-30		A7
4541	" "	8	SWNE	1882-03-30		A7
7900	ALSUP, Joseph	6	W½NE	1860-10-01		A1
4543	AMERMAN, William C	29	NE	1892-03-07		A7
4544	ARELL, Joseph A	25	S½NE	1895-08-01		A7
4550	ARNOLD, Susannah	13	SENE	1860-09-10		A6 G5
4549	" "	13	NESE	1860-09-10		A6 G5
4552	BAKER, Ebby	14	W½SE	1872-08-30		A6 G11
4551	" "	14	SESE	1872-08-30		A6 G11
7836	BARRETT, William L	18	N½SW	1885-03-20		A1
4556	BARROWS, Herbert P	18	SWSE	1913-01-31		A7
4555	" "	18	E½SE	1913-01-31		A7
7908	BARTHOLOMEW, Daniel	7	S½SW	1893-09-08		A7
4558	" "	7	SWSE	1893-09-08		A7
4557	" "	7	E½SE	1893-09-08		A7
7838	BINGAMAN, Andrew J	18	S½NW	1894-05-18		A7
4560	" "	18	NWSE	1894-05-18		A7
7839	" "	18	S½SW	1894-05-18		A7
4561	BISE, Henry A	7	SENE	1892-11-03		A7
4562	" "	8	SWNW	1892-11-03		A7
4563	BISSETT, Horatio	10	W½SW	1892-06-10		A7
4565	" "	10	SWNW	1892-06-10		A7
4564	" "	10	SESW	1892-06-10		A7
4566	BLACK, Francis M	28	SWSE	1886-11-19		A1
4567	BLACK, John F	31	SE	1885-12-19		A7
4568	BLACK, Simon	29	S½SW	1873-02-01		A7
4569	" "	32	N½NW	1873-02-01		A7
4571	BOLLINGER, Mathias H	35	S½NE	1877-06-04		A7
4572	" "	36	S½NW	1877-06-04		A7
4575	BOND, Newton	22	SESW	1871-12-06		A7
4573	" "	22	W½SE	1860-05-02		A6
4574	" "	22	SESE	1860-05-02		A6
4577	BOND, Riley	10	NWSE	1860-05-02		A6 G20
4576	" "	10	S½SE	1860-05-02		A6 G20
4578	BOND, Thomas J	10	SWNE	1882-05-10		A1
4579	" "	10	NESE	1875-02-15		A7
4580	" "	10	SENE	1875-02-15		A7
4581	" "	10	NESW	1880-10-01		A1
4582	" "	11	NWSW	1875-02-15		A7
4583	BRADFORD, John R	23	SESE	1871-11-01		A7
4584	" "	24	W½SW	1871-11-01		A7
4585	" "	26	NENE	1871-11-01		A7
4586	BRADFORD, Thomas G	15	S½NW	1860-11-12		A6

ID	Individual in Patent	Sec.	Sec. Part	Date Issued	Other Counties	For More Info . . .
4587	BRADFORD, Thomas G (Cont'd)	15	NWSW	1860-11-12		A6
4588	BRADSHAW, Elias	5	SWSW	1877-01-15		A7
4589	" "	6	SESE	1877-01-15		A7
4590	" "	7	NENE	1877-01-15		A7
4591	" "	8	NWNW	1877-01-15		A7
4592	BRAGG, Major	22	S½NE	1892-03-07		A7
4593	" "	22	NESE	1892-03-07		A7
7892	BREEDLOVE, John W	5	W21NW	1890-01-30		A1
7894	" "	6	2NE	1899-02-13		A7
7896	" "	6	E21NE	1899-02-13		A7
7893	BREEDLOVE, William M	5	W22NE	1908-11-19		A1
4595	BRENNER, Christian D	36	S½SE	1889-06-22		A7
4594	" "	36	E½SW	1889-06-22		A7
4596	BULLARD, Peter H	36	SENE	1859-09-01		A1
4597	" "	36	NWSE	1859-09-01		A1
4598	BURNWORTH, John H	13	SWNW	1891-05-25		A7
4599	" "	14	SENE	1891-05-25		A7
4601	BURTON, Sarah	32	SWNW	1888-12-08		A7 G30
4600	" "	32	NWSW	1888-12-08		A7 G30
4604	BURTON, Thomas D	32	SWNW	1888-12-08		A7 G30
4602	" "	32	NWSW	1888-12-08		A7 G30
4603	" "	32	S½SE	1861-07-01		A6
4605	" "	33	SWSW	1861-07-01		A6
4608	CAMBELL, David	27	NENW	1861-05-01		A1
7868	CAMPBELL, John H	30	S21SW	1900-08-09		A7
7873	" "	31	N21NW	1900-08-09		A7
4610	CHAPMAN, Carrol	27	W½NE	1862-10-10		A6 G42
4609	" "	27	SENW	1862-10-10		A6 G42
4612	CHAPMAN, Elizabeth	27	W½NE	1862-10-10		A6 G42
4611	" "	27	SENW	1862-10-10		A6 G42
4613	CHAPMAN, Joanna	27	SENW	1862-10-10		A6 G42
4614	" "	27	W½NE	1862-10-10		A6 G42
4617	CHESNUT, Abraham	9	E½SW	1892-06-21		A7
4618	" "	9	SWSW	1892-06-21		A7
4620	CHESTNUT, James L	8	SENE	1890-01-10		A7
4619	" "	8	N½SE	1890-01-10		A7
4621	" "	9	NWSW	1890-01-10		A7
7875	CLARK, Amanda	31	S21NW	1889-01-12		A7 G45
4622	" "	31	S½NE	1889-01-12		A7 G45
7877	" "	31	S22NW	1889-01-12		A7 G45
4623	CLARK, Isaac P	31	S½NE	1889-01-12		A7 G45
7878	" "	31	S22NW	1889-01-12		A7 G45
7876	" "	31	S21NW	1889-01-12		A7 G45
4624	CLARK, Wesley E	26	W½SW	1860-05-02		A6 G47
4625	" "	35	NWNW	1859-09-01		A1
4626	CLAYTON, William E	21	NWSW	1895-05-28		A7
4627	" "	21	S½SW	1895-05-28		A7
4628	CLEMENT, James J	35	E½NW	1890-01-10		A7
4629	" "	35	NWNE	1890-01-10		A7
4631	CLONINGER, Henry	2	W½SE	1892-01-20		A7 G50
4630	" "	2	E½SW	1892-01-20		A7 G50
4632	CLONINGER, James F	2	W½SE	1892-01-20		A7 G50
4633	" "	2	E½SW	1892-01-20		A7 G50
4635	CLONINGER, Lawson	2	E½SW	1892-01-20		A7 G50
4634	" "	2	W½SE	1892-01-20		A7 G50
4636	CLONINGER, Thomas F	11	NESE	1875-02-15		A7
4637	COCK, Anthony	32	SENE	1860-09-10		A6 G52
4638	" "	32	NESE	1860-09-10		A6 G52
4639	" "	33	NWSW	1860-09-10		A6 G52
4640	" "	33	SWNW	1860-09-10		A6 G52
4641	" "	33	SWNE	1860-08-01		A1
4642	COOK, Jackson D	6	NESE	1902-05-21		A7
4643	COOPER, George W	11	S½NE	1861-07-01		A6
4644	" "	11	SENW	1861-07-01		A6
4645	CRISP, Thomas E	12	SESW	1874-06-15		A1
4646	DAVIS, Ed	17	SW	1901-07-09		A7
4647	DAVIS, George R	20	NENW	1911-02-09		A7
7834	DAVIS, William C	18	2SW	1888-11-27		A7
7840	" "	18	S22NW	1888-11-27		A7
4648	DOOLEY, Joshua	25	SESE	1874-10-01		A1
4649	DORSEY, Thomas J	13	NESE	1860-09-10		A6 G5
4650	" "	13	SENE	1860-09-10		A6 G5
4651	" "	13	SWNE	1859-09-01		A1

ID	Individual in Patent	Sec.	Sec. Part	Date Issued	Other Counties	For More Info . . .
4652	DORSEY, Thomas J (Cont'd)	13	NWSE	1859-09-01		A1
4653	"	22	N½NE	1860-09-10		A6
4658	DUNKLEBARGER, Susan S	27	NWSW	1860-09-10		A6 G69
4659	" "	28	NWSE	1860-09-10		A6 G69
4661	" "	28	SWNE	1860-09-10		A6 G69
4660	" "	28	NESE	1860-09-10		A6 G69
4662	DURFEE, Charles T	4	SWSW	1892-01-20		A7
4664	" "	9	SWNW	1892-01-20		A7
4663	" "	9	N½NW	1892-01-20		A7
7833	DURST, Johan	1	W22NW	1901-08-24		A7
4667	FAUROT, Henry	8	SW	1891-05-25		A7
4668	FOREST, H	6	SWSE	1882-12-20		A1
4669	FOUST, Jacob	1	S½SW	1874-11-20		A1
4670	" "	12	N½NW	1874-11-20		A1
4671	" "	12	E½NE	1882-09-30		A1
4672	" "	12	W½NE	1876-01-10		A1
4673	FRAZIER, Davis A	12	N½SE	1882-11-10		A7
4674	FULS, Samuel	5	S½SE	1886-04-10		A7
4675	" "	5	NWSE	1886-04-10		A7
4676	" "	5	SESW	1886-04-10		A7
4682	GIBBS, Daniel W	27	NWSW	1860-09-10		A6 G69
4683	" "	28	NWSE	1860-09-10		A6 G69
4684	" "	28	NESE	1860-09-10		A6 G69
4685	" "	28	SWNE	1860-09-10		A6 G69
4686	GIBSON, Henry A	33	SENE	1898-12-01		A7
4687	GILBERT, Lewis	23	W½SE	1892-12-09		A7
4688	" "	23	NESE	1892-12-09		A7
4690	GILBERT, Mary A	26	SENE	1892-12-09		A7
4689	" "	26	W½NE	1892-12-09		A7
4691	" "	26	SENW	1892-12-09		A7
4692	GILMORE, Ernest L	19	SWSE	1904-12-29		A1
4695	" "	30	NESE	1904-12-29		A1
4693	" "	30	NWNE	1904-12-29		A1
4694	" "	30	SENE	1904-12-29		A1
4697	GIPSON, James	19	S½NE	1892-06-30		A7
4696	" "	19	N½SE	1892-06-30		A7
4698	GRAMMER, John W	25	NESE	1870-05-10		A1
4701	" "	36	NESE	1870-05-10		A1
4700	" "	36	SWNE	1871-10-20		A1
4699	" "	36	NENE	1870-05-10		A1
4702	GREEN, Emory W	33	SESW	1888-12-08		A7
4703	" "	33	W½SE	1888-12-08		A7
7846	HALKYARD, James	19	S22SW	1892-06-10		A7
7844	" "	19	S21SW	1892-06-10		A7
7865	" "	30	N21NW	1892-06-10		A7
7866	" "	30	N22NW	1892-06-10		A7
7906	HALSELL, John T	7	N21SW	1908-06-29		A1
7855	HARBER, Margaret M	2	W22NE	1888-05-07		A1
7853	" "	2	W21NE	1888-05-07		A1
7850	HARDESTY, Morgan M	2	E22NE	1896-09-25		A7
7881	HARREN, Elisha N	4	E22NW	1859-03-01		A1
7854	HARSCH, Emanuel C	2	W21NW	1894-11-15		A7
4704	" "	2	W½SW	1894-11-15		A7
4705	" "	3	NESE	1894-11-15		A7
4706	HARSCH, Lucy	11	SWNW	1892-04-23		A1
4707	HAWKINS, Benjamin	12	SWSW	1860-02-10		A6
4709	" "	13	NWNW	1860-02-10		A6
4711	HAWKINS, John B	13	SENW	1861-02-09		A1
4712	" "	15	W½NE	1860-05-02		A6
4714	" "	27	W½NE	1862-10-10		A6 G42
4717	" "	27	SWSE	1859-09-01		A1
4713	" "	27	SENW	1862-10-10		A6 G42
4716	" "	27	NESE	1860-09-10		A6 G111
4715	" "	27	SENE	1860-09-10		A6 G111
4719	HENDRICK, Elizabeth	27	W½NE	1862-10-10		A6 G42
4718	" "	27	SENW	1862-10-10		A6 G42
7882	HERRIN, Mary	4	W21NE	1877-05-15		A7
7883	" "	4	W22NE	1877-05-15		A7
4720	HIGLEY, James E	34	SWSW	1901-03-23		A7
4721	HILL, William A	27	NWSE	1882-05-10		A1
4722	HOLBROOK, Jacob	1	NWSW	1893-03-03		A7
7831	" "	1	W21NW	1893-03-03		A7
7847	" "	2	E21NE	1893-03-03		A7

ID	Individual in Patent	Sec.	Sec. Part	Date Issued	Other Counties	For More Info . . .
4723	HOLBROOK, Jacob (Cont'd)	2	NESE	1893-03-03		A7
4727	HORSMAN, Samuel H	21	SWNE	1878-04-05		A7
4726	" "	21	NESW	1878-04-05		A7
4728	" "	21	SENW	1878-04-05		A7
4729	" "	21	NWSE	1878-04-05		A7
4730	HOVEY, Aaron G	29	E½SE	1890-10-11		A7
4731	" "	32	NENE	1890-10-11		A7
4732	" "	33	NWNW	1890-10-11		A7
4733	HOVEY, Fernando A	33	NENE	1892-01-05		A7
4734	" "	34	NWNW	1892-01-05		A7
4735	" "	34	E½NW	1892-01-05		A7
4736	HUNT, Jesse	11	SESE	1871-11-01		A7
4738	" "	14	NENW	1871-11-01		A7
4737	" "	14	N½NE	1871-11-01		A7
4739	HUNTER, Nancy	22	N½SW	1861-07-01		A6 G126
4740	ING, Joseph	32	E½SW	1860-08-01		A1
7870	JOHNSON, Charles	30	S22SW	1905-03-30		A7
7874	"	31	N22NW	1905-03-30		A7
4741	JOHNSON, Larkin	22	NENW	1861-02-09		A1
4743	JOHNSTON, Joel D	29	W½SE	1892-06-10		A7
4742	" "	29	N½SW	1892-06-10		A7
7828	JUDKINS, William L	1	E22NE	1889-06-22		A7
4744	KEE, John S	18	SENE	1884-10-11		A1
4745	"	18	SWNE	1884-10-11		A1
7845	KENNEY, John B	19	S22NW	1921-01-06		A7
4746	KENSLOW, James H	19	N½NW	1879-12-15		A7
4747	KENSLOW, Joshua S	27	SESE	1883-08-13		A1
7872	" "	31	2SW	1892-06-30		A7
7871	" "	31	1SW	1892-06-30		A7
4748	KINCHLOE, James	32	NWSE	1889-01-12		A7
4750	" "	32	W½NE	1889-01-12		A7
4749	" "	32	SENW	1889-01-12		A7
4751	KING, James L	24	SENE	1895-05-28		A7
7904	KINSOLVING, Timothy F	7	1NW	1900-08-09		A7
4752	" "	7	W½NE	1900-08-09		A7
7905	KINSOLVING, William S	7	2NW	1892-03-07		A7
4753	KNOX, Edward L	20	N½NE	1892-01-25		A7
4754	" "	21	N½NW	1892-01-25		A7
4756	LEATHERS, Thomas H	4	SESE	1907-06-24		A1
4760	LEONARD, Margaret	22	W½NW	1861-07-01		A6 G140
4759	" "	22	SENW	1861-07-01		A6 G140
4761	LIGETH, Charles	35	NENE	1861-02-09		A1
4762	LINTHICUM, John	21	SWSE	1882-05-20		A7
4763	"	28	NWNE	1882-05-20		A7
7902	LIVINGSTON, A H	6	W21NW	1886-11-19		A1
7867	LOGAN, Alexander	30	N22SW	1891-05-05		A7
7869	" "	30	S22NW	1891-05-05		A7
7895	LYON, Samuel F	6	2SW	1892-03-07		A7
7899	" "	6	N21SW	1892-03-07		A7
7832	MAHONEY, Patrick	1	W22NE	1892-10-17		A7
7829	" "	1	E22NW	1892-10-17		A7
4764	MARRITT, John W	7	NWSE	1885-03-20		A1
4765	MASON, Robertson C	25	SW	1877-06-04		A7
4766	MCAFEE, Spencer	13	SESW	1875-05-10		A7
4768	" "	24	SWNE	1875-05-10		A7
4767	" "	24	E½NW	1875-05-10		A7
4770	MCDANIEL, Andrew J	22	SENW	1861-07-01		A6 G140
4769	" "	22	W½NW	1861-07-01		A6 G140
4771	MCDANIEL, John	33	E½NW	1860-02-15		A6
4775	MEYER, Nellie	19	SESE	1906-06-21		A7 G149
4776	" "	30	NENE	1906-06-21		A7 G149
4777	MEYER, Nicholas	19	SESE	1906-06-21		A7 G149
4778	" "	30	NENE	1906-06-21		A7 G149
4779	MIDDAUGH, Charles M	36	W½SW	1892-03-07		A7
4780	MILLER, Pattron	33	NWNE	1885-06-03		A1
4781	MOBACK, Carl A	17	NW	1892-12-09		A7
4782	MOBACK, Henry E	17	S½NE	1903-06-08		A7
4783	MOORE, Peter A	26	E½SE	1860-09-10		A6 G1
4784	" "	26	SWSE	1860-08-01		A1
4786	MORGAN, Henry	9	S½NE	1891-05-25		A7
4787	" "	9	SENW	1891-05-25		A7
4785	" "	9	NENE	1891-05-25		A7
7843	MORRIS, George N	19	S21NW	1899-02-25		A7

ID	Individual in Patent	Sec.	Sec. Part	Date Issued	Other Counties	For More Info . . .
7841	MORRIS, George N (Cont'd)	19	N21SW	1899-02-25		A7
4788	NASH, Isaac	24	S½SE	1894-12-19		A7
4789	" "	25	N½NE	1894-12-19		A7
4792	NICKS, Alfred H	34	SESW	1860-05-02		A6
4791	" "	34	SWSE	1860-05-02		A6
4793	" "	35	SWNW	1860-08-01		A1
4796	NICKS, Daniel W	34	SWNW	1860-12-10		A1
4798	" "	34	N½SE	1885-02-25		A7
4797	" "	34	NESW	1885-02-25		A7
4794	" "	34	SESE	1885-02-25		A7
4795	" "	34	NWSW	1860-12-10		A1
7842	PAYTON, Joe W	19	N22SW	1919-07-24		A7
4800	PENN, Mary	27	NESE	1860-09-10		A6 G111
4799	" "	27	SENE	1860-09-10		A6 G111
4803	PHILLIPS, Thomas	9	SE	1888-12-06		A7
7901	PITTS, P T	6	W21NW	1886-11-19		A1
4806	RAGSDALE, Thomas E	27	E½SW	1860-09-10		A6
7907	RAMSEY, Hiram E	7	N22SW	1904-11-22		A1
4807	RAMSEY, Jasper N	19	N½NE	1891-06-09		A7 G160
4808	" "	20	W½NW	1891-06-09		A7 G160
7837	RAMSEY, Noel	18	N22NW	1895-05-28		A7
7909	" "	7	S22SW	1895-05-28		A7
4809	RAMSEY, Rosannah	19	N½NE	1891-06-09		A7 G160
4810	" "	20	W½NW	1891-06-09		A7 G160
4811	RATLIFF, Joanna	27	SENW	1862-10-10		A6 G42
4812	" "	27	W½NE	1862-10-10		A6 G42
4814	REDMAN, Howard N	24	E½SW	1889-06-22		A7
4813	" "	24	NWSE	1889-06-22		A7
7897	REEVES, Jesse	6	E21NW	1860-08-01		A1
4815	REIGER, John R	3	E½SW	1888-12-08		A7
4816	RICE, Thomas	15	E½NE	1860-09-10		A6
4817	RILEY, Joseph	10	N½NW	1892-08-08		A7
4818	" "	10	SENW	1892-08-08		A7
4819	" "	3	SWSW	1892-08-08		A7
4820	RITCHEY, John W	28	E½NE	1901-03-23		A7
4821	RITCHEY, William A	21	SESE	1888-12-06		A7
4822	" "	22	SWSW	1888-12-06		A7
4823	" "	27	W½NW	1888-12-06		A7
4825	ROBERTS, Delila	15	E½SW	1875-04-15		A7 G166
4824	" "	15	SWSW	1875-04-15		A7 G166
4826	ROBERTS, Elizabeth J	17	N½NE	1879-12-15		A7
4827	" "	8	S½SE	1879-12-15		A7
4828	ROBERTS, John	15	SWSW	1875-04-15		A7 G166
4829	" "	15	E½SW	1875-04-15		A7 G166
4830	ROLLINS, Eliza E	4	NWSW	1902-03-07		A7
7879	ROLLINS, John W	4	1NW	1883-02-10		A7
7884	" "	4	W22NW	1883-02-10		A7
7889	ROLLINS, Mary E	5	E22NE	1892-01-25		A7
7886	" "	5	E21NE	1892-01-25		A7
4831	" "	5	NESE	1892-01-25		A7
7858	ROOT, Jared W	3	2NW	1888-12-06		A7
7880	" "	4	E22NE	1888-12-06		A7
4833	RYNERSON, Barnett	26	N½NW	1892-01-05		A7
4832	" "	26	SWNW	1892-01-05		A7
4834	" "	27	NENE	1892-01-05		A7
4835	SCHELL, Solomon	8	SENW	1886-11-19		A1
4836	SCOGGIN, Turpin G	25	W½SE	1865-02-10		A6
4837	" "	27	NWSW	1860-09-10		A6 G69
4838	" "	28	NWSE	1860-09-10		A6 G69
4839	" "	28	NESE	1860-09-10		A6 G69
4840	" "	28	SWNE	1860-09-10		A6 G69
4842	" "	33	NESE	1859-09-01		A1
4841	" "	33	SESE	1859-09-01		A1
4843	" "	36	NWNE	1865-02-10		A6
4844	" "	36	NENW	1865-02-10		A6
4845	SEAY, Josiah	6	NWSE	1859-09-01		A1
4846	SHARP, James M	11	SWSW	1889-06-22		A7 G169
4847	" "	14	W½NW	1889-06-22		A7 G169
4848	SHARP, Mary K	11	SWSW	1889-06-22		A7 G169
4849	" "	14	W½NW	1889-06-22		A7 G169
7826	SHEPARD, Jeremiah A	1	E21NE	1890-10-11		A7
4853	" "	1	NESE	1890-10-11		A7
4854	" "	1	S½SE	1890-10-11		A7

ID	Individual in Patent	Sec.	Sec. Part	Date Issued	Other Counties	For More Info . . .
4855	SHINKLE, Thomas J	33	NESW	1882-12-20		A1
4856	SMITH, John	11	N½NE	1892-03-07		A7
4857	" "	11	N½NW	1892-03-07		A7
7827	SMITH, John H	1	E21NW	1891-05-25		A7
7830	" "	1	W21NE	1891-05-25		A7
4858	" "	1	NESW	1891-05-25		A7
4859	" "	1	NWSE	1891-05-25		A7
4861	SNIDER, John F	20	SENW	1892-10-17		A7
4860	" "	20	S½NE	1892-10-17		A7
4862	" "	21	SWNW	1892-10-17		A7
4863	SPEAKER, William G	15	N½NW	1892-04-23		A1
4864	SPEARS, Joseph	12	S½SE	1860-05-02		A6
4865	SPEARS, Joseph T	13	SWSW	1872-08-30		A6 G173
4868	" "	14	SENW	1860-08-15		A6
4870	" "	14	SESE	1872-08-30		A6 G11
4871	" "	14	W½SE	1872-08-30		A6 G11
4869	" "	14	SWNE	1860-08-15		A6
4867	" "	14	NESE	1872-08-30		A1
4866	" "	14	SW	1872-08-30		A1
4872	" "	23	NENE	1872-08-30		A6 G173
4873	" "	24	NWNW	1872-08-30		A6 G173
4874	SPENCER, John A	13	NENW	1874-06-15		A1
4875	ST CLAIR, John B	24	NESE	1883-08-13		A1
7863	STAGGS, John W	3	W22NE	1905-11-03		A7
7864	STAGGS, Lucinda C	3	W22NE	1905-11-03		A7
4880	STEWART, Mary	32	SENE	1860-09-10		A6 G52
4881	" "	32	NESE	1860-09-10		A6 G52
4883	" "	33	SWNW	1860-09-10		A6 G52
4882	" "	33	NWSW	1860-09-10		A6 G52
4884	STROTHER, Richard	32	SWSW	1860-10-01		A1
4888	TABOR, John	27	NESE	1860-09-10		A6 G111
4887	" "	27	SENE	1860-09-10		A6 G111
4889	TAYLOR, Newton S	24	SWNW	1900-08-09		A7
4891	TEDDER, John	26	W½SW	1860-05-02		A6 G47
4892	THOMAS, Ann	10	NWSE	1860-05-02		A6 G20
4893	" "	10	S½SE	1860-05-02		A6 G20
7852	THORNTON, Charles W	2	E22NW	1890-01-10		A7
7849	" "	2	E21NW	1890-01-10		A7
7848	THORNTON, Christina	2	E21NW	1890-01-10		A7
7851	" "	2	E22NW	1890-01-10		A7
7856	UITTS, Benjamin F	2	W22NW	1886-11-19		A1
7890	UITTS, Johnson R	5	W21NE	1886-07-20		A1 G182
4897	" "	5	N½SW	1886-07-20		A1 G182
7888	" "	5	E21NW	1886-07-20		A1 G182
7887	UITTS, Margaret	5	E21NW	1886-07-20		A1 G182
7891	" "	5	W21NE	1886-07-20		A1 G182
4898	" "	5	N½SW	1886-07-20		A1 G182
4899	UPTON, Edward A	30	S½SE	1888-11-27		A7
4900	" "	31	N½NE	1888-11-27		A7
4901	VALENTINE, Aaron	13	S½SE	1889-01-12		A7
4902	" "	24	N½NE	1889-01-12		A7
4903	VALENTINE, Solomon	13	N½NE	1888-11-27		A7
4904	VAN VORHIS, Isaac M	13	N½SW	1892-01-05		A7
4905	WADLY, John B	6	SESW	1888-12-06		A1
4906	WALTERS, Caroline	27	SWSW	1872-08-30		A1
4907	" "	28	SESE	1872-08-30		A1
4909	WARD, Charity	21	NESE	1888-12-06		A7
4910	" "	21	E½NE	1888-12-06		A7
4908	" "	21	NWNE	1888-12-06		A7
4911	WEAVER, Emma	2	SESE	1891-12-26		A1
4912	WEAVER, Garret	36	NWNW	1860-08-01		A1
4913	WEAVER, William H	10	N½NE	1895-07-08		A7
4914	" "	3	S½SE	1895-07-08		A7
4915	WEIR, Rudolph	15	E½SE	1888-12-08		A7
7862	WELLS, John F	3	W21NW	1892-01-25		A7
7859	" "	3	E21NE	1892-01-25		A7
4916	" "	3	NWSW	1892-01-25		A7
4917	" "	4	NESE	1892-01-25		A7
4919	WEST, James	11	E½SW	1871-11-01		A7
4918	" "	11	W½SE	1871-11-01		A7

ID	Individual in Patent	Sec.	Sec. Part	Date Issued	Other Counties	For More Info . . .
4920	WEST, Margaret	12	N½SW	1875-09-10		A7 G188
4921	" "	12	S½NW	1875-09-10		A7 G188
4922	WEST, Nathan D	12	N½SW	1875-09-10		A7 G188
4923	" "	12	S½NW	1875-09-10		A7 G188
4924	WESTERN, Wardall E	18	N½NE	1903-10-01		A7
7835	" "	18	N21NW	1903-10-01		A7
4925	WICKER, Elisha H	17	SE	1877-08-01		A7
4926	WIKOFF, Sarah	13	SWSW	1872-08-30		A6 G173
4927	" "	23	NENE	1872-08-30		A6 G173
4928	" "	24	NWNW	1872-08-30		A6 G173
4933	WINTERS, Losinda	22	N½SW	1861-07-01		A6 G126
7861	WOODROME, Barton C	3	E22NE	1885-05-25		A1
7898	WOODSIDE, Emily H	6	E22NW	1859-09-01		A1
4934	WRIGHT, Adam S	26	NWSE	1875-11-01		A7
4935	" "	26	E½SW	1875-11-01		A7
4937	WRIGHT, Timothy	4	NWSE	1888-05-07		A1
4936	" "	4	E½SW	1888-11-27		A7
4938	" "	4	SWSE	1888-11-27		A7
4939	" "	9	NWNE	1888-11-27		A7
7885	WRIGHT, Willis M	5	2NW	1878-04-05		A7
4940	WYMAN, Schuyler C	29	NW	1904-03-19		A7
4941	YOUNGBLOOD, Jonathan	15	W½SE	1860-09-10		A6

Patent Map

T23-N R9-W
5th PM 23-N 9-W Meridian

Map Group 18

Township Statistics

Parcels Mapped	:	367
Number of Patents	:	208
Number of Individuals	:	239
Patentees Identified	:	208
Number of Surnames	:	177
Multi-Patentee Parcels	:	46
Oldest Patent Date	:	9/1/1859
Most Recent Patent	:	1/31/1913
Block/Lot Parcels	:	76
Cities and Town	:	2
Cemeteries	:	2

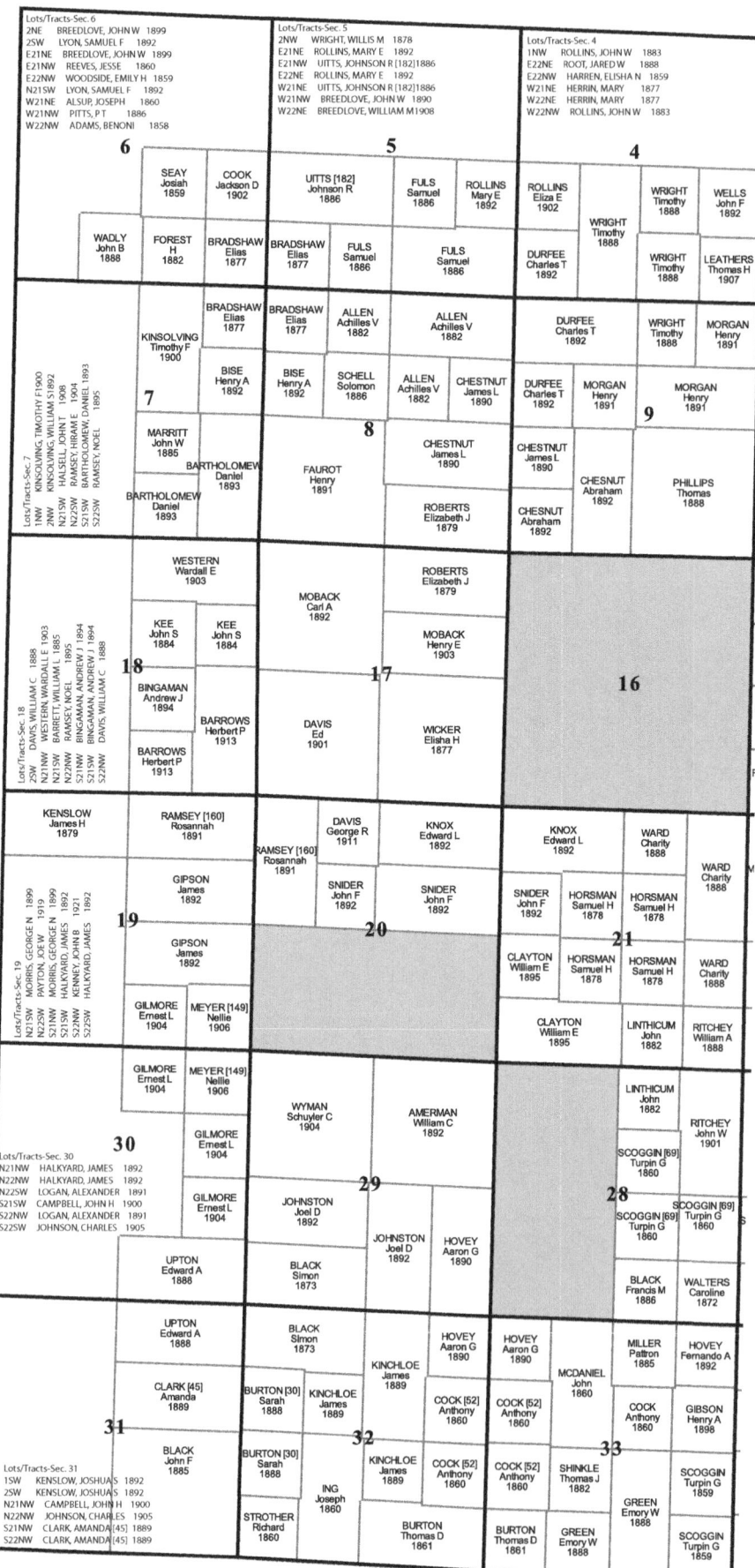

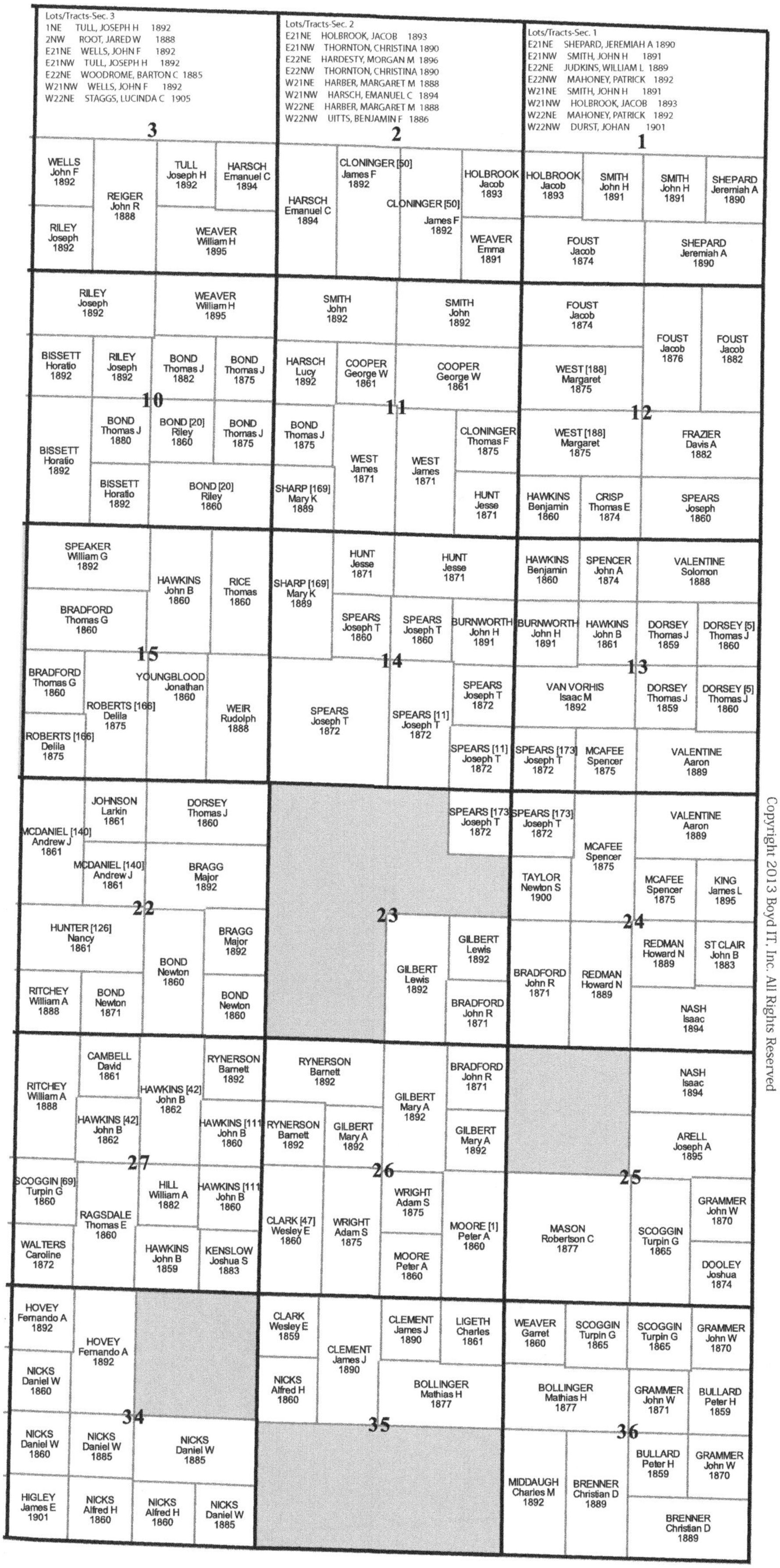

Lots/Tracts-Sec. 3
1NE TULL, JOSEPH H 1892
2NW ROOT, JARED W 1888
E21NE WELLS, JOHN F 1892
E21NW TULL, JOSEPH H 1892
E22NE WOODROME, BARTON C 1885
W21NW WELLS, JOHN F 1892
W22NE STAGGS, LUCINDA C 1905

Lots/Tracts-Sec. 2
E21NE HOLBROOK, JACOB 1893
E21NW THORNTON, CHRISTINA 1890
E22NE HARDESTY, MORGAN M 1896
E22NW THORNTON, CHRISTINA 1890
W21NE HARBER, MARGARET M 1888
W21NW HARSCH, EMANUEL C 1894
W22NE HARBER, MARGARET M 1888
W22NW UITTS, BENJAMIN F 1886

Lots/Tracts-Sec. 1
E21NE SHEPARD, JEREMIAH A 1890
E21NW SMITH, JOHN H 1891
E22NE JUDKINS, WILLIAM L 1889
E22NW MAHONEY, PATRICK 1892
W21NE SMITH, JOHN H 1891
W21NW HOLBROOK, JACOB 1893
W22NE MAHONEY, PATRICK 1892
W22NW DURST, JOHAN 1901

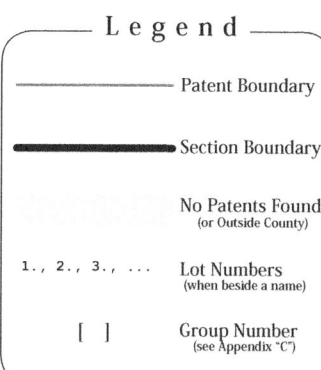

[Map grid of Township 23-N Range 9-W showing land patentee names organized by section numbers 1-3, 10-15, 22-27, 34-36]

Helpful Hints

1. This Map's INDEX can be found on the preceding pages.

2. Refer to Map "C" to see where this Township lies within Howell County, Missouri.

3. Numbers within square brackets [ ] denote a multi-patentee land parcel (multi-owner). Refer to Appendix "C" for a full list of members in this group.

4. Areas that look to be crowded with Patentees usually indicate multiple sales of the same parcel (Re-issues) or Overlapping parcels. See this Township's Index for an explanation of these and other circumstances that might explain "odd" groupings of Patentees on this map.

Legend

— Patent Boundary
— Section Boundary
No Patents Found (or Outside County)
1., 2., 3., ... Lot Numbers (when beside a name)
[ ] Group Number (see Appendix "C")

Scale: Section = 1 mile X 1 mile (generally, with some exceptions)

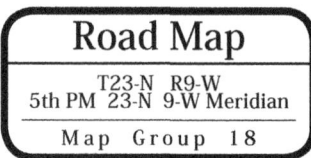

Road Map

T23-N R9-W
5th PM 23-N 9-W Meridian

Map Group 18

Cities & Towns

Homeland
South Fork

Cemeteries

Homeland Cemetery
Spears Graveyard

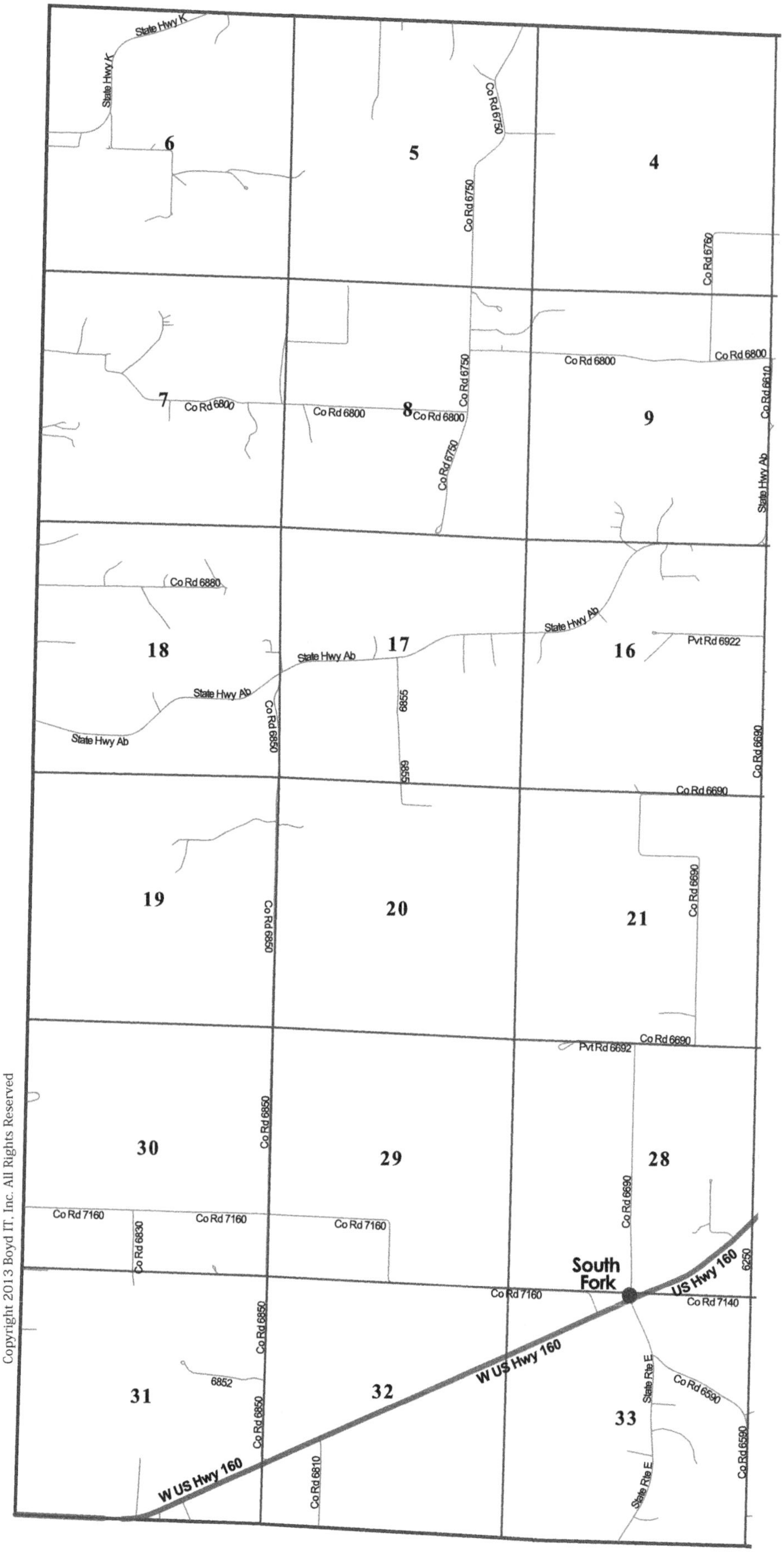

State Hwy K

Co Rd 6750

6

5

4

Co Rd 6750

Co Rd 6750

Co Rd 6750

Co Rd 6800

Co Rd 6800

7

Co Rd 6800

Co Rd 6800

8

Co Rd 6800

9

Co Rd 6750

Co Rd 6750

State Hwy Ab

Co Rd 6880

State Hwy Ab

Pvt Rd 6922

18

State Hwy Ab

17

State Hwy Ab

16

State Hwy Ab

6855

Co Rd 6850

Co Rd 6690

State Hwy Ab

6855

Co Rd 6690

19

Co Rd 6850

20

21

Co Rd 6690

Co Rd 6690

Co Rd 6690

Pvt Rd 6692

30

Co Rd 6850

29

28

Co Rd 6690

Co Rd 7160

Co Rd 7160

Co Rd 7160

Co Rd 6830

Co Rd 6850

South Fork

Co Rd 7160

US Hwy 160

6250

Co Rd 7140

W US Hwy 160

State Rte E

Co Rd 6590

31

6852

Co Rd 6850

32

W US Hwy 160

33

State Rte E

Co Rd 6590

W US Hwy 160

Co Rd 6810

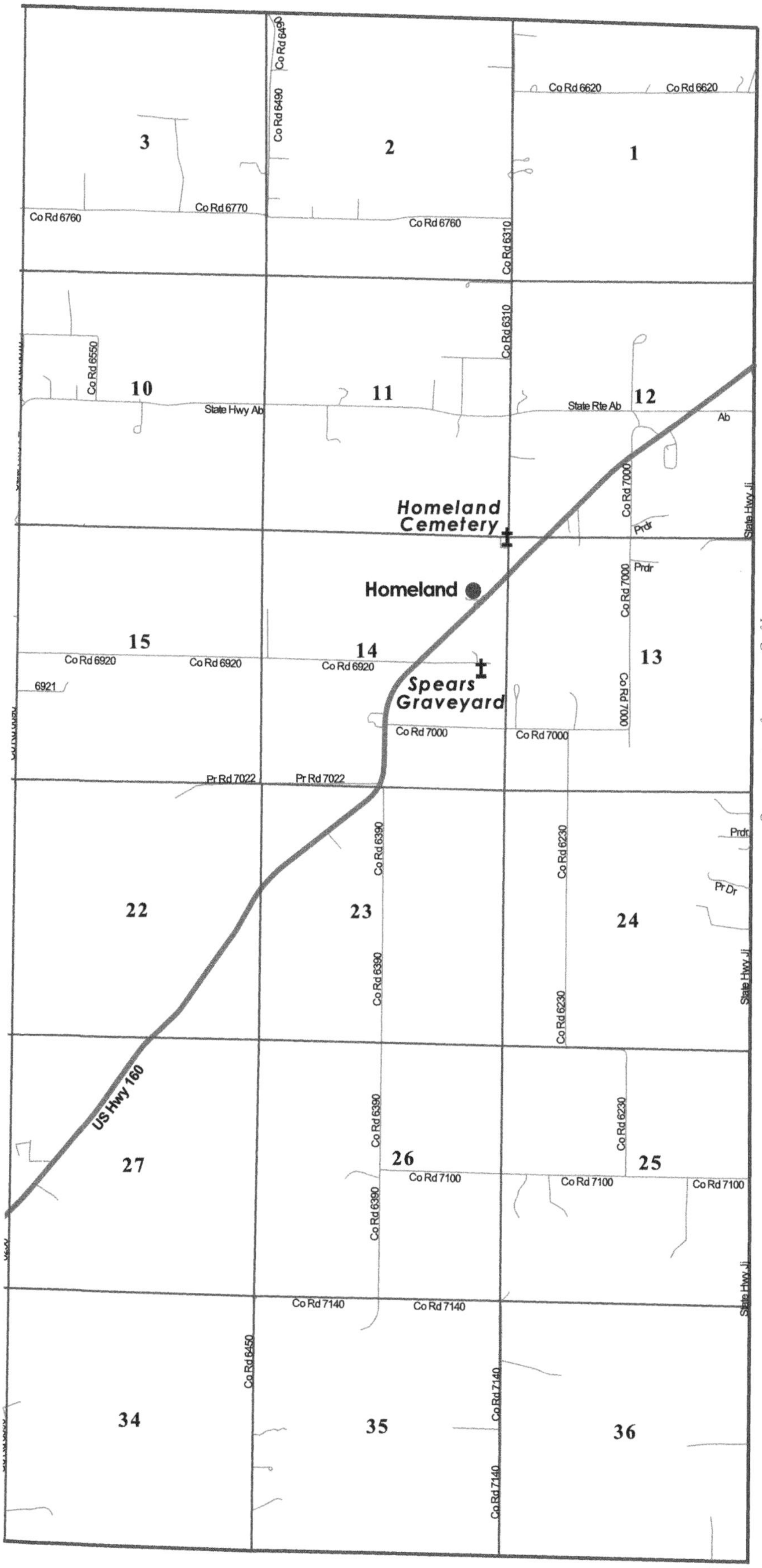

3

2

1

Co Rd 6490

Co Rd 6490

Co Rd 6620

Co Rd 6620

Co Rd 6760

Co Rd 6770

Co Rd 6760

Co Rd 6310

Co Rd 6310

10

11

12

Co Rd 6550

State Hwy Ab

State Rte Ab

Ab

Co Rd 7000

Homeland Cemetery

Prdr

Homeland

Co Rd 7000

Prdr

15

14

13

Co Rd 6920

Co Rd 6920

Co Rd 6920

Co Rd 7000

6921

Spears Graveyard

Co Rd 7000

Co Rd 7000

Pr Rd 7022

Pr Rd 7022

Prdr

Co Rd 6390

Co Rd 6230

22

23

24

Pr Dr

Co Rd 6390

Co Rd 6230

State Hwy JJ

US Hwy 160

27

Co Rd 6390

26

Co Rd 6230

25

Co Rd 7100

Co Rd 7100

Co Rd 7100

Co Rd 6390

Co Rd 7140

Co Rd 7140

Co Rd 8450

34

35

Co Rd 7140

36

Co Rd 7140

Helpful Hints

1. This road map has a number of uses, but primarily it is to help you: a) find the present location of land owned by your ancestors (at least the general area), b) find cemeteries and city-centers, and c) estimate the route/roads used by Census-takers & tax-assessors.

2. If you plan to travel to Howell County to locate cemeteries or land parcels, please pick up a modern travel map for the area before you do. Mapping old land parcels on modern maps is not as exact a science as you might think. Just the slightest variations in public land survey coordinates, estimates of parcel boundaries, or road-map deviations can greatly alter a map's representation of how a road either does or doesn't cross a particular parcel of land.

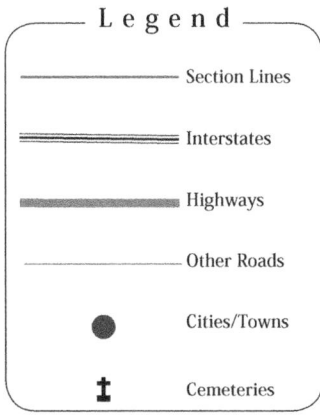

L e g e n d

————	Section Lines
═══════	Interstates
━━━━━	Highways
———	Other Roads
●	Cities/Towns
‡	Cemeteries

Scale: Section = 1 mile X 1 mile
(generally, with some exceptions)

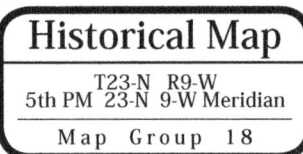

Historical Map

T23-N R9-W
5th PM 23-N 9-W Meridian

Map Group 18

Cities & Towns
Homeland
South Fork

Cemeteries
Homeland Cemetery
Spears Graveyard

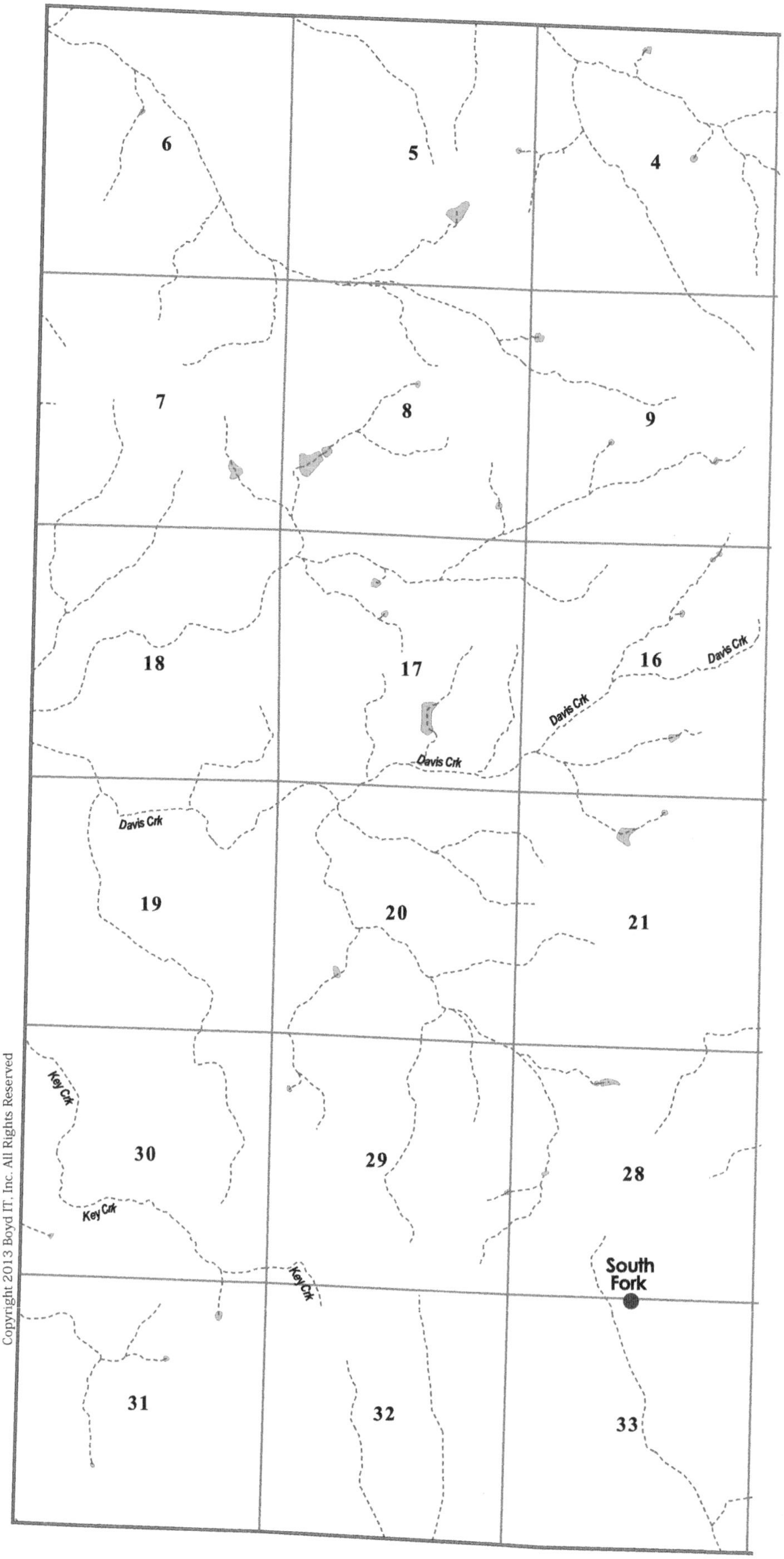

6

5

4

7

8

9

18

17

16   Davis Crk

Davis Crk

Davis Crk

Davis Crk

19

20

21

Key Crk

30

29

28

Key Crk

Key Crk

South Fork

31

32

33

Copyright 2013 Boyd IT, Inc. All Rights Reserved

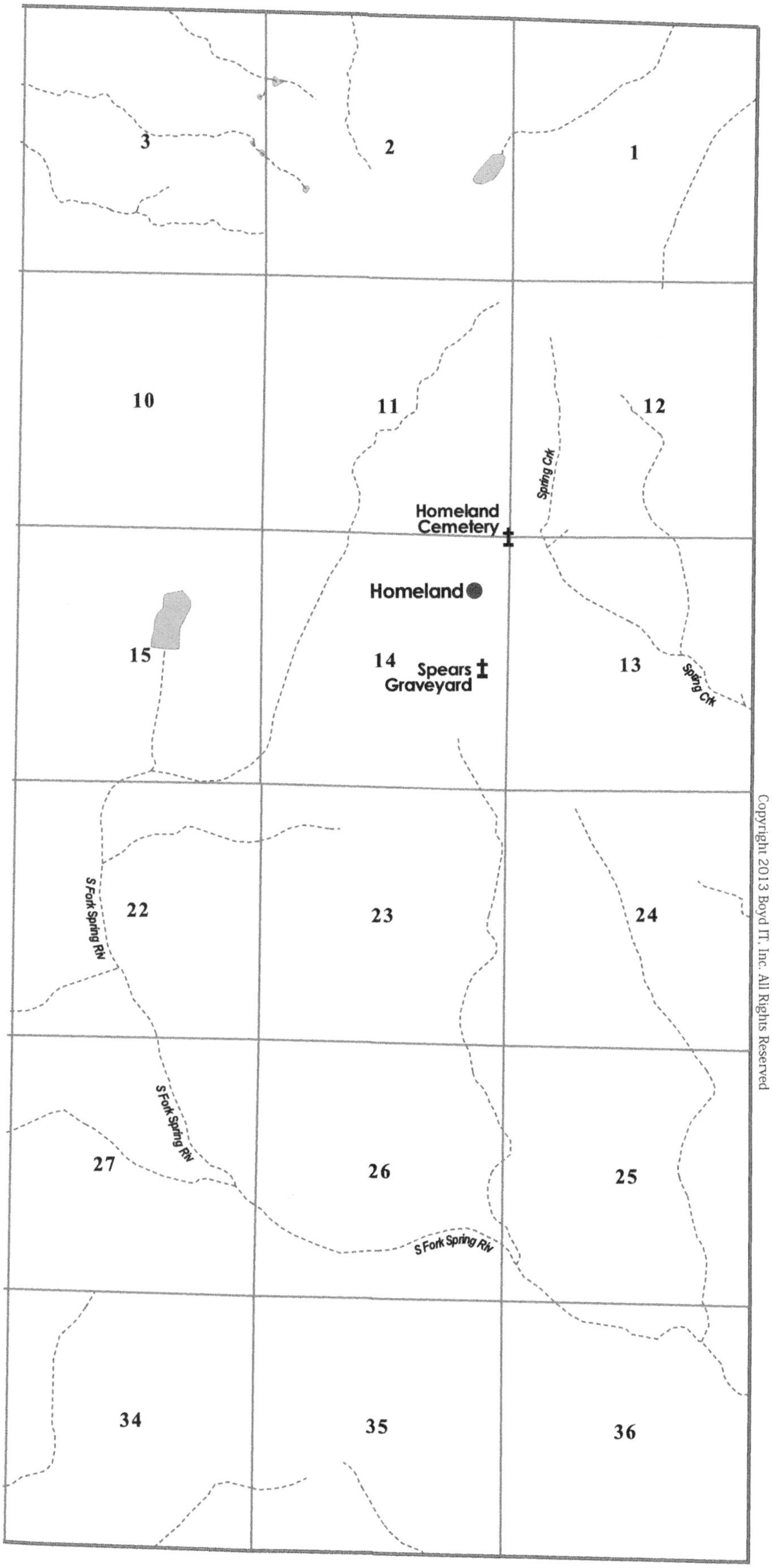

3

2

1

10

11

12

Spring Crk

Homeland
Cemetery ☨

Homeland ●

15

14 Spears ☨
Graveyard

13

Spring Crk

22

S Fork Spring Riv

23

24

27

S Fork Spring Riv

26

25

S Fork Spring Riv

34

35

36

Copyright 2013 Boyd IT, Inc. All Rights Reserved

Helpful Hints

1. This Map takes a different look at the same Congressional Township displayed in the preceding two maps. It presents features that can help you better envision the historical development of the area: a) Water-bodies (lakes & ponds), b) Water-courses (rivers, streams, etc.), c) Railroads, d) City/ town center-points (where they were oftentimes located when first settled), and e) Cemeteries.

2. Using this "Historical" map in tandem with this Township's Patent Map and Road Map, may lead you to some interesting discoveries. You will often find roads, towns, cemeteries, and waterways are named after nearby landowners: sometimes those names will be the ones you are researching. See how many of these research gems you can find here in Howell County.

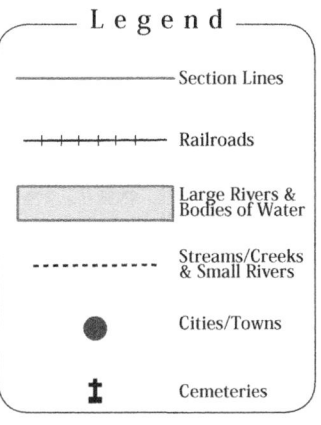

Legend

— Section Lines

+++++++ Railroads

▭ Large Rivers & Bodies of Water

- - - - - Streams/Creeks & Small Rivers

● Cities/Towns

☨ Cemeteries

Scale: Section = 1 mile X 1 mile
(there are some exceptions)

Map Group 19: Index to Land Patents

Township 23-North Range 8-West (5th PM 23-N 8-W)

After you locate an individual in this Index, take note of the Section and Section Part then proceed to the Land Patent map on the pages immediately following. You should have no difficulty locating the corresponding parcel of land.

The "For More Info" Column will lead you to more information about the underlying Patents. See the *Legend* at right, and the "How to Use this Book" chapter, for more information.

```
LEGEND
          "For More Info . . . " column
A = Authority (Legislative Act, See Appendix "A")
B = Block or Lot (location in Section unknown)
C = Cancelled Patent
F = Fractional Section
G = Group (Multi-Patentee Patent, see Appendix "C")
V = Overlaps another Parcel
R = Re-Issued (Parcel patented more than once)

(A & G items require you to look in the Appendixes referred
to above. All other Letter-designations followed by a number
require you to locate line-items in this index that possess
the ID number found after the letter).
```

ID	Individual in Patent	Sec.	Sec. Part	Date Issued	Other Counties	For More Info . . .
4942	ADEN, Solomon	3	NESW	1893-04-08		A7
7957	" "	3	W21NE	1893-04-08		A7
7954	" "	3	E21NW	1893-04-08		A7
7992	ALBRECHT, Frederick	7	S21NW	1888-12-08		A7
7993	" "	7	S22NW	1888-12-08		A7
7987	" "	7	1SW	1888-12-08		A7
4943	ALLEN, Mary	30	SE	1860-02-15		A6 G3
4946	ASHBROOK, William	28	SENW	1865-09-01		A6 G6
4944	" "	28	SWNE	1865-09-01		A6 G6
4945	" "	28	N½SW	1865-09-01		A6 G6
4947	ASHBY, Hannah	8	S½SW	1860-09-10		A6 G7
4948	" "	8	NWSW	1860-09-10		A6 G7
4951	BACHMANN, Christian H	15	SE	1875-11-01		A7
4952	BAILEY, William	26	SESE	1860-08-01		A1
4953	BARTHOLOMEW, Allen	9	N½SE	1893-04-29		A7
4954	BESS, William F	3	NESE	1890-10-11		A7
7953	" "	3	E21NE	1890-10-11		A7
7952	" "	3	2NE	1890-10-11		A7
4955	BISSEL, Mary L	11	S½SE	1892-06-30		A7 G17
4956	" "	14	NENE	1892-06-30		A7 G17
4957	BOOTMAN, Charles M	10	NENE	1893-12-19		A7
4958	" "	10	W½NE	1893-12-19		A7
4959	" "	3	SESE	1893-12-19		A7
4960	BOOTMAN, George W	10	NW	1894-05-18		A7
4961	BRIDENTHAL, Charlotte E	18	NE	1860-05-02		A6
4962	" "	30	SE	1860-02-15		A6 G3
4963	" "	34	SW	1860-05-02		A6 G22
4964	BROWN, James W	24	SENE	1897-04-02		A7
4965	BULARD, William C	31	E½NE	1861-07-01		A6
4966	BURNS, Jackson J	12	NENW	1859-09-01		A1
4969	BURRIS, Esther	23	E½SE	1882-08-30		A7 G29
4968	" "	23	SWSE	1882-08-30		A7 G29
4970	" "	26	NWNE	1882-08-30		A7 G29
4972	BURRIS, Tobias	23	SWSE	1882-08-30		A7 G29
4971	" "	23	E½SE	1882-08-30		A7 G29
4973	" "	26	NWNE	1882-08-30		A7 G29
4975	CANTLEY, Anna	23	SENE	1904-11-22		A1
4976	CANTLEY, Lafayette	23	NWSE	1891-05-25		A7
4977	CANTLEY, Silas B	22	S½SW	1881-10-06		A7
4978	" "	22	S½SE	1881-10-06		A7
4979	CASH, Eliza	21	NWNE	1860-05-02		A6 G40
4980	" "	21	N½NW	1860-05-02		A6 G40
4983	CATER, Mettides T	12	SWSW	1883-08-13		A1
4984	CAUTLEY, Silas B	27	NWNE	1882-05-10		A1
7951	CHAMBERS, George	2	W22NW	1892-03-07		A7
7949	" "	2	W21NW	1892-03-07		A7

ID	Individual in Patent	Sec.	Sec. Part	Date Issued	Other Counties	For More Info . . .
4985	CHAPIN, Silas J	27	SESE	1859-09-01		A1
4987	CHRISTENSEN, Andrew	4	S½SW	1892-06-10		A7
4986	" "	4	NWSW	1892-06-10		A7
7976	" "	4	W21NW	1892-06-10		A7
4990	CLARK, Patience	22	E½NW	1860-09-10		A6 G46
4991	" "	22	SWNE	1860-09-10		A6 G46
4994	CLAYTER, Sarah	19	SESE	1860-09-10		A6 G48
4995	" "	20	SWSW	1860-09-10		A6 G48
4996	COLDIRON, Wesley	12	SESW	1902-10-20		A7
7917	COLLIER, Frederick	1	W22NE	1867-08-20		A1
7912	" "	1	E22NE	1853-12-01		A1
7914	" "	1	W21NE	1860-03-01		A1
7926	COTTLE, Philip S	18	S21NW	1860-09-10		A6
7919	" "	18	1SW	1860-09-10		A6
4997	CRANE, Albert	25	E½SW	1885-03-20		A1
4998	" "	26	N½SW	1885-03-20		A1
4999	" "	27	NESE	1885-03-20		A1
5000	" "	34	SENE	1885-03-20		A1
5003	" "	35	SENE	1885-03-20		A1
5002	" "	35	N½SW	1885-03-20		A1
5001	" "	35	SWNW	1885-03-20		A1
5005	" "	36	S½	1885-05-25		A1
5006	" "	36	NW	1886-04-10		A7 G62
5004	" "	36	NE	1885-05-25		A1
5007	CRANE, Arch M	26	SWSW	1891-06-09		A7
5008	" "	34	NENE	1891-06-09		A7
5009	" "	35	NWNW	1891-06-09		A7
5011	CROW, John	28	N½NW	1892-03-07		A7
5012	" "	28	SWNW	1892-03-07		A7
5010	" "	28	NWNE	1892-03-07		A7
7966	CURRY, Perry A	31	N22SW	1893-09-01		A7
5014	DAVIDSON, Louisa A	22	N½SW	1877-10-10		A7 G64
5013	" "	22	SWNW	1877-10-10		A7 G64
5015	" "	22	NWSE	1877-10-10		A7 G64
5016	DELAY, James H	1	NWSE	1882-09-30		A1
5018	DOCKERY, James J	25	S½SE	1860-09-10		A6
5017	" "	25	NWSE	1860-09-10		A6
5021	DOCKEY, James J	25	SENW	1866-09-01		A1
7929	DOOLEY, Joshua	18	S22SW	1890-01-10		A7
5022	DOWNS, William H	13	NENE	1901-12-30		A7
5023	DRINNON, Joseph	12	S½SE	1889-01-12		A7
5025	" "	13	NENW	1889-01-12		A7
5024	" "	13	NWNE	1889-01-12		A7
5027	DUNEHEW, William C	29	SESW	1860-10-01		A1
5028	EVANS, Martha M	8	N½SE	1891-05-25		A7
5029	EWART, James	34	SE	1893-03-03		A7
5031	FARQUAR, James M	29	SWNW	1897-04-02		A7
5030	" "	29	NWSW	1897-04-02		A7
7971	FAST, George W	4	2NE	1896-10-13		A1
7974	FIELDS, Green	4	E22NE	1891-08-24		A1
7972	" "	4	E21NE	1891-08-24		A1
7981	" "	5	W22NW	1891-08-24		A1
5033	FOWLER, Sumner S	35	W½SE	1885-02-25		A7
5032	" "	35	SESW	1885-02-25		A7
5034	FREEZE, John L	5	SW	1879-12-15		A7
5037	GEISLER, Malinda	10	W½SE	1874-04-20		A7 G92
5036	" "	10	NESE	1874-04-20		A7 G92
5035	" "	10	SENE	1874-04-20		A7 G92
5038	GEISLER, William	10	W½SE	1874-04-20		A7 G92
5040	" "	10	NESE	1874-04-20		A7 G92
5039	" "	10	SENE	1874-04-20		A7 G92
5041	GIBSON, Levi	11	NESE	1890-10-11		A7
5043	" "	12	NWSW	1890-10-11		A7
5042	" "	12	S½NW	1890-10-11		A7
5044	GLENN, Charles H	23	S½SW	1890-10-11		A7
5045	" "	26	N½NW	1890-10-11		A7
5046	GOODGION, Orpha	15	NWNE	1859-09-01		A1
5047	GOODNO, Edgar E	32	SESW	1888-12-08		A7
5048	" "	32	SWSE	1888-12-08		A7
5049	GRANT, Emmett E	31	W½NE	1893-09-01		A7
5050	" "	31	N½SE	1893-09-01		A7
5051	GREEN, Benjamin F	27	W½NW	1888-12-08		A7
5052	GREEN, James H	28	E½NE	1889-01-12		A7

ID	Individual in Patent	Sec.	Sec. Part	Date Issued	Other Counties	For More Info . . .
5053	GREENSTREET, Moses A	29	SWSW	1882-05-10		A7
5054	" "	32	N½NW	1882-05-10		A7
5055	GRIESEL, Henry	8	NENW	1882-09-30		A7
5057	" "	8	S½NW	1882-09-30		A7
5056	" "	8	SWNE	1882-09-30		A7
5061	GRIFFITH, Martin	17	SWSW	1859-01-01		A1
5062	" "	18	S½SE	1860-02-15		A6
5063	" "	19	NENE	1858-11-10		A8
5064	" "	20	N½NW	1860-05-02		A6 G101
5065	" "	20	SWNW	1860-05-02		A6 G101
5066	" "	20	NWSW	1860-05-02		A6 G101
5067	GRIFFITH, Mary	1	NESE	1860-02-15		A6
5068	" "	1	S½SE	1860-02-15		A6
5069	" "	12	NENE	1860-02-15		A6
5070	GROTE, John C	27	SW	1860-09-10		A6
5071	GUTHRIE, Robert P	11	SESW	1882-09-30		A1
5074	HALL, Andrew L	35	E½NW	1892-03-07		A7
5073	" "	35	W½NE	1892-03-07		A7
5077	HALL, Henderson	32	NESE	1861-02-01		A1 G104
5076	" "	32	NESE	1853-12-01		A1 C G104
5075	" "	32	NWSE	1920-10-15		A1 G104
5078	" "	32	SENW	1860-08-01		A1
5081	HALL, James H	21	NESW	1875-05-10		A7
5080	" "	21	SENW	1875-05-10		A7
5079	" "	21	S½SW	1875-05-10		A7
5082	" "	32	SWNE	1882-09-30		A1
5083	HALL, Leonard	28	S½SW	1873-05-30		A7 G105
5084	" "	29	SESE	1873-05-30		A7 G105
5086	" "	32	NESE	1853-12-01		A1 C G104
5088	" "	32	NESE	1861-02-01		A1 G104
5087	" "	32	SESE	1859-01-01		A1
5085	" "	32	NWSE	1920-10-15		A1 G104
5089	" "	33	NENW	1873-05-30		A7 G105
5090	HALL, Thomas	28	E½SE	1873-11-01		A7
5091	" "	28	SWSE	1873-11-01		A7
5092	" "	33	NENE	1873-11-01		A7
5093	HALL, Thomas J	33	W½NW	1888-12-06		A7
7969	HARKINS, Hiram D	31	S22SW	1889-01-12		A7
5097	HARRIS, Joshua J	25	NESE	1885-02-25		A7
5098	" "	25	SENE	1885-02-25		A7
5099	HARRIS, William C	35	NENE	1889-09-27		A7
5100	HOCUTT, William C	4	S½SE	1890-10-11		A7
5101	" "	9	E½NE	1890-10-11		A7
5103	HOLZSCHEITER, Paul	1	S½SW	1878-06-24		A7
5104	" "	12	NWNW	1878-06-24		A7
5105	" "	2	SESE	1878-06-24		A7
5107	HUDDLESTON, Mary	15	S½NW	1873-05-30		A7
5106	" "	15	N½SW	1873-05-30		A7
7983	HULL, Gersham	6	2NE	1893-09-01		A7
7982	" "	6	1NE	1893-09-01		A7
5109	INGLE, Peter	32	W½SW	1882-05-20		A7
5111	" "	32	SWNW	1882-05-20		A7
5110	" "	32	NESW	1882-05-20		A7
5113	JAMES, Patience	34	SW	1860-05-02		A6 G22
5114	JAMES, William	13	SWNW	1884-03-10		A1
5115	" "	23	NENE	1884-03-10		A1
5116	JOHNSON, Everett S	12	NESW	1888-12-06		A1
5118	" "	17	S½NE	1882-09-30		A1
5119	" "	17	E½NW	1882-09-30		A1
5120	" "	17	NWSW	1882-09-30		A1
5117	" "	17	SESW	1882-09-30		A1
5121	" "	18	NWSE	1883-08-13		A1
7922	" "	18	N21NW	1883-08-13		A1
7933	" "	19	N21NW	1883-08-13		A1
5124	" "	19	NESE	1883-08-13		A1
5122	" "	19	SENE	1882-09-30		A1
5123	" "	19	NWNE	1882-09-30		A1
7936	" "	19	N22SW	1883-08-13		A1
5125	" "	20	E½SW	1882-09-30		A1
5126	" "	20	NWNE	1890-06-04		A1
5127	" "	20	SENW	1882-09-30		A1
5128	" "	8	NWNW	1883-08-13		A1
5129	JOHNSON, Hans	9	E½NW	1892-06-10		A7

ID	Individual in Patent	Sec.	Sec. Part	Date Issued	Other Counties	For More Info . . .
5130	JOHNSON, Hans (Cont'd)	9	W½NE	1892-06-10		A7
5133	JOHNSON, James	33	NWNE	1878-11-30		A7
5132	" "	33	S½NE	1878-11-30		A7
5131	" "	33	SENW	1878-11-30		A7
7934	JOHNSON, Rocla W	19	N21SW	1860-09-10		A6
5135	" "	19	SWNE	1860-09-10		A6
5134	" "	19	NWSE	1860-09-10		A6
5136	JOHNSON, Roda W	19	SESE	1860-09-10		A6 G48
5137	" "	20	SWSW	1860-09-10		A6 G48
5139	" "	8	S½SW	1860-09-10		A6 G7
5138	" "	8	NWSW	1860-09-10		A6 G7
5140	JOHNSON, Roela W	8	NESW	1860-08-01		A1
5141	JOHNSON, William H	17	SWNW	1859-09-01		A1
5142	" "	18	NESE	1859-09-01		A1
5143	JOHNSTON, William H	17	NWNW	1860-03-01		A1
7986	JUDKINS, William L	6	W22NW	1889-06-22		A7
7985	" "	6	W21NW	1889-06-22		A7
7962	KENNEY, Robert N	30	S22SW	1890-01-10		A7
7960	" "	30	1SW	1890-01-10		A7
7964	" "	31	N21NW	1890-01-10		A7
7911	KING, Martin L	1	E21NW	1889-01-12		A7
5144	" "	1	N½SW	1889-01-12		A7
5145	" "	2	NESE	1889-01-12		A7
5146	KIRKPATRICK, Benjamin S	26	SESW	1882-05-10		A1
5147	KISNER, Mary L	11	S½SE	1892-06-30		A7 G17
5148	" "	14	NENE	1892-06-30		A7 G17
5149	KNIGHT, Fanny	11	N½NW	1891-06-09		A7 G137
5150	" "	2	W½SW	1891-06-09		A7 G137
5151	KNIGHT, Samuel	11	N½NW	1891-06-09		A7 G137
5152	" "	2	W½SW	1891-06-09		A7 G137
5154	KNIGHT, William W	11	NESW	1894-05-18		A7
5153	" "	11	SENW	1894-05-18		A7
5156	KROHN, Fred	13	NESW	1899-02-13		A7
5155	" "	13	SENW	1899-02-13		A7
5157	KROHN, John H	14	N½SE	1892-03-07		A7
5158	" "	14	S½NE	1892-03-07		A7
5159	KROHN, William	14	SWSE	1901-11-08		A7
5162	LAMONS, James H	14	SWNW	1879-12-15		A7
5163	" "	15	E½NE	1879-12-15		A7
5164	" "	15	SWNE	1879-12-15		A7
5165	LAMONS, John W	22	NESE	1890-10-11		A7
5166	LAMONS, Peter	22	NWNE	1879-12-15		A7
5167	" "	22	SENE	1879-12-15		A7
5168	LANGSTON, Samuel J	24	NWSW	1884-03-10		A1
5169	LEMONS, Peter	22	E½NW	1860-09-10		A6 G46
5170	" "	22	SWNE	1860-09-10		A6 G46
5171	LOAGUE, Patrick	24	E½SE	1894-12-17		A7
5172	" "	25	N½NE	1894-12-17		A7
5173	LOGSTON, James W	26	S½NW	1898-04-06		A7
5176	LUDWIG, Charles T	22	NENE	1884-03-10		A1
5177	" "	23	NWNE	1877-10-10		A7
5179	" "	23	NENW	1877-10-10		A7
5178	" "	23	W½NW	1877-10-10		A7
5182	LUDWIG, Fritz W	26	W½SE	1890-06-06		A7
5180	" "	26	NESE	1890-06-06		A7
5181	" "	26	SWNE	1890-06-06		A7
5183	LUDWIG, Herman S	14	SW	1877-10-10		A7
5184	LUNG, John G	11	NE	1874-04-20		A7
5185	LUNG, Paul	2	E½SW	1889-01-12		A7
5186	" "	2	W½SE	1889-01-12		A7
5187	MAY, George E	32	N½NE	1897-06-11		A7
5188	" "	32	SENE	1897-06-11		A7
5190	MAYHEW, William C	5	SE	1893-03-03		A7
5192	MCANALLY, James L	21	E½NE	1875-11-01		A7
5191	" "	21	NESE	1875-11-01		A7
5193	MCCLAIN, Fergus J	30	NW	1888-12-06		A7
5195	MCCOMB, Samuel S	3	W½SE	1884-10-11		A1
5194	" "	3	S½SW	1884-10-11		A1
5196	MCMASTER, Sarah B	28	NWSE	1894-12-17		A7
7965	MEADOWS, Peter H	31	N21SW	1884-11-01		A7
7967	" "	31	S21NW	1884-11-01		A7
7963	" "	31	2NW	1884-11-01		A7
5198	MITCHELL, James W	21	SWNE	1888-12-08		A7

ID	Individual in Patent	Sec.	Sec. Part	Date Issued	Other Counties	For More Info . . .
5199	MITCHELL, James W (Cont'd)	21	W½SE	1888-12-08		A7
5197	" "	21	SESE	1888-12-08		A7
5201	MOORE, Thomas	12	NWNE	1875-11-01		A7
5207	MORRISON, Joseph	23	SWNE	1881-04-09		A7
5206	" "	23	N½SW	1881-04-09		A7
5205	" "	23	SENW	1881-04-09		A7
5209	MUSTION, Alfred	9	S½SE	1870-11-01		A1 G153
5208	" "	9	SESW	1870-11-01		A1 G153
5210	MUSTION, Alfred T	17	NESW	1882-06-01		A1
5211	MUSTION, John W	11	NWSE	1883-08-13		A1
5212	MUSTION, William D	9	S½SE	1870-11-01		A1 G153
5213	" "	9	SESW	1870-11-01		A1 G153
5215	NETTLETON, George W	22	N½SW	1877-10-10		A7 G64
5216	" "	22	NWSE	1877-10-10		A7 G64
5214	" "	22	SWNW	1877-10-10		A7 G64
5218	NETTLETON, Louisa A	22	SWNW	1877-10-10		A7 G64
5217	" "	22	NWSE	1877-10-10		A7 G64
5219	" "	22	N½SW	1877-10-10		A7 G64
5220	OLSON, Lars	29	N½SE	1894-05-18		A7
5221	" "	29	SWSE	1894-05-18		A7
5222	" "	29	NESW	1894-05-18		A7
5224	ORCHARD, James M	28	SWNE	1865-09-01		A6 G6
5225	" "	28	SENW	1865-09-01		A6 G6
5223	" "	28	N½SW	1865-09-01		A6 G6
5226	PACE, David T	10	S½SW	1860-09-10		A6 G156
5227	" "	15	N½NW	1860-09-10		A6 G156
5228	PALMER, Jeffrey	27	W½SE	1871-11-01		A7
5229	" "	34	W½NE	1871-11-01		A7
5230	PARRISH, Josiah W	12	NESE	1859-09-01		A1
7918	PENNINGTON, Dabner	1	W22NW	1882-08-30		A7
7916	" "	1	W21NW	1860-05-02		A6
7945	" "	2	E22NE	1860-05-02		A6
7943	" "	2	E21NE	1860-05-02		A6
5231	" "	35	NESE	1884-10-11		A1
5232	PEOPLES, John M	25	NWSW	1875-04-01		A7
5233	" "	25	SWSW	1866-09-01		A1
5234	PHILLIPS, Tilmon D	15	S½SW	1891-06-09		A7
7913	POMEROY, Thomas	1	E22NW	1860-03-01		A1
5235	POOL, John T	22	NWNW	1888-12-08		A7
5236	POPE, Henry T	10	S½SW	1860-09-10		A6 G156
5237	" "	15	N½NW	1860-09-10		A6 G156
5240	PRANTL, Joseph	13	S½SE	1889-01-12		A7
5241	" "	24	N½NE	1889-01-12		A7
7920	PROFFIT, John	18	1SW	1860-09-10		A6
7927	" "	18	S21NW	1860-09-10		A6
7924	PROFFITT, John	18	N22SW	1882-06-30		A7
7928	" "	18	S22NW	1880-06-30		A1
5243	REED, Ezekiel T	13	N½SE	1894-11-30		A7
5242	" "	13	S½NE	1894-11-30		A7
5244	RENFRO, Andrew	36	NW	1886-04-10		A7 G62
5245	RENFRO, George G	36	NW	1886-04-10		A7 G62
5246	RICE, David	17	SE	1860-09-10		A6
5247	RIGGS, Alvin	13	W½SW	1892-03-07		A7 G165
5248	" "	14	SESE	1892-03-07		A7 G165
5249	RIGGS, Mary	13	W½SW	1892-03-07		A7 G165
5250	" "	14	SESE	1892-03-07		A7 G165
5251	ROBARDS, Alfred	23	S½SE	1860-08-01		A1
5252	" "	29	E½NW	1860-08-01		A1
5253	ROBERDS, Alfred	29	NE	1860-03-01		A1
5255	ROBINS, John	27	E½NW	1892-01-25		A7
5254	" "	27	S½NE	1892-01-25		A7
5257	SEATT, John M	24	S½SW	1911-04-20		A7
5256	" "	24	SWSE	1911-04-20		A7
5258	" "	25	NENW	1911-04-20		A7
5259	SEUTEFF, Henrietta	28	S½SW	1873-05-30		A7 G105
5260	" "	29	SESE	1873-05-30		A7 G105
5261	" "	33	NENW	1873-05-30		A7 G105
5264	SHELTON, Tate	14	N½NW	1879-12-15		A7
5263	" "	14	NWNE	1879-12-15		A7
5262	" "	14	SENW	1879-12-15		A7
7910	SHEPPARD, Thomas	1	E21NE	1860-08-01		A1
7961	SHERWOOD, Pleasant M	30	N22SW	1888-12-06		A1
5265	SHEWBART, Henry H	17	N½NE	1888-12-06		A7

ID	Individual in Patent	Sec.	Sec. Part	Date Issued	Other Counties	For More Info . . .
5266	SHEWBART, Henry H (Cont'd)	8	S½SE	1888-12-06		A7
5267	SKINNER, John J	4	NESW	1888-12-08		A7
7973	" "	4	E21NW	1888-12-08		A7
7970	" "	4	1NE	1888-12-08		A7
5268	SMITH, Edward M	7	NE	1889-01-12		A7
5271	SMITH, Oscar R	10	N½SW	1894-12-17		A7
5272	SMITH, Sarah	20	SWNE	1860-09-10		A6 G172
5273	" "	20	E½NE	1860-09-10		A6 G172
7959	SMITH, Thomas	3	W22NW	1875-04-01		A7
7958	SMOTHERMON, Elbert	3	W21NW	1877-10-10		A7
5274	" "	3	NWSW	1877-10-10		A7
5275	" "	4	N½SE	1877-10-10		A7
5276	SNEAD, Austin	35	SESE	1897-11-10		A7
7923	SPEARS, Joseph	18	N22NW	1859-09-01		A1
7937	STANBERY, Philemon B	19	S21NW	1860-09-10		A6
7930	" "	19	2NW	1860-09-10		A6
7991	STEPHENSON, William E	7	N22NW	1892-03-07		A7
7990	" "	7	N21NW	1892-03-07		A7
7931	STOUT, Dolphin E	19	2NW	1860-09-10		A6
7939	" "	19	S21NW	1860-09-10		A6
5277	" "	20	SWNE	1860-09-10		A6 G172
5279	" "	20	N½SE	1865-09-01		A6
5278	" "	20	E½NE	1860-09-10		A6 G172
7989	" "	7	2SW	1865-09-01		A6
5281	STREET, John B	8	NWNE	1878-03-20		A7
5280	" "	8	E½NE	1878-03-20		A7
5282	" "	9	NWNW	1878-03-20		A7
5285	STREET, William	9	SWNW	1890-01-10		A7
5283	" "	9	NESW	1890-01-10		A7
5284	" "	9	W½SW	1890-01-10		A7
5286	SUETEFF, John C	28	S½SW	1873-05-30		A7 G105
5287	" "	29	SESE	1873-05-30		A7 G105
5288	" "	33	NENW	1873-05-30		A7 G105
5289	SUMMERS, George M	13	NWNW	1905-03-30		A7
5290	SUMMERS, Lawrence M	10	SESE	1892-09-15		A7
5291	" "	11	W½SW	1892-09-15		A7
5292	" "	11	SWNW	1892-09-15		A7
7980	TAYLOR, Henry A	5	W22NE	1889-01-12		A7
7979	" "	5	W21NE	1889-01-12		A7
5293	TERRY, Stephen	31	S½SE	1888-12-06		A7
7968	" "	31	S21SW	1888-12-06		A7
7975	THURMAN, Marshall	4	E22NW	1895-11-13		A1
5294	TURLEY, Dillard M	12	S½NE	1883-02-10		A7
5295	" "	12	NWSE	1883-02-10		A7
5296	WALKER, John A	25	W½NW	1892-01-05		A7
5297	" "	26	E½NE	1892-01-05		A7
5301	WALKER, John H	24	NESW	1893-03-03		A7
5300	" "	24	SENW	1893-03-03		A7
5298	" "	24	SWNE	1893-03-03		A7
5299	" "	24	NWSE	1893-03-03		A7
5302	WEIBEL, Herman	13	SESW	1891-05-25		A7
5303	" "	24	N½NW	1891-05-25		A7
5304	" "	24	SWNW	1891-05-25		A7
7977	WEST, John R	5	1NW	1891-05-25		A7
7978	" "	5	2NW	1891-05-25		A7
5305	WHITNEY, Sylvester H	27	NENE	1890-01-30		A1
5306	WILKERSON, Arta M	25	SWNE	1885-05-20		A7 G190
5307	WILKERSON, Fidelia	25	SWNE	1885-05-20		A7 G190
5308	WILKERSON, Ida E	25	SWNE	1885-05-20		A7 G190
5309	WILKERSON, Julian W	25	SWNE	1885-05-20		A7 G190
5310	WILKERSON, Mary J	25	SWNE	1885-05-20		A7 G190
7984	WILLIAMS, Alexander L	6	E21NW	1893-09-01		A7
5311	WINSTRAN, Niles J	35	SWSW	1892-01-05		A7
5312	WOODREL, Isaiah	29	NWNW	1873-11-01		A7
5314	" "	30	SENE	1873-11-01		A7
5313	" "	30	N½NE	1873-11-01		A7
7940	WOODREL, Mordica H	19	S21SW	1885-05-20		A7
7941	" "	19	S22SW	1885-05-20		A7
5315	" "	19	SWSE	1885-05-20		A7
5316	WOODRELL, William C	30	SWNE	1891-06-09		A7
5317	WOODS, Robert K	20	N½NW	1860-05-02		A6 G101
5318	" "	20	SWNW	1860-05-02		A6 G101
5319	" "	20	NWSW	1860-05-02		A6 G101

ID	Individual in Patent	Sec.	Sec. Part	Date Issued	Other Counties	For More Info . . .
7956	WOODSIDE, John R	3	E22NW	1860-05-02		A6
5321	WOODWORTH, Stephen R	21	NWSW	1860-05-02		A6
5320	" "	21	N½NW	1860-05-02		A6 G40
5322	" "	21	NWNE	1860-05-02		A6 G40
5323	" "	21	SWNW	1860-05-02		A6
7944	YOUNGS, George A	2	E21NW	1888-12-08		A7
7947	" "	2	E22NW	1888-12-08		A7
7948	" "	2	W21NE	1888-12-08		A7
7950	" "	2	W22NE	1888-12-08		A7

Patent Map

T23-N R8-W
5th PM 23-N 8-W Meridian

Map Group 19

Township Statistics

Parcels Mapped	:	361
Number of Patents	:	204
Number of Individuals	:	221
Patentees Identified	:	194
Number of Surnames	:	161
Multi-Patentee Parcels	:	44
Oldest Patent Date	:	12/1/1853
Most Recent Patent	:	10/15/1920
Block/Lot Parcels	:	70
Cities and Town	:	2
Cemeteries	:	2

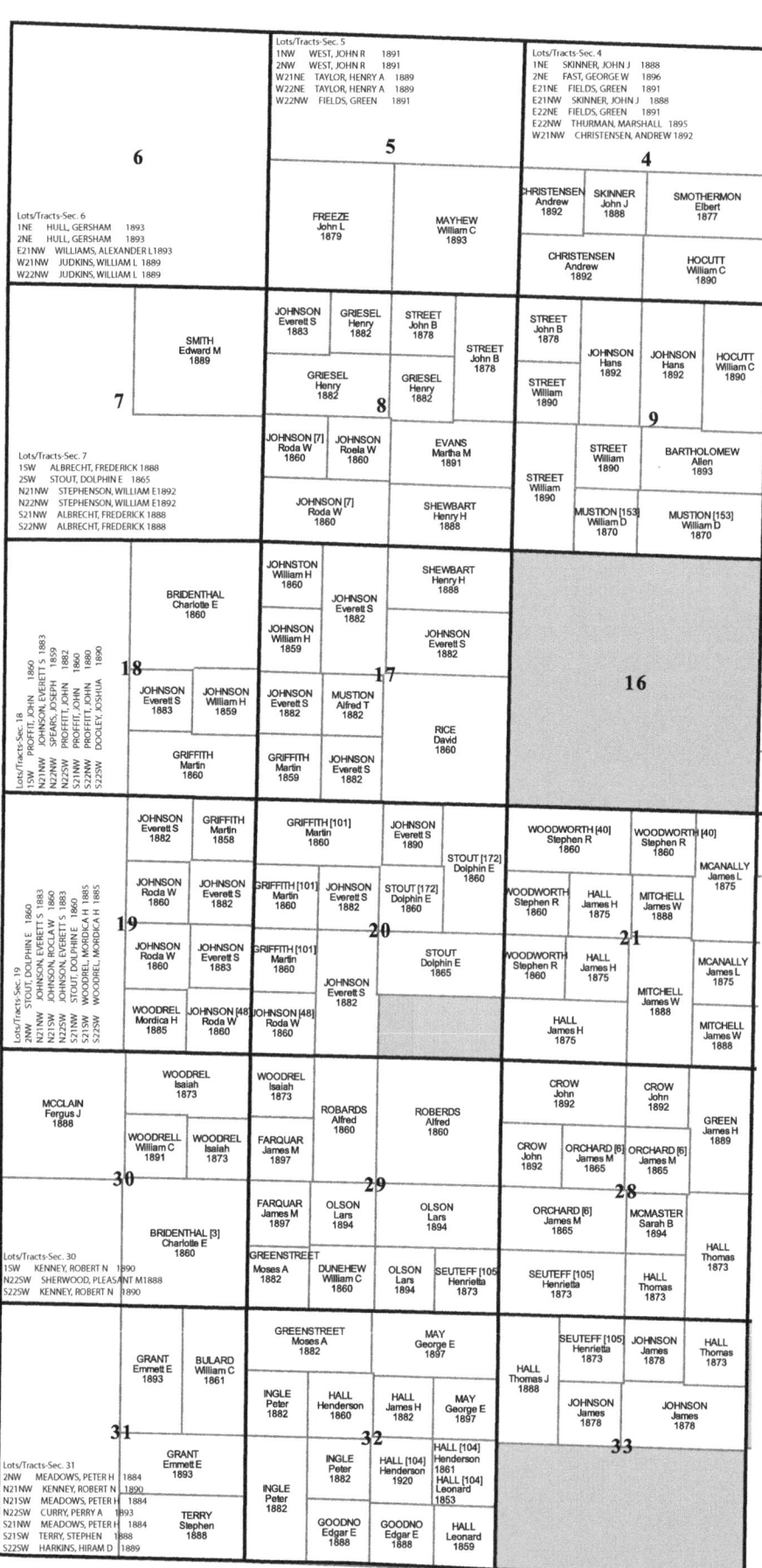

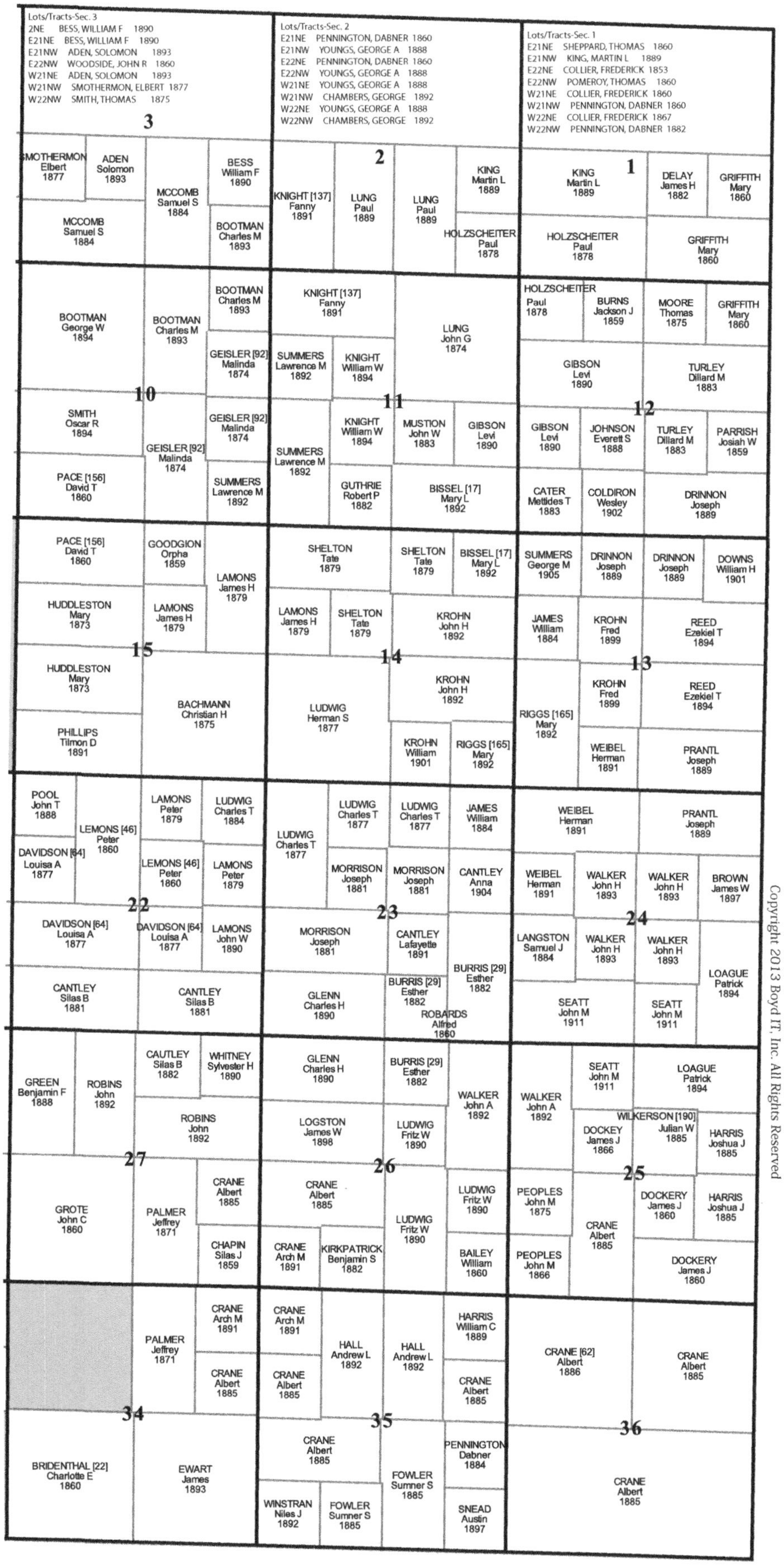

Lots/Tracts-Sec. 3
2NE   BESS, WILLIAM F   1890
E21NE   BESS, WILLIAM F   1890
E21NW   ADEN, SOLOMON   1893
E22NW   WOODSIDE, JOHN R 1860
W21NE   ADEN, SOLOMON   1893
W21NW   SMOTHERMON, ELBERT 1877
W22NW   SMITH, THOMAS   1875

Lots/Tracts-Sec. 2
E21NE   PENNINGTON, DABNER 1860
E21NW   YOUNGS, GEORGE A 1888
E22NE   PENNINGTON, DABNER 1860
E22NW   YOUNGS, GEORGE A 1888
W21NE   YOUNGS, GEORGE A 1888
W21NW   CHAMBERS, GEORGE 1892
W22NE   YOUNGS, GEORGE A 1888
W22NW   CHAMBERS, GEORGE 1892

Lots/Tracts-Sec. 1
E21NE   SHEPPARD, THOMAS 1860
E21NW   KING, MARTIN L   1889
E22NE   COLLIER, FREDERICK 1853
E22NW   POMEROY, THOMAS   1860
W21NE   COLLIER, FREDERICK 1860
W21NW   PENNINGTON, DABNER 1860
W22NE   COLLIER, FREDERICK 1867
W22NW   PENNINGTON, DABNER 1882

3

2

1

SMOTHERMON Elbert 1877

ADEN Solomon 1893

MCCOMB Samuel S 1884

BESS William F 1890

KNIGHT [137] Fanny 1891

LUNG Paul 1889

LUNG Paul 1889

KING Martin L 1889

KING Martin L 1889

DELAY James H 1882

GRIFFITH Mary 1860

MCCOMB Samuel S 1884

BOOTMAN Charles M 1893

HOLZSCHEITER Paul 1878

HOLZSCHEITER Paul 1878

GRIFFITH Mary 1860

BOOTMAN George W 1894

BOOTMAN Charles M 1893

BOOTMAN Charles M 1893

KNIGHT [137] Fanny 1891

LUNG John G 1874

HOLZSCHEITER Paul 1878

BURNS Jackson J 1859

MOORE Thomas 1875

GRIFFITH Mary 1860

GEISLER [92] Malinda 1874

SUMMERS Lawrence M 1892

KNIGHT William W 1894

GIBSON Levi 1890

TURLEY Dillard M 1883

10

11

12

SMITH Oscar R 1894

GEISLER [92] Malinda 1874

KNIGHT William W 1894

MUSTION John W 1883

GIBSON Levi 1890

GIBSON Levi 1890

JOHNSON Everett S 1888

TURLEY Dillard M 1883

PARRISH Josiah W 1859

GEISLER [92] Malinda 1874

SUMMERS Lawrence M 1892

GUTHRIE Robert P 1882

BISSEL [17] Mary L 1892

CATER Metildes T 1883

COLDIRON Wesley 1902

DRINNON Joseph 1889

PACE [156] David T 1860

PACE [156] David T 1860

GOODGION Orpha 1859

LAMONS James H 1879

SHELTON Tate 1879

SHELTON Tate 1879

BISSEL [17] Mary L 1892

SUMMERS George M 1905

DRINNON Joseph 1889

DRINNON Joseph 1889

DOWNS William H 1901

HUDDLESTON Mary 1873

LAMONS James H 1879

LAMONS James H 1879

SHELTON Tate 1879

KROHN John H 1892

JAMES William 1884

KROHN Fred 1899

REED Ezekiel T 1894

15

14

13

HUDDLESTON Mary 1873

BACHMANN Christian H 1875

LUDWIG Herman S 1877

KROHN John H 1892

KROHN Fred 1899

REED Ezekiel T 1894

PHILLIPS Tilmon D 1891

KROHN William 1901

RIGGS [165] Mary 1892

RIGGS [165] Mary 1892

WEIBEL Herman 1891

PRANTL Joseph 1889

POOL John T 1888

LAMONS Peter 1879

LUDWIG Charles T 1884

LUDWIG Charles T 1877

LUDWIG Charles T 1877

JAMES William 1884

WEIBEL Herman 1891

PRANTL Joseph 1889

LEMONS [46] Peter 1860

LUDWIG Charles T 1877

DAVIDSON [64] Louisa A 1877

LEMONS [46] Peter 1860

LAMONS Peter 1879

MORRISON Joseph 1881

MORRISON Joseph 1881

CANTLEY Anna 1904

WEIBEL Herman 1891

WALKER John H 1893

WALKER John H 1893

BROWN James W 1897

22

23

24

DAVIDSON [64] Louisa A 1877

DAVIDSON [64] Louisa A 1877

LAMONS John W 1890

MORRISON Joseph 1881

CANTLEY Lafayette 1891

LANGSTON Samuel J 1884

WALKER John H 1893

WALKER John H 1893

BURRIS [29] Esther 1882

LOAGUE Patrick 1894

CANTLEY Silas B 1881

CANTLEY Silas B 1881

GLENN Charles H 1890

BURRIS [29] Esther 1882

ROBARDS Alfred 1860

SEATT John M 1911

SEATT John M 1911

CAUTLEY Silas B 1882

WHITNEY Sylvester H 1890

GLENN Charles H 1890

BURRIS [29] Esther 1882

SEATT John M 1911

LOAGUE Patrick 1894

GREEN Benjamin F 1888

ROBINS John 1892

WALKER John A 1892

WALKER John A 1892

ROBINS John 1892

LOGSTON James W 1898

LUDWIG Fritz W 1890

WILKERSON [190] Julian W 1885

DOCKEY James J 1866

HARRIS Joshua L 1885

27

26

25

CRANE Albert 1885

CRANE Albert 1885

LUDWIG Fritz W 1890

PEOPLES John M 1875

DOCKERY James J 1860

HARRIS Joshua L 1885

GROTE John C 1860

PALMER Jeffrey 1871

LUDWIG Fritz W 1890

CRANE Albert 1885

CHAPIN Silas J 1859

CRANE Arch M 1891

KIRKPATRICK Benjamin S 1882

BAILEY William 1860

PEOPLES John M 1866

DOCKERY James J 1860

CRANE Arch M 1891

CRANE Arch M 1891

HARRIS William C 1889

PALMER Jeffrey 1871

HALL Andrew L 1892

HALL Andrew L 1892

CRANE [62] Albert 1886

CRANE Albert 1885

CRANE Albert 1885

CRANE Albert 1885

CRANE Albert 1885

34

35

36

BRIDENTHAL [22] Charlotte E 1860

EWART James 1893

CRANE Albert 1885

PENNINGTON Dabner 1884

FOWLER Sumner S 1885

CRANE Albert 1885

WINSTRAN Niles J 1892

FOWLER Sumner S 1885

SNEAD Austin 1897

Copyright 2013 Boyd IT, Inc. All Rights Reserved

Helpful Hints

1. This Map's INDEX can be found on the preceding pages.

2. Refer to Map "C" to see where this Township lies within Howell County, Missouri.

3. Numbers within square brackets [ ] denote a multi-patentee land parcel (multi-owner). Refer to Appendix "C" for a full list of members in this group.

4. Areas that look to be crowded with Patentees usually indicate multiple sales of the same parcel (Re-issues) or Overlapping parcels. See this Township's Index for an explanation of these and other circumstances that might explain "odd" groupings of Patentees on this map.

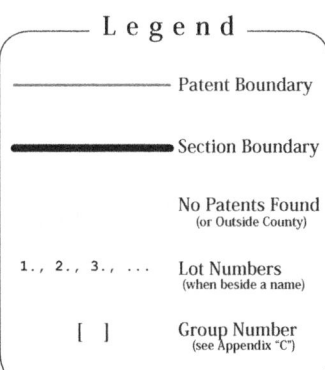

Legend

———— Patent Boundary

━━━━ Section Boundary

No Patents Found (or Outside County)

1., 2., 3., . . .   Lot Numbers (when beside a name)

[ ]   Group Number (see Appendix "C")

Scale: Section = 1 mile X 1 mile (generally, with some exceptions)

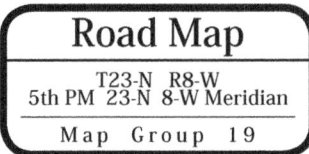

Road Map

T23-N   R8-W
5th PM 23-N 8-W Meridian

Map Group 19

Cities & Towns
Cottbus
Frankville

Cemeteries
Howell County Cemetery
Parker Cemetery

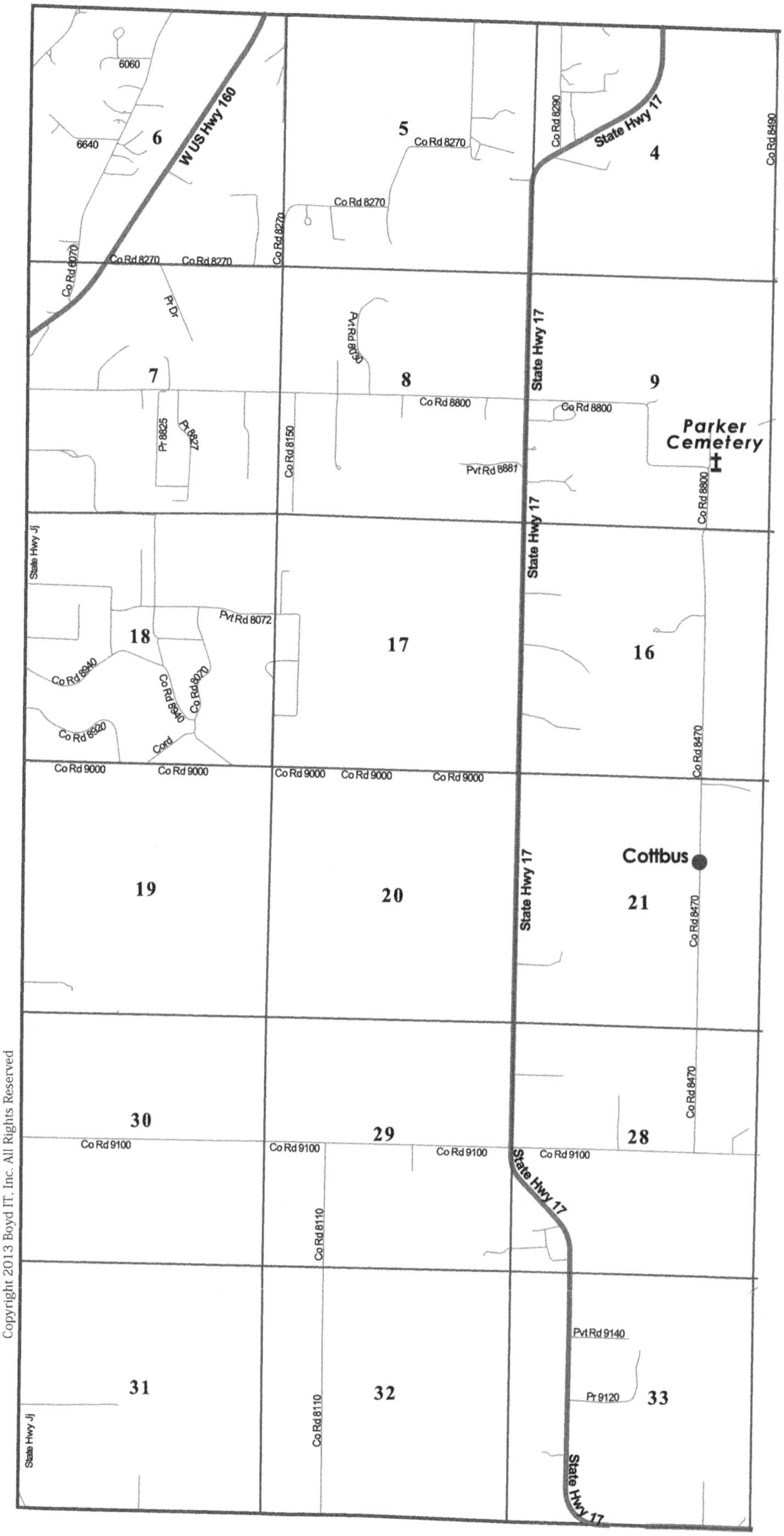

6060

6640

W US Hwy 160

6

5

Co Rd 8270

Co Rd 8290

State Hwy 17

4

Co Rd 8490

Co Rd 8270

Co Rd 8270

Co Rd 8270

Co Rd 8270

Pt Dr

Pvt Rd 809

7

8

Co Rd 8800

State Hwy 17

Co Rd 8800

9

Pr 8825

Pr 8827

Co Rd 8150

Pvt Rd 8881

Parker Cemetery

Co Rd 8800

State Hwy Jj

State Hwy 17

Pvt Rd 8072

18

17

16

Co Rd 8940

Co Rd 8970

Co Rd 8940

Co Rd 8920

Cord

Co Rd 9000

Co Rd 9000

Co Rd 9000

Co Rd 9000

Co Rd 9000

Co Rd 8470

19

20

State Hwy 17

Cottbus

21

Co Rd 8470

30

29

Co Rd 9100

Co Rd 9100

Co Rd 9100

State Hwy 17

Co Rd 9100

28

Co Rd 8470

Co Rd 8110

Pvt Rd 9140

State Hwy Jj

31

Co Rd 8110

32

Pr 9120

33

State Hwy 17

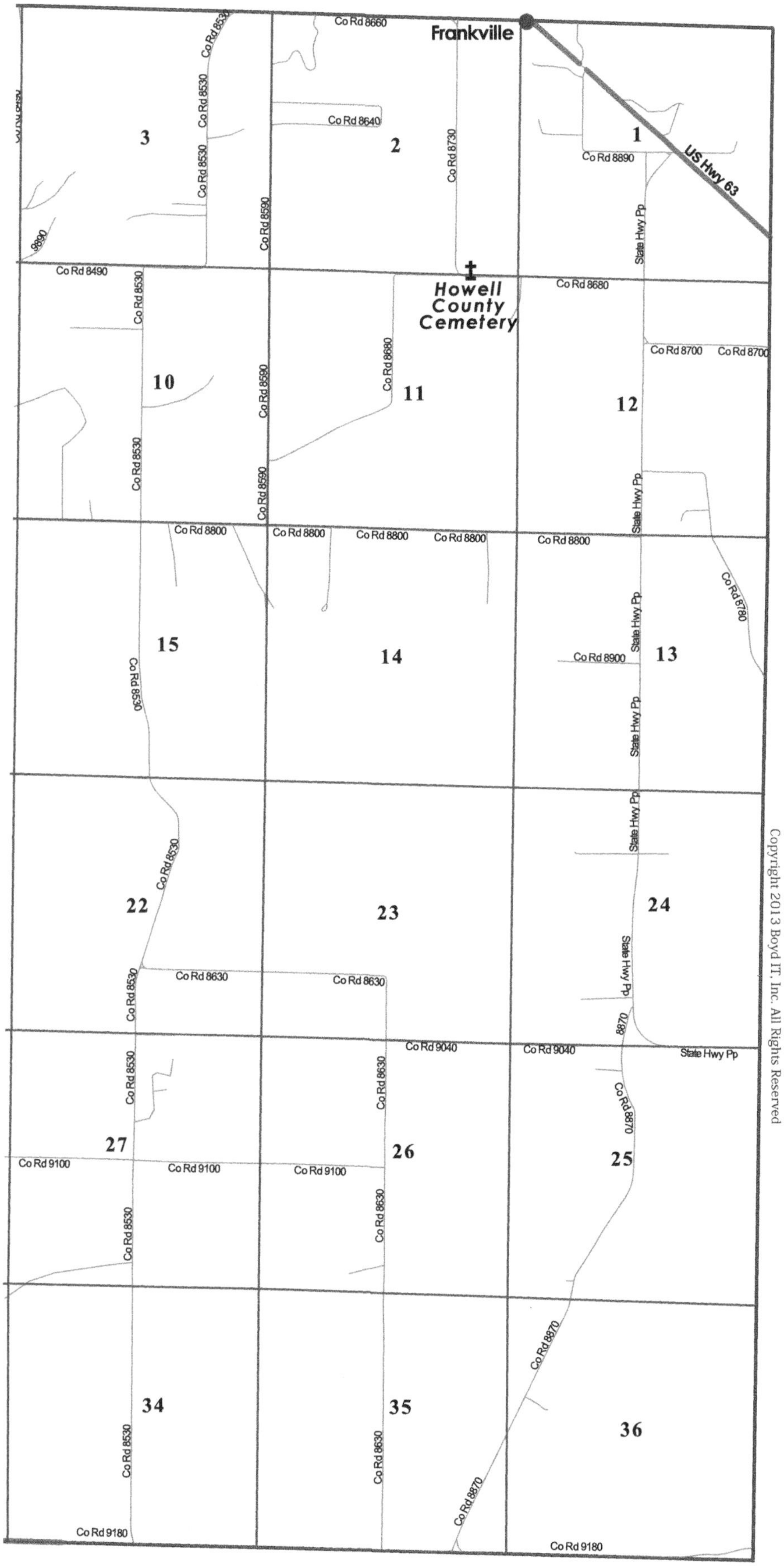

Co Rd 8530
Co Rd 8660
Frankville
Co Rd 8640
Co Rd 8730
8890

3

2

1
Co Rd 8890
US Hwy 63
State Hwy Pp

Co Rd 8490
Co Rd 8530
✝
Howell County Cemetery
Co Rd 8680

Co Rd 8590
Co Rd 8880
Co Rd 8700   Co Rd 8700

10
Co Rd 8530

11

12

Co Rd 8590
State Hwy Pp

Co Rd 8800   Co Rd 8800   Co Rd 8800   Co Rd 8800   Co Rd 8800
Co Rd 8780

15
Co Rd 8530

14

State Hwy Pp
Co Rd 8900   **13**

State Hwy Pp

Co Rd 8530

22

23

24
State Hwy Pp

Co Rd 8530   Co Rd 8630   Co Rd 8630
8870

Co Rd 8530   Co Rd 9040   Co Rd 9040   State Hwy Pp
Co Rd 8630
Co Rd 8870

27   **26**   **25**
Co Rd 9100   Co Rd 9100   Co Rd 9100

Co Rd 8530
Co Rd 8630

34   **35**   **36**
Co Rd 8530
Co Rd 8630
Co Rd 8870

Co Rd 9180
Co Rd 9180

Helpful Hints

1. This road map has a number of uses, but primarily it is to help you: a) find the present location of land owned by your ancestors (at least the general area), b) find cemeteries and city-centers, and c) estimate the route/roads used by Census-takers & tax-assessors.

2. If you plan to travel to Howell County to locate cemeteries or land parcels, please pick up a modern travel map for the area before you do. Mapping old land parcels on modern maps is not as exact a science as you might think. Just the slightest variations in public land survey coordinates, estimates of parcel boundaries, or road-map deviations can greatly alter a map's representation of how a road either does or doesn't cross a particular parcel of land.

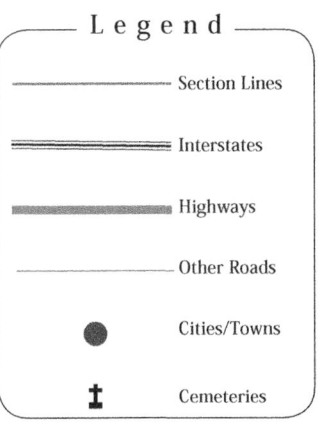

L e g e n d

——————————— Section Lines

═══════════ Interstates

▬▬▬▬▬▬▬ Highways

——————————— Other Roads

● Cities/Towns

✝ Cemeteries

Scale: Section = 1 mile X 1 mile
(generally, with some exceptions)

Cities & Towns
Cottbus
Frankville

Cemeteries
Howell County Cemetery
Parker Cemetery

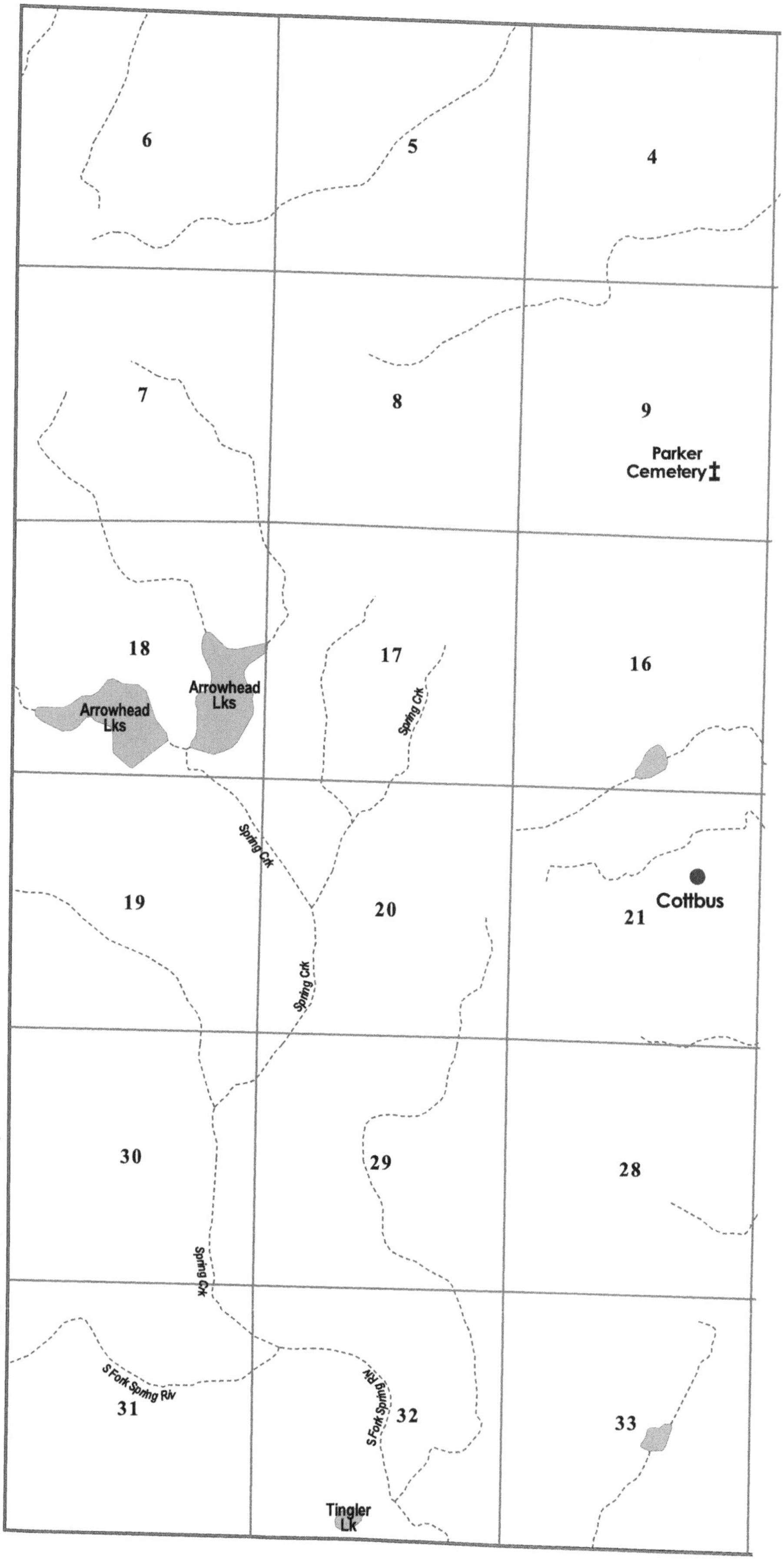

6

5

4

7

8

9

Parker
Cemetery ‡

18

Arrowhead
Lks

Arrowhead
Lks

17

Spring Crk

16

19

Spring Crk

20

Spring Crk

21 Cottbus

30

29

28

Copyright 2013 Boyd IT. Inc. All Rights Reserved

31 S Fork Spring Riv

Spring Crk

32 S Fork Spring Riv

33

Tingler
Lk

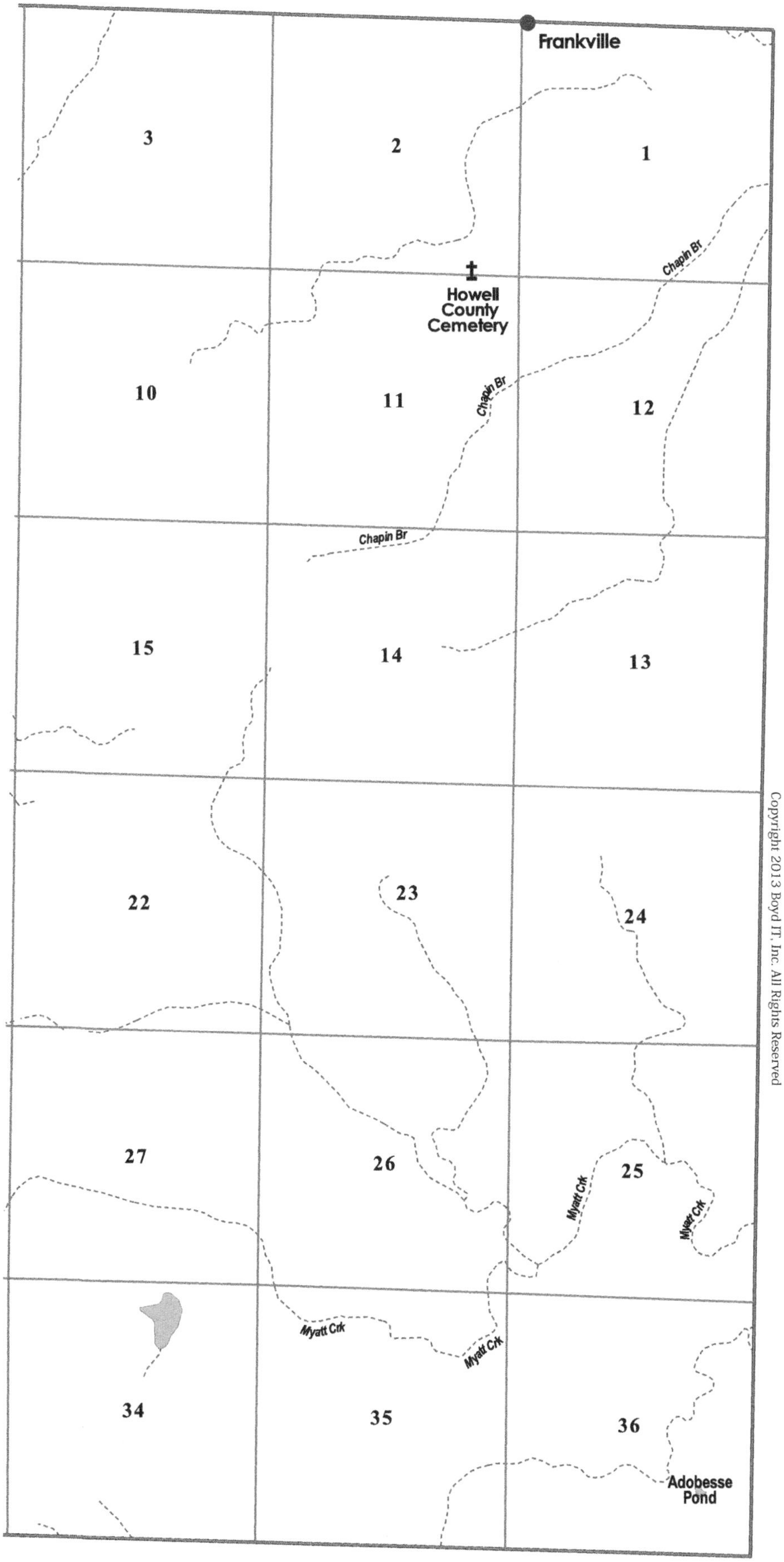

3

2

1

Frankville

✝
Howell
County
Cemetery

Chapin Br

10

11

Chapin Br

12

Chapin Br

15

14

13

22

23

24

27

26

Myatt Crk

25

Myatt Crk

34

Myatt Crk

35

Myatt Crk

36

Adobesse
Pond

Helpful Hints

1. This Map takes a different look at the same Congressional Township displayed in the preceding two maps. It presents features that can help you better envision the historical development of the area: a) Water-bodies (lakes & ponds), b) Water-courses (rivers, streams, etc.), c) Railroads, d) City/ town center-points (where they were oftentimes located when first settled), and e) Cemeteries.

2. Using this "Historical" map in tandem with this Township's Patent Map and Road Map, may lead you to some interesting discoveries. You will often find roads, towns, cemeteries, and waterways are named after nearby landowners: sometimes those names will be the ones you are researching. See how many of these research gems you can find here in Howell County.

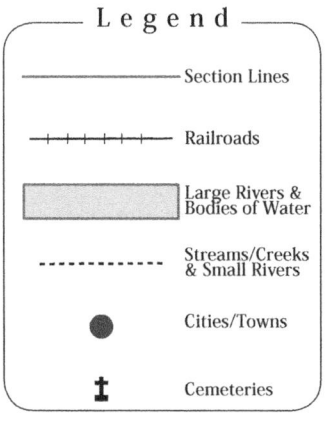

L e g e n d

———————— Section Lines

+++++++ Railroads

▭ Large Rivers & Bodies of Water

----------- Streams/Creeks & Small Rivers

● Cities/Towns

✝ Cemeteries

Scale: Section = 1 mile X 1 mile
(there are some exceptions)

Map Group 20: Index to Land Patents

Township 23-North Range 7-West (5th PM 23-N 7-W)

After you locate an individual in this Index, take note of the Section and Section Part then proceed to the Land Patent map on the pages immediately following. You should have no difficulty locating the corresponding parcel of land.

The "For More Info" Column will lead you to more information about the underlying Patents. See the *Legend* at right, and the "How to Use this Book" chapter, for more information.

```
                    LEGEND
              "For More Info . . . " column
A = Authority (Legislative Act, See Appendix "A")
B = Block or Lot (location in Section unknown)
C = Cancelled Patent
F = Fractional Section
G = Group  (Multi-Patentee Patent, see Appendix "C")
V = Overlaps another Parcel
R = Re-Issued (Parcel patented more than once)

(A & G items require you to look in the Appendixes referred
to above. All other Letter-designations followed by a number
require you to locate line-items in this index that possess
the ID number found after the letter).
```

ID	Individual in Patent	Sec.	Sec. Part	Date Issued	Other Counties	For More Info . . .
5324	ALEXANDER, Benjamin F	17	N½NW	1890-10-11		A7
7996	BEESLEY, Albert H	18	1SW	1902-12-30		A7
8038	BLACKBURN, Harvey	7	S21NW	1859-09-01		A1
8022	BOYD, Robert	6	2NE	1860-08-01		A1
8023	" "	6	E21NE	1860-08-01		A1
7995	BRAND, Michael	1	2NE	1894-09-18		A1
5326	" "	25	W½NW	1882-09-30		A1
5327	BRIMHALL, Joseph	6	NWSE	1853-11-01		A8
8028	" "	6	N22NW	1854-10-02		A8
5328	BUCHANAN, George W	9	SE	1859-09-01		A1
5330	" "	9	E½NE	1859-09-01		A1
5329	" "	9	E½SW	1859-09-01		A1
5331	CAPIN, John A	4	N½SW	1853-11-01		A8 G37
5332	CASWELL, Benjamin	34	S½	1859-09-01		A1
5333	CAY, William C	10	W½	1859-09-01		A1
5334	CHAPIN, Ely H	4	N½SW	1853-11-01		A8 G37
5335	CHAPIN, Franklin M	4	SESE	1859-09-01		A1
5336	CHAPIN, John A	6	SESW	1860-08-01		A1
8030	" "	6	S22SW	1859-09-10		A1
8029	" "	6	N22SW	1859-09-01		A1
5337	CHAPIN, Sarah	4	N½SE	1859-03-01		A1
5340	CLARK, Thomas M	25	SENE	1859-09-01	Oregon	A1
5341	" "	25	NENE	1859-09-01	Oregon	A1
5342	" "	25	NWNE	1859-09-01	Oregon	A1
5339	" "	25	NENW	1859-09-01	Oregon	A1
5338	" "	25	NESE	1859-09-01	Oregon	A1
5343	CLIFTON, John C	32	E½SW	1901-05-08		A7
5344	CLOONEY, Dennis	24	W½	1859-09-01		A1
8031	COLLIER, Frederick	6	SW2NW	1897-04-02		A1
5345	CORDILL, William	31	SE	1859-09-10		A1
8012	" "	31	S21SW	1859-09-10		A1
5346	" "	32	W½SW	1859-09-10		A1
5348	COX, John	8	N½NE	1859-09-01		A1
5347	" "	8	NWSE	1859-09-01		A1
5349	COX, Silas J	8	NESE	1892-07-11		A1
5352	COX, William R	17	NESE	1859-09-01		A1
5350	" "	17	E½NE	1859-09-01		A1
5351	" "	17	SWNE	1859-09-01		A1
5353	" "	17	NWNE	1859-09-01		A1
5354	" "	8	SESE	1859-09-01		A1
5355	" "	9	SWSW	1859-09-01		A1
5357	DAVISON, John	3	N½SW	1860-10-01		A1
5356	" "	3	SESW	1860-10-01		A1
5358	DEXTER, Matilda	32	SENW	1859-01-01		A1
5360	DICKSON, George	29	SENW	1859-09-01		A1
5359	" "	29	N½NW	1859-09-01		A1

ID	Individual in Patent	Sec.	Sec. Part	Date Issued	Other Counties	For More Info . . .
8004	DICKSON, George (Cont'd)	30	1NW	1859-09-01		A1
5362	" "	30	NENE	1859-09-01		A1
5361	" "	30	W½NE	1859-09-01		A1
5363	DOUGHERTY, Dermon	23	W½	1859-09-01		A1
5364	DUNNILL, Thomas D	15	E½	1859-09-01		A1
5365	EASTERLY, Beard H	30	SESE	1904-06-02		A7
8036	EDSON, Hannah	7	N21SW	1898-10-04		A7
5366	ELLIOTT, Thomas W	29	SWNW	1859-09-01		A1
5367	" "	30	SENE	1859-09-01		A1
5368	" "	30	NESE	1859-09-01		A1
5369	FLESHER, Andrew	34	N½	1859-09-01		A1
5370	FLESHER, John W	27	S½	1859-09-01		A1
5371	FLESHER, Ulysses W	15	W½	1859-09-01		A1
7994	FRAY, Jason C	1	1NE	1859-09-01		A1
5372	" "	1	E½SW	1859-09-01		A1
5373	" "	1	SE	1859-09-01		A1
5374	FRAYNER, Richard	21	SESW	1859-09-01		A1
5376	" "	28	E½NE	1859-09-01		A1
5375	" "	28	NW	1859-09-01		A1
5377	" "	28	NWNE	1859-09-01		A1
5379	GAGE, Warren A	25	SENE	1896-07-27		A1
5380	" "	25	SW	1896-07-27		A1
5378	" "	25	W½SE	1896-07-27		A1
5381	GARRET, Jacob	4	SWSE	1857-04-15		A1
5382	" "	9	W½NE	1857-04-15		A1
5383	" "	9	SENW	1857-04-15		A1
5384	GARRETT, Mary	9	SWNW	1859-01-01		A1
5385	" "	9	NWSW	1859-01-01		A1
5386	GIBBS, Harmon	3	SWSW	1859-09-01		A1
5387	GIBBS, John L	24	E½	1859-09-01		A1
5389	GODDARD, Franklin H	20	NWNE	1859-09-01		A1
5388	" "	20	S½NE	1859-09-01		A1
5392	" "	21	N½NE	1859-09-01		A1
5390	" "	21	W½NW	1859-09-01		A1
5391	" "	21	NENW	1859-09-01		A1
5396	GRISHAM, Archibald	28	SWNE	1859-09-01		A1
5394	" "	28	E½SW	1859-09-01		A1
5395	" "	28	NWSE	1859-09-01		A1
5393	" "	28	W½SW	1860-08-01		A1
5397	GRISHAM, Samuel	28	S½SE	1860-03-01		A1
5398	" "	28	NESE	1860-03-01		A1
8002	HALL, Thomas	2	W21NW	1859-03-01		A1
5399	" "	2	NWSW	1859-03-01		A1
8003	" "	2	W22NW	1859-03-01		A1
5401	HANNAH, William J	8	E½NW	1859-09-01		A1
5400	" "	8	NESW	1859-09-01		A1
5402	HARMON, Oliver A	33	E½	1859-09-01		A1
5403	HARRIS, Joseph S	21	S½NE	1859-09-01		A1
5404	" "	22	SWNW	1859-09-01		A1
5405	" "	22	NWSW	1859-09-01		A1
5406	" "	8	S½NE	1857-10-30		A1
5407	HARRIS, Robert H	21	E½SE	1860-08-01		A1
5408	" "	22	SWSW	1860-08-01		A1
5409	HARRIS, William	30	SWSE	1857-10-30		A1
5410	" "	31	N½NE	1857-10-30		A1
5411	" "	32	W½NW	1857-10-30		A1
8039	HAYT, Theodore M	7	S21SW	1859-09-01		A1
8034	" "	7	2SW	1859-09-01		A1
5412	" "	7	SE	1859-09-01		A1
5413	HELM, David	3	NW	1859-09-01		A1
5414	" "	4	NE	1859-09-01		A1
5415	HENDERSON, Richard N	19	E½	1859-09-01		A1
7997	HEWITT, Richard	18	2SW	1859-09-01		A1
5416	" "	18	NW	1859-09-01		A1
5418	HOMANS, Henry C	2	NE	1859-09-01		A1
8000	" "	2	E21NW	1859-09-01		A1
8001	" "	2	E22NW	1859-09-01		A1
5417	" "	2	N½SE	1859-09-01		A1
5419	HOYT, Myrom F	12	S½	1859-09-01		A1
5421	JOHNSON, Thomas	25	SENW	1882-09-30		A1
5425	KEIVER, Leonard M	22	NWNW	1859-09-01		A1
5422	" "	22	NE	1859-09-01		A1
5423	" "	22	NESW	1859-09-01		A1

ID	Individual in Patent	Sec.	Sec. Part	Date Issued	Other Counties	For More Info . . .
5424	KEIVER, Leonard M (Cont'd)	22	E½NW	1859-09-01		A1
5426	KING, George J	20	W½	1859-09-01		A1
5428	KING, Nelson	17	S½SE	1859-09-01		A1
5427	" "	17	NWSE	1859-09-01		A1
5429	" "	17	SW	1859-09-01		A1
5430	" "	20	NENE	1859-09-01		A1
5434	LOUTHEN, Vincent D	8	W½SW	1894-12-17		A7
5433	" "	8	SESW	1894-12-17		A7
5432	" "	8	SWSE	1894-12-17		A7
5436	LUMPS, Frederick	2	S½SW	1860-10-01		A1
5435	" "	2	NESW	1860-10-01		A1
5437	MARONEY, William W	17	S½NW	1859-09-01		A1
8007	MAVONEY, Sarah	30	2SW	1859-09-01		A1
8009	" "	31	2NW	1859-09-01		A1
5439	MAXEY, James H	7	SWNE	1890-06-04		A1
8035	MCCAMMAN, Jesse E	7	N21NW	1859-09-01		A1
5440	" "	7	NWNE	1859-09-01		A1
8025	MCCAMMAN, Matthew	6	E22NW	1859-09-01		A1
5441	MCCAMMON, James	7	E½NE	1859-01-01		A1
5442	" "	8	W½NW	1859-01-01		A1
5443	MCCAMMON, Jesse	6	S½SE	1859-01-01		A1
8032	" "	6	W21NE	1859-01-01		A1
8024	MCCAMMON, Mathew	6	E21NW	1857-10-30		A1
5444	MCCAMRON, James	5	W½SW	1853-11-01		A8
5445	" "	6	NESE	1853-08-01		A1
5446	MCELFATRICK, John B	22	SE	1859-09-01		A1
5447	" "	27	NE	1859-09-01		A1
5448	MEARS, Henry A	18	E½	1859-09-01		A1
5449	MILLARD, Thomas	12	N½	1859-09-01		A1
8040	MILLER, Joseph	7	S22NW	1859-09-01		A1
8037	" "	7	N22NW	1857-04-15		A1
5450	MUHL, Erastus	3	E½	1859-09-01		A1
5451	MURDOCK, Jane F	35	W½	1859-09-01		A1
8013	NEWBERRY, Henderson H	4	1NW	1859-09-01		A1
8021	NEWBERRY, Robert	5	W22NE	1859-09-01		A1
5452	ORIELLEY, Francis C	33	W½	1859-09-01		A1
5453	OROURKE, Thomas	11	E½	1859-09-01		A1
5454	OVERTON, Josiah E	36	N½	1859-09-01		A1
5455	PALMER, Henry F	13	N½	1859-09-01		A1
5456	PARKER, Elkana D	27	W½NW	1859-09-01		A1
8016	POOL, James H	5	2NW	1857-04-15		A1
5457	PURCHASE, Charles	26	W½	1859-09-01		A1
5458	PURCHASE, John	32	E½	1859-09-01		A1
8026	RALLS, Nathaniel	6	N21SW	1853-12-01		A1
5459	RAY, Simon P	14	W½	1859-09-01		A1
8014	REED, Malachi W	4	2NW	1860-08-01		A1
8015	" "	5	1NE	1860-08-01		A1
8019	" "	5	E22NE	1860-08-01		A1
5460	RIDDLE, John M	20	SE	1859-09-01		A1
5461	" "	29	NE	1859-09-01		A1
5462	ROOTES, Benjamin F	36	S½	1859-09-01		A1
5465	RUSSELL, Joseph H	5	SESW	1859-01-01		A1
8020	" "	5	W21NW	1859-01-01		A1
5463	" "	5	N½SE	1853-11-01		A8
5464	" "	5	NESW	1853-11-01		A8
5466	" "	5	S½SE	1859-01-01		A1
8018	" "	5	E21NW	1853-11-01		A8
5467	SARGENT, George R	10	E½	1859-09-01		A1
5468	SHEA, Michael	4	S½SW	1860-08-01		A1
5469	" "	9	N½NW	1860-08-01		A1
8033	SHEPPARD, Thomas	6	W21NW	1854-11-15		A1
5470	SICKLY, Henry	35	E½	1859-09-01		A1
5471	SNOWDEN, John L	19	NW	1859-09-01		A1
7999	" "	19	2SW	1859-09-01		A1
5472	STEININGER, Joseph H	21	W½SW	1892-03-07		A7
5473	SWAN, Hugh L	23	E½	1859-09-01		A1
5477	THOMPSON, Miranda	21	NESW	1859-09-01		A1
5475	" "	21	SENW	1859-09-01		A1
5476	" "	21	W½SE	1859-09-01		A1
8010	TUNE, John W	31	2SW	1899-05-12		A7
8006	TUNE, William R	30	2NW	1900-08-09		A7
5478	UNDERWOOD, Lawrence	14	E½	1859-09-01		A1
5479	WALKER, Milton	26	E½	1859-09-01		A1

ID	Individual in Patent	Sec.	Sec. Part	Date Issued	Other Counties	For More Info . . .
5480	WALL, John D	22	SESW	1889-01-12		A7
5481	" "	27	E½NW	1889-01-12		A7
5482	WATSON, James C	30	NWSE	1859-09-01		A1
8005	" "	30	1SW	1859-09-01		A1
8011	" "	31	N21SW	1859-09-01		A1
8008	" "	31	1NW	1859-09-01		A1
5483	" "	31	S½NE	1859-09-01		A1
5484	WILLIAMSON, William W	25	SESE	1882-09-30		A1
5485	WOOD, Aaron	29	S½	1859-09-01		A1
5486	WOOD, Frank W	1	W½SW	1859-09-01		A1
5487	" "	1	NW	1859-09-01		A1
5488	" "	2	S½SE	1859-09-01		A1
5489	WOOD, John	13	S½	1859-09-01		A1
5490	WOOD, Moses	11	W½	1859-09-01		A1
7998	YATES, James W	19	1SW	1900-08-09		A7

Patent Map

T23-N R7-W
5th PM 23-N 7-W Meridian

Map Group 20

Township Statistics

Parcels Mapped	:	206
Number of Patents	:	124
Number of Individuals	:	118
Patentees Identified	:	116
Number of Surnames	:	97
Multi-Patentee Parcels	:	1
Oldest Patent Date	:	8/1/1853
Most Recent Patent	:	6/2/1904
Block/Lot Parcels	:	45
Cities and Town	:	4
Cemeteries	:	2

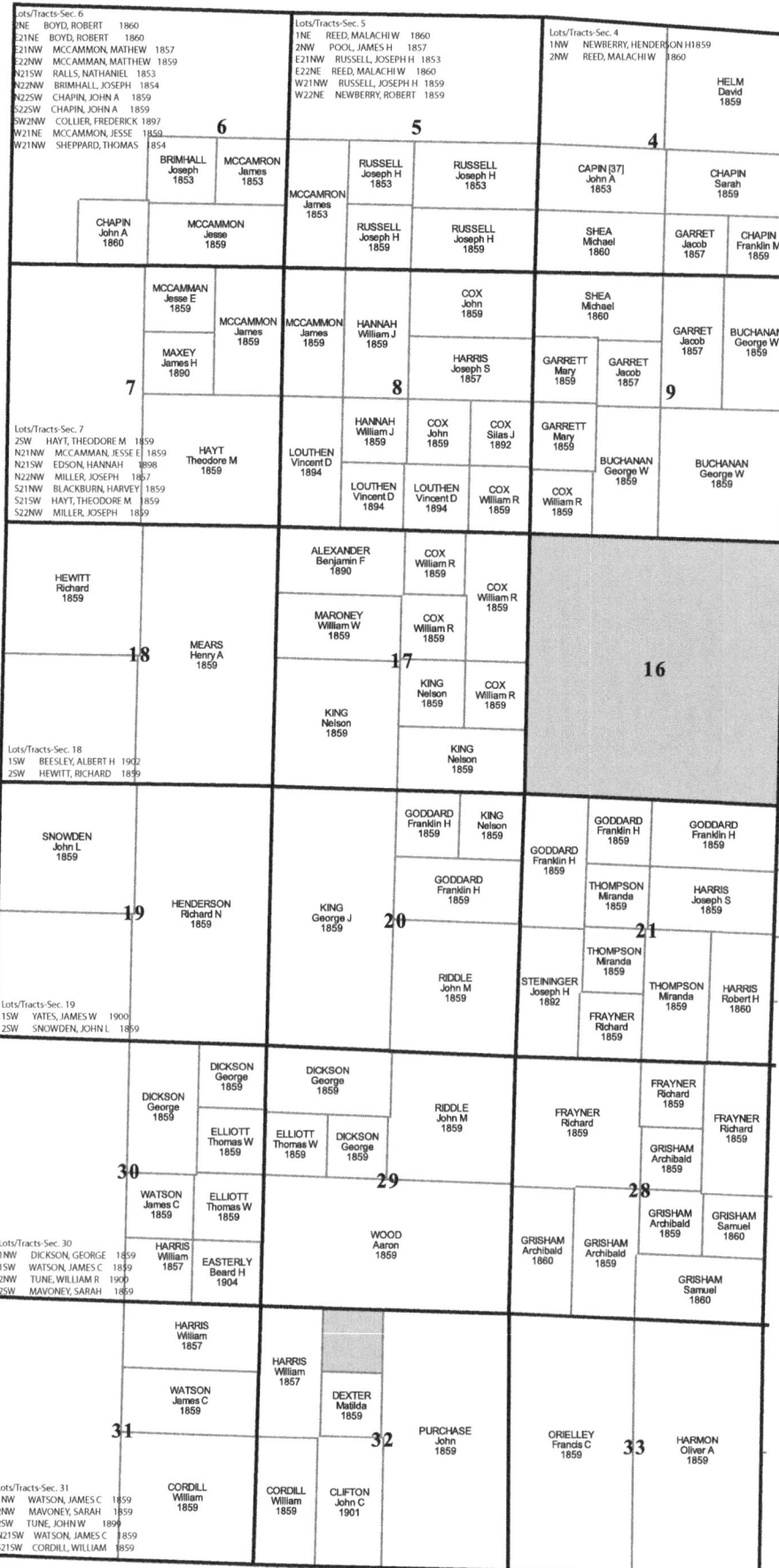

HELM
David
1859

3

MUHL
Erastus
1859

DAVISON
John
1860

GIBBS
Harmon
1859

DAVISON
John
1860

Lots/Tracts-Sec. 2
E21NW HOMANS, HENRY C 1859
E22NW HOMANS, HENRY C 1859
W21NW HALL, THOMAS   1859
W22NW HALL, THOMAS   1859

HOMANS
Henry C
1859

2

HALL
Thomas
1859

LUMPS
Frederick
1860

HOMANS
Henry C
1859

LUMPS
Frederick
1860

WOOD
Frank W
1859

Lots/Tracts-Sec. 1
1NE FRAY, JASON C   1859
2NE BRAND, MICHAEL   1894

WOOD
Frank W
1859

1

WOOD
Frank W
1859

FRAY
Jason C
1859

FRAY
Jason C
1859

CAY
William C
1859

10

SARGENT
George R
1859

WOOD
Moses
1859

11

OROURKE
Thomas
1859

MILLARD
Thomas
1859

12

HOYT
Myrom F
1859

FLESHER
Ulysses W
1859

15

DUNNILL
Thomas D
1859

RAY
Simon P
1859

14

UNDERWOOD
Lawrence
1859

PALMER
Henry F
1859

13

WOOD
John
1859

KEIVER
Leonard M
1859

KEIVER
Leonard M
1859

KEIVER
Leonard M
1859

HARRIS
Joseph S
1859

HARRIS
Joseph S
1859

KEIVER
Leonard M
1859

22

MCELFATRICK
John B
1859

HARRIS
Robert H
1860

WALL
John D
1889

DOUGHERTY
Dermon
1859

23

SWAN
Hugh L
1859

CLOONEY
Dennis
1859

24

GIBBS
John L
1859

PARKER
Elkana D
1859

WALL
John D
1889

MCELFATRICK
John B
1859

27

FLESHER
John W
1859

PURCHASE
Charles
1859

26

WALKER
Milton
1859

BRAND
Michael
1882

CLARK
Thomas M
1859

CLARK
Thomas M
1859

CLARK
Thomas M
1859

JOHNSON
Thomas
1882

GAGE
Warren A
1896

CLARK
Thomas M
1859

25

GAGE
Warren A
1896

GAGE
Warren A
1896

CLARK
Thomas M
1859

WILLIAMSON
William W
1882

FLESHER
Andrew
1859

34

CASWELL
Benjamin
1859

MURDOCK
Jane F
1859

35

SICKLY
Henry
1859

OVERTON
Josiah E
1859

36

ROOTES
Benjamin F
1859

Copyright 2013 Boyd IT, Inc. All Rights Reserved

Helpful Hints

1. This Map's INDEX can be found on the preceding pages.

2. Refer to Map "C" to see where this Township lies within Howell County, Missouri.

3. Numbers within square brackets [ ] denote a multi-patentee land parcel (multi-owner). Refer to Appendix "C" for a full list of members in this group.

4. Areas that look to be crowded with Patentees usually indicate multiple sales of the same parcel (Re-issues) or Overlapping parcels. See this Township's Index for an explanation of these and other circumstances that might explain "odd" groupings of Patentees on this map.

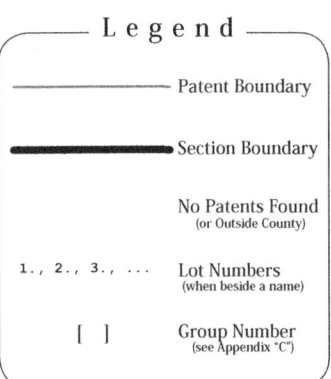

Legend

——————— Patent Boundary

━━━━━━━ Section Boundary

No Patents Found
(or Outside County)

1., 2., 3., ...   Lot Numbers
(when beside a name)

[ ]   Group Number
(see Appendix "C")

Scale: Section = 1 mile X 1 mile
(generally, with some exceptions)

Road Map

T23-N R7-W
5th PM 23-N 7-W Meridian

Map Group 20

Cities & Towns
Brandsville
Chapin
Fruitville
Pocohontas Crossing

Cemeteries
Chapin Cemetery
Meltabarger Cemetery

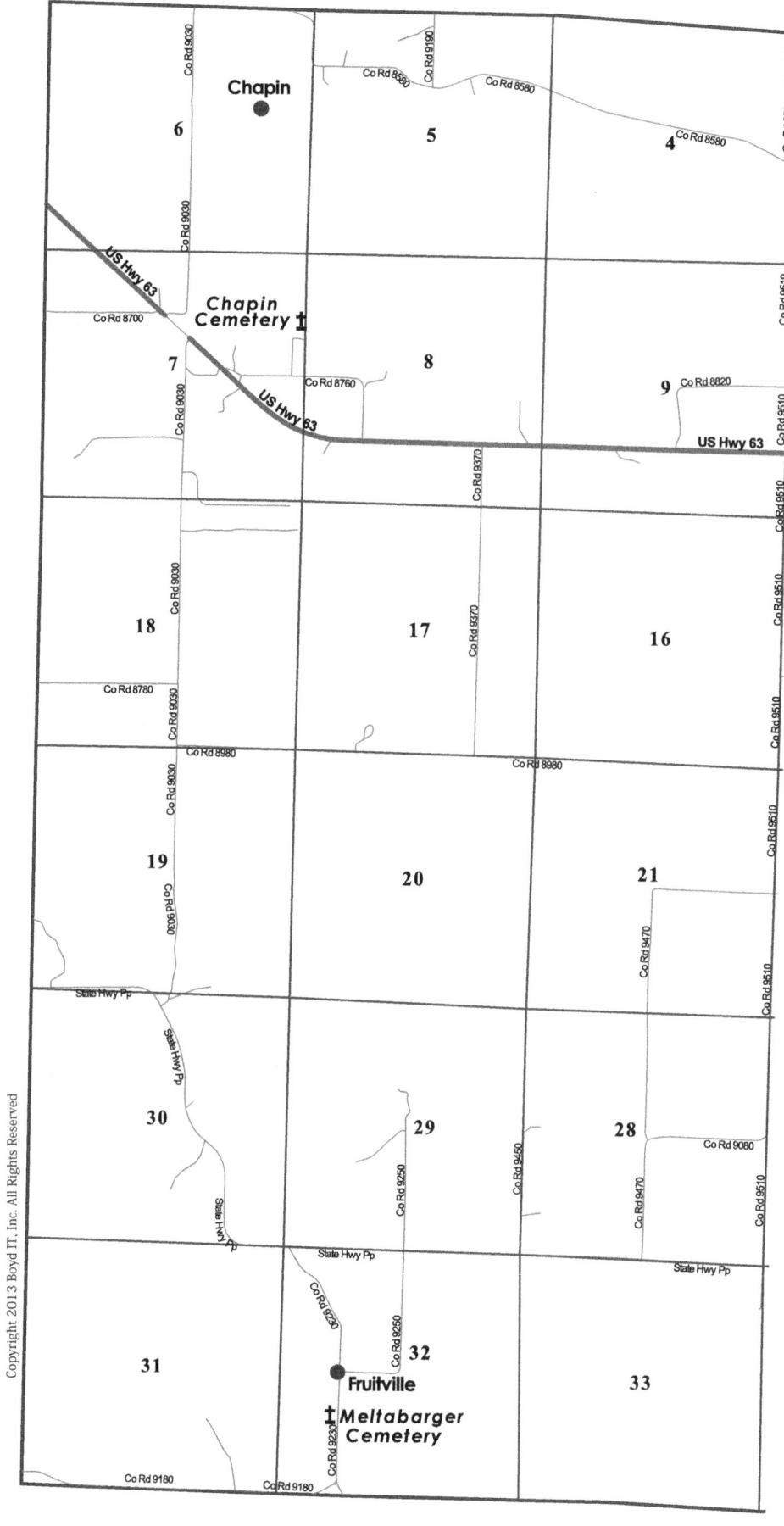

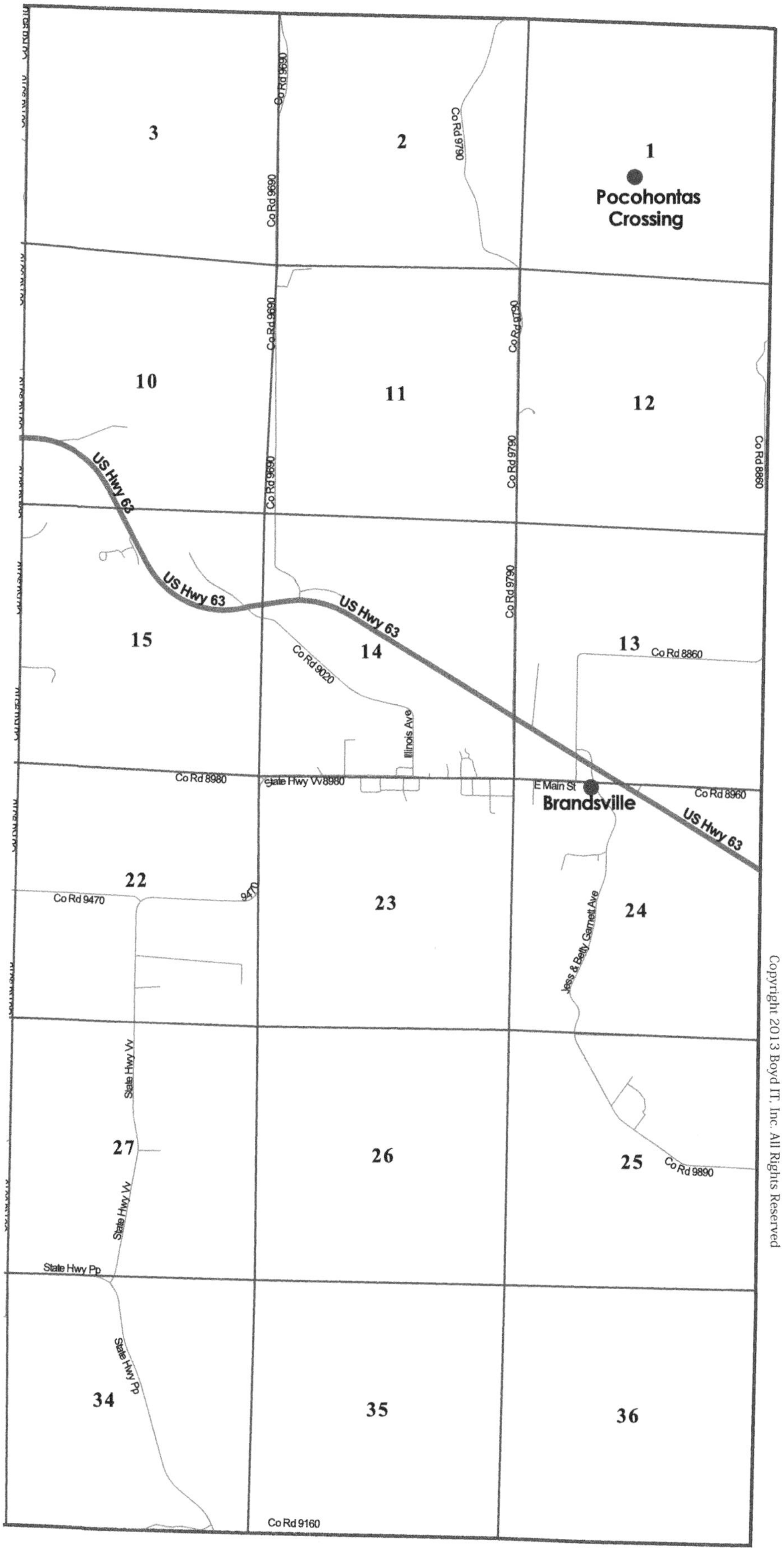

3

2

1

●
Pocohontas
Crossing

10

11

12

Co Rd 9690

Co Rd 9690

Co Rd 9790

Co Rd 9790

Co Rd 9790

Co Rd 8860

US Hwy 63

US Hwy 63

US Hwy 63

15

14

13   Co Rd 8860

Co Rd 9020

Illinois Ave

Co Rd 8980

State Hwy VV 8980

E Main St

●
Brandsville

Co Rd 8960

US Hwy 63

22

Co Rd 9470

23

24

Jess & Betty Garnett Ave

9470

27

26

25   Co Rd 9890

State Hwy VV

State Hwy VV

State Hwy Pp

34

35

36

State Hwy Pp

Co Rd 9160

Helpful Hints

1. This road map has a number of uses, but primarily it is to help you: a) find the present location of land owned by your ancestors (at least the general area), b) find cemeteries and city-centers, and c) estimate the route/roads used by Census-takers & tax-assessors.

2. If you plan to travel to Howell County to locate cemeteries or land parcels, please pick up a modern travel map for the area before you do. Mapping old land parcels on modern maps is not as exact a science as you might think. Just the slightest variations in public land survey coordinates, estimates of parcel boundaries, or road-map deviations can greatly alter a map's representation of how a road either does or doesn't cross a particular parcel of land.

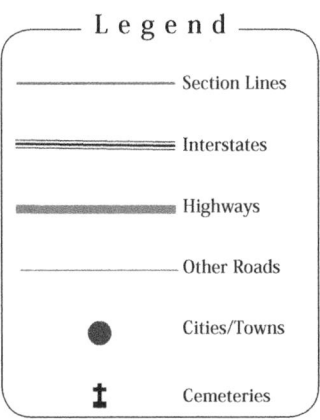

L e g e n d

——————— Section Lines

━━━━━━━ Interstates

━━━━━━━ Highways

——————— Other Roads

●   Cities/Towns

†   Cemeteries

Scale: Section = 1 mile X 1 mile
(generally, with some exceptions)

Historical Map

T23-N R7-W
5th PM 23-N 7-W Meridian

Map Group 20

Cities & Towns
Brandsville
Chapin
Fruitville
Pocohontas Crossing

Cemeteries
Chapin Cemetery
Meltabarger Cemetery

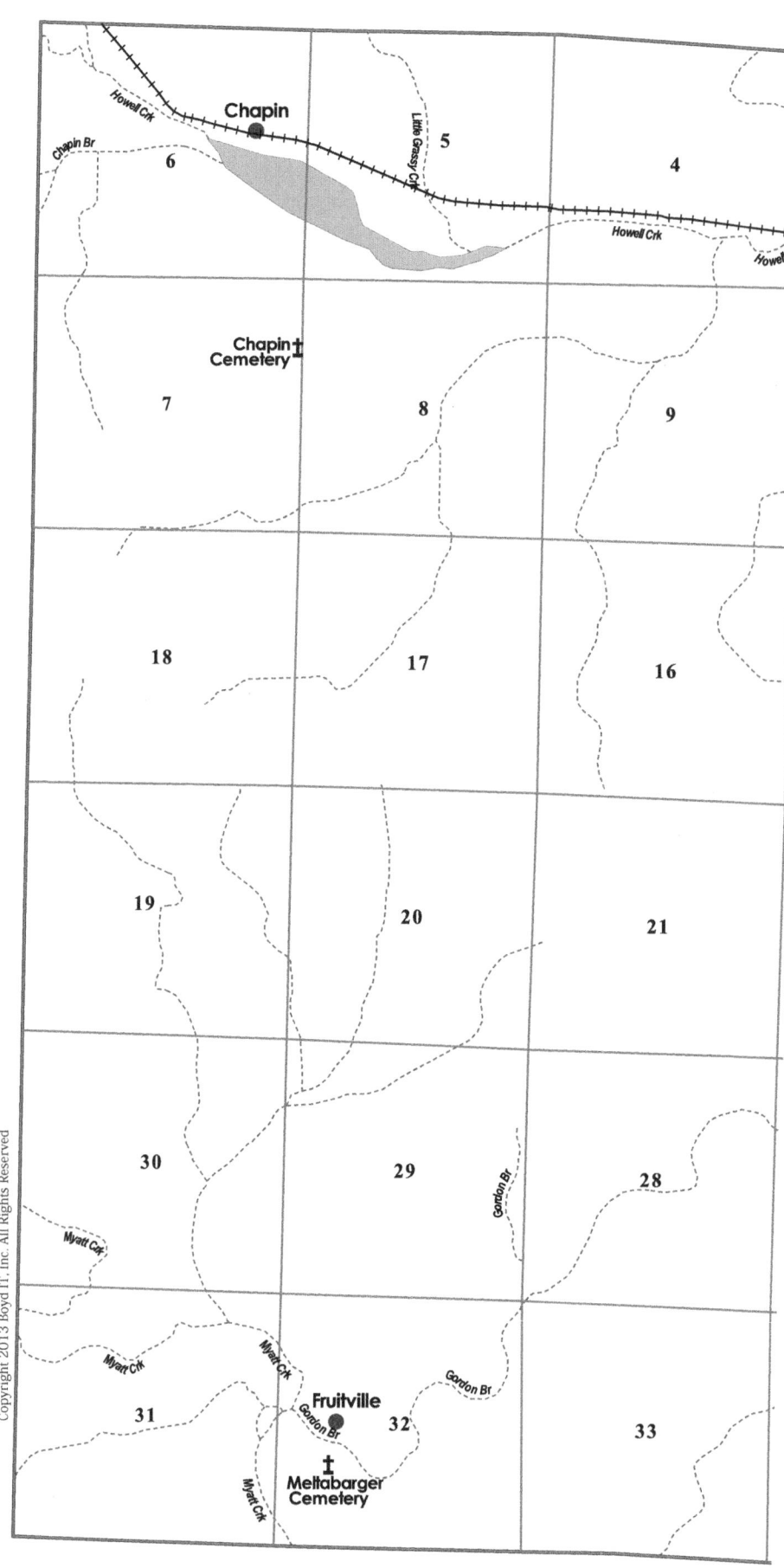

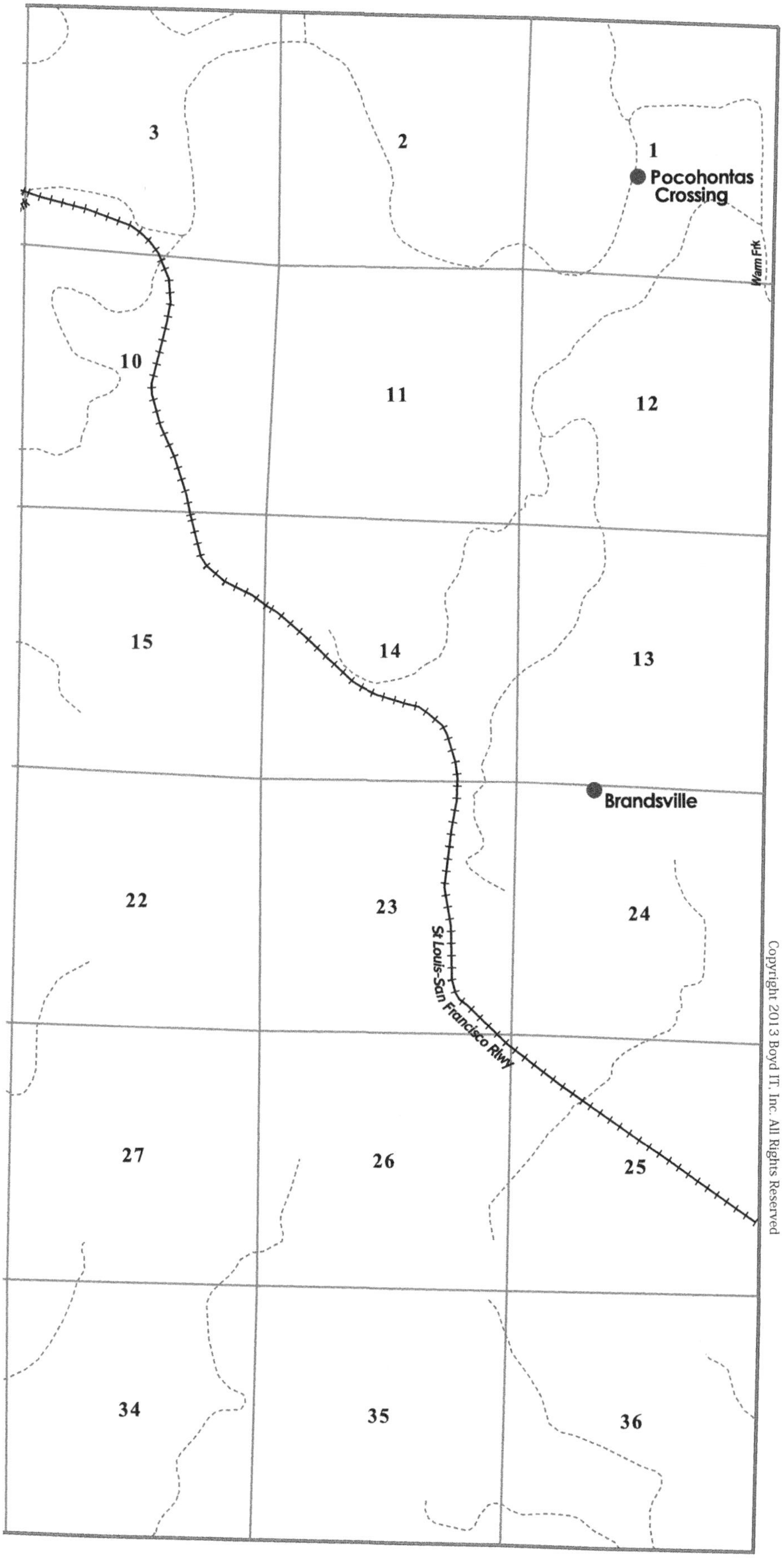

3

2

1

● Pocohontas
Crossing

Warm Frk

10

11

12

15

14

13

● Brandsville

22

23

24

St Louis-San Francisco Rlwy

27

26

25

34

35

36

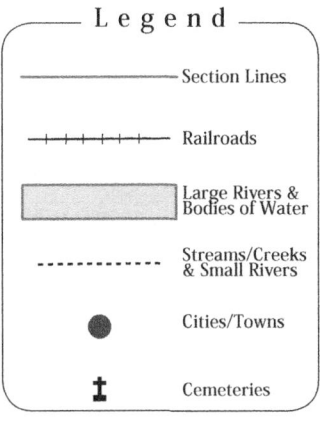

L e g e n d

———————— Section Lines

+++++++ Railroads

Large Rivers &
Bodies of Water

- - - - - - - Streams/Creeks
& Small Rivers

● Cities/Towns

‡ Cemeteries

Scale: Section = 1 mile X 1 mile
(there are some exceptions)

Map Group 21: Index to Land Patents

Township 22-North Range 10-West (5th PM 22-N 10-W)

After you locate an individual in this Index, take note of the Section and Section Part then proceed to the Land Patent map on the pages immediately following. You should have no difficulty locating the corresponding parcel of land.

The "For More Info" Column will lead you to more information about the underlying Patents. See the *Legend* at right, and the "How to Use this Book" chapter, for more information.

```
                    LEGEND
          "For More Info . . ." column
A = Authority (Legislative Act, See Appendix "A")
B = Block or Lot (location in Section unknown)
C = Cancelled Patent
F = Fractional Section
G = Group (Multi-Patentee Patent, see Appendix "C")
V = Overlaps another Parcel
R = Re-Issued (Parcel patented more than once)

(A & G items require you to look in the Appendixes referred
to above. All other Letter-designations followed by a number
require you to locate line-items in this index that possess
the ID number found after the letter).
```

ID	Individual in Patent	Sec.	Sec. Part	Date Issued	Other Counties	For More Info . . .
5493	ADKINS, Joseph M	29	SWSE	1890-10-11		A7
5492	" "	29	SESW	1890-10-11		A7
5491	" "	29	N½SE	1890-10-11		A7
5494	ALFORD, Catharine	28	S½NE	1865-09-01		A6 G2
5498	ALLEN, Tucker W	13	NWSW	1890-10-11		A7
5496	" "	13	SWNW	1890-10-11		A7
5497	" "	13	N½NW	1890-10-11		A7
5499	ANDERSON, Andy	27	W½SW	1860-02-15		A6
5500	" "	28	N½NE	1860-05-02		A6
5503	BAILY, Gamaliah H	21	NESE	1860-09-10		A6 G10
5505	" "	22	W½SW	1860-09-10		A6 G10
5504	" "	22	NESW	1860-09-10		A6 G10
8129	BAKER, Thomas W	30	N23SW	1860-08-01		A1
8144	" "	30	S24SW	1860-08-01		A1
8155	" "	31	5NW	1860-08-01		A1
5506	BALES, Samuel P	14	SENE	1898-07-25		A7
8208	BATTERTON, Alexander A	6	21NW	1894-05-18		A7
8194	BAZE, George	6	11NW	1860-06-01		A8
8191	" "	6	10NW	1860-06-01		A8
5507	BEAMAN, James H	11	NENW	1903-10-01		A7
5508	" "	2	SESW	1903-10-01		A7
5509	BEYER, Christian	20	N½SE	1902-12-30		A7
8164	BIFFLE, William D	31	N27NW	1860-10-01		A1
8162	" "	31	N26NW	1860-10-01		A1
8049	BLACK, Daniel W	1	W22NW	1886-11-19		A1
8047	" "	1	W21NE	1877-08-01		A7
8044	" "	1	E21NW	1877-08-01		A7
8045	BLACK, William C	1	E22NW	1860-10-01		A1
5510	BOSWELL, Frederick	10	SE	1894-01-24		A7
8230	BRIDGES, Orren S	7	1NW	1898-04-11		A7
5511	" "	7	NWNE	1898-04-11		A7
8238	" "	7	N21SW	1898-04-11		A7
8163	BRIDWELL, Peter Y	31	N26SW	1888-12-04		A7
8173	" "	31	S26NW	1888-12-04		A7
5512	BROWN, Andrew B	11	SESW	1882-05-10		A7
5514	" "	11	W½SE	1882-05-10		A7
5513	" "	11	SWNE	1882-05-10		A7
5515	BROWN, Daniel T	13	E½SW	1895-05-28		A7
5517	" "	13	NWSE	1895-05-28		A7
5516	" "	13	SWSW	1895-05-28		A7
5518	BURDEN, George C	3	S½SW	1891-05-05		A7
5519	" "	4	SESE	1891-05-05		A7
5520	BURDEN, John	10	NENE	1892-12-09		A7
5521	" "	11	NWNW	1892-12-09		A7
5522	" "	2	SWSW	1892-12-09		A7
5523	" "	3	SESE	1892-12-09		A7

ID	Individual in Patent	Sec.	Sec. Part	Date Issued	Other Counties	For More Info . . .
8150	CALLAHAN, John T	30	S27NW	1903-01-31		A7
8174	CANTRELL, Pinkney	31	S26SW	1889-01-12		A7
5524	CARRELL, Elizabeth	1	SWSW	1891-05-25		A7
5525	" "	11	E½NE	1891-05-25		A7
5526	" "	2	SESE	1891-05-25		A7
5527	CARRELL, Franklin S	13	E½NE	1891-06-09		A7
5528	CARRELL, Julius E	11	SESE	1888-12-06		A7
5530	" "	14	SWNE	1888-12-06		A7
5529	" "	14	N½NE	1888-12-06		A7
5531	CARRELL, Lavina C	1	SESW	1883-06-30		A7 G38
5532	" "	12	NENW	1883-06-30		A7 G38
5533	" "	12	W½NW	1883-06-30		A7 G38
5534	CARRELL, Lovely S	1	SESW	1883-06-30		A7 G38
5535	" "	12	W½NW	1883-06-30		A7 G38
5536	" "	12	NENW	1883-06-30		A7 G38
5538	CARRELL, Peter	12	SENW	1877-06-04		A7
5539	" "	12	S½NE	1877-06-04		A7
5537	" "	12	NWSE	1877-06-04		A7
8203	CARTER, William M	6	18NW	1892-01-25		A7
8207	" "	6	20NW	1892-01-25		A7
8204	" "	6	19NW	1892-01-25		A7
8235	CARTER, Williamson F	7	5SW	1900-02-02		A7
8119	CARTWRIGHT, Mary A	3	E23NW	1889-01-12		A7
8120	CARTWRIGHT, Wiley P	3	E23NW	1889-01-12		A7
8214	CHANDLER, John R	6	4NW	1888-12-08		A7
8216	" "	6	5NW	1888-12-08		A7
8222	" "	6	N25SW	1888-12-08		A7
8217	" "	6	6NW	1888-12-08		A7
8225	CHANDLER, William	6	S25SW	1888-12-08		A7
8226	" "	6	S26SW	1888-12-08		A7
8242	" "	7	N25NW	1888-12-08		A7
8243	" "	7	N26NW	1888-12-08		A7
8215	CHANDLER, William J	6	4SW	1888-12-08		A7
8241	" "	7	N24NW	1888-12-08		A7
8240	" "	7	N23NW	1888-12-08		A7
5544	CHENEY, Levi	23	S½NE	1860-05-02		A6
5543	" "	23	SW	1862-10-10		A6 G44
5541	" "	23	NENW	1860-09-10		A6
5542	" "	23	NWNE	1860-09-10		A6
5540	" "	23	NENE	1860-05-02		A6
8108	CLARK, Isaac	2	E21NW	1888-12-08		A7
8104	" "	2	2NE	1888-12-08		A7
8109	" "	2	E22NW	1888-12-08		A7
8048	COLLINS, James A	1	W21NW	1900-08-09		A7
5548	" "	1	NWSW	1900-08-09		A7
5549	COLLINS, John B	24	NESE	1860-09-10		A6 G54
5551	COLLINS, Peter H	13	S½SE	1875-04-01		A7
5550	" "	13	NESE	1861-02-09		A1
5552	" "	24	SWNE	1875-04-01		A7
5553	" "	24	NWNE	1861-02-09		A1
5555	COOPER, John T	35	W½SW	1860-09-10		A6
5556	" "	35	S½SE	1862-10-10		A6
5557	COOPER, Marcus A	26	NENE	1888-12-06		A1
5558	CRANE, Emerson F	28	SWSW	1908-03-02		A7
5559	CROWLEY, Lawrence N	17	SESW	1901-06-13		A1
5561	CRUMLEY, John A	4	SESW	1889-06-22		A7
5560	" "	4	W½SW	1889-06-22		A7
8182	" "	4	W21NW	1889-06-22		A7
5562	CULBERTSON, John C	36	SE	1860-06-01		A8
8088	CUNNINGHAM, James A	19	N27SW	1898-04-11		A7
8078	" "	19	7NW	1898-04-11		A7
8175	CUNNINGHAM, James P	31	S27NW	1875-11-01		A7
8165	" "	31	N27SW	1875-11-01		A7
5564	CUNNINGHAM, John W	31	W½SE	1892-01-25		A7
8169	" "	31	S22SW	1892-01-25		A7
8167	" "	31	S21SW	1892-01-25		A7
5569	CUTLER, William P	19	SESE	1902-10-01		A1
5570	" "	30	NENE	1902-10-01		A1
5571	DAVIS, Elizabeth	23	SW	1862-10-10		A6 G44
5572	DAVIS, Greer W	12	N½SW	1862-10-10		A6 G65
5573	" "	22	E½NW	1862-10-10		A6 G65
5575	DERRICK, Alfred C	9	SW	1882-08-30		A7
8149	DIELLE, Henry	30	S26SW	1861-06-27	Dunklin	A4

307

ID	Individual in Patent	Sec.	Sec. Part	Date Issued	Other Counties	For More Info . . .
5576	DODSON, Vernon M	31	SENE	1896-06-04		A7
5577	" "	31	W½NE	1896-06-04		A7
5578	" "	32	SWNW	1896-06-04		A7
5579	DORRIS, George M	24	E½NE	1888-11-27		A7
5580	DOWNING, James W	9	E½NW	1902-10-11		A7
5581	" "	9	W½NE	1902-10-11		A7
5582	EASLEY, Benjamin W	5	SESW	1905-03-30		A7
5583	" "	5	S½SE	1905-03-30		A7
5584	EASLEY, Francis H	36	S½NE	1860-09-10		A6 G71
5586	EASLEY, Woodson	21	NWSE	1885-02-25		A7
5585	" "	21	S½SE	1885-02-25		A7
5587	ELDER, William F	33	N½SE	1860-11-12		A6 G74
8123	ELLIOTT, Robert F	3	W23NW	1889-01-12		A7
8179	" "	4	3NE	1889-01-12		A7
5588	ENDECOTT, Joseph	19	SENE	1888-12-06		A1
8117	ENDICOTT, John F	3	E21NW	1905-08-26		A7
8118	" "	3	E22NW	1905-08-26		A7
5590	EPLEY, David W	15	E½NW	1888-12-06		A7
5589	" "	15	W½NE	1888-12-06		A7
5591	FAIR, Thomas R	7	NENE	1910-11-25		A7
8122	FARE, William M	3	W22NW	1907-12-05		A7
8177	" "	4	2NE	1907-12-05		A7
8180	" "	4	E21NE	1907-12-05		A7
5592	FEAMAN, Margaret	36	S½NE	1860-09-10		A6 G71
5595	FITE, George H	8	E½NE	1890-01-10		A7
5594	" "	8	W½NE	1890-01-30		A1
5596	" "	9	W½NW	1890-01-10		A7
5597	FORESTER, James B	20	S½SE	1900-02-08		A1
5598	FOWLER, Bassil G	6	N½SE	1892-03-07		A7
8220	" "	6	E21NE	1892-03-07		A7
8221	" "	6	E22NE	1892-03-07		A7
8229	FOWLER, George W	6	W22NE	1888-12-04		A7
8198	" "	6	14NW	1888-12-04		A7
8205	" "	6	1NW	1888-12-04		A7
5599	FOWLER, James S	8	NWSE	1897-06-11		A7
5601	" "	8	SWSW	1897-06-11		A7
5600	" "	8	N½SW	1897-06-11		A7
8218	FOWLER, William	6	7NW	1885-05-25		A1
5602	FOWLER, William R	8	NW	1901-07-09		A7
5603	FOX, Jacob B	4	SWSE	1910-04-14		A7
5604	FUDGE, Sarah C	27	N½NE	1860-05-02		A6 G89
8105	FUNK, Santford	2	3NW	1903-01-31		A7
8116	" "	2	W23NE	1903-01-31		A7
5606	GILL, Rebecca V	7	SWSE	1910-01-24		A1
8224	GOODWIN, Andrew J	6	N27SW	1861-02-09		A1
8223	" "	6	N26SW	1861-02-09		A1
5607	GREEN, Thomas	28	E½SW	1859-11-01		A6 G97
8126	HALSEY, Ralph	30	2SW	1892-01-20		A7
8125	" "	30	1SW	1892-01-20		A7
8082	HARDCASTLE, Walker	19	N25NW	1900-02-02		A7
8083	" "	19	N26NW	1900-02-02		A7
8151	HARDIN, Jesse	30	S27SW	1915-04-27		A7
5610	HEATON, William	27	N½NE	1860-05-02		A6 G89
5609	" "	27	S½NE	1860-05-02		A6
5611	" "	33	NE	1860-05-02		A6
5612	" "	34	N½NW	1860-05-02		A6
5613	" "	34	S½NW	1860-05-02		A6 G112
5614	HEINRICH, Jacob G	23	S½SE	1903-05-25		A7
5615	" "	24	SWSW	1903-05-25		A7
5618	HEMPHILL, Mary	32	SENW	1902-05-21		A7 G113
5616	" "	32	W½SE	1902-05-21		A7 G113
5617	" "	32	NESW	1902-05-21		A7 G113
5619	HEMPHILL, William P	32	SENW	1902-05-21		A7 G113
5621	" "	32	NESW	1902-05-21		A7 G113
5620	" "	32	W½SE	1902-05-21		A7 G113
8061	HENSLEY, Sherman H	18	N24NW	1910-01-20		A7
8050	HENSON, James M	17	N22SW	1860-08-01		A1
5623	HENSON, Solomon M	19	SWNE	1901-06-08		A7
5625	HIGH, Martha	34	S½NW	1860-05-02		A6 G112
8101	HINES, Sarah	19	S27SW	1861-07-01		A6
8100	" "	19	S26SW	1861-07-01		A6
8137	" "	30	N26NW	1861-07-01		A6
8249	HIXON, Joseph S	7	S23NW	1900-02-02		A7

ID	Individual in Patent	Sec.	Sec. Part	Date Issued	Other Counties	For More Info . . .
8233	HIXON, Joseph S (Cont'd)	7	3SW	1900-02-02		A7
5626	HIXON, Murry W	6	S½SE	1894-11-30		A7
8206	" "	6	1SW	1894-11-30		A7
5627	HOBBS, Green B	21	NESW	1897-10-28		A7
5628	" "	21	S½SW	1897-10-28		A7
5629	" "	21	SENW	1897-10-28		A7
5631	HOGGATT, Isaac B	35	SESW	1904-01-28		A1
5630	"	35	SENW	1894-06-09		A7
5632	HOLEMAN, James A	28	NENW	1880-11-20		A7
5633	" "	28	NWSW	1880-11-20		A7
5634	" "	28	S½NW	1880-11-20		A7
8069	HOLLAND, Bennett N	18	S24NW	1892-09-09		A7
8062	" "	18	N24SW	1892-09-09		A7
8072	" "	18	S26NW	1892-09-09		A7
8071	" "	18	S25NW	1892-09-09		A7
5636	HON, John S	17	NWNW	1903-08-25		A7
8075	HON, William	19	3NW	1892-09-27		A7
8080	" "	19	N24NW	1892-09-27		A7
5637	HORSMAN, Alexander R	35	S½NE	1895-05-28		A7
5638	" "	35	N½SE	1895-05-28		A7
5639	HORSMAN, Benjamin	35	NESW	1888-12-08		A7
8161	HOWARD, John A	31	N25SW	1897-08-16		A7
8171	HOWARD, Peter V	31	S23SW	1877-04-05		A7
8154	" "	31	4SW	1877-04-05		A7
8172	" "	31	S25SW	1877-04-05		A7
5640	HUFF, James W	20	NWNW	1901-06-08		A7
5641	HUFF, Paul E	14	NWSW	1904-11-15		A7
5642	HUFF, Thomas E	15	SENE	1907-06-26		A1
5644	HULS, William D	5	N½SW	1901-06-08		A7
5643	" "	5	SWSW	1901-06-08		A7
5645	HUNTER, James M	15	E½SE	1895-09-04		A7
5646	JOHNSON, Eli	22	E½SE	1860-05-02		A6
5647	" "	26	NWNW	1860-08-01		A1
8147	JOHNSON, Harlen	30	S25SW	1860-10-01		A1
8132	" "	30	N24SW	1860-10-01		A1
8176	JOHNSON, William C	31	S27SW	1908-07-27		A7
8232	JONES, Betsey J	7	2SW	1882-06-30		A7
8245	" "	7	S21SW	1882-06-30		A7
8247	" "	7	S22NW	1882-06-30		A7
8246	JONES, Stewart	7	S21SW	1882-06-30		A7
8248	" "	7	S22NW	1882-06-30		A7
8231	" "	7	2SW	1882-06-30		A7
8089	KILLION, Daniel W	19	S21SW	1888-12-08		A7
8141	" "	30	S22NW	1888-12-08		A7
8124	" "	30	1NW	1888-12-08		A7
5649	KILLION, Isaac N	29	SESE	1900-08-09		A7
5650	" "	32	N½NE	1900-08-09		A7
5651	" "	32	NENW	1900-08-09		A7
8142	KIMBROUGH, Robert D	30	S23SW	1893-12-19		A7
8159	" "	31	N23NW	1893-12-19		A7
8153	" "	31	4NW	1893-12-19		A7
8058	KING, Charlotte M	18	N22SW	1908-04-30		A7
5652	KINGDON, Samuel	4	NWSE	1895-06-28		A7
8190	" "	5	W21NE	1895-06-28		A7
8110	LAIR, Joseph	2	E23	1911-04-27		A7
8106	" "	2	4NE	1911-04-27		A7
5654	LAIR, Reuben	7	SENE	1882-06-30		A7
5655	" "	7	NWSE	1882-06-30		A7
5653	" "	7	E½SE	1882-06-30		A7
5656	LEEPER, William T	28	SESE	1859-11-01		A6
5659	" "	28	E½SW	1859-11-01		A6 G97
5657	" "	28	NESE	1860-08-01		A1
5658	" "	28	W½SE	1859-11-01		A6
5661	LETSINGER, John M	13	SWNE	1861-07-01		A6
5660	" "	13	SENW	1861-07-01		A6
5662	LINGO, Alexander A	14	SWSW	1898-04-11		A7
5665	LONG, Henry T	17	N½SW	1889-01-12		A7
5666	" "	17	SWNW	1889-01-12		A7
5667	" "	17	SWSW	1889-01-12		A7
5668	LONG, Isaac	18	SENE	1882-06-10		A1
8057	" "	18	N21NW	1873-04-10		A7
5670	" "	18	NENE	1860-08-01		A1
5669	" "	18	W½NE	1873-04-10		A7

ID	Individual in Patent	Sec.	Sec. Part	Date Issued	Other Counties	For More Info . . .
8090	LONG, John A	19	S22SW	1891-05-25		A7
8092	" "	19	S24SW	1891-05-25		A7
8076	" "	19	3SW	1891-05-25		A7
8227	LONG, Joseph	6	S27SW	1892-05-26		A7
8244	" "	7	N27NW	1892-05-26		A7
5672	LOVELACE, C P	32	S½NE	1890-10-11		A7
5671	" "	32	E½SE	1890-10-11		A7
8114	MALONE, Jake	2	W21NW	1908-07-27		A7
8115	" "	2	W22NW	1908-07-27		A7
5674	MARTIN, George G	17	E½NW	1898-01-26		A7
8131	MARTIN, Samuel H	30	N24NW	1903-07-01		A7
8146	" "	30	S25NW	1905-12-30		A7
8133	" "	30	N25NW	1903-07-01		A7
5675	MATLOCK, Lucinda F	25	SESE	1891-06-09		A7
5676	" "	36	N½NE	1891-06-09		A7
5677	MATLOCK, William H	25	NWSW	1895-05-28		A7
5678	" "	26	E½SE	1895-05-28		A7
5679	" "	35	NENE	1895-05-28		A7
5680	MATTHEWS, John T	11	SWSW	1900-02-02		A7
5681	" "	14	W½NW	1900-02-02		A7
5682	" "	15	NENE	1900-02-02		A7
5683	MATTHEWS, Julius	15	SWSE	1905-05-02		A7
5684	" "	15	SESW	1905-05-02		A7
8085	MCBRIDE, Mary Ann	19	N26SW	1860-09-10		A6
8094	" "	19	S26NW	1860-09-10		A6
8184	MCDANIEL, James J	5	1NE	1889-01-12		A7
5685	" "	5	N½SE	1889-01-12		A7
8181	MCDANIEL, John	4	E21NW	1861-02-09		A1
8199	" "	6	15NW	1860-09-10		A6
8202	" "	6	16NW	1860-09-10		A6
8197	" "	6	13NW	1860-09-10		A6
5686	MCDANIEL, John H	4	NESE	1905-03-30		A7
8107	MCDANIEL, John M	2	E21NE	1860-03-01		A1
8183	" "	4	W23NW	1860-08-01		A1
8189	MCDANIEL, John S	5	3NW	1896-07-23		A7
8211	" "	6	3NE	1896-07-23		A7
8186	MCDANIEL, Marian C	5	2NE	1888-12-08		A7
8188	" "	5	3NE	1888-12-08		A7
5687	MCDANIEL, Mary A	1	NESE	1875-05-01		A7
8043	" "	1	E21NE	1875-05-01		A7
5689	MCDANIEL, Samuel R	21	SENE	1860-08-01		A1
5688	" "	21	NESE	1860-09-10		A6 G10
5690	" "	22	W½SW	1860-09-10		A6 G10
5691	" "	22	NESW	1860-09-10		A6 G10
5692	" "	22	SWSE	1860-10-01		A8 G144
5693	" "	22	SESW	1860-10-01		A8 G144
8228	MCDANIEL, William C	6	W21NE	1860-03-01		A1
5694	MCELRATH, Jane	22	SWSE	1860-10-01		A8 G144
5695	" "	22	SESW	1860-10-01		A8 G144
5698	MCGEE, James A	24	SESE	1892-01-25		A7
5699	MCGUIRE, James M	34	SE	1860-11-12		A6
8178	MCMURTRY, John W	4	2NW	1892-03-07		A7
5700	MCNAY, James	27	SE	1860-05-02		A6 G147
5701	" "	34	W½NE	1860-05-02		A6
5704	" "	34	NENE	1860-05-02		A6
5706	MCTHOMPSON, Charles M	11	SWNW	1903-01-31		A7
5705	" "	11	NWSW	1903-01-31		A7
5707	MEDLOCK, Jesse	26	W½NE	1875-02-15		A7
5709	" "	26	SENE	1875-02-15		A7
5708	" "	26	NWSE	1875-02-15		A7
5710	MILLS, Samuel W	12	NESE	1884-03-10		A1
5711	MOODY, Joel W	23	S½NW	1857-06-15		A8
5713	MOORE, Margaret	27	SE	1860-05-02		A6 G147
5714	MOORE, Thomas	27	SE	1860-05-02		A6 G147
5715	MORELAND, Alexander L	24	NESE	1860-09-10		A6 G54
8195	MORRIS, William C	6	12NW	1897-04-10		A7
8209	" "	6	2NW	1897-04-10		A7
8212	" "	6	3NW	1897-04-10		A7
5716	MORTON, Jeremiah	25	SESW	1859-09-01		A1
5717	" "	33	N½SE	1860-11-12		A6 G74
5718	NEWBERRY, Richard C	23	NESE	1890-01-10		A7
5719	" "	24	NWSW	1890-01-10		A7
5720	NICHOLAS, Anthony W	11	NWNE	1859-09-01		A1

ID	Individual in Patent	Sec.	Sec. Part	Date Issued	Other Counties	For More Info . . .
5721	NICHOLAS, David	12	N½SW	1862-10-10		A6 G65
5722	" "	14	SESW	1859-09-01		A1
5723	" "	14	NESW	1860-05-02		A6
5724	" "	14	NWSE	1860-05-02		A6
5725	" "	15	SWSW	1860-08-01		A1
5727	" "	22	NWNW	1859-09-01		A1
5728	" "	22	E½NW	1862-10-10		A6 G65
5726	" "	22	NE	1860-05-02		A6
5729	" "	23	NWNW	1859-09-01		A1
5730	NICHOLAS, Elihu B	22	SWNW	1895-11-05		A7
5731	NICHOLAS, James E	19	N½SE	1860-09-10		A6
5732	NICHOLAS, John B	11	NESE	1872-08-30		A1
5733	" "	14	E½NW	1861-02-01		A1
5734	NICHOLAS, Thomas B	12	S½SW	1860-05-02		A6
5735	NICKS, Alexander	24	NW	1891-05-25		A7
5736	NICKS, Annis	23	NWSE	1879-09-23		A1
5737	NICKS, James	14	NESE	1888-12-04		A7
5738	" "	14	S½SE	1888-12-04		A7
5739	NICKS, William	22	NWSE	1861-02-01		A1
5741	PACKMAN, George J	19	SWSE	1906-06-30		A1
5742	" "	30	NWNE	1906-06-30		A1
8079	PENDERGRASS, Roye	19	N21SW	1952-05-16		A1
8251	RICHEY, Robert T	7	S25NW	1877-04-05		A7
8250	" "	7	S24NW	1877-04-05		A7
8234	" "	7	4SW	1877-04-05		A7
8219	RILEY, John H	6	8NW	1898-01-26		A7
8239	ROACH, Porter H	7	N22NW	1904-11-22		A1
5745	ROBERTS, James L	1	W½SE	1891-08-19		A7
5744	" "	1	NESW	1891-08-19		A7
5746	" "	12	NWNE	1891-08-19		A7
8053	ROBERTS, John	18	5SW	1879-12-15		A7
8070	" "	18	S24SW	1879-12-15		A7
8068	" "	18	S23SW	1879-12-15		A7
8055	ROBINSON, George W	18	7NW	1901-05-08		A7
8064	" "	18	N26NW	1901-05-08		A7
8063	" "	18	N25NW	1901-05-08		A7
8237	ROMANS, Mary J	7	7SW	1895-05-28		A7
8236	" "	7	6SW	1895-05-28		A7
5748	ROMINE, John W	24	W½SE	1875-09-10		A7
5747	" "	24	E½SW	1875-09-10		A7
5749	ROOP, Samuel	9	E½NE	1904-12-31		A7
5750	SAMPLE, Moses	4	NESW	1882-09-30		A1
5751	SAPP, Thomas A	35	SWNW	1861-02-01		A1
8145	SAPP, William S	30	S24SW	1860-08-01		A1
8130	" "	30	N23SW	1860-08-01		A1
8156	" "	31	5NW	1860-08-01		A1
5752	SAPPS, Thomas A	34	SENE	1859-01-01		A1
5753	SCOGGIN, Turpin G	27	E½NW	1860-09-10		A6 G168
8253	SCROGGINS, William J	7	S27NW	1872-08-30		A1
8054	SHARP, Benjamin E	18	6SW	1900-02-02		A7
8056	" "	18	7SW	1900-02-02		A7
5755	SHARP, Sarah	28	E½SW	1859-11-01		A6 G97
5761	SHURLEY, Thomas P	33	SESW	1877-08-01		A7
5760	" "	33	S½SE	1877-08-01		A7
8185	SINGLETON, Preston B	5	1NW	1892-03-07		A7
8187	" "	5	2NW	1892-03-07		A7
5768	SLAYBARK, Solomon	23	NWNE	'		A6
5769	" "	23	NENW	'		A6
8252	SLOAN, John P	7	S26NW	1895-05-28		A7
8213	SLOAN, Norman M	6	3SW	1894-05-18		A7
8210	" "	6	2SW	1894-05-18		A7
5772	SMITH, Ayres	27	W½NW	1859-01-01		A1
8143	SMITH, James M	30	S24NW	1880-11-20		A7
8134	" "	30	N25SW	1880-11-20		A7
8081	SMITH, John B	19	N24SW	1882-08-30		A7
8077	" "	19	5SW	1882-08-30		A7
8093	" "	19	S25NW	1882-08-30		A7
8139	" "	30	N27NW	1879-09-23		A1
8160	SMITH, Samuel M	31	N23SW	1883-02-10		A7
8157	" "	31	N21SW	1883-02-10		A7
8170	" "	31	S23NW	1883-02-10		A7
8158	" "	31	N22SW	1883-02-10		A7
5773	SMITH, William	28	S½NE	1865-09-01		A6 G2

311

ID	Individual in Patent	Sec.	Sec. Part	Date Issued	Other Counties	For More Info . . .
5774	SPARKS, Elizabeth J	18	E½SE	1876-05-15		A7
5775	"	19	N½NE	1876-05-15		A7
8067	SPARKS, Robert T	18	S23NW	1876-01-10		A7
8052	"	18	2NW	1876-01-10		A7
8060	"	18	N23SW	1876-01-10		A7
8051	SPARKS, William W	18	1SW	1883-02-10		A7
8073	"	19	1NW	1883-02-10		A7
8166	"	31	S21NW	1885-07-27		A1
8168	"	31	S22NW	1885-07-27		A1
5776	STARK, Jeremiah A	30	S½NE	1895-09-04		A7
5777	"	30	N½SE	1895-09-04		A7
8046	STARKEY, James N	1	E23NE	1888-12-08		A7
8041	"	1	2NE	1888-12-08		A7
5778	STARKEY, Lycurgus	1	SESE	1890-10-11		A7
5779	"	12	NENE	1890-10-11		A7
5780	STEPHENS, David C	10	W½NE	1903-11-24		A7
5781	STEPHENS, Esau M	26	E½NW	1878-06-24		A7
5782	"	26	SWNW	1878-06-24		A7
5783	STEPHENS, James W	25	SWSW	1919-07-01		A7
5784	STRAUSE, Bernhard	27	E½NW	1860-09-10		A6 G168
8042	STROTHER, Richard	1	4NE	1860-08-01		A1
5785	TALLEY, Charles M	33	NESW	1902-05-21		A7
5786	"	33	W½SW	1902-05-21		A7
8152	TALLY, Joseph	30	W22NW	1860-08-01		A1
8127	"	30	3NW	1860-09-10		A6
8138	TAYLOR, James	30	N26SW	1894-05-18		A7
8140	"	30	N27SW	1894-05-18		A7
8148	"	30	S26NW	1894-05-18		A7
5789	TAYLOR, Nero	20	SENW	1860-08-01		A1
5787	"	20	NENW	1876-01-10		A7
5788	"	20	SWNW	1876-01-10		A7
5791	THOMAS, Margaret	26	SW	1869-06-23		A8
8084	THOMPSON, Baxter	19	N26SW	1860-09-10		A6
8095	"	19	S26NW	1860-09-10		A6
8099	"	19	S26SW	1861-07-01		A6
8102	"	19	S27SW	1861-07-01		A6
8135	"	30	N26NW	1861-07-01		A6
8065	THOMPSON, William	18	S21NW	1860-10-01		A1
5794	UNGER, Amelia	36	S½NE	1860-09-10		A6 G71
5795	UNGER, Eli	36	S½NE	1860-09-10		A6
5797	UNGER, Henry W	36	S½NE	1860-09-10		A6 G71
5798	UNGER, Louisa	36	S½NE	1860-09-10		A6 G71
5799	UPTON, William R	12	SESE	1873-02-01		A7
5801	VAUGHAN, Richard M	3	N½SW	1892-04-01		A7
8121	"	3	W21NW	1892-04-01		A7
5800	"	3	NWSE	1892-04-01		A7
5802	VAUGHN, Sherwood	26	SWSE	1875-09-10		A7
5804	"	35	NWNE	1875-09-10		A7
5803	"	35	N½NW	1875-09-10		A7
5805	VENUS, David A	24	NESE	1860-09-10		A6 G54
5806	VERBICK, Andrew J	29	NW	1896-01-14		A7
5808	VERBICK, Oran V	21	NENE	1896-01-14		A7
5807	"	21	NENW	1896-01-14		A7
5809	"	21	W½NE	1896-01-14		A7
5810	VERBICK, Robert M	18	W½SE	1903-06-08		A7
5811	VERNON, Joel	27	E½SE	1860-05-02		A6
5813	VOEGELE, Charles H	3	SWSE	1902-02-07		A1
5812	"	3	NESE	1902-02-07		A1
5815	WALLACE, James T	13	NWNE	1859-09-01		A1
5816	WALLACE, William	34	SW	1860-05-02		A6 G185
5817	WALLICE, James T	12	SWSE	1860-08-01		A1
5820	"	2	SWSE	1860-08-01		A1
5821	"	2	NWSE	1860-08-01		A1
5818	"	2	NESW	1860-09-10		A6 G186
5822	"	2	NWSE	1860-09-10		A6 G186
8112	"	2	W21NE	1860-09-10		A6 G186
5819	"	2	NWSW	1860-08-01		A1
8091	WESCOTT, B R	19	S24NW	1902-02-21		A1
8059	WESTMORELAND, Joseph	18	N23NW	1900-08-09		A7
8066	WESTMORELAND, Shade	18	S22SW	1872-03-15		A7
8074	"	19	2NW	1872-03-15		A7
5823	WICKER, Andrew J	7	SWNE	1897-11-22		A1
5824	WILCOX, Joseph	10	SENE	1905-09-05		A7

ID	Individual in Patent	Sec.	Sec. Part	Date Issued	Other Counties	For More Info . . .
5825	WILCOX, Robert E	17	NE	1892-03-07		A7
5826	WILCOX, William J	11	SENW	1903-01-31		A7
5827	" "	11	NESW	1903-01-31		A7
8087	WILLIAMS, H H M	19	N26SW	1860-09-10		A6
8096	" "	19	S26NW	1860-09-10		A6
5829	WILLIAMS, Mary	34	SW	1860-05-02		A6 G185
8113	WISNER, Andrew	2	W21NE	1860-09-10		A6 G186
5831	" "	2	NWSE	1860-09-10		A6 G186
5830	" "	2	NESW	1860-09-10		A6 G186
5835	WRIGHT, William L	8	SESW	1892-03-07		A7
5836	" "	8	NESE	1892-03-07		A7
5834	" "	8	S½SE	1892-03-07		A7
5837	WRIGHT, William S	25	NESW	1873-04-10		A7
5839	" "	25	N½SE	1873-04-10		A7
5838	" "	25	SWSE	1873-04-10		A7

Patent Map

T22-N R10-W
5th PM 22-N 10-W Meridian

Map Group 21

Township Statistics

Parcels Mapped	:	451
Number of Patents	:	263
Number of Individuals	:	290
Patentees Identified	:	260
Number of Surnames	:	186
Multi-Patentee Parcels	:	27
Oldest Patent Date	:	
Most Recent Patent	:	7/1/1919
Block/Lot Parcels	:	186
Cities and Town	:	7
Cemeteries	:	4

Copyright 2013 Boyd IT. Inc. All Rights Reserved

Lots/Tracts-Sec. 5
1NE MCDANIEL, JAMES J 1889
1NW SINGLETON, PRESTON B 1892
2NE MCDANIEL, MARIAN C 1888
2NW SINGLETON, PRESTON B 1892
3NE MCDANIEL, MARIAN C 1888
3NW MCDANIEL, JOHN S 1896
W21NE KINGDON, SAMUEL 1895

Lots/Tracts-Sec. 4
2NE FARE, WILLIAM M 1907
2NW MCMURTRY, JOHN W 1892
3NE ELLIOTT, ROBERT F 1889
E21NE FARE, WILLIAM M 1907
E21NW MCDANIEL, JOHN 1861
W21NE CRUMLEY, JOHN A 1889
W23NW MCDANIEL, JOHN M 1860

6

Lots/Tracts-Sec. 6
0NW BAZE, GEORGE 1860
1NW BAZE, GEORGE 1860
2NW MORRIS, WILLIAM C 1897
3NW MCDANIEL, JOHN 1860
14NW FOWLER, GEORGE W 1888
15NW MORRIS, MARY J 1895
16NW MCDANIEL, JOHN 1860
17NW CARTER, WILLIAM M 1892
18NW CARTER, WILLIAM M 1892
19NW FOWLER, GEORGE W 1888
1NW HIXON, MURRY W 1894
15W CARTER, WILLIAM M 1888
20NW CARTER, WILLIAM M 1892
21NW CHANDLER, ALEXANDER A 1894
2NW MORRIS, WILLIAM C 1897
25W SLOAN, NORMAN M 1894
3NE MORRIS, MARY J 1895
3NW SLOAN, NORMAN M 1894
35W CHANDLER, WILLIAM 1888
4NW CHANDLER, JOHN R 1888
45W CHANDLER, WILLIAM 1888
5NW FOWLER, WILLIAM 1885
6NW CANDLOGEBIL 1892
7NW MCDANIEL, WILLIAM C 1860
8NW FOWLER, GEORGE W 1888

5

FOWLER
Bassil G
1892

HIXON
Murry W
1894

HULS
William D
1901

HULS
William D
1901

MCDANIEL
James J
1889

EASLEY
Benjamin W
1905

EASLEY
Benjamin W
1905

4

CRUMLEY
John A
1889

CRUMLEY
John A
1889

SAMPLE
Moses
1882

KINGDON
Samuel
1895

FOX
Jacob B
1910

MCDANIEL
John H
1905

BURDEN
George C
1891

Lots/Tracts-Sec. 7
1NW BRIDGES, ORREN S 1898
2SW JONES, BETSEY J 1882
3SW ROBERTS, JOHN 1879
4SW RICHEY, ROBERT T 1877
6SW CARTER, WILLIAMSON F 1900
7SW ROMANS, MARY J 1895
7SW LONG, ISAAC 1873
N21SW BRIDGES, CHARLOTTE M 1908
N22SW KING, CHARLOTTE M 1908
N23NW WESTMORELAND, JOSEPH 1900
N24NW CHANDLER, WILLIAM J 1888
N25NW CHANDLER, WILLIAM 1888
N26NW CHANDLER, WILLIAM 1888
N27NW CHANDLER, GEORGE W 1901
S21SW JONES, JOSEPH 1882
S22NW JONES, BETSEY J 1882
S23NW HIXON, JOSEPH S 1896
S24NW RICHEY, ROBERT T 1877
S25NW SLOAN, JOHN P 1895
S26NW SCROGGINS, WILLIAM J1872

7

BRIDGES
Orren S
1898

FAIR
Thomas R
1910

WICKER
Andrew J
1897

LAIR
Reuben
1882

LAIR
Reuben
1882

LAIR
Reuben
1882

GILL
Rebecca V
1910

FOWLER
William R
1901

FITE
George H
1890

FITE
George H
1890

FOWLER
James S
1897

FOWLER
James S
1897

FOWLER
James S
1897

WRIGHT
William L
1892

FITE
George H
1890

WRIGHT
William L
1892

WRIGHT
William L
1892

8

DOWNING
James W
1902

DOWNING
James W
1902

9

DERRICK
Alfred C
1882

ROOP
Samuel
1904

Lots/Tracts-Sec. 18
1SW SPARKS, WILLIAM W 1883
2SW WESTMORELAND, SHADE 1872
5SW ROBERTS, ROBERT T 1876
6SW SHARP, BENJAMIN E 1900
7SW ROBINSON, GEORGE W 1901
7SW LONG, ISAAC. 1873
N21NW LONG, ISAAC. 1873
N22SW HENSLEY, SHERMAN H 1910
N23NW SPARKS, ROBERT T 1876
N24NW ROBINSON, GEORGE W 1901
N25NW ROBINSON, GEORGE W 1901
N26NW THOMPSON, WILLIAM 1876
S21NW THOMPSON, SHADE 1872
S22SW ROBERTS, JOHN 1879
S23NW ROBERTS, JOHN 1879
S24NW HOLLAND, BENNETT N 1892
S25NW HOLLAND, BENNETT N 1892
S26NW HOLLAND, BENNETT N 1892

18

LONG
Isaac
1873

LONG
Isaac
1860

LONG
Isaac
1882

HON
John S
1903

LONG
Henry T
1889

LONG
Henry T
1889

MARTIN
George G
1898

WILCOX
Robert E
1892

17

VERBICK
Robert M
1903

SPARKS
Elizabeth J
1876

LONG
Henry T
1889

CROWLEY
Lawrence N
1901

Lots/Tracts-Sec. 17
N22SW HENSON, JAMES M 1860

16

Lots/Tracts-Sec. 19
1NW KILLION, DANIEL W 1888
1SW HALSEY, RALPH 1892
2SW LONG, JOHN A 1891
3NW TALLY, JOSEPH 1860
5SW BAKER, THOMAS W 1860
7SW CUNNINGHAM, JAMES A 1898
7SW MARTIN, SAMUEL H 1903
N21SW JOHNSON, HARLEN 1860
N24NW HON, WILLIAM 1897
N25SW SMITH, SAMUEL H 1883
N24SW SMITH, JOHN B 1882
N25NW THOMPSON, BAXTER 1861
N26NW HARDCASTLE, WALKER 1900
N26NW HARDCASTLE, WALKER 1900
N27NW TAYLOR, JAMES 1894
S21SW SMITH, JOHN B 1879
S22NW TAYLOR, JAMES 1894
S21SW KILLION, DANIEL W 1888
S22NW LONG, JOHN A 1891
S23NW WESCOTT, B R 1902
S24NW SMITH, JOHN B 1891
S25NW THOMPSON, BAXTER 1860
S26NW THOMPSON, BAXTER 1861
S27SW THOMPSON, BAXTER 1861

19

SPARKS
Elizabeth J
1876

HUFF
James W
1901

TAYLOR
Nero
1876

HENSON
Solomon M
1901

ENDECOTT
Joseph
1888

TAYLOR
Nero
1876

TAYLOR
Nero
1860

NICHOLAS
James E
1860

PACKMAN
George J
1906

CUTLER
William P
1902

20

BEYER
Christian
1902

FORESTER
James B
1900

VERBICK
Oran V
1896

VERBICK
Oran V
1896

HOBBS
Green B
1897

HOBBS
Green B
1897

HOBBS
Green B
1897

21

VERBICK
Oran V
1896

MCDANIEL
Samuel R
1860

EASLEY
Woodson
1885

EASLEY
Woodson
1885

MCDANIEL [10]
Samuel R
1860

Lots/Tracts-Sec. 30
4NW KIMBROUGH, ROBERT D 1893
1SW HOWARD, PETER V 1877
4SW BAKER, THOMAS W 1860
N21SW SMITH, SAMUEL M 1883
N22SW SMITH, SAMUEL M 1883
N23NW KIMBROUGH, ROBERT D 1893
N24SW SMITH, SAMUEL M 1883
N25SW HOWARD, JOHN A 1897
N26SW BIFFLE, WILLIAM D 1860
N26SW BRIDWELL, PETER V 1888
N27NW BIFFLE, WILLIAM D 1860
S21NW CUNNINGHAM, JOHN W 1892
S21SW SPARKS, WILLIAM W 1885
S22NW SPARKS, WILLIAM W 1885
S22SW CUNNINGHAM, JOHN W 1892
S23NW SMITH, SAMUEL M 1883
S24SW HOWARD, PETER V 1877
S25NW HOWARD, PETER V 1877
S26NW BRIDWELL, PETER V 1888
S26SW CANTRELL, PINKNEY 1889
S27NW CUNNINGHAM, JAMES P 1875
S27SW JOHNSON, WILLIAM C 1908

30

PACKMAN
George J
1906

CUTLER
William P
1902

STARK
Jeremiah A
1895

STARK
Jeremiah A
1895

VERBICK
Andrew J
1896

29

ADKINS
Joseph N
1890

ADKINS
Joseph M
1890

ADKINS
Joseph M
1890

KILLION
Isaac N
1900

KILLION
Isaac N
1900

KILLION
Isaac N
1900

HOLEMAN
James A
1880

HOLEMAN
James A
1880

HOLEMAN
James A
1880

LEEPER [97]
William T
1859

CRANE
Emerson F
1908

ANDERSON
Andy
1860

SMITH [2]
William
1865

LEEPER
William T
1859

LEEPER
William T
1859

LEEPER
William T
1859

28

Lots/Tracts-Sec. 31
4NW KIMBROUGH, ROBERT D 1893
4SW HOWARD, PETER V 1877
5NW BAKER, THOMAS W 1860
N21SW SMITH, SAMUEL M 1883
N22SW SMITH, SAMUEL M 1883
N23NW SMITH, SAMUEL M 1883
N24SW KIMBROUGH, ROBERT D 1893
N25SW SMITH, SAMUEL M 1883
N26SW HOWARD, JOHN A 1897
N26SW BIFFLE, WILLIAM D 1860
N27NW CUNNINGHAM, JOHN W 1892
S21SW SPARKS, WILLIAM W 1885
S21SW SPARKS, WILLIAM W 1885
S22SW CUNNINGHAM, JOHN W 1892
S23NW SMITH, SAMUEL M 1883
S24SW HOWARD, PETER V 1877
S25SW HOWARD, PETER V 1877
S26SW BRIDWELL, PETER V 1888
S26SW DIELLE, HENRY 1861
S27NW CALLAHAN, JOHN T 1903
S27SW HARDIN, JESSE 1915
W22NW TALLY, JOSEPH 1860

31

DODSON
Vernon M
1896

DODSON
Vernon M
1896

CUNNINGHAM
John W
1892

DODSON
Vernon M
1896

HEMPHILL [13]
Mary
1902

HEMPHILL [113]
Mary
1902

HEMPHILL [113]
Mary
1902

LOVELACE
C P
1890

LOVELACE
C P
1890

32

TALLEY
Charles M
1902

TALLEY
Charles M
1902

SHURLEY
Thomas P
1877

HEATON
William
1860

MORTON [74]
Jeremiah
1860

SHURLEY
Thomas P
1877

33

Lots/Tracts-Sec. 3
E21NW ENDICOTT, JOHN F 1905
E22NW ENDICOTT, JOHN F 1905
E23NW CARTWRIGHT, MARY A 1889
W21NW VAUGHAN, RICHARD M 1892
W22NW FARE, WILLIAM M 1907
W23NW ELLIOTT, ROBERT F 1889

Lots/Tracts-Sec. 2
2NE CLARK, ISAAC 1888
3NW FUNK, SANTFORD 1903
4NE LAIR, JOSEPH 1911
E21NE MCDANIEL, JOHN M 1860
E21NW CLARK, ISAAC 1888
E22NW CLARK, ISAAC 1888
E23 LAIR, JOSEPH 1911
W21NE WALLICE, JAMES T [186]1860
W21NW MALONE, JAKE 1908
W22NW MALONE, JAKE 1908
W23NE FUNK, SANTFORD 1903

Lots/Tracts-Sec. 1
2NE STARKEY, JAMES N 1888
4NE STROTHER, RICHARD 1860
E21NE MCDANIEL, MARY A 1875
E21NW BLACK, DANIEL W 1877
E22NW BLACK, WILLIAM C 1860
E23NE STARKEY, JAMES N 1888
W21NE BLACK, DANIEL W 1877
W21NW COLLINS, JAMES A 1900
W22NW BLACK, DANIEL W 1886

Section 3

VAUGHAN Richard M 1892
VAUGHAN Richard M 1892
VOEGELE Charles H 1902
BURDEN George C 1891
VOEGELE Charles H 1902
BURDEN John 1892
STEPHENS David C 1903
WILCOX Joseph 1905
BOSWELL Frederick 1894

10

Section 2

WALLICE [186] James T 1860
WALLICE James T 1860
WALLICE James T 1860
WALLICE [186] James T 1860
WALLICE James T 1860
BURDEN John 1892
BEAMAN James H 1903
BURDEN John 1892
BEAMAN James H 1903
NICHOLAS Anthony W 1859
MCTHOMPSON Charles M 1903
WILCOX William J 1903
BROWN Andrew B 1882
MCTHOMPSON Charles M 1903
WILCOX William J 1903
BROWN Andrew B 1882
MATTHEWS John T 1900
BROWN Andrew B 1882

2

11

Section 1

COLLINS James A 1900
ROBERTS James L 1891
ROBERTS James L 1891
MCDANIEL Mary A 1875
CARRELL Elizabeth 1891
CARRELL Elizabeth 1891
CARRELL Lavina C 1883
STARKEY Lycurgus 1890
CARRELL [38] Lavina C 1883
CARRELL Lavina C 1883
ROBERTS James L 1891
STARKEY Lycurgus 1890
CARRELL Peter 1877
CARRELL Peter 1877
NICHOLAS John B 1872
NICHOLAS David 1862
CARRELL Peter 1877
MILLS Samuel W 1884
NICHOLAS Thomas B 1860
WALLICE James T 1860
UPTON William R 1873

1

12

EPLEY David W 1888
EPLEY David W 1888
MATTHEWS John T 1900
HUFF Thomas E 1907
CARRELL Julius E 1888
ALLEN Tucker W 1890
WALLACE James T 1859
CARRELL Franklin S 1891

15

MATTHEWS John T 1900
NICHOLAS John B 1861
CARRELL Julius E 1888
BALES Samuel P 1898
ALLEN Tucker W 1890
LETSINGER John M 1861
LETSINGER John M 1861

HUFF Paul E 1904
NICHOLAS David 1860
NICHOLAS David 1860
NICKS James 1888
ALLEN Tucker W 1890
BROWN Daniel T 1895
BROWN Daniel T 1895
COLLINS Peter H 1861

NICHOLAS David 1860
LINGO Alexander A 1898
NICHOLAS David 1859
NICKS James 1888
BROWN Daniel T 1895
COLLINS Peter H 1875

14

13

NICHOLAS David 1860
MATTHEWS Julius 1905
MATTHEWS Julius 1905
HUNTER James M 1895

NICHOLAS David 1859
NICHOLAS David 1862
NICHOLAS David 1860
NICHOLAS [65] David 1862
NICHOLAS Elihu B 1895
NICHOLAS David 1859
CHENEY Levi 1860
CHENEY Levi 1860
CHENEY Levi 1860
SLAYBARK Solomon
SLAYBARK Solomon
CHENEY Levi 1860
COLLINS Peter H 1861
DORRIS George M 1888
MOODY Joel W 1857
CHENEY Levi 1860
NICKS Alexander 1891
COLLINS Peter H 1875

22

23

24

MCDANIEL [10] Samuel R 1860
NICKS William 1861
MCDANIEL [10] Samuel R 1860
MCDANIEL [144] Samuel R 1860
JOHNSON Eli 1860
MCDANIEL [144] Samuel R 1860
CHENEY [44] Levi 1862
NICKS Annis 1879
NEWBERRY Richard C 1890
NEWBERRY Richard C 1890
ROMINE John W 1875
ROMINE John W 1875
COLLINS [54] John B 1860
MCGEE James A 1892
HEINRICH Jacob G 1903
HEINRICH Jacob G 1903

HEATON [89] William 1860
SCOGGIN [168] Turpin G 1860
HEATON William 1860
JOHNSON Eli 1860
SMITH Ayres 1859
STEPHENS Esau M 1878
STEPHENS Esau M 1878
MEDLOCK Jesse 1875
COOPER Marcus A 1888
MEDLOCK Jesse 1875

27

26

25

ANDERSON Andy 1860
VERNON Joel 1860
MCNAY [147] James 1860
THOMAS Margaret 1869
MEDLOCK Jesse 1875
MEDLOCK William H 1895
MATLOCK William H 1895
VAUGHN Sherwood 1875
MATLOCK William H 1895
WRIGHT William S 1873
WRIGHT William S 1873
STEPHENS James W 1919
MORTON Jeremiah 1859
WRIGHT William S 1873
MATLOCK Lucinda F 1891

HEATON William 1860
MCNAY James 1860
MCNAY James 1860
VAUGHN Sherwood 1875
VAUGHN Sherwood 1875
MATLOCK William H 1895
MATLOCK Lucinda F 1891
HEATON [112] William 1860
SAPPS Thomas A 1859
SAPP Thomas A 1861
HOGGATT Isaac B 1894
HORSMAN Alexander R 1895
EASLEY [71] Francis H 1860

34

35

36

WALLACE [185] William 1860
MCGUIRE James M 1860
COOPER John T 1860
HORSMAN Benjamin 1888
HORSMAN Alexander R 1895
HOGGATT Isaac B 1904
COOPER John T 1862
CULBERTSON John C 1860

Helpful Hints

1. This Map's INDEX can be found on the preceding pages.

2. Refer to Map "C" to see where this Township lies within Howell County, Missouri.

3. Numbers within square brackets [ ] denote a multi-patentee land parcel (multi-owner). Refer to Appendix "C" for a full list of members in this group.

4. Areas that look to be crowded with Patentees usually indicate multiple sales of the same parcel (Re-issues) or Overlapping parcels. See this Township's Index for an explanation of these and other circumstances that might explain "odd" groupings of Patentees on this map.

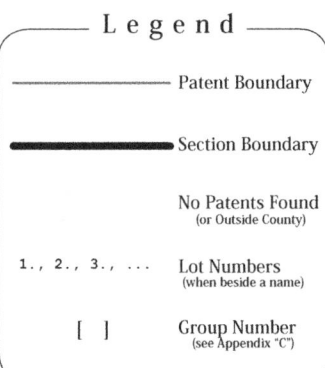

Legend

——— Patent Boundary

━━━ Section Boundary

No Patents Found (or Outside County)

1., 2., 3., ... Lot Numbers (when beside a name)

[ ] Group Number (see Appendix "C")

Scale: Section = 1 mile X 1 mile (generally, with some exceptions)

Road Map

T22-N R10-W
5th PM 22-N 10-W Meridian

Map Group 21

Cities & Towns

Amy
Caulfield
Egypt Grove
Hocomo
Leota
Moody
Wetherhill (historical)

Cemeteries

Big Spring Cemetery
Joyes Cemetery
Nicks Cemetery
Youngblood Cemetery

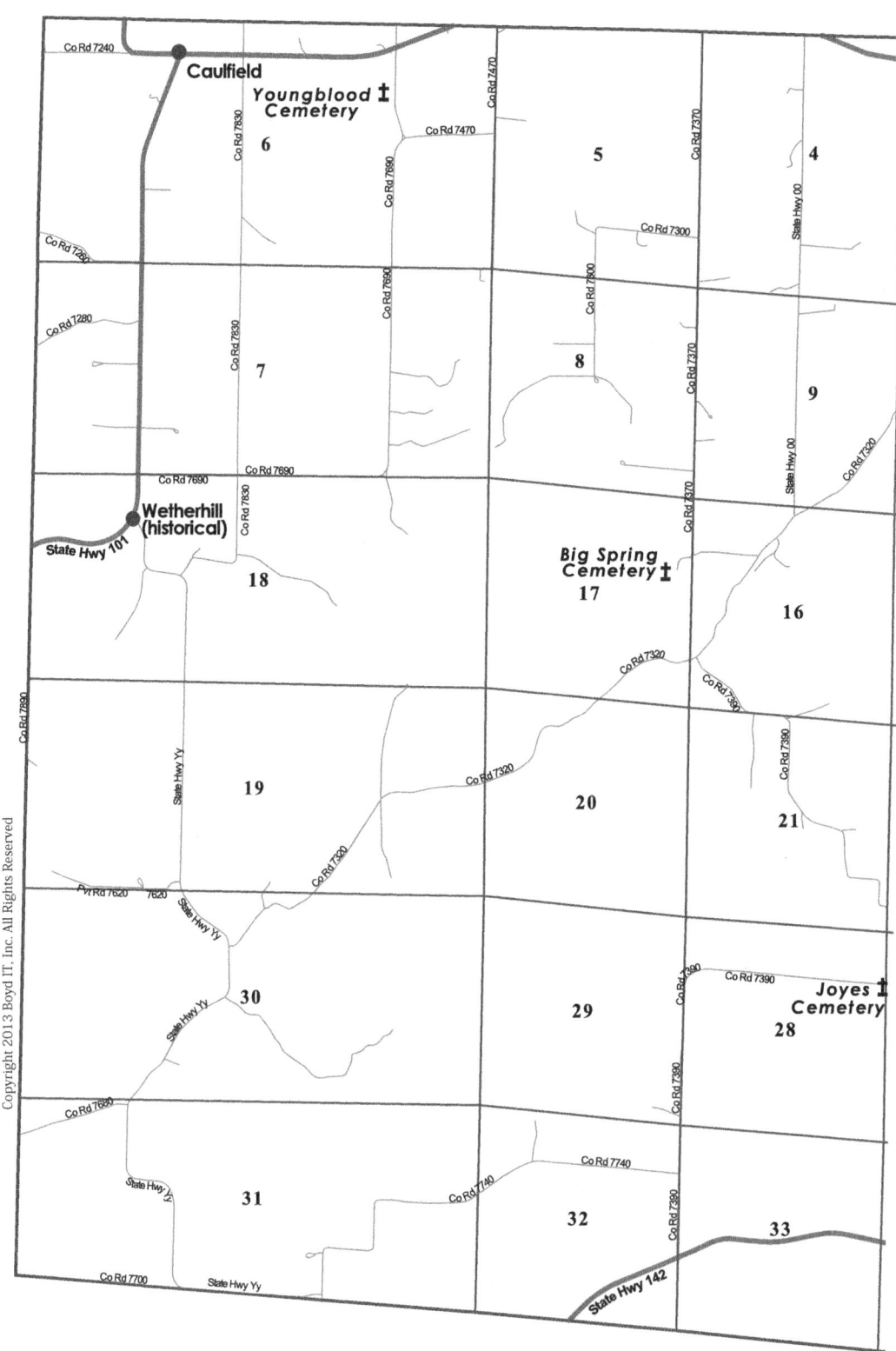

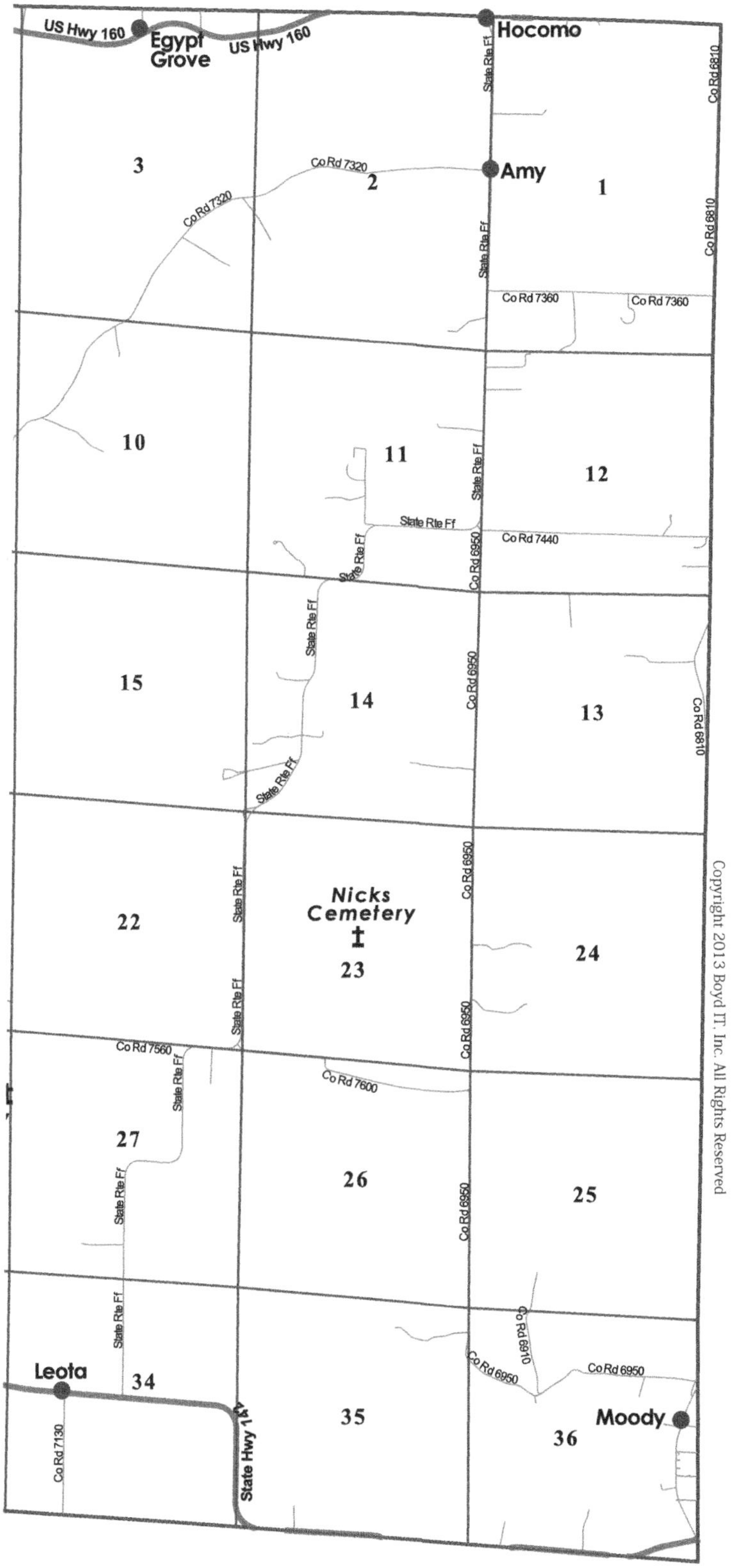

US Hwy 160

Egypt
Grove

US Hwy 160

Hocomo

State Rte Ff

Co Rd 6810

3

Co Rd 7320

2

Amy

1

Co Rd 7320

Co Rd 7360

Co Rd 7360

State Rte Ff

10

11

State Rte Ff

12

State Rte Ff

State Rte Ff

Co Rd 7440

Co Rd 6950

15

State Rte Ff

14

Co Rd 6950

13

Co Rd 6810

State Rte Ff

Co Rd 6950

22

Nicks
Cemetery
‡
23

24

State Rte Ff

Co Rd 6950

Co Rd 7560

State Rte Ff

Co Rd 7600

27

State Rte Ff

26

Co Rd 6950

25

State Rte Ff

State Hwy 19

Co Rd 6910

Leota

34

Co Rd 7130

35

Co Rd 6950

Co Rd 6950

Moody

36

Helpful Hints

1. This road map has a number of uses, but primarily it is to help you: a) find the present location of land owned by your ancestors (at least the general area), b) find cemeteries and city-centers, and c) estimate the route/roads used by Census-takers & tax-assessors.

2. If you plan to travel to Howell County to locate cemeteries or land parcels, please pick up a modern travel map for the area before you do. Mapping old land parcels on modern maps is not as exact a science as you might think. Just the slightest variations in public land survey coordinates, estimates of parcel boundaries, or road-map deviations can greatly alter a map's representation of how a road either does or doesn't cross a particular parcel of land.

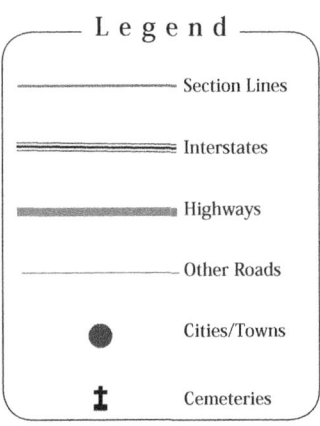

L e g e n d

———— Section Lines

═══════ Interstates

━━━━━━ Highways

———— Other Roads

● Cities/Towns

‡ Cemeteries

Scale: Section = 1 mile X 1 mile
(generally, with some exceptions)

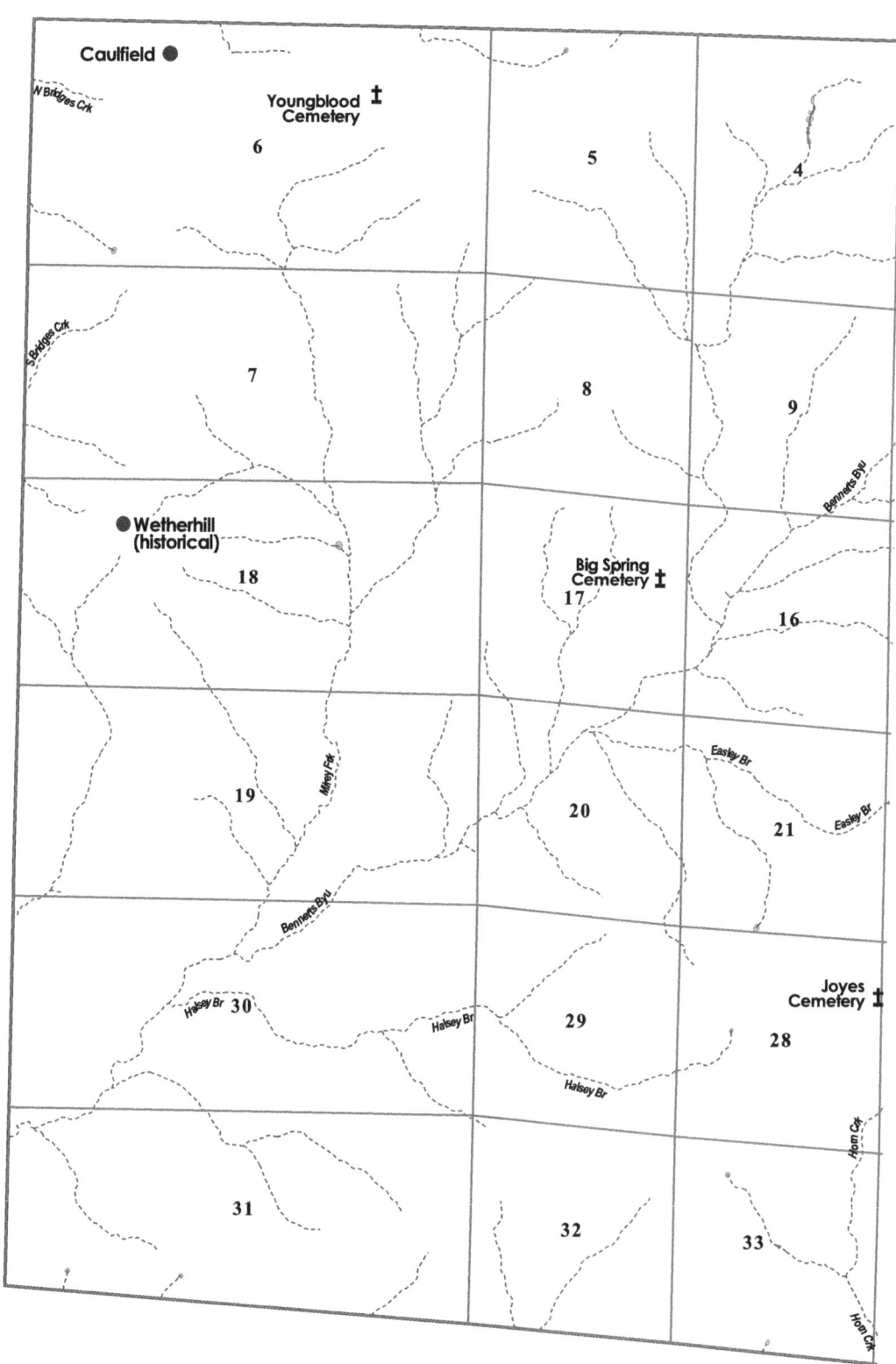

Historical Map

T22-N R10-W
5th PM 22-N 10-W Meridian

Map Group 21

Cities & Towns
Amy
Caulfield
Egypt Grove
Hocomo
Leota
Moody
Wetherhill (historical)

Cemeteries
Big Spring Cemetery
Joyes Cemetery
Nicks Cemetery
Youngblood Cemetery

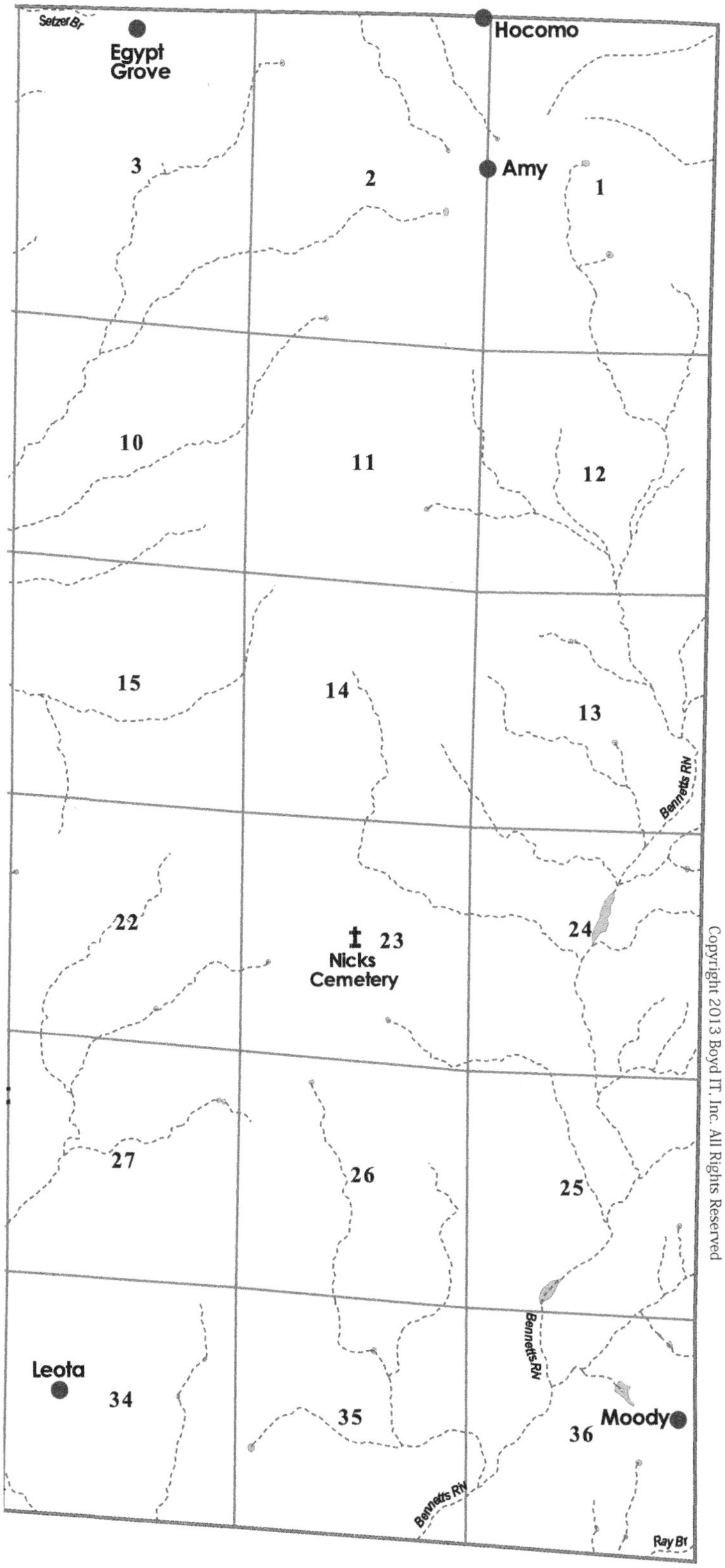

Setzer Br

● Egypt Grove

Hocomo ●

3

2

● Amy

1

10

11

12

15

14

13

Bennetts RN

22

✝ 23
Nicks
Cemetery

24

27

26

25

Bennetts RN

Leota
●

34

35

36

Moody ●

Bennetts RN

Ray Br

Helpful Hints

1. This Map takes a different look at the same Congressional Township displayed in the preceding two maps. It presents features that can help you better envision the historical development of the area: a) Water-bodies (lakes & ponds), b) Water-courses (rivers, streams, etc.), c) Railroads, d) City/ town center-points (where they were oftentimes located when first settled), and e) Cemeteries.

2. Using this "Historical" map in tandem with this Township's Patent Map and Road Map, may lead you to some interesting discoveries. You will often find roads, towns, cemeteries, and waterways are named after nearby landowners: sometimes those names will be the ones you are researching. See how many of these research gems you can find here in Howell County.

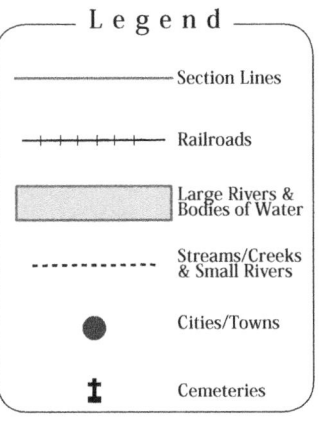

L e g e n d

——————— Section Lines

+–+–+–+–+– Railroads

Large Rivers &
Bodies of Water

- - - - - - - - Streams/Creeks
& Small Rivers

● Cities/Towns

✝ Cemeteries

Scale: Section = 1 mile X 1 mile
(there are some exceptions)

Map Group 22: Index to Land Patents

Township 22-North Range 9-West (5th PM 22-N 9-W)

After you locate an individual in this Index, take note of the Section and Section Part then proceed to the Land Patent map on the pages immediately following. You should have no difficulty locating the corresponding parcel of land.

The "For More Info" Column will lead you to more information about the underlying Patents. See the *Legend* at right, and the "How to Use this Book" chapter, for more information.

```
                        LEGEND
           "For More Info . . . " column
A = Authority (Legislative Act, See Appendix "A")
B = Block or Lot (location in Section unknown)
C = Cancelled Patent
F = Fractional Section
G = Group (Multi-Patentee Patent, see Appendix "C")
V = Overlaps another Parcel
R = Re-Issued (Parcel patented more than once)

(A & G items require you to look in the Appendixes referred
to above. All other Letter-designations followed by a number
require you to locate line-items in this index that possess
the ID number found after the letter).
```

ID	Individual in Patent	Sec.	Sec. Part	Date Issued	Other Counties	For More Info . . .
5840	ANDERSON, James E	18	S½SE	1891-05-05		A7
5841	" "	19	W½NE	1891-05-05		A7
5842	BALL, Gehazi R	32	SESE	1861-07-01		A6 G12
5843	BARGER, John J	13	E½SE	1895-05-28		A7
5844	BARKER, Thomas A	30	W½NE	1910-05-23		A7
5845	BEAN, Horace E	26	NE	1901-03-23		A7
5846	BERRY, James T	24	SESW	1892-03-07		A7
5847	" "	25	W½NW	1892-03-07		A7
5848	" "	25	NENW	1892-03-07		A7
5850	BINGHAM, John S	31	N½SE	1882-03-30		A7
5849	" "	31	S½NE	1882-03-30		A7
5851	BISE, John N	17	S½SE	1873-02-01		A7
5852	" "	20	N½NE	1873-02-01		A7
5853	BISE, W A	28	SWNW	1871-10-20		A1
5854	BISE, William R	20	SESE	1876-06-20		A7
5856	" "	21	S½SW	1876-06-20		A7
5855	" "	21	NWSW	1876-06-20		A7
8322	BLACK, James W	4	E21NE	1901-06-08		A7
5857	BLACK, John	7	NWNE	1877-04-05		A7
5858	BLACK, William C	6	SWSE	1860-09-10		A6
8367	" "	6	S21SW	1860-09-10		A6
8371	" "	7	N21NW	1860-09-10		A6
5859	BRADLEY, Russell	36	SENE	1901-05-08		A7
5861	BRYAN, Mary	19	E½NE	1860-09-10		A6 G25
8366	BURTON, Lemuel J	6	N21SW	1877-06-04		A7
5862	BURTON, Thomas D	20	N½SE	1860-09-10		A6
8362	" "	6	3NW	1861-07-01		A6
8369	" "	6	W22NE	1860-08-01		A1
5863	" "	6	SESE	1860-11-12		A6
8359	" "	6	2NW	1860-09-10		A6
8356	" "	6	1NW	1860-09-10		A6
5864	" "	7	NENE	1860-11-12		A6
5866	CAMPBELL, Hugh N	22	SWSE	1899-02-13		A7
5867	" "	22	SESW	1899-02-13		A7
5868	CAMPBELL, John S	14	N½NW	1903-03-17		A7
8255	CARR, Joseph	1	2NE	1884-11-01		A7
8272	CARRELL, Franklin S	18	S22NW	1891-06-09		A7
8269	" "	18	N22SW	1891-06-09		A7
5869	CARRINGTON, Ben	14	NE	1889-06-22		A7
5870	CARSON, David	12	NENE	1873-06-05		A1
8291	CHERRY, George W	2	1NW	1899-05-12		A7
8292	" "	2	2NW	1899-05-12		A7
8296	CHERRY, Isaac A	3	3NW	1893-12-19		A7
8302	" "	3	W23NE	1893-12-19		A7
8298	" "	3	E22NW	1893-12-19		A7
5873	CLARK, James	33	SESW	1878-06-24		A7

ID	Individual in Patent	Sec.	Sec. Part	Date Issued	Other Counties	For More Info . . .
5872	CLARK, James (Cont'd)	33	SWSE	1878-06-24		A7
8339	CLEMENT, Nathaniel C	5	E21NE	1885-12-19		A1
5874	CLIFFORD, Augustus	12	NWNE	1888-07-03		A1
5875	" "	12	NENW	1888-07-03		A1
8285	COLLINS, John B	19	S22NW	1860-09-10		A6 G54
8282	" "	19	S21NW	1860-09-10		A6 G54
8280	" "	19	N22SW	1860-09-10		A6 G54
5876	" "	20	SESW	1860-08-01		A1
5877	" "	24	NESW	1861-02-09		A1
5878	COLLINS, Lucy C	5	S½SW	1890-12-31		A7
5879	" "	8	N½NW	1890-12-31		A7
5880	COLLINS, Thomas A	19	E½NE	1860-09-10		A6 G25
8354	COLMERY, Robert C	6	1NE	1860-09-10		A6 G56
5881	" "	6	N½SE	1860-09-10		A6 G56
5882	COOPER, George H	9	NW	1891-05-25		A7
5883	COOPER, George W	12	N½SW	1860-09-10		A6
5884	" "	24	N½NW	1860-09-10		A6
8378	" "	7	S22NW	1861-02-01		A1
5885	CRAPO, Francis	10	SESW	1902-10-20		A7
5886	" "	15	N½NW	1902-10-20		A7
5887	" "	15	SENW	1902-10-20		A7
5888	DAVIS, Joseph	12	SENE	1911-12-11		A1
5889	" "	13	SENE	1906-06-30		A1
5890	" "	34	S½SE	1892-08-08		A7 G66
5891	DAVIS, Rebecca	34	S½SE	1892-08-08		A7 G66
8260	DEEMS, George W	1	W21NW	1891-08-19		A7
5892	" "	2	NESE	1891-08-19		A7
8290	" "	2	1NE	1891-08-19		A7
5893	DEJARNATH, Walter F	25	W½NE	1860-09-10		A6
8297	" "	3	E21NW	1861-02-01		A1
5894	" "	3	NWSW	1861-02-01		A1
5895	DENNY, Thomas J	27	SENW	1886-11-19		A1
5896	" "	27	SWNE	1886-11-19		A1
8276	DORRIS, George M	19	N22NW	1888-11-27		A7
8275	" "	19	N21NW	1888-11-27		A7
5897	DORRIS, Othello	17	NWNE	1905-03-30		A7
5899	DUNN, James M	21	N½NE	1882-06-30		A7
5898	" "	21	E½NW	1882-06-30		A7
8316	EASLEY, Francis H	31	S22NW	1860-09-10		A6 G71
5900	" "	4	S½SE	1861-07-01		A6
8320	EASLEY, William W	31	S22SW	1860-08-01		A1
5902	ENO, Eldon C	25	SWSW	1914-10-29		A7
5903	" "	26	E½SE	1914-10-29		A7
5904	" "	36	NWNW	1914-10-29		A7
8315	FEAMAN, Margaret	31	S22NW	1860-09-10		A6 G71
5905	FERGUSON, George W	27	NWNE	1883-06-30		A7
5907	" "	27	NENW	1883-06-30		A7
5906	" "	27	W½NW	1883-06-30		A7
5908	FOLEY, Tillman D	1	SWSE	1907-06-26		A1
5912	FRANK, Samuel	6	N½SE	1860-09-10		A6 G56
8351	" "	6	1NE	1860-09-10		A6 G56
8370	FRIEND, Alexander	6	W23NE	1860-08-01		A1
5917	GABBERT, John P	20	NW	1891-05-25		A7
5918	GADBERRY, John D	28	E½SW	1888-12-08		A7
5919	GADBERRY, Mandy	26	E½SW	1890-01-10		A7
5920	GEYER, John C	15	SWSE	1891-08-19		A7
5921	" "	15	SESW	1891-08-19		A7
5922	" "	22	N½NW	1891-08-19		A7
5923	GIBBS, Jonas G	32	E½NW	1880-11-20		A7
5924	" "	32	W½NE	1880-11-20		A7
5925	GILL, William F	24	SE	1875-05-01		A7
5926	GRAGG, Andrew	26	W½SE	1910-04-14		A7
8360	GRAVES, Delilah	6	2NW	1860-09-10		A6
8357	" "	6	1NW	1860-09-10		A6
8343	GREEN, Emory W	5	E23NW	1888-12-08		A7
5927	GREEN, John	12	SWNE	1875-07-20		A7
5928	" "	12	SENW	1875-07-20		A7
5929	" "	12	W½NW	1875-07-20		A7
5930	GUY, John	26	SWSW	1860-05-02		A6 G103
5931	" "	27	SESE	1860-05-02		A6 G103
5932	HAHN, John J	17	NENE	1877-04-05		A7
5933	" "	17	S½NE	1877-04-05		A7
5934	" "	8	SESE	1877-04-05		A7

ID	Individual in Patent	Sec.	Sec. Part	Date Issued	Other Counties	For More Info . . .
5935	HARDIN, Joseph C	35	E½SW	1895-05-28		A7
8261	HARKINS, Hiram D	1	W22NW	1889-01-12		A7
8257	"	1	3NW	1889-01-12		A7
5939	HARRIS, Mary A	34	NESW	1889-01-12		A7 G107
5937	"	34	NWSE	1889-01-12		A7 G107
5936	"	34	SENW	1889-01-12		A7 G107
5938	"	34	SWNE	1889-01-12		A7 G107
5943	HARRIS, William H	34	NWSE	1889-01-12		A7 G107
5940	"	34	SWNE	1889-01-12		A7 G107
5941	"	34	SENW	1889-01-12		A7 G107
5942	"	34	NESW	1889-01-12		A7 G107
5944	HAWKINS, William H	20	SWSE	1877-05-15		A7
5945	"	29	W½NE	1877-05-15		A7
5946	"	29	NENW	1877-05-15		A7
5948	HEINRICH, Phillip J	29	E½SW	1880-11-20		A7
5947	"	29	W½SE	1880-11-20		A7
5952	HENDERSON, Margaret B	25	SENE	1859-08-01		A8 G114
5951	"	25	NESE	1859-08-01		A8 G114
8310	HOLMAN, James T	31	N22SW	1889-06-22		A7
8258	HOLMES, James	1	E21NW	1879-12-15		A7
5954	"	1	E½SW	1879-12-15		A7
5953	"	1	NWSE	1879-12-15		A7
5955	HOOPER, William A	12	SWSW	1869-10-15		A1
5956	"	13	NWNW	1869-10-15		A1
8344	HOWARD, William	5	W21NE	1859-09-01		A1
5957	"	5	NESW	1859-09-01		A1
8346	"	5	W22NE	1859-09-01		A1
8340	"	5	E21NW	1859-09-01		A1
5958	JARRELL, Bert E	36	NWNE	1910-09-08		A1
5959	JOHNSON, Charles M	27	NENE	1890-08-13		A1
5961	JOHNSON, James M	20	N½SW	1892-06-21		A7
5960	"	20	SWSW	1892-06-21		A7
5962	"	29	NWNW	1892-06-21		A7
5963	JONES, Lizzie	32	SWSW	1877-10-10		A7
5964	JONES, William H	13	NWSE	1895-05-28		A7
5965	"	13	S½SW	1895-05-28		A7
5966	"	13	NESW	1895-05-28		A7
5967	KAY, Alexander	3	SWSE	1904-11-15		A7
5968	KEELE, Abraham M	17	N½SE	1860-09-10		A6
5969	KEIRN, Rebecca	34	S½SW	1892-08-08		A7 G66
5970	KELLY, Loid	25	NESE	1859-08-01		A8 G114
5971	"	25	SENE	1859-08-01		A8 G114
5972	KILLOUGH, John R	8	NWSW	1892-06-21		A7
5973	KILLOUGH, Milton A	29	SESE	1860-09-10		A6
5974	"	32	E½NE	1860-09-10		A6
5975	"	33	SWNW	1860-09-10		A6
5978	"	8	SWSW	1860-08-01		A1
5976	"	8	SWSE	1860-08-01		A1
5977	"	8	NESW	1860-08-01		A1
5979	"	9	SESE	1860-03-01		A1
5980	KRAUSE, John W	13	SWSE	1910-11-25		A7
5981	"	13	NWSW	1861-02-09		A1
5982	KRAUSE, Wilson P	13	SWNW	1860-08-01		A1
5983	LAMBE, William	13	NENE	1892-03-07		A7
8376	LANGLEY, George W	7	S21NW	1888-12-08		A7
8375	"	7	N22SW	1888-12-08		A7
8373	"	7	N21SW	1888-12-08		A7
5984	"	7	SWNE	1888-12-08		A7
5985	LANGLEY, Isaac N	30	SENE	1907-08-23		A7
5986	LAWHORN, Benjamin G	36	NENE	1907-05-10		A1
5987	LAWHORN, James L	36	SWNE	1892-10-17		A7
5988	"	36	SWNW	1892-10-17		A7
5989	"	36	E½NW	1892-10-17		A7
5990	LEFEVER, Mary Ann	6	N½SE	1860-09-10		A6 G56
8352	"	6	1NE	1860-09-10		A6 G56
5993	LEWEY, William P	18	SENE	1898-04-11		A7
8265	"	18	N21SW	1898-04-11		A7
5992	"	18	N½SE	1898-04-11		A7
5994	LEWIS, William B	8	N½SE	1885-08-20		A7
5995	"	9	W½SW	1885-08-20		A7
8333	LINTHICUM, John	4	W22NE	1872-02-05		A1
5996	"	4	N½SE	1871-10-20		A1
8336	"	4	W23NE	1873-04-01		A1

ID	Individual in Patent	Sec.	Sec. Part	Date Issued	Other Counties	For More Info . . .
5998	LOWREY, William P	3	NESW	1890-12-31		A7
5997	" "	3	E½SE	1890-12-31		A7
5999	" "	3	NWSE	1890-12-31		A7
6001	LOY, David	34	N½NE	1877-05-15		A7
6000	" "	34	N½NW	1877-05-15		A7
6002	LOY, George	27	W½SE	1886-04-10		A7 G142
6003	" "	28	W½SW	1877-05-15		A7
6004	" "	29	NESE	1877-05-15		A7
6006	" "	33	NENW	1886-11-19		A1
6005	" "	33	NWNW	1877-05-15		A7
8256	LOY, Martin L	1	3NE	1872-03-15		A7
6007	LOY, Sarah	27	W½SE	1886-04-10		A7 G142
6008	MASON, Charles F	15	N½SE	1892-06-10		A7
6009	" "	15	W½NE	1892-06-10		A7
6011	MASON, James D	10	E½NW	1877-04-05		A7
6010	" "	10	N½NE	1877-04-05		A7
6012	MATNEY, Solomon	35	SE	1885-02-25		A7
8267	MCCALLISTER, Mary	18	N22NW	1860-06-01		A8
8263	" "	18	N21NW	1860-06-01		A8
8311	MCCALLON, Newton F	31	S21NW	1897-08-09		A7
8308	" "	31	N21SW	1897-08-09		A7
6013	MCCOY, Francis M	12	SE	1895-05-28		A7
6014	MCCOY, James	33	SESE	1891-05-25		A7
8361	MCDANIEL, Mary A	6	2SW	1875-05-01		A7
6015	MCELMURRY, Charley E	20	S½NE	1897-08-18		A7
6016	" "	21	W½NW	1897-08-18		A7
6017	MCFADDIN, Isaac	26	SWSW	1860-05-02		A6 G103
6018	" "	27	SESE	1860-05-02		A6 G103
6019	" "	28	N½SE	1859-11-01		A8 G146
6020	" "	28	SWSE	1859-09-01		A1
6021	" "	28	S½NE	1859-11-01		A8 G146
6022	" "	33	NENE	1859-09-01		A1
8289	MCGEE, James A	19	S22SW	1892-01-25		A7
8274	" "	19	1SW	1892-01-25		A7
8293	MIDDAUGH, Charles M	2	3NW	1892-03-07		A7
6025	MILLER, Isaac N	30	NENE	1891-04-17		A1
8273	MILLS, Samuel W	18	S22SW	1885-03-20		A1
8271	" "	18	S21SW	1885-03-20		A1
6027	MONKS, William	11	SENW	1860-08-01		A1
6028	" "	11	NENW	1861-02-09		A1
6026	" "	11	NWNW	1894-09-18		A1
6030	" "	2	SESW	1872-02-05		A1
6029	" "	2	SWSW	1861-02-09		A1
6031	MONTGOMERY, William	29	E½NE	1861-07-01		A6
6034	" "	8	S½NW	1861-02-01		A8
8284	MORELAND, Alexander L	19	S21NW	1860-09-10		A6 G54
8279	" "	19	N22SW	1860-09-10		A6 G54
8287	" "	19	S22NW	1860-09-10		A6 G54
6036	MYRICK, Benjamin F	2	NWSE	1893-12-19		A7
6035	" "	2	N½SW	1893-12-19		A7
8299	NASH, Lavina	3	E23NE	1884-10-11		A1
8294	" "	3	1NE	1881-04-09		A7
8295	" "	3	2NE	1881-04-09		A7
6037	NELSON, Peter D	13	W½NE	1900-08-09		A7
6038	" "	13	E½NW	1900-08-09		A7
6039	NEWBERRY, Cyrus	21	SENE	1860-08-01		A1
6041	" "	28	NWNE	1860-05-02		A6
6040	" "	28	E½NW	1860-05-02		A6
6042	" "	28	NWNW	1860-05-02		A6
6044	NEWBERRY, Edward J	22	S½NW	1890-01-10		A7
6043	" "	22	N½SW	1890-01-10		A7
6045	NEWBERRY, John R	21	SWNE	1892-09-09		A7
6046	NEWBERRY, William B	21	W½SE	1873-02-01		A7
6047	NICHOLAS, Elihu B	29	SENW	1901-10-09		A1
6048	NICHOLAS, Sims	28	SESE	1888-07-03		A1
6049	NICHOLAS, Thomas B	5	NWSW	1859-09-01		A1
8345	" "	5	W21NW	1859-09-01		A1
8327	NICKS, Alfred H	4	E22NW	1860-09-10		A6
8330	" "	4	W21NE	1860-09-10		A6
8321	" "	4	3NW	1859-09-01		A1
8323	" "	4	E21NW	1860-09-10		A6
6050	" "	7	N½SE	1862-10-10		A6
6051	" "	7	SENE	1862-10-10		A6

ID	Individual in Patent	Sec.	Sec. Part	Date Issued	Other Counties	For More Info . . .
8335	NICKS, Samuel P	4	W2NW	1860-09-10		A6
8332	"	4	W21NW	1860-09-10		A6
6052	NORTON, Alexander P	14	NENW	1861-02-01		A1
6053	PALMER, Edward E	25	NWSW	1907-10-11		A1
6054	PARKER, Benjamin H	17	NW	1875-02-15		A7
6055	"	8	SESW	1883-08-13		A1
6058	PERRY, C C	11	W½NE	1876-03-15		A1
6059	PERRY, Christopher	11	NENE	1860-03-01		A1
6060	"	11	SENE	1861-02-01		A1
6061	PERRY, Christopher C	1	W½SW	1884-03-10		A1
6063	PERRY, Levi S	26	NWSW	1891-05-25		A7
6062	"	26	SWNW	1891-05-25		A7
6065	"	27	SENE	1891-05-25		A7
6064	"	27	NESE	1891-05-25		A7
6066	PERRY, Pinkney E	2	S½SE	1901-03-23		A7
8350	PHELAN, Stephen M	5	W23NW	1860-09-10		A6
8347	"	5	W22NW	1860-09-10		A6
8365	"	6	E23NE	1860-08-01		A1
8364	"	6	E22NE	1860-08-01		A1
6070	POWELL, James A	32	NESE	1877-05-15		A7
6071	"	33	W½SW	1877-05-15		A7
6072	POWELL, William L	31	N½NE	1896-06-04		A7
6073	PROFFITT, Andrew J	34	NESE	1888-11-27		A7
6074	"	34	SENE	1888-11-27		A7
6075	"	35	W½SW	1888-11-27		A7
6076	RANEY, George C	10	W½NW	1892-03-07		A7
6077	"	3	S½SW	1892-03-07		A7
6079	RENNER, George F	26	SENW	1895-07-08		A7
6078	"	26	N½NW	1895-07-08		A7
6081	RHOADS, Richard M	29	SWSW	1890-01-10		A7
6082	"	32	NWSW	1890-01-10		A7
6083	"	32	W½NW	1890-01-10		A7
6084	RICE, John W	12	SESW	1914-03-28		A1
6085	RISLEY, Carolile	10	SWSW	1891-06-09		A7
6086	"	9	S½SE	1891-06-09		A7
6087	"	9	SESW	1891-06-09		A7
6088	RISLEY, Enoch W	10	NWSW	1891-06-09		A7
6090	"	9	NESW	1891-06-09		A7
6089	"	9	N½SE	1891-06-09		A7
8312	ROADS, John	31	S21SW	1882-03-30		A7
6094	SCALES, Martha E	15	SESE	1907-05-10		A1
6095	SCALES, Minos W	10	SESE	1890-10-11		A7
6096	"	14	SWNW	1890-10-11		A7
6097	"	15	E½NE	1890-10-11		A7
6099	SCHAFLER, Jacob	10	S½NE	1886-04-10		A7
6098	"	10	NESE	1886-04-10		A7
6100	"	11	SWNW	1886-04-10		A7
6101	SCHALLER, Jacob	33	W½NE	1875-07-20		A7
6102	"	33	SENE	1875-07-20		A7
6103	"	34	SWNW	1875-07-20		A7
8337	SCOGGIN, Turpin G	5	3NE	1860-09-10		A6
8342	"	5	E22NE	1860-09-10		A6
6104	SHERLEY, George W	34	NWSW	1892-06-21		A7
6105	"	34	S½SW	1892-06-21		A7
6106	SMITH, Walker D	29	NWSW	1891-05-25		A7
6107	"	29	SWNW	1891-05-25		A7
6108	"	30	E½SE	1891-05-25		A7
6110	SPENCER, James S	33	SWNE	1860-03-01		A1
6109	"	33	SENW	1860-03-01		A1
8374	STARKEY, Lycurgus	7	N22NW	1890-10-11		A7
6111	STEUART, John W	25	NENE	1882-06-30		A7 C
6113	STEWART, Henry W	25	SESE	1888-11-27		A7 G175
6112	"	25	NWSE	1888-11-27		A7 G175
6115	STEWART, Miranda J	25	NWSE	1888-11-27		A7 G175
6114	"	25	SESE	1888-11-27		A7 G175
6117	STRANGE, Archelaus	31	S½SE	1878-04-05		A7
8305	STRICKLAND, William L	30	N22SW	1906-06-21		A7
6118	STUART, John W	25	NENE	1919-02-01		A7
6119	SUMMERS, Houston	1	E½SE	1891-11-23		A7
8254	"	1	1NE	1891-11-23		A7
6121	THRELKELD, William H	24	S½NW	1891-02-07		A7
6120	"	24	W½SW	1891-02-07		A7
8314	UNGER, Amelia	31	S22NW	1860-09-10		A6 G71

ID	Individual in Patent	Sec.	Sec. Part	Date Issued	Other Counties	For More Info . . .
8319	UNGER, Eli	31	S22NW	1860-09-10		A6 G71
8313	UNGER, Henry W	31	S22NW	1860-09-10		A6 G71
8318	UNGER, Louisa	31	S22NW	1860-09-10		A6 G71
8262	UPTON, Thomas E	18	N21NW	1860-06-01		A8
8266	" "	18	N22NW	1860-06-01		A8
8379	UPTON, William R	7	S22SW	1873-02-01		A7
6122	" "	7	SWSE	1873-02-01		A7
8377	" "	7	S21SW	1873-02-01		A7
6124	VANDERHOEF, Archie O	25	E½SW	1912-09-09		A7
6125	" "	25	SENW	1912-09-09		A7
6123	" "	25	SWSE	1912-09-09		A7
6126	VAUGHN, James M	21	NESW	1893-04-29		A7
8283	VENUS, David A	19	S21NW	1860-09-10		A6 G54
8286	" "	19	S22NW	1860-09-10		A6 G54
8278	" "	19	N22SW	1860-09-10		A6 G54
6127	WARNER, Christian	15	N½SW	1897-11-10		A7
6129	" "	15	SWNW	1897-11-10		A7
6128	" "	15	SWSW	1897-11-10		A7
6130	WARNER, William	10	NESW	1907-06-25		A7
6131	" "	10	W½SE	1907-06-25		A7
6133	WATERS, Caroline Black	28	S½NE	1859-11-01		A8 G146
6132	" "	28	N½SE	1859-11-01		A8 G146
6135	WATERS, Dorsey D	30	W½SE	1877-05-15		A7
6134	" "	30	E½SW	1877-05-15		A7
6138	WATERS, John H	28	S½NE	1859-11-01		A8 G146
6139	" "	28	N½SE	1859-11-01		A8 G146
8303	WATERS, John W	30	1NW	1897-11-10		A7
8304	" "	30	2NW	1897-11-10		A7
6141	WEBB, Doctor F	33	N½SE	1895-05-28		A7
6142	" "	33	NESW	1895-05-28		A7
6140	" "	33	SENW	1895-05-28		A7
6144	WELLINGTON, Matthew H	32	E½SW	1882-06-30		A7
6143	" "	32	W½SE	1882-06-30		A7
8259	WHITNEY, Frank M	1	E22NW	1886-07-20		A1
6145	WIGGINS, Samuel H	24	NE	1882-03-30		A7
6146	WILLIAMS, Elizabeth	32	SESE	1861-07-01		A6 G12
6148	WISEMAN, James R	14	SE	1882-09-30		A7
8270	WRIGHT, Erastus M	18	S21NW	1895-05-28		A7
6149	" "	18	SWNE	1895-05-28		A7
6150	" "	18	N½NE	1895-05-28		A7
6151	WRIGHT, Joseph L	21	E½SE	1891-05-25		A7
6152	" "	22	SWSW	1891-05-25		A7
6153	" "	28	NENE	1891-05-25		A7
8301	WRIGHT, Martha B	3	W22NW	1888-12-04		A7
8300	" "	3	W21NW	1888-12-04		A7
8328	" "	4	E23NE	1888-12-04		A7
8325	" "	4	E22NE	1888-12-04		A7
8306	WRIGHT, Richard N	30	S22SW	1892-03-07		A7
8309	" "	31	N22NW	1892-03-07		A7
8307	" "	31	N21NW	1892-03-07		A7

Patent Map

T22-N R9-W
5th PM 22-N 9-W Meridian

Map Group 22

Township Statistics

Parcels Mapped	:	350
Number of Patents	:	205
Number of Individuals	:	218
Patentees Identified	:	196
Number of Surnames	:	158
Multi-Patentee Parcels	:	22
Oldest Patent Date	:	8/1/1859
Most Recent Patent	:	2/1/1919
Block/Lot Parcels	:	88
Cities and Town	:	2
Cemeteries	:	3

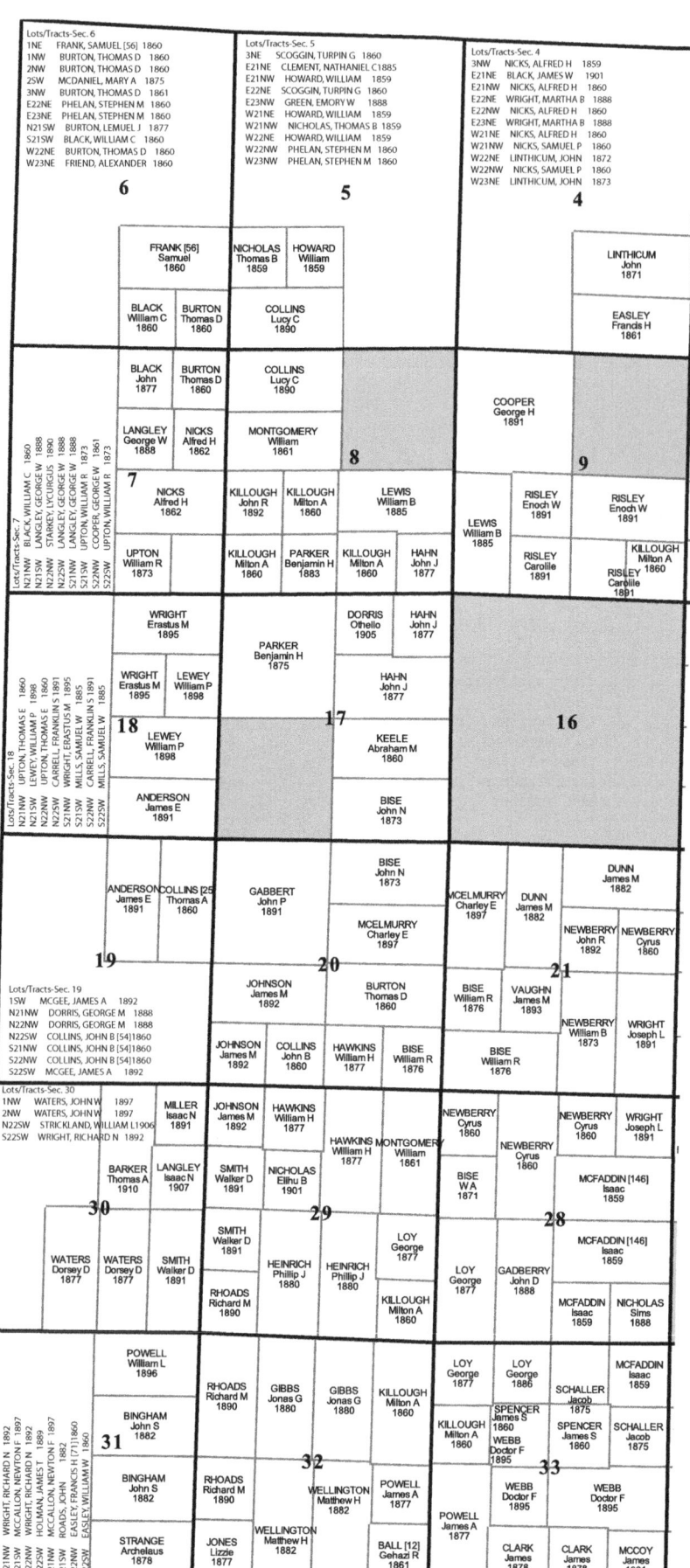

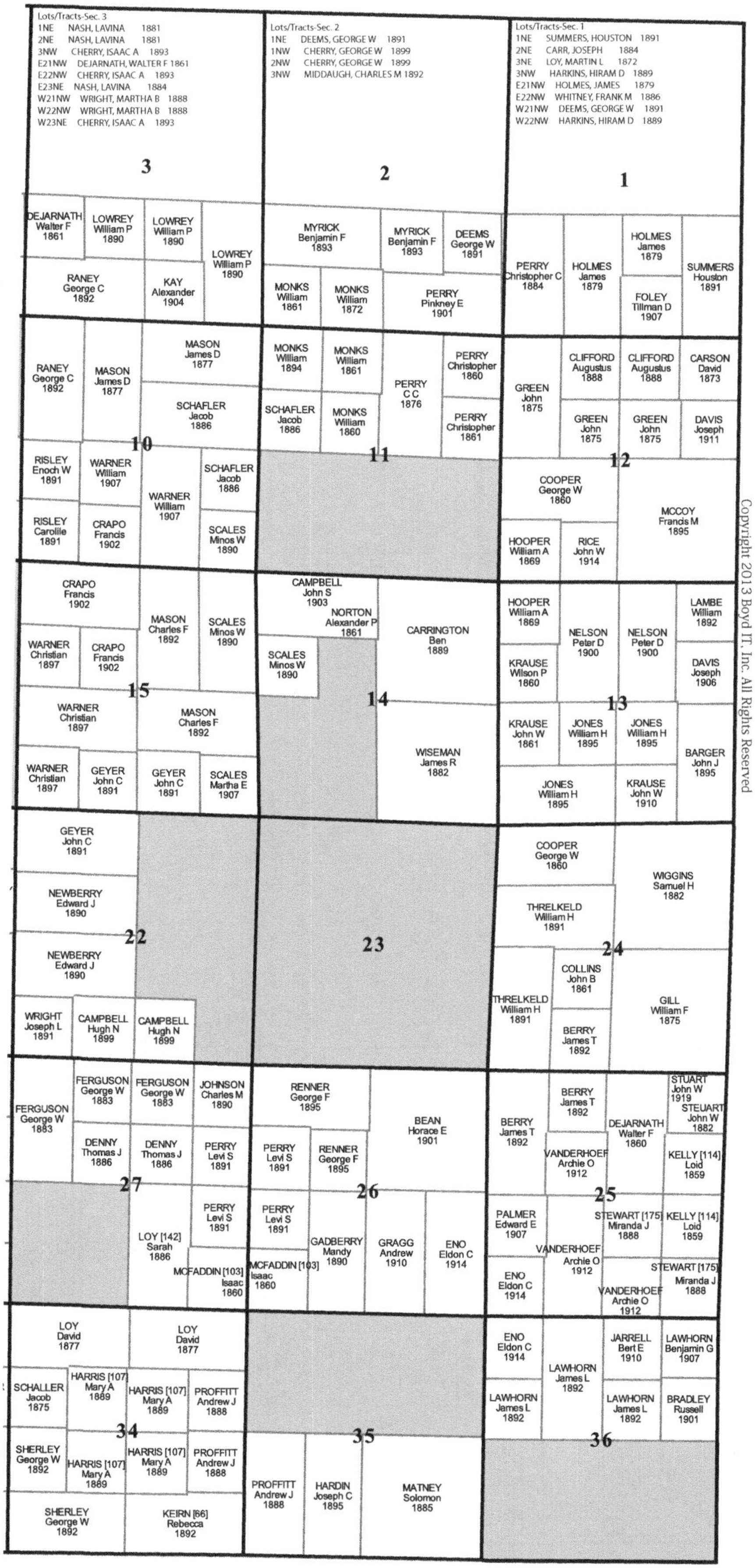

Lots/Tracts-Sec. 3
1NE NASH, LAVINA 1881
2NE NASH, LAVINA 1881
3NW CHERRY, ISAAC A 1893
E21NW DEJARNATH, WALTER F 1861
E22NW CHERRY, ISAAC A 1893
E23NE NASH, LAVINA 1884
W21NW WRIGHT, MARTHA B 1888
W22NW WRIGHT, MARTHA B 1888
W23NE CHERRY, ISAAC A 1893

Lots/Tracts-Sec. 2
1NE DEEMS, GEORGE W 1891
1NW CHERRY, GEORGE W 1899
2NW CHERRY, GEORGE W 1899
3NW MIDDAUGH, CHARLES M 1892

Lots/Tracts-Sec. 1
1NE SUMMERS, HOUSTON 1891
2NE CARR, JOSEPH 1884
3NE LOY, MARTIN L 1872
3NW HARKINS, HIRAM D 1889
E21NW HOLMES, JAMES 1879
E22NW WHITNEY, FRANK M 1886
W21NW DEEMS, GEORGE W 1891
W22NW HARKINS, HIRAM D 1889

Section 3

DEJARNATH Walter F 1861
LOWREY William P 1890
LOWREY William P 1890
LOWREY William P 1890
RANEY George C 1892
KAY Alexander 1904

Section 2

MYRICK Benjamin F 1893
MYRICK Benjamin F 1893
DEEMS George W 1891
MONKS William 1861
MONKS William 1872
PERRY Pinkney E 1901

Section 1

PERRY Christopher C 1884
HOLMES James 1879
HOLMES James 1879
SUMMERS Houston 1891
FOLEY Tilliman D 1907

Section 10

RANEY George C 1892
MASON James D 1877
MASON James D 1877
SCHAFLER Jacob 1886
RISLEY Enoch W 1891
WARNER William 1907
WARNER William 1907
SCHAFLER Jacob 1886
RISLEY Carolile 1891
CRAPO Francis 1902
SCALES Minos W 1890

Section 11

MONKS William 1894
MONKS William 1861
PERRY C C 1876
PERRY Christopher 1860
PERRY Christopher 1861
SCHAFLER Jacob 1886
MONKS William 1860

Section 12

GREEN John 1875
CLIFFORD Augustus 1888
CLIFFORD Augustus 1888
CARSON David 1873
GREEN John 1875
GREEN John 1875
DAVIS Joseph 1911
COOPER George W 1860
MCCOY Francis M 1895
HOOPER William A 1869
RICE John W 1914

Section 15

CRAPO Francis 1902
MASON Charles F 1892
SCALES Minos W 1890
WARNER Christian 1897
CRAPO Francis 1902
SCALES Minos W 1890
WARNER Christian 1897
MASON Charles F 1892
WARNER Christian 1897
GEYER John C 1891
GEYER John C 1891
SCALES Martha E 1907

Section 14

CAMPBELL John S 1903
NORTON Alexander P 1861
CARRINGTON Ben 1889
SCALES Minos W 1890
WISEMAN James R 1882

Section 13

HOOPER William A 1869
NELSON Peter D 1900
NELSON Peter D 1900
LAMBE William 1892
KRAUSE Wilson P 1860
DAVIS Joseph 1906
KRAUSE John W 1861
JONES William H 1895
JONES William H 1895
BARGER John J 1895
JONES William H 1895
KRAUSE John W 1910

Section 22

GEYER John C 1891
NEWBERRY Edward J 1890
NEWBERRY Edward J 1890
WRIGHT Joseph L 1891
CAMPBELL Hugh N 1899
CAMPBELL Hugh N 1899

Section 23

Section 24

COOPER George W 1860
WIGGINS Samuel H 1882
THRELKELD William H 1891
COLLINS John B 1861
THRELKELD William H 1891
GILL William F 1875
BERRY James T 1892

Section 27

FERGUSON George W 1883
FERGUSON George W 1883
FERGUSON George W 1883
JOHNSON Charles M 1890
DENNY Thomas J 1886
DENNY Thomas J 1886
PERRY Levi S 1891
PERRY Levi S 1891
LOY [142] Sarah 1886
MCFADDIN [103] Isaac 1860

Section 26

RENNER George F 1895
BEAN Horace E 1901
PERRY Levi S 1891
RENNER George F 1895
PERRY Levi S 1891
GADBERRY Mandy 1890
MCFADDIN [103] Isaac 1860
GRAGG Andrew 1910
ENO Eldon C 1914

Section 25

BERRY James T 1892
STUART John W 1919
STEUART John W 1882
BERRY James T 1892
DEJARNATH Walter F 1860
KELLY [114] Loid 1859
VANDERHOEF Archie O 1912
PALMER Edward E 1907
STEWART [175] Miranda J 1888
KELLY [114] Loid 1859
VANDERHOEF Archie O 1912
ENO Eldon C 1914
STEWART [175] Miranda J 1888
VANDERHOEF Archie O 1912

Section 34

SCHALLER Jacob 1875
HARRIS [107] Mary A 1889
HARRIS [107] Mary A 1889
PROFFITT Andrew J 1888
SHERLEY George W 1892
HARRIS [107] Mary A 1889
HARRIS [107] Mary A 1889
PROFFITT Andrew J 1888
SHERLEY George W 1892
KEIRN [66] Rebecca 1892

Section 35

PROFFITT Andrew J 1888
HARDIN Joseph C 1895
MATNEY Solomon 1885

Section 36

ENO Eldon C 1914
JARRELL Bert E 1910
LAWHORN Benjamin G 1907
LAWHORN James L 1892
LAWHORN James L 1892
LAWHORN James L 1892
BRADLEY Russell 1901

Loy Section (lower left)

LOY David 1877
LOY David 1877

Helpful Hints

1. This Map's INDEX can be found on the preceding pages.

2. Refer to Map "C" to see where this Township lies within Howell County, Missouri.

3. Numbers within square brackets [ ] denote a multi-patentee land parcel (multi-owner). Refer to Appendix "C" for a full list of members in this group.

4. Areas that look to be crowded with Patentees usually indicate multiple sales of the same parcel (Re-issues) or Overlapping parcels. See this Township's Index for an explanation of these and other circumstances that might explain "odd" groupings of Patentees on this map.

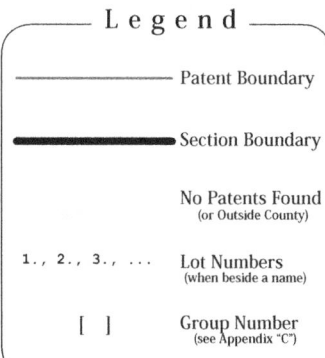

Legend

—————— Patent Boundary

━━━━━━ Section Boundary

No Patents Found (or Outside County)

1., 2., 3., ... Lot Numbers (when beside a name)

[ ] Group Number (see Appendix "C")

Scale: Section = 1 mile X 1 mile (generally, with some exceptions)

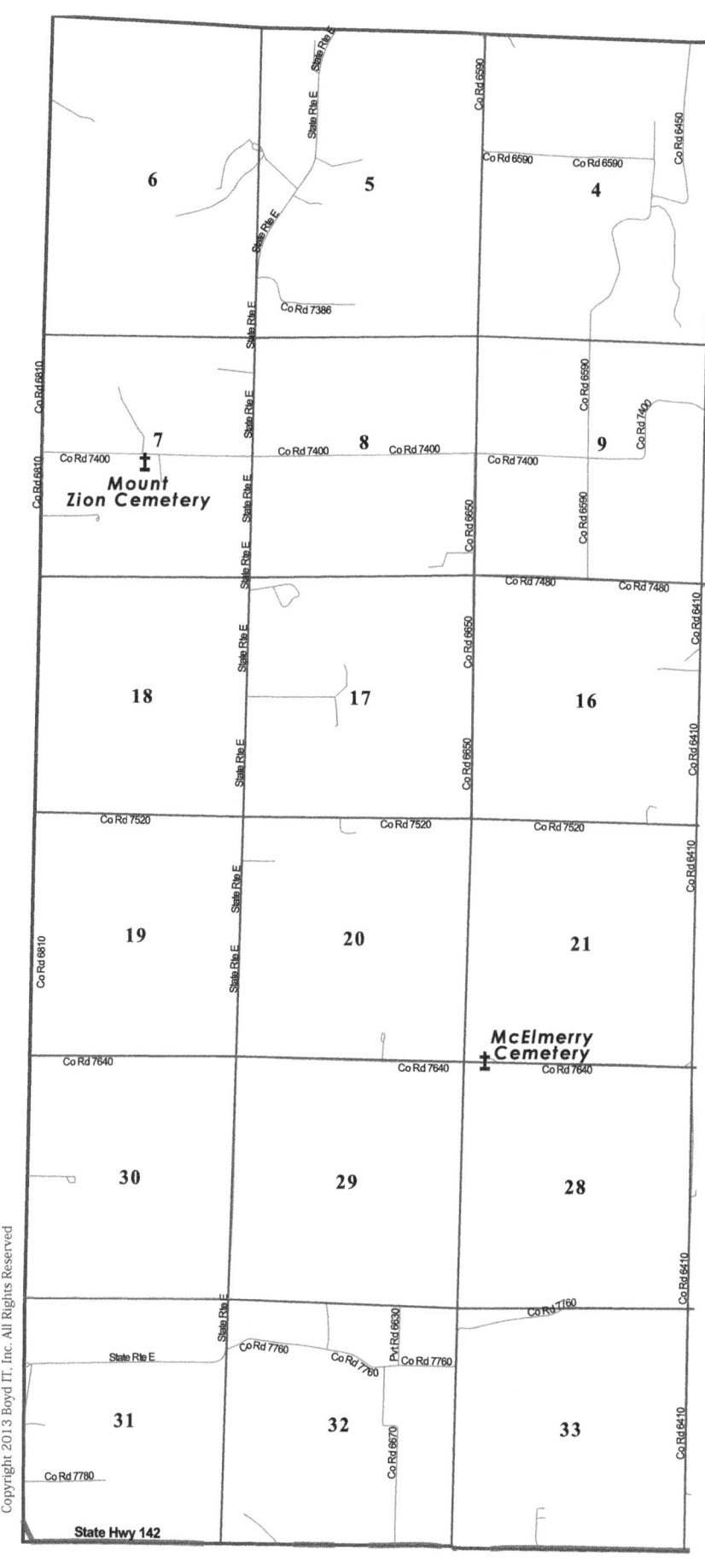

Road Map

T22-N R9-W
5th PM 22-N 9-W Meridian

Map Group 22

Cities & Towns
China
Lebo

Cemeteries
Davis Cemetery
McElmerry Cemetery
Mount Zion Cemetery

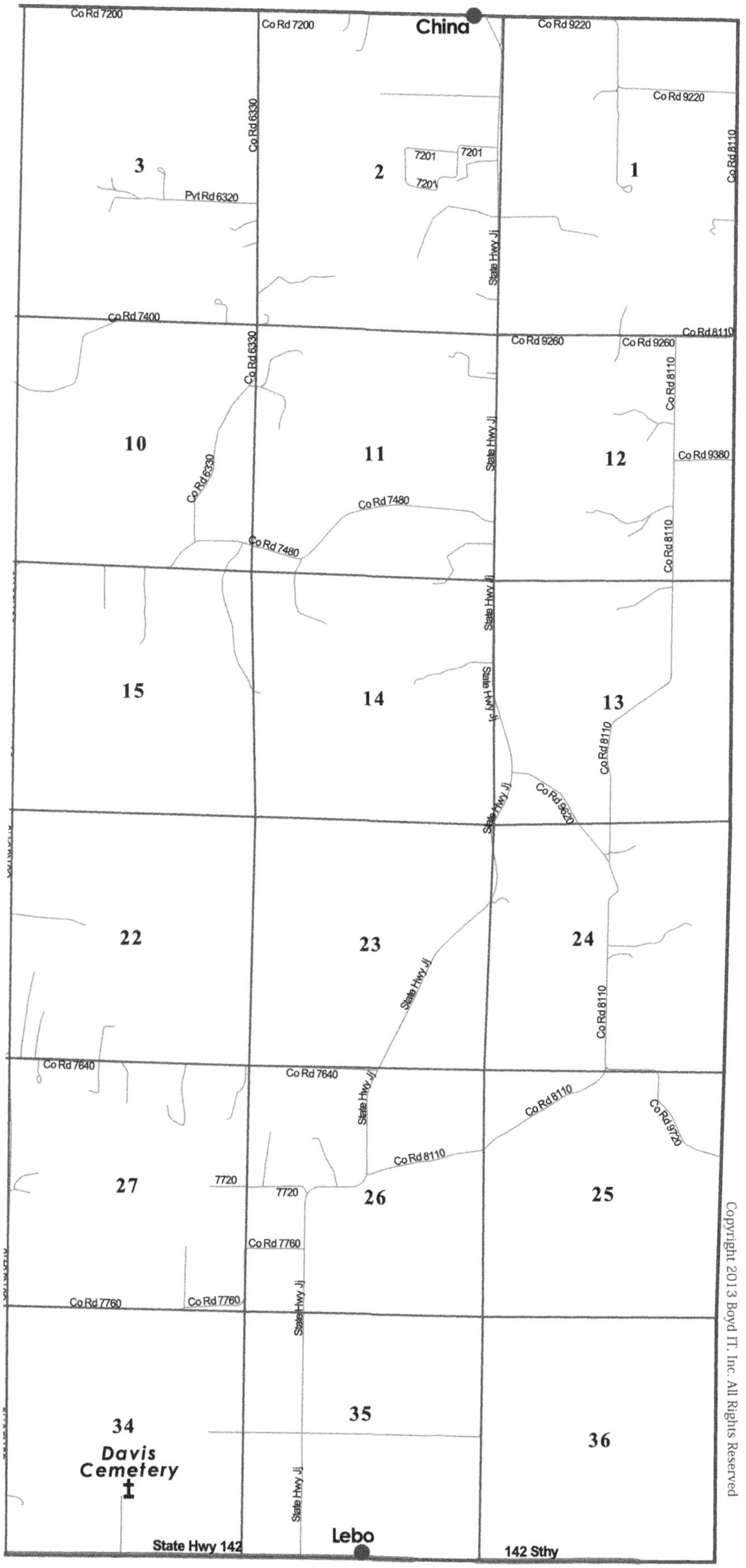

Co Rd 7200

Co Rd 7200

China

Co Rd 9220

Co Rd 9220

Co Rd 6330

Co Rd 8110

3

Pvt Rd 6320

2

7201 7201

7201

1

State Hwy Jl

Co Rd 7400

Co Rd 6330

Co Rd 9260

Co Rd 9260

Co Rd 8110

Co Rd 8110

10

11

12

State Hwy Jl

Co Rd 9380

Co Rd 6330

Co Rd 7480

Co Rd 7480

Co Rd 8110

15

14

State Hwy Jl

13

State Hwy Jl

Co Rd 8110

State Hwy Jl

Co Rd 9620

22

23

State Hwy Jl

24

Co Rd 8110

Co Rd 7640

Co Rd 7640

State Hwy Jl

Co Rd 8110

Co Rd 9720

27

7720

7720

Co Rd 8110

26

25

Co Rd 7760

Co Rd 7760

Co Rd 7760

State Hwy Jl

34

**Davis
Cemetery**

35

State Hwy Jl

36

State Hwy 142

Lebo

142 Sthy

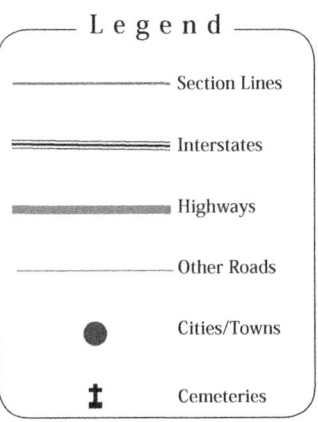

Helpful Hints

1. This road map has a number of uses, but primarily it is to help you: a) find the present location of land owned by your ancestors (at least the general area), b) find cemeteries and city-centers, and c) estimate the route/roads used by Census-takers & tax-assessors.

2. If you plan to travel to Howell County to locate cemeteries or land parcels, please pick up a modern travel map for the area before you do. Mapping old land parcels on modern maps is not as exact a science as you might think. Just the slightest variations in public land survey coordinates, estimates of parcel boundaries, or road-map deviations can greatly alter a map's representation of how a road either does or doesn't cross a particular parcel of land.

Legend

———— Section Lines

═══════ Interstates

━━━━━━ Highways

———— Other Roads

● Cities/Towns

‡ Cemeteries

Scale: Section = 1 mile X 1 mile
(generally, with some exceptions)

Historical Map

T22-N R9-W
5th PM 22-N 9-W Meridian

Map Group 22

Cities & Towns
China
Lebo

Cemeteries
Davis Cemetery
McElmerry Cemetery
Mount Zion Cemetery

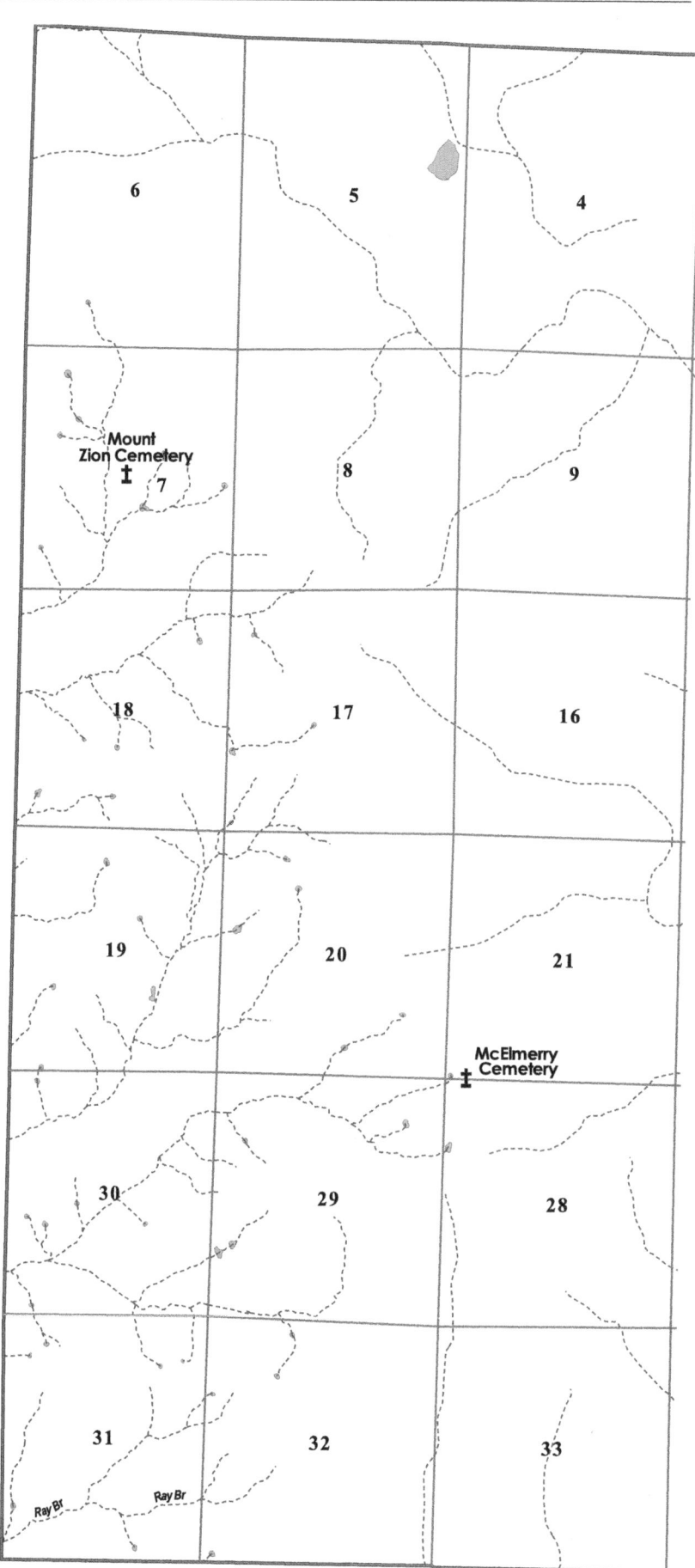

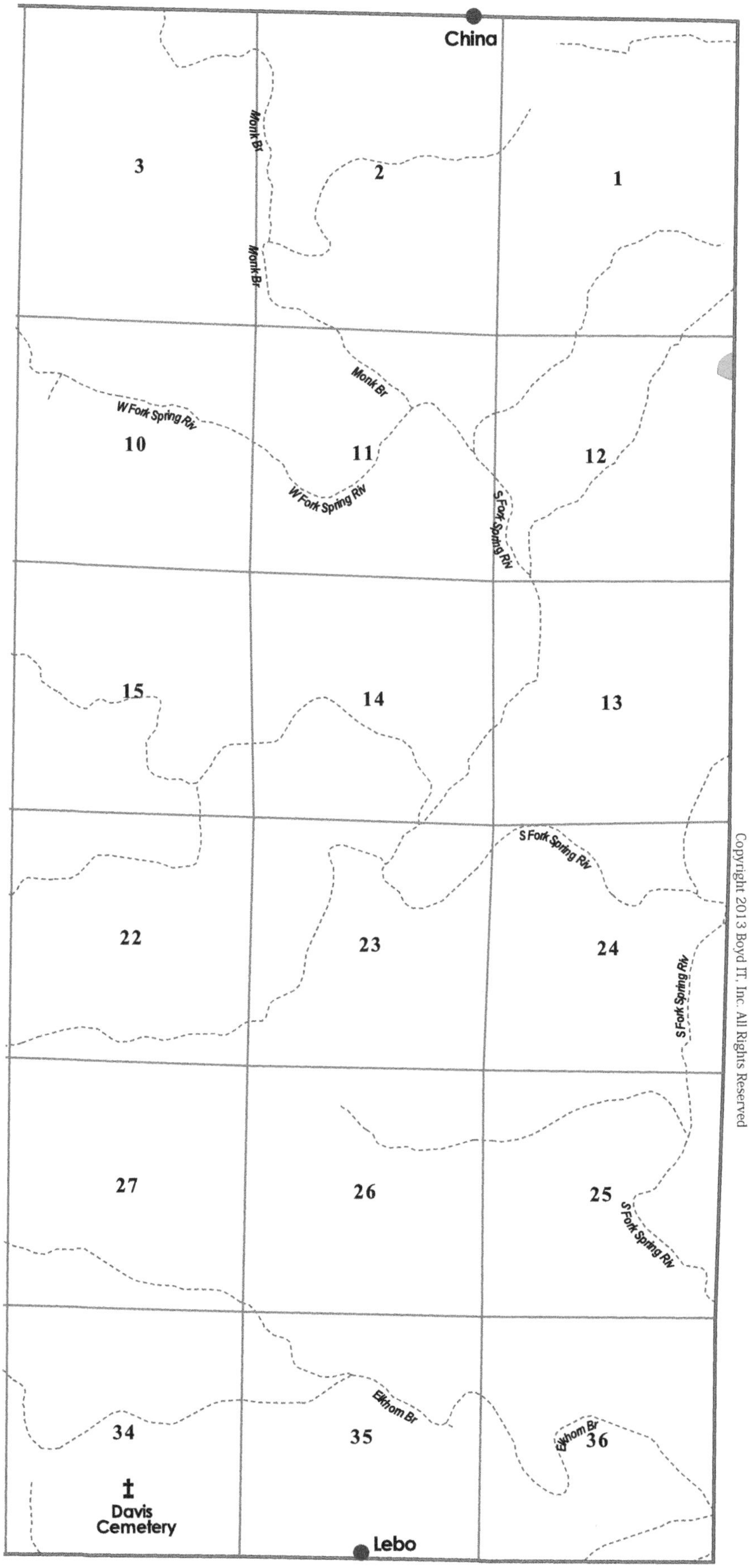

China

3

2

1

Monk Br

Monk Br

Monk Br

W Fork Spring Riv

10

11

W Fork Spring Riv

12

S Fork Spring Riv

15

14

13

S Fork Spring Riv

22

23

24

S Fork Spring Riv

27

26

25

S Fork Spring Riv

Elkhorn Br

34

35

36

Elkhorn Br

‡
Davis
Cemetery

● Lebo

Helpful Hints

1. This Map takes a different look at the same Congressional Township displayed in the preceding two maps. It presents features that can help you better envision the historical development of the area: a) Water-bodies (lakes & ponds), b) Water-courses (rivers, streams, etc.), c) Railroads, d) City/town center-points (where they were oftentimes located when first settled), and e) Cemeteries.

2. Using this "Historical" map in tandem with this Township's Patent Map and Road Map, may lead you to some interesting discoveries. You will often find roads, towns, cemeteries, and waterways are named after nearby landowners: sometimes those names will be the ones you are researching. See how many of these research gems you can find here in Howell County.

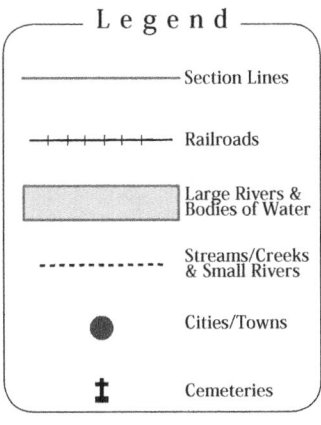

L e g e n d

——————— Section Lines

+–+–+–+–+– Railroads

Large Rivers &
Bodies of Water

- - - - - - - Streams/Creeks
& Small Rivers

● Cities/Towns

‡ Cemeteries

Scale: Section = 1 mile X 1 mile
(there are some exceptions)

Map Group 23: Index to Land Patents

Township 22-North Range 8-West (5th PM 22-N 8-W)

After you locate an individual in this Index, take note of the Section and Section Part then proceed to the Land Patent map on the pages immediately following. You should have no difficulty locating the corresponding parcel of land.

The "For More Info" Column will lead you to more information about the underlying Patents. See the *Legend* at right, and the "How to Use this Book" chapter, for more information.

```
                        LEGEND
            "For More Info . . . " column
A = Authority (Legislative Act, See Appendix "A")
B = Block or Lot (location in Section unknown)
C = Cancelled Patent
F = Fractional Section
G = Group  (Multi-Patentee Patent, see Appendix "C")
V = Overlaps another Parcel
R = Re-Issued (Parcel patented more than once)

(A & G items require you to look in the Appendixes referred
to above. All other Letter-designations followed by a number
require you to locate line-items in this index that possess
the ID number found after the letter).
```

ID	Individual in Patent	Sec.	Sec. Part	Date Issued	Other Counties	For More Info . . .
6154	ABRAMS, Joseph	34	E½NE	1860-05-02		A6
6157	" "	35	W½NW	1858-12-16		A8
6158	ARVIN, John B	32	N½SE	1888-12-06		A7
6159	" "	33	N½SW	1896-01-14		A7
6160	BAILEY, Betsey	15	W½NE	1861-07-01		A6 G8
6161	BAILEY, Campbell R	15	W½NE	1861-07-01		A6 G8
6162	" "	15	E½NE	1861-06-01		A8 G9
6164	BALEY, Betsy	15	E½NE	1861-06-01		A8 G9
8390	BARGER, John J	18	2SW	1895-05-28		A7
8392	" "	18	S21SW	1895-05-28		A7
6166	BATEMAN, James C	36	SESW	1890-01-10		A7
6167	BEHYMER, Anna E	9	N½NW	1892-09-09		A7
8387	BERRY, Lewis G	1	3NW	1879-12-15		A7
8384	" "	1	2NW	1879-12-15		A7
8383	BERRY, Sarah	1	2NW	1879-12-15		A7
8386	" "	1	3NW	1879-12-15		A7
6168	BLACKWELL, Thomas C	8	NWNE	1898-10-04		A7
8425	BRADLEY, Russell	31	N21S2	1901-05-08		A7
8427	" "	31	N22S2	1901-05-08		A7
8430	" "	31	S22N2	1901-05-08		A7
6170	BRENNER, Christian D	20	NENE	1883-08-13		A1
6171	BRISCOE, John H	11	SE	1895-05-28		A7
6172	BRISCOE, Thomas	10	S½SW	1882-06-30		A7
6174	BUNCE, Winfield S	20	SENE	1891-08-19		A7
6173	" "	20	NESE	1891-08-19		A7
6175	" "	21	W½NW	1891-08-19		A7
6176	CANNON, John	25	SWSW	1888-12-06		A7
6177	" "	35	NENE	1888-12-06		A7
6178	" "	36	W½NW	1888-12-06		A7
8450	CARR, Joseph	6	2N2	1884-11-01		A7
6179	CARSON, David	7	N½N½	1873-04-01		A1
6180	" "	7	S½N½	1873-04-01		A1
8426	CHAPIN, Hugh K	31	N22N2	1885-12-19		A1
6181	COCK, Anthony	32	SWSE	1860-11-12		A6
6182	" "	32	E½SW	1860-11-12		A6
6183	COLLIER, Oscar L	8	NESW	1912-11-20		A1
6184	COLLINS, Jesse	14	NWSW	1882-11-10		A7
6185	" "	14	S½SW	1882-11-10		A7
6186	" "	15	SESE	1882-11-10		A7
6188	COOK, William F	17	N½SE	1893-12-19		A7
6187	" "	17	E½NE	1893-12-19		A7
8381	CRANE, Albert	1	1NW	1885-03-20		A1
6189	" "	1	S½	1885-03-20		A1
8380	" "	1	1NE	1885-03-20		A1
6191	" "	10	NENW	1885-05-25		A1
6190	" "	10	NE	1885-03-20		A1

ID	Individual in Patent	Sec.	Sec. Part	Date Issued	Other Counties	For More Info . . .
6193	CRANE, Albert (Cont'd)	11	SW	1885-03-20		A1
6192	" "	11	N½	1885-03-20		A1
6194	" "	12		1885-03-20		A1
6195	" "	13		1885-03-20		A1
6197	" "	14	NESE	1885-03-20		A1
6198	" "	14	N½NW	1885-03-20		A1
6199	" "	14	W½SE	1885-03-20		A1
6196	" "	14	NE	1885-03-20		A1
6200	" "	15	W½SE	1885-03-20		A1
6202	" "	15	SW	1885-05-25		A1
6201	" "	15	NESE	1885-03-20		A1
6205	" "	17	W½	1885-05-25		A1
6204	" "	17	W½NE	1885-05-25		A1
6203	" "	17	S½SE	1885-05-25		A1
8402	" "	2	2NE	1885-03-20		A1
8403	" "	2	3NE	1885-03-20		A1
8405	" "	2	E23NW	1885-03-20		A1
8404	" "	2	E22NW	1885-03-20		A1
8398	" "	2	1NE	1885-03-20		A1
6206	" "	2	SE	1885-03-20		A1
6208	" "	20	W½NE	1885-05-25		A1
6209	" "	20	SESE	1885-05-25		A1
6210	" "	20	W½SE	1885-05-25		A1
6207	" "	20	W½	1885-05-25		A1
6212	" "	21	S½	1885-05-25		A1
6211	" "	21	E½NE	1885-05-25		A1
6213	" "	22	W½	1885-05-25		A1
6214	" "	22	W½SE	1885-05-25		A1
6219	" "	23	S½SE	1885-03-20		A1
6215	" "	23	SENE	1885-05-25		A1
6216	" "	23	SW	1885-05-25		A1
6217	" "	23	NESE	1885-03-20		A1
6218	" "	23	W½NE	1885-05-25		A1
6220	" "	24	E½	1885-03-20		A1
6222	" "	24	E½NW	1885-03-20		A1
6221	" "	24	SW	1885-03-20		A1
6224	" "	25	E½SW	1885-05-25		A1
6225	" "	25	SE	1885-05-25		A1
6226	" "	25	N½	1885-05-25		A1
6223	" "	25	NWSW	1885-05-25		A1
6228	" "	26	NESW	1885-05-25		A1
6227	" "	26	SWSE	1885-05-25		A1
6229	" "	26	N½SE	1885-05-25		A1
6230	" "	26	N½	1885-05-25		A1
6231	" "	27	W½	1885-05-25		A1
6232	" "	28		1885-05-25		A1
6234	" "	29	NESW	1885-05-25		A1
6233	" "	29	N½	1885-05-25		A1
6235	" "	29	SE	1885-05-25		A1
6236	" "	3	SE	1885-03-20		A1
8416	" "	3	W21NE	1885-03-20		A1
8417	" "	3	W22NE	1885-03-20		A1
6237	" "	30	W½SW	1885-05-25		A1
6238	" "	30	SESE	1885-05-25		A1
6240	" "	33	NE	1885-05-25		A1
6239	" "	33	N½SE	1885-05-25		A1
6241	" "	33	SWSE	1885-05-25		A1
6242	" "	33	S½SW	1885-05-25		A1
6243	" "	34	NWSW	1885-05-25		A1
6245	" "	34	NW	1885-05-25		A1
6244	" "	34	W½NE	1885-05-25		A1
6246	" "	35	NWSE	1885-05-25		A1
6247	" "	35	E½NW	1885-05-25		A1
6249	" "	35	W½NE	1885-05-25		A1
6248	" "	35	SW	1885-05-25		A1
6250	" "	36	E½	1885-05-25		A1
6252	" "	36	NESW	1885-05-25		A1
6251	" "	36	E½NW	1885-05-25		A1
8436	CRONER, Floyd J	4	E21NE	1904-11-01		A7
6253	DOTY, Townsand W	8	SENW	1888-12-06		A7
6255	" "	8	W½SE	1888-12-06		A7
6254	" "	8	SWNE	1888-12-06		A7
6256	DUCKERING, Thomas	5	S½SW	1894-05-23		A7

ID	Individual in Patent	Sec.	Sec. Part	Date Issued	Other Counties	For More Info . . .
6257	DUCKERING, Thomas (Cont'd)	8	N½NW	1894-05-23		A7
6258	DUNHAM, Daniel F	34	S½SW	1861-02-09		A1
8432	ELLIOTT, Melville	4	1NW	1866-05-15		A6
8440	" "	4	W21NE	1866-05-15		A6
8446	ENGLE, William E	5	E21NW	1891-05-25		A7
6259	" "	5	NESW	1891-05-25		A7
8391	ENO, Charles W	18	N21SW	1910-07-21		A1
6260	FAULCONER, Mumford N	35	SENE	1891-04-17		A1
8415	FOWLER, Sumner S	3	E23NE	1885-02-25		A7
8385	GALLOWAY, William	1	3NE	1888-07-03		A1
8382	" "	1	2NE	1888-07-03		A1
8445	GOODNO, Edgar E	5	3NW	1888-12-08		A7
8407	GUNDER, Sophia	2	W22NW	1872-04-23		A6
8400	" "	2	1NW	1872-04-23		A6
6261	GUNDY, Henry F	9	SWNW	1891-05-25		A7
6262	" "	9	E½SW	1891-05-25		A7
6263	" "	9	NWSW	1891-05-25		A7
6264	HALL, Leonard	10	NWSW	1860-09-10		A6
6265	" "	10	SWNW	1860-09-10		A6
6266	HAMILTON, William F	10	NWNW	1892-03-07		A7
6267	" "	3	W½SW	1892-03-07		A7
6268	" "	9	NENE	1892-03-07		A7
6274	HYLTON, Roberson H	26	W½SW	1874-01-10		A7
6273	" "	26	SESW	1860-08-01		A1
6276	JARGENSON, George	14	NESW	1871-11-01		A7 G130
6275	" "	14	S½NW	1871-11-01		A7 G130
6278	JARGENSON, Hannah	14	S½NW	1871-11-01		A7 G130
6277	" "	14	NESW	1871-11-01		A7 G130
8397	JARRELL, Bert E	19	S21NE	1910-09-08	Oregon	A1
8428	" "	31	S21NE	1910-09-08	Douglas	A1
8399	JUDD, Wallace A	2	1NW	1872-04-23		A6
8408	" "	2	W22NW	1872-04-23		A6
6281	" "	2	SW	1872-04-23		A6 G134
6282	KENSLOW, James H	34	SESE	1890-06-04		A1
6284	KURSEY, Annis	35	SWSE	1892-03-07		A7
8388	LAMBE, William	18	1N2	1892-03-07		A7
8389	" "	18	2N2	1892-03-07		A7
6285	LAMONS, Malcom	10	S½SE	1860-10-01		A1
6286	LAMONS, Peter J	9	E½SE	1882-09-30		A7
6287	" "	9	SWSE	1882-09-30		A7
6288	LAWHORN, Benjamin G	29	S½SW	1889-01-12		A7
6289	" "	29	NWSW	1889-01-12		A7
6290	" "	32	NENW	1889-01-12		A7
8451	LOY, Martin L	6	3	1872-03-15		A7
8444	MACK, Julia	5	2NW	1891-06-09		A7 G143
8447	" "	5	W21NW	1891-06-09		A7 G143
6292	" "	5	NWSW	1891-06-09		A7 G143
8443	MACK, Tyra	5	2NW	1891-06-09		A7 G143
8448	" "	5	W21NW	1891-06-09		A7 G143
6293	" "	5	NWSW	1891-06-09		A7 G143
6296	MANSFIELD, Robert E	8	SWNW	1896-12-08		A7
6294	" "	8	S½SW	1896-12-08		A7
6295	" "	8	NWSW	1896-12-08		A7
8453	MANZE, Donatus A	7	2S2	1898-12-01		A7
8452	" "	7	1S2	1898-12-01		A7
8429	MATNEY, Joseph L	31	S21SW	1882-09-30		A7
8431	" "	31	S22SW	1882-09-30		A7
6297	MCCRACKEN, Samuel M	5	SE	1888-12-08		A7
6299	MCGINTY, William C	10	SENW	1894-11-30		A7
6300	" "	10	NESW	1894-11-30		A7
6298	" "	10	N½SE	1894-11-30		A7
6302	MILLSAPS, Joseph	22	NENE	1865-02-10		A6 G150
6301	" "	22	W½NE	1865-02-10		A6 G150
6303	MINER, William M	26	SESE	1907-08-09		A7
6304	MONKS, William	22	SENE	1860-09-10		A6
6305	" "	22	NESE	1860-09-10		A6
6306	MYRES, Jacob	34	NESE	1860-08-01		A1
6307	OWEN, Elizabeth	2	SW	1872-04-23		A6 G134
6308	PETER, John	8	E½NE	1891-05-25		A7
6309	" "	8	E½SE	1891-05-25		A7
8449	PIETY, Robert	6	1NW	1892-11-03		A7
6310	" "	6	N½S½	1892-11-03		A7
6311	RANDEL, Amos P	35	NESE	1893-12-19		A7

ID	Individual in Patent	Sec.	Sec. Part	Date Issued	Other Counties	For More Info . . .
6312	RANDEL, Amos P (Cont'd)	36	NWSW	1893-12-19		A7
6315	REAVES, Celia	35	SESE	1861-07-01		A6 G163
6316	"	36	SWSW	1861-07-01		A6 G163
6320	REILEY, Robert	21	E½NW	1892-01-25		A7
6319	" "	21	W½NE	1892-01-25		A7
6321	RICE, Thomas	9	SENE	1860-08-01		A1
6322	ROBINS, Lewis A	3	E½SW	1893-12-09		A1
6323	ROMINE, Abraham	14	SESE	1885-08-20		A7
6324	" "	23	NENE	1885-08-20		A7
6325	" "	24	W½NW	1885-08-20		A7
6326	SCHRIVER, Justina	9	SWSW	1894-11-17		A1
6330	SLOAN, John	22	NENE	1865-02-10		A6 G150
6329	" "	22	W½NE	1865-02-10		A6 G150
6331	" "	35	SESE	1861-07-01		A6 G163
6332	" "	36	SWSW	1861-07-01		A6 G163
6333	SPAHR, Jacob	4	SW	1860-05-02		A6
6334	" "	4	SE	1860-05-02		A6
8423	SPEARS, Joseph	31	N21NE	1860-09-10		A6
6335	" "	32	SENW	1860-09-10		A6
6336	" "	32	W½NW	1860-09-10		A6
6337	SPENCER, Opie A	6	S½SE	1902-08-29		A7
8421	STEUART, John W	30	N22NE	1882-06-30		A7 C
6338	STEVENS, John	33	SESE	1885-05-25		A1
8393	STUART, Alvarado	19	1S2	1905-03-30		A7
8419	" "	30	1N2	1905-03-30		A7
8420	STUART, John W	30	N22N2	1919-02-01		A7
8422	STUART, Miranda J	30	S22N2	1882-09-30		A1
8395	STUART, Silas C	19	2S2	1890-06-06		A7
8394	" "	19	2N2	1890-06-06		A7
8396	" "	19	N21N2	1890-06-06		A7
8411	SUNDBYE, Andrew J	3	2NW	1885-02-25		A7
8410	" "	3	1NW	1885-02-25		A7
8437	SUNDBYE, Anthon	4	E22NW	1892-06-10		A7
8434	" "	4	2NE	1892-06-10		A7
8438	" "	4	E23NE	1892-06-10		A7
6341	TAINTER, Joel E	9	SENW	1873-05-30		A7 G177
6340	" "	9	W½NE	1873-05-30		A7 G177
6339	" "	9	NWSE	1873-05-30		A7 G177
6342	TAINTER, Nancy M	9	SENW	1873-05-30		A7 G177
6344	" "	9	NWSE	1873-05-30		A7 G177
6343	" "	9	W½NE	1873-05-30		A7 G177
6345	TURNER, Tilman P	22	SESE	1860-10-01		A1
6346	VERNON, James H	23	NWSE	1883-08-13		A1
8442	WATKINS, Benjamin R	4	W23NE	1898-12-01		A7
8441	" "	4	W22NW	1898-12-01		A7
8435	" "	4	3NW	1898-12-01		A7
8412	WINSTRAN, Niles J	3	3NW	1892-01-05		A7
8418	" "	3	W23NE	1892-01-05		A7
8409	WINSTRAN, Nils J	2	W23NW	1883-08-13		A1
8414	" "	3	E22NE	1883-08-13		A1
8413	" "	3	E21NE	1883-08-13		A1
6347	WIRE, James P	34	W½SE	1885-12-19		A7
6348	" "	34	NESW	1885-12-19		A7
6350	WYATT, Buford J	22	W½NE	1865-02-10		A6 G150
6349	" "	22	NENE	1865-02-10		A6 G150
6351	WYATT, Eliza J	22	NENE	1865-02-10		A6 G150
6352	" "	22	W½NE	1865-02-10		A6 G150
6354	WYATT, Francis H	22	NENE	1865-02-10		A6 G150
6353	" "	22	W½NE	1865-02-10		A6 G150
6356	WYATT, George W	22	W½NE	1865-02-10		A6 G150
6355	" "	22	NENE	1865-02-10		A6 G150
6358	WYATT, Marian M	22	W½NE	1865-02-10		A6 G150
6357	" "	22	NENE	1865-02-10		A6 G150

Patent Map

T22-N R8-W
5th PM 22-N 8-W Meridian

Map Group 23

Township Statistics

Parcels Mapped	:	226
Number of Patents	:	118
Number of Individuals	:	112
Patentees Identified	:	97
Number of Surnames	:	89
Multi-Patentee Parcels	:	15
Oldest Patent Date	:	12/16/1858
Most Recent Patent	:	11/20/1912
Block/Lot Parcels	:	63
Cities and Town	:	1
Cemeteries	:	0

Lots/Tracts-Sec. 6
1NW PIETY, ROBERT 1892
2N2 CARR, JOSEPH 1884
3 LOY, MARTIN L 1872

Lots/Tracts-Sec. 5
2NW MACK, JULIA [143] 1891
3NW GOODNO, EDGAR E 1888
E21NW ENGLE, WILLIAM E 1891
W21NW MACK, JULIA [143] 1891

Lots/Tracts-Sec. 4
1NW ELLIOTT, MELVILLE 1866
2NE SUNDBYE, ANTHON 1892
3NW WATKINS, BENJAMIN R 1898
E21NE CRONER, FLOYD J 1904
E22NW SUNDBYE, ANTHON 1892
E23NE SUNDBYE, ANTHON 1892
W21NE ELLIOTT, MELVILLE 1866
W22NW WATKINS, BENJAMIN R 1898
W23NE WATKINS, BENJAMIN R 1898

Section 6
PIETY Robert 1892
SPENCER Opie A 1902
CARSON David 1873
CARSON David 1873

Section 5
MACK [143] Julia 1891
ENGLE William E 1891
DUCKERING Thomas 1894
MCCRACKEN Samuel M 1888
DUCKERING Thomas 1894
BLACKWELL Thomas C 1898

Section 4
SPAHR Jacob 1860
SPAHR Jacob 1860
BEHYMER Anna E 1892
HAMILTON William F 1892

Section 7
Lots/Tracts-Sec. 7
1S2 MANZE, DONATUS A 1898
2S2 MANZE, DONATUS A 1898

MANSFIELD Robert E 1896
MANSFIELD Robert E 1896
MANSFIELD Robert E 1896

Section 8
DOTY Townsand W 1888
DOTY Townsand W 1888
COLLIER Oscar L 1912
DOTY Townsand W 1888
PETER John 1891
PETER John 1891

Section 9
GUNDY Henry F 1891
TAINTER [177] Nancy M 1873
GUNDY Henry F 1891
GUNDY Henry F 1891
SCHRIVER Justina 1894
TAINTER [177] Nancy M 1873
RICE Thomas 1860
TAINTER [177] Nancy M 1873
LAMONS Peter J 1882
LAMONS Peter J 1882

Section 18
Lots/Tracts-Sec. 18
1N2 LAMBE, WILLIAM 1892
2N2 LAMBE, WILLIAM 1892
2SW BARGER, JOHN J 1895
N21SW ENO, CHARLES W 1910
S21SW BARGER, JOHN J 1895

Section 17
CRANE Albert 1885
CRANE Albert 1885
COOK William F 1893
COOK William F 1893
CRANE Albert 1885

Section 16

Section 19
Lots/Tracts-Sec. 19
1S2 STUART, ALVARADO 1905
2N2 STUART, SILAS C 1890
2S2 STUART, SILAS C 1890
N21N2 STUART, SILAS C 1890
S21NE JARRELL, BERT E 1910

Section 20
CRANE Albert 1885
CRANE Albert 1885
BRENNER Christian D 1883
BUNCE Winfield S 1891
BUNCE Winfield S 1891
CRANE Albert 1885
CRANE Albert 1885

Section 21
BUNCE Winfield S 1891
REILEY Robert 1892
REILEY Robert 1892
CRANE Albert 1885
CRANE Albert 1885

Section 30
Lots/Tracts-Sec. 30
1N2 STUART, ALVARADO 1905
N22NE STUART, JOHN W 1919
N22N2 STUART, JOHN W 1882
S22N2 STUART, MIRANDA J 1882

CRANE Albert 1885
CRANE Albert 1885

Section 29
LAWHORN Benjamin G 1889
CRANE Albert 1885
CRANE Albert 1885
CRANE Albert 1885
LAWHORN Benjamin G 1889

Section 28
CRANE Albert 1885
CRANE Albert 1885

Section 31
Lots/Tracts-Sec. 31
N21NE SPEARS, JOSEPH 1860
N21S2 BRADLEY, RUSSELL 1901
N22N2 CHAPIN, HUGH K 1885
S21NE BRADLEY, RUSSELL 1901
S21SW JARRELL, BERT E 1910
S22N2 MATNEY, JOSEPH L 1882
S22S2 BRADLEY, RUSSELL 1901
S22SW MATNEY, JOSEPH L 1882

Section 32
SPEARS Joseph 1860
SPEARS Joseph 1860
LAWHORN Benjamin G 1889
COCK Anthony 1860
COCK Anthony 1860
ARVIN John B 1888

Section 33
ARVIN John B 1896
CRANE Albert 1885
CRANE Albert 1885
CRANE Albert 1885
STEVENS John 1885

Lots/Tracts-Sec. 3
1NW   SUNDBYE, ANDREW J   1885
2NW   SUNDBYE, ANDREW J   1885
3NW   WINSTRAN, NILES J   1892
E21NE WINSTRAN, NILS J   1883
E22NE WINSTRAN, NILS J   1883
E23NE FOWLER, SUMNER S   1885
W21NE CRANE, ALBERT   1885
W22NE CRANE, ALBERT   1885
W23NE WINSTRAN, NILES J   1892

Lots/Tracts-Sec. 2
1NE   CRANE, ALBERT   1885
1NW   JUDD, WALLACE A   1872
2NE   CRANE, ALBERT   1885
3NE   CRANE, ALBERT   1885
E22NW CRANE, ALBERT   1885
E23NW CRANE, ALBERT   1885
W22NW JUDD, WALLACE A   1872
W23NW WINSTRAN, NILES J   1883

Lots/Tracts-Sec. 1
1NE   CRANE, ALBERT   1885
1NW   CRANE, ALBERT   1885
2NE   GALLOWAY, WILLIAM   1888
2NW   BERRY, SARAH   1879
3NE   GALLOWAY, WILLIAM   1888
3NW   BERRY, SARAH   1879

3

2

1

HAMILTON
William F
1892

ROBINS
Lewis A
1893

CRANE
Albert
1885

JUDD [134]
Wallace A
1872

CRANE
Albert
1885

CRANE
Albert
1885

HAMILTON
William F
1892

CRANE
Albert
1885

CRANE
Albert
1885

CRANE
Albert
1885

CRANE
Albert
1885

HALL
Leonard
1860

MCGINTY
William C
1894

10

11

12

HALL
Leonard
1860

MCGINTY
William C
1894

MCGINTY
William C
1894

CRANE
Albert
1885

BRISCOE
John H
1895

CRANE
Albert
1885

BRISCOE
Thomas
1882

LAMONS
Malcom
1860

CRANE
Albert
1885

BAILEY [8]
Campbell R
1861

BAILEY [9]
Campbell R
1861

CRANE
Albert
1885

CRANE
Albert
1885

JARGENSON [130]
Hannah
1871

15

14

13

CRANE
Albert
1885

CRANE
Albert
1885

COLLINS
Jesse
1882

JARGENSON [130]
Hannah
1871

CRANE
Albert
1885

CRANE
Albert
1885

CRANE
Albert
1885

CRANE
Albert
1885

COLLINS
Jesse
1882

COLLINS
Jesse
1882

ROMINE
Abraham
1885

SLOAN [150]
John
1865

ROMINE
Abraham
1885

CRANE
Albert
1885

SLOAN [150]
John
1865

CRANE
Albert
1885

ROMINE
Abraham
1885

CRANE
Albert
1885

MONKS
William
1860

CRANE
Albert
1885

CRANE
Albert
1885

22

23

24

MONKS
William
1860

VERNON
James H
1883

CRANE
Albert
1885

CRANE
Albert
1885

CRANE
Albert
1885

CRANE
Albert
1885

CRANE
Albert
1885

TURNER
Tilman P
1860

CRANE
Albert
1885

CRANE
Albert
1885

CRANE
Albert
1885

CRANE
Albert
1885

27

26

25

CRANE
Albert
1885

CRANE
Albert
1885

CRANE
Albert
1885

HYLTON
Roberson H
1874

CRANE
Albert
1885

CRANE
Albert
1885

HYLTON
Roberson H
1860

CRANE
Albert
1885

MINER
William M
1907

CANNON
John
1888

CANNON
John
1888

CRANE
Albert
1885

CRANE
Albert
1885

ABRAMS
Joseph
1860

ABRAMS
Joseph
1858

CRANE
Albert
1885

CRANE
Albert
1885

CANNON
John
1888

CRANE
Albert
1885

34

35

36

CRANE
Albert
1885

WIRE
James P
1885

MYRES
Jacob
1860

FAULCONER
Mumford N
1891

CRANE
Albert
1885

CRANE
Albert
1885

WIRE
James P
1885

CRANE
Albert
1885

CRANE
Albert
1885

RANDEL
Amos P
1893

RANDEL
Amos P
1893

CRANE
Albert
1885

DUNHAM
Daniel F
1861

KENSLOW
James H
1890

KURSEY
Annis
1892

SLOAN [163]
John
1861

SLOAN [163]
John
1861

BATEMAN
James C
1890

Copyright 2013 Boyd IT, Inc. All Rights Reserved

Helpful Hints

1. This Map's INDEX can be found on the preceding pages.

2. Refer to Map "C" to see where this Township lies within Howell County, Missouri.

3. Numbers within square brackets [ ] denote a multi-patentee land parcel (multi-owner). Refer to Appendix "C" for a full list of members in this group.

4. Areas that look to be crowded with Patentees usually indicate multiple sales of the same parcel (Re-issues) or Overlapping parcels. See this Township's Index for an explanation of these and other circumstances that might explain "odd" groupings of Patentees on this map.

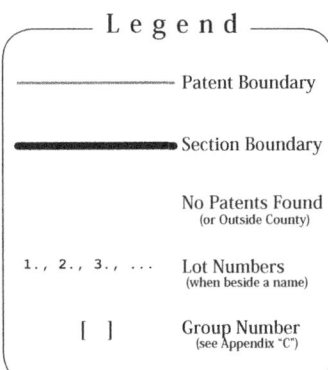

Legend

———————— Patent Boundary

━━━━━━━━ Section Boundary

No Patents Found
(or Outside County)

1., 2., 3., ...   Lot Numbers
(when beside a name)

[ ]   Group Number
(see Appendix "C")

Scale: Section = 1 mile X 1 mile
(generally, with some exceptions)

Road Map

T22-N R8-W
5th PM 22-N 8-W Meridian

Map Group 23

Cities & Towns
Mott (historical)

Cemeteries
None

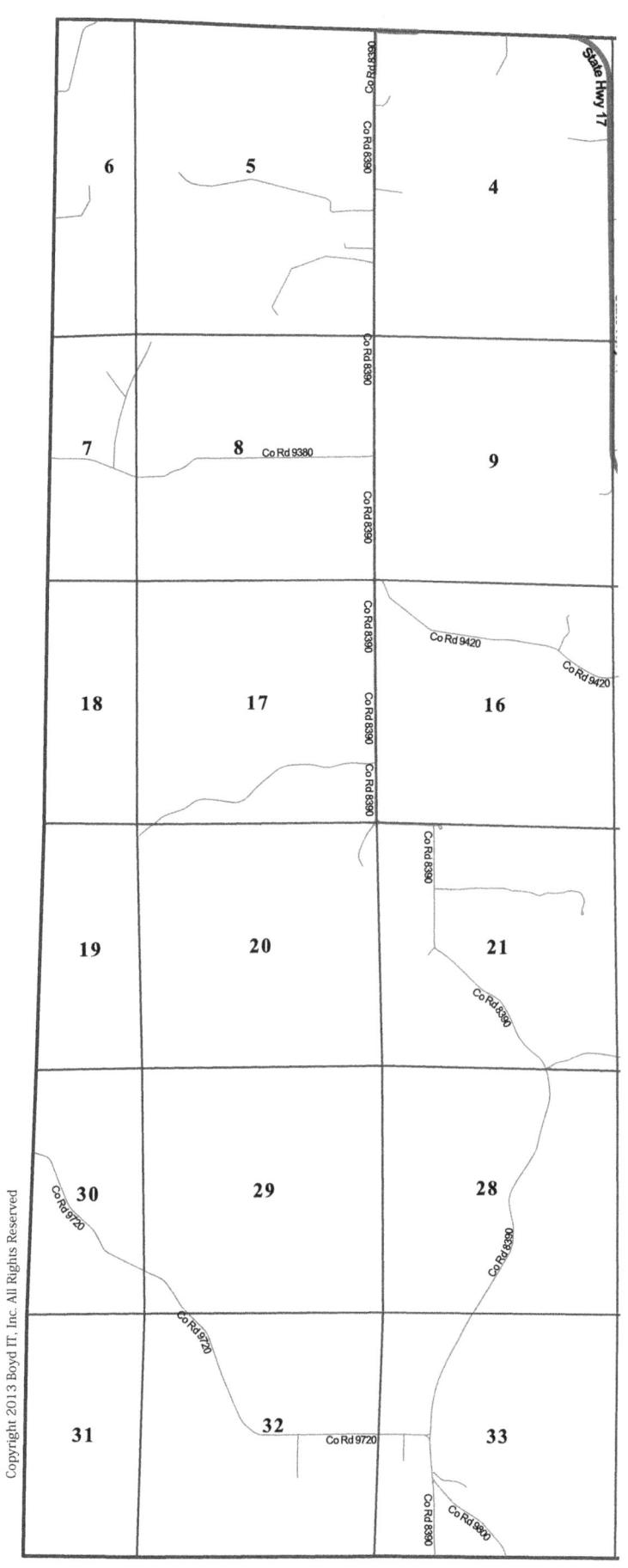

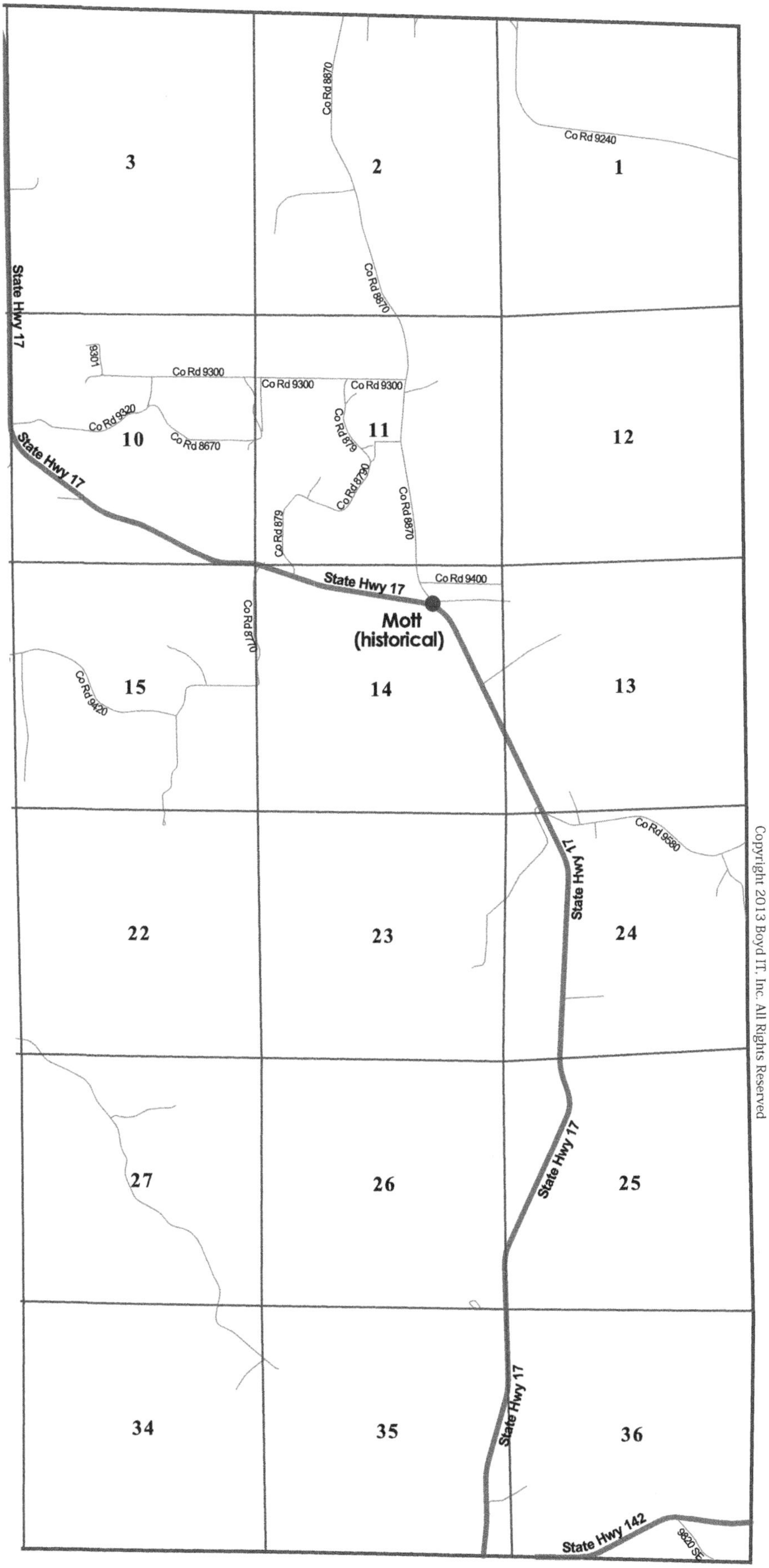

3

2

Co Rd 8870

Co Rd 9240

1

Co Rd 8870

State Hwy 17

9301

Co Rd 9300

Co Rd 9300

Co Rd 9300

10

Co Rd 9320

Co Rd 8670

11

Co Rd 879

Co Rd 8790

Co Rd 8870

12

State Hwy 17

State Hwy 17

Co Rd 9400

Mott
(historical)

Co Rd 870

15

Co Rd 9420

14

13

22

23

State Hwy 17

Co Rd 9580

24

27

26

State Hwy 17

25

State Hwy 17

34

35

State Hwy 17

36

State Hwy 142

9800 SE

Helpful Hints

1. This road map has a number of uses, but primarily it is to help you: a) find the present location of land owned by your ancestors (at least the general area), b) find cemeteries and city-centers, and c) estimate the route/roads used by Census-takers & tax-assessors.

2. If you plan to travel to Howell County to locate cemeteries or land parcels, please pick up a modern travel map for the area before you do. Mapping old land parcels on modern maps is not as exact a science as you might think. Just the slightest variations in public land survey coordinates, estimates of parcel boundaries, or road-map deviations can greatly alter a map's representation of how a road either does or doesn't cross a particular parcel of land.

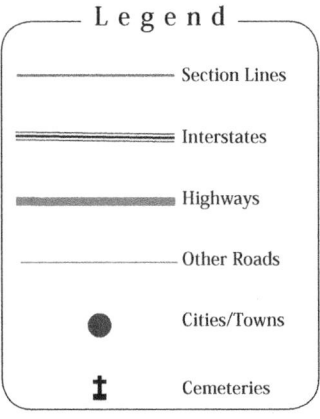

Legend

———— Section Lines

═══ Interstates

━━━ Highways

——— Other Roads

● Cities/Towns

† Cemeteries

Scale: Section = 1 mile X 1 mile
(generally, with some exceptions)

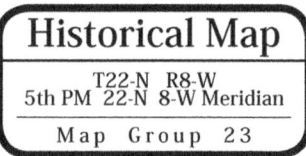

Historical Map

T22-N R8-W
5th PM 22-N 8-W Meridian

Map Group 23

Cities & Towns

Mott (historical)

Cemeteries

None

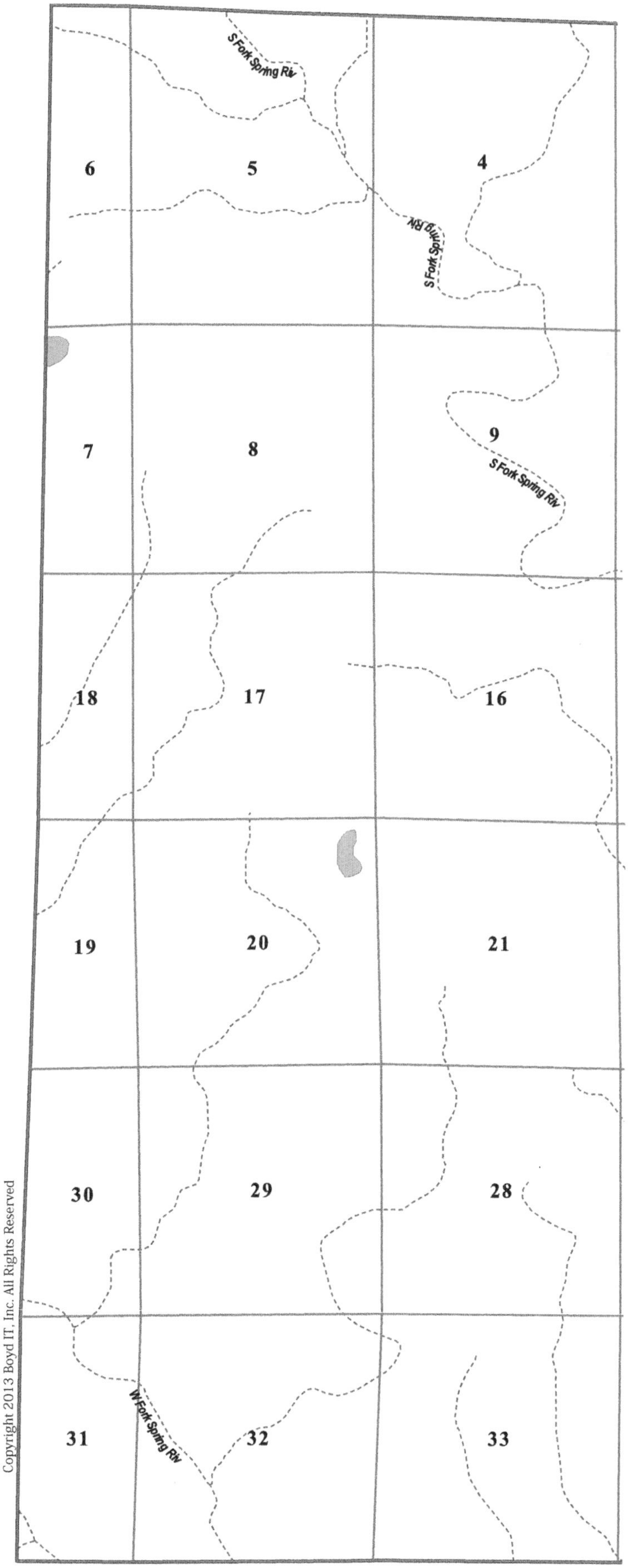

S Fork Spring Riv
6
5
4
S Fork Spring Riv
7
8
9
S Fork Spring Riv
18
17
16
19
20
21
30
29
28
31
W Fork Spring Riv
32
33

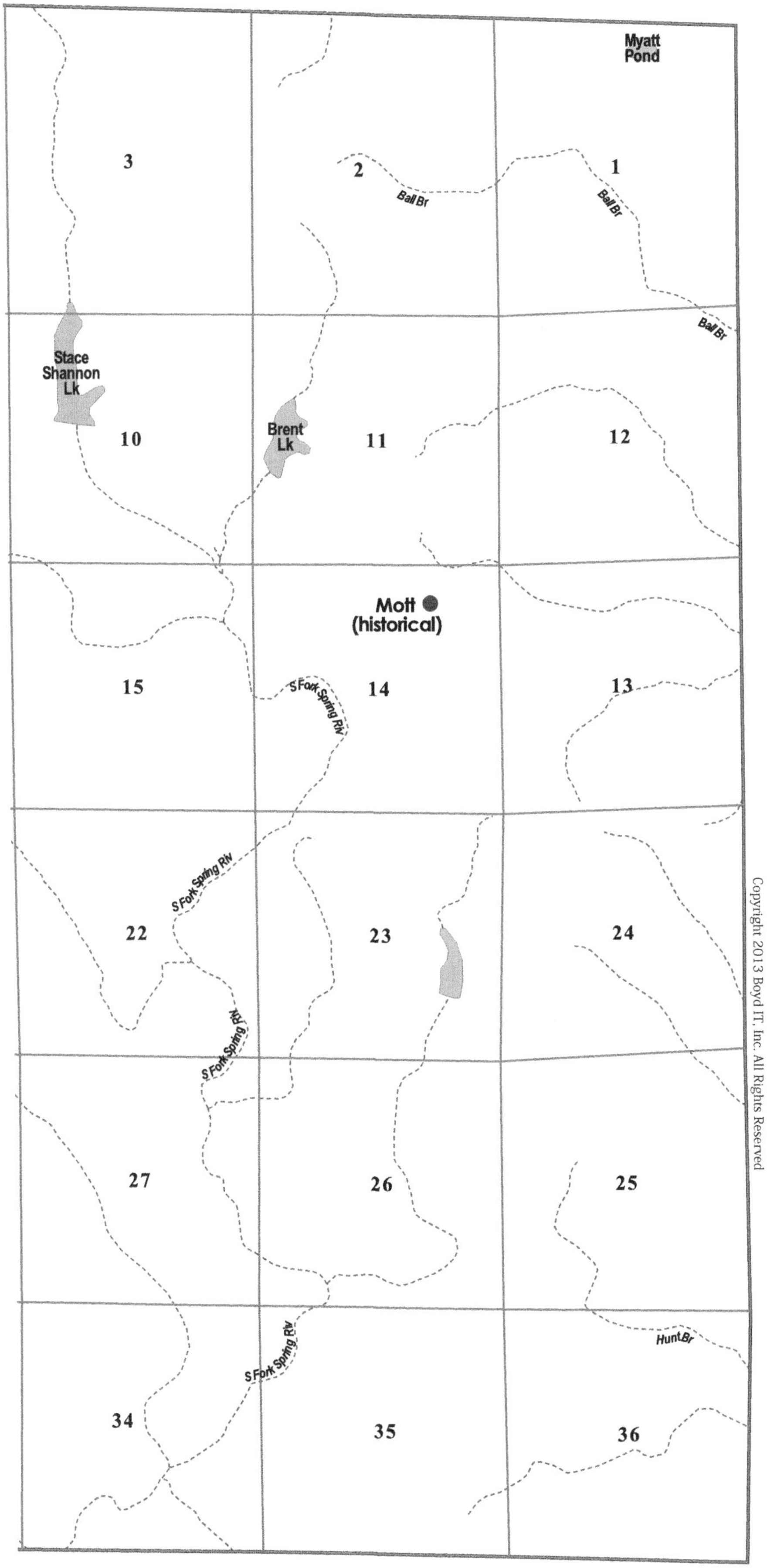

3

2

Ball Br

1

Ball Br

Myatt
Pond

Ball Br

Stace
Shannon
Lk

10

Brent
Lk

11

12

15

Mott ●
(historical)

14

S Fork Spring Riv

13

22

S Fork Spring Riv

23

24

S Fork Spring Riv

27

26

25

S Fork Spring Riv

34

35

36

Hunt Br

Helpful Hints

1. This Map takes a different look at the same Congressional Township displayed in the preceding two maps. It presents features that can help you better envision the historical development of the area: a) Water-bodies (lakes & ponds), b) Water-courses (rivers, streams, etc.), c) Railroads, d) City/ town center-points (where they were oftentimes located when first settled), and e) Cemeteries.

2. Using this "Historical" map in tandem with this Township's Patent Map and Road Map, may lead you to some interesting discoveries. You will often find roads, towns, cemeteries, and waterways are named after nearby landowners: sometimes those names will be the ones you are researching. See how many of these research gems you can find here in Howell County.

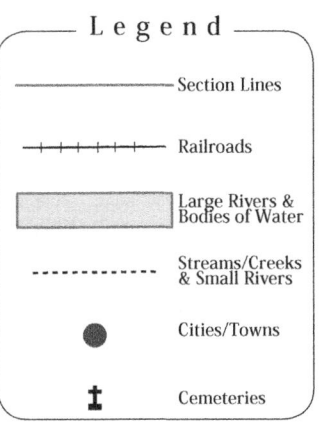

L e g e n d

——————— Section Lines

+++++++ Railroads

▭ Large Rivers &
Bodies of Water

- - - - - - - Streams/Creeks
& Small Rivers

● Cities/Towns

‡ Cemeteries

Scale: Section = 1 mile X 1 mile
(there are some exceptions)

Map Group 24: Index to Land Patents

Township 22-North Range 7-West (5th PM 22-N 7-W)

After you locate an individual in this Index, take note of the Section and Section Part then proceed to the Land Patent map on the pages immediately following. You should have no difficulty locating the corresponding parcel of land.

The "For More Info" Column will lead you to more information about the underlying Patents. See the *Legend* at right, and the "How to Use this Book" chapter, for more information.

```
                    LEGEND
          "For More Info . . . " column
A = Authority (Legislative Act, See Appendix "A")
B = Block or Lot (location in Section unknown)
C = Cancelled Patent
F = Fractional Section
G = Group  (Multi-Patentee Patent, see Appendix "C")
V = Overlaps another Parcel
R = Re-Issued (Parcel patented more than once)

(A & G items require you to look in the Appendixes referred
to above. All other Letter-designations followed by a number
require you to locate line-items in this index that possess
the ID number found after the letter).
```

ID	Individual in Patent	Sec.	Sec. Part	Date Issued	Other Counties	For More Info . . .
6361	ALLEN, Larkin	28	NWSW	1860-08-01		A1
6362	" "	29	NWSE	1860-08-01		A1
6363	" "	32	NENE	1859-01-01		A1
6364	" "	33	SWNW	1859-01-01		A1
6365	ALLEN, Sarah A	33	NWNW	1881-04-09		A7 G4
6366	ANGLE, Alfred A	12	E½SE	1889-06-22	Oregon	A7
6367	BALL, George W	7	SENE	1888-12-08		A7
6368	" "	7	W½NE	1888-12-08		A7
6369	" "	7	NESE	1888-12-08		A7
6370	" "	7	NWSE	1905-03-11		A1
6371	" "	8	SWNW	1885-12-19		A1
6372	BARGER, Samuel	22	E½SE	1892-12-20		A7
6373	" "	23	W½SW	1892-12-20		A7
6375	BATES, Edward	14	NENW	1892-01-05		A7
6374	" "	14	S½NW	1892-01-05		A7
6376	" "	15	SENE	1892-01-05		A7
6377	BATMAN, William J	25	SESE	1893-01-07		A7
6378	" "	36	SWNE	1893-01-07		A7
6379	" "	36	E½NE	1893-01-07		A7
6380	BENCH, Daniel	20	SWSW	1910-12-08		A7
6381	" "	29	N½NW	1910-12-08		A7
6382	BESS, George	23	SWNW	1908-08-17		A7
6383	BISSELL, Nora L	15	SENW	1904-01-28		A1
6384	BLEDSOE, Anderson M	13	NENW	1889-01-12		A7 G18
6385	" "	13	W½NE	1889-01-12		A7 G18
6386	" "	13	NWSE	1889-01-12		A7 G18
6389	BLEDSOE, Martha J	13	NWSE	1889-01-12		A7 G18
6387	" "	13	W½NE	1889-01-12		A7 G18
6388	" "	13	NENW	1889-01-12		A7 G18
8485	BOAK, Robert L	3	E22NW	1905-08-26		A7
8464	BOAK, Thomas J	1	W23NE	1892-01-25		A7
8463	" "	1	W22NW	1892-01-25		A7
8454	" "	1	3NW	1892-01-25		A7
6390	BOAK, William P	1	E½SE	1898-07-25		A7
8462	BOAK, Wright R	1	W22NE	1881-02-10		A7
6391	" "	1	NWSE	1881-02-10		A7
8456	" "	1	E21NW	1881-02-10		A7
8460	" "	1	W21NE	1881-02-10		A7
8480	BONBRIGHT, James	3	2NE	1860-05-02		A6
8478	" "	3	1NE	1860-05-02		A6
6396	BURTON, Samuel W	13	SESW	1889-01-12		A7
6395	" "	13	SWSE	1889-01-12		A7
6397	" "	13	W½SW	1889-01-12		A7
6398	BUSSELL, Elijah B	14	S½NE	1890-01-10		A7
6399	" "	14	N½NE	1890-01-10		A7
6400	BUSSELL, James	15	W½SE	1882-09-30		A7

ID	Individual in Patent	Sec.	Sec. Part	Date Issued	Other Counties	For More Info . . .
6401	BUSSELL, James (Cont'd)	15	E½SW	1882-09-30		A7
6402	BUSSELL, William	11	W½SE	1875-11-01		A7
6403	" "	14	N½NE	1875-11-01		A7
8477	CAMPBELL, Dorcas	3	1NE	1860-05-02		A6
8481	" "	3	2NE	1860-05-02		A6
6404	CAPSHAW, William H	25	SWSW	1895-09-04		A7
6406	" "	36	N½NW	1895-09-04		A7
6405	" "	36	NWNE	1895-09-04		A7
6407	CARSON, David	11	NE	1873-06-05		A1
6408	" "	12	NWNW	1873-06-05		A1
6409	" "	2	S½SE	1873-06-05		A1
6412	COOPER, Isaac	4	E½SE	1858-12-16		A8
6413	CRAIG, R L	15	SWSW	1886-07-20		A1
6418	" "	21	SESE	1886-07-20		A1
6417	" "	21	E½SW	1886-07-20		A1
6419	" "	21	W½SE	1886-07-20		A1
6415	" "	21	NW	1886-07-20		A1
6414	" "	21	W½NE	1886-07-20		A1
6416	" "	21	NENE	1886-07-20		A1
6420	" "	22	NWNW	1886-07-20		A1
6421	" "	22	W½SW	1886-07-20		A1
6423	" "	28	NENW	1886-07-20		A1
6422	" "	28	N½NE	1886-07-20		A1
8465	CRANE, Albert	18	1NW	1885-03-20		A1
8467	" "	18	2NW	1885-03-20		A1
8466	" "	18	1SW	1885-03-20		A1
8468	" "	18	2SW	1885-03-20		A1
6424	" "	18	SE	1885-03-20		A1
6425	" "	18	W½NE	1885-03-20		A1
6426	" "	19	N½	1885-03-20		A1
6429	" "	5	SESE	1886-10-29		A1
8505	" "	5	3NW	1886-10-29		A1
6427	" "	5	E½SW	1886-10-29		A1
6428	" "	5	N½SE	1886-10-29		A1
8504	" "	5	3NE	1886-10-29		A1
6431	" "	6	SESE	1885-07-27		A1
6430	" "	6	W½SE	1885-07-27		A1
8516	" "	6	W21NE	1885-07-27		A1
8514	" "	6	3NW	1885-07-27		A1
8512	" "	6	2SW	1885-07-27		A1
8511	" "	6	2NW	1885-07-27		A1
8509	" "	6	1SW	1885-07-27		A1
8508	" "	6	1NW	1885-07-27		A1
6433	" "	7	S½SE	1885-03-20		A1
8517	" "	7	1NW	1885-03-20		A1
8518	" "	7	1SW	1885-03-20		A1
8519	" "	7	2NW	1885-03-20		A1
8520	" "	7	2SW	1885-03-20		A1
6432	" "	7	NENE	1885-03-20		A1
6434	" "	8	NENE	1886-07-20		A1
8472	CURRY, Annie	2	3NE	1896-08-28		A7
8470	" "	2	2NE	1896-08-28		A7
6436	CURRY, Cornelius E	23	S½SE	1892-09-09		A7
6435	" "	23	SESW	1892-09-09		A7
6437	" "	26	NENW	1892-09-09		A7
8475	CURRY, Ida C	2	W21NE	1901-10-23		A7
8469	" "	2	1NW	1901-10-23		A7
6438	" "	2	NWSE	1901-10-23		A7
6439	CURRY, Lemuel H	24	SESW	1892-09-09		A7
6442	CURRY, Mary J	1	SWSE	1896-08-28		A7
6441	" "	1	NESW	1896-08-28		A7
6440	" "	1	S½SW	1896-08-28		A7
8502	DAVIS, Margaret	5	2NE	1861-07-01		A6
8499	" "	5	1NE	1861-07-01		A6
6443	DESITS, Malinda D	10	NWSE	1882-09-30		A1
6445	DYKES, James I	32	N½SE	1900-02-02		A7
6446	EASTRELY, John F	26	NWSE	1901-03-23		A7 G73
6447	" "	26	SWNE	1901-03-23		A7 G73
6449	EASTRELY, Nevada J	26	NWSE	1901-03-23		A7 G73
6448	" "	26	SWNE	1901-03-23		A7 G73
6451	EDELMAN, Jacob	17	N½NW	1877-01-15		A7
6450	" "	17	SWNW	1877-01-15		A7
6452	" "	18	SENE	1877-01-15		A7

ID	Individual in Patent	Sec.	Sec. Part	Date Issued	Other Counties	For More Info . . .
8461	EMMONS, Dallas	1	W21NW	1892-06-25		A7
6453	" "	1	NWSW	1892-06-25		A7
8458	" "	1	E22NW	1892-07-11		A1
8474	" "	2	E21NE	1892-06-25		A7
6454	" "	2	NESE	1892-06-25		A7
6455	EVANS, John L	28	SWNW	1879-12-15		A7
6457	" "	29	E½SE	1879-12-15		A7
6456	" "	29	SENE	1879-12-15		A7
8494	FEATHERSTON, John C	4	W22NW	1910-04-25		A7
8496	" "	4	W23NW	1910-04-25		A7
6458	FERGUSON, George W	10	NESE	1892-01-05		A7
6459	" "	11	E½SW	1892-01-05		A7
6460	" "	11	NWSW	1892-01-05		A7
6461	FILES, Jasper	25	NENE	1891-06-09	Oregon	A7
6462	FINEY, Samuel	11	NW	1862-10-10		A6 G83
6463	FINNEY, Samuel	10	NE	1860-05-02		A6 G85
6464	" "	11	NW	1862-10-10		A6 G83
6465	" "	2	SW	1860-05-02		A6 G85
6466	" "	3	SE	1860-05-02		A6 G84
6467	" "	3	SW	1860-05-02		A6 G85
6468	FORD, Charles P	15	W½NW	1860-05-02		A6
6469	" "	15	NWSW	1860-05-02		A6
6470	" "	22	NE	1860-05-02		A6
6472	FRITH, Margaret J	25	W½NE	1905-03-30		A7 G88
6471	" "	25	E½NW	1905-03-30		A7 G88
6473	FRITH, Mathias	25	W½NE	1905-03-30		A7 G88
6474	" "	25	E½NW	1905-03-30		A7 G88
6475	FULLER, Sarah A	33	NESW	1884-02-15		A7 G90
6476	" "	33	SENW	1884-02-15		A7 G90
6478	FULLER, William	33	SENW	1884-02-15		A7 G90
6477	" "	33	NESW	1884-02-15		A7 G90
8488	GAINES, James W	4	1NW	1901-10-08		A7
6479	" "	4	N½SW	1901-10-08		A7
8493	GAINES, Thomas B	4	W22NE	1889-06-22		A7
8495	" "	4	W23NE	1889-06-22		A7
8492	" "	4	E23NW	1889-06-22		A7
8490	" "	4	E22NW	1889-06-22		A7
8498	GLADDEN, Joseph	5	1NE	1861-07-01		A6
8500	" "	5	2NE	1861-07-01		A6
6481	GROFUSE, Jacob	17	E½NW	1879-12-15		A7
6482	HALSELL, John T	36	E½SE	1910-06-27		A1
6483	HANCOCK, Hiram H	10	SWSE	1888-12-08		A7
6484	" "	15	NENW	1888-12-08		A7
6485	" "	15	W½NE	1888-12-08		A7
8479	HANKINS, George A	3	1NW	1889-06-22		A7
8487	" "	4	1NE	1889-06-22		A7
6486	HARBINSON, Andrew J	9	NWSW	1884-10-11		A1
6487	HARBISON, Andrew J	4	SESW	1888-12-08		A7
6489	" "	9	SWNW	1888-12-08		A7
6488	" "	9	E½NW	1888-12-08		A7
8459	HARDY, George W	1	E23NE	1896-09-04		A7
6490	HARMON, Thomas L	27	SWNW	1899-02-13		A7
6491	" "	27	NWSW	1899-02-13		A7
6492	" "	28	E½SE	1899-02-13		A7
6493	HATFIELD, Francis M	29	SWSE	1888-12-08		A7
6495	" "	32	NWNE	1888-12-08		A7
6494	" "	32	S½NE	1888-12-08		A7
6496	HEALEY, John	3	SE	1860-05-02		A6 G84
6497	HILTON, James R	14	W½SW	1894-05-23		A7
6498	" "	15	E½SE	1894-05-23		A7
6499	HUNSPERGER, George W	23	NENE	1890-01-10		A7
6501	" "	24	SWNW	1890-01-10		A7
6500	" "	24	N½NW	1890-01-10		A7
6502	JEFFERY, Augustus C	32	N½SW	1903-10-01		A7
6503	JOHNSON, Lewis C	23	NESW	1893-12-19		A7
6505	JONES, John F	26	SENW	1914-03-07		A7
6504	" "	26	NESW	1914-03-07		A7
6506	JONES, William E	24	SE	1891-05-05		A7
8491	KIRKPATRICK, Hugh C	4	E23NE	1895-11-13		A1
8515	LAMONS, Solomon	6	E21NE	1866-09-01		A1
8510	" "	6	2NE	1879-12-15		A7
8513	" "	6	3NE	1879-12-15		A7
6507	LANCASTER, Elizabeth A	29	NESW	1888-12-08		A7

344

ID	Individual in Patent	Sec.	Sec. Part	Date Issued	Other Counties	For More Info . . .
6509	LANCASTER, Elizabeth A (Cont'd)	29	SENW	1888-12-08		A7
6508	" "	29	W½NE	1888-12-08		A7
6510	LANCASTER, James K	8	NESE	1886-07-20		A1
6512	" "	9	E½SW	1893-09-01		A7
6511	" "	9	S½SE	1893-09-01		A7
6513	LAWHEAD, George E	25	N½SW	1904-02-12		A1
6514	LUTHER, Josiah P	10	N½NW	1896-09-29		A7
6515	" "	10	SENW	1896-09-29		A7
6518	MADDEN, Albert M	13	NWNW	1891-05-05		A7
6516	" "	13	S½NW	1891-05-05		A7
6517	" "	13	NESW	1891-05-05		A7
6519	MAHORNEY, Mathew W	14	S½SE	1889-01-12		A7
6520	" "	14	E½SW	1889-01-12		A7
8506	MANNIX, Patrick	5	E21NW	1888-07-24		A1
8507	MARSHALL, Walter Y	5	W21NW	1884-02-15		A7
8503	" "	5	2NW	1884-02-15		A7
6521	MCCOY, Nancy	33	SESW	1858-01-15		A1
6522	MENDENHALL, John W	20	SWNW	1902-04-15		A7
6523	" "	20	N½NW	1902-04-15		A7
6525	MEREDITH, John	20	SESW	1882-09-30		A1
6526	MERIDETH, John M	20	E½SE	1892-10-26		A7
6527	" "	20	SENE	1892-10-26		A7
6528	" "	29	NENE	1892-10-26		A7
6529	MERIDETH, William M	8	NWSW	1896-10-13		A1
6530	MERIDITH, James	28	E½SW	1886-07-20		A1
6531	MERIDITH, W R	20	NWSE	1886-07-20		A1
6532	MERIEDITH, William R	20	N½SW	1882-09-30		A7
6534	" "	20	SENW	1882-09-30		A7
6533	" "	20	SWNE	1882-09-30		A7
8486	MILLER, Elijah	3	W22NW	1882-09-30		A7
8484	" "	3	3NW	1882-09-30		A7
8489	" "	4	E22NE	1882-09-30		A7
6535	MILLER, Ira	17	SESW	1882-05-20		A7
6536	" "	17	SWSE	1882-05-20		A7
6537	" "	20	N½NE	1882-05-20		A7
6538	MITTELSTETTER, Lisette	22	SESW	1886-10-29		A1
6539	" "	22	NENW	1886-10-29		A1
6540	" "	27	N½NW	1886-10-29		A1
6541	MUSE, William H	24	NWNE	1913-01-31		A7
6543	NALE, Hezekiah	32	S½SE	1879-12-15		A7
6542	" "	32	S½SW	1879-12-15		A7
6544	NICKS, Genings	24	NENE	1900-08-09	Oregon	A7
6545	OLDEN, Benjamin F	17	NWNW	1875-05-10		A7
6546	" "	18	NENE	1875-05-10		A7
6547	ONEY, Oscar G	10	SWNW	1889-06-22		A7
6548	" "	9	NWSE	1889-06-22		A7
6549	" "	9	S½NE	1889-06-22		A7
8483	PEASE, William A	3	3NE	1900-08-09		A7
6550	PHILLIPS, Peter S	23	N½NW	1898-04-06		A7
6551	POWELL, Catharine	10	SW	1892-03-07		A7 G158
6552	POWELL, George	10	SW	1892-03-07		A7 G158
6553	PRATT, Caroline D	17	E½SE	1886-07-20		A1
6554	" "	17	NE	1886-07-20		A1
6555	" "	21	W½SW	1886-07-20		A1
6556	" "	22	W½SE	1886-07-20		A1
6557	" "	22	NESW	1886-07-20		A1
6558	" "	26	SWSE	1886-07-20		A1
6562	" "	26	S½SW	1886-07-20		A1
6561	" "	26	E½SE	1886-07-20		A1
6560	" "	26	NWNE	1886-07-20		A1
6559	" "	26	NWSW	1886-07-20		A1
6564	" "	27	S½SW	1886-07-20		A1
6565	" "	27	N½NE	1886-07-20		A1
6563	" "	27	S½SE	1886-07-20		A1
6569	" "	28	SENW	1886-07-20		A1
6566	" "	28	S½NE	1886-07-20		A1
6567	" "	28	SWSW	1886-07-20		A1
6568	" "	28	NWNW	1886-07-20		A1
6570	" "	28	W½SE	1886-07-20		A1
6571	" "	33	NENW	1886-07-20		A1
6572	" "	34	N½	1886-11-04		A1
6573	" "	34	SW	1886-11-04		A1
6574	" "	35	SE	1886-11-04		A1

ID	Individual in Patent	Sec.	Sec. Part	Date Issued	Other Counties	For More Info . . .
6575	PRATT, Caroline D (Cont'd)	35	N½	1886-11-04		A1
6576	" "	36	W½SW	1886-07-20		A1
6577	" "	36	SWNW	1886-07-20		A1
6578	" "	4	SWSW	1886-07-20		A1
6579	" "	8	S½SE	1886-07-20		A1
6582	" "	9	NWNW	1886-07-20		A1
6580	" "	9	SWSW	1886-07-20		A1
6581	" "	9	NESE	1886-07-20		A1
8473	QUADE, Robert W	2	3NW	1900-08-09		A7
8471	" "	2	2NW	1900-08-09		A7
6583	RAYMOND, Albert L	17	SWSW	1886-11-19		A1
6584	" "	17	NWSE	1890-10-11		A7
6585	RAYMOND, Chance S	13	E½NE	1901-04-09		A7
6586	" "	13	E½SE	1901-04-09		A7
6587	RENNEKER, John R	10	SESE	1888-09-17		A7
6588	" "	11	SWSW	1888-09-17		A7
6589	" "	14	NWNW	1888-09-17		A7
6590	" "	15	NENE	1888-09-17		A7
6594	RICHARD, Auguste	27	SENW	1903-10-01		A7
6593	" "	27	NESW	1903-10-01		A7
6592	" "	27	SWNE	1903-10-01		A7
6591	" "	27	NWSE	1903-10-01		A7
6595	RIDEOUT, Henry	4	W½SE	1891-06-09		A7
6596	" "	9	N½NE	1891-06-09		A7
6597	ROBERTS, Alonzo P	21	NESE	1891-05-25		A7
6598	" "	21	SENE	1891-05-25		A7
6599	" "	22	S½NW	1891-05-25		A7
6600	SALMON, Henry H	26	W½NW	1890-01-30		A1
6602	" "	27	NESE	1890-01-30		A1
6601	" "	27	SENE	1890-01-30		A1
6603	SHAVER, John	5	SWSE	1886-10-29		A1
6605	" "	8	SENE	1880-10-01		A1
6609	" "	8	NESW	1873-02-01		A7
6608	" "	8	SWSW	1888-12-06		A1
6607	" "	8	W½NE	1873-02-01		A7
6606	" "	8	NESE	1873-02-01		A7
6604	" "	8	SESW	1866-09-01		A1
6610	SHAVER, William M	8	N½NW	1882-09-30		A1
6611	" "	8	SENW	1897-03-18		A1
6612	SHEARHEART, Sarah A	33	NWNW	1881-04-09		A7 G4
6613	SHERREY, Hugh P	36	SWSE	1903-06-08		A7
6614	SHOWERS, Andrew	11	E½SE	1885-03-20		A1
6619	" "	12	W½SE	1885-03-20		A1
6615	" "	12	SW	1885-03-20		A1
6618	" "	12	NE	1885-03-20		A1
6617	" "	12	SWNW	1885-03-20		A1
6616	" "	12	E½NW	1885-03-20		A1
6620	SMITH, Frances M	5	W½SW	1899-02-25		A7
6621	" "	6	NESE	1899-02-25		A7
6622	SMITH, James H	32	SENW	1908-06-25		A7
8455	SMITH, Jewell	1	E21NE	1901-01-10		A1
8457	" "	1	E22NE	1901-01-10		A1
6623	STEPHENS, Israel	20	SWSE	1860-08-01		A1
6624	" "	33	NWSW	1859-09-01		A1
6625	STEPHENS, James	33	SWSW	1894-08-14		A7
6626	SUTTON, James S	23	N½SE	1890-06-06		A7
6627	" "	24	W½SW	1890-06-06		A7
6630	SUTTON, William T	23	SENW	1889-01-12		A7
6629	" "	23	SENE	1889-01-12		A7
6628	" "	23	W½NE	1889-01-12		A7
6632	THOMAS, Charles M	10	NE	1860-05-02		A6 G85
6633	" "	11	NW	1862-10-10		A6 G83
6634	" "	2	SW	1860-05-02		A6 G85
6635	" "	3	SW	1860-05-02		A6 G85
6636	" "	3	SE	1860-05-02		A6 G84
6637	VANDIVER, James E	25	W½NW	1901-03-23		A7
6638	" "	26	E½NE	1901-03-23		A7
6639	VINCENT, Albert V	25	SENE	1896-10-13		A1
6641	VINCENT, Barbara L	25	SWSE	1890-10-11		A7 G183
6640	" "	25	SESW	1890-10-11		A7 G183
6642	" "	25	N½SE	1890-10-11		A7 G183
6643	" "	36	NWSE	1892-04-23		A1
6644	VINCENT, James A	25	SESW	1890-10-11		A7 G183

ID	Individual in Patent	Sec.	Sec. Part	Date Issued	Other Counties	For More Info . . .
6645	VINCENT, James A (Cont'd)	25	N½SE	1890-10-11		A7 G183
6646	"	25	SWSE	1890-10-11		A7 G183
6647	WADDLE, David	32	W½NW	1915-12-15		A7
6648	"	32	NENW	1915-12-15		A7
6650	WAID, Tilda M	36	E½SW	1881-04-09		A7 G184
6649	"	36	SENW	1881-04-09		A7 G184
6652	WAID, William P	36	E½SW	1881-04-09		A7 G184
6651	"	36	SENW	1881-04-09		A7 G184
6655	WILLBANKS, James E	29	NWSW	1901-05-08		A7
6653	"	29	S½SW	1901-05-08		A7
6654	"	29	SWNW	1901-05-08		A7
6658	YARNELL, Robert	24	S½NE	1892-03-07		A7 G191
6657	"	24	SENW	1892-03-07		A7 G191
6656	"	24	NESW	1892-03-07		A7 G191
6661	YARNELL, Sarah H	24	NESW	1892-03-07		A7 G191
6660	"	24	SENW	1892-03-07		A7 G191
6659	"	24	S½NE	1892-03-07		A7 G191

Patent Map

T22-N R7-W
5th PM 22-N 7-W Meridian

Map Group 24

Township Statistics

Parcels Mapped	:	325
Number of Patents	:	159
Number of Individuals	:	141
Patentees Identified	:	127
Number of Surnames	:	108
Multi-Patentee Parcels	:	24
Oldest Patent Date	:	1/15/1858
Most Recent Patent	:	12/15/1915
Block/Lot Parcels	:	59
Cities and Town	:	1
Cemeteries	:	0

Lots/Tracts-Sec. 6
1NW CRANE, ALBERT 1885
1SW CRANE, ALBERT 1885
2NE LAMONS, SOLOMON 1879
2NW CRANE, ALBERT 1885
2SW CRANE, ALBERT 1885
3NE LAMONS, SOLOMON 1879
3NW CRANE, ALBERT 1885
E21NE LAMONS, SOLOMON 1866
W21NE CRANE, ALBERT 1885

Lots/Tracts-Sec. 5
1NE GLADDEN, JOSEPH 1861
2NE GLADDEN, JOSEPH 1861
2NW MARSHALL, WALTER Y 1884
3NE CRANE, ALBERT 1886
3NW CRANE, ALBERT 1886
E21NW MANNIX, PATRICK 1888
W21NW MARSHALL, WALTER Y 1884

Lots/Tracts-Sec. 4
1NE HANKINS, GEORGE A 1889
1NW GAINES, JAMES W 1901
E22NE MILLER, ELIJAH 1882
E22NW GAINES, THOMAS B 1889
E23NE KIRKPATRICK, HUGH C 1895
E23NW GAINES, THOMAS B 1889
W22NE GAINES, THOMAS B 1889
W22NW FEATHERSTON, JOHN C 1910
W23NE GAINES, THOMAS B 1889
W23NW FEATHERSTON, JOHN C 1910

6

5

4

SMITH Frances M 1899

CRANE Albert 1885

SMITH Frances M 1899

CRANE Albert 1886

CRANE Albert 1885

CRANE Albert 1886

GAINES James W 1901

RIDEOUT Henry 1891

COOPER Isaac 1858

SHAVER John 1886

CRANE Albert 1886

PRATT Caroline D 1886

HARBISON Andrew J 1888

7

BALL George W 1888

CRANE Albert 1885

SHAVER William M 1882

CRANE Albert 1886

PRATT Caroline D 1886

RIDEOUT Henry 1891

BALL George W 1888

BALL George W 1885

SHAVER William M 1897

SHAVER John 1873

SHAVER John 1880

HARBISON Andrew J 1888

HARBISON Andrew J 1888

ONEY Oscar G 1889

8

9

BALL George W 1905

BALL George W 1888

MERIDETH William M 1896

SHAVER John 1873

LANCASTER James K 1886

HARBINSON Andrew J 1884

ONEY Oscar G 1889

PRATT Caroline D 1886

SHAVER John 1873

Lots/Tracts-Sec. 7
1NW CRANE, ALBERT 1885
1SW CRANE, ALBERT 1885
2NW CRANE, ALBERT 1885
2SW CRANE, ALBERT 1885

CRANE Albert 1885

SHAVER John 1888

SHAVER John 1866

PRATT Caroline D 1886

PRATT Caroline D 1886

LANCASTER James K 1893

LANCASTER James K 1893

CRANE Albert 1885

OLDEN Benjamin F 1875

OLDEN Benjamin F 1875

GROFUSE Jacob 1879

PRATT Caroline D 1886

EDELMAN Jacob 1877

EDELMAN Jacob 1877

18

17

16

EDELMAN Jacob 1877

RAYMOND Albert L 1890

Lots/Tracts-Sec. 18
1NW CRANE, ALBERT 1885
1SW CRANE, ALBERT 1885
2NW CRANE, ALBERT 1885
2SW CRANE, ALBERT 1885

CRANE Albert 1885

PRATT Caroline D 1886

RAYMOND Albert L 1886

MILLER Ira 1882

MILLER Ira 1882

MENDENHALL John W 1902

MILLER Ira 1882

CRAIG R L 1886

CRANE Albert 1885

MENDENHALL John W 1902

MERIEDITH William R 1882

MERIEDITH William R 1882

MERIDETH John M 1892

CRAIG R L 1886

CRAIG R L 1886

ROBERTS Alonzo P 1891

19

20

21

MERIEDITH William R 1882

MERIDITH W R 1886

ROBERTS Alonzo P 1891

MERIDETH John M 1892

PRATT Caroline D 1886

CRAIG R L 1886

CRAIG R L 1886

BENCH Daniel 1910

MEREDITH John 1882

STEPHENS Israel 1860

CRAIG R L 1886

BENCH Daniel 1910

MERIDETH John M 1892

PRATT Caroline D 1886

CRAIG R L 1886

CRAIG R L 1886

LANCASTER Elizabeth A 1888

WILLBANKS James E 1901

LANCASTER Elizabeth A 1888

EVANS John L 1879

EVANS John L 1879

PRATT Caroline D 1886

PRATT Caroline D 1886

30

29

28

WILLBANKS James E 1901

LANCASTER Elizabeth A 1888

ALLEN Larkin 1860

ALLEN Larkin 1860

MERIDITH James 1886

PRATT Caroline D 1886

HARMON Thomas L 1899

WILLBANKS James E 1901

EVANS John L 1879

HATFIELD Francis M 1888

PRATT Caroline D 1886

WADDLE David 1915

HATFIELD Francis M 1888

ALLEN Larkin 1859

SHEARHEART [4] Sarah A 1881

PRATT Caroline D 1886

WADDLE David 1915

SMITH James H 1908

HATFIELD Francis M 1888

ALLEN Larkin 1859

FULLER [90] Sarah A 1884

31

32

33

JEFFERY Augustus C 1903

DYKES James I 1900

STEPHENS Israel 1859

FULLER [90] Sarah A 1884

NALE Hezekiah 1879

NALE Hezekiah 1879

STEPHENS James 1894

McCOY Nancy 1858

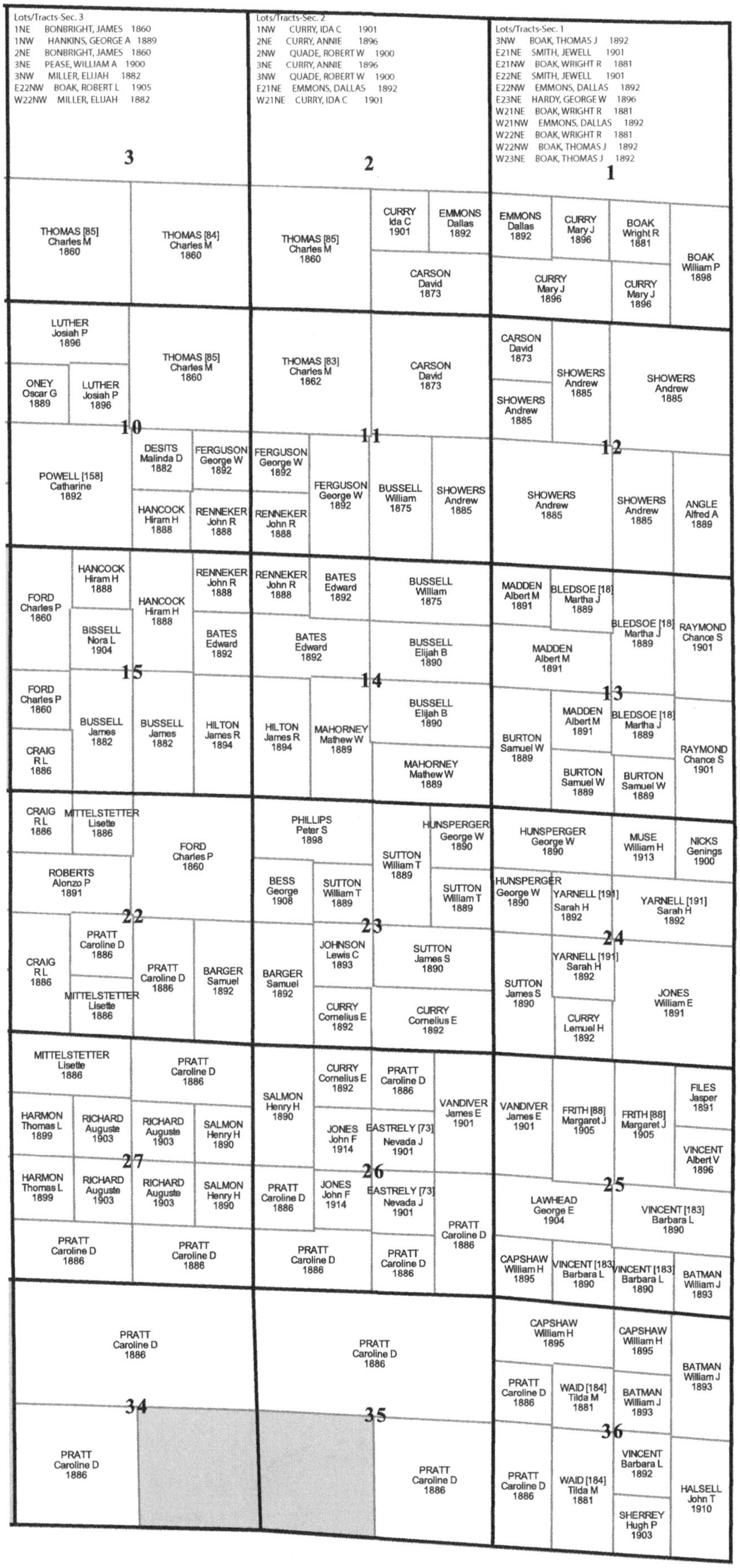

Lots/Tracts-Sec. 3
1NE BONBRIGHT, JAMES 1860
1NW HANKINS, GEORGE A 1889
2NE BONBRIGHT, JAMES 1860
3NE PEASE, WILLIAM A 1900
3NW MILLER, ELIJAH 1882
E22NW BOAK, ROBERT L 1905
W22NW MILLER, ELIJAH 1882

Lots/Tracts-Sec. 2
1NW CURRY, IDA C 1901
2NE CURRY, ANNIE 1896
2NW QUADE, ROBERT W 1900
3NE CURRY, ANNIE 1896
3NW QUADE, ROBERT W 1900
E21NE EMMONS, DALLAS 1892
W21NE CURRY, IDA C 1901

Lots/Tracts-Sec. 1
3NW BOAK, THOMAS J 1892
E21NE SMITH, JEWELL 1901
E21NW BOAK, WRIGHT R 1881
E22NE SMITH, JEWELL 1901
E22NW EMMONS, DALLAS 1892
E23NE HARDY, GEORGE W 1896
W21NE BOAK, WRIGHT R 1881
W21NW EMMONS, DALLAS 1892
W22NE BOAK, WRIGHT R 1881
W22NW BOAK, THOMAS J 1892
W23NW BOAK, THOMAS J 1892

3

2

1

THOMAS [85] Charles M 1860

THOMAS [84] Charles M 1860

THOMAS [85] Charles M 1860

CURRY Ida C 1901

EMMONS Dallas 1892

EMMONS Dallas 1892

CURRY Mary J 1896

BOAK Wright R 1881

BOAK William P 1898

CARSON David 1873

CURRY Mary J 1896

CURRY Mary J 1896

LUTHER Josiah P 1896

THOMAS [85] Charles M 1860

THOMAS [83] Charles M 1862

CARSON David 1873

CARSON David 1873

ONEY Oscar G 1889

LUTHER Josiah P 1896

SHOWERS Andrew 1885

SHOWERS Andrew 1885

SHOWERS Andrew 1885

10

11

12

DESITS Malinda D 1882

FERGUSON George W 1892

FERGUSON George W 1892

POWELL [158] Catharine 1892

FERGUSON George W 1892

BUSSELL William 1875

SHOWERS Andrew 1885

SHOWERS Andrew 1885

SHOWERS Andrew 1885

ANGLE Alfred A 1889

HANCOCK Hiram H 1888

RENNEKER John R 1888

RENNEKER John R 1888

FORD Charles P 1860

HANCOCK Hiram H 1888

RENNEKER John R 1888

HANCOCK Hiram H 1888

RENNEKER John R 1888

BATES Edward 1892

BUSSELL William 1875

MADDEN Albert M 1891

BLEDSOE [18] Martha J 1889

BISSELL Nora L 1904

BATES Edward 1892

BATES Edward 1892

BUSSELL Elijah B 1890

MADDEN Albert M 1891

BLEDSOE [18] Martha J 1889

RAYMOND Chance S 1901

15

14

13

FORD Charles P 1860

BUSSELL James 1882

BUSSELL James 1882

HILTON James R 1894

HILTON James R 1894

MAHORNEY Mathew W 1889

BUSSELL Elijah B 1890

MADDEN Albert M 1891

BLEDSOE [18] Martha J 1889

CRAIG R L 1886

MAHORNEY Mathew W 1889

BURTON Samuel W 1889

RAYMOND Chance S 1901

BURTON Samuel W 1889

BURTON Samuel W 1889

CRAIG R L 1886

MITTELSTETTER Lisette 1886

FORD Charles P 1860

PHILLIPS Peter S 1898

HUNSPERGER George W 1890

HUNSPERGER George W 1890

MUSE William H 1913

NICKS Genings 1900

ROBERTS Alonzo P 1891

BESS George 1908

SUTTON William T 1889

SUTTON William T 1889

HUNSPERGER George W 1890

YARNELL [191] Sarah H 1892

YARNELL [191] Sarah H 1892

22

23

24

PRATT Caroline D 1886

JOHNSON Lewis C 1893

SUTTON James S 1890

YARNELL [191] Sarah H 1892

CRAIG R L 1886

PRATT Caroline D 1886

BARGER Samuel 1892

BARGER Samuel 1892

SUTTON James S 1890

JONES William E 1891

MITTELSTETTER Lisette 1886

CURRY Cornelius E 1892

CURRY Cornelius E 1892

CURRY Lemuel H 1892

MITTELSTETTER Lisette 1886

PRATT Caroline D 1886

CURRY Cornelius E 1892

PRATT Caroline D 1886

FILES Jasper 1891

HARMON Thomas L 1899

RICHARD Auguste 1903

RICHARD Auguste 1903

SALMON Henry H 1890

SALMON Henry H 1890

VANDIVER James E 1901

VANDIVER James E 1901

FRITH [88] Margaret J 1905

FRITH [88] Margaret J 1905

VINCENT Albert V 1896

27

JONES John F 1914

EASTRELY [73] Nevada J 1901

26

25

HARMON Thomas L 1899

RICHARD Auguste 1903

RICHARD Auguste 1903

SALMON Henry H 1890

PRATT Caroline D 1886

JONES John F 1914

EASTRELY [73] Nevada J 1901

LAWHEAD George E 1904

VINCENT [183] Barbara L 1890

PRATT Caroline D 1886

PRATT Caroline D 1886

PRATT Caroline D 1886

PRATT Caroline D 1886

PRATT Caroline D 1886

CAPSHAW William H 1895

VINCENT [183] Barbara L 1890

VINCENT [183] Barbara L 1890

BATMAN William J 1893

CAPSHAW William H 1895

CAPSHAW William H 1895

BATMAN William J 1893

PRATT Caroline D 1886

PRATT Caroline D 1886

PRATT Caroline D 1886

CAPSHAW William H 1895

PRATT Caroline D 1886

WAID [184] Tilda M 1881

BATMAN William J 1893

34

35

36

VINCENT Barbara L 1892

PRATT Caroline D 1886

PRATT Caroline D 1886

PRATT Caroline D 1886

WAID [184] Tilda M 1881

HALSELL John T 1910

SHERREY Hugh P 1903

Helpful Hints

1. This Map's INDEX can be found on the preceding pages.

2. Refer to Map "C" to see where this Township lies within Howell County, Missouri.

3. Numbers within square brackets [ ] denote a multi-patentee land parcel (multi-owner). Refer to Appendix "C" for a full list of members in this group.

4. Areas that look to be crowded with Patentees usually indicate multiple sales of the same parcel (Re-issues) or Overlapping parcels. See this Township's Index for an explanation of these and other circumstances that might explain "odd" groupings of Patentees on this map.

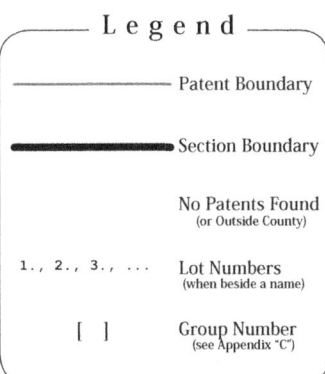

Legend

———— Patent Boundary

━━━━ Section Boundary

No Patents Found (or Outside County)

1., 2., 3., ... Lot Numbers (when beside a name)

[ ] Group Number (see Appendix "C")

Scale: Section = 1 mile X 1 mile (generally, with some exceptions)

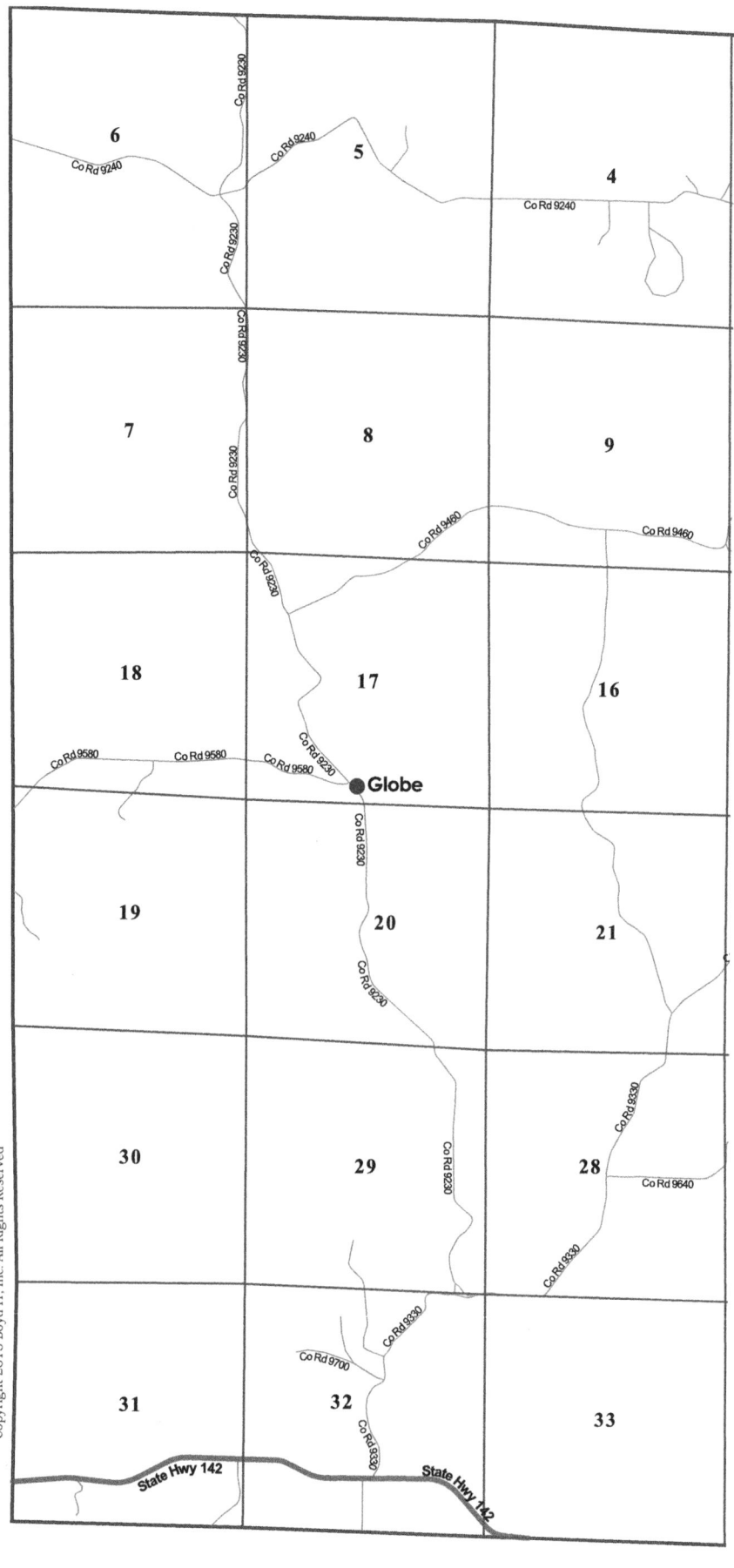

Road Map

T22-N R7-W
5th PM 22-N 7-W Meridian

Map Group 24

Cities & Towns
Globe

Cemeteries
None

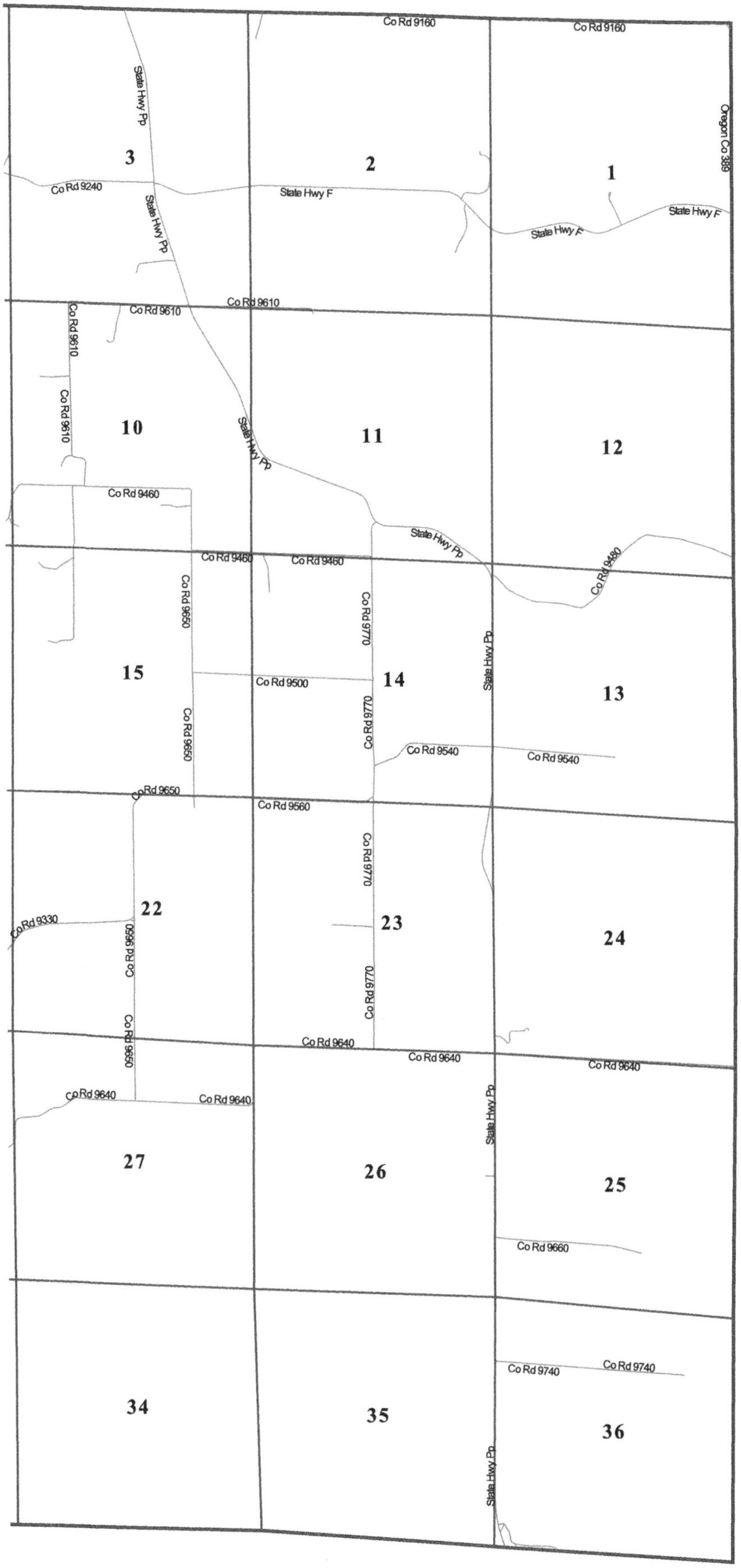

Co Rd 9160

Co Rd 9160

State Hwy Pp

Oregon Co 389

3

Co Rd 9240

State Hwy F

2

1

State Hwy Pp

State Hwy F

State Hwy F

Co Rd 9610

Co Rd 9610

Co Rd 9610

Co Rd 9610

State Hwy Pp

10

11

12

Co Rd 9460

Co Rd 9460

Co Rd 9460

State Hwy Pp

Co Rd 9460

Co Rd 9650

Co Rd 9770

State Hwy Pp

Co Rd 9480

15

Co Rd 9500

14

13

Co Rd 9650

Co Rd 9770

Co Rd 9540

Co Rd 9540

Co Rd 9650

Co Rd 9560

Co Rd 9770

Co Rd 9330

Co Rd 9650

22

23

24

Co Rd 9770

Co Rd 9650

Co Rd 9640

Co Rd 9640

Co Rd 9640

State Hwy Pp

Co Rd 9640

Co Rd 9640

Co Rd 9640

27

26

25

Co Rd 9660

Co Rd 9740

Co Rd 9740

34

35

36

State Hwy Pp

Helpful Hints

1. This road map has a number of uses, but primarily it is to help you: a) find the present location of land owned by your ancestors (at least the general area), b) find cemeteries and city-centers, and c) estimate the route/roads used by Census-takers & tax-assessors.

2. If you plan to travel to Howell County to locate cemeteries or land parcels, please pick up a modern travel map for the area before you do. Mapping old land parcels on modern maps is not as exact a science as you might think. Just the slightest variations in public land survey coordinates, estimates of parcel boundaries, or road-map deviations can greatly alter a map's representation of how a road either does or doesn't cross a particular parcel of land.

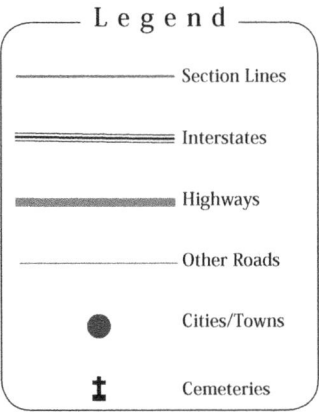

L e g e n d

———————— Section Lines

══════════ Interstates

━━━━━━━━━━ Highways

———————— Other Roads

● Cities/Towns

† Cemeteries

Scale: Section = 1 mile X 1 mile
(generally, with some exceptions)

Historical Map

T22-N R7-W
5th PM 22-N 7-W Meridian

Map Group 24

Cities & Towns
Globe

Cemeteries
None

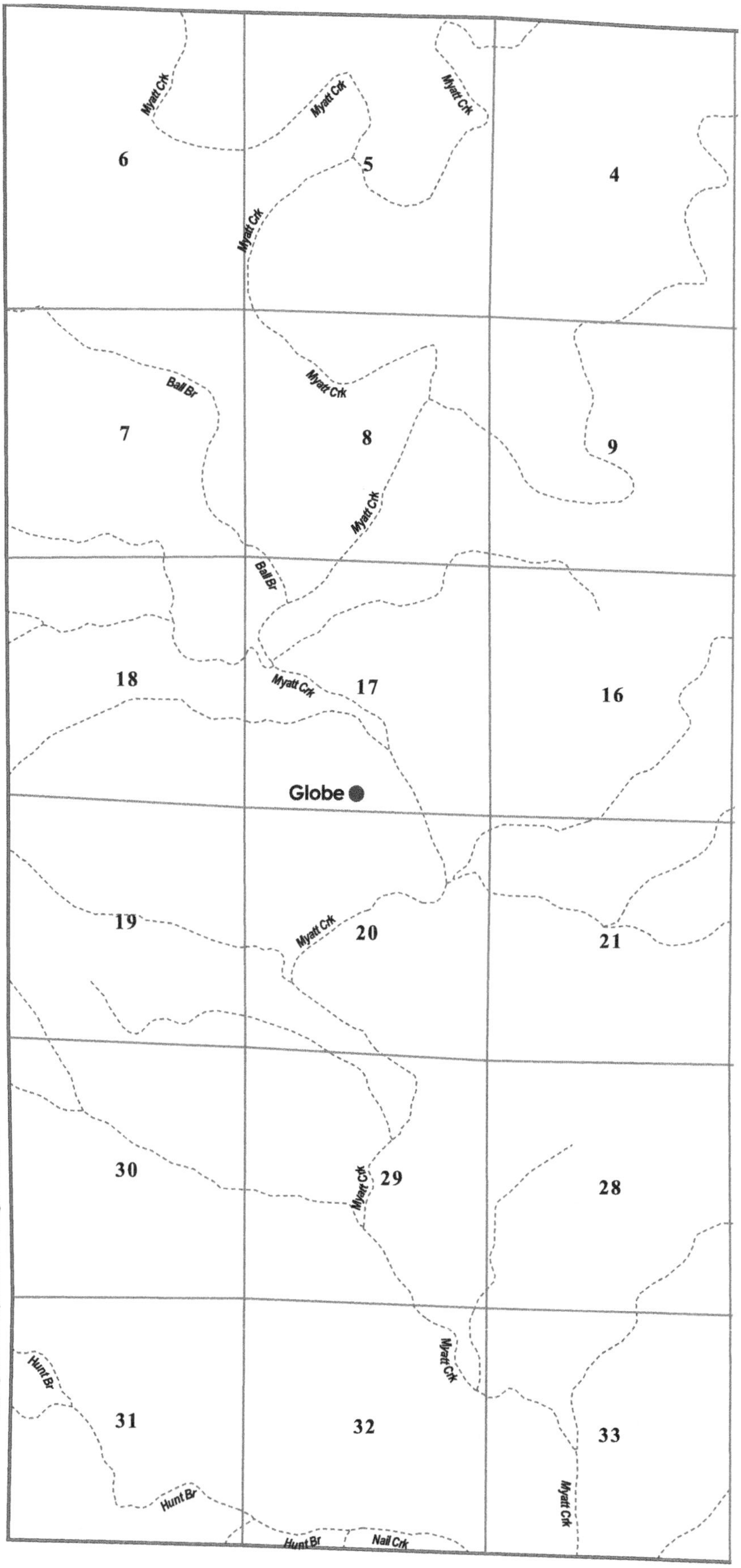

6	5	4
7	8	9
18	17	16
19	20	21
30	29	28
31	32	33

Globe ●

Myatt Crk
Ball Br
Hunt Br
Nail Crk

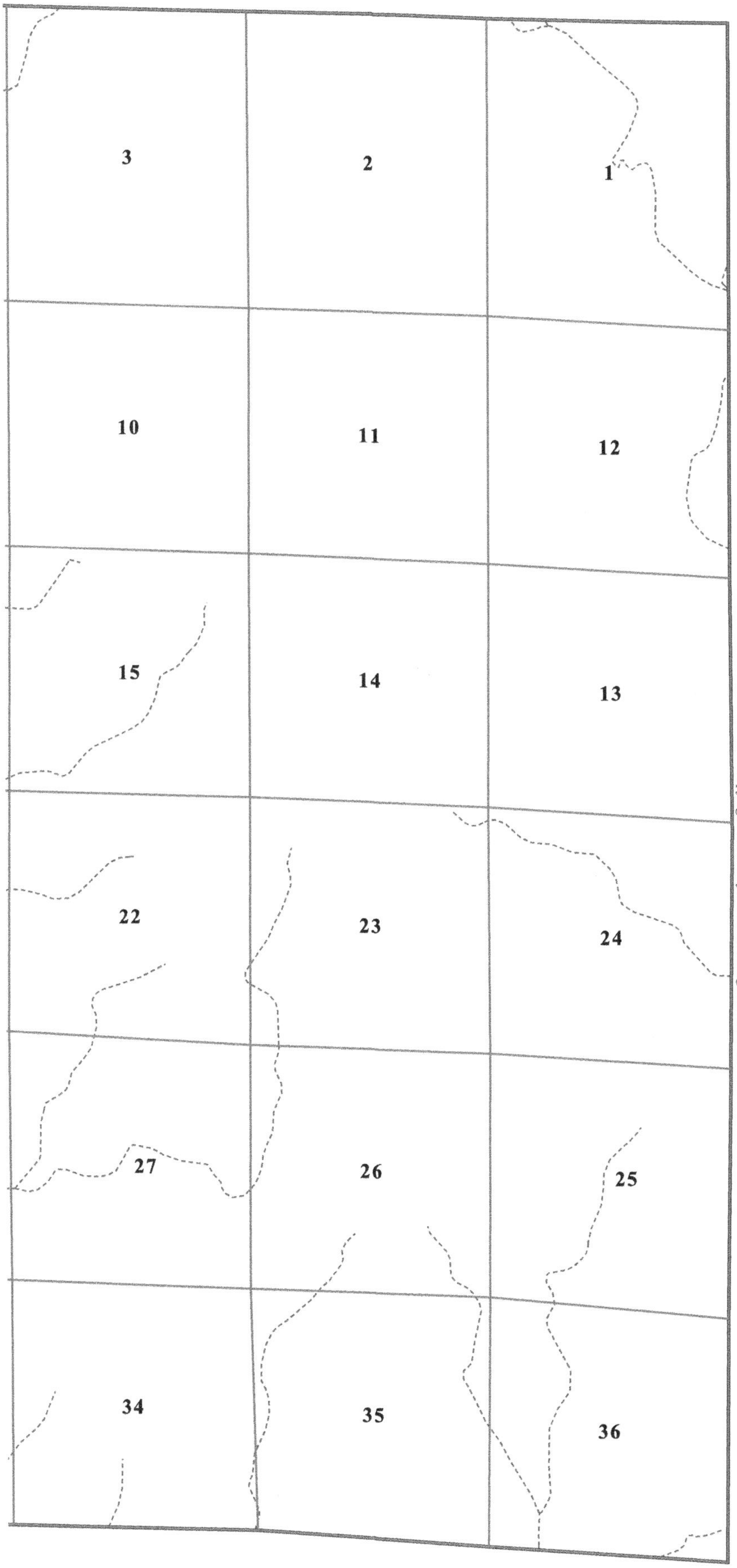

3	2	1
10	11	12
15	14	13
22	23	24
27	26	25
34	35	36

Helpful Hints

1. This Map takes a different look at the same Congressional Township displayed in the preceding two maps. It presents features that can help you better envision the historical development of the area: a) Water-bodies (lakes & ponds), b) Water-courses (rivers, streams, etc.), c) Railroads, d) City/ town center-points (where they were oftentimes located when first settled), and e) Cemeteries.

2. Using this "Historical" map in tandem with this Township's Patent Map and Road Map, may lead you to some interesting discoveries. You will often find roads, towns, cemeteries, and waterways are named after nearby landowners: sometimes those names will be the ones you are researching. See how many of these research gems you can find here in Howell County.

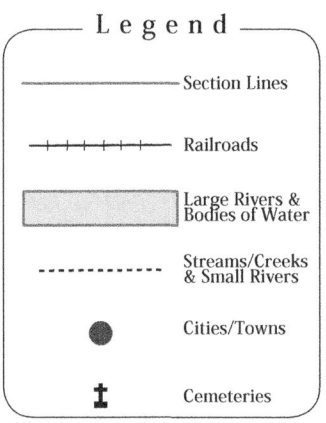

Legend

_____ Section Lines

+++++++ Railroads

Large Rivers & Bodies of Water

- - - - - Streams/Creeks & Small Rivers

● Cities/Towns

‡ Cemeteries

Scale: Section = 1 mile X 1 mile
(there are some exceptions)

Map Group 25: Index to Land Patents

Township 21-North Range 10-West (5th PM 21-N 10-W)

After you locate an individual in this Index, take note of the Section and Section Part then proceed to the Land Patent map on the pages immediately following. You should have no difficulty locating the corresponding parcel of land.

The "For More Info" Column will lead you to more information about the underlying Patents. See the *Legend* at right, and the "How to Use this Book" chapter, for more information.

ID	Individual in Patent	Sec.	Sec. Part	Date Issued	Other Counties	For More Info . . .
8579	ADKINS, Samuel A	8	W22SW	1891-05-25		A7
6662	" "	8	S½NW	1891-05-25		A7
8578	" "	8	W21SW	1891-05-25		A7
6663	BLACKWELL, Jesse B	6	SESE	1892-12-09		A7
6664	" "	7	N½NE	1892-12-09		A7
8537	CANTRELL, Pinkney	6	N27NW	1889-01-12		A7
8535	" "	6	N26NW	1889-01-12		A7
6665	CARTER, William V	3	W½SE	1898-01-26		A7
6671	COCHRAN, Joseph E	12	SENE	1860-09-10		A6 G51
6670	" "	12	W½NE	1860-09-10		A6 G51
6669	" "	12	NENW	1860-09-10		A6 G51
6672	COCHRAN, Wilson	12	SENE	1860-09-10		A6 G51
6673	" "	12	NENW	1860-09-10		A6 G51
6674	" "	12	W½NE	1860-09-10		A6 G51
6675	COLLINS, Thomas	11	SWNE	1893-04-29		A7
6676	" "	11	NWSE	1893-04-29		A7
6677	" "	11	N½SW	1893-04-29		A7
6678	COVALT, Abraham	2	SWNW	1895-07-08		A7
6680	" "	3	E½SE	1895-07-08		A7
6679	" "	3	SENE	1895-07-08		A7
8546	CROOM, John S	6	S26SW	1893-12-19		A7
8563	" "	7	N27NW	1893-12-19		A7
8561	" "	7	N26NW	1893-12-19		A7
6683	DAVIS, Jesse	2	NENW	1890-10-11		A7
6682	" "	2	N½NE	1890-10-11		A7
6681	" "	2	SWNE	1890-10-11		A7
6684	DEATHERAGE, William J	7	SWSE	1907-08-23		A7
6685	DODD, James A	4	E½SW	1875-09-10		A7
8576	DODD, Joseph F	8	E22SW	1911-12-04		A1
8573	" "	8	2SE	1911-12-04		A1
6686	DODD, Josiah	4	S½SE	1877-06-04		A7
6687	DODD, Nancy A	3	SESW	1870-11-01		A1
6688	" "	3	SWNE	1870-11-01		A1
6689	EASLEY, Francis H	12	SENE	1860-09-10		A6 G51
6690	" "	12	NENE	1861-02-01		A1
6691	" "	12	SENW	1861-02-01		A1
6693	" "	12	SWNW	1860-08-01		A1
6692	" "	12	NENW	1860-09-10		A6 G51
6694	" "	12	W½NE	1860-09-10		A6 G51
6695	EASLEY, Reuben B	3	E½NW	1880-11-20		A7
6696	" "	3	NWNE	1880-11-20		A7
6701	EASLEY, William W	1	S½NW	1861-07-01		A6
6700	" "	1	NWNW	1861-07-01		A6
6702	" "	2	SENE	1861-07-01		A6
8569	ENDICOTT, Samuel J	7	S26NW	1901-12-17		A7
8562	" "	7	N26SW	1901-12-17		A7

ID	Individual in Patent	Sec.	Sec. Part	Date Issued	Other Counties	For More Info . . .
8571	ENDICOTT, Samuel J (Cont'd)	7	S27NW	1901-12-17		A7
6703	GILLILAND, James	11	NESE	1893-03-03		A7
6704	" "	11	E½NE	1893-03-03		A7
6705	" "	12	NWNW	1893-03-03		A7
6706	HANEY, Susan	4	N½NW	1891-05-05		A7 G106
6707	" "	4	NWNE	1891-05-05		A7 G106
6708	" "	5	NENE	1891-05-05		A7 G106
6709	HANEY, Timothy	4	NWNE	1891-05-05		A7 G106
6710	" "	4	N½NW	1891-05-05		A7 G106
6711	" "	5	NENE	1891-05-05		A7 G106
6712	HARKINS, Benjamin F	1	E½SE	1879-12-15		A7
6713	" "	1	SWSE	1879-12-15		A7
6715	HART, Mary F	8	SWNE	1877-04-05		A7
6714	" "	8	E½NE	1877-04-05		A7
8577	" "	8	W21SE	1877-04-05		A7
8533	HEMPHILL, Robert E	6	N23SW	1905-11-03		A7
8527	" "	6	3NW	1905-11-03		A7
6716	HENSON, David	11	NWNE	1872-07-01		A7
6717	" "	2	SWSE	1872-07-01		A7
6718	" "	2	E½SE	1872-07-01		A7
8560	HINES, John W	7	N25SW	1892-01-25		A7
8567	" "	7	S23SW	1892-01-25		A7
8554	" "	7	4SW	1892-01-25		A7
6721	HOLEMAN, John C	4	NWSE	1892-04-23		A7
6722	HORSMAN, William L	1	NWNE	1881-10-06		A7
6723	" "	1	NENW	1881-10-06		A7
6724	HOWARD, Martin V	5	S½SW	1896-08-28		A7
6725	" "	8	N½NW	1896-08-28		A7
8549	HOWARD, William	6	S27SW	1874-06-15		A1
8552	HUGHES, James E	7	2NW	1889-01-12		A7
8556	" "	7	N21NW	1889-01-12		A7
8557	" "	7	N23NW	1889-01-12		A7
8558	KING, Elbert W	7	N23SW	1892-08-20		A7
8566	" "	7	S23SW	1892-08-20		A7
8568	" "	7	S24NW	1892-08-20		A7
8572	LOCH, George W	7	S27SW	1880-11-20		A7
8570	" "	7	S26SW	1884-10-11		A1
8529	MCLAIN, Frank	6	4SW	1891-05-25		A7
8530	" "	6	5SW	1891-05-25		A7
8523	MORROW, Margaret	3	W21NW	1860-09-10		A6
8525	" "	3	W22NW	1860-09-10		A6
6727	NICHOLAS, George T	6	S½NE	1877-04-05		A7
6726	" "	6	W½SE	1877-04-05		A7
8532	NICHOLAS, Lincoln	6	N22SW	1886-10-29		A1
8543	" "	6	S23SW	1878-04-05		A7
6728	NICKS, Charter N	7	N½SE	1888-12-08		A7
6729	" "	7	SWNE	1888-12-08		A7
6730	NICKS, Jefferson D	4	NWSW	1901-03-23		A7
6731	" "	5	NESE	1901-03-23		A7
6732	NICKS, Nancy E	5	SESE	1888-12-06		A7
6733	" "	9	NWNW	1888-12-06		A7
6734	NICKS, Robert H	4	SWNW	1901-03-23		A7
6735	" "	5	S½NE	1901-03-23		A7
6737	NICKS, Rodney D	4	SENW	1861-02-09		A1
6736	" "	4	SWSW	1861-02-09		A1
8555	PRICE, James B	7	5NW	1896-03-25		A7
8559	" "	7	N24NW	1896-03-25		A7
8565	QUEEN, William H	7	S21NW	1900-02-02		A7
6738	RAY, Anderson	12	SW	1904-07-15		A7
8536	RHOTON, Marion M	6	N26SW	1901-08-27		A1
6739	RICHEY, William F	2	NWNW	1888-12-08		A7
6740	" "	3	NENE	1888-12-08		A7
6741	RIGSBY, Millie A	10	N½NE	1897-10-28		A7
6742	" "	10	E½NW	1897-10-28		A7
6743	RIGSBY, William J	3	NWSW	1884-11-01		A7
6744	" "	4	NESE	1884-11-01		A7
6745	" "	4	S½NE	1884-11-01		A7
6746	ROADS, John	1	NENE	1882-03-30		A7
6747	ROMINE, James A	2	SENW	1901-07-09		A7
6748	SHIRL, William W	3	NESW	1861-02-01		A1
6749	SHURLEY, Thomas P	4	NENE	1877-08-01		A7
6750	SIGLER, Lewis A	5	N½SW	1892-01-05		A7
6752	" "	5	NWNW	1886-07-20		A1

ID	Individual in Patent	Sec.	Sec. Part	Date Issued	Other Counties	For More Info . . .
6751	SIGLER, Lewis A (Cont'd)	5	S½NW	1892-01-05		A7
6753	SMITH, Benjamin C	10	NWNW	1898-01-26		A7
6754	" "	3	SWSW	1898-01-26		A7
8548	SMITH, H S	6	S27SW	1874-06-15		A1
8544	SMITH, William R	6	S25NW	1885-02-25		A7
8528	" "	6	4NW	1885-02-25		A7
8534	" "	6	N25NW	1889-05-29		A1
6755	SOUTH, William B	9	SWNW	1891-05-25		A7
6756	" "	9	SW	1891-05-25		A7
8545	SPARKS, John S	6	S26NW	1888-12-08		A7
8547	" "	6	S27NW	1888-12-08		A7
8538	" "	6	N27SW	1888-12-08		A7
8531	SPEARS, Joseph T	6	N21SW	1860-08-01		A1
8542	" "	6	S22SW	1860-05-02		A6
8540	" "	6	S21SW	1860-05-02		A6
6757	SPRADLING, Dorsey H	1	NWSE	1861-07-01		A6
6759	" "	1	SWNE	1861-07-01		A6
6758	" "	1	SENE	1859-09-01		A1
8564	STACY, William D	7	N27SW	1859-09-01		A1
8553	" "	7	2SW	1859-09-01		A1
8551	" "	7	1SW	1859-09-01		A1
8522	TERRY, William M	3	W21NW	1860-09-10		A6
8526	" "	3	W22NW	1860-09-10		A6
6760	THOMPSON, Daniel G	10	SW	1908-07-27		A7
8550	TYREE, S W	6	S27SW	1874-06-15		A1
8574	UMPHREY, Michael A	8	E21SE	1888-12-04		A7
8575	" "	8	E21SW	1888-12-04		A7
6761	VAUGHAN, Anthony	10	S½NE	1891-05-25		A7
6762	" "	10	SE	1891-05-25		A7
6763	VAUGHAN, James M	5	W½SE	1905-08-26		A7
6764	" "	8	NWNE	1905-08-26		A7
6765	WILLIAMS, Stephen	2	NWSE	1861-02-01		A1
6766	YOUNG, Reuben	6	NESE	1886-10-29		A1

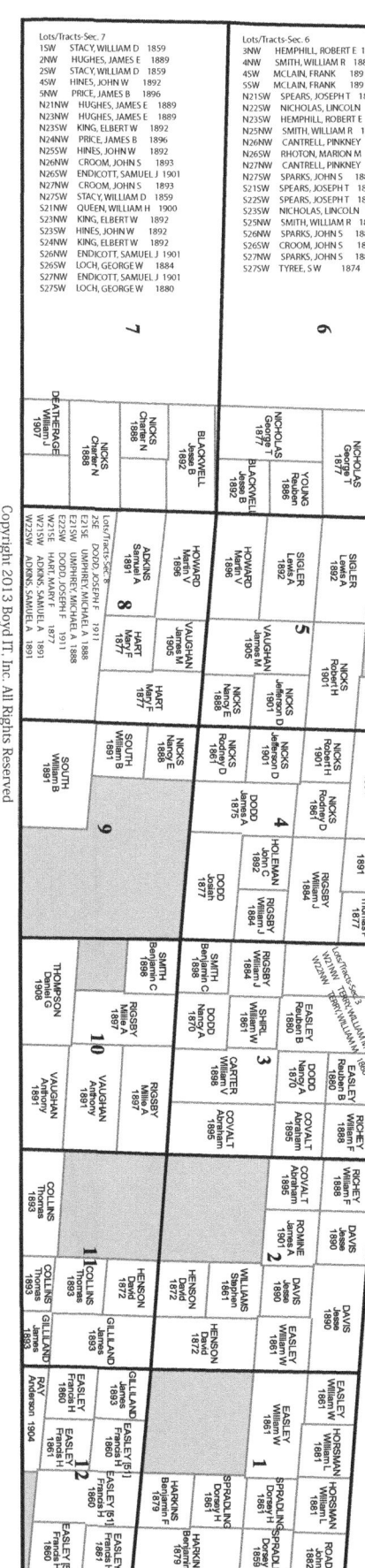

Lots/Tracts-Sec. 7
1SW	STACY, WILLIAM D	1859
2NW	HUGHES, JAMES E	1889
2SW	STACY, WILLIAM D	1859
4SW	HINES, JOHN W	1892
5NW	PRICE, JAMES B	1896
N21NW	HUGHES, JAMES E	1889
N23NW	HUGHES, JAMES E	1889
N23SW	KING, ELBERT W	1892
N24NW	PRICE, JAMES B	1896
N25SW	HINES, JOHN W	1892
N26NW	CROOM, JOHN S	1893
N26SW	ENDICOTT, SAMUEL J	1901
N27NW	CROOM, JOHN S	1893
N27SW	STACY, WILLIAM D	1859
S21NW	QUEEN, WILLIAM H	1900
S23NW	KING, ELBERT W	1892
S23SW	HINES, JOHN W	1892
S24NW	KING, ELBERT W	1892
S26NW	ENDICOTT, SAMUEL J	1901
S26SW	LOCH, GEORGE W	1884
S27NW	ENDICOTT, SAMUEL J	1901
S27SW	LOCH, GEORGE W	1880

Lots/Tracts-Sec. 6
3NW	HEMPHILL, ROBERT E	1905
4NW	SMITH, WILLIAM R	1885
4SW	MCLAIN, FRANK	1891
5SW	MCLAIN, FRANK	1891
N21SW	SPEARS, JOSEPH T	1860
N22SW	NICHOLAS, LINCOLN	1886
N23SW	HEMPHILL, ROBERT E	1905
N25NW	SMITH, WILLIAM R	1889
N26NW	CANTRELL, PINKNEY	1889
N26SW	RHOTON, MARION M	1901
N27NW	CANTRELL, PINKNEY	1889
N27SW	SPARKS, JOHN S	1888
S21SW	SPEARS, JOSEPH T	1860
S22SW	SPEARS, JOSEPH T	1860
S23SW	NICHOLAS, LINCOLN	1878
S25NW	SMITH, WILLIAM R	1885
S26NW	SPARKS, JOHN S	1888
S26SW	CROOM, JOHN S	1893
S27NW	SPARKS, JOHN S	1888
S27SW	TYREE, S W	1874

Copyright 2013 Boyd IT, Inc. All Rights Reserved

Patent Map

T21-N R10-W
5th PM 21-N 10-W Meridian

Map Group 25

Township Statistics

Parcels Mapped	:	139
Number of Patents	:	75
Number of Individuals	:	76
Patentees Identified	:	73
Number of Surnames	:	56
Multi-Patentee Parcels	:	6
Oldest Patent Date	:	9/1/1859
Most Recent Patent	:	7/27/1908
Block/Lot Parcels	:	51
Cities and Town	:	0
Cemeteries	:	0

Note: the area contained in this map amounts to far less than a full Township. Therefore, its contents are completely on this single page (instead of a "normal" 2-page spread).

Legend

—————— Patent Boundary

━━━━━━ Section Boundary

No Patents Found (or Outside County)

1., 2., 3., ... Lot Numbers (when beside a name)

[ ] Group Number (see Appendix "C")

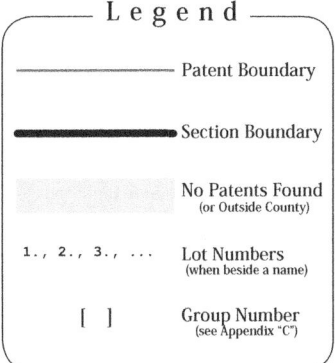

Scale: Section = 1 mile X 1 mile (generally, with some exceptions)

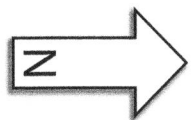

357

Road Map

T21-N R10-W
5th PM 21-N 10-W Meridian

Map Group 25

Note: the area contained in this map amounts to far less than a full Township. Therefore, its contents are completely on this single page (instead of a "normal" 2-page spread).

Cities & Towns
None

Cemeteries
None

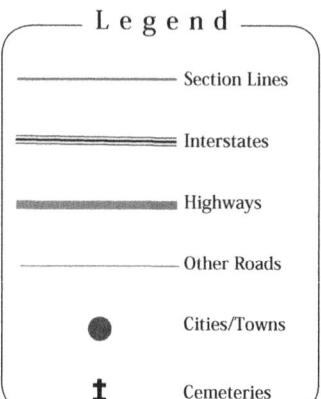

Legend

————————	Section Lines
═══════════	Interstates
▬▬▬▬▬▬	Highways
————————	Other Roads
●	Cities/Towns
♱	Cemeteries

Scale: Section = 1 mile X 1 mile
(generally, with some exceptions)

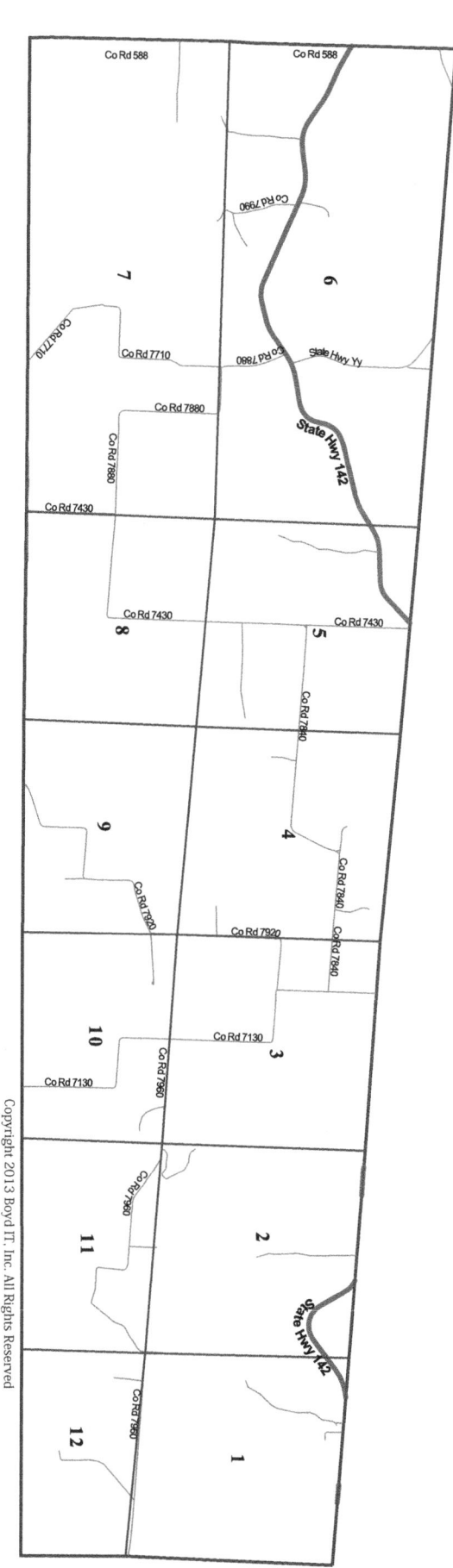

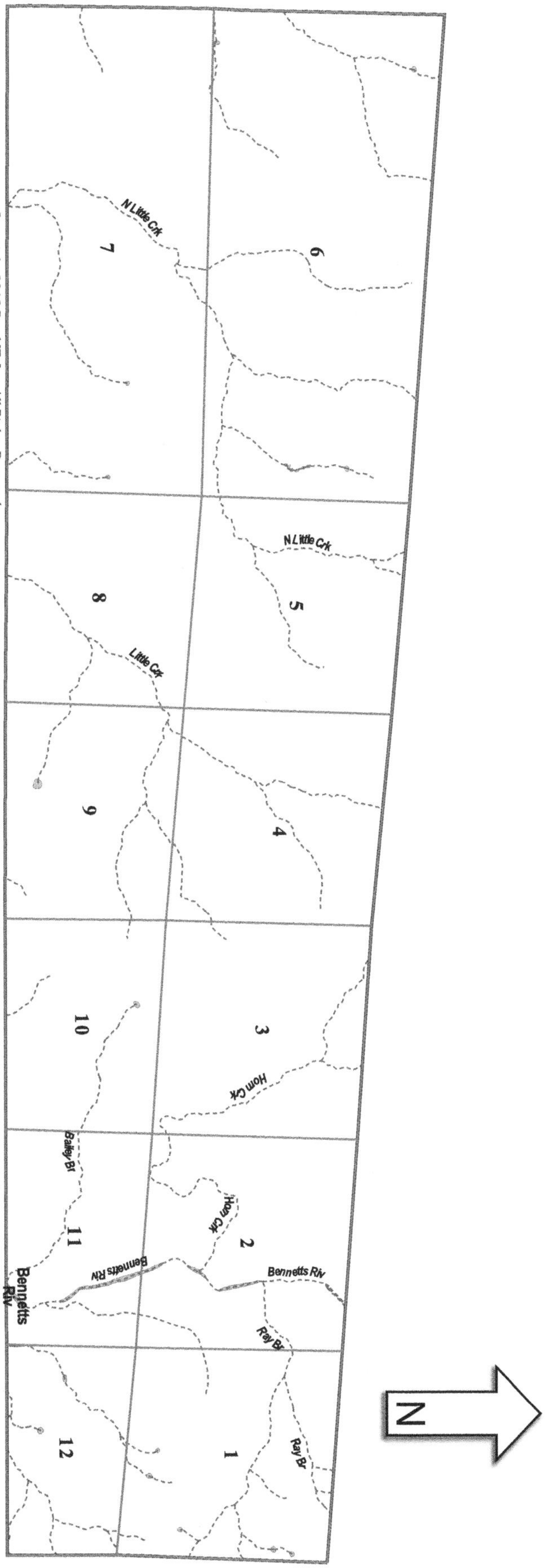

Historical Map

T21-N R10-W
5th PM 21-N 10-W Meridian

Map Group 25

Note: the area contained in this map amounts to far less than a full Township. Therefore, its contents are completely on this single page (instead of a "normal" 2-page spread).

Cities & Towns
None

Cemeteries
None

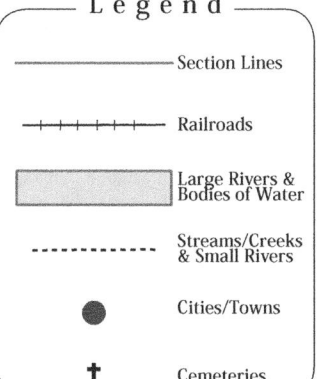

Legend

——————	Section Lines
—+—+—+—+—	Railroads
▭	Large Rivers & Bodies of Water
- - - - - - -	Streams/Creeks & Small Rivers
●	Cities/Towns
✝	Cemeteries

Scale: Section = 1 mile X 1 mile
(there are some exceptions)

N L Little Crk

N L Little Crk

Little Crk

Horn Crk

Bailey Br

Horn Crk

Bennetts Riv

Bennetts Riv

Bennetts Riv

Ray Br

Ray Br

7 6 8 5 9 4 10 3 11 2 1 12

Map Group 26: Index to Land Patents

Township 21-North Range 9-West (5th PM 21-N 9-W)

After you locate an individual in this Index, take note of the Section and Section Part then proceed to the Land Patent map on the pages immediately following. You should have no difficulty locating the corresponding parcel of land.

The "For More Info" Column will lead you to more information about the underlying Patents. See the *Legend* at right, and the "How to Use this Book" chapter, for more information.

```
                        LEGEND
            "For More Info . . . " column
A = Authority (Legislative Act, See Appendix "A")
B = Block or Lot (location in Section unknown)
C = Cancelled Patent
F = Fractional Section
G = Group (Multi-Patentee Patent, see Appendix "C")
V = Overlaps another Parcel
R = Re-Issued (Parcel patented more than once)

(A & G items require you to look in the Appendixes referred
to above. All other Letter-designations followed by a number
require you to locate line-items in this index that possess
the ID number found after the letter).
```

ID	Individual in Patent	Sec.	Sec. Part	Date Issued	Other Counties	For More Info . . .
6767	BALL, Gehazi R	4	SWNE	1872-07-01		A7
8628	" "	5	2NE	1861-07-01		A6 G12
8595	BALL, Robert	11	4	1891-08-24		A1
8589	BALL, Robert E	10	7NW	1872-07-01		A7
8590	" "	10	8NW	1872-07-01		A7
6768	" "	3	SWSW	1872-07-01		A7
6769	" "	4	SESE	1872-07-01		A7
8612	BALL, William E	3	E22NE	1903-07-29		A7
6770	BLACKWELL, Sidney	1	NESE	1908-06-25		A7
8660	CALDWELL, Robert H	8	8	1882-11-10		A7
8657	" "	8	5	1882-11-10		A7
8580	CATES, Solomon	1	2	1892-03-07		A7
8585	" "	1	W21NW	1892-03-07		A7
8586	" "	1	W22NE	1892-03-07		A7
8624	CLARK, James	4	E22NW	1878-06-24		A7
6771	CLAXTON, Francis M	4	S½SW	1878-06-24		A7
6772	" "	4	NWSW	1878-06-24		A7
8625	CLAXTON, William P	4	W21NW	1895-05-28		A7
8631	" "	5	E21NE	1895-05-28		A7
8655	CLAYTON, Hyrum M	8	3	1876-09-06		A7
8653	" "	8	1	1876-09-06		A7
8654	" "	8	2	1876-09-06		A7
8656	" "	8	4	1876-09-06		A7
8652	COLLINS, Perry C	7	8SW	1904-12-31		A7
6773	COVINGTON, Benjamin T	2	NW	1892-06-10		A7
8609	COVINGTON, Robert M	2	1NE	1892-06-10		A7
8610	" "	2	2NE	1892-06-10		A7
6774	COX, James	1	SESE	1890-01-10		A7
6775	" "	1	W½SE	1890-01-10		A7
8615	DAVIS, Joseph	3	W21NE	1892-08-08		A7 G66
8618	" "	3	W22NE	1892-08-08		A7 G66
8617	DAVIS, Rebecca	3	W22NE	1892-08-08		A7 G66
8614	" "	3	W21NE	1892-08-08		A7 G66
8633	DAVIS, Ulysses G	5	W21NE	1901-01-10		A1
8634	DIELLE, Henry	5	W21NW	1861-06-27	Dunklin	A4
8639	" "	6	E21NW	1861-06-27	Dunklin	A4
8640	" "	6	N21SW	1861-06-27	Dunklin	A4
8635	" "	6	1NE	1861-06-27	Dunklin	A4
6776	" "	6	N½SE	1861-06-27	Dunklin	A4
8649	EADES, Jessey F	7	5	1893-06-13		A7
8648	" "	7	4	1893-06-13		A7
8645	" "	7	1	1893-06-13		A7
6777	EASLEY, Francis H	6	SWSE	1880-03-05		A8 G72
8641	" "	6	S21SW	1880-03-05		A8 G72
8651	" "	7	7NW	1860-08-01		A1
6779	FELTS, Joseph J	3	NWSE	1892-03-07		A7

ID	Individual in Patent	Sec.	Sec. Part	Date Issued	Other Counties	For More Info . . .
6778	FELTS, Joseph J (Cont'd)	3	E½SE	1892-03-07		A7
6780	"	3	NESW	1892-03-07		A7
6781	GRAY, Obediah	6	SESE	1885-06-20		A7
8663	HAMMOND, Thomas F	9	3NE	1890-01-10		A7
8661	" "	9	1NE	1890-01-10		A7
8611	HARRIS, John	3	E21NE	1896-03-25		A7
6782	HIBBARD, Joseph	4	SWSE	1861-02-01		A1
8662	"	9	2NE	1860-12-10		A1
8630	JONES, Lizzie	5	2NW	1877-10-10		A7
8632	" "	5	E21NW	1877-10-10		A7
8616	KEIRN, Rebecca	3	W22NE	1892-08-08		A7 G66
8613	"	3	W21NE	1892-08-08		A7 G66
6783	KIMBALL, Richard	2	SW	1875-10-15		A7
8581	KING, James H	1	E21NE	1902-10-11		A7
8583	" "	1	E22NE	1902-10-11		A7
8594	MASON, Robert	11	3NE	1892-09-27		A7
8593	" "	11	2NE	1892-09-27		A7
6784	"	2	W½SE	1892-09-27		A7
8582	MATNEY, Eli	1	E21NW	1888-12-08		A7
8584	" "	1	W21NE	1888-12-08		A7
6785	" "	1	E½SW	1888-12-08		A7
8619	MCCOY, James	4	E21NE	1891-05-25		A7
8623	" "	4	E22NE	1891-05-25		A7
8587	MCKIM, William	10	5W2	1901-04-09		A7
8588	" "	10	6W2	1901-04-09		A7
6786	" "	3	SWSE	1901-04-09		A7
6787	" "	3	SESW	1901-04-09		A7
8622	MCNEELY, John	4	E21NW	1861-07-01		A6 G148
6788	" "	4	NWSE	1861-07-01		A6 G148
6789	" "	4	NESW	1861-07-01		A6 G148
8664	MORRIS, James L	9	4NE	1912-02-05		A1
6790	NELSON, James R	3	NWSW	1885-12-19		A7
6791	" "	4	NESE	1885-12-19		A7
8600	NEWKIRK, Braxton L	11	8	1891-06-09		A7
8597	" "	11	5	1891-06-09		A7
8598	" "	11	6	1891-06-09		A7
8599	" "	11	7	1891-06-09		A7
8626	PEARCE, Henry T	4	W22NE	1908-04-30		A7
6792	POWELL, James A	4	NWNW	1877-05-15		A7
8642	POWELL, Rebecca	6	S21SW	1880-03-05		A8 G72
6793	" "	6	SWSE	1880-03-05		A8 G72
6795	PUGH, Elizabeth	4	NWSE	1861-07-01		A6 G148
6796	" "	4	NESW	1861-07-01		A6 G148
8621	" "	4	E21NW	1861-07-01		A6 G148
8637	ROADS, John	6	2NW	1882-03-30		A7
8592	SHAW, Cora E	11	1	1911-05-11		A7
8607	" "	12	8	1911-05-11		A7
8605	" "	12	7	1911-05-11		A7
8602	" "	12	5	1911-05-11		A7
8603	" "	12	6	1911-05-11		A7
8646	SMITH, James	7	2NE	1888-12-08		A7
8650	" "	7	6NW	1888-12-08		A7
8647	" "	7	3NE	1888-12-08		A7
8638	SPRADLING, Dorsey H	6	2NW	1860-08-01		A1
8644	" "	6	W21NW	1859-09-01		A1
8636	STRANGE, Archelaus	6	2NE	1878-04-05		A7
6799	STUART, John F	1	W½SW	1892-06-10		A7
6800	" "	2	E½SE	1892-06-10		A7
8591	VAN DERNOEF, Cora E	11	1	1911-05-11		A7
8608	" "	12	8	1911-05-11		A7
8606	" "	12	7	1911-05-11		A7
8604	" "	12	6	1911-05-11		A7
8601	" "	12	5	1911-05-11		A7
8596	WHARTON, W E	11	4	1891-08-24		A1
8659	WHARTON, William E	8	7NW	1891-08-24		A1
8658	" "	8	6NW	1891-08-24		A1
8627	WILLIAMS, Elizabeth	5	2NE	1861-07-01		A6 G12

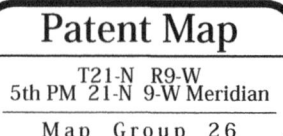

Patent Map

T21-N R9-W
5th PM 21-N 9-W Meridian

Map Group 26

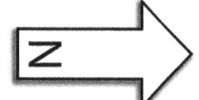

N

Township Statistics

Parcels Mapped	:	97
Number of Patents	:	49
Number of Individuals	:	55
Patentees Identified	:	49
Number of Surnames	:	43
Multi-Patentee Parcels	:	8
Oldest Patent Date	:	2/1/1861
Most Recent Patent	:	6/25/1908
Block/Lot Parcels	:	69
Cities and Town	:	0
Cemeteriesp	:	0

Note: the area contained in this map amounts to far less than a full Township. Therefore, its contents are completely on this single page (instead of a "normal" 2-page spread).

Legend

— Patent Boundary

— Section Boundary

No Patents Found (or Outside County)

1., 2., 3., ... Lot Numbers (when beside a name)

[ ] Group Number (see Appendix "C")

Scale: Section = 1 mile X 1 mile (generally, with some exceptions)

Section 6 — Lots/Tracts-Sec. 6
1NE DIELLE, HENRY 1861
2NE STRANGE, ARCHELAUS 1878
2NW ROADS, JOHN 1882
2NW SPRADLING, DORSEY H 1860
E2NW DIELLE, HENRY 1861
E2NW DIELLE, HENRY 1861
N21SW EASLEY, FRANCIS H [72]1880
S21SW EASLEY, FRANCIS H [72]1880
W21NW SPRADLING, DORSEY H 1859

6

DIELLE Henry 1861

Section 7 — Lots/Tracts-Sec. 7
1 EADES, JESSEY F 1893
2 SMITH, JAMES 1888
3NE SMITH, JAMES 1888
4 EADES, JESSEY F 1893
5 EADES, JESSEY F 1893
6WW SMITH, JAMES 1888
7NW EASLEY, FRANCIS H 1860
8SW COLLINS, PERRY C 1904

7

EASLEY [73] Francis H 1880
GRAY Obediah 1885

Section 5 — Lots/Tracts-Sec. 5
2NE BALL, GIHAZI R [12] 1861
2NW JONES, LIZZIE 1877
E2NE CLAXTON, WILLIAM P 1895
E2NW JONES, LIZZIE 1877
W21NE DAVIS, ULYSSES G 1901
W21NW DIELLE, HENRY 1861

5

Section 8 — Lots/Tracts-Sec. 8
1 CLAYTON, HYRUM M 1876
2 CLAYTON, HYRUM M 1876
3 CLAYTON, HYRUM M 1876
4 CLAYTON, HYRUM M 1876
5 CALDWELL, ROBERT H 1882
6WW WHARTON, WILLIAM E 1891
7NW WHARTON, WILLIAM E 1891
8 CALDWELL, ROBERT H 1882

8

Section 4 — Lots/Tracts-Sec. 4
E2NE MCCOY, JAMES 1891
E2NW MCNEELY, JOHN [148] 1861
E2NE MCCOY, JAMES 1891
E2NW CLARK, JAMES 1878
W21NW CLAYTON, WILLIAM P 1895
W2NE PEARCE, HENRY T 1908

POWELL James A 1877
CLAXTON Francis M 1878
MCNEELY John 1861
CLAXTON Francis M 1878
MCNEELY [148] John 1861
BALL Gihazi R 1872
HIBBARD Joseph 1861

4

Section 9 — Lots/Tracts-Sec. 9
1NE HAMMOND, THOMAS F 1890
2NE HIBBARD, JOSEPH 1860
3NE HAMMOND, THOMAS F 1890
4NE MORRIS, THOMAS L 1912

9

Section 3 — Lots/Tracts-Sec. 3
E2NE HARRIS, JOHN 1896
E2NE BALL, WILLIAM E 1903
W21NE KERR, REBECCA [60] 1892
W21NW KERR, REBECCA [60] 1892
W2NE KERR, REBECCA [60] 1892

COVINGTON Benjamin T 1892
NELSON James R 1885
BALL Robert E 1872
FELTS Joseph J 1892

3

MCKIM William 1901
FELTS Joseph J 1892

Section 10 — Lots/Tracts-Sec. 10
5W2 MCKIM, WILLIAM 1901
6W2 MCKIM, WILLIAM 1901
7NW BALL, ROBERT E 1872
8NW BALL, ROBERT E 1872

NELSON James R 1885
BALL Robert E 1872
MCKIM William 1901

10

Section 2 — Lots/Tracts-Sec. 2
1NE SHAW, CORA E 1911
2NE MASON, ROBERT 1892
3NE WHARTON, W E
1NE COVINGTON, ROBERT M 1892
2NE COVINGTON, ROBERT M 1892

KIMBALL Richard 1875
COVINGTON Benjamin T 1892
MASON Robert 1892
STUART John F 1892

2

Section 11 — Lots/Tracts-Sec. 11
1 SHAW, CORA E 1911
2NE MASON, ROBERT 1892
3NE NEWKIRK, BRAXTON L 1891
4 NEWKIRK, BRAXTON L 1891
5 NEWKIRK, BRAXTON L 1891
6 NEWKIRK, BRAXTON L 1891
7 NEWKIRK, BRAXTON L 1891
8 NEWKIRK, BRAXTON L 1891

11

Section 1 — Lots/Tracts-Sec. 1
1 CATES, SOLOMON 1892
2NE KING, JAMES H 1902
2NE MATNEY, ELI 1888
E2NE KING, JAMES H 1902
W21NE MATNEY, ELI 1888
W21NW CATES, SOLOMON 1892
W2NE CATES, SOLOMON 1892

STUART John F 1892
MATNEY Eli 1888
COX James 1880

1

BLACKWELL Sidney 1908
COX James 1880

Section 12 — Lots/Tracts-Sec. 12
1 SHAW, CORA E 1911
5 SHAW, CORA E 1911
6 SHAW, CORA E 1911
7 SHAW, CORA E 1911
8 SHAW, CORA E 1911

12

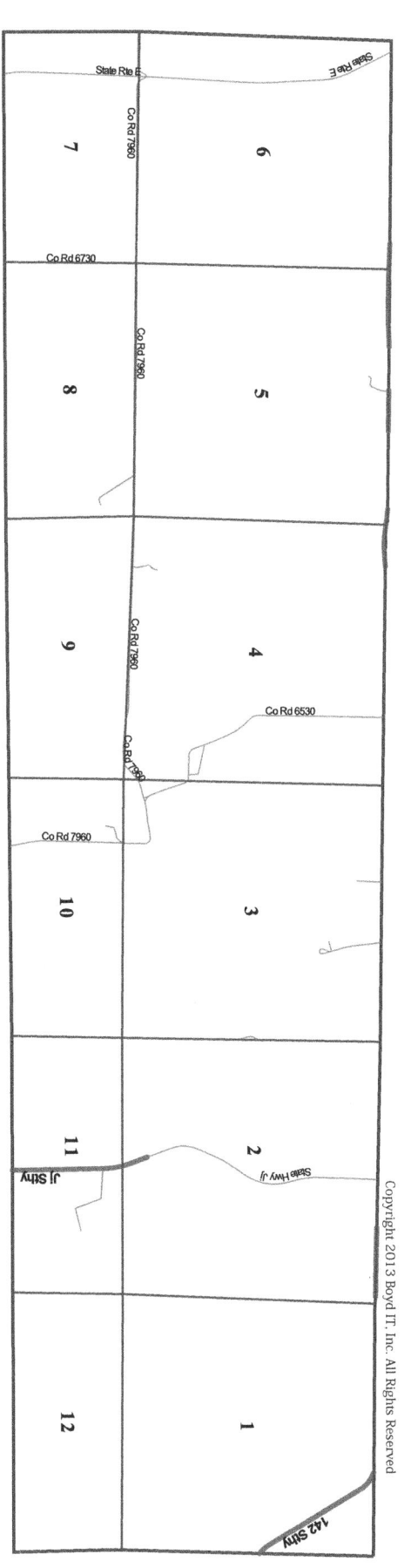

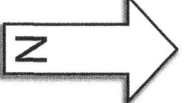

Road Map

T21-N R9-W
5th PM 21-N 9-W Meridian

Map Group 26

Note: the area contained in this map amounts to far less than a full Township. Therefore, its contents are completely on this single page (instead of a "normal" 2-page spread).

Cities & Towns
None

Cemeteries
None

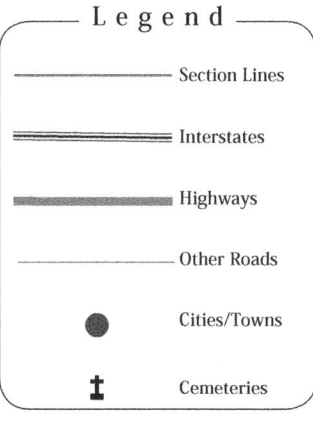

Legend

— Section Lines

= Interstates

— Highways

— Other Roads

● Cities/Towns

✝ Cemeteries

Scale: Section = 1 mile X 1 mile
(generally, with some exceptions)

Historical Map

T21-N R9-W
5th PM 21-N 9-W Meridian

Map Group 26

Note: the area contained in this map amounts to far less than a full Township. Therefore, its contents are completely on this single page (instead of a "normal" 2-page spread).

Cities & Towns
None

Cemeteries
None

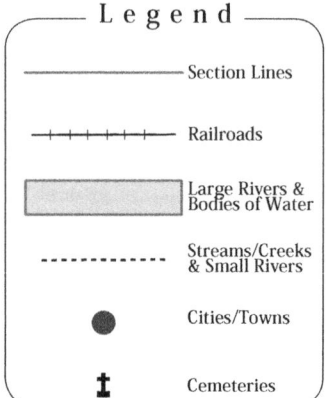

L e g e n d

——————— Section Lines

+++++++ Railroads

▭ Large Rivers & Bodies of Water

----------- Streams/Creeks & Small Rivers

● Cities/Towns

† Cemeteries

Scale: Section = 1 mile X 1 mile
(there are some exceptions)

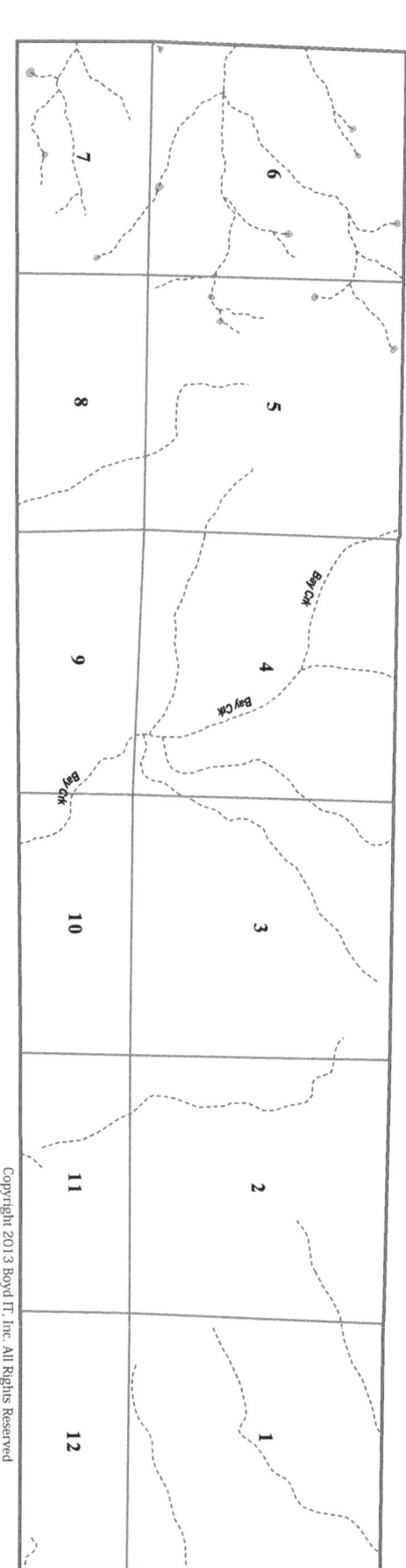

Map Group 27: Index to Land Patents

Township 21-North Range 8-West (5th PM 21-N 8-W)

After you locate an individual in this Index, take note of the Section and Section Part then proceed to the Land Patent map on the pages immediately following. You should have no difficulty locating the corresponding parcel of land.

The "For More Info" Column will lead you to more information about the underlying Patents. See the *Legend* at right, and the "How to Use this Book" chapter, for more information.

```
                    LEGEND
         "For More Info . . . " column
A = Authority (Legislative Act, See Appendix "A")
B = Block or Lot (location in Section unknown)
C = Cancelled Patent
F = Fractional Section
G = Group  (Multi-Patentee Patent, see Appendix "C")
V = Overlaps another Parcel
R = Re-Issued (Parcel patented more than once)

(A & G items require you to look in the Appendixes referred
to above. All other Letter-designations followed by a number
require you to locate line-items in this index that possess
the ID number found after the letter).
```

ID	Individual in Patent	Sec.	Sec. Part	Date Issued	Other Counties	For More Info . . .
6801	ALSUP, Ben M	7		1907-12-02		A1
6802	" "	8	W½W½	1907-12-02		A1
6803	ALSUP, Elijah	12	E½	1898-04-11		A7
8671	BATEMAN, James C	1	W22NE	1890-01-10		A7
8668	" "	1	E22NW	1890-01-10		A7
8667	BENCH, Henry	1	E22NE	1897-11-10		A7
8698	BLACKWELL, Sidney	6	N22SW	1908-06-25		A7
6804	CANNON, Granville	11	E½W½	1905-03-30		A7
6805	" "	11	E½	1905-03-30		A7
6806	CANNON, James	8	E½NE	1860-08-01		A1
6808	CANNON, James A	8	NWNE	1890-01-10		A7
6807	" "	8	E½NW	1892-03-07		A7
6809	CATES, James C	4	SWSW	1885-12-19		A7
6810	" "	9	W½NW	1885-12-19		A7
8669	CATES, James E	1	W21NE	1903-03-17		A7
8666	" "	1	E21NW	1903-03-17		A7
6811	CHAPIN, William A	9	E½NW	1906-05-16		A1
6812	COLE, Rachel	4	NWSE	1876-01-10		A7
6813	" "	4	E½SW	1876-01-10		A7
6814	COTHRAN, Thomas	4	NENE	1860-08-01		A1
8699	COX, James	6	S22S2	1890-01-10		A7
8684	CROWDER, John W	3	1NW	1890-10-11		A7
6815	" "	3	NESW	1890-10-11		A7
8688	" "	4	E21NE	1890-10-11		A7
6816	CROWDER, William R	3	NWSW	1902-11-25		A7
6817	" "	4	NESE	1902-11-25		A7
6818	DUNAVIN, Marion F	5	SWSE	1885-12-19		A7
6819	" "	5	N½SE	1885-12-19		A7
6820	ENGLAND, Joel W	1	W½SE	1890-01-10		A7 G76
6822	" "	1	E½SW	1890-01-10		A7 G76
6821	" "	1	E½SE	1888-12-06		A7
6824	ENGLAND, Mahaley	1	W½SE	1890-01-10		A7 G76
6823	" "	1	E½SW	1890-01-10		A7 G76
6825	EZELL, James W	4	SWSE	1900-11-12		A7
6826	" "	9	W½NE	1900-11-12		A7
8683	EZELL, Thomas	3	1NE	1895-08-01		A7
6827	" "	3	N½SE	1895-08-01		A7
6829	HARDIN, Marion S	2	NESW	1893-06-13		A7
6828	" "	2	S½SW	1893-06-13		A7
6830	HEATH, George O	10	W½NW	1902-10-20		A7
6831	" "	4	SESE	1902-10-20		A7
6832	" "	9	E½NE	1902-10-20		A7
8687	HOGAN, Robert S	3	W22NE	1907-08-06		A1
6833	HOLLOWAY, James M	10	E½NW	1892-01-05		A7
6834	" "	3	S½SW	1892-01-05		A7
8685	HOLLOWAY, Sydney	3	2NW	1877-06-04		A7

ID	Individual in Patent	Sec.	Sec. Part	Date Issued	Other Counties	For More Info . . .
6835	HOLLOWAY, Thomas A	2	NWSW	1892-09-15		A7
8676	" "	2	1NW	1892-09-15		A7
8682	HOLLOWAY, William	2	W22NW	1880-11-20		A7
8686	" "	3	E22NE	1880-11-20		A7
6836	HOLLOWAY, William H	10	W½NE	1892-01-05		A7
6837	" "	3	S½SE	1892-01-05		A7
6838	HOWERTON, Mary A	2	SE	1891-05-05		A7
8680	KURSEY, Annis	2	E22NW	1892-03-07		A7
8681	" "	2	W22NE	1892-03-07		A7
6839	LAMONS, John M	1	SWSW	1892-06-10		A7
6840	" "	12	W½	1892-06-10		A7
8695	LOCK, Granville W	6	1N2	1914-03-31		A7
8696	" "	6	1S2	1914-03-31		A7
8697	MATNEY, Joseph L	6	2NW	1882-09-30		A7
8692	MCCOMICK, Charles A	5	E22NE	1896-09-29		A7
6841	MYERS, Jacob	5	SESE	1860-10-01		A1
6842	NICKS, Alfred H	4	NWSW	1861-02-01		A1
8691	" "	5	E21NE	1861-02-01		A1
6843	PEARSON, Wilfred	10	E½E½	1905-03-30		A7
6844	" "	11	W½W½	1905-03-30		A7
8672	REAVES, Celia	1	W22NW	1861-07-01		A6 G163
8678	" "	2	E22NE	1861-07-01		A6 G163
8674	SLOAN, John	1	W22NW	1861-07-01		A6 G163
8679	" "	2	E22NE	1861-07-01		A6 G163
8689	STEVENS, John	4	W21NE	1879-12-15		A7
8690	" "	4	W22NE	1879-12-15		A7
8694	THOMAS, Woodley A	5	W22NE	1861-08-01		A1
8693	" "	5	W21NE	1861-08-01		A1
8665	THOMPSON, Willis A	1	E21NE	1892-06-10		A7
8670	VERNON, William S	1	W21NW	1891-06-09		A7
6845	" "	1	NWSW	1891-06-09		A7
8675	" "	2	1NE	1891-06-09		A7

Patent Map

T21-N R8-W
5th PM 21-N 8-W Meridian

Map Group 27

Township Statistics

Parcels Mapped	:	74
Number of Patents	:	45
Number of Individuals	:	45
Patentees Identified	:	43
Number of Surnames	:	33
Multi-Patentee Parcels	:	4
Oldest Patent Date	:	8/1/1860
Most Recent Patent	:	12/2/1907
Block/Lot Parcels	:	31
Cities and Town	:	1
Cemeteries	:	1

Note: the area contained in this map amounts to far less than a full Township. Therefore, its contents are completely on this single page (instead of a "normal" 2-page spread).

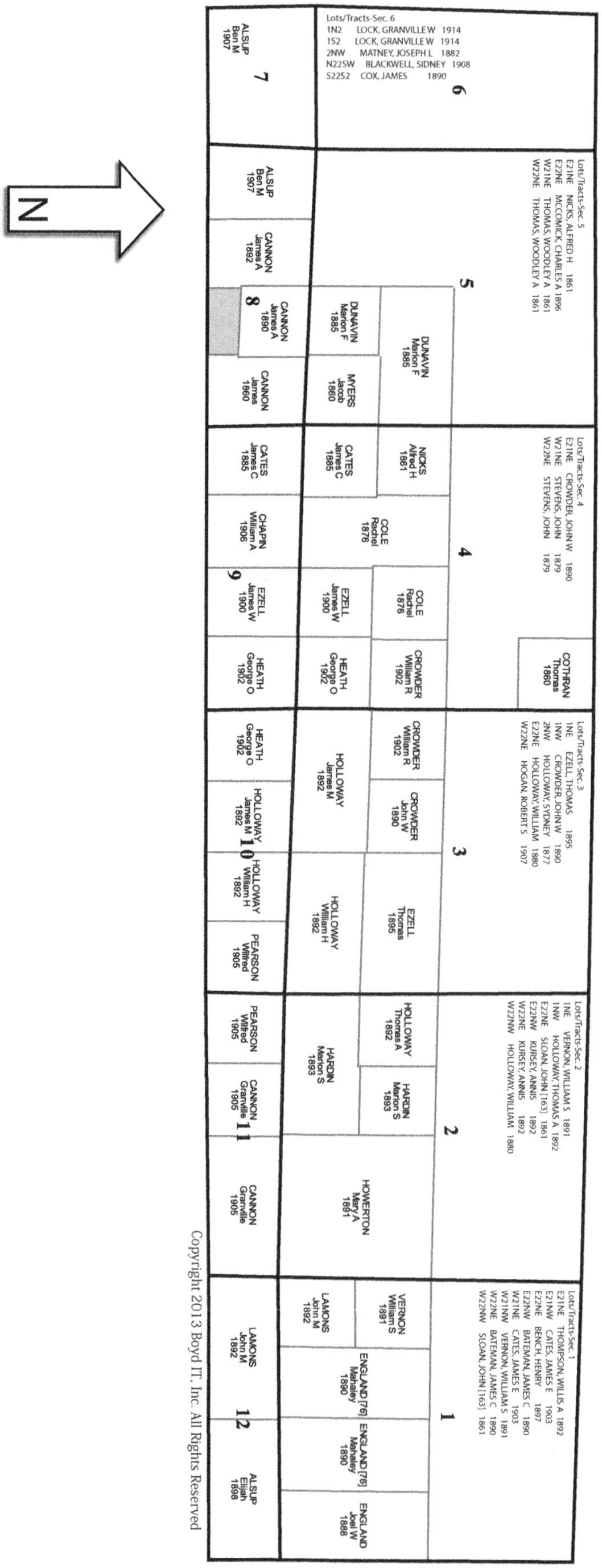
N
7
ALSUP Ben M 1907
6
Lots/Tracts-Sec. 6
1N2 LOCK, GRANVILLE W 1914
1S2 LOCK, GRANVILLE W 1914
2NW MATNEY, JOSEPH L 1882
N22SW BLACKWELL, SIDNEY 1908
S22S2 COX, JAMES 1890
8
ALSUP Ben M 1907
CANNON James A 1892
CANNON James A 1890
CANNON James 1860
5
Lots/Tracts-Sec. 5
E21NE NICKS, ALFRED H 1861
E22NE MCCOMICK, CHARLES A 1896
W21NE THOMAS, WOODLEY A 1861
W22NE THOMAS, WOODLEY A 1861
DUNAVIN Marion F 1885
DUNAVIN Marion F 1885
MYERS Jacob 1860
9
CATES James C 1885
CHAPIN William A 1906
EZELL James W 1900
HEATH George O 1902
4
Lots/Tracts-Sec. 4
E21NE CROWDER, JOHN W 1890
W21NE STEVENS, JOHN 1879
W22NE STEVENS, JOHN 1879
CATES James C 1885
NICKS Alfred H 1861
COLE Rachel 1876
EZELL James W 1900
COLE Rachel 1876
HEATH George O 1902
CROWDER William R 1902
COTHRAN Thomas 1860
10
HEATH George O 1902
HOLLOWAY James M 1882
HOLLOWAY William H 1892
PEARSON Wilfred 1905
3
Lots/Tracts-Sec. 3
1NE EZELL, THOMAS 1895
1NW CROWDER, JOHN W 1890
2NW HOLLOWAY, SYDNEY 1877
E22NE HOLLOWAY, WILLIAM 1880
W22NE HOGAN, ROBERT S 1907
HOLLOWAY James M 1892
CROWDER William R 1902
CROWDER John W 1890
HOLLOWAY William H 1892
EZELL Thomas 1895
11
PEARSON Wilfred 1905
CANNON Granville 1905
CANNON Granville 1905
2
Lots/Tracts-Sec. 2
1NE VERNON, WILLIAM S 1891
1NW HOLLOWAY, THOMAS A 1892
E22NE SLOAN, JOHN [163] 1861
E22NW KURSEY, ANNIS 1892
W22NE KURSEY, ANNIS 1892
W22NW HOLLOWAY, WILLIAM 1880
HOLLOWAY Thomas A 1892
HARDIN Marion S 1893
HARDIN Marion S 1893
HOWERTON Mary A 1891
12
LAMONS John M 1892
ALSUP Elijah 1898
1
Lots/Tracts-Sec. 1
E21NE THOMPSON, WILLIS A 1892
E21NW CATES, JAMES E 1903
E22NE BENCH, HENRY 1897
E22NW BATEMAN, JAMES C 1890
W21NE CATES, JAMES E 1903
W21NW VERNON, WILLIAM S 1891
W22NE BATEMAN, JAMES C 1890
W22NW SLOAN, JOHN [163] 1861
LAMONS John M 1892
VERNON William S 1891
ENGLAND [76] Mahaley 1890
ENGLAND [76] Mahaley 1890
ENGLAND Joel W 1888

Legend

- Patent Boundary
- Section Boundary
- No Patents Found (or Outside County)
- 1., 2., 3., ... Lot Numbers (when beside a name)
- [ ] Group Number (see Appendix "C")

Scale: Section = 1 mile X 1 mile
(generally, with some exceptions)

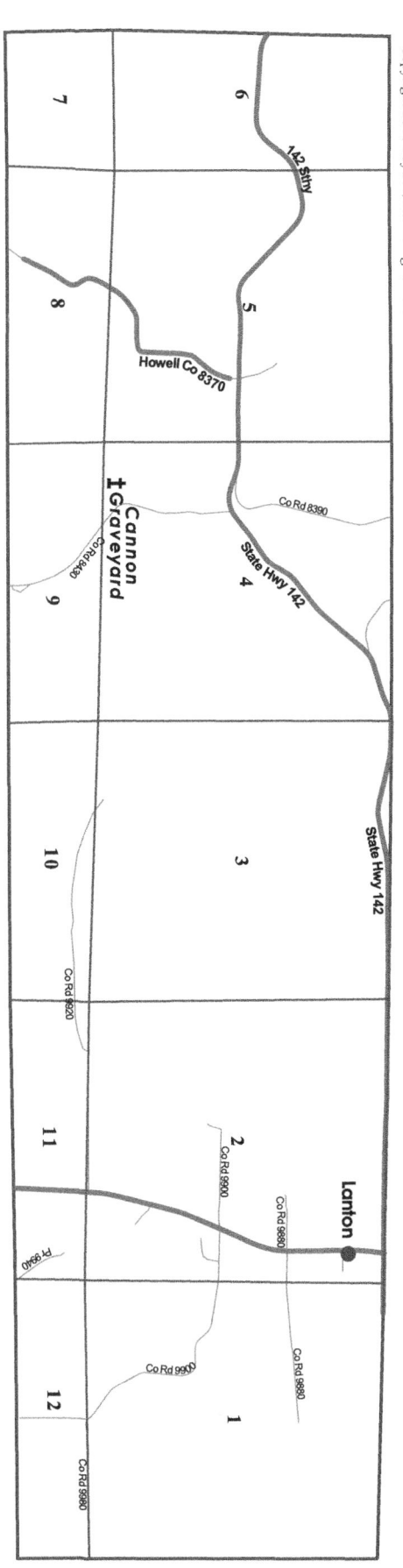

Road Map
T21-N R8-W
5th PM 21-N 8-W Meridian
Map Group 27

Note: the area contained in this map amounts to far less than a full Township. Therefore, its contents are completely on this single page (instead of a "normal" 2-page spread).

Cities & Towns
Lanton

Cemeteries
Cannon Graveyard

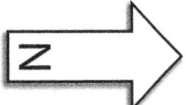

Legend

————	Section Lines
════	Interstates
▬▬▬	Highways
————	Other Roads
●	Cities/Towns
✝	Cemeteries

Scale: Section = 1 mile X 1 mile
(generally, with some exceptions)

Historical Map

T21-N   R8-W
5th PM 21-N 8-W Meridian

Map Group   27

Note: the area contained in this map amounts to far less than a full Township. Therefore, its contents are completely on this single page (instead of a "normal" 2-page spread).

Cities & Towns
Lanton

Cemeteries
Cannon Graveyard

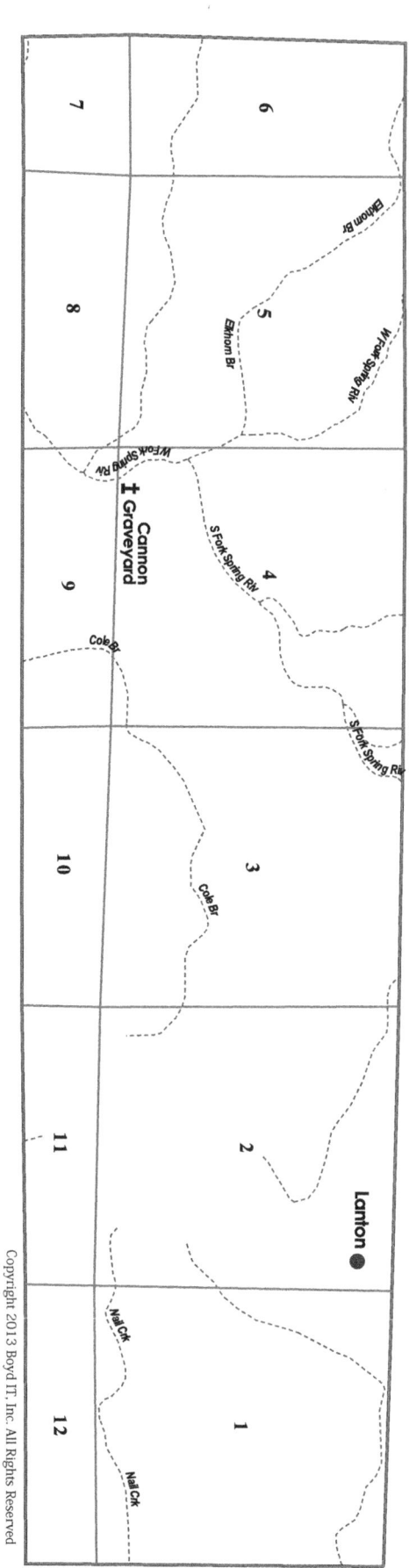

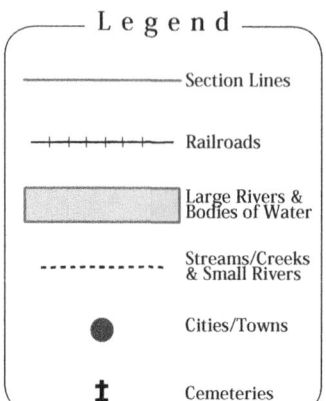

Legend

——————— Section Lines

+++++++ Railroads

▨ Large Rivers & Bodies of Water

- - - - - - - Streams/Creeks & Small Rivers

● Cities/Towns

‡ Cemeteries

Scale: Section = 1 mile X 1 mile
(there are some exceptions)

Map Group 28: Index to Land Patents

Township 21-North Range 7-West (5th PM 21-N 7-W)

After you locate an individual in this Index, take note of the Section and Section Part then proceed to the Land Patent map on the pages immediately following. You should have no difficulty locating the corresponding parcel of land.

The "For More Info" Column will lead you to more information about the underlying Patents. See the *Legend* at right, and the "How to Use this Book" chapter, for more information.

```
              LEGEND
        "For More Info . . . " column
A = Authority (Legislative Act, See Appendix "A")
B = Block or Lot (location in Section unknown)
C = Cancelled Patent
F = Fractional Section
G = Group  (Multi-Patentee Patent, see Appendix "C")
V = Overlaps another Parcel
R = Re-Issued (Parcel patented more than once)

(A & G items require you to look in the Appendixes referred
to above. All other Letter-designations followed by a number
require you to locate line-items in this index that possess
the ID number found after the letter).
```

ID	Individual in Patent	Sec.	Sec. Part	Date Issued	Other Counties	For More Info . . .
6846	ALSUP, Elijah	7	W½	1898-04-11		A7
6847	ALSUP, Martin S	10	N½NW	1886-10-29		A1
8707	" "	3	1NW	1886-07-20		A1
6848	ANTHONY, Amos	4	S½SW	1902-04-15		A7
6849	" "	9	NW	1902-04-15		A7
6850	BENCH, Christopher	2	S½SW	1877-04-05		A7
8731	BENCH, Henry	6	W22NW	1897-11-10		A7
8716	BENCH, Levi	5	1NE	1904-08-26		A7
6852	" "	5	NWSE	1904-08-26		A7
6851	" "	5	NESW	1904-08-26		A7
6853	BLAGG, Samuel A	1	SWSW	1895-05-28		A7
6854	" "	11	NE	1895-05-28		A7
6855	" "	12	NW	1895-05-28		A7
6857	BUMPASS, John H	3	SESE	1859-09-01		A1
6856	" "	3	SWSE	1860-08-01		A1
6858	" "	4	SESE	1860-08-01		A1
6859	" "	4	SWSE	1859-09-01		A1
6860	" "	4	NWSE	1860-08-01		A1
8723	CARNER, Jacob N	6	2NE	1900-02-02		A7
8725	" "	6	E22NW	1900-02-02		A7
6861	DAWSON, Robert M	8	E½	1891-08-24		A1
8728	DENGLER, George	6	S21SW	1895-04-06		A1
6862	DRIVER, James B	3	NWSW	1875-11-01		A7
6863	" "	4	NESE	1875-11-01		A7
8715	DYKES, William H	4	W22NW	1885-06-20		A7
8729	ENGLAND, Joel W	6	S22SW	1888-12-06		A7
6864	EVANS, Ambrose F	7		1911-05-11		A7
8717	EVANS, James T	5	2NE	1905-05-02		A7
6865	FARIS, Rebecca J	3	SESW	1867-05-01		A1
8706	FULLER, Robert E	1	W22NW	1898-04-11		A7
8718	GUNN, George W	5	E21NW	1892-06-10		A7
8719	" "	5	E22NW	1892-06-10		A7
8721	" "	5	W22NW	1980-01-29		A7
6866	HOWELL, Ruth	5	W½SW	1904-11-15		A7
6867	" "	8	N½NW	1904-11-15		A7
8713	JUERN, Charles H	4	1NW	1892-06-10		A7
6868	" "	4	N½SW	1892-06-10		A7
6869	KOLLING, William	9	N½NE	1892-12-09		A7
6870	MELTON, Noah	3	SWSW	1860-03-01		A1
6871	NALE, Lee R	5	SESW	1898-01-26		A7
6872	" "	5	NESE	1898-01-26		A7
6873	" "	5	S½SE	1898-01-26		A7
6874	PICKLE, Martha J	1	SESE	1901-03-23	Oregon	A7
6875	" "	12	N½NE	1901-03-23	Oregon	A7
6876	PRATT, Caroline D	1	NWSW	1886-07-20		A1
6877	" "	2	N½	1886-11-19		A1

ID	Individual in Patent	Sec.	Sec. Part	Date Issued	Other Counties	For More Info . . .
6879	PRATT, Caroline D (Cont'd)	2	SE	1886-11-19		A1
6878	" "	2	N½SW	1886-11-19		A1
8712	" "	3	W22NE	1886-07-20		A1
8708	" "	3	2NW	1886-07-20		A1
8711	" "	3	W21NE	1886-07-20		A1
6880	PRESLEY, Aley C	3	NESE	1891-10-06		A7
8709	" "	3	E21NE	1891-10-06		A7
8710	" "	3	E22NE	1891-10-06		A7
8702	PRESSLEY, John S	1	E21NE	1892-06-10		A7
6882	" "	1	NESE	1892-06-10		A7
6881	" "	1	W½SE	1892-06-10		A7
8700	PRESSLEY, Milas P	1	1NW	1881-04-09		A7
6883	" "	1	E½SW	1881-04-09		A7
8701	SHERREY, Hugh P	1	2NE	1903-06-08		A7
8705	" "	1	W21NE	1903-06-08		A7
8714	STEPHENS, Israel	4	E22NW	1860-08-01		A1
6884	STEVENS, Israel	11	W½	1874-06-15		A1
6885	THOMPSON, John W	6	SE	1892-03-07		A7
8726	THOMPSON, Willis A	6	N21SW	1892-06-10		A7
8730	" "	6	W21NW	1892-06-10		A7
8727	" "	6	N22SW	1892-06-10		A7
8720	THOMPSON, Willis M	5	W21NW	1895-05-28		A7
8724	" "	6	E21NW	1895-05-28		A7
8722	" "	6	1NE	1895-05-28		A7
8704	WAID, Tilda M	1	E22NW	1881-04-09		A7 G184
8703	WAID, William P	1	E22NW	1881-04-09		A7 G184
6886	WILLIAMS, J H	3	NWSE	1873-06-05		A1
6887	WILLIAMS, John H	10	N½NE	1882-06-10		A1
6888	" "	3	NESW	1883-06-30		A7

Patent Map

T21-N R7-W
5th PM 21-N 7-W Meridian

Map Group 28

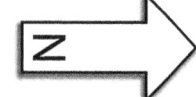

Township Statistics

Parcels Mapped	:	74
Number of Patents	:	46
Number of Individuals	:	39
Patentees Identified	:	38
Number of Surnames	:	30
Multi-Patentee Parcels	:	1
Oldest Patent Date	:	9/1/1859
Most Recent Patent	:	5/11/1911
Block/Lot Parcels	:	31
Cities and Town	:	0
Cemeteries	:	1

Note: the area contained in this map amounts to far less than a full Township. Therefore, its contents are completely on this single page (instead of a "normal" 2-page spread).

Legend

———————	Patent Boundary
━━━━━━━	Section Boundary
░░░░░░░	No Patents Found (or Outside County)
1., 2., 3., ...	Lot Numbers (when beside a name)
[ ]	Group Number (see Appendix "C")

Scale: Section = 1 mile X 1 mile
(generally, with some exceptions)

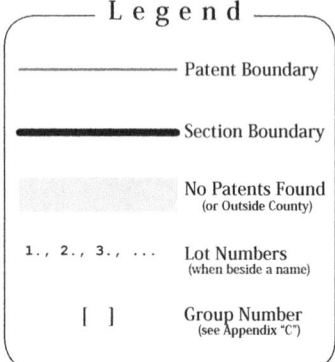

Section 6

Lots/Tracts-Sec. 6
1NE THOMPSON, WILLIS M 1895
2NE CARNER, JACOB N 1900
2NE THOMPSON, WILLIS M 1895
E2INW CARNER, JACOB N 1900
N21SW CARNER, GEORGE W 1892
N21SW THOMPSON, WILLIS A 1892
N25SW THOMPSON, WILLIS A 1892
S21SW DENGLER, GEORGE 1895
S25SW ENGLAND, JOEL W 1888
W21NW THOMPSON, WILLIS A 1892
W22NW BENCH, HENRY 1897

Section 5

Lots/Tracts-Sec. 5
1NE BENCH, LEVI 1904
2NE EVANS, JAMES T 1905
E21NW GUNN, GEORGE W 1892
E22NW GUNN, GEORGE W 1892
W21NW THOMPSON, WILLIS M 1895
W22NW GUNN, GEORGE W 1900

Section 4

Lots/Tracts-Sec. 4
1NW JUERN, CHARLES H 1892
E22NW STEPHENS, ISRAEL 1860
W22NW DYKES, WILLIAM H 1885

Section 3

Lots/Tracts-Sec. 3
1NW ALSUP, MARTIN S 1886
2NW PRATT, CAROLINE D 1886
E21NE PRESLEY, ALEY C 1891
E22NE PRESLEY, ALEY C 1891
W21NE PRATT, CAROLINE D 1886
W22NE PRATT, CAROLINE D 1886

Section 1

Lots/Tracts-Sec. 1
1NW PRESSLEY, MILAS P 1881
2NE SHERBEY, HUGH P 1903
E21NE PRESSLEY, JOHN S 1892
E22NW WARD, TILDA M [1844] 1881
W21NE SHERBEY, HUGH P 1903
W22NW FULLER, ROBERT E 1898

6
ALSUP Elijah 1898
EVANS Ambrose F 1911
7
THOMPSON John W 1892

5
HOWELL Ruth 1904
HOWELL Ruth 1904
8
NALE Lee R 1898
BENCH Levi 1904
BENCH Levi 1904
DAWSON Robert M 1891
NALE Lee R 1898
NALE Lee R 1898

4
ANTHONY Amos 1902
9
ANTHONY Amos 1902
JUERN Charles H 1892
KOLLING William 1892
BUMPASS John H 1859
BUMPASS John H 1860
BUMPASS John H 1860
DROVER James B 1875

3
ALSUP Martin S 1886
10
MELTON Noah 1860
FARIS Rebecca J 1867
WILLIAMS John H 1882
DROVER James B 1875
WILLIAMS John H 1883
WILLIAMS J H 1873
BUMPASS John H 1860
WILLIAMS J H 1873
PRESLEY Aley C 1891
BUMPASS John H 1859

2
PRATT Caroline D 1886
11
STEVENS Israel 1874
BENCH Christopher 1877
PRATT Caroline D 1886
BLAGG Samuel A 1895
PRATT Caroline D 1886

1
PRATT Caroline D 1886
12
BLAGG Samuel A 1895
BLAGG Samuel A 1895
PRESSLEY Milas P 1881
PRESSLEY John S 1892
PICKLE Martha J 1901
PRESSLEY John S 1892
PICKLE Martha J 1901

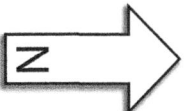

Road Map

T21-N R7-W
5th PM 21-N 7-W Meridian

Map Group 28

Note: the area contained in this map amounts to far less than a full Township. Therefore, its contents are completely on this single page (instead of a "normal" 2-page spread).

Cities & Towns
None

Cemeteries
Koellings Graveyard

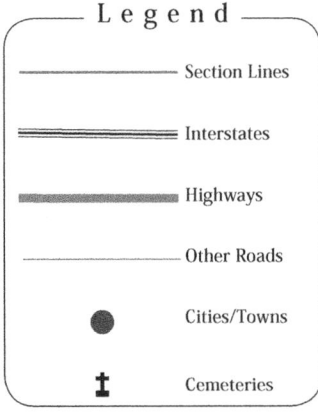

Legend

———— Section Lines

═══════ Interstates

▬▬▬▬ Highways

———— Other Roads

● Cities/Towns

☨ Cemeteries

Scale: Section = 1 mile X 1 mile
(generally, with some exceptions)

Historical Map

T21-N R7-W
5th PM 21-N 7-W Meridian

Map Group 28

Note: the area contained in this map amounts to far less than a full Township. Therefore, its contents are completely on this single page (instead of a "normal" 2-page spread).

Cities & Towns

None

Cemeteries

Koellings Graveyard

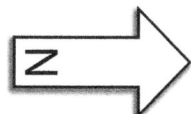

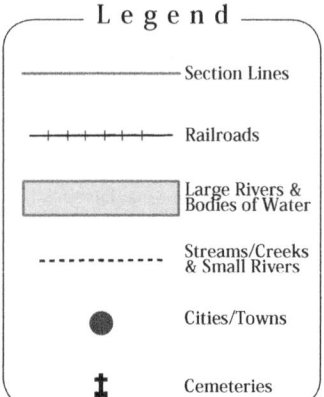

Legend

——————— Section Lines

+–+–+–+–+ Railroads

▭ Large Rivers & Bodies of Water

- - - - - - - Streams/Creeks & Small Rivers

● Cities/Towns

✝ Cemeteries

Scale: Section = 1 mile X 1 mile
(there are some exceptions)

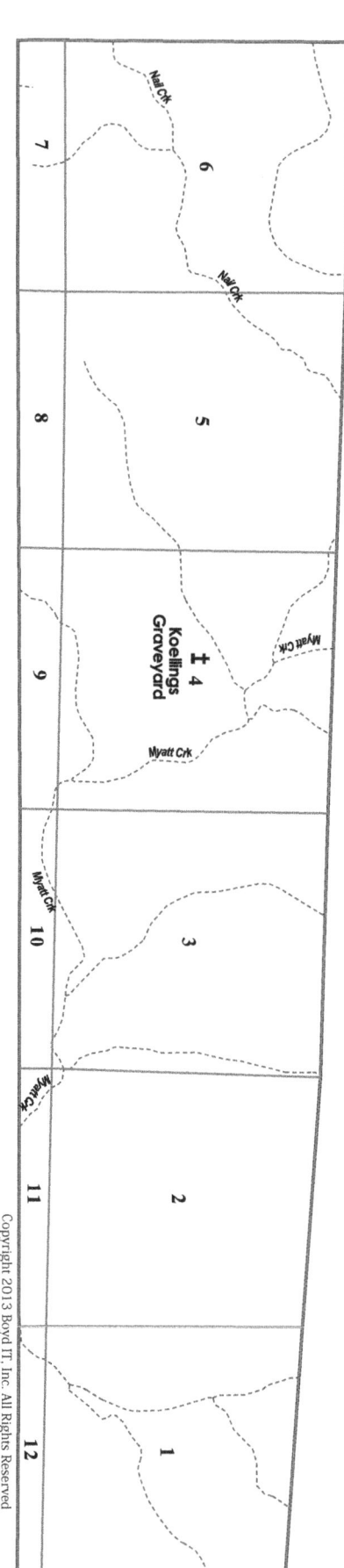

Appendices

Appendix A - Acts of Congress Authorizing the Patents Contained in this Book

The following Acts of Congress are referred to throughout the Indexes in this book. The text of the Federal Statutes referred to below can usually be found on the web. For more information on such laws, check out the publishers's web-site at *www.arphax.com*, go to the "Research" page, and click on the "Land-Law" link.

Ref. No.	Date and Act of Congress	Number of Parcels of Land
1	April 24, 1820: Sale-Cash Entry (3 Stat. 566)	1800
2	February 11, 1847: ScripWarrant Act of 1847 (9 Stat. 123)	8
3	July 2, 1862: State Grant-Agri College (12 Stat. 503)	3
4	March 17, 1842: Scrip or Nature of Scrip (5 Stat. 607)	1
5	March 22, 1852: ScripWarrant Act of 1852 (10 Stat. 3)	1
6	March 3, 1855: ScripWarrant Act of 1855 (10 Stat. 701)	322
7	May 20, 1862: Homestead EntryOriginal (12 Stat. 392)	3826
8	September 28, 1850: ScripWarrant Act of 1850 (9 Stat. 520)	52

Appendix B - Section Parts (Aliquot Parts)

The following represent the various abbreviations we have found thus far in describing the parts of a Public Land Section. Some of these are very obscure and rarely used, but we wanted to list them for just that reason. A full section is 1 square mile or 640 acres.

Section Part	Description	Acres
\<none\>	Full Acre (if no Section Part is listed, presumed a full Section)	640
\<1-??\>	A number represents a Lot Number and can be of various sizes	?
E½	East Half-Section	320
E½E½	East Half of East Half-Section	160
E½E½SE	East Half of East Half of Southeast Quarter-Section	40
E½N½	East Half of North Half-Section	160
E½NE	East Half of Northeast Quarter-Section	80
E½NENE	East Half of Northeast Quarter of Northeast Quarter-Section	20
E½NENW	East Half of Northeast Quarter of Northwest Quarter-Section	20
E½NESE	East Half of Northeast Quarter of Southeast Quarter-Section	20
E½NESW	East Half of Northeast Quarter of Southwest Quarter-Section	20
E½NW	East Half of Northwest Quarter-Section	80
E½NWNE	East Half of Northwest Quarter of Northeast Quarter-Section	20
E½NWNW	East Half of Northwest Quarter of Northwest Quarter-Section	20
E½NWSE	East Half of Northwest Quarter of Southeast Quarter-Section	20
E½NWSW	East Half of Northwest Quarter of Southwest Quarter-Section	20
E½S½	East Half of South Half-Section	160
E½SE	East Half of Southeast Quarter-Section	80
E½SENE	East Half of Southeast Quarter of Northeast Quarter-Section	20
E½SENW	East Half of Southeast Quarter of Northwest Quarter-Section	20
E½SESE	East Half of Southeast Quarter of Southeast Quarter-Section	20
E½SESW	East Half of Southeast Quarter of Southwest Quarter-Section	20
E½SW	East Half of Southwest Quarter-Section	80
E½SWNE	East Half of Southwest Quarter of Northeast Quarter-Section	20
E½SWNW	East Half of Southwest Quarter of Northwest Quarter-Section	20
E½SWSE	East Half of Southwest Quarter of Southeast Quarter-Section	20
E½SWSW	East Half of Southwest Quarter of Southwest Quarter-Section	20
E½W½	East Half of West Half-Section	160
N½	North Half-Section	320
N½E½NE	North Half of East Half of Northeast Quarter-Section	40
N½E½NW	North Half of East Half of Northwest Quarter-Section	40
N½E½SE	North Half of East Half of Southeast Quarter-Section	40
N½E½SW	North Half of East Half of Southwest Quarter-Section	40
N½N½	North Half of North Half-Section	160
N½NE	North Half of Northeast Quarter-Section	80
N½NENE	North Half of Northeast Quarter of Northeast Quarter-Section	20
N½NENW	North Half of Northeast Quarter of Northwest Quarter-Section	20
N½NESE	North Half of Northeast Quarter of Southeast Quarter-Section	20
N½NESW	North Half of Northeast Quarter of Southwest Quarter-Section	20
N½NW	North Half of Northwest Quarter-Section	80
N½NWNE	North Half of Northwest Quarter of Northeast Quarter-Section	20
N½NWNW	North Half of Northwest Quarter of Northwest Quarter-Section	20
N½NWSE	North Half of Northwest Quarter of Southeast Quarter-Section	20
N½NWSW	North Half of Northwest Quarter of Southwest Quarter-Section	20
N½S½	North Half of South Half-Section	160
N½SE	North Half of Southeast Quarter-Section	80
N½SENE	North Half of Southeast Quarter of Northeast Quarter-Section	20
N½SENW	North Half of Southeast Quarter of Northwest Quarter-Section	20
N½SESE	North Half of Southeast Quarter of Southeast Quarter-Section	20

Section Part	Description	Acres
N½SESW	North Half of Southeast Quarter of Southwest Quarter-Section	20
N½SESW	North Half of Southeast Quarter of Southwest Quarter-Section	20
N½SW	North Half of Southwest Quarter-Section	80
N½SWNE	North Half of Southwest Quarter of Northeast Quarter-Section	20
N½SWNW	North Half of Southwest Quarter of Northwest Quarter-Section	20
N½SWSE	North Half of Southwest Quarter of Southeast Quarter-Section	20
N½SWSE	North Half of Southwest Quarter of Southeast Quarter-Section	20
N½SWSW	North Half of Southwest Quarter of Southwest Quarter-Section	20
N½W½NW	North Half of West Half of Northwest Quarter-Section	40
N½W½SE	North Half of West Half of Southeast Quarter-Section	40
N½W½SW	North Half of West Half of Southwest Quarter-Section	40
NE	Northeast Quarter-Section	160
NEN½	Northeast Quarter of North Half-Section	80
NENE	Northeast Quarter of Northeast Quarter-Section	40
NENENE	Northeast Quarter of Northeast Quarter of Northeast Quarter	10
NENENW	Northeast Quarter of Northeast Quarter of Northwest Quarter	10
NENESE	Northeast Quarter of Northeast Quarter of Southeast Quarter	10
NENESW	Northeast Quarter of Northeast Quarter of Southwest Quarter	10
NENW	Northeast Quarter of Northwest Quarter-Section	40
NENWNE	Northeast Quarter of Northwest Quarter of Northeast Quarter	10
NENWNW	Northeast Quarter of Northwest Quarter of Northwest Quarter	10
NENWSE	Northeast Quarter of Northwest Quarter of Southeast Quarter	10
NENWSW	Northeast Quarter of Northwest Quarter of Southwest Quarter	10
NESE	Northeast Quarter of Southeast Quarter-Section	40
NESENE	Northeast Quarter of Southeast Quarter of Northeast Quarter	10
NESENW	Northeast Quarter of Southeast Quarter of Northwest Quarter	10
NESESE	Northeast Quarter of Southeast Quarter of Southeast Quarter	10
NESESW	Northeast Quarter of Southeast Quarter of Southwest Quarter	10
NESW	Northeast Quarter of Southwest Quarter-Section	40
NESWNE	Northeast Quarter of Southwest Quarter of Northeast Quarter	10
NESWNW	Northeast Quarter of Southwest Quarter of Northwest Quarter	10
NESWSE	Northeast Quarter of Southwest Quarter of Southeast Quarter	10
NESWSW	Northeast Quarter of Southwest Quarter of Southwest Quarter	10
NW	Northwest Quarter-Section	160
NWE½	Northwest Quarter of Eastern Half-Section	80
NWN½	Northwest Quarter of North Half-Section	80
NWNE	Northwest Quarter of Northeast Quarter-Section	40
NWNENE	Northwest Quarter of Northeast Quarter of Northeast Quarter	10
NWNENW	Northwest Quarter of Northeast Quarter of Northwest Quarter	10
NWNESE	Northwest Quarter of Northeast Quarter of Southeast Quarter	10
NWNESW	Northwest Quarter of Northeast Quarter of Southwest Quarter	10
NWNW	Northwest Quarter of Northwest Quarter-Section	40
NWNWNE	Northwest Quarter of Northwest Quarter of Northeast Quarter	10
NWNWNW	Northwest Quarter of Northwest Quarter of Northwest Quarter	10
NWNWSE	Northwest Quarter of Northwest Quarter of Southeast Quarter	10
NWNWSW	Northwest Quarter of Northwest Quarter of Southwest Quarter	10
NWSE	Northwest Quarter of Southeast Quarter-Section	40
NWSENE	Northwest Quarter of Southeast Quarter of Northeast Quarter	10
NWSENW	Northwest Quarter of Southeast Quarter of Northwest Quarter	10
NWSESE	Northwest Quarter of Southeast Quarter of Southeast Quarter	10
NWSESW	Northwest Quarter of Southeast Quarter of Southwest Quarter	10
NWSW	Northwest Quarter of Southwest Quarter-Section	40
NWSWNE	Northwest Quarter of Southwest Quarter of Northeast Quarter	10
NWSWNW	Northwest Quarter of Southwest Quarter of Northwest Quarter	10
NWSWSE	Northwest Quarter of Southwest Quarter of Southeast Quarter	10
NWSWSW	Northwest Quarter of Southwest Quarter of Southwest Quarter	10
S½	South Half-Section	320
S½E½NE	South Half of East Half of Northeast Quarter-Section	40
S½E½NW	South Half of East Half of Northwest Quarter-Section	40
S½E½SE	South Half of East Half of Southeast Quarter-Section	40

Section Part	Description	Acres
S½E½SW	South Half of East Half of Southwest Quarter-Section	40
S½N½	South Half of North Half-Section	160
S½NE	South Half of Northeast Quarter-Section	80
S½NENE	South Half of Northeast Quarter of Northeast Quarter-Section	20
S½NENW	South Half of Northeast Quarter of Northwest Quarter-Section	20
S½NESE	South Half of Northeast Quarter of Southeast Quarter-Section	20
S½NESW	South Half of Northeast Quarter of Southwest Quarter-Section	20
S½NW	South Half of Northwest Quarter-Section	80
S½NWNE	South Half of Northwest Quarter of Northeast Quarter-Section	20
S½NWNW	South Half of Northwest Quarter of Northwest Quarter-Section	20
S½NWSE	South Half of Northwest Quarter of Southeast Quarter-Section	20
S½NWSW	South Half of Northwest Quarter of Southwest Quarter-Section	20
S½S½	South Half of South Half-Section	160
S½SE	South Half of Southeast Quarter-Section	80
S½SENE	South Half of Southeast Quarter of Northeast Quarter-Section	20
S½SENW	South Half of Southeast Quarter of Northwest Quarter-Section	20
S½SESE	South Half of Southeast Quarter of Southeast Quarter-Section	20
S½SESW	South Half of Southeast Quarter of Southwest Quarter-Section	20
S½SESW	South Half of Southeast Quarter of Southwest Quarter-Section	20
S½SW	South Half of Southwest Quarter-Section	80
S½SWNE	South Half of Southwest Quarter of Northeast Quarter-Section	20
S½SWNW	South Half of Southwest Quarter of Northwest Quarter-Section	20
S½SWSE	South Half of Southwest Quarter of Southeast Quarter-Section	20
S½SWSE	South Half of Southwest Quarter of Southeast Quarter-Section	20
S½SWSW	South Half of Southwest Quarter of Southwest Quarter-Section	20
S½W½NE	South Half of West Half of Northeast Quarter-Section	40
S½W½NW	South Half of West Half of Northwest Quarter-Section	40
S½W½SE	South Half of West Half of Southeast Quarter-Section	40
S½W½SW	South Half of West Half of Southwest Quarter-Section	40
SE	Southeast Quarter Section	160
SEN½	Southeast Quarter of North Half-Section	80
SENE	Southeast Quarter of Northeast Quarter-Section	40
SENENE	Southeast Quarter of Northeast Quarter of Northeast Quarter	10
SENENW	Southeast Quarter of Northeast Quarter of Northwest Quarter	10
SENESE	Southeast Quarter of Northeast Quarter of Southeast Quarter	10
SENESW	Southeast Quarter of Northeast Quarter of Southwest Quarter	10
SENW	Southeast Quarter of Northwest Quarter-Section	40
SENWNE	Southeast Quarter of Northwest Quarter of Northeast Quarter	10
SENWNW	Southeast Quarter of Northwest Quarter of Northwest Quarter	10
SENWSE	Souteast Quarter of Northwest Quarter of Southeast Quarter	10
SENWSW	Southeast Quarter of Northwest Quarter of Southwest Quarter	10
SESE	Southeast Quarter of Southeast Quarter-Section	40
SESENE	SoutheastQuarter of Southeast Quarter of Northeast Quarter	10
SESENW	Southeast Quarter of Southeast Quarter of Northwest Quarter	10
SESESE	Southeast Quarter of Southeast Quarter of Southeast Quarter	10
SESESW	Southeast Quarter of Southeast Quarter of Southwest Quarter	10
SESW	Southeast Quarter of Southwest Quarter-Section	40
SESWNE	Southeast Quarter of Southwest Quarter of Northeast Quarter	10
SESWNW	Southeast Quarter of Southwest Quarter of Northwest Quarter	10
SESWSE	Southeast Quarter of Southwest Quarter of Southeast Quarter	10
SESWSW	Southeast Quarter of Southwest Quarter of Southwest Quarter	10
SW	Southwest Quarter-Section	160
SWNE	Southwest Quarter of Northeast Quarter-Section	40
SWNENE	Southwest Quarter of Northeast Quarter of Northeast Quarter	10
SWNENW	Southwest Quarter of Northeast Quarter of Northwest Quarter	10
SWNESE	Southwest Quarter of Northeast Quarter of Southeast Quarter	10
SWNESW	Southwest Quarter of Northeast Quarter of Southwest Quarter	10
SWNW	Southwest Quarter of Northwest Quarter-Section	40
SWNWNE	Southwest Quarter of Northwest Quarter of Northeast Quarter	10
SWNWNW	Southwest Quarter of Northwest Quarter of Northwest Quarter	10

Section Part	Description	Acres
SWNWSE	Southwest Quarter of Northwest Quarter of Southeast Quarter	10
SWNWSW	Southwest Quarter of Northwest Quarter of Southwest Quarter	10
SWSE	Southwest Quarter of Southeast Quarter-Section	40
SWSENE	Southwest Quarter of Southeast Quarter of Northeast Quarter	10
SWSENW	Southwest Quarter of Southeast Quarter of Northwest Quarter	10
SWSESE	Southwest Quarter of Southeast Quarter of Southeast Quarter	10
SWSESW	Southwest Quarter of Southeast Quarter of Southwest Quarter	10
SWSW	Southwest Quarter of Southwest Quarter-Section	40
SWSWNE	Southwest Quarter of Southwest Quarter of Northeast Quarter	10
SWSWNW	Southwest Quarter of Southwest Quarter of Northwest Quarter	10
SWSWSE	Southwest Quarter of Southwest Quarter of Southeast Quarter	10
SWSWSW	Southwest Quarter of Southwest Quarter of Southwest Quarter	10
W½	West Half-Section	320
W½E½	West Half of East Half-Section	160
W½N½	West Half of North Half-Section (same as NW)	160
W½NE	West Half of Northeast Quarter	80
W½NENE	West Half of Northeast Quarter of Northeast Quarter-Section	20
W½NENW	West Half of Northeast Quarter of Northwest Quarter-Section	20
W½NESE	West Half of Northeast Quarter of Southeast Quarter-Section	20
W½NESW	West Half of Northeast Quarter of Southwest Quarter-Section	20
W½NW	West Half of Northwest Quarter-Section	80
W½NWNE	West Half of Northwest Quarter of Northeast Quarter-Section	20
W½NWNW	West Half of Northwest Quarter of Northwest Quarter-Section	20
W½NWSE	West Half of Northwest Quarter of Southeast Quarter-Section	20
W½NWSW	West Half of Northwest Quarter of Southwest Quarter-Section	20
W½S½	West Half of South Half-Section	160
W½SE	West Half of Southeast Quarter-Section	80
W½SENE	West Half of Southeast Quarter of Northeast Quarter-Section	20
W½SENW	West Half of Southeast Quarter of Northwest Quarter-Section	20
W½SESE	West Half of Southeast Quarter of Southeast Quarter-Section	20
W½SESW	West Half of Southeast Quarter of Southwest Quarter-Section	20
W½SW	West Half of Southwest Quarter-Section	80
W½SWNE	West Half of Southwest Quarter of Northeast Quarter-Section	20
W½SWNW	West Half of Southwest Quarter of Northwest Quarter-Section	20
W½SWSE	West Half of Southwest Quarter of Southeast Quarter-Section	20
W½SWSW	West Half of Southwest Quarter of Southwest Quarter-Section	20
W½W½	West Half of West Half-Section	160

Appendix C - Multi-Patentee Groups

The following index presents groups of people who jointly received patents in Howell County, Missouri. The Group Numbers are used in the Patent Maps and their Indexes so that you may then turn to this Appendix in order to identify all the members of the each buying group.

Group Number 1
ALEXANDRIA, John G; MOORE, Peter A

Group Number 2
ALFORD, Catharine; SMITH, William

Group Number 3
ALLEN, Mary; BRIDENTHAL, Charlotte E

Group Number 4
ALLEN, Sarah A; SHEARHEART, Sarah A

Group Number 5
ARNOLD, Susannah; DORSEY, Thomas J

Group Number 6
ASHBROOK, William; ORCHARD, James M

Group Number 7
ASHBY, Hannah; JOHNSON, Roda W

Group Number 8
BAILEY, Betsey; BAILEY, Campbell R

Group Number 9
BAILEY, Campbell R; BALEY, Betsy

Group Number 10
BAILY, Gamaliah H; MCDANIEL, Samuel R

Group Number 11
BAKER, Ebby; SPEARS, Joseph T

Group Number 12
BALL, Gehazi R; WILLIAMS, Elizabeth

Group Number 13
BARKING, Herman; BARKING, Johannah

Group Number 14
BECKETT, Wiley H; BECKETT, William H

Group Number 15
BECKETT, Wiley H; WALKER, Mary

Group Number 16
BECKETT, Wiley H; WOODARD, Sally

Group Number 17
BISSEL, Mary L; KISNER, Mary L

Group Number 18
BLEDSOE, Anderson M; BLEDSOE, Martha J

Group Number 19
BLYTHE, Martha J; CROWDER, Joshua T; CROWDER, Martha

Group Number 20
BOND, Riley; THOMAS, Ann

Group Number 21
BRAY, Emily; BRAY, Jesse; WRIGHT, Emily

Group Number 22
BRIDENTHAL, Charlotte E; JAMES, Patience

Group Number 23
BRIDGES, Sarah L; MONTGOMERY, Sarah L

Group Number 24
BROWN, Elizabeth; BROWN, Harden

Group Number 25
BRYAN, Mary; COLLINS, Thomas A

Group Number 26
BUCK, Phoebe A; BUCK, W G

Group Number 27
BURGESS, Gabriel; BURGESS, Serila A

Group Number 28
BURNHAM, Charles M; CUNNINGHAM, Wilson V

Group Number 29
BURRIS, Esther; BURRIS, Tobias

Group Number 30
BURTON, Sarah; BURTON, Thomas D

Group Number 31
CALLAHAN, Charles W; CALLAHAN, Sarah E

Group Number 32
CALLAHAN, John L; SMITH, Martin L

Group Number 33
CAMPBELL, George W; CAMPBELL, Harriett

Group Number 34
CAMPBELL, J J; CAMPBELL, Mary J

Group Number 35
CAMPBELL, Susan E; CAMPBELL, William

Group Number 36
CANNON, Martha; MARTIN, John L

Group Number 37
CAPIN, John A; CHAPIN, Ely H

Group Number 38
CARRELL, Lavina C; CARRELL, Lovely S

Group Number 39
CARTMILL, Charles; CARTMILL, Emma E

Group Number 40
CASH, Eliza; WOODWORTH, Stephen R

Group Number 41
CASTLEMAN, Ann; HOWARD, Harmon

Group Number 42
CHAPMAN, Carrol; CHAPMAN, Elizabeth; CHAPMAN, Joanna; HAWKINS, John B; HENDRICK, Elizabeth; RATLIFF, Joanna

Group Number 43
CHEEK, Nan; CHEEK, Thomas J

Group Number 44
CHENEY, Levi; DAVIS, Elizabeth

Group Number 45
CLARK, Amanda; CLARK, Isaac P

Group Number 46
CLARK, Patience; LEMONS, Peter

Group Number 47
CLARK, Wesley E; TEDDER, John

Group Number 48
CLAYTER, Sarah; JOHNSON, Roda W

Group Number 49
CLICK, George W; CLICK, Nancy C; MODRALL, Nancy C

Group Number 50
CLONINGER, Henry; CLONINGER, James F; CLONINGER, Lawson

Group Number 51
COCHRAN, Joseph E; COCHRAN, Wilson; EASLEY, Francis H

Group Number 52
COCK, Anthony; STEWART, Mary

Group Number 53
COLLINS, Henry; COLLINS, Polly A

Group Number 54
COLLINS, John B; MORELAND, Alexander L; VENUS, David A

Group Number 55
COLLINS, Martha J; COLLINS, William

Group Number 56
COLMERY, Robert C; FRANK, Samuel; LEFEVER, Mary Ann

Group Number 57
COOK, George N; COOK, John L

Group Number 58
COOK, William D; GRIFFITH, Elizabeth

Group Number 59
COOK, William D; SIMS, Elizabeth

Group Number 60
COVERT, Jane E; COVERT, John R

Group Number 61
CRABTREE, Mary; HULL, James; WILSON, G P

Group Number 62
CRANE, Albert; RENFRO, Andrew; RENFRO, George G

Group Number 63
DAVIDSON, Caroline; DAVIDSON, William

Group Number 64
DAVIDSON, Louisa A; NETTLETON, George W; NETTLETON, Louisa A

Group Number 65
DAVIS, Greer W; NICHOLAS, David

Group Number 66
DAVIS, Joseph; DAVIS, Rebecca; KEIRN, Rebecca

Group Number 67
DEBOARD, Mary J; DEBOARD, Wiley

Group Number 68
DENZEL, Catherine; DENZEL, Edward; ROHR, Catherine

Group Number 69
DUNKLEBARGER, Susan S; GIBBS, Daniel W; SCOGGIN, Turpin G

Group Number 70
DUNLAP, Delila; DUNLAP, R M

Group Number 71
EASLEY, Francis H; FEAMAN, Margaret; UNGER, Amelia; UNGER, Eli; UNGER, Henry W; UNGER, Louisa

Group Number 72
EASLEY, Francis H; POWELL, Rebecca

Group Number 73
EASTRELY, John F; EASTRELY, Nevada J

Group Number 74
ELDER, William F; MORTON, Jeremiah

Group Number 75
ELLINGTON, William; HOWELL, Thomas J

Group Number 76
ENGLAND, Joel W; ENGLAND, Mahaley

Group Number 77
EVANS, Narcissa M; EVANS, William

Group Number 78
FEATHER, Nancy L; MCMURTRY, Nancy L

Group Number 79
FERGUSON, Elizabeth; FERGUSON, William M

Group Number 80
FILLMAN, Celia B; STEPP, Celia B

Group Number 81
FINDLEY, Jemima O; FINDLEY, Samuel H

Group Number 82
FINDLEY, Lavada M; FINDLEY, William A

Group Number 83
FINEY, Samuel; FINNEY, Samuel; THOMAS, Charles M

Group Number 84
FINNEY, Samuel; HEALEY, John; THOMAS, Charles M

Group Number 85
FINNEY, Samuel; THOMAS, Charles M

Group Number 86
FORD, Charles P; JORDAN, Margaret Ann

Group Number 87
FRAZIER, Jonathan; SISSON, Robert G

Group Number 88
FRITH, Margaret J; FRITH, Mathias

Group Number 89
FUDGE, Sarah C; HEATON, William

Group Number 90
FULLER, Sarah A; FULLER, William

Group Number 91
GATTON, Anne; TOOMEY, Andrew J

Group Number 92
GEISLER, Malinda; GEISLER, William

Group Number 93
GIBSON, George M; HORSTEN, Leo

Group Number 94
GIBSON, George W; HORSTEN, Leo

Group Number 95
GLASS, Nancy; TOBLER, Jacob; WATSON, Jas S

Group Number 96
GODSY, Emily; GODSY, John

Group Number 97
GREEN, Thomas; LEEPER, William T; SHARP, Sarah

Group Number 98
GREGORY, Julia A; GREGORY, Sheriff

Group Number 99
GRIFFITH, Lewis; MONKS, Francis M; MONKS, James Q; MONKS, William

Group Number 100
GRIFFITH, Martin; MURPHEY, Jane

Group Number 101
GRIFFITH, Martin; WOODS, Robert K

Group Number 102
GUILLIAMS, Mary L; GUILLIAMS, William M

Group Number 103
GUY, John; MCFADDIN, Isaac

Group Number 104
HALL, Henderson; HALL, Leonard

Group Number 105

HALL, Leonard; SEUTEFF, Henrietta; SUETEFF, John C

Group Number 106
HANEY, Susan; HANEY, Timothy

Group Number 107
HARRIS, Mary A; HARRIS, William H

Group Number 108
HARROD, Jehu; HARROD, John

Group Number 109
HARTMAN, John A; REID, John

Group Number 110
HARVEY, William B; HOWELL, Josephus M; KEISTER, George W; KEISTER, Martha C; KEISTER, Mary M; KEISTER, Susanna

Group Number 111
HAWKINS, John B; PENN, Mary; TABOR, John

Group Number 112
HEATON, William; HIGH, Martha

Group Number 113
HEMPHILL, Mary; HEMPHILL, William P

Group Number 114
HENDERSON, Margaret B; KELLY, Loid

Group Number 115
HENRY, Elizziebeth; HENRY, Osburne

Group Number 116
HERNDON, Catharine; HOWELL, Josiah

Group Number 117
HINDS, Joel; HINDS, Viann

Group Number 118
HOOSE, Lydia; KNOWLTON, Levi W

Group Number 119
HOSHOUR, Samuel H; SUTTLE, Maria

Group Number 120
HOWELL, George W; HOWELL, Mary C

Group Number 121
HOWELL, Wilie; MCKNIGHT, Arabella W

Group Number 122
HUDSON, Jesse F; HUDSON, Susan G

Group Number 123
HUFFHINES, Jacob; MARTIN, St George

Group Number 124
HUNT, John M; HUNT, Lulu L

Group Number 125
HUNT, Margret T; HUNT, William C

Group Number 126
HUNTER, Nancy; WINTERS, Losinda

Group Number 127
INGOLD, Louisa; TILSON, Louisa

Group Number 128
JACKSON, A J; JACKSON, Susan

Group Number 129
JACKSON, Jancey M; JONES, Jancey M

Group Number 130
JARGENSON, George; JARGENSON, Hannah

Group Number 131
JENKINS, Mary; JENKINS, Thomas M

Group Number 132
JOHNS, Richard C; JOHNS, Susan J

Group Number 133
JONES, Murrey; THEOBALD, E S

Group Number 134
JUDD, Wallace A; OWEN, Elizabeth

Group Number 135
KILE, Martha; KILE, Walter L

Group Number 136
KING, Wilsey P; SPENCE, Nancy

Group Number 137
KNIGHT, Fanny; KNIGHT, Samuel

Group Number 138
LASSWELL, Julia A; LASSWELL, William H

Group Number 139
LEE, Susan; WILLIAMS, D H

Group Number 140
LEONARD, Margaret; MCDANIEL, Andrew J

Group Number 141
LORD, Tamson A; OKES, Tamson A

Group Number 142
LOY, George; LOY, Sarah

Group Number 143
MACK, Julia; MACK, Tyra

Group Number 144
MCDANIEL, Samuel R; MCELRATH, Jane

Group Number 145
MCDONAL, Rhoda; SEAL, Rhoda

Group Number 146
MCFADDIN, Isaac; WATERS, Caroline Black; WATERS, John H

Group Number 147
MCNAY, James; MOORE, Margaret; MOORE, Thomas

Group Number 148
MCNEELY, John; PUGH, Elizabeth

Group Number 149
MEYER, Nellie; MEYER, Nicholas

Group Number 150
MILLSAPS, Joseph; SLOAN, John; WYATT, Buford J; WYATT, Eliza J; WYATT, Francis H; WYATT, George W; WYATT, Marian M

Group Number 151
MIRES, J W; WILLIAMS, H M

Group Number 152
MODRALL, Flora B; OVERMAN, Flora B

Group Number 153
MUSTION, Alfred; MUSTION, William D

Group Number 154
NEWTON, Jonathan R; NEWTON, Lucy J; TERRY, Lucy J

Group Number 155
ODOM, Isaac; ODOM, Mary J

Group Number 156
PACE, David T; POPE, Henry T

Group Number 157
PAUL, Mary V; SISSON, Brown

Group Number 158
POWELL, Catharine; POWELL, George

Group Number 159
PROFFITT, Nancy J; PROFFITT, Riley M

Group Number 160
RAMSEY, Jasper N; RAMSEY, Rosannah

Group Number 161
RANKIN, Lorin; RANKIN, Luther

Group Number 162
RAY, Sarah J; RAY, William R

Group Number 163
REAVES, Celia; SLOAN, John

Group Number 164
REED, Frances; VASSAW, Frances

Group Number 165
RIGGS, Alvin; RIGGS, Mary

Group Number 166
ROBERTS, Delila; ROBERTS, John

Group Number 167
SCHAUB, George D; SCHAUB, Tina

Group Number 168
SCOGGIN, Turpin G; STRAUSE, Bernhard

Group Number 169
SHARP, James M; SHARP, Mary K

Group Number 170
SMITH, Mary; SMITH, William

Group Number 171
SMITH, Orlena; SMITH, Philip

Group Number 172
SMITH, Sarah; STOUT, Dolphin E

Group Number 173
SPEARS, Joseph T; WIKOFF, Sarah

Group Number 174
SRIVER, Irena; SRIVER, Peter M

Group Number 175
STEWART, Henry W; STEWART, Miranda J

Group Number 176
SWIFT, Clara C; SWIFT, Franklin B

Group Number 177
TAINTER, Joel E; TAINTER, Nancy M

Group Number 178
THOMAS, Adam; THOMAS, Janey

Group Number 179
TILSON, John A; TILSON, Theodore W

Group Number 180
TREVOR, Mathew R; TUPPER, Sally

Group Number 181
TUCKER, Delpha; TUCKER, Peterson

Group Number 182
UITTS, Johnson R; UITTS, Margaret

Group Number 183
VINCENT, Barbara L; VINCENT, James A

Group Number 184
WAID, Tilda M; WAID, William P

Group Number 185
WALLACE, William; WILLIAMS, Mary

Group Number 186
WALLICE, James T; WISNER, Andrew

Group Number 187
WARCUM, Nancy E; WARCUM, William H

Group Number 188
WEST, Margaret; WEST, Nathan D

Group Number 189
WHITE, Josie F; YOUNG, George; YOUNG, Josie F

Group Number 190
WILKERSON, Arta M; WILKERSON, Fidelia;
WILKERSON, Ida E; WILKERSON, Julian W;
WILKERSON, Mary J

Group Number 191
YARNELL, Robert; YARNELL, Sarah H

Group Number 192
YENNEY, George; YENNEY, Martha

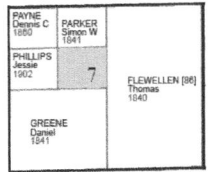

Extra! Extra! (about our Indexes)

We purposefully do not have an all-name index in the back of this volume so that our readers do not miss one of the best uses of this book: finding misspelled names among more specialized indexes.

Without repeating the text of our "How-to" chapter, we have nonetheless tried to assist our more anxious researchers by delivering a short-cut to the two county-wide Surname Indexes, the second of which will lead you to all-name indexes for each Congressional Township mapped in this volume :

For your convenience, the "How To Use this Book" Chart on page 2 is repeated on the reverse of this page.

We should be releasing new titles every week for the foreseeable future. We urge you to write, fax, call, or email us any time for a current list of titles. Of course, our web-page will always have the most current information about current and upcoming books.

Arphax Publishing Co.
2210 Research Park Blvd.
Norman, Oklahoma 73069
(800) 681-5298 toll-free
(405) 366-6181 local
(405) 366-8184 fax
info@arphax.com

www.arphax.com

How to Use This Book - A Graphical Summary

Part I
"The Big Picture"

Map A	*Counties in the State*
Map B	*Surrounding Counties*
Map C	*Congressional Townships (Map Groups) in the County*
Map D	*Cities & Towns in the County*
Map E	*Cemeteries in the County*
Surnames in the County	*Number of Land-Parcels for Each Surname*
Surname/Township Index	*Directs you to Township Map Groups in Part II*

The <u>*Surname / Township Index*</u> *can direct you to any number of* **Township Map Groups**

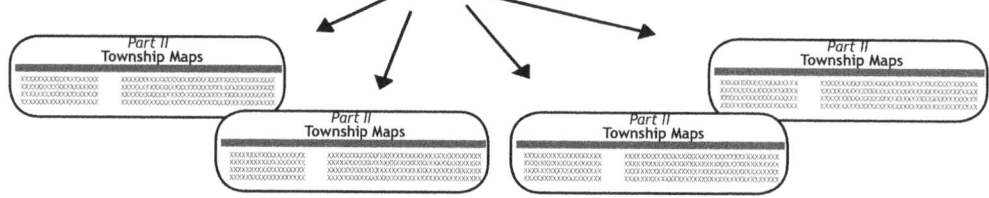

Part II
Township Map Groups
(1 for each Township in the County)

Each Township Map Group contains all four of of the following tools . . .

Land Patent Index	*Every-name Index of Patents Mapped in this Township*
Land Patent Map	*Map of Patents as listed in above Index*
Road Map	*Map of Roads, City-centers, and Cemeteries in the Township*
Historical Map	*Map of Railroads, Lakes, Rivers, Creeks, City-Centers, and Cemeteries*

Appendices

Appendix A	*Congressional Authority enabling Patents within our Maps*
Appendix B	*Section-Parts / Aliquot Parts (a comprehensive list)*
Appendix C	*Multi-patentee Groups (Individuals within Buying Groups)*

Made in the USA
Monee, IL
29 June 2022